THE BEST OF
ORIENTAL
COOKING

THE BEST OF
ORIENTAL
COOKING

Edited and adapted by
ALISON GRANGER

BLACK CAT

Based upon AZIATISCH KOKEN – ZO DOE JE DATI
© Kluwerpers B.V., The Netherlands, 1984/1987

This English language edition
© Macdonald & Co (Publishers) Ltd 1987

First published in Great Britain in 1987
by Macdonald & Co (Publishers) Ltd
Reprinted 1991 by Macdonald & Co (Publishing) Ltd
under the Black Cat imprint

A member of Maxwell Macmillan Pergamon Publishing Corporation

British Library Cataloguing in Publication Data

ISBN 0 7481 0305 8

Printed and bound in Czechoslovakia by Aventinum

AZIATISCH KOKEN
Editorial concept: Hans Belterman
Editor: Matjan J. J. Oleff
Editorial advisers: Kwee Siok Lan (China, Japan); Kim Manhave (India
& Pakistan, Sri Lanka); Lia Warani (Indonesia, Malaysia)
General advisers: Wies van Linge; Conimex/Baarn
Photography: Florian Lem; Philip Mechanicus; Paul van Riel; Ed
Suister; Koninklijk Instituut voor de Tropen/Amsterdam
Illustrations: Elisabeth Koelman; Wouter van Leeuwen
Art director: Gerard Reichart
Culinary realization: Wolf Anholt

A TASTE OF THE ORIENT
Compiled and designed by
Mander Gooch Callow
7 Hanover Street, London W1

Half-title: Anthony Blake Photo Library

Macdonald & Co (Publishers) Ltd
Orbit House
1 New Fetter Lane
London EC4A 1AR

CONTENTS

Symbols

The symbols will enable you to see at a glance how easy a recipe is, and the preparation and cooking times

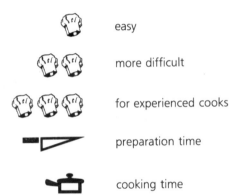

	easy
	more difficult
	for experienced cooks
	preparation time
	cooking time

When using the recipes in this book, remember the following points:

All quantities are for four people, unless otherwise stated.

Use only one set of measurements for the recipes, since American, imperial and metric measurements are not exact equivalents.

In the text of the recipes, American quantities and ingredients are listed first, with the British equivalents in brackets.

INTRODUCTION

A Taste of the Orient offers many of the classic dishes from the cuisines of China, Indonesia, Malaysia, The Philippines, Thailand, Vietnam, Korea, Singapore, Sri Lanka, Burma, India and Pakistan and Japan, presented so that they can be prepared easily and cooked in Western kitchens and served in the authentic style of their country of origin.

The accident of geography, climate, cultural traditions and religion has resulted in an enormous variety of cuisines, techniques and exquisite flavors. Imperial patronage has influenced the style of one cuisine, proximity to trade routes, another. Colonialism, conquest, famine and plenty, all have played their part in creating the richest, most exciting culinary history in the world.

Many experts believe that the art of cooking originated in China, and it is here that we begin a culinary journey. China has as many schools of cooking as there are regions, kept alive by government sponsorship but ever changing as new and better quality varieties of vegetables become available, as electricity supplies become more widespread, and as long as the Chinese maintain their enormous enthusiasm for cooking and experimentation.

From China, we travel to Indonesia. It is not surprising that there is a great Chinese influence here. Perhaps more surprisingly the cuisine has maintained a strong identity that is all its own despite its colonial history and like that of China, is still growing and developing.

Malaysia shares a common (unofficial) language with Indonesia, the peoples are related and its cooks' have the same ingredients available to them. Although prepared in a similar style Malaysian dishes are distinctive in their presentation and garnishing.

In the Philippines there are signs of colonial history, many of the dishes still have Spanish names, but this influence is declining as a very strong national identity emerges.

The Thais prepare even everyday meals, mainly based on a variety of fish, with almost ritual care. Chicken and meat dishes are rarely found here. Thai cooking could hardly be more different from that of Vietnam.

Vietnamese cuisine is regarded by some experts as the richest in Asia, despite the wars and political upheavals it too continues to grow and change, influenced by both East and West.

In Korea, once again the influence of China can be seen in the food and its preparation but the creativity of its sauces and spices is all its own, and placed as Korea is between China and Japan, Japanese cuisine has also had its effects.

The gigantic metropolis that is Singapore has fallen completely under the influence of Chinese culture, and is a true culinary paradise, because nowhere else in Asia will you find as many different kinds of eating houses as in Singapore. Famous curry dishes from India, specialities from Sri Lanka or examples of Japanese cuisine, you will find them all in Singapore. Although the once so famous cuisine of the nonyas (cooks employed by British families) has faded somewhat into the background.

In Sri Lanka, the cuisine still bears the signs of its colonial history but like all Asian cooking shows an ability to change and develop with its ever changing culture. Many dishes still bear their Dutch names, for example they eat ''lompa'' rice and ''frikadelle'', while a traditional pastry which is eaten by many Christian families at Christmas is called ''breuder'', which is none other than the ''broeder'' still eaten in West Friesland today.

After Burma, which is different yet again as Chinese, Indian and Malaysian influences are perceptible, we travel to India and Pakistan. The cuisine in these countries is highly developed and differs in many ways from that in other parts of Asia, partly because of its geographical situation, but the diverse religions and traditions also play an important role.

Finally we reach Japan where we encounter a unique cuisine and discover sushi, tempura, sashimi and tofu and learn the special techniques of cutting, which enable us to prepare Japanese dishes to perfection, and to serve them in an authentic and traditional style.

Health

In preparing dishes, the peoples of nearly all the Asian countries dealt with in this book, take account of the well- being of the mind and body, with the emphasis on health. In general, people in Asia eat less than we do in the West. In nearly all Asian countries meat and poultry play a much less significant role in the diet than in the West. An average Chinese meal contains no more than 2½ oz (75 g) of meat, 3½ oz (100 g) of chicken or poultry or 6½ oz (175 g) of fish per person. In Japan they eat even less but every dish, however small the portions, is prepared with care and attention. Food experts in the West have been pointing to Japan for a number of years as a country where meals have been traditionally prepared which also contain much less fat, sugar and salt than we are accustomed to in the West.

Scientific research has shown that the diseases associated with prosperity, which are so common in the West, occur rarely in Japan, except among people who have a preference for Western foods and lifestyle.

In the Chinese People's Republic, where the government is consciously encouraging healthy eating, great value is attached to having the widest possible variety of ingredients. Here, too, Western dietary experts point to the relatively low fat consumption and point out that this is largely determined by the technique of stir frying in a wok, which enables the tastiest of meals to be prepared with a minimum of oil or fat. Many ingredients that are used in Asian cooking can also be obtained in the West. Herbs and spices and different varieties of rice, cereals, pulses and fruit and vegetables are in the main all available, although they may be used and prepared in a different way in Western cuisine. For example: special attention is given in this book to the soybean, not only because it is the most widely cultivated pulse in the world, but because of its versatilty. Among the foods which can be made from it is soybean curd (tofu), which as it is rich in protein can take the place in the menu of all sources of animal protein such as fish, meat, game and poultry. Soybeans also form the basis of many sauces, which are widely obtainable in the West. In many Asian countries, such as China, Japan, Malaysia and Indonesia, there are many different kinds of soy sauce. They range from nearly black to fairly light in color and differ in taste not only from country to country, but from from manufacturer to manufacturer. Some soy sauces are quite salty, while others are almost syrupy sweet.

Besides the Chinese and Japanese soy sauces, the sweeter Indonesian soy sauces are popular and should be readily obtainable from Asian stores. Many ingredients have Western origins. Maize, which is being grown increasingly in areas where the climate is favorable, was introduced there during the last century. It is now regarded as a native cereal and is used in many dishes. Many vegetables do not originate from this part of the world, either, but were introduced by the colonial rulers a century or two ago. There are of course also ingredients, which are unobtainable in the West, including different varieties of fish. In A Taste of the Orient we have given readily available alternatives which have the same or very similar taste and texture. There are also differences in the meat and poultry since in many Asian countries the animals forage for food themselves and Western animal feed is not available, thus the same meat tastes quite different. Bread is, in general, much less eaten than in the West and this is because wheat does not grow in the tropics. Dairy products, such as milk, cheese and butter, are also not consumed very much. Many Asians have a strong aversion to dairy products. As in so many other respects India and Pakistan, are exceptions to this. Butter is widely made and is also used for frying and roasting. Flavorings are used on a large scale in the various Asian cuisines.

They can almost all be bought in the West and we give recipes for home-made spice mixtures, sauces and sambals in the chapters on each country. The short glossary at the end of the book explains any that are a little more difficult to obtain and offers substitutes if necessary. At the end of the glossary a list of addresses is given where ingredients should be obtainable by mail order.

A glance at the map of Asia shows the important place occupied in that continent by China and India. Both countries have a high population density and both lead the way in the art of cooking. Geographically Japan is also very important but its influence on the cuisines of other countries is small. China occupies a central position because of its place on the map of Asia. It is bordered by eleven countries, while Japan, the Philippines and Indonesia are not so very far away across the sea. It is the differences in soil and climate that play a decisive part in the comparison of one country's cuisine with that of another. Traditions and religions also play an

A map of Asia, showing the central position of China in relation to her neighbors.

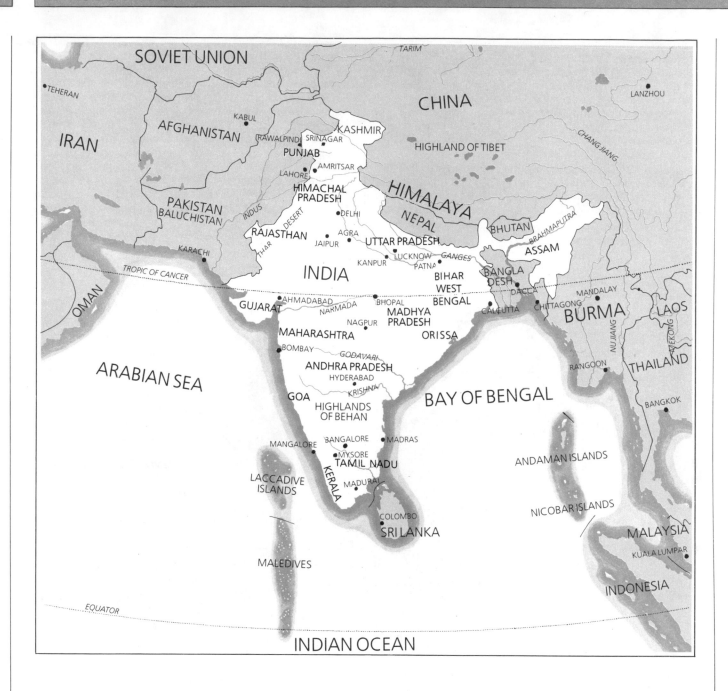

*A detail of a map of Asia
showing the position of India in
relation to her neighbors.*

important part. In India, Pakistan and Bangladesh you will find many contrasts. Such contrasts are not to be found in China, although that country still has typical Moslem and Buddhist cuisines. A disadvantage of the Chinese Buddhist cuisine is that so many different ingredients have to be used as flavorings. The vegetarian cuisine of India not only has a more immediate appeal to us in the West, but it is gradually extending its influence to parts of Asia where Buddhism is unknown. As you travel from one country to another, you will find that in Malaysia and Indonesia an increasing number of vegetarian dishes are being added to the repertoire of recipes. This influence is also noticeable in the Philippines and even in Japan.

This map shows very clearly the central location of China. It divides China into four major sectors, corresponding with the

different schools of cookery. The northern school, which is centered on Peking, comprises Manchuria and Korea.

Peking is also known for its imperial cuisine, as it was the residence of the Chinese emperors for many centuries. After the fall of the Chinese empire in 1912 many dishes from the imperial kitchen were democratised. The actual recipes from the imperial kitchen are made only on very rare occasions in Peking, because the high cost is not regarded as justified.

The eastern school, of which Shanghai is an important culinary center, is located in a particularly fertile area, from which the supply of produce is much greater and more varied than in Peking. The western school consists of the province of Szechwan and the bordering areas.

Szechwan was isolated for centuries and its isolation has only really been broken during the past few decades. This isolation is the reason why a special school of cookery has developed there which is unknown elsewhere in China. The Szechwan style of cookery is being threatened, however, by all the other Chinese cookery styles, because the government is actively encouraging migration to these areas in the heart of China. The Szechwan cookery style is incidentally very popular in Japan, and an increasing number of restaurants are being opened in the U.S.A where dishes from the western school are served.

The best known cookery styles are to be found in the southern school. Canton is, without any exaggeration, the culinary capital of the whole of China. The Cantonese kitchen offers greater variety in its dishes than any other school. The Cantonese cooks are famous for their creativity and inventiveness. It must be remembered here that this region is situated in a highly favorable sub-tropical climatic zone, from which more ingredients can be obtained than anywhere else in China.

Influences from other countries can be seen in the cuisine of Canton and it also contains 'translations' of dishes originating from other Chinese schools of cookery. Of all the schools of Chinese cookery, the cuisine of Canton has spread most widely throughout the world. The Cantonese cuisine is famous, for example, for its dim sum snacks and its roast pork and duck dishes. Besides the Cantonese cuisine, the southern school boasts another cuisine which is quite popular in other countries. This is the cuisine of the Hakkas, originally from the north of the country, in which the natural flavor of the main ingredients of a dish are brought out much more distinctly than in the majority of most typically Cantonese dishes.

A map of China, showing the different schools of regional cooking and the distribution of produce.

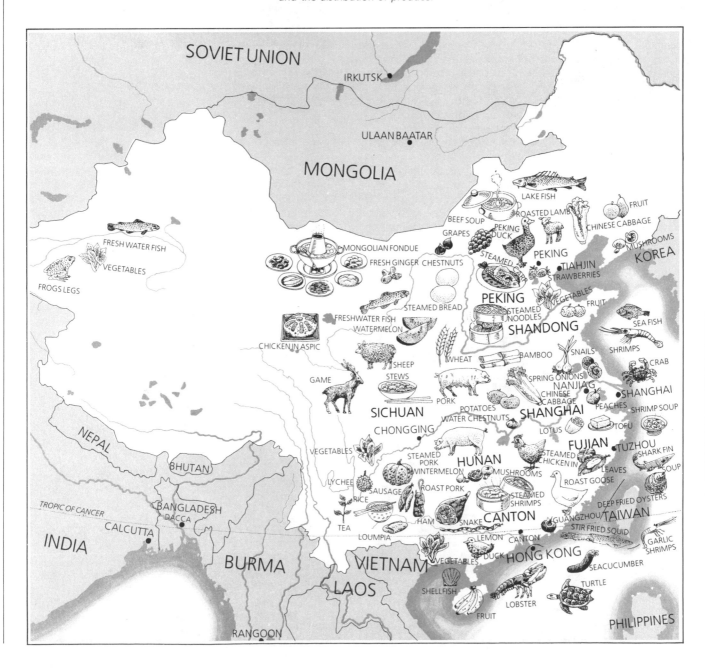

CHINA

The Chinese themselves refer to 'the country in the middle', which is not surprising when we look at the map of Asia. Nor is it surprising that the Chinese, irrespective of the regime they live under, have always regarded themselves as the center of the world, with their eleven neighbors and Japan, the Philippines and Indonesia lying very close across the sea. Bearing this in mind and remembering that the Chinese have been leaving their country for centuries to try to make a good living elsewhere, the extent of the influence of the Chinese cuisine in Asia becomes clear. To emphasize the influence of Chinese culture even further many of the peoples living in South East Asia, lived originally in the area which has now formed part of the Chinese territory for many centuries. China is one of the largest countries in the world, it is the country with the largest population, over 1,000 million, followed by India and the Soviet Union. The distance between east and west is over 3105 miles (5,000 km) and from north to south more than 2018 miles (3,250 km). Several climates can be distinguished there. In some regions it is warm throughout the year, while in others the summers are short and the winters long and quite cold. The greater part of the country however is situated in a moderate zone, where the seasons can be clearly distinguished. The combination of hot summers and fairly humid springs and autumns with not excessively low temperatures creates favorable conditions for agriculture and livestock farming. China also possesses rich water resources. There are countless rivers – including the world's longest the Yangtse, and lakes, which are important not only for the country's water economy, but which also yield a large quantity of freshwater fish and shellfish.

Many lakes and ponds support fish nurseries and there are many duck breeding farms. China's 8694 mile (14,000 km) coastline, makes the sea a great provider of fish and shellfish. The mountains in the south, the vast deserts in the west and north, and the seas in the east protected the Chinese territory for many centuries against invasion and thus they developed a strong, individual culture. It is not certain when the Chinese first went outside their natural frontiers.

It is believed that it was not earlier than during the famous Han dynasty (206BC – 220AD), which was characterized by a tremendous expansion. This brought Chinese traders into

Above: Eating in the street is becoming more common again in Chinese cities. Below: Sweet bread rolls are eaten as snacks between meals.

contact with their neighbors and they traveled even further in the direction of the Arabian Sea. It is assumed that, at that time, the Chinese became acquainted with products which had hitherto been unknown such as many kinds of pulses, grapes, nuts, seeds, and onions. Traders who passed westwards along the famous 'silk route' through Central Asia made the acquaintance en route of new spices, eg aniseed and cumin, and brought them back to China and the great barriers between the different great civilisations in the West and East were broken down. This was one of the factors which made it possible for Chinese cuisine to develop into one of the most important in the world and from this point of view, it is not so strange that the Chinese cuisine may be counted among the most important cuisines known to us.

INDONESIA

The cuisine of Indonesia has been shaped not by its isolation but by the history of incursions, invasions, conversions and colonialism into and of its territories. The first foreign visitors have been traced to the first century A.D. They are assumed to have come from India and China, for trade and commerce. Both Hindus and Chinese came and settled on the larger Indonesian islands bringing their cultures, traditions and indeed cuisines with them. It seems however that the native population resisted adopting the customs of their immigrants until the 7th or 8th centuries when the first adaptations of Indonesian culture are discernable. In the sphere of cuisine this is perhaps in part due to the fact that Indonesia was not closely bound by religious custom and taboo and had a greater range of ingredients than the foreiners were used to in their home lands. From the Hindu cuisine the Indonesians, adopted the practice of cooking in coconut milk and from the Chinese they learnt the technique of stir frying and the eating of noodles. They held on to their own traditions of spicing and flavoring foods. These three cultures seem to have co-existed

forced the influence of Indian cooking, and encouraged the making of spices, relishes and pickles. Once again the Indonesian cuisine borrowed from its 'visitors', but maintained its individuality and continued to preserve most foods by salting rather than pickling. The British incursion is the origin of the famous Java curry, the mildness of which distinguishes it from all other curry mixtures in this part of Asia.

The British also did much work in the pioneering of a better food supply for the native inhabitants, introducing the cultivation of rice and other crops.

This necessarily brief history of Indonesian cuisine does little justice to the fascinating history of the country and its culture but merely serves to point to some interesting features for the modern cook.

Left: Preserving in salt or pickling is traditional in Indonesia and jars of produce are often on sale. Right: Fresh fish, sold in the street in coastal towns is plentiful and varied.

peacefully learning from one another until the arrival of the Arabs in the 13th century. They came for trade and as evangelists for Islam. The success of their mission may be judged by the large Moslem population in Indonesia today.

They met nonetheless with resistence from convinced Hindus and the resistence of Majohapit king of the Javanese kingdom resulted in his voluntary death and the flight of his son and followers to Bali where Hinduism still flourishes today.

Bali has a rich culinary history and unbound by Islamic dietary law has maintained an interesting and varied cuisine. Marco Polo is considered to have been the first European to visit Indonesia, followed by the Portuguese. They were ejected by the Dutch who established their colonial empire there in 1596. Dutch rule lasted well into the 20th century.

Interestingly, the brief interruption to this rule by the British (1811-1814) had a powerful influence on Indonesian cuisine. The British brought many Indians into Indonesia which rein-

MALAYSIA

Malaysia is characterized by a tropical rain climate with monsoon influences. The soil is very fertile and produces the best fruit and vegetables under the tropical sun, including kiwi, pineapple, papaw, chayote, jack fruit, limes, dates, yams, paksoi, Chinese leaves, winter melon - in short too many to mention. Dried Chinese mushrooms are available in abundance and generous use is also made of oyster, hoisin and prawn sauces in Malaysian cuisine, where the sauces are thickened to be more like pastes. Light or dark soy sauces are also worked into nearly every dish. The enormous variety of fresh fruits and vegetables makes Malaysian cuisine specially impressive and colorful and the Malays present their dishes in the most attractive way, garnished with Chinese parsley, cut out fresh fruits in intricate shapes, and real flowers such as lotus and chrysanthemum.

Transport facilities are good in Malaya and people are now able to take advantage of more frozen foods like lamb from New Zealand, which are unavailable elsewhere. The Malaysian, eats rather simply. A meal is usually composed of one main dish and two vegetable dishes. Rice is the staple food, both long and short grain and is usually dry steamed. In Malaysia particularly in Malaya and Peneng, traces of the traditional 'nonya' cuisine are still to be found.

Street stall snacks of all kinds are enjoyed, particularly the delicious wafer thin pancakes containing diced radish, cabbage, shrimp (prawns), crab, chicken, bean sprouts or soy bean curd (tofu) wrapped in a lettuce leaf. Malaya contains a large number of provinces, each of which has its own culinary specialities: Hot spices in Perlis, rice in Kedah, curries in Penang, flat rice noodles and spiced stews in Perak, fish and rice in Kelantang, highly peppered dishes in Negri Sembilan, Portuguese specialities in Malacca, Javanese influenced dishes in Johore and Thai in Tregganu with much chicken and grilled fish, not to mention the specialities of Pahang, Sabah, Sarawak and Delangoor.

THE PHILIPPINES

The Republic of the Philippines is a country made up of 7107 islands in the Pacific Ocean and the China Sea between Indonesia and Taiwan. The islands are divided into three groups, from North to South, first the Luzon islands, named after Luzon the largest island in the group. More than half the inhabitants of the Philippines live on this island, and it is here that the most important cities are located -the capital Quezon City and the government center Manila. The second group is the Visayas Islands, with Cebu, the oldest city in the Philippines. The third is the Mindanao islands with Mindanao the most important island and on it Davao the largest city.

The Philippines have been at the center of various colonial incursions since before Christ. The first came from Central Asia, the Indonesians followed and about 200 BC the Malays arrived. In subsequent centuries, trade with China, Arabia, and in the 14th century the whole of South East Asia have all influenced Filipino culture. The West arrived in 1521 and the Spaniards ruled for 300 years. Their influence is still to be seen in the architecture, in religion, in names and in cookery. In 1850 the struggle for liberation began under Jose Rizal, resulting in the Philippines being sold to America in 1898. In 1946

the Philippines became independent, although they still maintain close ties with America.

Not surprisingly, cooking in the Philippines is a reflection of the islands' history. In the 17th and 18th centuries the original cuisine and that of the Spanish colonialists merged and it is characteristic of the Filipinos that they selected the best of both. In the past 10 years the Filipinos have begun to reintroduce original cuisine, ranging from highly spiced but slightly sour to extremely sweet dishes. Fish is a mainstay of Filipino cuisine, which they prepare very plainly and serve with boiled rice and soy sauce and more pork is eaten than in other parts of Asia.

THAILAND

Thai means free and Thailand's name reflects the fact that it is the only country in South East Asia that has never been under colonial rule. It has however been exposed to outside influences. Until the end of the 13th century it had come under different dominions. Like the Vietnamese and many other peoples of South East Asia, much of the original population of

The Buddha gallery at the ruins of the temple of Ayuthaya, to the north of Bangkok.

Thai food is mainly more highly spiced than in China and where the Chinese use soy sauce and oyster sauce, the Thais use their nam pla, a fish sauce. Thai cuisine remained largely unnoticed by the West until the beginning of the sixties when American soldiers began spending their leave in Bangkok and the Thai royal family went on tour to all the major cities in the West. This was also the time when tourism began to open up the paradise of Thailand to the Western world. Although the national religion in Thailand is Buddhism, Mohammedan influences are playing an increasingly important role in Thai cuisine. Many Thais prefer lamb and mutton to pork (Mohammedans do not eat pork) and it is disappearing from Thai dishes. It is extraordinary how easily new ingredients such as bell peppers have been incorporated into traditional Thai cuisine. Now grown in Thailand people prepare dishes using these new ingredients as if they had been a part of the standard repertoire of Thai cuisine for centuries.

VIETNAM

The part of South East Asia which has been known as Vietnam since 1954 was already inhabited as far as is known, roughly 4000 years ago. In the West we still know relatively little about this country except that the horrific Vietnam war brought it to the world's attention.

The strong unity with their land and their determination to defend it are like continuous threads running through the history of the Vietnamese people. This country seems always to have had to defend itself against invading powers. As a result of the huge migrations which took place throughout Asia, at the end of the 8th century B.C., a people settled in the north who were mainly agrarians who moved further and further South as the lands became exhausted. As developments made it possible for settlement in one place to happen the Champa kingdom came into being at the end of the 2nd century B.C. in the north of Annam, the region with Tonkin in the north and Cochin-China in the south, which would be the Socialist Republic of Vietnam in our time. The Chinese during the Han dynasty of 212 B.C.-220 A.D. expanded their territory by invading the kingdom which was then under Chinese rule from 11 B.C. to 939 A.D. The majority of the original population moved into the mountains or further south along the coast. This expansion continued until the 18th century and forms the basis of the modern Vietnam area.

Until the arrival of the French in 1883 the Chinese tried time and again to regain lost territory, but it was defended and they never succeeded. Vietnam nonetheless has kept Chinese culture for centuries. Once again as food often reflects the history of a nation so Vietnam reflects its Chinese influence in its cuisine. It is actually surprising that the French who ruled from 1883 to 1954, French Indo-China (Vietnam, Laos and Cambodia) had little influence at all on the food and cuisine of Vietnam. Vietnamese cuisine was at its height during the latter part of the last century and many of the dishes served outside Vietnam reflect this period. Typically Vietnamese is the spicing of its dishes with a great deal of garlic, red chilies and spicy sambals based on chilies and the use of Nuoc mam, Vietnamese fish sauce, which is as important to Vietnamese cuisine as soy sauce is to Chinese. They also eat a lot of pork, chicken, duck and fish, although cattle are kept as work animals, so little beef or dairy products are eaten. Nowadays Vietnamese cuisine in Vietnam is much simpler though highly nutritious, and the dishes described will largely be found outside that country.

Some of the best of Asian cuisine is available everywhere, from street vendors.

Thailand came from the heart of China. After 10 centuries, the Chinese way of life was interrupted when Thailand came under the rule of Java, Sumatra and partly under that of Khmer. At the end of the 13th century independent realms began to appear, together forming Thailand (then Siam). Thailand has maintained its independence to this day, but it is hardly surprising that the Chinese influence on Thai cooking should be so great. Stir frying in the wok and the use of the moh fai, an originally Mongolian stewing kettle has never disappeared from Thai cuisine.

Rice noodles, more highly spiced than Chinese noodles and of course rice itself, figure largely in Thai cooking too. The country is extremely fertile and the climate is such that rice can be harvested 3 or 4 times a year. Thailand is one of the largest rice suppliers in the world and Thai rice is of the highest quality. Even the words for expressing hunger in Thai, reflect the importance of this food, they are 'Hiu kao' which means 'I have an appetite for rice'. The word 'kao' means both rice and food. In Thailand rice is even served as an accompaniment to rice noodles.

KOREA

The peninsula of Korea, is situated in the Northern part of Asia and because of its position forms a natural bridge between China and Japan. An old Korean legend has it that a local hero founded the kingdom of Jeo-Son (morning rest) in about 300 B.C. Sadly this land of morning rest has known little peace in its history. Until the present day Korea has seen a continuous flow of monarchs, feudal lords, tribes and conquerors, whether Chinese, Mongolian, Japanese or Western missionaries and businessmen, Russians or Americans. This has influenced Korea's politics and culture for 2000 years.

Until the middle of the seventeenth century, Korea was a kind of Chinese protectorate and that country's influence has been enormous. Korea was attacked by Japan at the end of the sixteenth century, destroying much Korean cultural heritage. A century later Korea fell prey to Manchus, but like the Chinese they left the ruling of the land to the Korean kings. In the 19th century Korea was the center of a struggle between China, Japan and Russia and was officially annexed to Japan. Sadly its modern history is known all too well. If it can be said that any advantages can have been gained for this land by its

history, its literature is one and its cuisine, influenced as it has been by both China and Japan is another. The Chinese influences were a grafting onto the Peking cuisine already in existence in Korea of Mongolian cuisine. The Koreans copied the fire pot, a special pot in which a spicy sauce is prepared at the table using different ingredients, from the Mongolians, and the eating of beef. The meals in Korea are generally heavier than in other parts of Asia and they specialize in thick soups and pickled vegetables also borrowed from Mongolian cooking. Korean cuisine boasts numerous fish dishes, fried or roasted with batter or without, as the Yellow Sea and the Japanese Sea by which it is surrounded yield a great deal of fresh fish, shell fish and crustaceans. The seasons in Korea are very important for agriculture. In Summer, the Koreans have a greater variety of fresh fruit and vegetables than in Winter when there can be severe frosts. In the bigger cities in South Korea the influence of American cuisine is noticable. In North Korea, people live far more modestly and the old traditions are maintained.

SINGAPORE

Since Singapore became an independent state it has changed a great deal. The Chinese brought to Singapore in the 19th Century to work in the docks and ports, now constitute the majority of the population. So Singapore may nowadays be regarded as a genuinely Chinese city. Singapore is also a cosmopolitan city, however, since in this part of Asia it would be difficult to find another city with so many nationalities, besides Chinese.

There are of course still many Malays living in Singapore, and Indians and Pakistanis. There are also people from Japan, Taiwan, Indonesia and the Philippines, Thais and Vietnamese. A colorful combination who value their individual identities highly. One way in which this is expressed is in their cookery. Singapore has many high class restaurants where the preparation of food is unequalled, but it is more fun to eat in the

street. This is one of Singapore's great attractions. As well as the best of oriental cuisine you will find, Mexican, Italian and Norwegian food and even American style fast food snacks.

What is difficult to find now is the nonya cuisine. Nonya cuisine originated in the time of the British, when the Chinese settled among the Malay residents and carried over their eating habits into Malay cuisine. Nonya meals consist of a unique combination of Chinese ingredients and Malay methods of preparation. Malay Moslem cuisine has been adapted for the Chinese, allowing even their much loved pork to be used. Nonya cuisine is in its way the forerunner of many oriental cuisines prepared in Western kitchens. A combination of experimentation with ingredients and the methods familiar to the cook.

Singapore is justifiably famous for the high standard of cuisine in its restaurants, both Asian and Western foods are represented.

SRI LANKA

Although Sri Lanka is called the pearl in India's ear and there are close resemblances to the cuisines of the states of Southern India, there are nevertheless marked differences and the cuisine of Sri Lanka is outstanding for its diversity, a characteristic which is absent elsewhere, particularly in India. This is not surprising because Sri Lanka is surrounded by seas rich in fish and the relatively cool climate of the elevated interior makes it possible to grow a wide variety of vegetables and fruit. In addition Sri Lanka's population is divided into distinct groups each with their own preferences. Remember too, that Sri Lanka was dominated for centuries by Arabs, Moors, Malaysians, Portuguese, Dutch and British. Each conqueror has left something behind and it is that which makes the cuisine of modern Sri Lanka so interesting. The true cuisine of Sri Lanka is to be found in the small coastal villages where fresh fish is landed daily and in the plantations of the interior where fresh vegetables and fruit form the basis of so many tasty dishes. Here we discover that the curries of Sri Lanka look and taste quite different from those of India. A Sri Lankan meal consists of rice, preferably long grain, which is spiced and every Sri Lankan cook does it her own way. The rice is served with curries, four, five or more different dishes, each varied in color and flavor. Color forms an important part of Sri Lankan cuisine. They have attractive red and yellow curries and one must not be alarmed when a black curry is placed alongside for contrast.

The other side dishes which are served contain eggs and vegetables and are also full of contrast. Sri Lanka's history is also one of contrast and the many influences are reflected in the foods. The effects of the Moors and Arabs are found in the sweets which are eaten between meals. One finds fish dishes which might also be found in Portugal, simply spiced and cooked over charcoal or fried in hot oil.

Dutch dishes such as lampries and breuder are still to be found and so are British Christmas cakes.

Sri Lanka is still famous for high quality tea.

The traditional manner of Sri Lankan eating is reminiscent of India, where food is eaten from the right hand in banana leaves and where similar ingredients are used it is the individual approach of the Sri Lankan cook that makes this cuisine so distinctive.

BURMA

You will soon realise in Rangoon, Burma's capital that Burma is the land of curries that are nonetheless quite different from those in India and Pakistan. Burma's curries are exciting and almost always highly spiced. Yet their distinctive flavor is not derived from the the complex mixture of spices as in India. The heart of Burmese curries is their fresh ingredients: onions, garlic and root ginger, plus dried shrimp (prawn) paste.

Burmese cuisine is to be found everywhere, on the streets, in the bazaars and wherever you might expect to find people. Street vendors are also to be seen at bus stations and in the interior you will find them at every bus stop. It is the love and care with which Burmese dishes are prepared that will impress you time and time again. In Burma it is mainly the men who sell the prepared foods and the women who sell the fresh ingredients, such as fruits. There are also sweets, which the Burmese eat as snacks at any time of day.

Burmese cuisine like that of Indonesia is one in which you will find dishes from all over South East Asia. The influence of nearby India is considerable as is that of China and Malaysia. Burmese dishes are always 'free interpretations' however as the Burmese nearly always add extra fresh ingredients and leave out the complex spice mixtures. The basis of most

Burmese meals is boiled or steamed rice, always served hot. This is accompanied by side dishes (curries) which with few exceptions are always served lukewarm. Three or four small dishes are always served with a meal and often one or two side salads. There are also single dishes served as a complete meal which usually have a Chinese flavor to them and virtually always include or are accompanied by rice vermicelli or egg noodles. Like Sri Lanka, color plays an important part in the presentation of Burmese food and most dishes have colorful garnishes.

Vegetables have a different role to play in meals than in the West. The Burmese for vegetables also includes most fruits. Vegetable dishes are often served just warm or cold. Three or four vegetables are often combined to make salads, and prepared with a dressing of lemon or lime juice and oil, seasoned with a little salt and pepper. Vegetables which are not prepared for salads are cut into 2 in (5 cm) strips rather than thin strips and are lightly fried and seasoned with fish sauce. Rice is also very important in Burmese cuisine as it is in most Asian cuisines. The Burmese prefer long grain varieties and the rice is always boiled except for special occasions when it is cooked in coconut milk.

INDIA AND PAKISTAN

For several centuries Pakistan and India were linked together. The two states became independent in 1947 and in 1971 the eastern region of Pakistan separated from the mother country and the state of Bangladesh was born. The countries in this part of Asia can look back on prehistory of over 50 centuries. An estimated 700 million people live in this part of the world. Mainly Moslems live in Pakistan, while the majority of the inhabitants of India follow the religion of Brahmanism; they are Hindus. There are however important Moslem and Buddhist minorities. It is not really possible to speak of a national cuisine in India and Pakistan, since the internal differences are too great, which is not surprising as India and Pakistan are countries with four different climates and very different foods are available. The climate even determines the thickness of the sauces prepared there. In Northern India and in Pakistan, where wheat grows well and chapatis (flat bread individually and freshly made from a thick dough of flour and water) are eaten with the meal, the food is drier and the sauces are thicker the chapatis are used to mop up the sauce. In the south, rice is almost always eaten with the meal and the sauces can be thinner, because they are partly absorbed by the rice. Even more important than the geographical and climatic conditions are the differences in religion and tradition. Islam forbids the eating of pork. Hindus regard the cow as a sacred animal and will certainly not eat beef, instead they eat vegetarian food. Vegetarianism is particularly prevalent among the better-off, where there is strong social control. The Buddhists are also vegetarians and particularly strict ones, because they refuse to eat any animal products and will not even break an egg. Besides these there are other minorities in India who are trying to protect their cultures; they often practise a cuisine which differs from the others. Among these are Christians who, under the influence of the former British rule, prepare dishes bearing a clearly British stamp. Other Christians, such as the Roman Catholics in the former Portuguese colony of Goa, produce dishes marked by a clearly Portuguese influ-

Above: Complex spice mixtures are a feature of Indian and Pakistani cuisine. Left: As elsewhere in Asia, street vendors sell snacks and produce.

ence. In northern and parts of central India the eating of meat is not unusual for those people who do not refuse it on religious grounds and here are to be found the best meat dishes in the whole of India.

Meat and poultry were introduced here by the Mogul invasion of the 16th century bringing the cuisine of Asia. There are, however, other reasons why the eating of meat is not regarded as so important in the south of India. As a result of the favorable climate, the supply of different kinds of vegetables and fruit is much greater than in the north of India and Pakistan. India is washed by seas which are particularly rich in fish. In the coastal areas fish is preferably eaten fresh. The fish intended for consumption in the interior is nearly always dried before being sent there.

India and Pakistan have little refrigerated transport. In the interior of India, however, there are quite a lot of fish farms where freshwater fish are being bred on an increasingly large scale. The Hindus of Kashmir readily eat the lamb and mutton which the Mohammedans, who form the majority in that region, traditionally eat, while those same Mohammedans refuse to eat beef because the Hindus do not eat it. The Hindus of Madras, Mangalore and Bombay eat fish, which they see the Christian communities of those cities eating.

Spices lie at the heart of cooking in India, Pakistan and Bangladesh. Nearly every family cherishes the recipes for spice mixtures which are often hundreds of years old and have been passed from mother to daughter over the generations.

Japan

When the geographical position of Japan is considered it is not surprising that generations of Japanese fishermen have sailed the seas around their homeland for centuries to supply the needs of their countrymen for fresh fish and sea food. One reason for the national need for huge supplies of fish is the lack of a large cattle stock in Japan.

As most fish and seafood is eaten raw and as fresh as possible the fish are kept alive until the last possible moment. It is not just fish but other products of the sea which play an important role in Japanese cuisine, seaweed plays a very important part in flavoring many dishes, iziki, 'crumb ' seaweed, wakame, long curly seaweed, nori, black green sheets, kombu, sea grape all have different roles to play. Seaweed can also be eaten as a vegetable. Dried fish (katsuobushi) is used as the basis for dashi a bouillon (stock) which forms the basis of most Japanese sauces.

There is a huge variety of vegetables available in Japan and they are presented as a part of every meal. All the varieties we know in the West are found in Japan as well as others which are known only in Asia. Daikon or giant radish is a good example of this but we can substitute radish or turnip for recipes requiring these. Spring onions are also a good substitute for dishes needing negi a sort of thin leek.

Japan is also the country of the lotus root, chrysanthemum leaves, burdock, bamboo shoots, ginger root and aromatic toadstools such as shiitake. Many varieties of peas, beans and lettuce are also grown in Japan. Fruit too is available in abundance, thanks to the ideal climate in the Southern islands and excellent transport facilities, people in northern Japan enjoy all the sub tropical fruits such as kiwis, kakis, mangos and melons as well as raspberries and strawberries. The Japanese are also very fond of apricots and plums and plums are often used to make delicious pastes.

There are lychees, peaches and bananas in abundance and Japan is famous not only for its cherry blossom but for the sweet and juicy cherries that follow.

Oranges grown in Japan are more fragrant than any in the world and they have a fruit called the mikan which is like our kumquat, a cross between an orange and a mandarin and this is widely eaten as a dessert.

Desserts as we know them are scarcely ever eaten in Japan, although desserts used to be served at imperial banquets. They almost always included fruit as the Japanese have always eaten fruit after a meal.

The Japanese are famous both for their meals, cooked at the table, with a variety of beautifully prepared ingredients cooked by the guest in boiling stock and/or the raw fish of sashimi. Sushi snacks based on spiced rice are delicious for luncheons or cocktail snacks and Tempura can be made with any combination of ingredients as long as it is prepared in the Japanese style. Japanese meals are generally very quick to cook but until the cook becomes practised the preparation time can be quite lengthy. The harmony and beauty of Japanese meals is very hard to better and the combination of ingredients and techniques, makes Japanese cuisine very healthy indeed.

Sweet soybean curd (tofu) is fried in oil and served with fresh fruit.

COOKING TECHNIQUES

In the past few decades there have been many cross cultural exchanges in cooking techniques between Asia and the West. These have effected both eating habits and the development of the art of cooking all over the the world. From the West, famous chefs have been happy to be influenced by their colleagues in China and Japan, and many have derived ideas, by traveling even further into Asia to gain experience in Malaysia, India and, particularly, Thailand. Certain techniques, such as stir frying, steaming and the cooking of dishes in a "wrapping", are now the center of attention. Stir frying, a Chinese technique originally, is already very popular and much has been published about it during the past few decades. This method of cooking in a wok is regarded as a great

Street cuisine is a feature of all the countries covered in this book.

contribution to modern cooking because dishes can be prepared very quickly, using fresh produce and preserving the maximum vitamin and nutrient content. This is also true of steaming as opposed to boiling, particularly of vegetables.

The influence of the West on the art of cooking in all parts of Asia is not only very great, but may even constitute a threat to the further development of the local cuisine. The most important developments have much to do with the introduction of extensive electricity supply networks, allowing for the installation of refrigerators and other electrical equipment in Asian kitchens. In the refrigerator such ingredients as fish, meat and vegetables can be kept fresh for longer, which means that certain Asian cooking techniques, originally preserving methods, may eventually disappear.

The cuisines of Indonesia and Malaysia for example, where many dishes containing highly perishable ingredients are highly spiced and flavored, have been radically effected by the coming of the refrigerator. Some of the spices and flavorings are used not only because of their delicious flavor, but to disguise the taste of spoiled ingredients and to preserve them for longer. The refrigerator and education on food and health, have resulted in the creation of a new cuisine in those countries. The flavor of the actual ingredients has become more important and the use of spices and other flavorings is being reduced so that they enhance those flavors rather than disguise them. This trend was set some decades ago in the large cities of Indonesia and Malaysia. The once so popular pot roasts and the sambal gorengs now have a completely different flavor. Similarly in the urbanised areas of India and in the major cities of Thailand, the Philippines and China great changes can be seen. However, although these changes are apparent, it will be a very long time before the "blessings" of modern technology become universally familiar.

Science has as much to offer both East and West as technology. Many Asian governments have recruited nutrition experts trained in the West, whilst in the West the enormous benefits to health from the use of less fat, more pulses and vegetables, high fiber and a reduction in processing of foodstuffs has been learned from the East. Most of the cooking techniques offered here will be familiar, but sometimes they are applied in a different way and with different ingredients. For example, the Chinese are unlikely to adopt frying in butter, because they have a cultural aversion to dairy products. However there is enormous emphasis on stir frying in low cholesterol groundnut oil, and in the West the use of such oils for flavor and health has become much more widespread. The following guidelines to techniques give many further examples and all in all cooks new to Asian cooking will find little with which they are not already familar.

Cooking

Cooking is making food suitable for consumption. In Asia nearly all foods are made suitable for consumption by heating. Heating alters the structure, consistency, color, form and usually the taste of nearly all foods. Cooking in water modifies the starches in many foods such as rice and flour. They absorb moisture and increase in volume. Animal proteins will coagulate, as is seen with frying, baking and roasting meat and boiling eggs. In meat the protein in the connective tissue is converted into gelatin, which tenderizes the meat. In Indonesia for example pot roasts use the least tender cuts. The making of broth is also a good example of this, as the gelatin and flavoring essences are withdrawn from the meat and taken up in the water.

Many of the fruits and vegetables used in oriental cooking are familiar and available both in Asia and the West.

Fruit and vegetables

In the West most fruits and vegetables are now grown to such uniform standards that they are almost all suitable for consumption without the need for cooking. When fruit and vegetables are cooked the pectin which holds the walls of the plant cells together is dissolved, so that they become soft and digestible. Vegetables are very rarely served raw and even many fruits are cooked in most Asian kitchens because of the quality of the produce. These practical considerations have resulted in unusual combinations of flavors and textures which have given us many of the delicious classic dishes of eastern cuisine.

In the West, marrying high quality ingredients with eastern recipes has modified traditional techniques. We have also taken produce originating in the East and introduced it into our own cuisine. A perfect example of this is Chinese leaves which are now grown in the West and which have been improved by agriculturalists, so that the vegetable can be served raw as a salad. In China where the leaves originate, they are still always cooked, but it is certain that there, too, improvements in the varieties will lead to changes in the cuisine. It is possible that such vegetables will appear as salads and will be replaced by others in cooked dishes.

The improvement in the variety and quality of produce in Asia will mean that in the future, fruit and vegetables will have a very fine texture and be suitable for serving raw or only lightly cooked.

Fats

In the cooking process fats in meat are released. In Asian cooking very little commercial use is made of this because in hot climates where refrigeration is still not widespread, it is recognized that fats go rancid quickly and spoil the meat. Butcher's meat and other foods contain little fat and that which is released during cooking, in making broths, for example is nearly always used for frying and roasting.

Acids

In order to speed the cooking process acids are used in Asia just as they are in the West, to attack the structure of meat and other ingredients so that they become more tender. In the West, wine, vinegar, lemon juice and the juice of other acid fruits is used. In many Asian countries the juice of the tamarind is also used for this purpose. The pulp of the fruit is dried, when needed it is soaked in water to produce an acid juice which is strained. Called asem in Indonesia it gives a unique flavor to the dish.

Sugar

Sugar (cane or palm) is used in some Asian cuisines, e.g. Malaysia, Indonesia and the Philippines, as a sweetener and to speed the cooking process. Sugar effects the structure of many ingredients, attacking the cell walls of tough vegetable substances. It is also used, in Chinese cooking, to tenderize meats, fish and shellfish. If cane or palm sugars are available they should be dissolved in a little boiling water and strained through wet muslin. Soft brown sugar or treacle are suitable substitutes.

Kitchen equipment

Most of the equipment needed for oriental cooking will be part of every cook's general kitchenware. The possible exceptions will be a wok and some steamers and a fondue pan or other means of cooking at the table. The Chinese cook also makes great use of cleavers of various sizes, and a selection of knives is useful for creating garnishes and in Japanese cuisine for the preparation of fish for sashimi. Saucepans including woks, can be made of different materials, such as:
– aluminum
– stainless steel
– sheet steel
– cast iron
Cooking equipment of glass, china and earthenware is also used to a lesser extent.

Woks

A wok is a spherically based pan, usually made of heavy material such as cast iron and used for the stir frying of all ingredients, in a little oil at high temperatures. As will be seen the ingredients are cut into very small pieces for cooking in a wok and the pan is sufficiently deep for liquids to be added and brought to the boil. Many different kinds of woks are now available from the traditional to the electrically heated. Woks which can be used with gas are supplied with a ring to be placed under the wok, thus ensuring that it remains upright, despite its rounded base. Woks which can be used both over a gas ring or an electric hot plate are also available from specialist kitchenware stores. A wok with double handles is known as a wadjan. In general, serving ladles, wooden stirring sticks and ladles used when frying food items in oil are used with a wok.

Cooking by heating in oil or fat

There are several methods of cooking in oil or fat which are used in Asian cooking:
– stir frying
– rendering down
– shallow frying
– frying
– roasting
– deep-frying

Stir Frying

Cooking by heating in oil or fat covers one of the main techniques used in the East – stir frying, for which a wok is required. Stir frying originated in China and is widely used in all other countries where Chinese cooking has had a marked influence.

There are many advantages in preparing food in a wok, as food that is stirred and tossed continuously whilst heating, cooks much faster. The semi-spherical base allows the fat to flow easily in all directions, giving a greater cooking surface than a flat based pan and less oil is used than in conventional

frying. The resultant even, high temperature of the oil quickly seals the ingredients, retaining their juices. The ingredients are added in order, according to their degree of toughness, so that everything can finish cooking at the same time, and is consequently crunchy. The relatively short cooking times are achieved by first cutting the ingredients into very small pieces and ensure that vitamins, minerals and trace elements are retained.

Rendering down

Rendering down butter, for example, to prepare ghee (clarified butter) for Indian, Pakistani and Sri Lankan cooking, is carried out at an extremely low temperature. Once the butter has turned to liquid and the surface foam has disappeared, remove the pan from the heat. Leave the pan to stand for about 10 minutes, then pour off the clarified butter (fat). The residue left at the bottom of the pan is then generally used to toss vegetables etc.

The butter used in Asia is generally not completely pure and therefore it is generally strained through a piece of linen or muslin. This technique is also used in various countries to remove fat from poultry skin. This fat, clarified in exactly the same way as ghee, is only rarely used in cooking food. This type of fat is generally added to dishes to impart a particular flavor.

Shallow frying

The difference between shallow frying and stir frying is that the temperature is generally lower and the ingredients are stirred less intensively. Shallow frying is often used in Asia, mostly for onions, garlic, root ginger and other fresh spices and vegetables used in dishes as flavorings.

Frying

The frying pan is also used in Asia, although this frying technique is not used everywhere, or to the same extent in places where it is used. Certain ingredients are less easy to cook in a wok — fried eggs, or omelettes, for example The Japanese cook omelettes in special rectangular omelette pans. A frying pan is always used for cooking tender large pieces of meat such as slices of beef (steaks), slices of pork (schnitzels), and certain sliced shellfish. Large fish or large pieces of fish are also better cooked in a frying pan. Just as in stir frying, it is generally oil that is used, or ghee in India and Pakistan.

A selection of woks and wadjans (double handled). The wok featured on the far left is an electric model, the others can be used on both gas and electric hobs. Ladles and Skimmers are usually used with the wok.

Roasting

Roasting is a method of cooking used for relatively large pieces of meat, game and poultry. Food can be roasted in a roasting pan either in the oven or on the hob. This method of cooking is known throughout Asia although it is used much less frequently than in the West. In Asia, it is more common for ingredients to be cut into small pieces. It is in fact only on high days and holidays, for special celebrations or family gatherings that large pieces of meat, game or poultry are roasted. Before being roasted, the meat is carefully dried, and is then sealed in the oil or ghee. It may then be roasted in a roasting pan or oven tray at a relatively high temperature, basting regularly, until cooked to the required degree. In Asia, as here, red meat is roasted at a high temperature, whilst meat that has·to be done right through is cooked at a much lower temperature. Some countries also have special forms of roasting – India, for example, where food can be roasted in the tandoor, a small oven.

Deep frying

Frying by immersing an ingredient in hot oil is a very popular method of cooking in Asia. Each country has a number of deep fried specialities – one example is the fritters of China. The temperature of the oil can vary from 325°F/160 °C to 350°F 180°C. It is extremely important not to cook too large a quantity at one time, otherwise the temperature of the oil drops and the oil is absorbed into the food.

Heating food in a liquid

In Asian cuisine, heating a food in a liquid includes:
– simmering
– poaching
– poaching "au bleu"
– steaming
– cooking with a "bain marie "(double boiler)
– blanching
– boiling
– evaporation
– extraction
– pot roasting
– braising

A selection of modern and traditional steamers and steaming baskets.

Steamed bread rolls are sold from carts, in the streets.

Poaching

Poaching is a means of cooking foods which, because of their structure, can easily fall apart through the agitation of the cooking liquid when this is heated to 200°F/100°C. Poaching is really nothing more than the cooking of a food in a liquid kept just below that temperature. Poaching is used for the cooking of fish, eggs and many kinds of fruit. In Asia this technique is used mainly for the cooking of fish, particularly in Japanese cookery. In nearly all the other countries dishes with poached fish are not popular.

Poaching "au bleu"

When acids such as vinegar, wine vinegar or lemon or lime juice are added to the liquid in which the fish is to be poached, the mucous layer on the skin of the fish turns a misty blue. A good example of this in the West is truite au bleu. This technique is also known in Asia. It is used in China and in those countries most influenced by Chinese cuisine. For poaching au bleu the whole fish should be cooked, it must be very fresh, and the skin must be damaged as little as possible when the fish is cooked. It should be carefully drawn through the vinegar and then slipped into the water, which should be bubbling gently.

Steaming

Steaming is a widely used technique in Asia. In Chinese, Vietnamese, Korean and Japanese cooking in particular, steaming plays an extremely important role in the preparation of food, special steaming baskets and steaming pans being used (see illustration). In most Asian countries cooks prefer to finish cooking rice by steaming rather than boiling it until completely cooked. The rice is usually soaked after rinsing, then boiled without salt for 7-8 minutes. It is then transferred to a steamer until it is fully cooked. The boiling is necessary so that the rice can absorb as much liquid as possible. In Japanese cuisine, a short steaming period is used to warm cooked noodles (udon, soba and somen). Many fish dishes are also cooked over steam as are vegetables, potatoes and other tubers. One of the latest forms of steaming in many Asian countries is by means of specially designed, tall pressure cookers, which enable the steaming period to be considerably shortened, taking about a third of the time.

Cooking with a 'bain marie' (double boiler)

This technique is used for cooking dishes which definitely cannot tolerate boiling temperatures. These dishes include sauces thickened with egg yolk. In Asia, this technique is used only rarely, if at all, as they use agar agar or arrowroot in place of egg yolks for thickening; sauces are thickened with a little flour. This technique has been introduced by Westerners. In Japan, however, light sauces containing sesame oil, dashi and egg yolks are cooked in a 'bain marie' (double boiler). Ideally, this technique requires a specially designed saucepan, but it is also possible to get by with a large saucepan in which the water is kept just at boiling point. A second saucepan or bowl containing the ingredients is then placed in the water, taking care not to get any water in the second pan. This technique can also be used in the oven, for example, for the cooking of pâtés or hot custards. In Vietnam fish pâtés and certain kinds of sausage are cooked in this manner.

Simmering

Simmering is the means by which food is cooked in a liquid at a temperature well below 200°F/100°C, the boiling point of water. Simmering is used mainly to cook those foods which have to absorb moisture. These include in the first place many dried fruits, mushrooms and some kinds of dried vegetables. This technique is also used in the West for the cooking of sausages, such as smoked sausage. In Asia simmering is used almost exclusively for cooking dried fish, meat, fruit, beans etc. Dried mushrooms are not simmered but are placed in a bowl with boiling water to cover. They soak for 30 minutes and can then be prepared further. This form of simmering occurs frequently in this book and is reflected in the cooking times, particularly in the chapter on Chinese cooking.

Blanching

Blanching is a technique – it should really be called a preliminary operation – much used in the West to prepare fruit and vegetables for deep freezing. In Asia, where vegetables are rarely served raw, blanching is frequently used. In the West, the ingredient to be blanched is placed in plenty of cold water, which is then brought to the boil. After a few minutes the ingredient is removed from the hot water and generally transferred to a colander and cold water poured over it until the cooking process is brought to a halt. In Asia the vegetable is first drained in a colander after it has been washed. Then a large quantity of boiling water is poured over it, fairly slowly, after which it is drained again. Although the two techniques do not greatly resemble each other, the same goal is achieved: keeping a food white (calve's or lamb's sweetbreads), more or less neutralising the taste (calve's or lamb's kidneys) or rendering particular enzymes inoperable (important where products have to be frozen). You will come across the Asian manner of blanching in many recipes, particularly when bean sprouts are included in a dish. Use of this technique maintains the crispness of the bean sprouts and they retain most of their natural flavor.

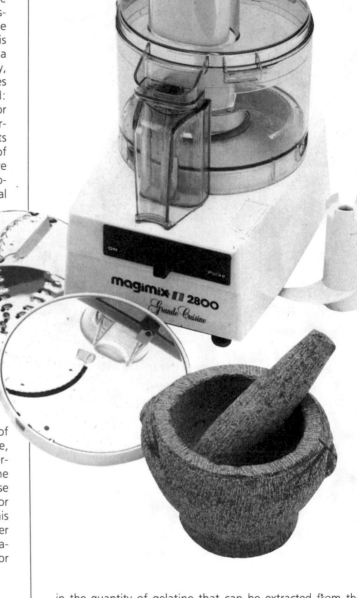

Traditionally, a pestle and mortar is used to grind and purée foods. A food processor is a great time saver however.

Boiling

Boiling is the cooking of food in a liquid at a temperature of 200°F/100°C. In Asia boiling is used for the cooking of rice, pasta, vegetables, potatoes and other tubers, eggs and certain kinds of meat. Fish is rarely boiled. An exception are the soups which contain shellfish as well as white fish, because such soups should always be boiled. The cooking times for Asian dishes are generally much shorter than in the West. This is because the ingredients are cut up into small pieces after being boiled and further prepared in various ways in combination with other ingredients, the whole having to be warmed or heated again.

Evaporation

The method of evaporation, which is used for example, to obtain a concentrated broth, is unknown in Asia. Western chefs have introduced the technique to Japan. In many leading Japanese restaurants concentrated broths or fondues are used for the preparation of sauces. Evaporation can best be carried out in a deep saucepan placed over moderate heat. The saucepan should obviously not be covered.

Extraction

Extraction is the distilling in a liquid of essences and flavorings. In extracting meat the gelatinous constituents also play a part. Extraction may be done in various ways. A boiling liquid is poured over dried ingredients, which are then left to stand for a short time, for example in the infusion of tea. Extraction can also take place in water which has been kept just below boiling point for quite a long time as in the making of broths. In Asia exactly the same method is used, although generally less time is allowed, because the Asian cook is less interested in the quantity of gelatine that can be extracted from the meat. Moreover, in Asian cuisine many of the flavorings such as ginger, lose most of the flavor they have imparted to the broth if they are heated for too long at a particular temperature.

Pot Roasting

Pot roasting is a cooking method which is known in all the Asian countries, but varies in the degree to which it is used. It is seldom found in China, Japan and Korea, but in Malaysia, Indonesia, India and Pakistan it is frequently employed. Curries from India, Pakistan and Sri Lanka and Indonesian and Malaysian pot roasts are particularly popular in Europe. In pot roasting the added flavorings always play an important part. The main ingredient is usually browned very quickly together with the spices and other flavorings in a wok or frying pan. Liquid, such as water, stock or a marinade, is then added, after which the dish is cooked in a closed saucepan very slowly at a low temperature for quite a long time.

Braising

Braising or stewing is very similar to pot roasting. In general, more liquid is used with braising and stewing than with pot roasting and the cooking temperature is somewhat higher and therefore the cooking time is shorter. Both techniques are used on the hob as well as in the oven. With both methods the cook must check occasionally to see whether too much liquid has evaporated. If this has happened, warm liquid (water or stock) must be added while the dish is still cooking.

Cooking with radiant heat

The two ways of cooking food by radiant heat are:
– barbecuing
– broiling (grilling)

Barbecuing

This is the oldest known cooking technique. Food is often still roasted in many parts of Asia, particularly in remote regions, in the same way as it has been for thousands of years. Large pieces of meat, game, poultry and fish are cooked slowly on a spit over a glowing bed of wood, charcoal or other combustible material until they are more or less tender. Barbecuing is the cooking of food making use of the radiation of glowing charcoal from below. Barbecues offer a unique possibility for cooking certain Asian dishes as authentically as possible and this is indicated in the individual recipes. More conventional roasting in an oven where the heat is circulated around the dish is known in the cities and towns in Asia.

Broiling (Grilling)

Broiling (Grilling)is the roasting of food, without the use of much fat and/or oil, until it is brown and tender. Broiling (grilling) is very suitable for the cooking of small pieces of tender meat, game, poultry and fish. The fierce radiant heat quickly sears the pores of the meat, thus sealing in the flavor and the juices. Food to be grilled is usually basted once with oil before broiling (grilling) and again a couple of times during cooking. Food should not be salted as salt draws out the juices, so that the meat cannot seal quickly and brown more slowly.

Preparatory operations

In Asian cuisine, the preparation of ingredients often takes much longer than the cooking. Usually it involves nothing more complicated than the cutting up of ingredients into very small pieces and the conventional, peeling, washing, seeding etc of vegetables and fruits. However, Asian cooking in a western kitchen may involve other processes if the ingredients are to be made ready for the Asian cooking techniques.

Thawing

Before frozen meat and game are cooked, they must be thawed until they are soft and supple but they should not be allowed to thaw completely. If meat is completely thawed, too much moisture will be released and it will become dry and will not brown. Very small pieces of meat, such as steak and chops, should be fully thawed beforehand, because the frying time is too short for the meat to thaw out during cooking. It is best to allow meat to thaw in the refrigerator. Poultry should be thawed if large pieces are being cooked. It is not necessary to thaw fish completely as long as care is taken that the fish is not too thick to cook through in the cooking time suggested.

Marinating

The purpose of marinating is to soften the fibrous tissue by means of acids. The technique is used mainly with less tender cuts of meat. Marinades are acidic liquids to which spices are often added. In most Asian cuisines use is made of soy sauces in marinating. Meat must be coated on all sides with a layer of marinade. The time allowed for the meat to remain in the marinade depends very much on the structure of the meat and the personal taste of the cook. It should be remembered that marinading affects the natural flavor of the ingredient. Poultry and fish are usually marinaded in a mixture of soy sauce and lemon or tamarind juice.

Cutting

In all Asian cuisines the meat, game, poultry, fish and vegetables are normally cut into the desired shapes before cooking. These are usually cubes or strips. This will always be indicated in the recipes.

Chicken and poultry are rarely cooked whole as in the West but are cut into small pieces. Fish can be served whole but is generally cut up after being filletted and cleaned thoroughly. If this is done by the fishmonger, it is useful to ask to keep the trimmings to make the bouillon (stock) needed for many fish recipes.

Grinding (Mincing)

Meat and game can be finely ground or minced. Ground (minced) meat, poultry and fish are also used in Asia in large quantities in all kinds of stuffed dishes or as a filling. A food processor is a very important addition to the cook's kitchen in preparing many of the ingredients, which were traditionally pounded in a pestle and mortar and indeed for the grinding of nuts and vegetables for purées and pastes.

Larding

Wrapping meat or poultry and game with rashers of bacon to prevent drying out is done in China and Korea, where it has been learned from the West, but its use is not widespread and is done mainly with lean meat which would otherwise dry out. It is more usual to baste the meat with oil or fat.

Incision

Making an incision in meat, poultry or fish is done in order to insert herbs and/or garlic cloves into the incision or to allow the speedy absorbtion of marinades or spice pastes. Incisions are always made into the rim of fat on thin slices of meat in order to stop them curling up during frying or grilling.

Stuffing

By stuffing is meant the filling of meat with a mixture of, for example, finely ground (minced) meat with herbs etc. This is much less common in Asian cooking although it does occur with fish.

Coating

The Western method of coating is also known in Asia, although Asian cooks do not always use bread crumbs or coating meal. They often use finely ground roasted rice or besan (flour of roasted chick-peas). They also have a method of preparation by which the ingredient is dipped in a simple batter of water and flour and/or egg before being fried in hot oil.

Salting

In most Asian cuisines salt is rubbed into poultry before cooking. Generally less salt is used than in the West. This is because, besides salt, use is made of flavorings, such as soy sauce, which contain salt.

Garnishing

In a Taste of the Orient you will find many references to garnishing with flowers, fans etc. Instructions for these are usually given in the relevant chapters but on the following pages we offer brief instructions on the attractive garnishes used in Japanese and other cuisines. In countries such as the Philippines, Malaysia, Burma and Thailand quite simple garnishings are used. They nevertheless radiate a refinement which lends the dish a particular attraction. In those countries, in contrast to Japan, it is a question of small touches such as a red pepper flower, a tomato flower or a radish flower.

A special knife is need to give carrots an interesting shape.

If you cannot obtain a cutter, pinking shears cut the skin of a citrus fruit into a toothed shape.

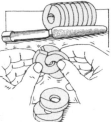

Making interlocking cucumber rings.

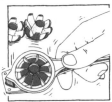

You need a special cutter to make radish flowers.

Radish chrysanthemums, can be made with a sharp knife.
To ensure that you do not cut too deeply into the radish, place it between two matchsticks.

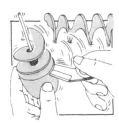

Using a special knife to make a cucumber spiral.

This is how to incise a leek to obtain a decorative plume.

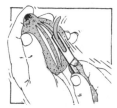

To improve the appearance of slices of lemon, first remove strips from the peel.

Then cut the lemon into thin slices.

Gherkin fans can be made by first cutting the gherkin lengthwise into thin slices, which are then carefully fanned out.

Mushrooms look more attractive with cross-like incisions or grooves in the caps.

Cut a slice of lotus root into an attractive shape.

Make a cucumber fan by first cutting the cucumber into slices which remain attached on the underside. A stick is used for this purpose.

Then use the flat side of the knife to flatten the slices of cucumber.

CHINA

Ching choong chow fan
Fried Rice with Scallions (Spring Onions)

	00.02 Serves 4	00.05

American	Ingredients	Metric/Imperial
3 cups	cold, dry cooked rice	350 g/12 oz
2 tbsp	groundnut oil	2 tbsp
2 tbsp	Chinese soy sauce, light or dark, as preferred	2 tbsp
6-8	coarsely chopped scallions (spring onions)	6-8

1. Heat the oil in a wok and add the rice.
2. Stir fry the rice until it begins to color.
3. Sprinkle the soy sauce over the rice and add the scallions (spring onions) and stir fry for another minute.
4. Serve immediately.

Cook's tip: Fried rice with scallions (spring onions) can be served with almost all Chinese dishes. By adding different ingredients the character of the dish can be changed and it can be served as a main course. Other ingredients can be added, such as coarsely chopped cooked ham, freshly peeled shrimp (prawn), cooked crab or lobster cut into pieces, lightly beaten eggs, chopped cooked beans and cooked peas. Serve with an omelette or scrambled egg or stir in cubes of soybean curd (tofu) fried in oil.

Chai chow fan I
Fried Rice with Vegetables (I)

	00.15 plus soaking time	00.05

American	Ingredients	Metric/Imperial
6	dried Chinese mushrooms	6
2 cups	bean sprouts	125 g/4 oz
2 tbsp	groundnut oil	2 tbsp
1 tbsp	sesame oil	1 tbsp
1-2	finely chopped garlic cloves	1-2
1 tsp	grated fresh root ginger	1 tsp
2	medium size leeks	2
8	coarsely chopped scallions (spring onions)	8
2-3	sticks celery, cut into thin strips	2-3
¼ lb	canned bamboo shoots cut into thin strips	125 g/4 oz
3 cups	cold, dry cooked rice	350 g/12 oz
2 tbsp	Chinese light soy sauce	2 tbsp

1. Place the mushrooms in a bowl and pour 1 cup (250 ml/8 fl oz) boiling water over them. Leave to stand for 30 minutes.
2. Wash the bean sprouts in cold running water. Remove as many skins as possible. Drain the bamboo shoots for 10 minutes.
3. Drain the soaked mushrooms. Strain and reserve the soaking liquid. Remove the stalks and cut the caps into thin strips or cubes.

4. Heat both oils in a wok. Stir fry the garlic and grated root ginger over low heat for 30 seconds.
5. Increase the heat. Add ¾ of the leeks or scallions (spring onions) and the celery. Stir fry for 1 minute then add the bean sprouts and bamboo shoots. Stir fry for 1 minute then add the rice.
6. Stir in the soy sauce and add 3-4 tbsp of the strained mushroom liquid to the mixture.
7. Stir well and stir fry until the rice is hot. Transfer to a warmed serving dish.
8. Sprinkle the reserved leek or scallion (spring onion) over the rice and serve immediately.

Chai chow fan II
Fried Rice with Vegetables (II)

	00.15 Serves 4	00.08

American	Ingredients	Metric/Imperial
6	large fresh mushrooms	6
½ lb	haricots verts or very thin string beans	250 g/8 oz
2 cups	bean sprouts	125 g/4 oz
¼ lb	Chinese leaves, iceberg lettuce or paksoi	125 g/4 oz
2 tbsp	groundnut oil	2 tbsp
1 tbsp	sesame oil	1 tbsp
2	finely chopped garlic cloves	2
1 tsp	grated fresh root ginger	1 tsp
1	medium size leek cut into thin strips	1
3 cups	cold, dry cooked rice	350 g/12 oz
4 tbsp	cooked peas	4 tbsp
2 tbsp	Chinese light soy sauce	2 tbsp
2-3	coarsely chopped scallions (spring onions)	2-3

1. Wipe the mushrooms clean with a moist cloth. Trim the stalks. Cut the mushrooms into thin slices and then into thin strips.
2. Trim the beans, string them if necessary and cut them into pieces 1-1½in (2-3 cm) long.
3. Wash the bean sprouts in cold water. Remove as many skins as possible. Drain well.
4. Cut the washed Chinese leaves, iceberg lettuce or paksoi into very thin strips.
5. Heat both the oils in a wok. Add the garlic and root ginger and stir fry over low heat for 30 seconds.
6. Add the mushrooms, leeks and beans, increase the heat and stir fry for 2 minutes.
7. Add the Chinese leaves or iceberg lettuce, bean sprouts rice and peas. Stir fry until the rice is hot.
8. Sprinkle the soy sauce and 3-4 tbsp hot water or vegetable bouillon (stock) over the rice mixture. Stir well then transfer to a warmed dish.
9. Sprinkle chopped scallions (spring onions) over the top and serve.

Hung shiu yue har guen

Fish Rolls with Shrimp (Prawns)

■━━━▷ 00.10
Serves 4

00.10 🍲

American	Ingredients	Metric/Imperial
12	large shrimp (prawns) thawed if frozen	12
6 (1½ lb)	small fish fillets eg cod, haddock, plaice	6 (700 g/1½ lb)
2 tbsp	groundnut oil	2 tbsp
2	slices fresh root ginger	2
1 tbsp	Chinese light soy sauce	1 tbsp
2 tbsp	Chinese rice wine or dry sherry	2 tbsp
1½ tsp	cornstarch (cornflour)	1½ tsp
3	scallions (spring onions) or small pieces of chopped leek	3

1. Peel the shrimp (prawns).
2. Cut the fish fillets in half, lengthwise.
3. Place a shrimp (prawn) on each slice of fish. Roll up the slices of fish and secure them with wooden cocktail picks.
4. Heat the oil in a wok and stir fry the slices of ginger over low heat for 30 seconds.
5. Add the fish rolls and stir fry for 2 minutes.
6. Add ½ cup (100 ml/4 fl oz) hot water or fish bouillon (stock) if available.
7. Add soy sauce and rice wine or sherry.
8. Leave the ingredients to cook gently for 3 minutes.
9. Mix the cornstarch (cornflour) with 1 tbsp cold water.
10. Push the fish rolls to one side of the wok, remove the slices of ginger and stir the cornstarch (cornflour) mixture into the liquid in the wok. Stir well and bring to the boil. Simmer until the sauce has thickened.
11. Push the fish rolls into the sauce and stir the contents of the wok once more.
12. Transfer the rolls to a warmed dish.
13. Remove the cocktail picks and pour over the sauce.
14. Sprinkle the dish with chopped scallion (spring onion) or leek.

Ho Nan jum choa yue

Fish on a Bed of Vegetables (Hunan)

■━━━▷ 00.15
Serves 4

00.12 🍲

American	Ingredients	Metric/Imperial
1½ lb	filleted white fish (sole, haddock, plaice)	700 g/1½ lb
	salt	
¾ lb	washed Chinese leaves or iceberg lettuce or paksoi	350 g/12 oz
8	young, peeled carrots	8
2	sticks of celery	2
2 tbsp	groundnut oil	2 tbsp
2	peeled garlic cloves	2
2	slices fresh root ginger	2
1 tbsp	sesame oil	1 tbsp
2 tbsp	Chinese light soy sauce	2 tbsp
4	coarsely chopped scallions (spring onions)	4

1. Cut the fish into 8 equal pieces, rinse under cold running water and place them in a saucepan.
2. Pour in enough cold water to just cover the fish, salt lightly and bring slowly to near boiling point. Cook the fish gently for 7 minutes.
3. Remove the fish pieces from the saucepan, drain very briefly on kitchen paper and keep warm.
4. Cut the Chinese leaves, lettuce or paksoi into very thin strips.
5. Cut the carrots and celery sticks into very thin strips.
6. Spread the Chinese leaves, iceberg lettuce or paksoi over a large, shallow, warmed dish, top with the carrot and celery strips.
7. Heat the groundnut oil in a wok. Add the garlic and root ginger and stir fry over low heat for 2 minutes. Remove from the pan.
8. Remove the wok from the heat and add the sesame oil and soy sauce to the groundnut oil.
9. Place the warm fish pieces on the bed of vegetables. Stir the contents of the wok a few times and then pour over the fish.
10. Sprinkle the chopped scallion (spring onion) over the top and serve immediately with dry cooked or steamed rice.

Cook's tip: fish on a bed of vegetables can have many variations. The bed of vegetables should always be made up of one main variety and two others. The variety first mentioned in these examples is always the main one: Strips of iceberg lettuce, carrot and cucumber. Strips of iceberg lettuce, carrot and leek. Strips of Chinese leaves, cucumber, and red bell pepper. Strips of Chinese leaves, leek and sweetcorn.

Peeling Shrimp (prawns)

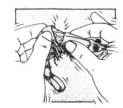

1. With one hand, hold the shrimp (prawn) just behind the head. Pull off the head with the other hand.

2. Using kitchen scissors, cut off the tail and the legs.

3. Peel off the snell, opening it from the underside of the shrimp (prawn).

Gwoo lo yue lau

Fish in Batter with Sweet and Sour Sauce

00.15 Serves 4   **00.30**

American	Ingredients	Metric/Imperial
1½ lb	filleted sea fish (turbot, brill, cod or catfish).	700 g/1 ½ lb
½ tsp	salt	½ tsp
½ tsp	five spice powder	½ tsp
2	lightly beaten eggs	2
6 tbsp	cornstarch (cornflour)	6 tbsp
6-8 tbsp	groundnut oil	6-8 tbsp
3	young carrots	3
2	small onions	2
½	cucumber or piece of unripe melon or pumpkin	½
2 tbsp	Chinese light soy sauce	2 tbsp
4 tbsp	Chinese tomato sauce	4 tbsp
2 tbsp	Chinese rice wine or dry sherry	2 tbsp
1 tbsp	vinegar	1 tbsp
1 tbsp	cornstarch (cornflour)	1 tbsp
1	crushed garlic clove	1
½ tsp	grated root ginger	½ tsp
4 tbsp	boiled peas	4 tbsp
1-2 tsp	sugar	1-2 tsp
2-3	scallions (spring onions) or a leek	2-3

1. Rinse the fish under cold running water. Dry with kitchen paper and cut the fish into pieces of about 1½×2 in (3×5 cm).
2. Mix the salt and five spice powder. Rub into the fish.
3. Dip the fish in the lightly beaten egg and roll in cornstarch (cornflour). Make sure that the pieces of fish are fully coated with cornstarch (cornflour).
4. Heat the oil in a wok and fry the fish 6-7 pieces at a time until golden. Remove the fish pieces. Leave to drain, and cool on kitchen paper.
5. Immediately before serving, fry the pieces once more in the hot oil until golden brown, giving a crisp batter.
6. Cut the carrots into julienne strips.
7. Cut each onion into 8 segments, separate each segment.
8. Peel the cucumber, melon or pumpkin. Remove the seeds and cut the flesh into small chunks.
9. Prepare the sauce by mixing the soy sauce with the tomato sauce, the rice wine or sherry and vinegar. Bring to the boil in a small saucepan stirring constantly. Add ¾ cup (200 ml/7 fl oz) water and simmer gently for 2 minutes.
10. Mix the cornstarch (cornflour) with 2-3 tbsp cold water. Stir into the sauce, cooking until the sauce thickens.
11. Add the garlic and ginger. Stir well and add the strips of carrot and pieces of onion. Simmer gently for 2 minutes.
12. Immediately before serving, stir the cucumber, melon or pumpkin and cooked peas into the sauce. Sample and add 1-2 tsp of sugar to taste.
13. Place the fish in a warmed dish. Pour over the sauce, sprinkle with scallions (spring onions) or leek and serve.

Sichuan chow har kau

Fried Shrimp (Prawns) Szechwan

00.15 plus standing time   **00.10**

American	Ingredients	Metric/Imperial
16-20	large shrimp (prawns) thawed if frozen	16-20
2 tsp	cornstarch (cornflour)	2 tsp
1	lightly beaten egg white	1
	pinch salt	
	pinch freshly ground black pepper	
2	peeled garlic cloves	2
1 tbsp	Chinese light soy sauce	1 tbsp
1 tbsp	Chinese rice wine or dry sherry	1 tbsp
1 tbsp	honey	1 tbsp
½ tbsp	vinegar	½ tbsp
3 tbsp	groundnut oil	3 tbsp
8	seeded dried chilies	8
2	chopped scallions (spring onions)	2
1 tsp	grated root ginger	1 tsp

1. Remove the shrimp (prawn) tails. Rinse under cold running water. Drain and dry with kitchen paper.
2. Mix the cornstarch (cornflour) with 1 tbsp cold water. Beat in the egg white and a little salt and continue beating until the mixture is smooth.
3. Place the shrimp (prawns) in a dish. Pour over the cornstarch (cornflour) and egg white mixture and turn the shrimp (prawns) in the mixture. Leave to stand for about 30 minutes, turning the shrimp (prawns) occasionally.
4. Add the soy sauce, Chinese rice wine or sherry, honey, vinegar, pepper and a little salt to the fish.
5. Heat the oil in a wok and stir fry the garlic until golden brown. Remove the garlic from the pan.
6. Fry the dried chilies golden brown. Remove from the oil with a slotted spoon, and set aside.
7. Remove the shrimp (prawns) from the egg white mixture and drain.
8. Fry the shrimp (prawns) for one minute in the remaining oil.
9. Add the scallions (spring onions) and grated root ginger. Stir fry for 30 seconds then slide the shrimp (prawns) to one side of the wok.
10. Stir the cornstarch (cornflour) mixture into the contents of the wok. Cook until the sauce thickens.
11. Draw the shrimp (prawns) through the sauce and immediately transfer the entire contents of the wok to a warmed platter.
12. Sprinkle with the fried chilies and serve immediately.

Cook's tip: Szechwan cooking is known for its very highly spiced dishes. It can be an acquired taste and may seem to overwhelm the delicate flavor of fish dishes in particular. When serving a dish for the first time, it may be a good idea to halve the specified quantities of soy sauce.

Ching yu chow loon joo

Fried Lobster in a Piquant Sauce

00.10 00.12

Serves 4

American	Ingredients	Metric/Imperial
1 ½ lb	*peeled lobster or crayfish tails, thawed if frozen*	*700 g/1 ½ lb*
1	*red bell pepper*	*1*
1	*green bell pepper*	*1*
3 tbsp	*groundnut oil*	*3 tbsp*
2	*crushed garlic cloves*	*2*
½ tsp	*grated fresh root ginger*	*½ tsp*
2 tbsp	*yellow bean sauce*	*2 tbsp*
⅔ cup	*chicken or fish bouillon (stock)*	*150 ml/¼ pint*
2 tbsp	*Chinese rice wine or dry sherry*	*2 tbsp*
1	*lightly beaten egg*	*1*
2 tbsp	*cornstarch (cornflour)*	*2 tbsp*
	few drops sesame oil	

1. Cut the lobster or crayfish tails into pieces.
2. Wash the peppers, remove the stalk ends. Halve and remove the pith and the seeds. Cut the flesh into squares.
3. Heat the oil in a wok and stir fry the lobster or crayfish pieces for 1 minute. Remove with a skimmer and drain over the wok for a few seconds. Keep warm.
4. Stir fry the bell pepper pieces for 1 minute. Remove with a skimmer. Drain and keep warm.
5. Add the garlic and ginger to the remaining oil and fry for a few seconds.
6. Add the yellow bean sauce, bouillon (stock) and rice wine or sherry, stirring constantly. Bring to the boil.
7. Add the lightly beaten egg very slowly, stirring constantly, so that it forms threads in the sauce.
8. Mix the cornstarch (cornflour) with 2 tbsp cold water and add to the sauce. Cook, stirring until it thickens.
9. Add the lobster or crayfish and bell pepper and stir in a few drops of sesame oil. Cook gently for 2-3 minutes.
10. Transfer to a warmed platter and serve immediately.

Hu lan du chow tsi tsei

Shellfish with Snow Peas (Mange-tout)

00.15 00.10

Serves 4

American	Ingredients	Metric/Imperial
1 lb	*shelled scallops or large mussels*	*450 g/1 lb*
¾ lb	*snow peas (mange-tout)*	*350 g/12 oz*
3 tbsp	*groundnut oil*	*3 tbsp*
½ tsp	*grated fresh root ginger*	*½ tsp*
2	*medium size leeks white and light green parts cut into narrow strips*	*2*
2 tsp	*cornstarch (cornflour)*	*2 tsp*
2 tsp	*Chinese light soy sauce*	*2 tsp*
	pinch salt	
2	*chopped scallions (spring onions) (optional)*	*2*

1. Rinse the shellfish and dry with kitchen paper.
2. Trim the snow peas (mange-tout).
3. Heat the oil in a wok and stir fry the shellfish for 1 minute. Remove them with a skimmer, drain over the wok and keep warm.
4. Fry the root ginger in the remaining oil for 30 seconds. Add the strips of leek and the snow peas (mange-tout) and stir well.
5. Push everything to one side of the wok and add 1 cup (250 ml/8 fl oz) water.
6. Mix the cornstarch (cornflour) with 2 tbsp cold water and stir into the liquid in the wok. Cook, stirring until the sauce thickens.
7. Stir in the soy sauce and add a little salt to taste. Stir the snow peas (mange-tout) and shellfish into the sauce. Bring to the boil, then remove the wok from the heat.
8. Divide the contents of the wok between four warmed plates. Sprinkle with some chopped scallion (spring onion) and serve immediately.

Shellfish with snow peas (mange-tout)

The Szechwan method of frying fish is particularly suitable for small mackerel or whiting. In China, fish are generally left with the head and tail intact. To be really authentic, dishes should be prepared in this way. If preferred, however, the head and tail can be removed, it makes no difference to the flavor or aroma of the dish.

Sichuan yaujar yue

Fried Fish Szechwan style

	00.20	00.20	
	plus standing time		

American	Ingredients	Metric/Imperial
4	small fresh mackerel or whiting	4
4 tbsp	Chinese rice wine or dry sherry	4 tbsp
2 tbsp	Chinese light soy sauce	2 tbsp
2 tsp	cornstarch (cornflour)	2 tsp
2 tbsp	Chinese dark soy sauce	2 tbsp
6 tbsp	groundnut oil	6 tbsp
1 tbsp	finely grated root ginger	1 tbsp
1 tbsp	crushed garlic about 4 cloves	1 tbsp
2 tbsp	Chinese bean sauce	2 tbsp
3	scallions (spring onions) or piece of chopped leek	3

1. Rinse the fish under cold running water. Dry with kitchen paper. Using a sharp knife, make 3 or 4 incisions in the fish on either side.

2. Mix 2 tbsp Chinese rice wine or sherry with 2 tbsp Chinese light soy sauce. Rub the mixture over the outside of the fish then leave the fish to stand for about 10 minutes.

3. Mix the cornstarch (cornflour) with 1 tbsp cold water, and add the dark soy sauce and the remaining rice wine or sherry. Stir well.

4. Heat the oil in a large wok and fry the fish for about 4 minutes each side turning carefully, until golden brown.

5. Remove the fish from the pan. Drain well and keep hot.

6. Remove all but 2 tbsp of oil from the wok. Add the ginger and garlic and fry for 30 seconds. Add the bean sauce and 1¼ cups (300 ml/½ pint) hot water. Stir well.

7. Stir the cornstarch (cornflour) mixture into the liquid in the wok until the sauce thickens. Simmer and cook for 1 minute.

8. Return the fish to the wok and simmer gently in the sauce for 2-3 minutes.

9. Transfer the fish and sauce to a warmed platter, sprinkle with a little chopped scallion (spring onion) or leek and serve immediately.

Left: Fried fish Szechwan style
Right: Fried fish with Hoisin sauce

Hoi seen jeung boon yue lau

Fried Fish with Hoisin Sauce

00.05 Serves 4		00.12
American	**Ingredients**	**Metric/Imperial**
4	small mackerel fillets or filleted whiting	4
3 tbsp	groundnut oil	3 tbsp
4	peeled garlic cloves	4
1 tbsp	Chinese light soy sauce	1 tbsp
½ tsp	finely grated fresh root ginger	½ tsp
1 tsp	hoisin sauce	1 tsp
2-3	scallions (spring onions)	2-3

1. Rinse the fish fillets under cold running water. Dry with kitchen paper.

2. Heat the oil in a wok, add the garlic and fry until golden brown, turning frequently. Remove from the oil.

3. Fry the fish fillets for 2-3 minutes each side.

4. Slide the fish fillets to one side of the wok and add the soy sauce and the root ginger.

5. Slide the fish fillets back to the middle of the wok. Cover with a closely fitting lid and cook for 1-2 minutes over moderate heat.

6. Transfer to warmed plates. Stir the hoisin sauce into the mixture in the wok and spoon over the fish.

7. Sprinkle with chopped scallion (spring onion) and serve.

Ching chow ho yau har yan

Fried Shrimp (Prawns) with Oyster Sauce

00.10 Serves 4		00.00
American	**Ingredients**	**Metric/Imperial**
16-20	large shrimp (prawns) thawed if frozen	16-20
2 tbsp	groundnut oil	2 tbsp
2	peeled garlic cloves	2
2	slices fresh root ginger	2
1 tbsp	oyster sauce	1 tbsp
2 tbsp	Chinese rice wine or dry sherry	2 tbsp
1½ tsp	cornstarch (cornflour)	1½ tsp

1. Remove the tails from the shrimp (prawns). Dry tails with kitchen paper.

2. Heat the oil in a wok and stir fry the garlic and root ginger until golden brown.

3. Remove the garlic and ginger from the wok, add the shrimp (prawns) and stir fry until they change color.

4. Add the oyster sauce, rice wine or sherry, and ¾ cup (200 ml/7 floz) boiling water. Cook gently for 1 minute.

5. Mix the cornstarch (cornflour) with 1½ tbsp cold water. Slide the shrimp (prawns) to one side of the wok and pour in the cornstarch (cornflour) mixture. Stir well and cook until the sauce thickens.

6. Draw the shrimp (prawns) through the sauce and serve.

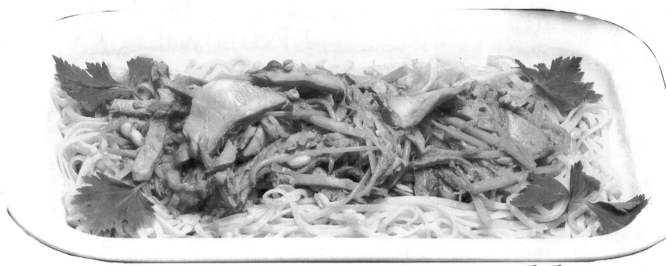

Yee wui chow meen

Chow Mein

| 00.30 plus drying time | 00.08 |

American	Ingredients	Metric/Imperial
4-6	nests of egg noodles	4-6
4-6 tbsp	groundnut oil	4-6 tbsp
1	finely chopped garlic clove	1
½ tsp	finely grated root ginger	½ tsp
½ lb	roasted streaky pork cut into thin strips	225 g/8 oz
½ lb	poached chicken breasts cut into thin strips	225 g/8 oz
3-4	canned, sliced abalones (Chinese shellfish)	3-4
½ lb	Chinese leaves or white cabbage, shredded very thin	225 g/8 oz
2 cups	washed, well drained bean sprouts	125 g/4 oz
8	scallions (spring onions) cut into pieces 1½-2 in (4-5 cm) long	8
1	can bamboo shoots cut into narrow strips	1
⅔ cup	bouillon (stock) (or water)	150 ml/¼ pint
2 tbsp	Chinese light soy sauce	2 tbsp
2 tsp	cornstarch (cornflour)	2 tsp

1. Cook the noodles as directed on the packet. Drain and leave for 15 minutes to dry.
2. Heat 2-3 tbsp of oil in a large wok. Stir fry the noodles over moderate heat until golden brown. Keep warm.
3. Heat a further 2-3 tbsp of oil in the wok and stir fry the garlic and root ginger for 10 seconds.
4. Add the pork, chicken, abalones, Chinese leaves or white cabbage, bean sprouts, scallions (spring onions) and bamboo shoots. Stir fry for 2 minutes.
5. Push all the ingredients to one side of the wok. Pour the bouillon (stock) (or water) and the soy sauce into the wok and bring to the boil.
6. Mix the cornstarch (cornflour) with 2 tbsp cold water. Stir into the wok and cook, stirring until the sauce thickens.
7. Stir all of the ingredients into the sauce.
8. Spoon the noodles on to a large warmed dish and spread the meat and vegetable mixture over the top and serve.

Nyu juk du kow chow mee fun

Rice Vermicelli with Beef and Beans

| 00.15 Serves 4 | 00.15 |

American	Ingredients	Metric/Imperial
½ lb	rice vermicelli	225 g/8 oz
¾ lb	lean beef eg silverside or entrecote	350 g/12 oz
¾ lb	haricots verts or thin French beans	350 g/12 oz
2 tbsp	groundnut oil	2 tbsp
1 tbsp	sesame oil	1 tbsp
1	finely chopped garlic clove	1
½ tsp	freshly grated root ginger	½ tsp
⅔ cup	beef bouillon (stock)	150 ml/¼ pint
	generous pinch salt	
2 tbsp	Chinese light soy sauce	2 tbsp

1. Cook the rice vermicelli as directed on the packet. Drain well. Cut into 2-3 in (5-7 cm) lengths.
2. Cut the meat into strips.
3. Trim the beans and cut into 2 in (5 cm) pieces.
4. Heat both the oils in a wok and stir fry the beans for 2 minutes. Remove them from the wok with a skimmer, leave to drain over the wok for a moment and then keep warm.
5. Fry the garlic and root ginger in the remaining oil for 30 seconds.
6. Add the strips of meat and stir fry until the meat has changed color. Push the meat to one side of the wok.
7. Add the bouillon (stock), salt and soy sauce. Stir well. Stir in the rice vermicelli and cook very gently for 1-2 minutes.
8. Stir in the meat and the beans and continue cooking until very hot. Serve immediately.

Mei du fu

Soybean Curd (Tofu) with Ground (Minced) Meat

◣▱	00.10 Serves 4	00.15 ⌷

American	Ingredients	Metric/Imperial
2 (3 in)	cubes of soybean curd (tofu)	2 (7.5 cm/3 in)
3 tbsp	groundnut oil	3 tbsp
1 tbsp	black bean sauce	1 tbsp
2	chopped scallions (spring onions)	2
1	very finely chopped garlic clove	1
6 oz	lean ground (minced) beef	175 g/6 oz
1 tbsp	Chinese light soy sauce	1 tbsp
⅔ cup	beef bouillon (stock)	150 ml/¼ pint

1. Cut the soybean curd (tofu) into 1 in (1.25 cm) cubes.
2. Heat the oil in a wok and add the black bean sauce, scallions (spring onions), garlic and ground (minced) beef. Stir fry until the meat changes color and crumbles.
3. Add the soy sauce, bouillon (stock) and cubes of soybean curd (tofu). Stir carefully. Simmer very gently for 10 minutes.
4. Serve on a warmed shallow dish.

Chu hwa jiong mun du fu

Soybean Curd (Tofu) and Savory Sauce

◣▱	00.05 Serves 4	00.08 ⌷

American	Ingredients	Metric/Imperial
2 (3 in)	cubes of soybean curd (tofu)	2 (7.5 cm/3 in)
2 tbsp	groundnut oil	2 tbsp
1 tbsp	Chinese light soy sauce	1 tbsp
1 tsp	Chinese tomato sauce	1 tsp
1 tsp	oyster sauce	1 tsp
¾ cup	bouillon (stock), liquid from vegetables or water	200 ml/7 fl oz
¾ cup	cooked peas fresh or frozen	125 g/4 oz
4	coarsely chopped scallions (spring onions)	4

1. Cut the soybean curd (tofu) into ½ in (1.25 cm) cubes.
2. Heat the oil in a wok and stir fry the soybean curd (tofu) cubes very lightly on all sides.
3. Mix together the soy sauce, tomato sauce, oyster sauce and bouillon (stock) and pour the mixture into the wok. Boil very gently for 3 minutes.
4. Stir in the peas and half the chopped scallion (spring onion).
5. Leave to come briefly to the boil, then serve on four warmed plates. Sprinkle the remainder of the chopped scallion (spring onion) on top.

Hwa juk du fu

Soybean Curd (Tofu) with Crab Sauce

◣▱	00.10 Serves 4	00.10 ⌷

American	Ingredients	Metric/Imperial
2 (3 in)	cubes of soybean curd (tofu)	2 (7.5 cm/3 in)
6 oz	crabmeat, thawed if frozen	175 g/6 oz
2 tbsp	groundnut oil	2 tbsp
6	coarsely chopped scallions (spring onions) or a medium size leek	6
½ tsp	grated fresh root ginger	½ tsp
1 tsp	Chinese tomato sauce	1 tsp
1 cup	chicken or fish bouillon (stock)	250 ml/8 fl oz
	ground black pepper	
	salt	
1 tsp	Chinese light soy sauce	1 tsp
2 tsp	cornstarch (cornflour)	2 tsp

1. Cut the soybean curd (tofu) into ½ in (1.25 cm) cubes.
2. Pick over the crabmeat and cut into small pieces.
3. Heat the oil in a wok and stir fry the scallions (spring onions) or leek and root ginger for 30 seconds.
4. Mix the tomato sauce with the bouillon (stock), add a little pepper and salt to taste and the Chinese light soy sauce.
5. Pour the bouillon (stock) into the wok, stir well and leave to boil gently for 3 minutes.
6. Add the crab and stir until the liquid comes to the boil again.
7. Mix the cornstarch (cornflour) with 2 tbsp cold water and stir into the contents of the wok. Cook until the sauce thickens.
8. Add the cubes of soybean curd (tofu) and stir gently a few times to make sure that the cubes are coated with the sauce.
9. Serve on warmed plates with dry boiled or steamed rice.

Soybean curd (tofu) and savory sauce

Chia du fu
Soybean Curd (Tofu) with Pork

▬▭ 00.20 Serves 4   00.12 🍲

American	Ingredients	Metric/Imperial
2 (3 in)	cubes of soybean curd (tofu)	2 (7.5 cm/3 in)
6 oz	lean pork	175 g/6 oz
½ cup	canned, drained bamboo shoots	75 g/3 oz
4-6 tbsp	groundnut oil	4-6 tbsp
1	seeded finely chopped red chili	1
2	coarsely chopped scallions (spring onions)	2
2 tbsp	Chinese light soy sauce	2 tbsp
1 tsp	sugar	1 tsp
1 tbsp	Chinese rice wine or dry sherry	1 tbsp
⅔ cup	chicken bouillon (stock)	150 ml/¼ pint
½ cup	fresh peeled shrimp (prawns)	75 g/3 oz

1. Cut the soybean curd (tofu) into 1 in (2.5 cm) rectangles.
2. Slice the pork very thinly against the grain.
3. Cut the bamboo shoots into thin slices about the same size as the slices of meat.
4. Heat 4-6 tbsp of oil in a wok fry the slices of soybean curd (tofu) golden brown. Remove from the wok and drain on kitchen paper.
5. Add enough oil to the oil remaining in the wok to bring the total quantity to about 3 tbsp. Heat the oil and stir fry the meat, bamboo shoots, strips of red chili and scallions (spring onions) for 3 minutes.
6. Add the soy sauce, sugar, rice wine or sherry and bouillon (stock). Stir and add the fried soybean curd (tofu).
7. Leave ingredients to warm through then transfer the whole contents of the wok to a warmed, shallow dish and sprinkle the shrimp (prawns) on top.

Sie kwee du fu
Soybean Curd (Tofu) with Cucumber

▬▭ 00.15 Serves 4   00.05 🍲

American	Ingredients	Metric/Imperial
2 (3 in)	cubes of soybean curd (tofu)	2 (7.5 cm/3 in)
2	small cucumbers or a large one	2
3 tbsp	groundnut oil	3 tbsp
2 tbsp	Chinese light soy sauce	2 tbsp
2 tsp	sugar	2 tsp
4	coarsely chopped scallions (spring onions) or a small leek	4
⅔ cup	chicken bouillon (stock)	150 ml/¼ pint
2 tsp	cornstarch (cornflour)	2 tsp

1. Cut the soybean curd (tofu) into 1 in (1.25 cm) cubes.
2. Peel the cucumber(s) or scrub under cold running water. Halve lengthwise, remove the ends and scoop out the seeds with a spoon. Cut the halves once again lengthwise and then cut the strips into small cubes.
3. Heat the oil in a wok and stir fry the pieces of cucumber for 2 minutes.
4. Add the soy sauce, sugar, scallions (spring onions) and bouillon (stock).
5. Mix the cornstarch (cornflour) with 2 tbsp cold water and stir into of the wok. Cook until the sauce thickens.

Cook's tip: the pork given in the recipe can be replaced by an equivalent quantity of lean lamb or chicken and the bamboo shoots by 2-3 sticks of celery, cut into very thin strips.

6. Add the soybean curd (tofu) cubes. Stir carefully a few times and simmer for 1 minute.

7. Serve immediately with egg noodles which have been boiled and then fried in oil.

Fan dwa swa du fu

Soybean Curd (Tofu) with Tomatoes

	00.15	00.07
	Serves 4	

American	Ingredients	Metric/Imperial
2 (3 in)	cubes of soybean curd (tofu)	2 (7.5 cm/3 in)
6	skinned, seeded, drained tomatoes	6
2 tbsp	groundnut oil	2 tbsp
⅔ cup	chicken bouillon (stock)	150 ml/¼ pint
1 tsp	sugar	1 tsp
1 tbsp	Chinese light soy sauce	1 tbsp
1 tbsp	Chinese tomato sauce	1 tbsp
	salt	
	ground black pepper	
1 tbsp	cornstarch (cornflour)	1 tbsp
2	chopped scallions (spring onions)	2

1. Cut the soybean curd (tofu) into 3×½ in (1.25 cm) rectangular pieces ½ in (1.25 cm) thick.

2. Cut the tomatoes into large pieces.

Soybean curd (tofu) with tomatoes

3. Heat the oil in a wok and stir fry the tomatoes for 30 seconds.

4. Add the bouillon (stock), sugar, soy sauce, tomato sauce and a little salt and pepper to taste. Stir well and bring to the boil.

5. Mix the cornstarch (cornflour) with 3 tbsp cold water and stir into the contents of the wok. Cook until the sauce thickens.

6. Add the pieces of soybean curd (tofu). Stir a few times and leave to simmer for 3 minutes.

7. Serve the dish on warmed deep plates, sprinkled with a little chopped scallion (spring onion).

Chow fu chee

Dried Soybean Curd (Tofu) with Mushrooms

	00.20	00.15
	plus soaking time	

American	Ingredients	Metric/Imperial
5 oz	dried soybean curd sticks	150 g/5 oz
12	Chinese dried mushrooms	12
½ cup	canned, drained bamboo shoots	50 g/2 oz
3 tbsp	groundnut oil	3 tbsp
1	very finely chopped garlic clove	1
3	washed, trimmed sticks of celery	3
3 tbsp	Chinese light soy sauce	3 tbsp
2 tbsp	Chinese rice wine or sherry	2 tbsp
1½ tsp	cornstarch (cornflour)	1½ tsp
1	chopped scallion (spring onion)	1

1. Place the soybean sticks in a bowl and pour on warm water (40°C) to cover them well. Soak for 30 minutes.

2. Place the dried mushrooms in a bowl and pour on boiling water to cover them well. Soak for 30 minutes.

3. Cut the bamboo shoots into 2×2 in (5 cm) pieces.

4. Cut the sticks of celery into 2×2 in (5 cm) pieces.

5. Cut the soaked soybean curd (tofu) sticks into 2 in (5 cm) pieces. Drain well.

6. Remove the stalks from the soaked mushrooms. Cut the caps into thin strips. Strain the liquid in which the mushrooms have been soaked.

7. Heat the oil in a wok, add the garlic and celery. Stir fry for 2 minutes.

8. Add the mushrooms, bamboo shoots and soybean curd (tofu). Stir fry for a further 2 minutes.

9. Add the soy sauce, rice wine and ¾ cup (200 ml/7 fl oz) of the mushroom liquid. Stir well and bring to the boil. Reduce the heat and simmer for 4 minutes.

10. Mix the cornstarch (cornflour) with 2 tbsp cold water and stir the mixture into the contents of the wok. Cook until the sauce has thickened slightly. Simmer for a few minutes longer.

11. Serve in warmed deep plates sprinkled with a little chopped scallion (spring onion).

Cook's tip: home-made soybean curd (tofu) can be made quite easily see page 48.

Du fu

Soybean Curd (Tofu)

00.30
plus soaking time

00.10

American	Ingredients	Metric/Imperial
1¾ lb	soybeans	800 g/1¾ lb
1½ tbsp	calcium sulfate	1½ tbsp

Soybean curd (tofu)

1. Rinse the soybeans in plenty of water. Put them in a large glazed or glass jar and pour on enough water to cover them well. Soak the beans for at least 12 hours.
2. Wash them again in plenty of water.
3. Make the soybeans into a soft paste with 2 quarts (2 litres/3½ pints) water in a food processor or large blender.
4. Strain the paste through a piece of damp muslin, folded double. Wring out all the liquid from it.
5. Bring the liquid very slowly to the boil. Stir well and boil gently for 10 minutes.
6. Dissolve the calcium sulfate in ¾ cup (200 ml/7 fl oz) cold water and strain it through a piece of damp muslin.
7. Add the calcium sulfate to the soybean mixture. Stir well then pour into a large mould which has been lined with a piece of wet muslin.
8. When the soybean curd (tofu) begins to set cover the surface with a piece of wet muslin.
9. After 10 minutes put a suitable board or plate on top and place a weight of not more than 11lb (5 kg) on the board.
10. Leave the curd to set for no more than 40 minutes then cut the soybean curd (tofu) into pieces and wrap in foil.
11. Store in a large jar with enough cold water to cover and chill.

Tsie bei tse

Paper Wrapped Chicken

00.30
plus standing time

00.15

American	Ingredients	Metric/Imperial
1¼ lb	boneless, skinless chicken breasts	575 g/1¼ lb
1 tbsp	Chinese light soy sauce	1 tbsp
1 tsp	oyster sauce	1 tsp
2 tsp	sesame oil	2 tsp
2 tsp	Chinese rice wine or dry sherry	2 tsp
1 tsp	sugar	1 tsp
2 tsp	coarsely grated fresh root ginger	2 tsp
1	packet of rice paper	1
	oil for deep frying	

1. Dry the chicken breasts with kitchen paper. Cut them into strips not more than 2 in (5 cm) long.
2. Mix the soy sauce, oyster sauce, sesame oil, rice wine or sherry, sugar and root ginger in a bowl.
3. Spoon the mixture over the strips of chicken and leave to stand for 30 minutes. Turn over occasionally.
4. Lay out 12 sheets of rice paper on a work surface and spoon some of the chicken mixture on to each sheet.
5. Fold the sheets like envelopes round the fillings. Moisten the edges of the paper and press them firmly together.
6. Heat the oil until very hot. Fry 4 or 5 packets at a time until golden brown. Remove them from the hot oil with a skimmer, drain for a moment then arrange on a warmed serving dish.

Cook's tip: serve with a dip made by mixing 2 parts of Chinese tomato sauce with 1 part of Chinese light soy sauce and 1 part of Chinese rice wine or dry sherry. Add a pinch of five spice powder and mix well.

Sha ng hiong tse

Roasted, Spiced Chicken Legs

00.10
plus standing time

00.40

American	Ingredients	Metric/Imperial
8	chicken legs	8
2	finely crushed garlic cloves	2
6 tbsp	Chinese light soy sauce	6 tbsp
6 tbsp	groundnut oil	6 tbsp
2 tbsp	Chinese rice wine or dry sherry	2 tbsp
½ tsp	salt	½ tsp
	pinch five spice powder	
	pinch ground root ginger	
5 tsp	honey	5 tsp

1. Dry the chicken legs with kitchen paper.
2. Mix together all the ingredients except the honey.
3. Pour the mixture over the chicken legs and leave to stand for 1 hour.
4. Preheat the oven to 180°C/350°F/Gas mark 4.
5. Grease an oven rack with a little oil.
6. Remove the chicken legs from the marinade, drain for a moment above the marinade and place them on the rack.
7. Place an oven dish or baking sheet under the rack to catch the dripping fat.
8. Roast the chicken legs for 30-35 minutes until golden brown. Baste them a few times with the marinade and turn them over after 15 minutes.
9. Use the remainder of the marinade to make a sauce. Heat it in a small saucepan and add 1 tsp of honey and 1 tsp of water for each tbsp of marinade.
10. Arrange the chicken legs on a warmed dish and serve the sauce separately.

Paper wrapped chicken

Koe loe joek

Sweet and Sour Pork

00.30 plus standing time   00.20

American	Ingredients	Metric/Imperial
1½ lb	pork tenderloin (fillet)	575 g/1½ lb
1½ tbsp	Chinese light soy sauce	1½ tbsp
1½ tbsp	Chinese rice wine or dry sherry	1½ tbsp
¼ tsp	five spice powder	¼ tsp
1 tsp	salt	1 tsp
1¾ cups	flour	200 g/7 oz
1 tbsp	sesame oil	1 tbsp
1	stiffly whisked egg white	1
8 tbsp	groundnut oil	8 tbsp
1¼ cups	sweet and sour sauce	300 ml/½ pint
½ cup	sliced water chestnuts	50 g/2 oz
3-4 tbsp	cooked peas, fresh or frozen	3-4 tbsp
4 tbsp	seeded cucumber or under-ripe melon, cut into strips	4 tbsp

Sweet and sour pork

1. Cut the meat into 1 in (2.5 cm) cubes.
2. Mix together the soy sauce, rice wine or sherry, five spice powder and salt. Stir until the salt is dissolved.
3. Toss the cubes of meat in this mixture. Leave to stand for about 1 hour, turning occasionally.
4. Make a batter by first sifting the flour into a bowl. Add ⅔ cup (150 ml/¼ pint) water and continue stirring until the batter is smooth. Stir in the sesame oil, then fold in the egg white as lightly as possible.
5. Heat the groundnut oil in a wok until very hot.
6. Using a fork, dip the cubes of meat in the batter. Fry a few at a time until golden.
7. Remove the cubes of meat with a slotted spoon. Leave to drain, then cool.
8. Immediately before serving, fry the meat in the hot oil once more until the batter is golden brown and very crisp.
9. Heat the sweet and sour sauce and add the water chestnuts and peas. Cook for a minute then add the cucumber or melon.
10. Place the meat on a warmed dish and pour over the sauce. Serve immediately.

Goe jiet foen joem

Salt and Pepper Mixture

00.05   00.00

American	Ingredients	Metric/Imperial
3 tbsp	black peppercorns	3 tbsp
4 tbsp	salt	4 tbsp

1. Heat a small frying pan, add the peppercorns and roast, shaking constantly until the pepper gives off an aroma.
2. Cool the peppercorns on a large plate until completely cold. Pound to a powder in a mortar.
3. Mix in the salt.

Cook's tip: this mixture will keep for years if stored in a tightly sealed container. This salt and pepper mixture can be used for all meat and poultry dishes. A small quantity is often placed on the table. Variations include:- 6 parts salt, 1 part five spice powder, 1 part black pepper from the mill (for preparation, see recipe for Goe jiet foen joem) – 6 parts salt, 1 part curry (mild flavor) – 6 parts salt, 1 part ground root ginger, 1 part finely milled or crushed 'gingko' nuts – 6 parts salt, 1 part milled black pepper (for preparation, see recipe for Goe jiet foen joem), 1 part finely milled or crushed coriander seeds – 6 parts salt, 2 parts lightly roasted then finely crushed or ground black mustard seeds. In mixtures in which five spice powder plays an important role, it is quite common to add, as a little extra, a small quantity of one of the spices contained in the five spice powder. This addition is largely determined by personal taste and preference. Five spice powder as made in China consists of almost equal parts of finely ground star anise, fennel seeds, cinnamon, cloves and Szechwan pepper. This Chinese pepper is also known as aniseed pepper. The peppercorns, which are brown in color, are prepared in exactly the same way as for Goe jiet foen joem.

Tim soen tsijoen

Traditional Sweet and Sour Sauce

00.15   00.10

American	Ingredients	Metric/Imperial
1 tbsp	Chinese light soy sauce	1 tbsp
1 tbsp	Chinese rice wine or dry sherry	1 tbsp
4 tbsp	tomato sauce or	4 tbsp
2 tbsp	tomato purée	2 tbsp
2 tbsp	mild vinegar	2 tbsp
1-2 tbsp	sugar	1-2 tbsp
1 tbsp	cornstarch (cornflour)	1 tbsp
1	onion	1
2 tbsp	groundnut oil	2 tbsp
4-6	peeled garlic cloves halved lengthwise	4-6
4	slices of root ginger	4
1 tsp	grated fresh root ginger	1 tsp
1	seeded chili cut into strips	1
1-2 tbsp	ginger syrup	1-2 tbsp

1. Mix together the soy sauce, rice wine or sherry, tomato sauce or tomato purée, vinegar and sugar. Stir until the sugar dissolves. Add ¾ cup (200 ml/7 fl oz) water.
2. Mix the cornstarch (cornflour) with 3 tbsp cold water.
3. Peel the onion, cut into 8 segments and separate the layers.
4. Heat the oil in a wok and add the garlic and slices of root ginger and stir fry until the garlic is golden brown. Remove the garlic and root ginger.
5. Add the onion, grated root ginger, chili and ginger syrup to the remaining oil. Stir fry for 2 minutes.
6. Add the tomato sauce mixture and bring to the boil.
7. Stir in the cornstarch (cornflour) mixture and continue stirring until the sauce thickens. Simmer gently for a few minutes.

Wah yim

Five Spice Salt

00.05   00.00

American	Ingredients	Metric/Imperial
6 tbsp	salt	6 tbsp
1 tbsp	five spice powder	1 tbsp

1. Mix the two ingredients together.

Cook's tip: five spice salt is used with roast poultry and pork. as well as with many other dishes.

Disi chuanwei zhi

Szechwan Sauce

00.10   00.02
Serves 4

American	Ingredients	Metric/Imperial
2 tbsp	groundnut oil	2 tbsp
4	crushed garlic cloves	4
1 tbsp	coarsely grated fresh root ginger	1 tbsp
2 tbsp	Chinese light soy sauce	2 tbsp
1 tbsp	Chinese dark soy sauce	1 tbsp
1 tbsp	hoisin sauce	1 tbsp
1 tbsp	oyster sauce	1 tbsp
2 tbsp	Chinese rice wine or dry sherry	2 tbsp
2 tbsp	brown cane sugar	2 tbsp
2 tsp	red chili oil	2 tsp
1½ tbsp	mild Chinese vinegar	1½ tbsp
⅔ cup	hot beef bouillon (stock)	150 ml/¼ pint
1½ tsp	cornstarch (cornflour)	1½ tsp
½ tsp	sesame oil	½ tsp

1. Heat the oil in a wok and stir fry the garlic for 30 seconds.
2. Add the ginger and fry for another 30 seconds.
3. Add both types of soy sauce, the hoisin and oyster sauces, rice wine or sherry, sugar, red chili oil, vinegar and hot bouillon (stock). Bring slowly to the boil stirring all the time. Boil vigorously for 20 seconds.
4. Mix the cornstarch (cornflour) with 1½ tbsp cold water. Stir this into the wok and cook over fairly high heat for 10 seconds.
5. Add a few drops of sesame oil before removing the wok.

Cook's tip: this light and spicy sweet and sour sauce makes a delicious accompaniment to beef, veal and chicken as well as pork and can be substituted for traditional sweet and sour sauce in any of the recipes calling for the former. In Szechwan, strips of fried beef are added to this sauce and it is sprinkled with finely chopped scallions (spring onions) or shallots. When it is served with roast meat, half the sauce is poured over the meat just before serving and the remainder is served separately in a warmed sauce boat.

Joe joek ma t'ai tsjow

Pork Rolls and Vegetables in a Sweet and Sour Sauce

American	Ingredients	Metric/Imperial
	00.20 Serves 4	01.45
1 lb	lean, very finely ground (minced) pork	450 g/1 lb
¾ cup	canned, very finely chopped water chestnuts, drained	75 g/3 oz
2	crushed garlic cloves	2
⅓ tsp	five spice powder	⅓ tsp
2 tsp	cornstarch (cornflour)	2 tsp
1	lightly beaten egg	1
	salt	
1¾ cups	flour	200 g/7 oz
1	lightly beaten egg	1
1 tbsp	sesame oil	1 tbsp
1¼ cups	sweet and sour sauce	300 ml/½ pint
1	small can pineapple in light syrup, drained	1
1	small can Chow Chow (mixed Chinese vegetables)	1
8 tbsp	groundnut oil	8 tbsp
	few tomato 'roses'	
2 tbsp	finely chopped parsley	2 tbsp

1. Mix the meat with the water chestnuts, garlic, five spice powder, cornstarch (cornflour) and the lightly beaten egg. Beat to form a stiff mixture, then add salt to taste.
2. Shape the meat into a thick roll 3-4in (8-10 cm) in diameter.
3. Line a steamer with aluminum foil, oil lightly. Place the meat roll on top. Steam for 40-45 minutes, until the meat roll is cooked. Leave to cool.
4. Make the batter by sifting the flour into a bowl and stirring in 1 cup (250 ml/8 fl oz) water and 1 lightly beaten egg. Add the sesame oil once the batter is smooth.
5. Bring the sweet and sour sauce to the boil and add the chopped pineapple and the entire contents of the can of vegetables.
6. Bring the sauce back to the boil and cook gently for 2 minutes.
7. Cut the meat roll into 1-2 in (2-3 cm) slices.
8. Heat the oil in the wok until very hot.
9. Carefully dip the meat roll slices in the batter, then slide 2-3 slices at a time into the hot oil. Fry until golden brown.
10. Pour half the sauce on to a large warm dish. Arrange the slices of meat, overlapping, in the middle of the dish. Garnish with tomato roses and chopped parsley.
11. Serve the rest of the sauce separately.

Tsjia sjioe

Roast Pork with Sweet and Sour Sauce

American	Ingredients	Metric/Imperial
	00.15 plus standing time	00.50
1¼ lb	lean pork, eg loin	575 g/1¼ lb
4	crushed garlic cloves	4
⅓ tsp	five spice powder	⅓ tsp
1 tsp	salt	1 tsp
1 tsp	grated fresh root ginger	1 tsp
3 tsp	Chinese dark soy sauce	3 tsp
2 tbsp	honey	2 tbsp
1-2 tbsp	Chinese rice wine or dry sherry	1-2 tbsp
1¼ cups	sweet and sour sauce	300 ml/½ pint

1. Dry the meat with kitchen paper and cut into finger width strips.
2. Pound the garlic to a smooth paste in a mortar.
3. Mix with remaining ingredients, except the sweet and sour sauce. Stir well.
4. Dip the strips of meat in the mixture and leave to stand for 1-2 hours.
5. Fill a roasting tin with water and place on the oven floor. Heat the oven to 220°C/425°F/Gas mark 7. Brush an oven rack with a little oil and lay the strips of meat on the rack. Place in the middle of the preheated oven and roast for about 40 minutes. Turn the meat after 20 minutes, and brush with the remaining marinade.
6. Meanwhile, heat the sweet and sour sauce.
7. Immediately before serving, slice the meat.
8. Pour half the sauce on to a warmed plate.
9. Arrange the pieces of meat in the middle and pour the rest of the sauce over the top.
10. Serve immediately with boiled or steamed rice.

Jing ng few nam

Steamed Pork with Sweet and Sour Sauce

American	Ingredients	Metric/Imperial
	00.20 plus standing time	02.00
1½ lb	lean pork, eg loin	700 g/1½ lb
2 tbsp	soft brown sugar or honey	2 tbsp
2 tbsp	Chinese rice wine or dry sherry	2 tbsp
½ tsp	five spice powder	½ tsp
3	crushed garlic cloves	3
4 tbsp	Chinese dark soy sauce	4 tbsp
¾ cup	rice	175 g/6 oz
	sweet and sour sauce	

1. Dry the meat with kitchen paper. Cut into 1 in (2.5 cm) cubes.

2. Add the sugar or honey, rice wine or sherry, five spice powder and garlic to the soy sauce. Stir until the sugar has dissolved.

3. Add the meat to the marinade and leave to stand for 1 hour, stirring occasionally.

4. Heat a dry frying pan or wok. Add the rice and dry roast until golden in color. Tip the rice on to a large plate and leave to cool.

5. Crush the rice coarsely in a mortar.

6. Roll the pieces of meat in the coarsely crushed rice and place in a dish to fit a steamer or steaming pan. Steam the meat for 2 hours.

7. Serve the meat in the dish, with a sweet and sour sauce, served separately.

Ngoe joek hoe hoek yin
Steamed Beef Balls in Rice Jackets

	00.40	00.45
	plus soaking time	

American	Ingredients	Metric/Imperial
1 cup	short grain rice	225 g/8 oz
6	large dried Chinese mushrooms	6
¾ lb	lean ground (minced) beef	350 g/12 oz
4	finely chopped scallions (spring onions)	4
½ tsp	finely grated root ginger	½ tsp
1-2	crushed garlic cloves	1-2
¼ cup	finely chopped water chestnuts	50 g/2 oz
	salt	
1	lightly beaten egg	1
	sesame oil	

1. Soak the rice in cold water for 2-3 hours. Leave to drain in a colander and roll in a teacloth to dry.

2. Place the mushrooms in a bowl with boiling water to cover. Soak for 30 minutes. Remove the stalks and cut the caps into very thin strips.

3. Mix the strips of mushroom with the beef, scallions (spring onions), root ginger, garlic, water chestnuts, a little salt to taste and the egg. Stir well. Leave to stand for 15 minutes then shape into walnut size balls.

4. Roll the balls through the dry rice, pressing the rice grains in firmly.

5. Brush a dish with a little sesame oil and place the balls in the dish.

6. Set the dish in a steaming pan or steamer and steam for 40-45 minutes until cooked.

Ng hioeng joek sie
Beef with Five Spice Sauce

	00.25	00.06
	plus standing time	

American	Ingredients	Metric/Imperial
¾ lb	lean beef	350 g/12 oz
1	crushed garlic clove	1
½ tsp	salt	½ tsp
½ tsp	grated fresh root ginger	½ tsp
1 tbsp	Chinese dark soy sauce	1 tbsp
1 tsp	sugar	1 tsp
	pinch five spice powder	
1-2 tbsp	groundnut oil	1-2 tbsp
⅔ cup	beef bouillon (stock)	150 ml/¼ pint
1 tsp	cornstarch (cornflour)	1 tsp

1. Dry the meat with kitchen paper. Cut crosswise into thin slices, then into strips, then small squares.

2. Mix the garlic with salt, root ginger, soy sauce, sugar and five spice powder. Stir until the sugar has dissolved.

3. Mix the meat into the mixture and leave to stand for 10-15 minutes.

4. Heat the oil in a wok and add the meat mixture. Stir fry for 2 minutes until the meat has changed color.

5. Add the bouillon (stock) and bring to the boil.

6. Mix the cornstarch (cornflour) with 1 tbsp cold water and stir into the contents of the wok. Cook stirring until the sauce has thickened slightly.

7. Serve immediately, with boiled or steamed rice.

Cook's tip: another delicious combination is with egg noodles, boiled and then fried. Serve the noodles on to a large warm plate, spread the meat mixture evenly over the top and sprinkle with a little finely chopped shallot or scallion (spring onion).

Making tomato flowers

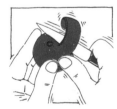

Waterlilies: push the point of a small sharp-knife into the tomato in a zig-zag pattern. Twist the two halves slightly to separate.

Roses: peel the tomato skin in a spiral with a small, very sharp knife. Roll up the skin, secure with a cocktail pick and chill for 30 minutes. Remove the cocktail pick to release the rose shape.

Lien ngoe tsjow ngoe joek

Beef with Lotus Root

	OO. 15	OO.O8
	Serves 4	

American	Ingredients	Metric/Imperial
¾ lb	lean beef	350 g/12 oz
2 tbsp	Chinese dark soy sauce	2 tbsp
	good pinch salt	
1	crushed garlic clove	1
½ tsp	finely grated root ginger	½ tsp
1	pinch of five spice powder	1
2-3 tbsp	groundnut oil	2-3 tbsp
⅔ cup	beef bouillon (stock)	150 ml/¼ pint
1 tsp	cornstarch (cornflour)	1 tsp
2	slices canned lotus root drained	2

1. Dry the meat with kitchen paper. Cut into 3-4 in (4-5 cm) strips then into extra thin slices.
2. Mix together the soy sauce, salt, garlic, root ginger and five spice powder. Stir until the salt has dissolved.
3. Mix the mixture with the meat making sure that every slice of meat is coated. Leave to stand for a few minutes.
4. Heat the oil in a wok, add the meat and stir fry until the meat has changed color.
5. Add the bouillon (stock) and bring to the boil.
6. Mix the cornstarch (cornflour) with 1 tbsp cold water and stir into the contents of the wok. Cook, stirring until the sauce thickens. Stir in the lotus root and leave to heat through thoroughly.
7. Serve into 4 warmed plates.

Doeng doe tsjow ngoe joek

Beef with Mushrooms and Onions

	OO. 15	OO. 1O
	plus standing time	

American	Ingredients	Metric/Imperial
6-8	dried Chinese mushrooms	6-8
¾ lb	lean beef	350 g/12 oz
	pinch five spice powder	
½ tsp	salt	½ tsp
1	crushed garlic clove	1
½ tsp	grated fresh root ginger	½ tsp
4	small onions	4
2-3 tbsp	groundnut oil	2-3 tbsp
2 tbsp	Chinese dark soy sauce	2 tbsp
1 tbsp	Chinese light soy sauce	1 tbsp
1 tsp	sugar	1 tsp
¾ cup	beef bouillon (stock)	200 ml/7 fl oz
1 tsp	cornstarch (cornflour)	1 tsp
3-4	chopped shallots or scallions (spring onions)	3-4

1. Place the mushrooms in a bowl with boiling water to cover. Soak the mushrooms for 30 minutes. Remove the stalks and cut the caps into narrow strips.

Left to right: Beef with lotus root; Beef with mushrooms and onions

2. Dry the meat with kitchen paper. Cut into strips the thickness of the little finger and then into cubes.
3. Place the meat in a bowl and add the five spice powder, salt, garlic and root ginger. Stir well and leave to stand for 15 minutes.
4. Peel the onions and cut each into 8 segments. Separate the layers.
5. Heat the oil in a wok, add the onions and stir fry until transparent.
6. Add the strips of mushroom and continue frying until the onions have turned a pale golden color.
7. Add the soy sauces, sugar and bouillon (stock). Stir well and bring to the boil.
8. Mix the cornstarch (cornflour) with 2 tbsp cold water and stir into the wok until the sauce thickens. Cook for a further minute.
9. Transfer to a warmed, shallow dish and sprinkle with sliced shallots or scallions (spring onions).

Sie joe ngoe joek
Red Cooked Beef

◢	00.05 plus cooling time	03.00 🍲

American	Ingredients	Metric/Imperial
3½ lb	lean braising beef	1.5 kg/3½ lb
5 tbsp	Chinese dark soy sauce	5 tbsp
5 tbsp	Chinese light soy sauce	5 tbsp
5 tbsp	oyster sauce	5 tbsp
3 tbsp	Chinese rice wine or dry sherry	3 tbsp
2	thin slices root ginger cut into thin strips	2
2	peeled garlic cloves, cut through lengthwise	2
2	small segments of star anise	2
2 tbsp	sesame oil	2 tbsp

1. Place all the ingredients except the meat in a pan just large enough to hold the meat. Pour in 1½ cups (350 ml/12 fl oz) water. Stir well, then add the meat to the pan. The meat should be completely covered by the liquid.
2. Bring quickly to the boil. Reduce the heat, cover the pan and simmer gently for 2½-3 hours.
3. Turn the meat at 30 minute intervals. Remove lid for the last fifteen minutes of the cooking time.
4. Remove the pan from the heat and leave the meat in the sauce until cold. Remove the meat from the sauce, drain and cut into slices.
5. Place the slices on a plate, and serve as a starter or side dish.

Cook's tip: the sauce, which is quite gelatinous when cooled, can be strained and used as a basis for many other sauces. It is also a good base for a number of soups.

Sie joe ngoe joek
Beef with Black Bean Sauce

◢	00.15 Serves 4	00.10 🍲

American	Ingredients	Metric/Imperial
¾ lb	lean beef	350 g/12 oz
1-1½ tbsp	canned black beans	1-1½ tbsp
2½ tbsp	Chinese dark soy sauce	2½ tbsp
½ tbsp	oyster sauce	½ tbsp
1 tsp	sugar	1 tsp
5 tbsp	beef bouillon (stock)	5 tbsp
3-4 tbsp	groundnut oil	3-4 tbsp
2	peeled garlic cloves	2
1 tsp	cornstarch (cornflour)	1 tsp
1 tsp	sesame oil	1 tsp

1. Dry the meat with kitchen paper. Cut into thin slices, then into thin strips.
2. Rinse the black beans in a strainer (sieve) under cold running water. Mash the beans finely with a fork and mix with the soy sauce, oyster sauce, sugar and bouillon (stock).
3. Heat the groundnut oil in a wok, fry the garlic until golden brown and remove from the pan.
4. Fry the meat, turning constantly, until it has changed color. Add the black bean mixture. Stir well and bring to the boil.
5. Mix the cornstarch (cornflour) with 1 tbsp cold water and stir into the contents of the wok. Cook, stirring until the sauce thickens.
6. Add the sesame oil. Continue cooking gently for another minute.
7. Serve immediately on warmed plates.

Beef with snow peas (mange tout)

Hoelan doe tsjow ngoe joek
Beef with Snow Peas (Mange-tout)

	00.20	
	plus standing and soaking time	00.15

American	Ingredients	Metric/Imperial
¾ lb	lean beef	350 g/12 oz
3 tbsp	Chinese dark soy sauce	3 tbsp
1 tbsp	Chinese light soy sauce	1 tbsp
	good pinch of salt	
	good pinch of sugar	
6-8	large dried Chinese mushrooms	6-8
⅔ cup	beef bouillon (stock)	150 ml/¼ pint
½ lb	snow peas (mange-tout)	225 g/8 oz
4-5 tbsp	groundnut oil	4-5 tbsp
6	shallots or scallions (spring onions) cut into 1 in (2.5 cm) pieces	6
1 tbsp	Chinese rice wine or dry sherry	1 tbsp
1½ tsp	cornstarch (cornflour)	1½ tsp

1. Dry the meat with kitchen paper. Cut into thin slices, then into thin strips.
2. Mix the soy sauces with the salt and sugar. Stir well, until the sugar is dissolved.
3. Put the meat into the mixture, stir to coat then leave to stand for 30 minutes, turning the meat.
4. Place the mushrooms in a bowl with boiling water to cover and leave to soak for 30 minutes. Remove the stalks and cut the caps into extremely thin strips. Strain the liquid and add 4 tbsp of this liquid to the bouillon (stock).
5. Trim the snow peas (mange-tout), wash them and put into a pan with salted boiling water to cover. Cook for 2-3 minutes. Drain and rinse with cold water to cool them.
6. Heat 3 tbsp of oil in a wok, add the strips of meat and fry, turning constantly, until they have changed color. Remove from the wok with a slotted spoon and set aside.

7. Add 1-2 tbsp of oil to the oil remaining in the pan and stir fry the strips of mushroom and shallots or scallions (spring onions) for exactly 1 minute.
8. Add the rice wine or sherry and bouillon (stock) and bring to the boil.
9. Mix the cornstarch (cornflour) with 2 tbsp cold water and stir into the contents of the wok. Cook, stirring until the sauce thickens. Simmer for 1 minute.
10. Add the meat and snow peas (mange-tout). Leave to heat through thoroughly then serve immediately.

Lo han tsjai
Braised Vegetables

	00.15	
	plus soaking time	00.25

American	Ingredients	Metric/Imperial
1 (3 in)	cube soybean curd (tofu)	1 (7.5 cm/3 in)
6	large dried Chinese mushrooms	6
20	dried lily buds	20
¼ cup	dried Chinese cloud ears or wood mushrooms	50 g/2 oz
1 (8 oz)	can bamboo shoots	1 (225 g/8 oz)
1 (8 oz)	can sliced lotus roots	1 (225 g/8 oz)
¼ cup	washed bean sprouts drained	50 g/2 oz
5-6 tbsp	groundnut oil	5-6 tbsp
2 tbsp	Chinese light soy sauce	2 tbsp
2 tbsp	hoisin sauce	2 tbsp
1	piece star anise	1
2 tsp	sesame oil	2 tsp
2 tsp	cornstarch (cornflour)	2 tsp
2 tsp	sugar	2 tsp
2	sliced scallions (spring onions)	2

1. Cut the soybean curd (tofu) into ½ in (1.25 cm) cubes.
2. Place the large dried mushrooms in a bowl with boiling water to cover. Leave to soak for 30 minutes. Remove the stalks and cut the caps into thin strips. Strain the liquid and set aside.
3. Soak the lily buds in boiling water for 30 minutes. Turn the ends to form a button.
4. Soak the cloud ears or wood mushrooms in hot water for 10 minutes. Cut large ears in half. Drain and cut into pieces.
5. Cut the drained bamboo shoots and lotus root slices into thin strips.
6. Heat the oil in a large wok and add the cubes of soybean curd, the large mushrooms and lily buds and stir fry for 4 minutes.
7. Add the soy sauce, hoisin sauce and star anise, stir well and add 1¼ cups (300 ml/½ pint) of the strained mushroom liquid.
8. Add the bamboo shoots, the lotus root and sesame oil. Cover the pan and simmer for 10 minutes.
9. Mix the cornstarch (cornflour) with 2 tbsp cold water and stir into the wok and cook until the sauce thickens.
10. Add the sugar, bean sprouts and cloud ears or wood mushrooms. Stir well and bring back to the boil.
11. Serve in a warmed shallow dish, sprinkle with sliced scallions (spring onions) and serve.

Jing tsijoen bok koe

Stuffed Mushrooms

◼▷ 00.30   00.30
Serves 4

American	Ingredients	Metric/Imperial
20-24	large cup mushrooms	20-24
½ lb	lean ground (minced) pork	225 g/8 oz
4	finely chopped canned water chestnuts, drained	4
¼ cup	finely chopped bamboo shoots	50g/2 oz
1-2 tsp	cornstarch (cornflour)	1-2 tsp
2-3 tbsp	Chinese light soy sauce	2-3 tbsp
½ tsp	grated fresh root ginger	½ tsp
1	crushed garlic clove	1
	good pinch of sugar	
2 tbsp	Chinese dark soy sauce	2 tbsp
1 tbsp	Chinese light soy sauce	1 tbsp
1 tsp	cornstarch (cornflour)	1 tsp
	good pinch salt	
	freshly ground pepper	
1 tsp	sesame oil	1 tsp

1. Wipe the mushrooms with a moist cloth and trim away the base of the stalk, then carefully remove the remainder of the stalk from the cap. Chop the stalks finely.
2. Mix the finely chopped mushroom stalks with the meat, water chestnuts, bamboo shoots, 1-2 tsp cornstarch (cornflour), 2-3 tbsp light soy sauce, root ginger, garlic and sugar.
3. Fill the mushroom caps with a ball of this mixture.
4. Brush a little sesame oil over a dish to fit into a steaming pan or steamer.
5. Place the mushroom caps, with the filling on top, on the dish. Cover the dish with a sheet of foil.
6. Place the dish in the steaming pan or steamer and steam for 20-25 minutes.
7. Place the mushrooms in a warmed shallow dish.

8. Pour the liquid (about ⅔ cup 150 ml/¼ pint) left in the mushroom steaming dish into a small pan. Bring to the boil and add the light and dark soy sauce.
9. Mix the remaining cornstarch (cornflour) with 1 tbsp cold water and stir into the liquid. Cook until the sauce has thickened slightly then leave to simmer for 2 minutes.
10. Add a little salt, pepper and sesame oil, to taste and pour the sauce over the stuffed mushrooms. Serve immediately.

Hoen sjoee doeng doe

Braised Chinese Mushrooms

◼▷ 00.05   00.30
plus soaking time

American	Ingredients	Metric/Imperial
¼ cup	large dried Chinese mushrooms	50 g/2 oz
2 tbsp	Chinese dark soy sauce	2 tbsp
1 tbsp	sugar	1 tbsp
1 tsp	sesame oil	1 tsp
3 tbsp	groundnut oil	3 tbsp
4	thinly sliced shallots or scallions (spring onions)	4

1. Place the mushrooms in a bowl with boiling water to cover and soak for 30 minutes. Remove the stalks. Carefully press the mushroom caps between the palms of the hands, collecting the liquid expressed and adding it to the soaking liquid. Strain the soaking liquid, and pour 1¼ cups (300 ml/10 fl oz) of this liquid into a bowl.
2. Add the soy sauce, sugar and sesame oil. Stir until the sugar is dissolved.
3. Heat the oil in a wok and add the mushroom caps. Stir fry for 4 minutes.
4. Add the liquid from the bowl and bring to the boil. Reduce the heat and simmer for 30 minutes. The liquid should evaporate and be absorbed by the mushrooms. Transfer to a serving dish and sprinkle with shallots or scallions (spring onions). Serve immediately as an accompaniment to an omelette, or serve cold as a starter.

Stuffed mushrooms

Tsjow seng tsjoi
Braised Lettuce

00.10 · Serves 4 as side dish · **00.10**

American	Ingredients	Metric/Imperial
1 (1 lb)	iceberg lettuce	1 (450 g/1 lb)
3 tbsp	groundnut oil	3 tbsp
1	peeled garlic clove	1
1	slice fresh root ginger	1
½ cup	bouillon (stock), vegetable juice or water	100 ml/4 fl oz
2 tbsp	Chinese light soy sauce	2 tbsp
1 tbsp	Chinese rice wine or dry sherry	1 tbsp
½ tsp	sugar	½ tsp
½ tsp	cornstarch (cornflour)	½ tsp
1 tsp	sesame oil	1 tsp

1. Trim the lettuce. Cut into four pieces. Remove part of the stalk, without breaking the leaves apart. Wash between leaves in cold water. Drain well.
2. Heat the groundnut oil in a wok and add the garlic and root ginger, stirring constantly. Remove from the oil.
3. Add the lettuce and stir fry for 2 minutes.
4. Add the bouillon (stock), soy sauce, rice wine or sherry and sugar.
5. Slide the lettuce to one side of the wok.
6. Mix the cornstarch (cornflour) with 2 tsp cold water and stir into the liquid in the wok. Cook, until the sauce thickens.
7. Add the sesame oil and draw the lettuce through the sauce several times. Serve immediately.

Joe sek tsjoi
Vegetable Salad

00.05 · plus chilling time · **00.05**

American	Ingredients	Metric/Imperial
½ lb	Chinese cabbage, iceberg lettuce or paksoi	225 g/½ lb
1 cup	fresh bean sprouts washed, drained	125 g/4 oz
2 cups	bamboo shoots, cut into thin strips	450 g/1 lb
½ lb	canned lychees, drained or peeled and stoned fresh lychees	225 g/½ lb
2	crushed garlic cloves	2
½ tsp	grated fresh root ginger	½ tsp
3 tbsp	Chinese dark soy sauce	3 tbsp
3 tbsp	Chinese light soy sauce	3 tbsp
4 tbsp	mild vinegar	4 tbsp
2 tbsp	Chinese rice wine or dry sherry	2 tbsp
3 tbsp	groundnut oil	3 tbsp
1 tbsp	sesame oil	1 tbsp
2 tbsp	lightly roasted sesame seeds	2 tbsp

1. Trim the cabbage, iceberg lettuce or paksoi. Remove most of the stalk, cut the cabbage or lettuce into very thin strips.

Wash and dry thoroughly. Put the cabbage or lettuce into a large bowl.
2. Arrange the bean sprouts on top in a large ring.
3. Arrange a ring of bamboo shoots round the outside of the ring of bean sprouts, and arrange the lychees in the middle. Cover the dish and chill until needed.
4. Mix together the garlic, root ginger, soy sauces, vinegar and rice wine or sherry. Stir and beat for 5 minutes.
5. Gradually add the oils, beating the mixture constantly. Chill the sauce until the salad is to be served.
6. Pour the sauce over the salad, sprinkle with sesame seeds and serve.

Cook's tip: salads of this type have been very popular in China for many years using as many fresh vegetables and fruits as possible.
Variations:
Iceberg lettuce – oranges – scallions (spring onions) – bean sprouts
Lettuce – grapefruit – bean sprouts - white celery
Chinese cabbage – mangoes – bean sprouts - green bell peppers

So joe tse joen
Golden Blossoms

00.30 · plus standing time · **00.15**

American	Ingredients	Metric/Imperial
½ lb	fresh peeled shrimp (prawns)	225 g/8 oz
½ lb	chicken breast fillets	225 g/8 oz
¼ lb	very finely ground (minced) pork	125 g/4 oz
3	very finely chopped scallions (spring onions)	3
½ tsp	salt	½ tsp
2½ tsp	cornstarch (cornflour)	2½ tsp
½ cup	canned sweetcorn, drained	50 g/2 oz
1 cup	flour	125 g/4 oz
½ cup	cornstarch (cornflour)	50 g/2 oz
	good pinch of salt	
2 tsp	groundnut oil	2 tsp
½ tsp	grated fresh root ginger	½ tsp
1	stiffly beaten egg white	1
¾ cup	groundnut oil	200 ml/7 fl oz

1. Grind (mince) or chop the shrimp (prawns) and chicken meat very finely.
2. Mix with the ground (minced) pork and rub the mixture through a very fine strainer (sieve). Add the scallions (spring onions), salt, cornstarch (cornflour) and sweetcorn.
3. Shape the mixture into 12 balls.
4. Make the batter by mixing the flour with the cornstarch (cornflour) and salt in a bowl. Make a well in the middle and pour in ¾ cup (200 ml/7 fl oz) cold water. Stir well, working from the middle and continue stirring until the mixture forms a smooth batter that runs off the spoon in a thick stream.
5. Stir in the oil and root ginger, leave the batter to stand for 30 minutes, then stir well.
6. Immediately before using, fold in the egg white.
7. Heat the oil in a wok. Coat the balls in the batter and fry 3-4 at a time, until golden brown. Drain on kitchen paper.
8. Serve with a sauce made by mixing 2 parts Chinese light soy sauce with 1 part Chinese plum sauce.

Joe tsjioe hwa goen

Fish Rolls with Shrimp (Prawns)

00.15 00.05

makes 12 as snack or starter

American	Ingredients	Metric/Imperial
12	large Chinese shrimp (prawns) thawed if frozen	12
	salt	
½ lb	filleted saltwater fish eg turbot or brill	225 g/8 oz
4 tbsp	sifted flour	4 tbsp
1	lightly beaten egg	1
½ cup	lightly dry roasted finely crushed rice	125 g/4 oz
6-8 tbsp	groundnut oil	6-8 tbsp

1. Peel the shrimp (prawns) and sprinkle with a little salt.
2. Cut the fish into 12 equal, very thin slices.
3. Lay a peeled shrimp (prawn) on each slice of fish. Roll the slice of fish round the shrimp (prawn) and secure with a wooden cocktail pick.
4. Toss the rolled fish in the flour.
5. Roll in the lightly beaten egg to coat.
6. Toss in the finely crushed rice.
7. Heat the oil in a wok and quickly fry the fish rolls 2-3 at a time until golden brown. Drain on kitchen paper, remove the cocktail pick and serve.

Cook's tip: serve with a sauce made by mixing 3 parts Chinese tomato sauce with 1 part dark soy sauce and 1 part Chinese rice wine or dry sherry. Add a touch of five spice powder to taste, or, for a slightly more piquant sauce, add ½ tsp of Chinese chili sauce.

So joe hwa joen

Lotus Flowers

00.15 00.05

makes 12 as snack or starter

American	Ingredients	Metric/Imperial
1 lb	fresh peeled shrimp (prawns)	450 g/1 lb
6	canned, finely chopped water chestnuts, drained	6
2	extremely finely chopped shallots or scallions (spring onions)	2
½ tsp	grated fresh root ginger	½ tsp
½ tsp	salt	½ tsp
2 tsp	Chinese rice wine or dry sherry	2 tsp
2 tsp	oyster or shrimp sauce	2 tsp
2 tsp	Chinese light soy sauce	2 tsp
1	stiffly beaten egg white	1
2 tsp	cornstarch (cornflour)	2 tsp
	groundnut oil for deep frying	

1. Finely chop the shrimp (prawns).
2. Mix with the water chestnuts, shallots or scallions (spring onions), root ginger, salt, rice wine or sherry, oyster or shrimp sauce and soy sauce.
3. Add the egg white and cornstarch (cornflour) and fold in as lightly as possible.
4. Shape the mixture into balls, the size of a walnut.
5. Heat the oil in a wok, add the shrimp (prawn) balls and fry for 2-3 minutes, until golden brown.
6. Remove the balls using a slotted spoon. Drain over the wok then lay on kitchen paper.
7. Serve as hot as possible on a warm dish.

Cook's tip: a mixture of finely minced or chopped shrimp (prawn) to which 1 lightly beaten egg is added in place of the white of one egg is an interesting variation.

1. Shape the mixture into rolls 1in (2.5 cm) thick and 3in (7.5 cm) long.
2. Toss the rolls in a little cornstarch (cornflour).
3. Draw them through the lightly beaten egg and roll them in finely chopped nuts (eg walnuts), sesame seeds or ground roasted rice.
4. Fry the rolls in hot oil until brown all over.
5. After removing the rolls from the oil, cut into 4 or 5 equal sized pieces.

Woe die hwa

Butterfly Shrimp (Prawns)

00.30 00.12

makes 12 as snack or starter

American	Ingredients	Metric/Imperial
12	large Chinese shrimp (prawns) partly thawed if frozen	12
2-3 tbsp	Chinese rice wine or dry sherry	2-3 tbsp
3 tbsp	Chinese light soy sauce	3 tbsp
2	crushed garlic cloves	2
½ tsp	finely grated fresh root ginger	½ tsp
4 tbsp	rice flour or cornstarch (cornflour)	4 tbsp
1	lightly beaten egg	1
½ cup	lightly dry roasted finely crushed rice	125 g/4 oz
¾ cup	groundnut oil	200 ml/7 fl oz

1. Peel the shrimp (prawns) but leave on the bottom part of the tail. Using the tip of a sharp knife, cut lengthwise down into the back of each shrimp (prawn) so that the back is neatly cut almost in two.
2. Mix the rice wine with the soy sauce, garlic and root ginger. Stir well.
3. Brush over the shrimp (prawns), coating them all over. Leave to stand for 15 minutes.
4. Toss the shrimp (prawns) in the rice flour or cornstarch (cornflour).
5. Coat with the lightly beaten egg, then coat with the finely crushed rice. Press the rice firmly into the surface.
6. Heat the oil in a wok and fry the shrimp (prawns) 2-3 at a time, turning constantly, until golden brown. The shrimp (prawns) should not be fried for more than 2 minutes, otherwise they will become tough and lose flavor.
7. After frying, drain on kitchen paper and arrange on a warmed dish. Serve immediately.

Sjoi mai

Steamed Shrimp (Prawn) Parcels

	00.15	00.30
	makes 12 as snack or starter	

American	Ingredients	Metric/Imperial
8	large Chinese shrimp (prawns) thawed if frozen	8
½ lb	very finely ground (minced) pork	225 g/8 oz
1½ oz	finely chopped water chestnuts drained	40 g/1½ oz
1½ oz	finely chopped bamboo shoots drained	40 g/1½ oz
1 tbsp	oyster sauce	1 tbsp
1 tbsp	hoisin sauce	1 tbsp
1 tbsp	Chinese light soy sauce	1 tbsp
1 tbsp	Chinese rice wine or dry sherry	1 tbsp
1 tbsp	sesame oil	1 tbsp
1	lightly whisked egg white	1
1 tbsp	rice flour or cornstarch (cornflour)	1 tbsp
1	packet 12 wonton wrappers thawed if frozen	1

1. Peel the shrimp (prawns) and chop them very finely.
2. Mix them with the pork, water chestnuts, bamboo shoots, oyster sauce, hoisin sauce, soy sauce, rice wine or sherry, sesame oil, egg white and rice flour or cornstarch (cornflour).
3. Lay out the wonton wrappers on a work surface.
4. Spoon some of the shrimp (prawn) mixture into the middle of each wrapper. Fold the wrapper round the filling to make a little bundle in which the filling is still clearly visible from the top.

5. Put a piece of aluminum foil on the base of a steamer.
6. Brush with a little sesame oil, and lay the bundles on top.
7. Steam the bundles for 20-30 minutes until cooked.
8. Serve the shrimp (prawn) bundles from the steamer with a piquant sauce separately.

Hwa koe

Steamed Shrimp (Prawn) Crescents

	00.30	00.20
	plus resting time	

American	Ingredients	Metric/Imperial
12	large Chinese shrimp (prawns), thawed if frozen	12
2 tbsp	very finely chopped cooked ham or cooked lean ground (minced) pork	2 tbsp
2 tbsp	very finely chopped bamboo shoots	2 tbsp
2 tbsp	very finely chopped shallots or scallions (spring onions)	2 tbsp
1	lightly beaten egg white	1
½ tsp	salt	½ tsp
½ tsp	sugar	½ tsp
1 cup + 2 tbsp	flour	150 g/5 oz
½ cup + 1 tbsp	cornstarch (cornflour)	75 g/3 oz
2 tsp	sesame oil	2 tsp
1 tbsp	rice flour or cornstarch (cornflour)	1 tbsp

Steamed shrimp (prawn) parcels

1. Peel the shrimp (prawns) and chop very finely. Add the ham or pork, bamboo shoots, shallots or scallions (spring onions), egg white, salt and sugar. Mix together thoroughly and set aside in a cool place.

2. To make the pastry, sift the flour with the cornstarch (cornflour) into a bowl. Make a well in the middle and pour in ⅔ cup (150 ml/¼ pint) boiling water and 1 tsp sesame oil. Mix together quickly with the fingers, and knead the dough until firm and elastic.

3. Shape the dough into a roll 2 in (5 cm) in diameter, wrap in a sheet of foil and leave to rest for 15 minutes.

4. Cut the dough into 12 slices.

5. On a board sprinkled with rice flour or cornstarch (cornflour) roll out the dough into thin rounds 6-8 in (8-10 cm) across.

6. Put a little of the filling on to each round. Moisten the edges with water, fold the pastry over the filling, and press the edges together firmly, shaping the filled parcels into half moons.

7. Put a sheet of aluminum foil on the base of a steamer.

8. Brush the foil with 1 tsp sesame oil, and put the shrimp (prawn) crescents on top.

9. Steam for 20 minutes. Serve in the steamers with one of the sauces on page 66.

Hwa koe
Variations

00.30 plus resting time   **00.20**

American	Ingredients	Metric/Imperial
¾ lb	finely chopped, peeled fresh small shrimp (prawns)	350 g/¾ lb
¼ lb	finely chopped raw salmon	125 g/¼ lb
2 tbsp	finely chopped broccoli	2 tbsp
2 tbsp	finely chopped parsley	2 tbsp
	or	
¾ lb	finely chopped, peeled fresh small shrimp (prawns)	350 g/¾ lb
¼ lb	ground (minced) pork	125 g/¼ lb
2 tbsp	finely chopped blanched celery	2 tbsp
2 tbsp	finely chopped shallots or onion	2 tbsp
	or	
¾ lb	finely chopped, peeled fresh small shrimp (prawns)	350 g/¾ lb
¼ lb	finely chopped tuna fish	125 g/¼ lb
1 tbsp	finely chopped celery	1 tbsp
2 tbsp	finely chopped scallions (spring onions)	2 tbsp
	or	
¾ lb	finely chopped white fish fillets	350 g/¾ lb
¼ lb	finely chopped crabmeat or lobster	125 g/¼ lb
2 tbsp	finely chopped paksoi	2 tbsp
2 tbsp	finely chopped scallions (spring onions)	2 tbsp
	or	
¾ lb	finely chopped white fish fillet	350 g/¾ lb
¼ lb	finely pounded scallop roes	125 g/¼ lb
1 tbsp	finely chopped parsley	1 tbsp
2 tbsp	finely chopped leek or scallion (spring onion)	2 tbsp

Jigan zhemgjiao
Steamed Chicken Liver Crescents

00.30 makes 24   **00.15**

American	Ingredients	Metric/Imperial
1 cup	sifted flour	125 g/4 oz
½ tsp	salt	½ tsp
1	beaten egg	1
½ lb	chicken livers	225 g/8 oz
3 oz	lean smoked bacon or ham	75 g/3 oz
2 tbsp	cornstarch (cornflour)	2 tbsp
2 tsp	finely ground fresh ginger	2 tsp
2-3 tbsp	chopped shallot or scallion (spring onion)	2-3 tbsp
2 tbsp	Chinese light soy sauce	2 tbsp
2 tbsp	Chinese dark soy sauce	2 tbsp
2 tbsp	Chinese rice wine or sherry	2 tbsp
1 tbsp	ginger syrup	1 tbsp
1½ tsp	red chili oil	1½ tsp
1½ tsp	sesame oil	1½ tsp
1 tbsp	palm sugar	1 tbsp
2 tsp	honey	2 tsp
2 tbsp	cornstarch (cornflour)	2 tbsp
1	egg yolk	1
	oil or soft butter	
	salt	
1	skinned tomato (optional)	1

1. Make the dough cases as described in the previous recipe.

2. Trim the chicken livers and rinse with cold water. Dry with kitchen paper and chop them into small pieces.

3. Chop the smoked bacon or ham. Grind (mince) the liver and bacon in a food processor.

4. Mix 2 tbsp cornstarch (cornflour) with 1 tbsp cold water. Stir into the meat mixture with the remaining ingredients except the remaining 2 tbsp cornstarch (cornflour), egg yolk, oil or soft butter, salt and garnish. Mix thoroughly.

5. Leave the mixture to stand for 15 minutes in a cool place and then mix again using dampened fingers.

6. Place about 1½ tbsp filling on each dough case. Moisten the uncovered area of each case with beaten egg yolk. Fold the case round the filling to form a crescent.

7. Rub a little soft butter or oil over the trivet of a steamer and place the half-moons on it. Bring a few pints/litres of water to the boil in the pan. Place the trivet over the boiling water, cover the pan and steam the crescents for 12-15 minutes until soft.

8. Serve on a warmed dish or small plates garnished with a tomato 'flower'.

Steamed dumplings with chicken liver.

Shu mai

Steamed Dumplings with Chicken Liver

American	Ingredients	Metric/Imperial
	00.30 makes 12	**00.20**
¼ lb	pork	125 g/4 oz
¼ lb	chicken livers	125 g/4 oz
1½ tsp	cornstarch (cornflour)	1½ tsp
1	egg white	1
2 tbsp	chopped shallot, or scallion (spring onion)	2 tbsp
3 oz	cleaned and chopped fresh mushrooms	75 g/3 oz
2-3 oz	sliced bamboo shoots	50-75 g/2-3 oz
½ tsp	Chinese light soy sauce	½ tsp
½ tsp	Chinese dark soy sauce	½ tsp
2 tsp	hoisin sauce	2 tsp
1 tbsp	Chinese rice wine or sherry	1 tbsp
1½ tsp	sugar	1½ tsp
1 tsp	sesame oil	1 tsp
	salt	
	freshly ground pepper	
12	wonton wrappers thawed if frozen	12
1	egg yolk	1
	butter or sesame oil	
	salt	

1. Dry the pork with kitchen paper and cut into small pieces.
2. Wash and trim the chicken livers. Dry with kitchen paper.
3. Coarsely grind (mince) the pork and chicken livers.
4. Beat the egg white with 1 tbsp of water. Stir in the cornstarch (cornflour) and add this mixture to the meat before adding all the other ingredients, except the wonton wrappers,

egg yolk, butter or sesame oil and remaining salt. Mix together to form a fairly smooth mixture.
5. Lay out the wonton wrappers on a chopping board or worktop and place about 1 tbsp of filling in the middle of each. Dampen the edges with a little beaten egg yolk or water. Make each one into a round dumpling with the top slightly open so that the filling is visible.
6. Rub the top section of a steaming pan with a little soft butter or oil and place the dumplings on top. Bring a few pints/litres of salted water to the boil in the pan. Place the trivet in the pan and cover. Steam the dumplings for 15-20 minutes until soft. Use a fork or skewer to test the filling. If none of the filling sticks to it, the dumplings are ready. Serve from the steamer with tomato sauce.

Zha zhurov jiao

Wonton with Pork, Shrimp (Prawns) and Green Chilies

American	Ingredients	Metric/Imperial
	00.15 makes 12	**00.15**
¼ lb	pork	125 g/4 oz
¼ lb	fresh, peeled, cooked shrimp (prawn)	125 g/4 oz
2 tbsp	cornstarch (cornflour)	2 tbsp
1	beaten egg	1
2	seeded, shredded green chilies	2
3 tbsp	chopped shallot or scallion (spring onion)	3 tbsp
½ tbsp	Chinese light soy sauce	½ tbsp
½ tbsp	Chinese dark soy sauce	½ tbsp
1½ tsp	shrimp sauce	1½ tsp
1 tbsp	Chinese rice wine or dry sherry	1 tbsp
1½ tsp	hoisin sauce	1½ tsp
1½ tsp	sugar	1½ tsp
12	wonton wrappers, thawed if frozen	12
1	beaten egg yolk	1
	oil for frying	

1. Coarsely chop or grind (mince) the pork and shrimp (prawns)
2. Mix the cornstarch (cornflour) with 1 tbsp cold water and stir this mixture into the egg.
3. Add to the pork and shrimp (prawn) mixture, then add chilies, shallots or scallions (spring onions), soy sauces, shrimp sauce, rice wine or sherry, hoisin sauce and sugar.
4. Mix together with wetted finger tips.
5. Put the wonton wrappers on a chopping board or worktop and place about 1 tbsp filling in the middle of each. Brush the wrappers with a little water or egg yolk, then fold each one into a triangle using the base of a fork to press it flat.
6. Heat the oil in a wok until very hot, then fry the triangles three at a time until golden brown.
7. Drain the triangles on kitchen paper then serve on a warmed dish.
8. Accompany with a sauce made by mixing equal parts of Chinese tomato or barbecue sauce and Chinese dark soy sauce. For each tbsp of soy sauce, add ½ tsp sugar.

Zha jiaozi

Half-moon Snacks with Pork and Vegetables

⬤⬤ 00.30
makes 24

00.30 ⬤

American	Ingredients	Metric/Imperial
1 cup	sifted flour	125 g/4 oz
½ tsp	salt	½ tsp
1	beaten egg	1
¾ lbs	lightly fatty pork	350 g/12 oz
2 tbsp	cornstarch (cornflour)	2 tbsp
4 tbsp	finely chopped Chinese cabbage	4 tbsp
2-3 tbsp	chopped shallot or scallion· (spring onion)	2-3 tbsp
4 tbsp	washed, drained, coarsely chopped bean sprouts	4 tbsp
2 tbsp	Chinese light soy sauce	2 tbsp
2 tbsp	Chinese dark soy sauce	2 tbsp
½ tbsp	oyster sauce	½ tbsp
1 tbsp	hoisin sauce	1 tbsp
1½ tbsp	Chinese rice wine or sherry	1½ tbsp
1 tbsp	sugar	1 tbsp
1	beaten egg yolk	1
2 tbsp	cornstarch (cornflour)	2 tbsp
8-10 tbsp	groundnut oil	8-10 tbsp
	few sprigs of coriander or parsley	

1. Mix the flour and salt together in a bowl. Make a well in the center and add the beaten egg and 5 tbsp hot water. Knead with wet fingers to make a light, elastic dough.
2. Sprinkle a worktop with flour, take half the dough and roll it into a square of about 20 in (33 cm), about 1/16 in (1.5 mm) thick. Cut this into circles 4 in (10 cm) across or 3½ in (8 cm) squares. Do the same with the other half of the dough.
3. Grind (mince) or chop the meat finely.
4. Mix the cornstarch (cornflour) with 1 tbsp cold water. Add this mixture to the meat and mix together well. Add all the remaining ingredients except the egg yolk, 2 tbsp cornstarch (cornflour), groundnut oil and the garnish and mix well.
5. Place the squares or circles of dough on a worktop or chopping board which has been sprinkled with cornstarch (cornflour) and place 1½ tbsp filling in the middle of each.
6. Brush areas of each case which are not covered by filling with egg yolk. Fold each one into a half moon shape using the base of a fork to press it flat.
7. Heat the oil until very hot then fry four of the half-moons at a time until golden brown. Drain on a piece of kitchen paper and serve garnished with sprigs of coriander or parsley.

Cook's tip: serve with a sauce made by mixing 4 tbsp light and 2 Chinese dark soy sauce, 2 tbsp Chinese rice wine or dry sherry, 1 tsp brown cane sugar and 1 tsp sesame oil.

Making crescents

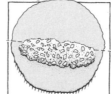
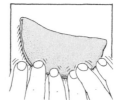

1. Place filling in the middle of each round

2. Dampen the edges and press firmly together.

Half-moon snacks with pork and vegetables

Xiaren chunjuan

Spring Rolls with Shrimp (Prawns) and Leek

00.12
plus standing time

00.25

American	Ingredients	Metric/Imperial
½ lb	fresh peeled shrimps (prawns)	225 g/8 oz
¼ lb	finely ground (minced) pork	125 g/4 oz
1	beaten egg white	1
1 tbsp	cornstarch (cornflour)	1 tbsp
1	finely chopped small leek (white and yellow parts)	1
1-2	crushed garlic cloves	1-2
1 tbsp	Chinese dark soy sauce	1 tbsp
1 tbsp	shrimp sauce	1 tbsp
1 tbsp	Chinese rice wine or dry sherry	1 tbsp
½ tsp	white sugar	½ tsp
	pinch allspice	
2 tbsp	Chinese tomato or barbecue sauce	2 tbsp
1 tsp	sesame oil	1 tsp
12	small spring roll or wonton wrappers	12
1	beaten egg white	1
	oil for frying	
	sprigs coriander or parsley	

1. Finely chop half of the shrimps (prawns). Cut the rest into small pieces. Mix the shrimps (prawns) with the ground (minced) pork.

2. Stir one egg white into the cornstarch (cornflour) and mix this with the shrimp mixture. Add all the remaining ingredients except the wonton wrappers, remaining egg white, oil for frying and coriander or parsley. Knead them together.

3. Leave the mixture to stand for 15 minutes in a cool place.

4. Place the spring roll or wonton wrappers on a worktop or chopping board. Make the shrimp (prawn) mixture into 12 small rolls of equal size. Place one on each wrapper. Brush the uncovered part of each wrapper with egg white. Roll up the wrappers round the filling and fold tightly, tucking in the ends to enclose the filling securely.

5. Heat the oil until very hot and fry 3-4 spring rolls at a time. Turn the rolls occasionally using a skimmer or slotted spoon.

6. Drain the spring rolls on kitchen paper and serve very hot garnished with sprigs of coriander or parsley.

Cook's tip: there are many delicious variations on spring rolls. The recipes given here are made to the same method as that above.

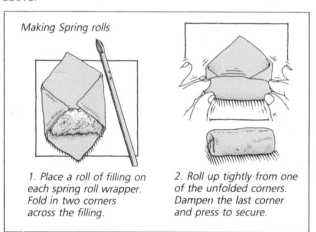

Making Spring rolls

1. Place a roll of filling on each spring roll wrapper. Fold in two corners across the filling.

2. Roll up tightly from one of the unfolded corners. Dampen the last corner and press to secure.

Spring rolls with shrimp (prawns) and leeks

Jisi chunjuan
Chicken Spring Rolls

00.12 makes 12   **00.25**

American	Ingredients	Metric/Imperial
¾ lb	ground (minced) chicken breasts	350 g/12 oz
2 tbsp	chopped shallot, scallion (spring onion)	2 tbsp
1 tbsp	grated fresh root ginger	1 tbsp
1	crushed garlic clove	1
2 tsp	Chinese light soy sauce	2 tsp
1 tsp	Chinese dark soy sauce	1 tsp
½ tbsp	oyster sauce	½ tbsp
½ tsp	red chili oil	½ tsp
1 tsp	sugar	1 tsp
½ tsp	hoisin sauce	½ tsp
1 tbsp	cornstarch (cornflour)	1 tbsp
1 tbsp	Chinese rice wine or sherry	1 tbsp

1. Mix together all the ingredients and then complete as recipe above.

Niurou Chunjuan
Beef Spring Rolls

00.12 makes 12   **00.25**

American	Ingredients	Metric/Imperial
2	small finely chopped onions	2
2	finely chopped garlic cloves	2
¾ lb	lean ground (minced) beef	350 g/12 oz
2 tbsp	chopped shallot, scallion (spring onion)	2 tbsp
1 tsp	sugar	1 tsp
1 tsp	grated fresh root ginger	1 tsp
1 tsp	Chinese light soy sauce	1 tsp
2 tsp	Chinese dark soy sauce	2 tsp
1½ tbsp	Chinese tomato or barbecue sauce	1½ tbsp
1 tsp	sesame oil	1 tsp
1 tbsp	cornstarch (cornflour)	1 tbsp
1 tbsp	Chinese rice wine or sherry	1 tbsp

1. Fry the onions, stirring constantly, until they are transparent.
2. Add the garlic and continue stirring until the onions begin to change color.
3. Mix all the remaining ingredients together and complete the recipe as above.

Haixian Chunjuan
Fish Spring Rolls

00.12 makes 12   **00.25**

American	Ingredients	Metric/Imperial
½ lb	ground (minced) white fish fillets	225 g/8 oz
¼ lb	finely chopped fresh peeled shrimp (prawns)	125 g/4 oz
1	beaten egg	1
1½ tsp	cornstarch (cornflour)	1½ tsp
½ tsp	grated fresh root ginger	½ tsp
1 tsp	Chinese light soy sauce	1 tsp
2 tsp	crab sauce	2 tsp
1 tbsp	Chinese tomato or barbecue sauce	1 tbsp
1 tbsp	Chinese rice wine or sherry	1 tbsp
2 tsp	lemon juice	2 tsp
2 tbsp	chopped shallot, scallion (spring onion) or leek	2 tbsp

1. Mix together all the ingredients above and complete recipe as above.

Donggu chunjuan
Mushroom Spring Rolls

00.12 plus soaking time   **00.25**

American	Ingredients	Metric/Imperial
6	dried Chinese mushrooms	6
¾ lb	fresh mushrooms	350 g/12 oz
1	beaten egg white	1
1 tbsp	cornstarch (cornflour)	1 tbsp
3 oz	crumbled soybean curd (tofu)	75 g/3 oz
1 tbsp	finely grated carrot	1 tbsp
1 tbsp	finely grated fresh root ginger	1 tbsp
1	crushed garlic clove	1
1 tbsp	Chinese light soy sauce	1 tbsp
½ tbsp	Chinese dark soy sauce	½ tbsp
2 tsp	hoisin sauce	2 tsp
1 tsp	sesame oil	1 tsp
1 tsp	sugar	1 tsp
1 tbsp	Chinese rice wine or sherry	1 tbsp
2-3 tbsp	chopped shallot, scallion (spring onion) or leek	2-3 tbsp

1. Soak the dried Chinese mushrooms for 30 minutes in hot water to cover.
2. Wipe and trim the fresh mushrooms and discard the stalks.
3. Finely chop both the fresh and dried mushrooms.
4. Mix all the remaining ingredients together.
5. Complete as for recipe above.

Jiangwei jiangyou

Soy Sauce with Ginger

00.10 00.00

makes a dip for 12 small snacks

American	Ingredients	Metric/Imperial
1½-2 tbsp	*finely ground fresh root ginger*	*1½-2 tbsp*
1½ tbsp	*raw cane sugar*	*1½ tbsp*
5 tbsp	*Chinese light soy sauce*	*5 tbsp*
5 tbsp	*Chinese dark soy sauce*	*5 tbsp*
1 tbsp	*ginger syrup*	*1 tbsp*
2 tbsp	*Chinese rice wine or sherry*	*2 tbsp*
1 tsp	*sesame oil*	*1 tsp*

1. Blend the ginger and sugar to a fine paste in a pestle and mortar.
2. Mix with the soy sauces and the ginger syrup then stir in all the remaining ingredients.
3. Serve the sauce in small individual dishes.

Liang fanqui zhi

Tomato Sauce

00.02 00.05

makes a dip for 12 small snacks

American	Ingredients	Metric/Imperial
5 tbsp	*Chinese tomato or barbecue sauce*	*5 tbsp*
2 tbsp	*Chinese plum sauce*	*2 tbsp*
1 tbsp	*Chinese light soy sauce*	*1 tbsp*
1 tbsp	*Chinese dark soy sauce*	*1 tbsp*
1 tbsp	*sugar*	*1 tbsp*
1 tbsp	*ginger syrup*	*1 tbsp*
1 tbsp	*finely chopped shallot or scallion (spring onion)*	*1 tbsp*

1. Bring the tomato or barbecue sauce to the boil. Add the remaining ingredients and stir until the sugar has dissolved.
2. Stir in 1 tbsp of finely chopped shallot or scallion (spring onions).
3. Serve the sauce in individual bowls.

Fanquie zhi

Hot Tomato Sauce

00.00 00.10

American	Ingredients	Metric/Imperial
¾ cup	*Chinese tomato or barbecue sauce*	*200 ml/7 fl oz*
1 tbsp	*Chinese light soy sauce*	*1 tbsp*
½ tbsp	*Chinese dark soy sauce*	*½ tbsp*
3 tbsp	*Chinese rice wine or dry sherry*	*3 tbsp*
1 tsp	*ginger syrup*	*1 tsp*
2 tsp	*hoisin sauce*	*2 tsp*
1 tbsp	*sugar*	*1 tbsp*

1. Mix all the ingredients with 4 tbsp water and bring slowly to the boil in a small pan, stirring until the sugar has dissolved. Simmer until reduced by one quarter.
2. Serve as a dipping sauce in individual bowls.

Jiang zhi

Hot Ginger Sauce

00.10 00.10

American	Ingredients	Metric/Imperial
1 tbsp	*finely grated fresh ginger*	*1 tbsp*
1 tsp	*coarsely grated fresh ginger*	*1 tsp*
1 tbsp	*finely chopped shallot, scallion (spring onion) or leek*	*1 tbsp*
4 tbsp	*Chinese light soy sauce*	*4 tbsp*
2 tbsp	*Chinese dark soy sauce*	*2 tbsp*
4 tbsp	*Chinese rice wine or dry sherry*	*4 tbsp*
3 tbsp	*sugar*	*3 tbsp*
	pinch allspice	
½ tsp	*hoisin sauce*	*½ tsp*

1. Place all the ingredients in a heavy-based saucepan. Add 3 tbsp water and stir well.
2. Bring slowly to the boil, stirring constantly, until the sugar has dissolved then simmer until the sauce is quite thick and syrupy.
3. Serve as a dipping sauce in individual small bowls.

Sumei zhi

Hot Plum Sauce

00.05 00.10

American	Ingredients	Metric/Imperial
6 tbsp	*Chinese plum sauce*	*6 tbsp*
1 tbsp	*red chili oil*	*1 tbsp*
1 tbsp	*Chinese light soy sauce*	*1 tbsp*
2 tbsp	*Chinese dark soy sauce*	*2 tbsp*
4 tbsp	*Chinese rice wine or dry sherry*	*4 tbsp*
2 tbsp	*sugar*	*2 tbsp*
1 tbsp	*ginger syrup*	*1 tbsp*
1 tbsp	*finely chopped shallot, scallion (spring onion) or leek*	*1 tbsp*
1½ tbsp	*lemon juice*	*1½ tbsp*

1. Put all the ingredients in a small heavy-based saucepan with 4 tbsp water. Bring to the boil, stirring constantly, until the sugar has dissolved.
2. Simmer until the sauce has thickened.
3. Serve as a dipping sauce in individual small bowls.

Mogu jiding
Diced Chicken and Mushrooms in Oyster Sauce

◢ 00.05
plus standing time

00.30 🍲

American	Ingredients	Metric/Imperial
1¼ lb	boneless chicken breasts	575 g/1¼ lb
	salt	
	freshly ground pepper	
2 tbsp	groundnut oil	2 tbsp
2	crushed garlic cloves	2
1 tsp	finely ground fresh ginger	1 tsp
2 tbsp	Chinese light soy sauce	2 tbsp
1 tbsp	Chinese dark soy sauce	1 tbsp
2 tbsp	hoisin sauce	2 tbsp
2-3 tbsp	Chinese rice wine or sherry	2-3 tbsp
¾ cup	chicken bouillon (stock)	200 ml/7 fl oz
1 tsp	sugar (optional)	1 tsp
1½-2 tsp	cornstarch (cornflour)	1½-2 tsp
1 tbsp	sesame oil	1 tbsp
1	medium size, seeded red bell pepper	1
3 oz	bean sprouts	75 g/3 oz
¼ lb	small, trimmed, wiped mushrooms	125 g/4 oz
4 tbsp	chopped shallot or scallion (spring onion)	4 tbsp
12	washed lettuce leaves from the heart of the lettuce	12
1-2 tbsp	finely chopped coriander leaves or parsley (optional)	1-2 tbsp

1. Dry the chicken with kitchen paper and season it with equal amounts of salt and pepper.
2. Heat the oil in a frying pan and fry the chicken for 10-12 minutes until golden brown on both sides. Remove from the pan and drain on kitchen paper. Leave to cool then cut into ½ in (1.25 cm) cubes.
3. Make the sauce by mixing the garlic, ginger, soy sauces, hoisin sauce, rice wine or sherry, bouillon (stock) and sugar together. Bring gradually to the boil.
4. Mix the cornstarch (cornflour) with 1 tbsp cold water. Stir this into the boiling sauce and cook until it starts to thicken. Simmer for 2-3 minutes, then remove the pan from the heat and leave to cool. Stir in the sesame oil.
5. Cut the bell pepper into strips and then into very small cubes.
6. Wash the bean sprouts in cold water and remove as many of the seed cases as possible. Drain in a colander.
7. Add the bell pepper to the bean sprouts and slowly pour a few pints/litres of boiling water over. Dry in a colander.
8. Cut the mushrooms into paper thin slices.
9. Mix together the diced chicken, shallot or scallion (spring onion), diced bell pepper, bean sprouts and mushrooms. Pour the sauce over them and carefully stir once more. Cover and leave to stand for 30 minutes in a cool place, stirring occasionally. Arrange the lettuce leaves on a large plate. Top with the salad and sauce.
10. Serve, sprinkled with the coriander or parsley.

Ningmeng jiding
Diced Chicken with Lemon and Coriander

◢ 00.10
plus cooling time

00.25 🍲

American	Ingredients	Metric/Imperial
1¼ lb	boneless chicken breasts	575 g/1¼ lb
	salt	
	freshly ground pepper	
2 tbsp	groundnut oil	2 tbsp
2-3	small onions	2-3
4-5 tbsp	lemon juice	4-5 tbsp
2 tsp	grated lemon zest	2 tsp
2	crushed garlic cloves	2
2-3 tbsp	Chinese rice wine or sherry	2-3 tbsp
2 tbsp	honey	2 tbsp
1 tbsp	Chinese light soy sauce	1 tbsp
1 tbsp	Chinese dark soy sauce	1 tbsp
1 tbsp	ginger syrup	1 tbsp
2 tsp	hoisin sauce	2 tsp
1½ tsp	cornstarch (cornflour)	1½ tsp
1 tbsp	sesame oil	1 tbsp
2	green bell peppers	2
1	red bell pepper	1
2 tbsp	finely chopped coriander or parsley	2 tbsp
12	lettuce leaves from the heart of the lettuce	12
	few sprigs of coriander or parsley (optional)	

1. Dry the chicken with kitchen paper and season with equal amounts of salt and pepper.
2. Heat the oil in a frying pan and fry the chicken for 10-12 minutes until golden brown on both sides. Remove the chicken from the pan and drain and leave to cool on kitchen paper. Cut into ½ in (1.25 cm) cubes.
3. Cut each onion into 6 or 8 slices. Put the lemon juice in a pan and add the grated lemon zest, garlic, slices of onion, rice wine or sherry, honey, soy sauces, ginger syrup and hoisin sauce. Mix well and bring slowly to the boil.
4. Mix the cornstarch (cornflour) with 2 tbsp cold water and stir this into the boiling sauce. Stir until the sauce begins to thicken. Simmer gently for 2-3 minutes.
5. Remove from the heat and leave the sauce to cool. Stir in the sesame oil.
6. Wash, halve, trim and seed the bell peppers. Cut into very thin slices all the same length.
7. Bring 1 quart (1 litre/2 pints) water to the boil, adding 2 tsp of salt. Add the bell pepper and boil for exactly 1½ minutes. Drain in a strainer (sieve), then leave under cold running water to get cold.
8. Mix the diced chicken, slices of bell pepper and coriander or parsley leaves in a bowl. Stir in the sauce then chill for 1 hour.
9. Wash and dry the lettuce leaves and arrange them on a large dish. Top with the salad and garnish with a few sprigs of coriander or parsley.

Cha je dan

Marbled or Tea Eggs (Canton)

	00.00 plus cooling time	01.00

American	Ingredients	Metric/Imperial
6	new laid eggs	6
3 tbsp	black China tea leaves	3 tbsp
1 tbsp	salt	1 tbsp
3-4 tbsp	Chinese dark soy sauce	3-4
2 tsp	five spice powder or whole star anise	2 tsp

1. Put the eggs in a saucepan and pour on enough water to cover them well. Bring very slowly to the boil and simmer gently for 7 minutes after the water has come to the boil. Stir constantly with a small wooden spoon during the first 3 or 4 minutes of cooking so that the egg yolks move to the center of the eggs. Cool under cold running water for a few minutes then, pressing lightly, dry them with kitchen paper and roll them carefully over a hard surface with the flat of the hand to crack the shell all over. Alternatively the eggs may also be tapped gently with a small spoon.
2. Bring 2 cups (450 ml/¾ pint) water to the boil in a saucepan. Add the tea leaves, salt, soy sauce and the five spice powder or star anise. Stir well.
3. Put the eggs in the saucepan cover and simmer very gently for 45-50 minutes checking that the eggs remain under water throughout the cooking time.
4. Remove the saucepan from the heat and leave to cool for at least 2 hours.
5. Shell the eggs very carefully immediately before use.

Cook's tip: the eggs may be used as a garnish with various dishes or as a snack between meals. They are usually halved or cut into sections. They can be served whole in a sauce which may be a mixture of dark soy sauce, oyster sauce and chili sauce.

Fu yong shi

Eggs with Crab (Shanghai)

	00.15 plus standing time	00.05

American	Ingredients	Metric/Imperial
½ lb	crabmeat thawed if frozen	225 g/8 oz
6-7	eggs	6-7
1½ tbsp	Chinese light soy sauce	1½ tbsp
1½ tbsp	Chinese dark soy sauce	1½ tbsp
2 tsp	oyster or crab sauce	2 tsp
	pinch sugar	
2 tsp	sesame oil	2 tsp
	salt	
1½ lb	spinach	700 g/1½ lb
2 tbsp	groundnut oil	2 tbsp

1. Remove all cartilage from the crabmeat and then shred the meat with two forks.

2. Lightly beat the eggs. Add the crabmeat, 1 tbsp of light and 1 tbsp of dark Chinese soy sauce, the oyster or crab sauce, a pinch of sugar, 1 tsp of sesame oil and a little salt. Leave to stand for 15 minutes.
3. Clean the spinach, wash it in plenty of water and drain it. Remove any thick stalks.
4. Bring a few quarts/litres of water to the boil. Add all the spinach at the same time and bring the water to the boil again. Drain the spinach in a colander and pour over plenty of cold water to cool it completely. Drain well.
5. Heat the groundnut oil in a wok and turn the pan round so that the sides are coated with oil.
6. Beat or stir the egg mixture lightly. Pour half into the wok. Leave to set and then lift the sides with a spatula or pancake knife and pour the rest of the mixture under the egg which has already set.
7. Remove the wok from the heat and wait for one minute until all the contents have set. Transfer to a warmed plate and cover with a second warmed plate.
8. Return the wok to the heat and add the spinach. Add the remainder of the two soy sauces and stir until hot. Add the remaining sesame oil and heat for a further 30 seconds.
9. Make a bed of spinach on a warmed plate. Cut the omelette into 2in (5 cm) diamonds and arrange on the spinach. Serve immediately.

Jang chong show dan

Scrambled Eggs with Scallions (Spring Onions) (Canton)

00.10 Serves 4 as side dish **00.05**

American	Ingredients	Metric/Imperial
4	eggs	4
	sugar	
1 tsp	sesame oil	1 tsp
1 tsp	Chinese light soy sauce	1 tsp
1 tsp	Chinese dark soy sauce	1 tsp
1 tsp	ginger syrup	1 tsp
6	chopped scallions (spring onions)	6
⅔ cup	chicken bouillon (stock)	150 ml/¼ pint
	salt	
2 tbsp	groundnut oil	2 tbsp
2	large, skinned tomatoes cut into segments	2
	few sprigs of parsley	

1. Lightly beat the eggs. Add a pinch of sugar, the sesame oil, soy sauces, ginger syrup, scallions (spring onions) and chicken bouillon (stock) and salt to taste.
2. Heat the oil in a wok and turn the pan so that the sides are coated with oil.
3. Add all the egg mixture at once and stir fry until it has set, but still looks moist on top.
4. Serve immediately in a warmed dish, garnished with sprigs of curled parsley.

Left to right: Scrambled eggs with scallions (spring onions); Marbled or tea eggs; Eggs with crab

Du ja show dan

Scrambled Eggs and Bean Sprouts (Peking)

00.10   00.08

Serves 4 as side dish

American	Ingredients	Metric/Imperial
1-2 oz	bean sprouts	30-40 g/1-2 oz
4	eggs	4
4 tbsp	chicken bouillon (stock)	4 tbsp
2 tsp	Chinese light soy sauce	2 tsp
2 tsp	Chinese dark soy sauce	2 tsp
	pinch of salt	
	sugar	
1 tsp	ginger syrup	1 tsp
2 tbsp	groundnut oil	2 tbsp
1	skinned, diced tomato	1

1. Wash the bean sprouts and remove as many of the seed cases as possible. Drain in a colander. Place the colander in a draughty place to dry the bean sprouts as much as possible.
2. Lightly beat the eggs and add the chicken bouillon (stock), soy sauces, a pinch of salt, a pinch of sugar and the ginger syrup.
3. Heat the oil in a wok and turn the pan so that the sides are coated with oil.
4. Add the bean sprouts and turn them over once. Fry for 30 seconds without turning over.
5. Add the egg mixture, turning over the contents of the wok constantly until the eggs have set.
6. Remove the wok from the heat, cover with a lid and leave to stand for 3 minutes.
7. Cut the scrambled eggs into four portions and serve on warmed plates garnished with diced tomatoes.

Hwo chu show dan

Scrambled Eggs with Ham and Tree Onions (Canton)

00.05   00.05

Serves 4 as side dish

American	Ingredients	Metric/Imperial
4	eggs	4
	pinch of salt	
	sugar	
4 tbsp	chicken bouillon (stock)	4 tbsp
1 tsp	sesame oil	1 tsp
2 tsp	Chinese light soy sauce	2 tsp
2 tsp	Chinese dark soy sauce	2 tsp
1 tsp	oyster sauce	1 tsp
¼ lb	thick slices boiled ham, cut into small diamonds	125 g/4 oz
3	chopped tree onions	3
2 tbsp	groundnut oil	2 tbsp

1. Lightly beat the eggs. Add the salt, a pinch of sugar, bouillon (stock), sesame oil, soy sauces, oyster sauce, ham and tree onions.

2. Heat the oil in a wok and turn the pan so that the sides are coated with oil.
3. Pour the egg mixture into the pan and stir fry until the eggs have set but still look moist on top. Serve immediately in a warmed dish.

Jee gan show dan

Scrambled Egg with Chicken Livers and Bean Sprouts

00.15   00.10

Serves 4 as side dish

American	Ingredients	Metric/Imperial
¼ lb	bean sprouts	125 g/4 oz
¼ lb	fresh chicken livers	125 g/4 oz
	salt	
4 tbsp	groundnut oil	4 tbsp
4	eggs	4
1 tbsp	Chinese light soy sauce	1 tbsp
1 tbsp	Chinese dark soy sauce	1 tbsp
1 tsp	ginger syrup	1 tsp
1 tbsp	oyster sauce	1 tbsp
	sugar	
	pinch of five spice powder	
2 tbsp	Chinese rice wine or dry sherry	2 tbsp
1 tsp	cornstarch (cornflour)	1 tsp
1	chopped onion or leek	1
1	crushed garlic clove	1
1 tsp	grated fresh root ginger	1 tsp
1 tbsp	finely chopped celery	1 tbsp
2	skinned tomatoes (optional)	2

1. Wash the bean sprouts, removing as many seed cases as possible. Drain the bean sprouts thoroughly in a colander. Slowly pour several quarts/litres of boiling water over them and drain again.
2. Trim the chicken livers, wash them and dry with kitchen paper. Sprinkle with a little salt.
3. Heat 2 tbsp of oil in a wok and stir fry the livers for 3 minutes.
4. Remove from the wok and drain on kitchen paper. After they have cooled a little, cut into ¼ in/5 mm slices.
5. Lightly beat the eggs, add the soy sauces, ginger syrup, oyster sauce, a pinch of sugar, five spice powder, rice wine or sherry, cornstarch (cornflour), a little salt and 2 tbsp water. Stir well.
6. Heat the remaining oil in a wok and fry the onion or leek, garlic and root ginger for 30 seconds.
7. Add the chicken liver slices and a few seconds later, the egg mixture. Immediately sprinkle the celery and bean sprouts over the egg mixture and continue stir frying until the eggs have set, but still look moist on top.
8. Transfer to a round, warmed dish and garnish with a few slices of skinned tomato.

4. Wash the spinach. Drain in a colander and remove any thick stalks.
5. Bring the remaining chicken bouillon (stock) to the boil.
6. Add the spinach and the sesame oil or chicken fat. Stir once and remove the pan from the heat.
7. Heat ½ tbsp of oil in a small frying pan. Make sure that the oil completely covers the bottom of the pan.
8. Pour a quarter of the egg mixture into the pan and leave until the surface begins to set. Spread a quarter of the minced chicken mixture over it with a spatula or pancake knife.
9. Immediately slide the omelette on to a plate and fold it in half.
10. Fry 3 more omelettes in exactly the same manner.
11. Place the omelettes in the saucepan with the chicken bouillon (stock) and spinach.
12. Very slowly bring almost to the boil. Place the lid on the saucepan and simmer for 4 minutes.
13. Serve the omelettes on warmed deep plates and spoon over the bouillon (stock) and spinach.

Jee lan fu rong

Scrambled Egg with Crab, Tomato and Broccoli

◢▽ 00.10   00.15 ◱
Serves 4 as side dish

American	Ingredients	Metric/Imperial
¼ lb	crabmeat, frozen or canned	125 g/4 oz
¼ lb	broccoli sprigs	125 g/4 oz
	salt	
4	eggs	4
1 tbsp	Chinese light soy sauce	1 tbsp
1 tbsp	Chinese dark soy sauce	1 tbsp
1 tbsp	crab sauce	1 tbsp
1 tsp	ginger syrup	1 tsp
1 tbsp	Chinese rice wine or dry sherry	1 tbsp
1 tsp	cornstarch (cornflour)	1 tsp
	pinch sugar	
3 tbsp	groundnut oil	3 tbsp
1	small chopped onion or shallot	1
1 tsp	grated fresh root ginger	1 tsp
2	skinned diced tomatoes	2

1. Defrost the frozen or drain canned crabmeat thoroughly.
2. Pick over and cut the crabmeat into small pieces.
3. Bring 1 quart (1 litre/1¾ pints) water to the boil add a little salt and the broccoli sprigs.
4. Bring to the boil again and boil for 4 minutes. Drain and keep warm between 2 warmed plates or wrapped in a sheet of aluminum foil.
5. Lightly beat the eggs, add the soy sauces, crab sauce, ginger syrup, rice wine or sherry, cornstarch (cornflour), a little salt, sugar and 2 tbsp water. Stir well.
6. Heat the oil in a wok and turn the pan so that the sides are coated with oil.
7. Fry the onion or shallot and the root ginger for 30 seconds.
8. Add the egg mixture, turn everything over once and sprinkle the crabmeat on top. Turn over again and sprinkle on the diced tomato.
9. Continue stirring until the eggs have set then spoon the scrambled egg into the middle of a round, warmed dish and arrange the broccoli sprigs around it.

Small omelettes with chicken and spinach

Bochai dan zjian

Small Omelettes with Chicken and Spinach (Peking)

◢▽ 00.15   00.25 ◱
Serves 4

American	Ingredients	Metric/Imperial
6	eggs	6
	salt	
	pinch of sugar	
3¼ cups	chicken bouillon (stock)	750 ml/1 ¼ pints
½ lb	chicken breasts	225 g/8 oz
2	chopped scallions (spring onions)	2
2 tsp	cornstarch (cornflour)	2 tsp
2 tsp	Chinese light soy sauce	2 tsp
2 tsp	Chinese dark soy sauce	2 tsp
1 tbsp	Chinese rice wine or dry sherry	1 tbsp
1 lb	spinach	450 g/1 lb
1 tsp	sesame oil or chicken fat	1 tsp
2 tbsp	groundnut oil	2 tbsp

1. Lightly beat the eggs. Add a little salt, the sugar and 5 tbsp chicken bouillon (stock) and stir well.
2. Chop the chicken very finely in a food processor.
3. Mix the chopped chicken with the scallions (spring onions), cornstarch (cornflour), soy sauces, rice wine or sherry and 3 tbsp of bouillon (stock).

Shee hong sh'ee show dan

Scrambled Eggs with Tomato and Meat Sauce (Peking)

00.10 00.15

Serves 4 as side dish

American	Ingredients	Metric/Imperial
2	*large, skinned tomatoes*	*2*
	salt	
4 tbsp	*groundnut oil*	*4 tbsp*
1	*peeled garlic clove*	*1*
¼ lb	*lean ground (minced) beef or pork*	*75-125 g/3-4 oz*
2 tbsp	*Chinese tomato sauce,*	*2 tbsp*
2 tbsp	*Chinese light soy sauce*	*2 tbsp*
2 tbsp	*Chinese dark soy sauce*	*2 tbsp*
2 tbsp	*Chinese rice wine or dry sherry*	*2 tbsp*
1 tbsp	*ginger syrup*	*1 tbsp*
	sugar	
	pinch five spice powder	
1 tsp	*cornstarch (cornflour)*	*1 tsp*
4	*lightly beaten eggs*	*4*
1 tbsp	*finely chopped celery or coriander leaves*	*1 tbsp*
2 tbsp	*cooked peas*	*2 tbsp*
½	*cucumber (optional)*	*½*
	few sprigs of curled parsley (optional)	

1. Cut each tomato into 8 segments. Remove the seeds and drain. Sprinkle the segments with a little salt.
2. Heat 2 tbsp of oil in a wok and stir fry the garlic clove until golden brown. Remove the garlic from the pan.
3. Add the meat to the hot oil and stir fry using a large fork until the meat has changed color and falls apart.
4. Sprinkle on a little salt and add the tomato sauce, 1 tbsp of light and 1 tbsp of dark Chinese soy sauce and 5 tbsp of water. Turn over well a few times and then add the tomato segments. Reduce the heat and cover the wok with a lid. Simmer gently for 2 minutes.
5. Add the remaining soy sauce, Chinese rice wine or sherry, ginger syrup, a little salt, sugar and five spice powder.
6. Mix the cornstarch (cornflour) with 2 tbsp water and stir into the wok.
7. Heat the remaining oil in another wok, or frying pan.
8. Pour in the beaten eggs and sprinkle with the celery or coriander. Stir in the cooked peas.
9. Stir fry until the eggs have set.
10. Transfer to a large, warmed dish. Make a hole in the middle and spoon in the meat and tomato mixture.
11. Garnish with cucumber fans and curled parsley and serve immediately.

Scrambled egg with chicken and green and red bell peppers

Jee see show dan

Scrambled Egg with Chicken and Green and Red Bell Peppers

00.10 00.10

Serves 4 as side dish

American	Ingredients	Metric/Imperial
¼ lb	*chicken, preferably breast*	*125 g/4 oz*
1	*small green bell pepper*	*1*
1	*small red bell pepper*	*1*
4	*eggs*	*4*
1 tbsp	*Chinese light soy sauce*	*1 tbsp*
1 tbsp	*Chinese dark soy sauce*	*1 tbsp*
1 tbsp	*Chinese rice wine or sherry*	*1 tbsp*
1 tsp	*ginger syrup*	*1 tsp*
1 tsp	*cornstarch (cornflour)*	*1 tsp*
	salt	
	pinch sugar	
2½ tbsp	*groundnut oil*	*2½ tbsp*
1	*chopped onion or leek*	*1*
1 tsp	*grated fresh root ginger*	*1 tsp*
1-2	*skinned tomatoes (optional)*	*1-2*
	few sprigs curled parsley (optional)	

1. Dry the chicken with kitchen paper and cut it into thin strips.
2. Wash the bell peppers, remove the stalk ends, halve and remove the seeds and seed cases. Cut the flesh into very thin strips.
3. Lightly beat the eggs, add soy sauces, rice wine or sherry, ginger syrup, cornstarch (cornflour), a little salt, sugar and 4 tbsp water. Stir thoroughly.
4. Heat the oil in a wok and turn the pan round so that the sides are coated with oil.
5. Stir fry the onion or leek and root ginger for 30 seconds.
6. Add the chicken and the peppers and continue stir frying for a further 2 minutes.

7. Pour in the egg mixture and cook, stirring until set.
8. Press the mixture together with a wooden spoon and slide it on to a warmed dish.
9. Garnish with one or more tomato 'roses' and sprigs of curled parsley and serve immediately.

Cook's tip: for a delicious variation, substitute lean rump steak cut into small diamonds for the chicken. Omit the green bell pepper and chop the red bell pepper very finely. Stir fry the beef and bell pepper very briefly then follow the method given in the recipe above.

Bee chee hey du show dan

Scrambled Egg with Snow Peas (Mange-tout) and Peanuts (Peking)

◄▭▽ 00.15   00.15 ◖▭
plus soaking time

American	Ingredients	Metric/Imperial
½ lb	snow peas (mange-tout)	225 g/8 oz
4	Chinese mushrooms	4
3 tbsp	shelled, skinned raw peanuts	3 tbsp
4-5 tbsp	groundnut oil	4-5 tbsp
2	chopped onions or thin leek	2
	salt	
2 tbsp	Chinese light soy sauce	2 tbsp
1 tbsp	Chinese dark soy sauce	1 tbsp
4	eggs	4
1 tbsp	ginger syrup	1 tbsp
2 tbsp	Chinese rice wine or dry sherry	2 tbsp
1 tsp	superfine (caster) sugar	1 tsp
1-2 tsp	cornstarch (cornflour)	1-2 tsp

1. Trim the snow peas (mange-tout), wash and drain well.
2. Soak the Chinese mushrooms in warm water for 20-30 minutes. Remove the stalks and cut the caps into strips.
3. Roast the peanuts in a small dry frying pan, stirring until they color evenly all over. Pour on to a large cold plate and leave to cool. Chop coarsely.
4. Heat 1 tbsp of oil in a wok, add the snow peas (mange-tout), mushrooms and onion or leek. Stir fry for 2 minutes.
5. Add a little salt and 1 tbsp each of the soy sauces. Stir well then reduce the heat. Leave to stand for a further 2 minutes. Pour off as much liquid and oil as possible and keep the contents of the pan warm.
6. Lightly beat the eggs, add the remaining soy sauce, the ginger syrup, rice wine or sherry, a little salt and sugar. Mix the cornstarch (cornflour) with 4 tbsp of water. Stir into the wok.
7. Heat the remaining oil in a wok, add the egg mixture and stir fry until the eggs have set.
8. Put the scrambled egg mixture on a large, warmed plate. Make a hole in the middle and pour the snow peas (mange-tout) into it.
9. Sprinkle chopped peanuts over the snow peas (mange-tout) and serve with a cold sauce made by mixing together equal parts of light and dark Chinese soy sauce, Chinese tomato sauce and Chinese rice wine or sherry.

Show fu rong

Scrambled Egg with Cultivated Mushrooms

◄▭▽ 00.05   00.06 ◖▭
Serves 4

American	Ingredients	Metric/Imperial
5	eggs	5
2-3 tbsp	chicken bouillon (stock)	2-3 tbsp
2 tbsp	Chinese light soy sauce	2 tbsp
1 tbsp	Chinese dark soy sauce	1 tbsp
2 tbsp	Chinese rice wine or dry sherry	2 tbsp
1 tbsp	ginger syrup	1 tbsp
1 tbsp	shrimp sauce	1 tbsp
2 tsp	cornstarch (cornflour)	2 tsp
	salt	
	five spice powder	
1 tsp	superfine (caster) sugar	1 tsp
4-5 tbsp	groundnut oil	4-5 tbsp
2	chopped onions	2
1	crushed garlic clove	1
1 tsp	grated fresh root ginger	1 tsp
¼ lb	peeled shrimp (prawns)	125 g/4 oz
2-3 tbsp	cooked peas	2-3 tbsp
½ lb	canned cultivated mushrooms	225 g/8 oz

1. Lightly beat the eggs. Stir in the bouillon (stock), the two soy sauces, rice wine or sherry, ginger syrup and shrimp sauce.
2. Mix the cornstarch (cornflour) with 1 tbsp cold water and add to the lightly beaten egg with salt, a pinch of five spice powder and sugar to taste.
3. Heat 2 tbsp of oil in a wok and turn the pan round to coat the sides with oil. Fry the onion with the garlic and the root ginger for 1 minute until transparent.
4. Add the shrimp (prawns) and peas and fry for 1 minute.
5. Spoon the contents of the wok on to a plate. Heat the remaining oil in the wok until very hot.
6. Pour half of the egg mixture into the wok and stir fry until the eggs are partly set. Add the mushrooms and the remaining egg mixture. Cook until set but moist on top.
7. Slide the egg on to a warmed dish.

Scrambled egg with snow peas (mange-tout) and peanuts

Wan du show dan

Scrambled Egg with Braised Peas (Peking)

	00.05 Serves 4	00.12

American	Ingredients	Metric/Imperial
5 tbsp	groundnut oil	5 tbsp
½ lb	shelled peas fresh or frozen	225 g/8 oz
3 oz	canned bamboo shoots	75 g/3 oz
¾ cup	chicken bouillon (stock)	200 ml/7 fl oz
4 tbsp	Chinese rice wine or dry sherry	4 tbsp
	salt	
	pinch sugar	
4	eggs	4
1 tbsp	Chinese light soy sauce	1 tbsp
1 tbsp	Chinese dark soy sauce	1 tbsp
1 tbsp	ginger syrup	1 tbsp
2 tsp	cornstarch (cornflour)	2 tsp
2 tbsp	finely chopped celery or coriander leaves	2 tbsp
2	very finely chopped onions or thin leek	2

1. Heat 2 tbsp of oil in a wok and stir fry the peas and bamboo shoots for 1 minute.
2. Add the hot bouillon (stock), 2 tbsp of rice wine or sherry, a little salt and the pinch of sugar. Leave to boil for 2 minutes then reduce the heat. Cover the wok with a lid and braise gently for a further 3-4 minutes.
3. Lightly beat the eggs in a bowl, add the rest of the rice wine or sherry, soy sauces, ginger syrup, a little salt, cornstarch (cornflour) and 2 tbsp of water. Stir well once more.
4. Heat the remainder of the oil in a wok. Add the egg mixture, sprinkle the celery or coriander leaves on top and stir fry until the eggs have set.
5. Put the scrambled egg on to a round, warmed dish, make a hole in the middle and spoon in the braised peas.
6. Sprinkle the onion or leek over the peas and serve immediately.

Sharen tzeng dan

Steamed Egg and Shrimp (Prawns) (Peking)

	00.05 Serves 4 as side dish	00.30

American	Ingredients	Metric/Imperial
3-4	eggs	3-4
¾ cup	chicken bouillon (stock)	200 ml/7 fl oz
1 tsp	Chinese light soy sauce	1 tsp
1 tsp	Chinese dark soy sauce	1 tsp
1 tbsp	oyster or shrimp sauce	1 tbsp
1 tbsp	Chinese rice wine or medium sherry	1 tbsp
	salt	
	pinch of sugar	
1 tbsp	chopped scallion (spring onion) or leek	1 tbsp
1 tsp	sesame oil or chicken fat	1 tsp
3 oz	fresh peeled shrimp (prawns)	75 g/3 oz
1	skinned, finely diced tomato	1

1. Lightly beat the eggs and add bouillon (stock), soy sauces, oyster or shrimp sauce, rice wine or sherry, salt, sugar, scallion (spring onion) or leek and sesame oil or chicken fat, stirring constantly.
2. Put the egg mixture in a smooth bowl and stand on the perforated section of a steamer.
3. Cover the bowl with aluminum foil.
4. Bring a generous quantity of water to the boil in the pan. Place perforated section on top and cover the pan. Leave to steam for 25 minutes. After 15 minutes, remove the lid from the pan, fold back the aluminum foil and sprinkle the shrimp (prawns) over the egg mixture. Replace the foil. Replace the lid on the pan and continue steaming for a further 10 minutes.

Left to right: Steamed egg with fish; Steamed egg with shrimp (prawns)

5. Test the egg with a skewer to see if it has set. Check the water level occasionally and top up if necessary. At the end of the steaming time remove the dish from the steamer.
6. Sprinkle on the diced tomato and serve immediately.

Steamed Egg with Fish

	00.10	00.30
	Serves 4 as side dish	

American	Ingredients	Metric/Imperial
3-4	eggs	3-4
¾ cup	chicken bouillon (stock)	200 ml/7 fl oz
1 tsp	Chinese light soy sauce	1 tsp
1 tsp	Chinese dark soy sauce	1 tsp
1 tsp	oyster sauce	1 tsp
2 tbsp	chopped leek or scallion (spring onion)	2 tbsp
1 tbsp	Chinese rice wine or medium sherry	1 tbsp
	salt	
¼ lb	filleted fish, eg sole	125 g/4 oz
1 tbsp	finely chopped parsley or celery	1 tbsp
1	tomato	1

1. Lightly beat the eggs and add the chicken bouillon (stock), soy sauces, oyster sauce, leek or scallion (spring onion), rice wine or sherry and salt to taste. Stir well.
2. Put all the ingredients in a smooth bowl of suitable size and follow the method given for Sharen tzeng dan, allowing a steaming time of 30 minutes.
3. Wash the fish under cold running water. Dry with kitchen paper and cut into thin strips. Sprinkle with a little salt.
4. Add the fish to the egg mixture after it has been steaming for 15 minutes.
5. Sprinkle with parsley or celery immediately before serving and garnish with tomato.

Steamed Egg with Ham

	00.10	00.30
	Serves 4 as side dish	

American	Ingredients	Metric/Imperial
3-4	eggs	3-4
¾ cup	chicken bouillon (stock)	200 ml/7 fl oz
1 tsp	Chinese light soy sauce	1 tsp
1 tsp	Chinese dark soy sauce	1 tsp
1 tsp	oyster sauce	1 tsp
	salt	
	sugar	
2 tbsp	chopped red bell pepper	2 tbsp
3 oz	thick sliced, cooked ham cut into tiny diamonds	75g/3 oz
1 tsp	sesame oil or chicken fat	1 tsp
2	very finely chopped onions or scallions (spring onions) (optional)	2
1	tomato (optional)	1

1. Lightly beat the eggs, add all the other ingredients and stir well.
2. Pour into a bowl of suitable size and follow the method given in the previous recipe, allowing 30 minutes steaming time.
3. Sprinkle with a little chopped onion or scallion (spring onion) immediately before serving, or place a tomato 'flower' in the middle.

Zjintza dan pian

Gold Coins (Hunan)

	00.10	00.50
	Serves 4 as side dish	

American	Ingredients	Metric/Imperial
4	large eggs	4
1 tbsp	rice flour	1 tbsp
3 tbsp	groundnut oil	3 tbsp
1 tbsp	Chinese light soy sauce	1 tbsp
1 tbsp	Chinese dark soy sauce	1 tbsp
1 tbsp	ginger syrup	1 tbsp
3	drops red pepper oil	3
2 tbsp	Chinese rice wine or dry sherry	2 tbsp
1 tbsp	chopped onion or leek	1 tbsp
1 tbsp	finely grated fresh root ginger	1 tbsp
6 tbsp	chicken bouillon (stock)	6 tbsp
2 tsp	cornstarch (cornflour)	2 tsp
1 tsp	sesame oil	1 tsp
1	piece of cucumber to garnish (optional)	1

1. Put the eggs in a saucepan with a generous quantity of cold water. Bring them to the boil and cook (boil) for 6 minutes.
2. Cool the eggs under cold running water for at least 5 minutes.
3. Prepare the sauce by mixing all the ingredients, except the cornstarch (cornflour), in a small saucepan and bringing them to the boil. Simmer gently for 30 minutes.
4. Mix the cornstarch (cornflour) with 1 tbsp cold water and stir into the sauce and cook until the sauce thickens. Keep the sauce warm over a very moderate heat.
5. Shell the cold eggs and cut each one into 3 or 4 slices. Press both sides of each slice in the rice flour.
6. Heat the two oils in a small frying pan and fry the slices of egg until golden brown on both sides. Carefully remove them from the pan, with a spatula or pancake knife, and drain on kitchen paper.
7. Add the sesame oil to the hot sauce, divide the sauce between small warmed dishes or saucers and place the egg slices on top.
8. Garnish with small cucumber fans.

Jun see ling ju leng tse

Cold Lemon Chicken

▬◣▱   **00. 10**   **00.20**
plus cooling time

American	Ingredients	Metric/Imperial
1½ lb	boneless, skinless chicken breasts	700 g/1½ lb
1 tbsp	cornstarch (cornflour)	1 tbsp
1 tsp	five spice powder	1 tsp
1 tsp	salt	1 tsp
4 tbsp	groundnut oil	4 tbsp
2	lightly crushed garlic cloves	2
2	slices fresh root ginger	2
1 cup	chicken bouillon (stock)	250 ml/8 fl oz
2 tsp	cornstarch (cornflour)	2 tsp
2 tbsp	Chinese lemon sauce	2 tbsp
1 tbsp	Chinese light soy sauce	1 tbsp
1 tbsp	strained lemon juice	1 tbsp
1	large iceberg lettuce	1
1	Chinese cabbage	1
3 tbsp	finely chopped coriander leaves	3 tbsp
1 tsp	finely grated fresh root ginger	1 tsp
	lemon or lime segments	

1. Dry the chicken breasts with kitchen paper. Cut them into cubes of equal size.
2. Mix the cornstarch (cornflour) with the five spice powder and salt. Sprinkle over the pieces of chicken. Make sure that the pieces are coated.
3. Heat the oil in a wok and stir fry the garlic and slices of root ginger for 30 seconds, then remove them.
4. Stir fry the pieces of chicken until golden brown all over. Push the chicken to one side of the wok.
5. Add the bouillon (stock) and bring to boiling point.
6. Mix the cornstarch (cornflour) with 3 tbsp cold water and stir into the bouillon (stock). Cook until the sauce thickens and simmer gently for a further 2 minutes.
7. Add the lemon sauce, soy sauce and lemon juice. Stir well and simmer very gently for 1 minute.
8. Remove the wok from the heat, stir the chicken into the sauce and leave to get cold.
9. Shred the lettuce or Chinese leaves very finely and spread on a large, flat dish.
10. Sprinkle on half the coriander leaves and root ginger.
11. Spoon the cold chicken and sauce into the middle of the dish and sprinkle the remainder of the coriander leaves and root ginger on top. Garnish the dish with segments of lemon or lime.

Hu ju moon tse

Cold Chicken with Oyster Sauce

▬◣▱   **00. 10**   **00.40**
plus cooling time

American	Ingredients	Metric/Imperial
3	coarsely chopped sprigs coriander or parsley	3
1	coarsely chopped onion	1
12	lightly bruised black peppercorns	12
1½ lb	boneless, skinless chicken breasts	700 g/1½ lb
3 tbsp	honey	3 tbsp
1 tbsp	oyster sauce	1 tbsp
1 tbsp	Chinese light soy sauce	1 tbsp
	pinch five spice powder	
	pinch salt	
2 tbsp	sesame seeds	2 tbsp
½ lb	washed bean sprouts well-drained	225 g/8 oz
4	chopped scallions (spring onions)	4
1 tbsp	grated fresh root ginger	1 tbsp
	tomato segments or red bell pepper	

1. Bring 2 quarts (2 litres/3½ pints) water to the boil in a saucepan. Add the coriander or parsley, onion and peppercorns and simmer for 20 minutes.
2. Add the chicken breasts to the liquid and simmer for 6 minutes. Remove the pan from the heat and leave the chicken to cool in the liquid.
3. Mix the honey, oyster sauce, soy sauce, five spice powder and salt in a bowl and add 1 tbsp of the cooled liquid from the chicken breasts.
4. Heat a small frying pan and dry roast the sesame seeds shaking the pan until the seeds begin to change color. Transfer the seeds to a large cold plate and leave to cool.
5. Cut the chicken breasts obliquely into thin slices. Pour over the sauce and turn over carefully a few times. Cover and chill for 1 hour.
6. Spread the bean sprouts on a large flat dish. Spoon the chicken breasts and sauce into the middle of the dish.
7. Sprinkle the scallions (spring onions), root ginger and sesame seeds over the top and garnish the dish with tomato segments or strips of red bell pepper.

Chu hwa jiung mun tse

Chicken and Smoked Oysters

	00.05		00.15
	Serves 4		

American	Ingredients	Metric/Imperial
1½ lb	chicken breast fillets	700 g/1½ lb
2 tsp	cornstarch (cornflour)	2 tsp
1 tsp	five spice powder	1 tsp
½ tsp	salt	½ tsp
4 tbsp	groundnut oil	4 tbsp
1	crushed garlic clove	1
1 cup	chicken bouillon (stock)	250 ml/8 fl oz
¼ lb	canned smoked oysters	125 g/4 oz
1 tbsp	chopped scallion (spring onion)	1 tbsp
2	skinned, sliced tomatoes	2

Left to right: Cold chicken with oyster sauce; cold lemon chicken

1. Dry the chicken breasts with kitchen paper. Cut into ½ in (1.25 cm) strips.
2. Mix together the cornstarch (cornflour), five spice powder and salt and coat the chicken with the mixture.
3. Heat the oil in a wok and stir fry the garlic for 30 seconds.
4. Add the strips of chicken and stir fry until golden brown.
5. Push the chicken to one side of the wok, add the chicken bouillon (stock) and bring to the boil.
6. Mix the cornstarch (cornflour) with 2 tbsp cold water and stir this mixture into the wok. Cook, stirring until the sauce thickens. Simmer briefly.
7. Push the chicken back into the sauce and add the smoked oysters, stir well.
8. Transfer to a warmed dish and serve garnished with a little chopped scallion (spring onion) and decorated with slices of tomato.

Sei lien fei tse pien hwa kau

Chicken with Shrimp (Prawns) and Broccoli

	00.15		00.15
	Serves 4		

American	Ingredients	Metric/Imperial
¾ lb	boneless, skinless chicken breasts	350 g/12 oz
½ tsp	five spice powder	½ tsp
1	good pinch salt	1
1 tsp	cornstarch (cornflour)	1 tsp
¼ lb	broccoli sprigs	125 g/4 oz
2 tbsp	groundnut oil	2 tbsp
1	garlic clove	1
2	slices fresh root ginger	2
1 tbsp	Chinese light soy sauce	1 tbsp
1 tbsp	Chinese rice wine or dry sherry	1 tbsp
5 tbsp	chicken bouillon (stock) or cooking liquid from the broccoli	5 tbsp
¼ lb	freshly peeled shrimp (prawns)	125 g/4 oz

1. Dry the chicken breasts with kitchen paper. Cut them into ½ in (1.25 cm) cubes.
2. Mix together the five spice powder, salt and cornstarch (cornflour) and sprinkle over the cubes of chicken, making sure that they are thinly coated on all sides.
3. Cook the broccoli sprigs in a little lightly salted boiling water for 3 minutes. Drain in a colander and rinse under cold running water. Drain well.
4. Heat the oil in a wok and stir fry the garlic and slices of root ginger for 30 seconds. Remove from the oil.
5. Stir fry the chicken for 2-3 minutes until golden brown. Push the cubes of chicken to one side of the wok.
6. Add the soy sauce, rice wine or sherry and bouillon (stock) or cooking liquid from the broccoli. Stir the cubes of chicken into the liquid. Bring to the boil and stir well.
7. Add the broccoli sprigs and 30 seconds later, the shrimp (prawns). Mix well and serve immediately on 4 warmed plates.

Cha tse
Oven Cooked Chicken (Canton)

	00.15 plus drying time	01.00

American	Ingredients	Metric/Imperial
1 (2½ lb)	roasting chicken	1 (1.2kg/2½ lb)
3 tsp	salt	3 tsp
1 tsp	five spice powder	1 tsp
3 tbsp	Chinese rice vinegar	3 tbsp
2 tbsp	Chinese rice wine or sherry	2 tbsp
1 tbsp	honey	1 tbsp
1 tsp	cornstarch (cornflour)	1 tsp
1 tbsp	groundnut oil	1 tbsp
	parsley sprigs to garnish	

1. Bring a few pints (litres) of water to the boil. Put the chicken in a colander and slowly pour the boiling water over it. Dry the chicken inside and out with kitchen paper then place it on a wire tray in a draughty place to dry further.
2. Place the salt and five spice powder in a dry saucepan and heat, stirring until it begins to brown. Transfer to a cold plate and leave to cool. Rub this mixture inside the chicken and close up both ends of the chicken with skewers.
3. Place the vinegar, rice wine or sherry and honey into a pan. Bring to the boil, stirring well until the honey has dissolved.
4. Mix the cornstarch (cornflour) with 1½ tbsp cold water and stir into the vinegar mixture. Brush the chicken on all sides with the mixture and leave to stand for 2 minutes then brush it again. Repeat until all the mixture is used.
5. Hang the chicken up in a dry, draughty place for 4-6 hours.
6. Preheat the oven to 180°C/350°F/Gas Mark 4. Brush a wire rack with oil. Place a baking sheet under the rack just below the center of the oven.
7. Roast the chicken on the rack with the breast upward. After 30 minutes turn the chicken over and roast for 10-15 minutes more. Turn off the heat and leave the chicken in the closed oven for a further 10 minutes.
8. Cut the chicken into 8 equal pieces and arrange them on a warmed dish in approximately the shape of the whole original chicken.
9. Serve, garnished with sprigs of parsley.

Sie yu hiung tse
Spiced Chicken with Soy Sauce (Canton)

	00.10 plus drying time	01.15

American	Ingredients	Metric/Imperial
1 (2½ lb)	roasting chicken	1 (1.2 kg/2½ lb)
2	whole nutmegs	2
2 (2 in)	sticks of cinnamon	2 (5 cm/2 in)
½ tsp	crushed black peppercorns	½ tsp
4	cloves	4
1 tsp	five spice powder	1 tsp
1 tsp	fennel seeds	1 tsp
¾ cup	Chinese light soy sauce	200 ml/7 fl oz
¾ cup	Chinese dark soy sauce	200 ml/7 fl oz
5 tbsp	Chinese rice wine or sherry	5 tbsp
3 tbsp	soft brown sugar	3 tbsp
1 (1½ oz)	piece peeled, thinly sliced fresh root ginger	1 (40 g/1½ oz)
4	shallots or thin leeks, quartered	4
2	coarsely chopped garlic cloves	2
1 tbsp	sesame oil	1 tbsp
	tomato flower and coriander leaves to garnish	

1. Bring a few pints/litres water to the boil. Put the chicken in a colander and slowly pour the boiling water over it. Dry the chicken inside and out with kitchen paper. Place it on a wire tray, in a draughty place to dry further.
2. Place the nutmeg, cinnamon, peppercorns, cloves, five spice powder and fennel seeds into a pan, add 3¼ cups (750

Left to right: Oven cooked chicken; Spiced chicken with soy sauce

ml/1¼ pints) boiling water and bring to the boil. Reduce the heat and simmer until the liquid is reduced to 1 cup (250 ml/9 fl oz). Strain the liquid through a strainer lined with a piece of wet muslin.

3. Add the soy sauces, rice wine or sherry, sugar, root ginger, shallots or leek and the garlic. Bring to the boil, stirring.

4. Place the chicken in the spicy sauce making sure that it is completely submerged. Bring to the boil again, reduce the heat, cover the pan and simmer for 35-45 minutes. Turn the chicken over several times and spoon some sauce into the cavity.

5. Remove the chicken from the pan, drain briefly over the pan then stand on a wire tray. When cooled brush it with sesame oil.

6. Bring the sauce to the boil, then strain it through the muslin.

7. Cut the chicken into 12-16 equal pieces and arrange on a warmed dish, approximately in the shape of the whole chicken. Pour a little of the sauce over the chicken and serve the remainder in warmed bowls. Garnish with a tomato flower and coriander leaves and serve.

Hu ju tsi yiung mun tse

Chicken with Ginger in Oyster Sauce

00.10 plus standing time   01.00

American	Ingredients	Metric/Imperial
1 (2½ lb)	roasting chicken	1 (1.2 kg/2½ lb)
2 tbsp	Chinese rice wine or dry sherry	2 tbsp
3 tbsp	ginger syrup	3 tbsp
2 tbsp	Chinese light soy sauce	2 tbsp
1 tsp	salt	1 tsp
5 tbsp	chicken bouillon (stock)	5 tbsp
2 tsp	soft brown sugar	2 tsp
2 tbsp	oyster sauce	2 tbsp
2 tsp	cornstarch (cornflour)	2 tsp
2 tsp	sesame oil	2 tsp
2	finely chopped scallions (spring onions)	2
1 tbsp	finely chopped coriander leaves or parsley	1 tbsp

1. Dry the chicken with kitchen paper.

2. Mix the rice wine or sherry with the ginger syrup, soy sauce and salt. Stir until the salt has dissolved.

3. Put the chicken in a bowl. Pour over the marinade and leave to stand for 2 hours, turning the chicken occasionally.

4. Bring the chicken bouillon (stock) to the boil in a steamer and place the chicken in the perforated section of the pan. Cover and steam the chicken for 35-40 minutes. Leave it to cool slightly.

5. Add the sugar and oyster sauce to the liquid in the steamer and simmer for a few minutes.

6. Mix the cornstarch (cornflour) with 2 tbsp cold water and stir into the sauce. Simmer briefly then add the sesame oil.

7. Cool the chicken and cut into pieces removing all the bones. Return the chicken pieces to the perforated section of the steamer. Cover and steam for 5 minutes.

8. Place the chicken on a warmed dish and pour the sauce over. Sprinkle with the scallion (spring onion) and coriander or parsley leaves. Serve immediately.

Ling mung tse

Chicken with Lime (Canton)

00.20 plus standing time   00.40

American	Ingredients	Metric/Imperial
1 (2½ lb)	roasting chicken cut into 8 pieces	1 (1.2 kg/2½ lb)
2 tbsp	Chinese rice wine or sherry	2 tbsp
2 tbsp	Chinese dark soy sauce	2 tbsp
1 tbsp	Chinese light soy sauce	1 tbsp
1 tsp	ginger syrup	1 tsp
	salt	
2	limes or lemons	2
2-3 tbsp	soft brown sugar	2-3 tbsp
1¼ cups	chicken bouillon (stock)	300 ml/½ pint
1 (1 oz)	piece fresh root ginger	1 (25 g/1 oz)
5 tbsp	groundnut oil	5 tbsp
4	finely chopped scallions (spring onions) or 1 thin leek	4
2	finely chopped garlic cloves	2
1 tbsp	sesame oil	1 tbsp
2 tsp	cornstarch (cornflour)	2 tsp
1	tomato cut in wedges (optional)	1
	few sprigs curly leafed parsley (optional)	

1. Dry the chicken with kitchen paper.

2. Mix the rice wine or sherry, soy sauces, ginger syrup, and salt. Stir until the salt has completely dissolved. Coat each piece of chicken with the marinade and leave to stand for 1 hour. Set aside the remainder of the marinade.

3. Wash the limes or lemons then remove the zest. Squeeze the fruit. Add the zest to the juice and then add the sugar and bouillon (stock). Stir until the sugar has dissolved.

4. Peel the ginger root, thinly and grate very finely.

5. Heat 4 tbsp groundnut oil in a wok and stir fry the chicken pieces over moderate heat until golden brown. Remove from the wok and keep hot.

6. Add a further tbsp groundnut oil to the wok. Add the root ginger, scallions (spring onions) or leek and garlic and stir fry for 1 minute.

7. Add the remaining marinade and return the chicken to the wok. Reduce the heat, cover and simmer for 20-25 minutes. Turn the chicken pieces occasionally to make sure they do not burn. Add 1 or more tbsp water or bouillon (stock) if necessary.

8. Remove the chicken pieces from the wok. Drain on kitchen paper and place on a warmed serving dish. Brush them with half the sesame oil.

9. Bring the mixture of lemon juice and chicken bouillon (stock) to the boil.

10. Mix the cornstarch (cornflour) with 2 tbsp cold water and stir into the contents of the wok. Cook, until the sauce thickens. Simmer for 30 seconds then add the remaining sesame oil. Taste the sauce, add salt if necessary.

11. Pour the sauce over the the chicken pieces and garnish with tomato wedges and sprigs of curly leafed parsley.

Gung bao ding tse

Chicken with Soy Sauce and Peanuts

▬▭ 00.15 00.15 🍲
plus standing time

American	Ingredients	Metric/Imperial
1¼ lb	chicken breast fillets	575 g/1¼ lb
2 tsp	cornstarch (cornflour)	2 tsp
1	lightly beaten egg white	1
2 tbsp	Chinese dark soy sauce	2 tbsp
2 tbsp	Chinese light soy sauce	2 tbsp
	pinch salt	
1 tbsp	red Chinese rice vinegar	1 tbsp
1 tbsp	brown sugar	1 tbsp
1 tsp	Chinese dark soy sauce	1 tsp
1 tsp	cornstarch (cornflour)	1 tsp
¾ cup	groundnut oil	200 ml/7 fl oz
¼ lb	shelled, skinned peanuts	125 g/4 oz
4	small, crumbled dried red chilies	4
2	crushed garlic cloves	2
1 tbsp	fresh grated root ginger	1 tbsp
1 tbsp	Chinese rice wine or dry sherry	1 tbsp
2	medium size onions cut into quarters	2
2 tsp	sesame oil	2 tsp
	sprigs curly leafed parsley (optional)	

1. Dry the chicken with kitchen paper and cut it into ¾ in (2 cm) cubes.
2. Mix 2 tsp cornstarch (cornflour) with 2 tbsp Chinese light soy sauce, 2 tbsp Chinese dark soy sauce and the salt.
3. Add to the egg white and stir until smooth.
4. Add the chicken cubes and stir several times. Leave to stand for 1 hour, stirring ocasionally.
5. Mix together the vinegar, brown sugar, 1 tsp Chinese dark soy sauce and 1 tsp cornstarch (cornflour).
6. Heat the oil in a wok and stir fry the peanuts until golden brown. Remove with a skimmer. Drain over the wok and put them on to a large plate lined with kitchen paper. Roll to rub off the oil and discard the paper.
7. Reheat the oil in the wok and add the diced chicken. Stir fry for 2 minutes, then transfer to a colander and drain.
8. Remove all but 2 tbsp oil from the wok. Reheat the remaining oil and add the crumbled chilies. Stir well.
9. Immediately add the garlic, root ginger, chicken, onion, rice wine or sherry. Stir fry for 2 minutes.
10. Push the contents of the wok to one side and add the mixture for the sauce to the oil in the bottom of the pan, stirring continuously.
11. Move the ingredients back to the center of the pan and cook for 1 minute, stirring well.
12. Add the sesame oil and transfer to a warmed dish.
13. Sprinkle the peanuts over and garnish with a few sprigs of curly leafed parsley.

Chow tse shan

Fifteen-minute Chicken (Shanghai)

▬▭ 00.05 00.15 🍲
Serves 4

American	Ingredients	Metric/Imperial
1¼ lb	chicken breast fillets	575 g/1¼ lb
4 tbsp	groundnut oil	4 tbsp
1	crushed garlic clove	1
1 tbsp	Chinese rice wine or sherry	1 tbsp
1 tbsp	grated fresh root ginger	1 tbsp
2 tbsp	Chinese dark soy sauce	2 tbsp
2 tbsp	Chinese light soy sauce	2 tbsp
1 tbsp	brown sugar	1 tbsp
¾ cup	chicken bouillon (stock)	200 ml/7 fl oz
6	finely chopped scallions (spring onions)	6

1. Dry the chicken fillets with kitchen paper and cut them into ½×1½ in (1.25×4 cm) strips.
2. Heat the oil in a wok and stir fry the pieces of chicken for 4-5 minutes until golden brown. Add the garlic and root ginger, stir, then mix in the remaining ingredients.
3. Add ¾ cup (200 ml/7 fl oz) boiling water or chicken bouillon (stock), stir thoroughly and simmer for 10 minutes.
4. Transfer to a warmed dish and serve sprinkled with scallions (spring onions).

Sien gu tse lu to yan

Chicken with Almonds

▬▭ 00.15 00.15 🍲
plus standing time

American	Ingredients	Metric/Imperial
1¼ lb	chicken breast fillets	575 g/1¼ lb
2 tbsp	Chinese dark soy sauce	2 tbsp
2 tbsp	Chinese light soy sauce	2 tbsp
1 tbsp	Chinese rice wine or dry sherry	1 tbsp
1	egg white	1
1 tsp	sesame oil	1 tsp
	pinch of soft brown sugar	
	pinch salt	
2 tsp	cornstarch (cornflour)	2 tsp
6-8	large dried Chinese mushrooms	6-8
1	red bell pepper	1
1	green bell pepper	1
¾ cup	groundnut oil	200 ml/7 fl oz
½ lb	blanched almonds	225 g/8 oz
2	thinly sliced garlic cloves	2
1	small leek, cut into thin strips	1
¼ lb	bamboo shoots cut into thin strips	125 g/¼ lb
1 tbsp	Chinese light soy sauce	1 tbsp
	salt	
1 tsp	sugar	1 tsp
1 tbsp	Chinese rice wine or sherry	1 tbsp

1. Dry the chicken with kitchen paper and cut into 1 in (2.5 cm) cubes.

2. Put the soy sauces, rice wine or sherry, egg white, sesame oil, brown sugar, salt and cornstarch (cornflour) in a bowl and stir until smooth and the salt and sugar have dissolved.

3. Mix in the diced chicken and leave to stand in a cool place for 30 minutes, stirring occasionally.

4. Put the mushrooms in a bowl with boiling water to cover. Soak for 30 minutes, then discard the stalks and cut the caps into thin strips. Strain the mushroom liquid through a strainer (sieve) lined with wet muslin.

5. Wash, halve and seed the bell peppers and and cut the flesh into thin strips.

6. Heat half the oil in a wok and stir fry the almonds until golden brown. Remove from the pan with a skimmer, drain over the pan for a few moments and put on a large plate lined with kitchen paper. Leave to cool.

7. Pour the remaining oil into the wok, add the garlic and stir fry for 30 seconds. Remove the garlic from the oil with a skimmer. Add the leek and diced chicken and stir fry for 3 minutes.

8. Push the ingredients to one side of the wok and remove all but 2 tbsp of the oil. Add the mushrooms, bamboo shoots and bell peppers. Add 1 tbsp soy sauce, salt and sugar, stir fry for another 3 minutes.

9. Stir in the rice wine or sherry, transfer to a warmed dish and scatter the cooled almonds over the top. Serve immediately.

Chow tse

Chicken with Papaw

American	Ingredients	Metric/Imperial
1¼ lb	chicken breast fillets	575 g/1¼ lb
1 tbsp	Chinese rice wine or dry sherry	1 tbsp
2 tbsp	Chinese light soy sauce	2 tbsp
2 tbsp	Chinese dark soy sauce	2 tbsp
1 tsp	fresh grated root ginger	1 tsp
	pinch of salt	
	pinch of soft brown sugar	
1	egg white	1
5 tbsp	chicken bouillon (stock)	5 tbsp
1 tsp	cornstarch (cornflour)	1 tsp
	freshly ground pepper	
1 tsp	sesame oil	1 tsp
1 tbsp	Chinese light soy sauce	1 tbsp
1 tbsp	Chinese dark soy sauce	1 tbsp
6 tbsp	groundnut oil	6 tbsp
6	finely chopped scallions (spring onions)	6
1	thinly sliced carrot	1
2	under-ripe papaws flesh cut into thin strips	2

1. Dry the chicken fillets with kitchen paper then slice and cut into thin strips.

2. Place the rice wine or sherry, soy sauces, root ginger, salt, sugar, and egg white into a bowl and stir until smooth and the salt and sugar have dissolved. Stir the chicken pieces into the marinade and leave the bowl in a cool place for 30 minutes.

3. Put the bouillon (stock), cornstarch (cornflour), pepper, sesame oil and soy sauces in a pan and stir until smooth. Stir in

3 tbsp water and bring to the boil. Simmer for a few moments then remove the pan from the heat.

4. Heat the oil in a wok and stir fry the strips of chicken until golden brown. Remove from the pan with a skimmer and drain briefly before transferring everything to a deep warmed serving platter. Cover with aluminum foil to keep hot.

5. Remove all but 2 tbsp of the oil from the wok. Reheat the oil, add the scallions (spring onions), carrot and papaw and carefully stir fry the mixture. Pour the sauce over it, spoon in the chicken and very briefly bring the mixture to the boil.

6. Return to the warmed dish and serve.

Moen tse du si

Chicken with Black Beans

American	Ingredients	Metric/Imperial
1¼ lb	boneless, skinless chicken breasts	575 g/1¼ lb
2 tbsp	Chinese light soy sauce	2 tbsp
1 tbsp	Chinese dark soy sauce	1 tbsp
1 tbsp	cornstarch (cornflour)	1 tbsp
	pinch salt	
4 tbsp	black beans	4 tbsp
1 tbsp	coarsely grated root ginger	1 tbsp
3 tbsp	Chinese rice wine or dry sherry	3 tbsp
1 tbsp	soft brown sugar	1 tbsp
5 tbsp	groundnut oil	5 tbsp
1	finely chopped large onion	1
2	crushed garlic cloves	2
2 tsp	sesame oil	2 tsp
⅔ cup	chicken bouillon (stock)	150 ml/¼ pint
2 tbsp	cornstarch (cornflour)	2 tbsp
1-2	skinned tomatoes (optional)	1-2
	few sprigs curly leafed parsley (optional)	

1. Dry the chicken with kitchen paper and cut it into ¾ in (2 cm) cubes.

2. Mix together the light and dark soy sauces, 1 tbsp cornstarch (cornflour) and salt. Stir in the diced chicken and leave to stand for 15 minutes, stirring occasionally.

3. Place the black beans in a strainer (sieve) and rinse them under cold water. Drain then place in a small flame-proof bowl with the root ginger, rice wine or sherry and sugar. Stir thoroughly.

4. Bring some water to the boil in the base of a steamer. Place the bowl on the perforated section and steam for 20 minutes.

5. Put the bouillon (stock) and 2 tbsp cornstarch (cornflour) in a pan. Add the liquid from the bowl of steamed beans. Stir thoroughly.

6. Heat the oil in a wok and stir fry the cubes of chicken for 2 minutes. Remove all but 2 tbsp of oil from the wok and add all ingredients except the bean mixture. Stir well.

7. Spoon in the black bean mixture and stir fry for 2 minutes then push the mixture to one side.

8. Pour the sauce over the oil in the bottom of the pan and bring to the boil. Bring the ingredients into the center of the wok and stir well.

9. Transfer to a warmed serving dish. Garnish with tomato wedges or sprigs of curly leafed parsley.

Hunan chicken with egg noodles

Hunan tse chow mie fun

Hunan Chicken with Egg Noodles (Szechwan)

00.10 Serves 4 — 01.15

American	Ingredients	Metric/Imperial
1 (2½ lb)	*roasting chicken*	*1 (1.2 kg/2½ lb)*
	salt	
2 tbsp	*sesame paste or peanut butter*	*2 tbsp*
1 tbsp	*Chinese rice vinegar*	*1 tbsp*
1 tbsp	*sesame oil*	*1 tbsp*
1 tbsp	*plum sauce*	*1 tbsp*
1 tbsp	*ginger syrup*	*1 tbsp*
1 tbsp	*crushed Szechwan peppercorns*	*1 tbsp*
1 tsp	*fresh grated root ginger*	*1 tsp*
2	*finely chopped scallions (spring onions)*	*2*
1	*crushed garlic clove*	*1*
4 tbsp	*finely chopped coriander leaves or parsley*	*4 tbsp*
¼ lb	*canned, drained, sliced water chestnuts*	*125 g/4 oz*
2 tbsp	*groundnut oil*	*2 tbsp*
½ lb	*cooked, drained egg noodles*	*225 g/8 oz*
1	*peeled, sliced cucumber*	*1*

1. In a pan bring several quarts/litres water to the boil. Add a few tsp of salt and put the chicken in the boiling water. After 2 minutes, reduce the heat, cover the pan and simmer the chicken for just under an hour.
2. Drain the chicken in a colander and leave to cool.
3. Remove the skin and cut the chicken into pieces, removing the bones.
4. In a bowl mix together the sesame paste or peanut butter, vinegar, sesame oil, plum sauce, ginger syrup, peppercorns, root ginger, scallions (spring onions), garlic and coriander leaves or parsley. Add the chicken and the water chestnuts and stir well.
5. Heat the groundnut oil in a wok and stir fry the egg noodles. Add the chicken and sauce mixture and warm through.
6. Transfer to a warmed serving dish, garnish with cucumber slices and serve immediately.

Chow cheng tse

Crisply-fried Chicken (Szechwan)

00.15 plus standing time — 00.15

American	Ingredients	Metric/Imperial
1 (2½ lb)	*roasting chicken*	*1 (1.2 kg/2½ lb)*
1-2 tsp	*five spice powder*	*1-2 tsp*
1 tbsp	*Chinese rice wine or sherry*	*1 tbsp*
2 tbsp	*Chinese dark soy sauce*	*2 tbsp*
2 tbsp	*hoisin sauce*	*2 tbsp*
1 tbsp	*cornstarch (cornflour)*	*1 tbsp*
1¼ cups	*groundnut oil*	*300 ml/½ pint*
1 tsp	*sesame oil*	*1 tsp*
	large sprigs of curly leafed parsley (optional)	

1. Dry the chicken inside and out with kitchen paper. Stir the five spice powder into the rice wine or sherry and rub this mixture into the chicken. Leave the chicken in a cool place for 1 hour.
2. Pour a generous quantity of water into a steamer and bring it to the boil.
3. Brush the perforated section of the pan with oil, put the chicken on to it, cover and steam for 1 hour.
4. Remove the pan from the heat and leave the chicken to cool in the closed pan. Remove the chicken and dry inside and out with kitchen paper.
5. Brush the chicken on all sides with soy sauce and hoisin sauce then put it on a wire rack in a draughty place for about 15 minutes to dry.
6. Sieve the cornstarch (cornflour) over the chicken to give it a very light covering all over.
7. Heat the groundnut oil in a wok and fry the chicken, turning frequently, until golden brown on all sides. Use 2 skimmers to lift the chicken from the wok, letting the oil drain back into the pan.
8. Reheat the oil and fry the chicken for another 2-3 minutes, turning it frequently. This will make the skin very crisp.
9. Cut the chicken into 8 or more pieces and arrange on a warmed dish, approximately in the shape of a whole chicken.
10. Sprinkle with sesame oil, garnish with large sprigs of curly leafed parsley and serve.

Cha liu shiu tse

Chicken with Bamboo Shoots (Peking)

▶━━▷ 00.15   00.08 🍲
      Serves 4

American	Ingredients	Metric/Imperial
1 lb	chicken breast fillets	450 g/1 lb
1	egg white	1
1 tbsp	cornstarch (cornflour)	1 tbsp
2 tbsp	Chinese light soy sauce	2 tbsp
2 tbsp	Chinese dark soy sauce	2 tbsp
¾ cup	groundnut oil	200 ml/7 fl oz
2 tbsp	lard	2 tbsp
½ lb	canned, drained sliced bamboo shoots	225 g/8 oz
1 tbsp	finely grated fresh root ginger	1 tbsp
	pinch of five spice powder	
	salt	
	freshly ground pepper	
5 tbsp	chicken bouillon (stock)	5 tbsp

1. Dry the chicken with kitchen paper. Slice thinly then cut into matchstick strips.
2. Lightly beat the egg white with the cornstarch (cornflour) and soy sauces. Stir until smooth. Fold in the strips of chicken.
3. Heat the oil in a wok, spoon in the strips of chicken and stir fry making sure they do not stick together. After 1½ minutes remove the chicken from the pan with a skimmer. Drain over the pan for a few moments. Place in a strainer (sieve) or colander to drain completely.
4. Remove oil from the wok and heat the lard. Add the bamboo shoots and root ginger and sprinkle on five-spice powder, salt and pepper to taste. Stir well and add 5 tbsp boiling water or bouillon (stock).
5. Bring to the boil, add the chicken and stir. Transfer to a warmed platter and serve.

Pai cheng tse hwo

Steamed Chicken with Ham (Hunan)

▶━━▷ 00.15   02.45 🍲
      Serves 4

American	Ingredients	Metric/Imperial
1 (2½ lb)	roasting chicken	1 (1.2 kg/2½ lb)
¼ lb	thickly sliced cooked ham	125 g/4 oz
2 tbsp	soft brown sugar	2 tbsp
2 tbsp	Chinese light soy sauce	2 tbsp
2 tbsp	Chinese dark soy sauce	2 tbsp
2 tbsp	Chinese rice wine or dry sherry	2 tbsp
1 tbsp	coarsely grated fresh root ginger	1 tbsp
½ tsp	crushed Szechwan peppercorns	½ tsp
3	finely chopped scallions (spring onions)	3
2	skinned tomatoes	2

1. Dry the chicken inside and out and cut it into 24 pieces.
2. Cut the ham into ¼ in (5 mm) squares.
3. Place the chicken in a steamer lined with aluminum foil and sprinkle with the chopped ham.
4. Mix together all the other ingredients and pour them over the chicken. Cover and steam for 2½ hours.
5. Transfer to a warmed shallow serving platter, garnish with scallions (spring onions) and sliced tomato.

Left to right: Chicken with bamboo shoots; Steamed chicken with ham

Mian bao ya (I)

Duck with Vegetables and Croûtons (Peking)

	00.20 Serves 4	00.20

American	Ingredients	Metric/Imperial
1 lb	boneless duck meat	450 g/1 lb
½ lb	snow peas (mange-tout) green beans, haricot beans or peas	225 g/8 oz
4	shallots or scallions (spring onions)	4
6-8	slices white bread	6-8
2½ cups	duck or chicken bouillon (stock)	600 ml/1 pint
3 tbsp	Chinese rice wine or dry sherry	3 tbsp
2 tbsp	Chinese dark soy sauce	2 tbsp
2 tbsp	Chinese light soy sauce	2 tbsp
2 tbsp	rice flour or cornstarch (cornflour)	2 tbsp
1¼ cups	sunflower oil	300 ml/½ pint
2 tsp	sesame oil	2 tsp
	salt	

1. Dry the duck meat with kitchen paper, then chop it very finely.
2. Wash the vegetables and cut into 1 in (2.5 cm) pieces.
3. Finely chop the shallots or scallions (spring onions). Remove the crusts from the bread and cut it into ½ in (1.25 cm) squares.
4. Bring the bouillon (stock) to the boil, add the chopped duck and bring to the boil again. Skim the surface several times then add the vegetables, rice wine or sherry and soy sauces. Reduce the heat and simmer for 2 minutes.
5. Mix the rice flour or cornstarch (cornflour) with 4 tbsp cold water. Stir into the contents of the pan and add the shallots or scallions (spring onions). Bring to the boil again, reduce the heat and simmer gently for 3-5 minutes covered.
6. Heat the oil in a wok and stir fry the pieces of bread until golden brown and crisp. Remove from the oil, drain over the pan and then on kitchen paper.

7. Just before serving, stir the sesame oil into the duck mixture and add salt to taste. Transfer to warmed plates and garnish with croûtons.

Mian bao ya (II)

Duck with Bell Pepper, Celery and Croûtons

	00.10 Serves 4	00.10

American	Ingredients	Metric/Imperial
1 lb	duck fillet, chopped into small pieces	450 g/1 lb
2 cups	duck or chicken bouillon (stock)	450 ml/¾ pint
½ lb	celery cut into thin strips	225 g/8 oz
1	trimmed, seeded red bell pepper, cut into strips	1
1 tbsp	finely chopped shallots	1 tbsp
3 tbsp	Chinese light soy sauce	3 tbsp
3 tbsp	Chinese rice wine or dry sherry	3 tbsp
2 tbsp	cornstarch (cornflour)	2 tbsp
1¼ cups	sunflower or corn oil	300 ml/½ pint
6-8	slices white bread crusts removed, cut into small squares	6-8
1 tbsp	sesame oil	1 tbsp
	salt	

1. Put the duck in a pan with the bouillon (stock) and bring to the boil. Skim the surface several times.
2. Add the celery, bell pepper and shallots, stir well. Mix in the soy sauce and rice wine or sherry. Simmer for 4-5 minutes.
3. Mix the cornstarch (cornflour) with 4 tbsp cold water and stir this into the duck and vegetable mixture.
4. Heat the oil in a wok and fry the bread until golden brown and crisp. Remove from the oil and drain over the pan then put the bread on kitchen paper to drain.
5. Stir in the sesame oil, adding salt to taste. Divide the duck and the croûtons between warmed plates and serve.

Duck with bell pepper, celery and croûtons

Mian bao ya (III)
Duck with Paksoi, Shallots and Croûtons

⏱ 00.10
Serves 4
🍲 00.15

American	Ingredients	Metric/Imperial
1 lb	finely ground (minced) duck fillet	450 g/1 lb
2 cups	duck or chicken bouillon (stock)	450 ml/¾ pint
1	washed, thinly sliced, Chinese cabbage or paksoi	1
2 tbsp	finely chopped shallots	2 tbsp
3 tbsp	Chinese rice wine or dry sherry	3 tbsp
3 tbsp	Chinese light soy sauce	3 tbsp
2 tbsp	cornstarch (cornflour)	2 tbsp
¾ cup	groundnut oil	200 ml/7 fl oz
6-8	slices white bread crusts removed, cut into small squares	6-8
1 tbsp	sesame oil	1 tbsp
	salt	

1. Put the duck in a pan with the bouillon (stock) and bring to the boil. Skim the surface several times and add the Chinese cabbage or paksoi and the shallots.
2. Stir in the rice wine or sherry and the soy sauce and simmer for 2 minutes.

3. Mix the cornstarch (cornflour) with 4 tbsp cold water and stir this into the duck and vegetable mixture. Simmer for a further 3 minutes.
4. Heat the oil in a wok and stir fry the bread until golden brown and crisp. Remove from the oil, drain over the pan then on kitchen paper.
5. Stir the sesame oil into the duck mixture, adding salt to taste. Transfer to 4 warmed plates, adding the croûtons. Serve hot.

Mian bao ya (IV)
Duck with Mushrooms and Bell Pepper

⏱ 00.10
plus soaking time
🍲 00.10

American	Ingredients	Metric/Imperial
6-8	dried Chinese mushrooms	6-8
1 lb	finely ground (minced) duck fillet	450 g/1 lb
2 cups	duck or chicken bouillon (stock)	450 ml/¾ pint
2	finely chopped medium size onions	2
1	trimmed, seeded green bell pepper cut into thin strips	1
3 tbsp	Chinese rice wine or dry sherry	3 tbsp
2 tbsp	Chinese light soy sauce	2 tbsp
2 tbsp	Chinese dark soy sauce	2 tbsp
1½ tbsp	rice flour or cornstarch (cornflour)	1½ tbsp
1 tbsp	sesame oil	1 tbsp
	salt	
2	skinned tomatoes cut into wedges (optional)	2
2	pickled gherkins (optional)	2

1. Soak the mushrooms in a bowl of lukewarm water for 1 hour 30 minutes, discard the stalks and cut the caps into very fine strips.
2. Put the duck and the bouillon (stock) in a saucepan and bring to the boil. Skim the surface several times and add the mushrooms, onions and green bell pepper. Pour in the rice wine or sherry and the soy sauces, stir well and simmer for 4 minutes.
3. Mix the rice flour or cornstarch (cornflour) with 3 tbsp cold water and add this mixture to the contents of the pan, stirring until the sauce has thickened slightly. Simmer for a further 2 minutes.
4. Just before serving stir in the sesame oil, adding salt to taste.
5. Transfer the mixture to a warmed serving dish and garnish with tomato wedges or gherkins cut into fans.

Duck with mushrooms and bell pepper

Kwingchong dun ya
Braised Duck with Shallots

▟ 00.15 plus drying time		02.15 ◗

American	Ingredients	Metric/Imperial
1 (4 lb)	duck	1 (1.8 kg/4 lb)
3 tbsp	Chinese kao-liang wine or vodka	3 tbsp
2 tbsp	Chinese light soy sauce	2 tbsp
2 tbsp	Chinese dark soy sauce	2 tbsp
2 tbsp	plum sauce	2 tbsp
	pinch five spice powder	
2 tbsp	grated fresh root ginger	2 tbsp
	salt	
8 tbsp	corn or sunflower oil	8 tbsp
1 lb	scallions (spring onions)	450 g/1 lb
1	large peeled garlic clove	1
1¼ cups	duck or chicken bouillon (stock)	300 ml/½ pint
2 tbsp	oyster sauce	2 tbsp
1 tbsp	honey	1 tbsp
1 tbsp	rice flour or cornstarch (cornflour)	1 tbsp
1 tbsp	sesame oil	1 tbsp

1. Dry the duck inside and out with kitchen paper.
2. Mix the kao-liang wine or vodka, soy sauces, plum sauce, five spice powder, root ginger and salt in a small bowl and rub the mixture into the duck.
3. Place the duck on a wire rack and leave to dry for 2-3 hours at room temperature, in a draughty place.
4. Heat 5 tbsp of oil in a wok and sauté the scallions (spring onions) for 3 minutes until golden brown. Remove from the oil with a skimmer, drain over the pan briefly and leave to cool slightly.
5. Stuff the duck with the onions, then close the cavity with wooden skewers.
6. Reheat the oil in the wok adding the remaining oil and sauté the garlic for 1 minute. Remove the garlic and fry the duck in the oil over moderate heat for about 20 minutes, turning regularly, until golden brown on all sides.
7. In a pan bring the bouillon (stock) to the boil and add the oyster sauce and honey. Stir until the honey has dissolved, then place the duck in the mixture, cover the pan and simmer for 1½ hours. Turn the duck over occasionally, spooning some sauce over it.
8. Carefully remove the duck from the pan and cut it into 12-16 pieces. Arrange the duck on a warmed plate approximately in the shape of the whole duck. Arrange the scallions (spring onions) from inside, around the bird. Cover the dish with aluminum foil to keep the duck warm.
9. Mix the rice flour or cornstarch (cornflour) with 2 tbsp cold water and stir into the hot liquid. Simmer the sauce for 1 minute, stirring in the sesame oil just before serving. Pour the sauce over the duck and serve.

Hong shu ya
Red Cooked Duck (Shanghai)

▟ 00.15 Serves 4		01.45 ◗

American	Ingredients	Metric/Imperial
2 quarts	duck or chicken bouillon (stock)	2 litres/3½ pints
1	finely chopped medium size onion	1
½	washed, sliced carrot	½
4	sticks celery	4
1 (4 lb)	duck	1 (1.8 kg/4 lb)
1 (2 oz)	peeled, sliced piece fresh root ginger	1 (50 g/2 oz)
¼ lb	coarsely shredded fennel root with leaves	125 g/4 oz
5 tbsp	Chinese rice wine or dry sherry	5 tbsp
3 tbsp	Chinese light soy sauce	3 tbsp
3 tbsp	Chinese dark soy sauce	3 tbsp
1 tbsp	cane sugar	1 tbsp
	salt	
	pinch of five spice powder	
1 tsp	chili oil	1 tsp
2½ tbsp	rice flour or cornstarch (cornflour)	2½ tbsp
	a few drops of red food coloring (optional)	
½	cucumber or 2 pickled gherkins (optional)	½

1. In a pan into which the duck fits comfortably bring the bouillon (stock) to the boil with the chopped onion, carrot and celery. Place the duck in the liquid with the breast downward, making sure that it is covered by the liquid.
2. Bring the bouillon (stock) to the boil again and skim the surface several times. Add the ginger, fennel, rice wine or sherry, soy sauces, sugar, salt to taste, a pinch of five spice powder and the chili oil.
3. Bring back to the boil, then reduce the heat and cover the pan. Leave to simmer for 1 hour. Remove the lid and simmer for a further 30 minutes, so that some of the liquid evaporates.
4. Carefully remove the cooked duck from the sauce. Drain over the pan and cut it into pieces.
5. Arrange the pieces on a warmed dish, approximately in the shape of the whole duck. Cover the dish with aluminum foil to keep the duck warm.
6. Strain the remaining liquid through a strainer (sieve) lined with wet muslin. Keep 2¼ cups (500 ml/18 fl oz) of the strained liquid and bring this to the boil.
7. Mix the rice flour or cornstarch (cornflour) with 4 tbsp cold water and pour this mixture into the boiling sauce, stirring until the sauce has thickened. Add salt to taste and a few drops of red food coloring. (optional)
8. Pour the hot sauce over the duck, garnish with cucumber 'fans' or pickled gherkins and serve.

4. Reheat the oil and add the remaining rice wine or sherry, soy sauces and sugar. Stir well then add the strained lime juice and simmer very briefly.

5. Place the duck in the sauce, stir and transfer it to a warmed dish.

6. Serve garnished with tomato 'flowers' and sprigs of curly leafed parsley.

Deep-fried duck

Shanghai yu yian ya

Deep-fried Duck (Shanghai)

▬▷	00.15	00.40 🍲
	Serves 4	

American	Ingredients	Metric/Imperial
1 (4 lb)	duck cut into 12 pieces	1 (1.8 kg/4 lb)
4 tbsp	Chinese rice wine or dry sherry	4 tbsp
4 tbsp	Chinese light soy sauce	4 tbsp
4 tbsp	Chinese dark soy sauce	4 tbsp
4 tbsp	cane sugar	4 tbsp
1 tbsp	fresh ground root ginger	1 tbsp
1	large crushed garlic clove	1
	pinch of five spice powder	
	sunflower oil for deep-frying	
	strained juice of 2 limes	
2	skinned tomatoes cut into 'flowers'	2
	few sprigs of curly leafed parsley	

1. Dry the pieces of duck with kitchen paper. In a small bowl mix 2 tbsp rice wine or sherry, 2 tbsp light and 2 tbsp dark soy sauce and 2 tbsp cane sugar. Stir the mixture until the sugar has dissolved, then add the root ginger, garlic and five spice powder. Stir well.

2. Rub the mixture into the pieces of duck and place them on the perforated section of a steamer. In the bottom half of the pan bring some water to the boil and place the perforated section on top (it must not touch the water). Cover the steamer and steam the duck for about 20 minutes. Leave the duck to cool and then dry it thoroughly with kitchen paper.

3. Heat the oil in a wok and fry the duck pieces until golden brown all over. Remove them from the oil with a skimmer. Drain over the pan, then on kitchen paper. Dry with kitchen paper as thoroughly as possible.

Wu xiang ya

Duck with Five Spice Powder (Canton)

▬▷	00.05	01.45 🍲
	plus soaking time	

American	Ingredients	Metric/Imperial
2 quarts	duck or chicken bouillon (stock)	2 litres/ 3½ pints
1 (4 lb)	duck	1 (1.8 kg/4 lb)
1 (1½ oz)	piece peeled, sliced fresh root ginger	1 (40 g/1½ oz)
6	sliced shallots	6
4 tbsp	Chinese light soy sauce	4 tbsp
4 tbsp	Chinese dark soy sauce	4 tbsp
4 tbsp	Chinese rice wine or dry sherry	4 tbsp
4 tbsp	cane sugar	4 tbsp
1 tsp	five spice powder	1 tsp
6	dried Chinese mushrooms	6
6	young carrots	6
1½ lb	Chinese cabbage	700 g/1½ lb
1½ tbsp	rice flour or cornstarch (cornflour)	1½ tbsp

1. Bring the bouillon (stock) to the boil. Place the duck in the bouillon (stock) and bring back to the boil. Skim the surface several times and add the root ginger, shallots, soy sauces, rice wine or sherry, sugar and five spice powder. Stir well and bring the mixture to the boil again. Reduce the heat, cover the pan and simmer for 1 hour.

2. Put the mushrooms in a bowl with boiling water to cover. Leave to soak for 30 minutes. Discard the stems and cut the caps into strips.

3. Cut the carrots into thin slices. Wash the cabbage and cut it into strips.

4. Carefully remove the duck from the bouillon (stock) mixture and strain the liquid through a strainer (sieve) lined with wet muslin. Bring the liquid to the boil again and boil to reduce to about 3¼ cups (750 ml/1¼ pints). Add the mushrooms, carrots and cabbage and simmer for 30 minutes, allowing the liquid to evaporate a little more.

5. Cut the duck into 8 pieces and cook with the vegetable mixture for the last 10 minutes of the cooking time.

6. Just before serving transfer the vegetables and the duck with a skimmer to a warmed serving dish.

7. Bring 1¼ cups (300 ml/½ pint) of the remaining liquid to the boil. Mix the rice flour or cornstarch (cornflour) with 2 tbsp cold water and pour into the boiling liquid, stirring until the mixture has thickened slightly. Simmer gently for 2 minutes, then spoon a little over the duck and serve the rest separately in a bowl.

Joe tsjoe ja roe

Duck Fillets in Mandarin Sauce

⏱ 00.30
plus marinating

00.15 🍲

American	Ingredients	Metric/Imperial
1½ lb	duck breast fillets	700 g/1½ lb
1 tbsp	sesame oil	1 tbsp
2 tbsp	mandarin juice, fresh or canned	2 tbsp
1 tbsp	lemon juice	1 tbsp
2 tbsp	honey	2 tbsp
1 tbsp	cornstarch (cornflour)	1 tbsp
	pinch five spice powder	
	salt	
	freshly ground pepper	
4 tbsp	groundnut oil	4 tbsp
4	scallions (spring onions) cut into 1 in (2.5 cm) pieces	4
¾ cup	duck or chicken bouillon (stock)	200 ml/7 fl oz
1	large mandarin	1
2	sugar lumps	2
	some mandarin segments	
	some sprigs of parsley	

1. Dry the fillets with kitchen paper. Cut into ½ in (1.25 cm) slices, then into strips.
2. Mix together the sesame oil, mandarin juice, lemon juice, honey, cornstarch (cornflour), five spice powder and a little salt and pepper. Stir until smooth.
3. Stir in the duck and leave to marinate for 15 minutes (or longer).
4. Remove the duck with a slotted spoon, drain thoroughly. Set the marinade aside.
5. Heat the oil in a wok until very hot.
6. Add all of the duck strips and stir fry for 3 minutes until the meat has changed color. If necessary, separate with chopsticks during frying.
7. Add the scallion (spring onion), marinade and bouillon (stock) and bring to the boil.
8. Rub the mandarin rind with 2 lumps of sugar so that they absorb the oil.
9. Add the sugar lumps to the bouillon (stock) and stir until dissolved.
10. Transfer to a warmed dish, garnish with mandarin segments and a few sprigs of parsley and serve.

Left to right: Duck fillets in mandarin sauce;
Duck fillets with mangoes;
Duck fillets with hoisin sauce

Manggoeo tsjoe japiean
Duck Fillets with Mangoes

◼▭▷ 00.15   00.15 🍲
plus standing time

American	Ingredients	Metric/Imperial
1½ lb	duck breast fillets	700 g/1 ½ lb
2 tbsp	groundnut oil	2 tbsp
1 tbsp	Chinese light soy sauce	1 tbsp
1 tbsp	Chinese dark soy sauce	1 tbsp
1 tbsp	hoisin sauce	1 tbsp
1	lightly beaten egg white	1
	pinch of five spice powder	
	freshly ground pepper	
2	large ripe mangoes	2
3-4 tbsp	groundnut oil	3-4 tbsp
3	scallions (spring onions)	3
¾ cup	duck or chicken bouillon (stock)	200 ml/7 fl oz
	salt	
2 tbsp	lime or lemon juice	2 tbsp
1 tbsp	honey	1 tbsp

1. Dry the fillets with kitchen paper. Cut into slices and then into strips.
2. Mix together 2 tbsp oil, the soy sauces, hoisin sauce, beaten egg white, five spice powder and freshly ground pepper. Stir until smooth.
3. Stir in the duck and leave to marinate for 25 minutes.
4. Halve the mangoes, stone and peel the halves and cut the flesh into strips ½ in (1.25 cm) thick.
5. Remove the duck from the marinade.
6. Heat 3-4 tbsp oil in a wok, add the duck and stir fry for 2 minutes. Separate with chop sticks during frying.
7. Sprinkle the meat with finely chopped scallion (spring onion) as soon as it changes color and add ¾ cup (200 ml/7 fl oz) bouillon (stock). Stir well and bring to the boil.
8. Add salt to taste and carefully stir in the mango slices, lime or lemon juice and honey. As soon as the mango slices are hot, transfer to a warmed dish and serve.

Hai xiang tsjie ja roe
Duck Fillets with Hoisin Sauce (Canton)

◼▭▷ 00.20   00.30 🍲
plus soaking and cooling time

American	Ingredients	Metric/Imperial
1 lb	small duck breast fillets	450 g/1 lb
8	large dried mushrooms	8
¾ cup	drained bamboo shoots	150 g/5 oz
1	beaten egg white	1
½ tbsp	cornstarch (cornflour)	½ tbsp
2 tbsp	Chinese light soy sauce	2 tbsp
2 tbsp	Chinese dark soy sauce	2 tbsp
2 tbsp	yellow bean paste	2 tbsp
	salt	
	pinch of five spice powder	
	freshly ground pepper	
4	chopped scallions (spring onions) or shallots	4
½ tbsp	grated root ginger	½ tbsp
4	large, washed lettuce leaves	4
4 tbsp	corn oil or sunflower oil	4 tbsp
8 tbsp	hoisin sauce	8 tbsp

1. Place the duck fillets in a pan with boiling water to just cover them. Bring the water to the boil and simmer for 15 minutes. Leave the fillets to cool in the water until cold. Remove from the pan, drain and dry with kitchen paper.
2. Cut the duck into small cubes.
3. Put the mushrooms in a small bowl with boiling water to cover. Leave to soak for 30 minutes. Remove the stalks, cut the caps into small cubes.
4. Cut the bamboo shoots into small cubes.
5. Put the duck in a bowl with the mushrooms and bamboo shoots. Stir together.
6. Beat the egg white in another bowl and add the cornstarch (cornflour), soy sauces and bean paste. Stir until smooth. Stir in the salt, five spice powder, pepper, scallion (spring onion) and ginger. Lay the lettuce on a dish.
7. Heat the oil in a wok, add the duck, mushrooms and bamboo shoots and stir for 4 minutes on high heat.
8. Add the sauce mixture and stir fry for a further 3-4 minutes and serve the hoisin sauce separately.

Woe xiang shoe ja 👨‍🍳👨‍🍳👨‍🍳
Roasted and Braised Duck (Canton)

▃▃▷ 00.30 01.30 🍲
plus drying time

American	Ingredients	Metric/Imperial
1 (4 lb)	duck	1 (1.8 kg/4 lb)
	salt	
	freshly ground pepper	
½ tsp	five spice powder	½ tsp
1-1½ tbsp	groundnut oil	1-1½ tbsp
3-4 tbsp	honey	3-4 tbsp
1 tbsp	hoisin sauce	1 tbsp
1 tbsp	yellow bean paste	1 tbsp
3 tbsp	Kao-liang wine rice wine or sherry	3 tbsp
1 tbsp	finely chopped fresh root ginger	1 tbsp
2	chopped shallots	2
	five spice powder	
2 cups	duck or chicken bouillon (stock)	450 ml/¾ pint
2-3	sugar lumps	2-3
3	oranges	3
1 tbsp	cornstarch (cornflour)	1 tbsp
1 tbsp	sesame oil	1 tbsp
2	scallions (spring onions)	2

1. Dry the duck inside and out with kitchen paper and rub it with the salt, pepper and five spice powder. Leave to stand for 15 minutes.
2. Bring enough water to the boil in a large pan and dip the duck into this for 15 seconds. Remove the duck and drain it on a cake or oven rack. Dry the duck again with kitchen paper.
3. Heat the oil in a heavy based pan. Add honey, hoisin sauce, bean paste, Kao-liang wine or rice wine or sherry, finely chopped root ginger, shallots and five spice powder to taste, stirring constantly. Stir continuously until smooth and take care not to let it come to the boil.
4. Remove the pan from the heat and leave the paste to cool.
5. Rub the duck with this paste inside and out, massaging the skin so that the aromatic flavor is absorbed into the skin and the meat will stay aromatic after drying.
6. Close the opening at the neck by tying it, or use pins. Hang the duck from a hook next to an open window and leave to dry overnight.
7. The next day, preheat the oven to 220°C/425°F/Gas Mark 7.
8. Brush an oven shelf with oil. Place the shelf a little below the middle of the oven and place a roasting tin on the bottom of the oven to catch the liquid.
9. Place the duck on the shelf and roast for about 20 minutes.
10. Bring the bouillon (stock) to the boil in a pan.
11. Add the remaining paste, stirring until it has dissolved.
12. Remove the duck from the oven and reduce the heat to 160°C/325°F/Gas Mark 3.
13. Place the duck and the spicy bouillon (stock) in a casserole and cook in the oven for 1 hour.
14. Turn the duck after 30 minutes and baste it repeatedly with the braising liquid. After 1 hour, remove the duck from the pan and cut or chop it into neat pieces for serving.
15. Cover with aluminum foil and keep the duck warm in the oven while the sauce is prepared.

16. Strain the braising liquid and boil to reduce to half the original quantity.
17. Rub the sugar lumps over the rind of the well scrubbed orange so that they absorb the oils from the rind.
18. Add the sugar to the simmering braising liquid.
19. Peel the oranges and remove the segments from the membranes.
20. Mix the cornstarch (cornflour) with 2 tbsp cold water and thicken the sauce with this, stirring constantly.
21. Add the orange segments and leave them to warm up in the sauce.
22. Remove the duck from the oven and remove the foil.
23. Stir a little sesame oil into the sauce to give it a gloss.
24. Pour some of the sauce over the duck and sprinkle with the chopped scallion (spring onion). Slice the remaining orange and use to garnish the duck. Serve the remaining sauce separately.

Liang noe ja roe 👨‍🍳👨‍🍳👨‍🍳
Duck Fillets with Lotus Root

▃▃▷ 00.20 00.15 🍲
plus standing time

American	Ingredients	Metric/Imperial
1 lb	duck breast fillets	450 g/1 lb
1	beaten egg white	1
1 tbsp	Chinese light soy sauce	1 tbsp
1 tbsp	Chinese dark soy sauce	1 tbsp
2 tbsp	hoisin sauce	2 tbsp
2 tbsp	Kao-liang wine, rice wine or medium sherry	2 tbsp
1 tbsp	finely grated root ginger	1 tbsp
1 tbsp	sesame oil	1 tbsp
	pinch of five spice powder	
	salt	
	freshly ground pepper	
¼ lb	canned lotus root	125 g/4 oz
4 tbsp	groundnut oil	4 tbsp
2	halved garlic cloves	2
¾ cup	duck or chicken bouillon (stock)	200 ml/7 fl oz
1 tsp	sesame oil	1 tsp

1. Dry the fillets with kitchen paper and cut into 1 in (1.25 cm) cubes.
2. Mix the beaten egg white, soy sauces, hoisin sauce, Kao-liang wine or rice wine or sherry, root ginger and sesame oil, adding five spice powder, salt and pepper to taste.
3. Stir in the duck and leave to marinate for 15 minutes (or longer).
4. Remove the duck, drain well and set the marinade aside.
5. Drain the lotus root and cut it into thin slices.
6. Heat the oil in a wok until very hot and stir fry the garlic until golden brown. Remove from the wok.
7. Add the duck cubes and lotus root to the oil and stir fry for 2 minutes. If necessary, separate the cubes of meat during frying with chop sticks.
8. Add the marinade and the duck or chicken bouillon (stock) and bring to the boil. Stir well, leave to simmer for 2 minutes and if necessary, add salt to taste.
9. Immediately before serving, stir in the sesame oil and transfer into a warmed dish.

Hoe joe jielan ja

Duck Drumsticks in Oyster Sauce with Broccoli (Canton)

00.15 plus standing time — 01.30

American	Ingredients	Metric/Imperial
8	duck drumsticks	8
2	green shallots or scallions (spring onions)	2
1 tsp	coarsely grated fresh root ginger	1 tsp
9-10 tbsp	groundnut oil	9-10 tbsp
2 tbsp	Chinese rice wine or dry sherry	2 tbsp
2 tbsp	Chinese dark soy sauce	2 tbsp
2 tbsp	ginger syrup	2 tbsp
	salt	
¼ tsp	five spice powder	¼ tsp
½ lb	broccoli	225 g/8 oz
6-8	dried Chinese mushrooms	6-8
3 tbsp	oyster sauce	3 tbsp
1 tbsp	hoisin sauce	1 tbsp
1 tbsp	cornstarch (cornflour)	1 tbsp
2 tsp	sesame oil	2 tsp

1. Dry the duck drumsticks with kitchen paper and chop each into 4 equal pieces.
2. Chop the green and white part of the green shallots or chop the scallions (spring onions) very finely. Add the root ginger. Grind to a paste in a pestle and mortar.
3. Heat about 6 tbsp groundnut oil in a wok and fry the duck pieces stirring constantly, until golden brown.
4. Stir in the onion paste then add the rice wine or sherry, soy sauce and ginger syrup.
5. Transfer the contents of the wok to a flameproof casserole.
6. Add a generous pinch of salt, the five spice powder and 1½ cups (350 ml/12 fl oz) boiling water. Stir well, cover the casserole with a lid and bring to the boil. Reduce the heat and leave to simmer very gently for 1-1½ hours until tender. Stir occasionally and add a little boiling water if too much liquid evaporates.
7. Wash the broccoli. Cut the stalks into thin slices, divide the tops into small florets and keep separate.
8. Put the dried mushrooms in a bowl with boiling water to cover generously and leave to soak for 30 minutes. Remove the stalks and cut the caps into thin strips.
9. Strain the mushroom soaking liquid through wet muslin.
10. Heat the remaining oil in a wok and stir fry the sliced broccoli stalks and mushroom strips for 2 minutes.
11. Add the broccoli and stir fry for a further 2 minutes.
12. Sprinkle with a little salt and 4 tbsp of the soaking liquid from the mushrooms. Bring to the boil.
13. Remove the broccoli and mushrooms from the wok with a slotted spoon and spread on a warmed dish.
14. Place the tender pieces of duck drumsticks on bed of vegetables.
15. Strain the braising liquid and add to the wok.
16. Add 4 tbsp of the mushroom soaking liquid, oyster sauce and hoisin sauce. Bring to the boil, stirring constantly.
17. Mix the cornstarch (cornflour) with 3 tbsp cold water and stir into the liquid. Cook until the sauce thickens.
18. Taste the sauce and add some salt if necessary.
19. Stir in the sesame oil, pour the sauce over the duck. Serve immediately.

Bit tsjie sjoe ja

Fried Duck with Water Chestnuts (Shanghai)

00.20 plus standing time — 00.35

American	Ingredients	Metric/Imperial
1 (2½ lb)	duck	1 (1.25 kg/2½ lb)
1 tbsp	Chinese light soy sauce	1 tbsp
1 tbsp	Chinese dark soy sauce	1 tbsp
1 tbsp	yellow bean paste	1 tbsp
1 tbsp	oyster sauce	1 tbsp
2 tbsp	Kao-liang wine, rice wine or medium sherry	2 tbsp
2 tbsp	honey	2 tbsp
	freshly ground pepper	
	salt	
⅔ cup	groundnut oil	150 ml/¼ pint
¾ lb	canned water chestnuts	350 g/12 oz
1 cup	duck or chicken bouillon (stock)	250 ml/8 fl oz
1 tbsp	cornstarch (cornflour)	1 tbsp
1 tsp	sesame oil	1 tsp
2	sour-sweet gherkins	2
2-3	chopped green shallots	2-3

1. Divide the duck into 16 or 8 pieces.
2. Simmer the pieces of duck in boiling water to cover for 4-5 minutes. Drain in a colander and leave to cool.
3. Stir together the soy sauces, yellow bean paste, oyster sauce, Kao-liang wine or rice wine or sherry, honey, freshly ground pepper and salt until mixed.
4. Rub the duck pieces with this mixture and leave them to stand for 15 minutes (or longer).
5. Heat the groundnut oil in a wok, add the pieces of duck and water chestnuts and stir fry for 3 minutes.
6. Add the bouillon (stock) and bring to the boil. Cover and simmer for 6 minutes.
7. Mix the cornstarch (cornflour) with 2 tbsp cold water.
8. Transfer the duck and water chestnuts to a warmed dish and stir the cornstarch (cornflour) mixture into the liquid in the pan. Cook, stirring, until the sauce thickens.
9. Taste the sauce and add salt if necessary. Stir in the sesame oil and pour the sauce over the duck immediately. Garnish with the gherkins cut into fans and chopped green shallots.

Tzentzoe wanzie
Steamed Pearls (Peking)

00.45 plus soaking time

00.30

American	Ingredients	Metric/Imperial
1 cup	short grain rice	225 g/8 oz
1 lb	ground (minced) pork	450 g/1 lb
½ cup	canned, drained water chestnuts or bamboo shoots	125 g/4 oz
1	egg	1
1 tbsp	Chinese light soy sauce	1 tbsp
2 tbsp	Chinese dark soy sauce	2 tbsp
1 tbsp	Chinese rice wine or dry sherry	1 tbsp
1 tbsp	oyster sauce	1 tbsp
	salt	
	freshly ground pepper	
	five spice powder	
2	chopped green shallots or scallions (spring onions)	2
1 tsp	ground root ginger	1 tsp
1 tsp	cornstarch (cornflour)	1 tsp
1 tbsp	groundnut oil	1 tbsp

1. Wash the rice several times in plenty of cold water until the rinsing water stays nearly clear. Leave to soak for 6-8 hours in cold water to cover. Drain the soaked rice in a colander and leave to dry for 30 minutes. Stir occasionally to help it to dry further.
2. Put the mince on a chopping board and spread it out into a thin layer several times, with the flat blade of a chopping knife, until the mince becomes sticky.
3. Chop the water chestnuts or bamboo shoots very finely.
4. Beat the egg. Add the soy sauces, rice wine or dry sherry, oyster sauce, some salt and pepper, a pinch five spice powder, green shallots or scallions (spring onions), ground root ginger and cornstarch (cornflour).
5. Add the meat and knead until very sticky.
6. Shape into balls the size of walnuts.
7. Spoon the drained rice on to a large plate and roll the mince balls through the rice, exerting pressure so that the balls are coated on all sides with a layer of rice.
8. Bring a generous quantity of water to the boil in a steamer.
9. Brush the perforated part of the pan with some oil.
10. Place the mince balls on to this part, cover and steam for 15 minutes, until the rice is tender. Serve immediately.

Hwang gwa roewan

Mince Balls in Sweet and Sour Sauce with Cucumber (Peking)

00.20 Serves 4   **00.15**

American	Ingredients	Metric/Imperial
1 lb	ground (minced) pork	450 g/1 lb
1	cucumber	1
1 tbsp	Chinese light soy sauce	1 tbsp
1 tbsp	Chinese dark soy sauce	1 tbsp
1	large beaten egg	1
3 tbsp	Chinese rice wine or dry sherry	3 tbsp
1 tbsp	ginger syrup	1 tbsp
1 tbsp	oyster sauce	1 tbsp
1 tbsp	finely grated root ginger	1 tbsp
	salt	
	five spice powder	
2 tbsp	cornstarch (cornflour)	2 tbsp
½ lb	spinach or paksoi	225 g/8 oz
¾ cup	groundnut oil	200 ml/7 fl oz
1¼ cups	chicken bouillon (stock)	300 ml/½ pint
1 tbsp	mild vinegar preferably cider vinegar	1 tbsp
1-1½ tbsp	confectioners' (icing) sugar	1-1½ tbsp
2 tbsp	finely chopped chives	2 tbsp
2	skinned tomatoes (optional)	2

1. Place the pork on a chopping board and spread it out into a thin layer several times with the flat blade of a chopping knife, until the meat becomes sticky.
2. Wash the cucumber and cut in half lengthwise. Remove the seeds from both halves with a small spoon. Cut each half lengthwise and cut into ½ in (1.25 cm) pieces.
3. Add half of each soy sauce to the beaten egg with 1 tbsp Chinese rice wine or dry sherry, the ginger syrup, oyster sauce, 1 tsp root ginger, a little salt, a pinch five spice powder and 1 tbsp cornstarch (cornflour).
4. Mix well and add the mince.
5. Knead with wet hands until the meat is very sticky. Shape this into balls the size of walnuts.
6. Pick over the spinach or paksoi and wash it in cold water. Place the wet vegetable in a pan. Sprinkle with a little salt and bring to the boil. Boil for 2-3 minutes, turning constantly for spinach, 5 minutes for paksoi. Drain and press out more liquid with a saucer. Keep warm.
7. Heat the oil in a wok and stir fry the mince balls until golden brown. Remove with a slotted spoon. Drain briefly over the wok and keep warm.

8. Remove all but 2 tbsp of oil from the wok and stir fry the cucumber pieces for 1 minute.
9. Add the remaining root ginger and stir well.
10. Add the bouillon (stock), the remaining soy sauces and the Chinese rice wine or dry sherry. Stir well and add the vinegar and sugar.
11. Mix 1 tbsp cornstarch (cornflour) with 3 tbsp cold water and stir into the contents of the wok. Cook until the sauce thickens. Add salt and sugar to taste.
12. Put the spinach or paksoi in a warmed dish.
13. Warm the pork balls in the sauce and arrange them on the spinach.
14. Sprinkle with chives just before serving and garnish with slices or pieces of tomato.

Cook's tip: for a variation, replace the cucumber with ¾ lb (350 g/12 oz) pumpkin. Remove the skin and seed from the pumpkin and cut it into ½ in (1.25 cm) cubes. Prepare as for the recipe above.

Joe mie sjizitoe

Steamed Meat Balls, Wax Beans and Corn (Peking)

00.30 Serves 4   **00.40**

American	Ingredients	Metric/Imperial
1 lb	ground (minced) pork	450 g/1 lb
1	egg white	1
1 tbsp	Chinese light soy sauce	1 tbsp
2 tbsp	Chinese dark soy sauce	1 tbsp
1 tbsp	Chinese rice wine or dry sherry	1 tbsp
1 tbsp	ginger syrup	1 tbsp
	pinch five spice powder	
	salt	
2 tsp	cornstarch (cornflour)	2 tsp
3¼ cups	chicken bouillon (stock)	750 ml/1¼ pints
1 tbsp	groundnut oil	1 tbsp
¾ lb	cleaned wax beans	350 g/12 oz
½ lb	cooked corn kernels	225 g/8 oz
4	sticks celery (optional)	4

1. Place the ground (minced) pork on a chopping board and spread it out into a thin layer several times with the flat blade of a chopping knife until it becomes sticky.
2. Beat the egg white and add the soy sauces, rice wine or sherry, ginger syrup, five spice powder, a pinch of salt and 1 tsp cornstarch (cornflour).
3. Add the meat and knead until very sticky. Shape into 4 large balls and flatten slightly.
4. Bring the bouillon (stock) to the boil in a steamer. Brush the perforated part of the pan with oil and place the mince balls on this. Place over the bouillon (stock), cover and steam for 20-25 minutes. Keep warm.
5. Boil the wax beans for 7-8 minutes in the bouillon (stock). Pour some bouillon (stock) out of the pan until about ¾ cup (200 ml/7 fl oz) remain. Add the corn kernels.
6. Mix the remaining cornstarch (cornflour) with 1 tbsp cold water and stir into the contents of the pan. Cook until the sauce thickens.
7. Put the mince balls on warmed plates and spoon over the vegetables and the sauce. Garnish with sticks of celery.

Top: Steamed meat balls, wax beans and corn; Steamed pearls

Mie tzie niang gwa
Stuffed Cucumbers with Honey Sauce (Canton)

00.30 Serves 4   **00.12**

American	Ingredients	Metric/Imperial
½ lb	ground (minced) pork	225 g/8 oz
1	beaten egg white	1
½ tsp	rice flour	½ tsp
1½ tbsp	Chinese light soy sauce	1½ tbsp
1 tbsp	oyster sauce	1 tbsp
½ tbsp	chili sauce	½ tbsp
1½ tbsp	Chinese rice wine or dry sherry	1½ tbsp
1 tbsp	ginger syrup	1 tbsp
½ tbsp	confectioners' (icing) sugar	½ tbsp
1 tbsp	extremely finely chopped green shallot, scallion (spring onion) or leek	1 tbsp
	salt	
2	small cucumbers	2
2½ tbsp	cornstarch (cornflour)	2½ tbsp
⅔ cup	oil for frying	150 ml/¼ pint
1¼ cups	chicken bouillon (stock)	300 ml/½ pint
2 tbsp	clear honey	2 tbsp

1. Place the pork on a chopping board and spread it out into a thin layer several times with the flat blade of a chopping knife, until it becomes sticky.
2. Mix the pork with the egg white, rice flour, ½ tbsp soy sauce, oyster sauce, chili sauce, ½ tbsp rice wine or sherry, ginger syrup, ½ tsp sugar, green shallot or scallion (spring onion) or leek and a little salt.
3. Knead until it is very sticky.
4. Wash the cucumbers, remove the ends and cut each into 8 equal pieces. Remove the seeds with a small spoon. Dry on all sides with kitchen paper. Fill the pieces with the meat mixture packing it tightly and keeping it level with the cucumber.
5. Press the cut sides into 1½ tbsp cornstarch (cornflour).
6. Heat the oil until very hot and fry the cucumber pieces 3-4 at a time for 3 minutes. Remove from the oil with a slotted spoon and drain over the pan. Dry with kitchen paper and place on a warmed dish.
7. Prepare the sauce by bringing the chicken bouillon (stock) to the boil and stirring in the remaining soy sauce and the rice wine or sherry. Add the honey. Boil steadily.
8. Mix 1 tbsp cornstarch (cornflour) with 3 tbsp cold water and stir into the bouillon (stock). Cook, until the sauce thickens and add a little salt to taste.
9. Pour the sauce over the cucumber pieces and serve.

Jang tjong zjiauroe
Braised Mince with Green Shallots (Peking)

00.10 Serves 4   **00.40**

American	Ingredients	Metric/Imperial
3-4 tbsp	groundnut oil	3-4 tbsp
1	halved garlic clove	1
1 lb	chopped or coarsely ground (minced) lean pork	450 g/l lb
1 tbsp	finely grated root ginger	1 tbsp
2 tbsp	Chinese light soy sauce	2 tbsp
1 tbsp	Chinese dark soy sauce	1 tbsp
1 tbsp	oyster sauce	1 tbsp
2 tbsp	Chinese rice wine or dry sherry	2 tbsp
1¼ cups	chicken bouillon (stock)	300 ml/½ pint
12	green shallots, cut into 1 in (2.5 cm) pieces	12
1 tbsp	cornstarch (cornflour)	1 tbsp
1 tsp	sesame oil	1 tsp
1 tbsp	finely chopped celery	1 tbsp

1. Heat the oil in a wok and stir fry the garlic until golden brown. Remove garlic from the pan.
2. Stir fry the meat until it separates into crumbs and has changed color.
3. Add the root ginger, stir, and after 30 seconds, add the soy sauces, oyster sauce, rice wine or sherry and half the bouillon (stock). Stir well then cover the wok and reduce the heat. Leave to simmer for 20 minutes.
4. Add the green shallots and bring to the boil again.
5. Add the remaining bouillon (stock) and salt to taste.
6. Mix the cornstarch (cornflour) with 2 tbsp cold water and stir into the contents of the wok. Cook, until the sauce thickens slightly.
7. Immediately before serving, stir in the sesame oil and celery.

Tsjjie tzie tsgin zjiauroe

Pork Rolls in Tomato Sauce with Bell Pepper (Canton)

00.20
Serves 4

00.20

American	Ingredients	Metric/Imperial
¾ lb	ground (minced) pork	350 g/12 oz
3 tbsp	Chinese light soy sauce	3 tbsp
3 tbsp	Chinese rice wine or dry sherry	3 tbsp
2 tbsp	very finely chopped green shallot, scallion (spring onion) or leek (white part only)	2 tbsp
	salt	
	pinch of five spice powder	
4 tbsp	cornstarch (cornflour)	4 tbsp
3-4 tbsp	groundnut oil	3-4 tbsp
2	medium size red bell peppers, trimmed, seeded, cut into thin strips	2
8	skinned tomatoes cut into pieces	8
⅔ cup	groundnut oil for frying	150 ml/¼ pint
1¼ cups	chicken bouillon (stock)	300 ml/½ pint
2 tbsp	confectioners' (icing) sugar	2 tbsp
1 tbsp	ginger syrup	1 tbsp
2 tbsp	Chinese tomato sauce or Chinese barbecue sauce	2 tbsp
1 tbsp	chopped celery	1 tbsp

1. Place the pork on a chopping board and spread it out into a thin layer, several times with the flat blade of a chopping knife, until it becomes sticky.
2. Mix the pork with 1 tbsp soy sauce, 1 tbsp rice wine or sherry, the green shallot, scallion (spring onion) or leek, a little salt, five spice powder and 1 tbsp cornstarch (cornflour).
3. Shape the meat into rolls 2 in×1 in (5×2.5 cm).
4. Sprinkle 2 tbsp cornstarch (cornflour) into a deep plate and roll the mince rolls in this, coating all sides.
5. Heat 3-4 tbsp oil in a wok and stir fry the bell pepper strips for 1 minute.
6. Add the bell pepper and tomato pieces and stir several times. Cover the wok, reduce the heat and leave to simmer for 5 minutes.
7. Heat the oil in a deep frying pan until very hot.
8. Fry the pork rolls, 4-5 at a time until golden brown. Remove from the oil. Drain briefly. Dry with kitchen paper and keep warm.
9. Add the remaining soy sauce and rice wine or sherry to the contents of the wok. Stir vigorously and add the bouillon (stock), sugar, ginger syrup and tomato or barbecue sauce. Leave to cook steadily.
10. Mix 1 tbsp cornstarch (cornflour) with 3 tbsp cold water and stir into the contents of the wok. Cook, until the sauce thickens.
11. Place the pork rolls on a warmed dish, pour over the sauce and sprinkle with the chopped celery.

Left to right: Braised mince with green shallots; Stuffed cucumbers with honey sauce; Pork rolls in tomato sauce with bell pepper

Tsjien tjai zjiauroe
Mince with Leek and Asparagus

◖═▷ 00.10   00.20 **◖╸═**
Serves 4

American	Ingredients	Metric/Imperial
2	medium size leeks	2
1 lb	asparagus	450 g/1 lb
4-5 tbsp	groundnut oil	4-5 tbsp
½ lb	ground (minced) beef or pork	225 g/8 oz
2 tbsp	Chinese light soy sauce	2 tbsp
½ tsp	Chinese chili sauce	½ tsp
3 tbsp	Chinese rice wine or dry sherry	3 tbsp
3 tbsp	Chinese tomato sauce	3 tbsp
1¼ cups	bouillon (stock)	300 ml/½ pint
1 tbsp	cornstarch (cornflour)	1 tbsp

1. Clean the leeks. Thinly slice the white and light yellow-green parts.
2. Trim the asparagus and cut into 1 in (2.5 cm) pieces.
3. Heat the oil in a wok and stir fry the meat until it separates and has changed color.
4. Add both vegetables and stir fry for 2 minutes.
5. Add the soy sauce, chili sauce, rice wine or sherry and tomato sauce. Stir well several times and add the bouillon (stock). Stir well. Cover the wok, simmer for 5 minutes.
6. Mix the cornstarch (cornflour) with 2 tbsp cold water and push the ingredients to one side of the wok. Stir the cornstarch (cornflour) mixture into the liquid in the wok. Cook, until the sauce thickens slightly.
7. Stir the ingredients into the sauce, add salt to taste.
8. Serve in a warmed dish

Zjie lau zjiauroe
Mince with Crab and Broccoli

◖═▷ 00.15   00.25 **◖╸═**
Serves 4

American	Ingredients	Metric/Imperial
6 oz	crabmeat, thawed if frozen	175 g/6 oz
6 oz	broccoli florets	175 g/6 oz
3 tbsp	groundnut oil	3 tbsp
¾ lb	ground (minced) pork	350 g/12 oz
1	small chopped onion or shallot	1
1 tbsp	Chinese light soy sauce	1 tbsp
2 tbsp	Chinese rice wine or dry sherry	2 tbsp
½ tsp	oyster sauce	½ tsp
1 tbsp	crab sauce	1 tbsp
1 tsp	confectioners' (icing) sugar	1 tsp
¾ cup	bouillon (stock)	200 ml/7 fl oz
1 tbsp	cornstarch (cornflour)	1 tbsp
2	skinned tomatoes, cut into thin strips	2

1. Pick over the crabmeat and cut into small pieces.
2. Bring the broccoli florets to the boil in boiling, salted water and cook for 5 minutes. Drain and keep warm.
3. Heat the oil in a wok and stir fry the meat until it separates and changes color.
4. Add the onion or shallot and stir well. Cook until the onion or shallot gain some color.
5. Add the soy sauce, rice wine or dry sherry, oyster sauce, crab sauce, and salt. Stir well and add the bouillon (stock). Stir well, cover the wok and simmer for 5 minutes.
6. Mix the cornstarch (cornflour) with 2 tbsp cold water.
7. Push the ingredients in the wok to one side and stir the cornstarch (cornflour) mixture into the liquid. Cook, until the sauce thickens.
8. Stir the crabmeat into the sauce.
9. Transfer to a warm dish, arrange the broccoli on top in a circle. Serve sprinkled with the tomato strips.

Bai thai sjizitoe
Steamed Mince Balls with Chinese Leaves

◖═▷ 00.30   00.30 **◖╸═**
Serves 4

American	Ingredients	Metric/Imperial
1 lb	ground (minced) pork	450 g/1 lb
1	egg white	1
1 tbsp	Chinese light soy sauce	1 tbsp
1 tbsp	oyster sauce	1 tbsp
1 tbsp	ginger syrup	1 tbsp
1 tbsp	Chinese rice wine or dry sherry	1 tbsp
	five spice powder	
	salt	
2 tsp	cornstarch (cornflour)	2 tsp
¾ lb	Chinese leaves	350 g/12 oz
3¼ cups	chicken bouillon (stock)	750 ml/1¼ pints
1 tbsp	groundnut oil	1 tbsp
	drop Chinese dark soy sauce	

1. Put the ground (minced) pork on a chopping board. Spread it out into a thin layer several times with the flat blade of a knife, until it becomes sticky.
2. Beat the egg white. Add the soy sauce, oyster sauce, ginger syrup, rice wine or sherry, five spice powder, salt and 1 tsp cornstarch (cornflour). Mix thoroughly and add the pork.
3. Knead, until it is very sticky. Shape into 8 balls.
4. Rinse the Chinese leaves and cut into finger width strips.
5. Bring the bouillon (stock) to the boil in a steamer. Brush the perforated part of the steamer with oil and place the mince balls on to it. Place over the pan with the bouillon (stock), cover and steam for 20 minutes over moderate heat. Keep warm wrapped in aluminum foil.
6. Add the Chinese leaves to the boiling bouillon (stock). Boil for 4-5 minutes.
7. Pour some bouillon (stock) out of the pan until about ¾ cup (200 ml/7 fl oz) remain.
8. Mix the remaining cornstarch (cornflour) with 1 tbsp cold water and stir into the remaining bouillon (stock) in the pan. Cook until the sauce thickens.
9. Add salt and a few drops dark soy sauce to taste.
10. Place the meat balls on a warmed deep plate and add the Chinese leaves and the sauce.

Steamed mince balls and shrimp sauce

Sjia mie roewan

Steamed Mince Balls and Shrimp Sauce (Peking)

00.40 Serves 4   **00.30**

American	Ingredients	Metric/Imperial
¾ lb	ground (minced) pork	350 g/12 oz
½ lb	peeled shrimps (prawns)	225 g/8 oz
1 tbsp	Chinese rice wine or dry sherry	1 tbsp
1 tbsp	Chinese light soy sauce	1 tbsp
½-1 tbsp	shrimp sauce	½-1 tbsp
	salt	
	pinch confectioners' (icing) sugar	
2	chopped scallions (spring onions)	2
1 tsp	cornstarch (cornflour)	1 tsp
1	beaten egg	1
1 tsp	sesame oil	1 tsp
1 cup	chicken bouillon (stock)	250 ml/8 fl oz
2 tbsp	Chinese rice wine or dry sherry	2 tbsp
1 tbsp	Chinese light soy sauce	1 tbsp
1 tbsp	Chinese dark soy sauce	1 tbsp
	salt	
1 tsp	oyster sauce	1 tsp
½ tsp	grated fresh ginger root	½ tsp
2 tsp	cornstarch (cornflour)	2 tsp
	few sticks celery (optional)	
2	skinned tomatoes (optional)	2

1. Place the ground (minced) pork on a chopping board and spread it out several times into a thin layer with the flat blade of a chopping knife, until it becomes sticky.
2. Cut the shrimp (prawns) lengthwise on the back and remove the black thread. Chop half the shrimp (prawns) very finely and cut the other half into small pieces.
3. Add 1 tbsp rice wine or sherry, 1 tbsp light soy sauce, shrimp sauce, some salt, 1 pinch of sugar, scallions (spring onions) and 1 tbsp cornstarch (cornflour) to the beaten egg.

4. Knead the pork and the chopped shrimp (prawn) into the mixture until very sticky. Shape into 8 balls.
5. Brush the perforated part of the steamer with oil and place the mince balls on to this.
6. Steam for 18-22 minutes until tender.
7. Bring the sesame oil, chicken bouillon (stock), remaining rice wine or sherry, soy sauces, salt, oyster sauce and root ginger to the boil in a pan.
8. Mix 2 tsp cornstarch (cornflour) with 2 tbsp cold water and stir into the pan. Cook until the sauce thickens.
9. Warm the shrimp (prawns) in the sauce just before serving.
10. Place the mince balls on a warmed dish, pour over the sauce and serve garnished with celery or a tomato flower.

Moe'er roewan

Steamed Mince Balls with Chinese Mushrooms (Canton)

00.30 plus standing time   **00.30**

American	Ingredients	Metric/Imperial
1 lb	ground (minced) pork	450 g/1 lb
20	large dried Chinese mushrooms	20
1 tbsp	Chinese light soy sauce	1 tbsp
1 tbsp	Chinese dark soy sauce	1 tbsp
1	beaten egg	1
2 tbsp	Chinese rice wine or dry sherry	2 tbsp
2	chopped scallions (spring onions)	2
1 tsp	ground root ginger	1 tsp
2 tsp	cornstarch (cornflour)	2 tsp
4 tbsp	groundnut oil	4 tbsp
1 cup	chicken bouillon (stock)	250 ml/8 fl oz
1 tbsp	ginger syrup	1 tbsp
½ tbsp	oyster sauce	½ tbsp
1 tsp	confectioners' (icing) sugar	1 tsp
1 tsp	sesame oil	1 tsp

1. Place the ground (minced) pork on a chopping board and spread it out into a thin layer several times with the flat blade of a chopping knife, until the meat becomes sticky.
2. Place the mushrooms in a bowl with boiling water to cover. Leave to stand for 30 minutes. Remove the stalks from the soaked mushrooms and cut the caps into thin strips.
3. Add the soy sauces to the beaten egg with 1 tbsp rice wine or sherry, the root ginger and 1 tsp cornstarch (cornflour).
4. Add the meat and knead until very sticky.
5. Shape the mince mixture into 8 balls.
6. Heat the groundnut oil in a wok and stir fry the meat balls in this oil, until golden brown on all sides.
7. Pour as much oil as possible out of the wok and add the bouillon (stock), ginger syrup, oyster sauce and confectioners' (icing) sugar. Bring to the boil, reduce the heat and leave to braise for 7-10 minutes.
8. Taste the cooking liquid and add salt to taste.
9. Mix the remaining cornstarch (cornflour) with 1½ tbsp cold water and stir into the contents of the wok. Cook until the sauce thickens.
10. Stir in the sesame oil just before serving.

Mince with onion and bell pepper

Botjae sjizitoe

Steamed Pork Balls with Spinach

	00.20 Serves 4	00.20

American	Ingredients	Metric/Imperial
1 lb	ground (minced) pork	450 g/1 lb
1 tbsp	canned black beans	1 tbsp
2	chopped green shallots or scallions (spring onions)	2
1	beaten egg	1
1 tsp	grated fresh root ginger	1 tsp
	salt	
1 tsp	confectioners' (icing) sugar	1 tsp
1 tbsp	ginger syrup	1 tbsp
1 tbsp	oyster sauce	1 tbsp
2½ tsp	cornstarch (cornflour)	2½ tsp
3 tbsp	groundnut oil	3 tbsp
2 tbsp	Chinese light soy sauce	2 tbsp
1 tbsp	Chinese dark soy sauce	1 tbsp
2 tbsp	Chinese rice wine or dry sherry	2 tbsp
1¼ cups	chicken bouillon (stock)	300 ml/½ pint
1½ lb	washed, picked over spinach	700 g/1½ lb
1 tsp	sesame oil	1 tsp

1. Place the ground (minced) pork on a chopping board and spread it out into a thin layer several times with the flat blade of a chopping knife until it becomes sticky.
2. Mash the beans with a fork. Spread out as for the mince.
3. Add the green shallots or scallions (spring onions) to the beaten egg with the root ginger, a little salt, sugar, ginger syrup, oyster sauce and 1 tsp cornstarch (cornflour).
4. Stir well and add the meat and mashed black beans. Knead with wet hands until very sticky. Shape into 8 balls.
5. Heat the oil in a wok and stir fry the mince balls in this oil until golden brown on all sides. Remove from the oil with a slotted spoon. Drain briefly and keep warm.
6. Pour as much oil as possible out of the wok. Add the soy sauces, rice wine or sherry and the bouillon (stock) and bring to the boil. Reduce the heat and leave to boil steadily until half the original quantity has evaporated.
7. Bring the wet spinach to the boil. Add a little salt. Stir constantly and cook for 2-3 minutes. Drain the spinach in a colander and press out as much liquid as possible.
8. Mix the remaining cornstarch (cornflour) with 2 tbsp cold water and stir into the contents of the wok. Cook until the sauce thickens.
9. Add the pork balls, cook for a further few seconds and stir in the sesame oil just before serving.
10. Transfer the spinach to warmed plates. Place the pork balls on top and then spoon the sauce over.

Jang tjong tsing zjiauroe

Mince with Onion and Bell Pepper

	00.15 Serves 4	00.20

American	Ingredients	Metric/Imperial
6	green shallots or small onions	6
2	medium size green bell peppers	2
1	red bell pepper	1
4-5 tbsp	groundnut oil	4-5 tbsp
1	garlic clove	1
¾ lb	ground (minced) beef	350 g/12 oz
1 tbsp	Chinese dark soy sauce	1 tbsp
1 tbsp	oyster sauce	1 tbsp
2 tbsp	Chinese rice wine or dry sherry	2 tbsp
2 tbsp	Chinese tomato sauce or Chinese barbecue sauce	2 tbsp
	five spice powder	
	pinch confectioners' (icing) sugar	
¾ cup	bouillon (stock)	200 ml/7 fl oz
1 tbsp	cornstarch (cornflour)	1 tbsp
	salt	
1-2	skinned tomatoes (optional)	1-2

1. Clean the shallots or onions. Cut each shallot or onion into 6 parts and then separate the layers.
2. Wash and trim the bell peppers and cut into thin strips or small diamonds.
3. Heat the oil in a wok, add the garlic and onions and stir fry until the onion is transparent.
4. Add the strips or diamonds of bell pepper and stir fry until the onion has gained some color.
5. Remove the onion and bell pepper with a slotted spoon, drain over the wok and keep warm.
6. Stir fry the meat in the remaining oil until is separates and changes color.
7. Add the soy sauce, oyster sauce, rice wine or sherry, tomato sauce or barbecue sauce, a pinch of five spice powder and the sugar. Stir well several times.
8. Add the bouillon (stock) and stir well. Cover the wok, reduce the heat and simmer gently for 5 minutes.
9. Push the ingredients to one side of the wok.
10. Mix the cornstarch (cornflour) with 2 tbsp cold water and stir into the liquid. Cook, until the sauce thickens. Add salt to taste.
11. Stir in the shallot or onion and the bell pepper.
12. Serve in a warmed dish garnished with tomatoes.

Tiean soean roewan

Mince Balls in Sweet and Sour Sauce (Peking)

➤ 00.20
Serves 4
00.15

American	Ingredients	Metric/Imperial
1 lb	ground (minced) pork	450 g/1 lb
1 tsp	cornstarch (cornflour)	1 tsp
1	beaten egg	1
1 tsp	grated fresh root ginger	1 tsp
4	finely chopped green shallots, scallions (spring onions) or 2 thin leeks	4
1	crushed garlic clove	1
	salt	
¾ cup	groundnut oil	200 ml/7 fl oz
1 tbsp	Chinese light soy sauce	1 tbsp
2 tbsp	Chinese dark soy sauce	2 tbsp
1½ tbsp	oyster sauce	1½ tbsp
2 tbsp	tomato purée	2 tbsp
2 tbsp	Chinese rice wine or dry sherry	2 tbsp
2 tbsp	mild vinegar, preferably rice vinegar	2 tbsp
5 tbsp	chicken bouillon (stock)	5 tbsp
1 tbsp	ginger syrup	1 tbsp
1 tbsp	cornstarch (cornflour)	1 tbsp
2 tbsp	sugar	2 tbsp

1. Place the pork on a chopping board and spread it out into a thin layer several times with the flat blade of a chopping knife until it becomes sticky.
2. Add 1 tsp cornstarch (cornflour) to the beaten egg with the root ginger, half of the shallots, scallions (spring onions) or leeks, and the garlic and salt.
3. Mix well and add the meat. Knead until very sticky.

4. Shape into balls the size of walnuts.
5. Heat the oil in a wok and stir fry the pork balls until golden brown all over.
6. Put the soy sauces, oyster sauce, tomato purée, rice wine or sherry, vinegar, bouillon (stock) and ginger syrup in a small pan. Bring slowly to the boil, stirring constantly. Keep warm over very low heat.
7. Remove as much oil as possible from the wok.
8. Push the pork balls to one side and add the remainder of the shallots, scallions (spring onions) or leeks. Stir fry for 1 minute.
9. Mix the remaining cornstarch (cornflour) with 4 tbsp cold water and stir into the liquid in the wok. Cook, until the sauce thickens. Add sugar to taste.
10. Stir the sauce well and stir the pork balls into the sauce. Serve as soon as the pork balls are hot.

Baitjai zjiauroe

Ground (Minced) Meat with Chinese Leaves

➤ 00.15
Serves 4
00.20

American	Ingredients	Metric/Imperial
1½ lb	Chinese leaves	700 g/1½ lb
3 tbsp	groundnut oil	3 tbsp
1 lb	chopped or coarsely ground (minced) pork	450 g/1 lb
1	large chopped onion or a few shallots	1
1	very finely chopped garlic clove	1
1 tsp	grated fresh root ginger	1 tsp
2 tbsp	Chinese light soy sauce	2 tbsp
2-3 tbsp	Chinese rice wine or dry sherry	2-3 tbsp
	salt	
	pinch five spice powder	
1 tsp	confectioners' (icing) sugar	1 tsp
⅔ cup	chicken bouillon (stock)	150 ml/¼ pint
1 tbsp	cornstarch (cornflour)	1 tbsp
2	hard-cooked (boiled) eggs (optional)	2

1. Clean the Chinese leaves. Remove the thickest stalks and cut the leaves into finger width strips.
2. Heat the oil in a wok, add the mince and stir fry until it separates into crumbs and has changed color.
3. Add the chopped onion or shallots, garlic and ginger. Stir several times and leave the onion to gain some color.
4. Add the soy sauce, rice wine or sherry, a pinch of salt, the five spice powder and sugar.
5. Stir in the bouillon (stock), bring to the boil and boil steadily for 3 minutes.
6. Add the Chinese leaves and boil for 3 minutes.
7. Mix the cornstarch (cornflour) with 2 tbsp cold water. Push the ingredients to one side of the wok and stir the cornstarch (cornflour) mixture into the liquid. Cook, until the sauce thickens slightly.
8. Push all the ingredients into the sauce and simmer for 1-2 minutes.
9. Serve in a warmed dish garnished with slices of egg.

Doefoe zjiauroe

Mince with Soybean Curd (Tofu)

◗▷ 00.15
Serves 4
00.35 🍲

American	Ingredients	Metric/Imperial
2	cakes soybean curd (tofu)	2
3 tbsp	groundnut oil	3 tbsp
1	large chopped onion	1
½ lb	ground (minced) beef or pork	225 g/8 oz
1	very finely chopped garlic clove	1
1 tsp	grated fresh root ginger	1 tsp
	few chopped shallots	
1	seeded, shredded red chili	1
2 tbsp	mashed black beans	2 tbsp
2 tbsp	Chinese light soy sauce	2 tbsp
1 tbsp	oyster sauce	1 tbsp
2 tbsp	Chinese rice wine or dry sherry	2 tbsp
¾ cup	bouillon (stock)	200 ml/7 fl oz
4	chopped scallions (spring onions)	4
1 tbsp	cornstarch (cornflour)	1 tbsp
	salt	
	freshly ground pepper	
1 tsp	confectioners' (icing) sugar	1 tsp
	some sticks celery (optional)	
1-2	skinned tomatoes (optional)	1-2

1. Cut the soybean curd (tofu) into 1 in (1.25 cm) cubes.
2. Heat the oil in a wok and stir fry the onion until it has gained some color.
3. Add the meat and stir fry until it separates into crumbs and has changed color.
4. Add the garlic, root ginger, shallots and red chili. Stir well several times.
5. Add the black beans, soy sauce, oyster sauce and rice wine or dry sherry. Stir well several times and add the bouillon (stock). Stir well.
6. Stir in the cubes of soybean curd (tofu) and scallions (spring onions). Reduce the heat, cover the wok with a lid and simmer for 15 minutes.
7. Push the ingredients to one side of the wok.
8. Mix the cornstarch (cornflour) with 2 tbsp cold water and stir into the liquid in the wok. Cook, until the sauce thickens slightly.
9. Stir the ingredients into the sauce. Taste the sauce and add salt and/or freshly ground pepper and sugar to taste.
10. Pour into a warmed dish, add sticks of celery or the pieces of skinned tomato and serve.

Cook's tip: the authentic recipe is for soybean curd (tofu) stuffed with mince. The soybean curd (tofu) is cut lengthwise diagonally. The cut side of each is then hollowed out and then stuffed with the mince.

Tzoe sjoen doeja zjiauroe

Mince with Bamboo Shoots and Bean Sprouts

◗▷ 00.20
plus cooling time
00.25 🍲

American	Ingredients	Metric/Imperial
¼ lb	canned bamboo shoots	125 g/4 oz
1 cup	bean sprouts	75 g/3 oz
4 tbsp	groundnut oil	4 tbsp
¾ lb	ground (minced) or coarsely chopped beef	350 g/12 oz
1	trimmed, seeded, small red bell pepper cut into thin strips	1
1	trimmed seeded, small green bell pepper cut into thin strips	1
2 tbsp	Chinese light soy sauce	2 tbsp
1 tbsp	oyster sauce	1 tbsp
1 tbsp	Chinese rice wine or dry sherry	1 tbsp
	salt	
1 tsp	confectioners' (icing) sugar	1 tsp
	five spice powder	
1 tbsp	cornstarch (cornflour)	1 tbsp
	celery strips (optional)	

1. Drain the bamboo shoots well. Cut into thin strips.
2. Wash the bean sprouts and remove as many seed cases as possible. Drain well.
3. Very slowly, pour a few quarts/litres of boiling water over the bean sprouts then drain again in a colander. Place the colander in a draughty place, to dry them quickly.
4. Heat the oil in a wok and stir fry the meat until it separates and changes color.
5. Add the bamboo shoots, bell pepper strips, soy sauce, oyster sauce and Chinese rice wine or sherry. Stir well and add ¾ cup (200 ml/7 fl oz) boiling water. Stir and add salt, sugar and five spice powder to taste. Cover the wok, reduce the heat and simmer for 5-7 minutes.
6. Push all ingredients to one side of the wok.
7. Mix the cornstarch (cornflour) with 3 tbsp cold water and stir into the liquid. Cook, until the sauce thickens.
8. Stir the ingredients into the sauce and add the bean sprouts. Heat, stirring constantly and add salt to taste.
9. Transfer to a warmed dish and serve garnished with celery strips.

Cook's tip: dishes in which minced beef or pork are combined with vegetables and or soybean curd are typical examples of dishes which are sold from small stalls in the streets of Chinese towns. They can best be served as lunch snacks, which is how they are eaten in China.

Niang ganqie

Stuffed Tomatoes (Canton)

▬▭ 00.30
plus standing time

00.30 🍲

American	Ingredients	Metric/Imperial
4	large, firm skinned tomatoes	4
	salt	
1 tbsp	Chinese rice wine or dry sherry	1 tbsp
2 tsp	Chinese light soy sauce	2 tsp
1 tbsp	Chinese dark soy sauce	1 tbsp
1 tsp	oyster sauce	1 tsp
1	beaten egg white	1
1 tsp	cornstarch (cornflour)	1 tsp
½ lb	lean ground (minced) pork	225 g/8 oz
1	chopped onion	1
2 tbsp	groundnut oil	2 tbsp
2 tsp	confectioners' (icing) sugar	2 tsp
2 tbsp	Chinese light soy sauce	2 tbsp
1 tbsp	Chinese dark soy sauce	1 tbsp
1 tbsp	ginger syrup	1 tbsp
1½ tsp	cornstarch (cornflour)	1½ tsp
4 tbsp	chicken bouillon (stock)	4 tbsp
2	green shallots or scallions (spring onions)	2

1. Halve the tomatoes and hollow them out. Sprinkle salt inside and out and drain on kitchen paper with the cut sides facing down, for at least 1 hour.

2. Mix the rice wine or sherry, 2 tsp light and 1 tbsp dark soy sauce, oyster sauce, egg white and 1 tsp cornstarch (cornflour) into a smooth paste. Beat for 10 seconds.
3. Add the pork and chopped onion and mix quickly with (wetted) fingers. Leave to stand for 30 minutes then knead again.
4. Turn the hollowed tomatoes over. Sprinkle the insides with some cornstarch (cornflour) through a small strainer.
5. Shape the mixture into 8 balls and firmly place 1 ball into each tomato half.
6. Heat the oil in a large frying pan and place the tomatoes in it with the stuffed sides downward. Fry for 3 minutes.
7. Place the tomatoes in a flame-proof dish, with the stuffed sides downward.
8. Mix the sugar, remaining soy sauces, ginger syrup and bouillon (stock) in a small pan. Bring to the boil, stirring constantly.
9. Mix 1-1½ tsp cornstarch (cornflour) with 2 tbsp cold water and stir into the pan. Cook, until the sauce thickens. Simmer for 2 minutes.
10. Preheat the oven to 200°C/400°F/Gas Mark 6.
11. Pour the sauce over the tomatoes, cover the dish with a lid and cook in the oven for 20 minutes.
12. Sprinkle with some chopped green shallot or scallion (spring onion) and serve immediately.

Meiwei xianggu

Monks' Caps

▬▭ 00.05
plus soaking time

00.25 🍲

American	Ingredients	Metric/Imperial
16-20	large dried Chinese mushrooms	16-20
1 tbsp	groundnut oil	1 tbsp
2 tsp	finely grated root ginger	2 tsp
2 tbsp	Chinese rice wine or dry sherry	2 tbsp
3 tbsp	soft brown sugar or brown candy sugar	3 tbsp
2 tbsp	Chinese light soy sauce	2 tbsp
1½ tsp	cornstarch (cornflour)	1½ tsp
	salt	
1 tsp	sesame oil	1 tsp

1. Place the dried mushrooms in a bowl with hot water to cover generously. Soak until the water has become completely cold. Remove the stalks from the caps. Cut or chop the caps into small pieces. Transfer the soaking liquid and the pieces into the steamer. Cover the pan and steam for 15-20 minutes. Strain the liquid through a piece of wet muslin. Keep warm.
2. Heat the oil in a wok and stir fry the root ginger for one minute.
3. Add the rice wine or sherry, sugar, soy sauce and ¾ cup (200 ml/8 fl oz) of the strained steaming liquid. Stir until the sugar has dissolved.
4. Mix the cornstarch (cornflour) with 1½ tbsp cold water and stir into the wok. Cook, until the sauce thickens. Bring to the boil.
5. Add salt and stir in the sesame oil just before serving.
6. Place the caps on a warmed dish with the rounded sides facing upward. Pour over the hot sauce and serve.

Stuffed tomatoes

Dong goe botjai sjau doe foe

Braised Spinach with Mushrooms and Soybean Curd (Tofu)

00.15 plus soaking time   **00.20**

American	Ingredients	Metric/Imperial
2	cakes soybean curd (tofu)	2
6	large dried Chinese mushrooms	6
¾ lb	young spinach	350 g/12 oz
1	small paksoi	1
3 tbsp	groundnut oil	3 tbsp
1½ tbsp	Chinese light soy sauce	1½ tbsp
1 tbsp	Chinese dark soy sauce	1 tbsp
1 tbsp	oyster sauce	1 tbsp
1 tsp	confectioners' (icing) sugar	1 tsp
2 tsp	sesame oil	2 tsp
2 tsp	cornstarch (cornflour)	2 tsp
1	finely chopped green shallot or scallion (spring onion)	1

1. Cut the soybean curd (tofu) into ½ in (1.25 cm) cubes.
2. Place the mushrooms in a bowl with boiling water to just cover. Leave to soak for 30 minutes. Remove the stalks. Cut the caps into strips.
3. Strain the mushroom soaking liquid through a piece of wet muslin and measure out ⅔ cup (150 ml/¼ pint).
4. Wash the spinach and remove any thick stalks.
5. Make small stacks of spinach by placing 12-16 leaves on top of each other, secured with wooden cocktail picks.
6. Wash the paksoi. Cut into ½ in (1.25 cm) strips.
7. Heat the oil in a wok and stir fry the soybean curd (tofu) cubes for 1 minute.
8. Add the mushroom strips. Stir fry for 2 minutes.
9. Add the strained mushroom soaking liquid. Stir several times then add the soy sauces, oyster sauce, sugar and sesame oil. Simmer very gently for 8 minutes.

10. Mix the cornstarch (cornflour) with 2 tbsp cold water.
11. Push ingredients to one side of the wok and stir the cornstarch (cornflour) mixture into the liquid and cook until the sauce thickens. Simmer gently for 2 minutes.
12. Stir in the vegetables and bring to the boil.
13. Remove the cocktail picks from the spinach and serve sprinkled with some finely chopped shallot or scallion (spring onion).

Lo han tsjai

Braised Vegetables with Mushrooms and Lily Buds

00.40 plus soaking time   **00.30**

American	Ingredients	Metric/Imperial
8	large dried Chinese mushrooms	8
12	dried lily buds	12
16	small dried Chinese mushrooms	16
1	zucchini (courgette)	1
1	small cucumber	1
	salt	
6	young carrots	6
2	cakes soybean curd (tofu)	2
5 tbsp	groundnut oil	5 tbsp
½ lb	bamboo shoots cut into ¼ in (5 mm) slices	225 g/½ lb
2 tbsp	Chinese light soy sauce	2 tbsp
1 tbsp	Chinese dark soy sauce	1 tbsp
2 tbsp	hoisin sauce	2 tbsp
2	segments star anise	2
2 tsp	sesame oil	2 tsp
2 tsp	confectioners' (icing) sugar	2 tsp
2 tsp	cornstarch (cornflour)	2 tsp
2	skinned tomatoes (optional)	2
1	green shallot or scallion (spring onion)	1

Braised spinach with mushrooms and soybean curd (tofu)

1. Place each dried vegetable in a separate bowl. Add enough warm water to each to just cover the ingredients. Soak for 15 minutes.
2. Wash the zucchini (courgette) and cucumber. Trim and cut both into ½ in (1.25 cm) slices.
3. Sprinkle with salt and drain well in a colander.
4. Clean the carrots and cut them obliquely into ¼ in (5 mm) slices.
5. Cut the drained mushrooms into thin slices. Remove the stalks from the large mushrooms. Cut the caps into thin strips. Strain the mushroom soaking liquid through a piece of wet muslin and measure out ⅔ cup (150 ml/¼ pint).
6. Twist the lily buds into a knot.
7. Cut the soybean curd (tofu) into ½ in (1.25 cm) cubes.
8. Heat the groundnut oil in a wok and stir fry the soybean curd (tofu) cubes for 1 minute.
9. Add the mushrooms, lily buds, carrots and bamboo shoots.
10. Add the soy sauces and hoisin sauce. Stir well and add the strained mushroom soaking liquid. Stir well again.
11. Add the star anise and bring to the boil. Reduce the heat and simmer for 10 minutes.
12. Add the slices of zucchini (courgette) and cucumber and the sesame oil and sugar. Stir carefully several times. Simmer for a further 5 minutes.
13. Mix the cornstarch (cornflour) with 2 tbsp cold water.
14. Push the ingredients to one side of the wok and stir the cornstarch (cornflour) mixture into the liquid. Cook, until the sauce thickens. Simmer gently for 2 minutes.
15. Stir all the ingredients into the sauce, remove the star anise and bring to the boil again.
16. Serve in a large warmed dish garnished with tomato' flowers' and chopped green shallot or scallion (spring onion).

Mogoe tsing sjau doe foe

Braised Vegetables with Mushrooms and Soybean Curd (Tofu)

| | 00.20 plus soaking time | 00.20 |

American	Ingredients	Metric/Imperial
6	large dried Chinese mushrooms	6
2	cakes soybean curd (tofu)	2
4	green shallots	4
½ lb	small fresh mushrooms	225 g/8 oz
4	sticks celery	4
1	small cucumber	1
¼ lb	canned lotus root slices	125 g/4 oz
4 tbsp	groundnut oil	4 tbsp
1½ tbsp	Chinese dark soy sauce	1½ tbsp
½ tsp	chili sauce	½ tsp
2 tbsp	hoisin sauce	2 tbsp
	five spice powder	
2 tsp	sesame oil	2 tsp
2 tsp	confectioners' (icing) sugar	2 tsp
2 tsp	cornstarch (cornflour)	2 tsp
1	young leek	1

1. Place the dried mushrooms in a bowl with warm water to just cover. Soak for 30 minutes.
2. Cut the soybean curd (tofu) into ½ in (1.25 cm) cubes.

Braised vegetables with mushrooms and lily buds

3. Clean the shallots and chop them.
4. Wipe the mushrooms, trim and cut each into 4 pieces.
5. Clean the celery and slice the stalks widthwise into ¼ in (5 mm) strips.
6. Wash the cucumber, remove the ends, cut lengthwise. Remove the seeds from both halves and cut each half into ¼ in (5 mm) slices.
7. Drain the lotus slices thoroughly.
8. Remove the stalks from the soaked mushrooms. Cut the caps into thin strips. Strain the mushroom soaking liquid through a piece of wet muslin and measure out ⅔ cup (150 ml/¼ pint).
9. Heat the groundnut oil in a wok and stir fry the soybean curd (tofu) cubes for 1 minute.
10. Add the strips of soaked mushrooms, pieces of fresh mushrooms and the celery strips. Stir fry for 3 minutes.
11. Add the soy sauce, chili sauce, hoisin sauce and a pinch of five spice powder. Stir again and pour in the strained mushroom soaking liquid. Stir well and simmer for 8 minutes over moderate heat.
12. Add the cucumber slices, lotus root slices, sesame oil and sugar. Simmer for a further 3 minutes.
13. Mix the cornstarch (cornflour) with 2 tbsp cold water.
14. Push the ingredients to one side of the wok and stir the cornstarch (cornflour) mixture into the liquid. Cook, until the sauce thickens. Boil gently for 2 minutes.
15. Stir the vegetables into the sauce. Bring to the boil briefly.
16. Serve immediately in a warmed dish garnished with plumes of leek.

Braised bell peppers with mushrooms and soybean curd (tofu)

Dong goe tsing zjiau doe foe

Braised Bell Peppers with Mushrooms and Soybean Curd (Tofu)

00.15 plus soaking time　　00.15

American	Ingredients	Metric/Imperial
2	red bell peppers	2
1	green bell pepper	1
6	large dried Chinese mushrooms	6
2	medium size very firm onions	2
2	cakes soybean curd (tofu)	2
5 tbsp	groundnut oil	5 tbsp
1 tsp	grated fresh root ginger	1 tsp
1 tbsp	Chinese light soy sauce	1 tbsp
1 tbsp	Chinese dark soy sauce	1 tbsp
1 tbsp	oyster sauce	1 tbsp
2 tsp	sesame oil	2 tsp
2 tsp	confectioners' (icing) sugar	2 tsp
2 tsp	cornstarch (cornflour)	2 tsp
1	young leek or green shallot	1

1. Wash, trim and seed the bell peppers. Halve them and cut the flesh into ½ in (1.25 cm) squares.
2. Place the mushrooms in a bowl with hot water to just cover. Leave to soak for 30 minutes. Remove the stalks and cut the caps into thin strips.
3. Strain the soaking liquid through a piece of wet muslin and measure out ⅔ cup (150 ml/¼ pint).
4. Cut each onion into 8 pieces. Separate the layers.
5. Cut the soybean curd (tofu) into ½ in (1.25 cm) cubes.
6. Heat the groundnut oil in a wok and stir fry the soybean curd (tofu) cubes for 1 minute.

7. Add the onion, root ginger and mushroom strips. Stir fry for 2 minutes.
8. Add the mushroom liquid, soy sauces, oyster sauce, sesame oil, sugar and bell pepper. Stir well. Reduce the heat and simmer for 6 minutes.
9. Mix the cornstarch (cornflour) with 2 tbsp cold water.
10. Push the vegetables to one side of the wok and stir the cornstarch (cornflour) mixture into the liquid in the wok. Cook until the sauce thickens. Simmer for 2 minutes.
11. Stir in the vegeatbles and bring to the boil briefly.
12. Serve immediately in a large warmed dish, sprinkled with chopped leek or shallot.

Dong goe jangtjong sjau doe foe

Braised Green Shallot with Mushrooms and Soybean Curd (Tofu)

00.10 plus soaking time　　00.10

American	Ingredients	Metric/Imperial
1¼ lb	green shallots or young leek	575 g/1¼ lb
6	large dried Chinese mushrooms	6
2	cakes soybean curd (tofu)	2
5 tbsp	groundnut oil	5 tbsp
1 tbsp	Chinese light soy sauce	1 tbsp
2 tbsp	Chinese dark soy sauce	2 tbsp
1 tbsp	hoisin sauce	1 tbsp
1 tbsp	confectioners' (icing) sugar	1 tbsp
2 tsp	sesame oil	2 tsp
2	skinned tomatoes, cut into pieces (optional)	2
1-2	red chilies	1-2

1. Clean the green shallots or leek. Cut into ½ in (1.25 cm) slices, separate the rings.
2. Place the mushrooms in a bowl with hot water to just cover. Leave them to soak for 30 minutes. Remove the stalks from the caps. Cut the caps into thin strips.
3. Strain the liquid through a piece of wet muslin and measure out ⅔ cup (150 ml/¼ pint).
4. Cut the soybean curd (tofu) into ½ in (1.25 cm) cubes.
5. Heat the groundnut oil in a wok and stir fry the soybean curd (tofu) cubes for 1 minute.
6. Add the green shallot or leek and mushrooms. Stir fry gently for 4 minutes until the green shallot or leek gain some color.
7. Add the soy sauces, hoisin sauce, sugar and sesame oil, and strained liquid. Simmer over moderate heat until most of the soaking liquid has evaporated.
8. Add the tomato pieces, stir several times and serve immediately in a warmed dish, garnished with one or more red chili 'flowers'.

Tsjau hoeang gwa

Braised Cucumber

◀▱ 00.15   00.05 ⌷

Serves 4 as side dish

American	Ingredients	Metric/Imperial
1	cake soybean curd (tofu)	1
¼ lb	peeled shrimp (prawns)	125 g/4 oz
1	large or 2 small cucumbers	1
4 tbsp	groundnut oil	4 tbsp
1	coarsely chopped large onion	1
1	very finely chopped garlic clove	1
1 tsp	finely grated fresh root ginger	1 tsp
2 tbsp	Chinese light soy sauce	2 tbsp
1 tbsp	hoisin sauce	1 tbsp
1 tbsp	tomato purée	1 tbsp
1 tsp	confectioners' (icing) sugar	1 tsp
	salt	
1 tsp	sesame oil (optional)	1 tsp
1	chopped green shallot or scallion (spring onion) (optional)	1
1 tbsp	finely chopped chives (optional)	1 tbsp

1. Cut the soybean curd (tofu) into ½ in (1.25 cm) cubes.
2. Rinse the shrimp (prawns) under cold running water and leave to drain.
3. Wash the cucumber(s), remove the ends and halve lengthwise. Remove the seeds with a small spoon. Cut the halves into ½ in (1.25 cm) slices.
4. Heat the groundnut oil in a wok and stir fry the onion for 30 seconds.
5. Add the garlic and root ginger, stir well.
6. Add the cucumber, soy sauce, hoisin sauce, tomato purée, shrimp (prawns), soybean curd (tofu), sugar, salt and sesame oil.
7. Stir in 3 tbsp boiling water. Simmer gently over moderate heat until most of the liquid has evaporated.
8. Serve in a warmed dish sprinkled with some chopped green shallot, scallion (spring onion) or chives.

Tsjau sjeng tjai

Braised Lettuce

◀▱ 00.10   00.12 ⌷

Serves 4

American	Ingredients	Metric/Imperial
2	medium size iceberg lettuces	2
4-5 tbsp	groundnut oil	4-5 tbsp
2	very finely chopped garlic cloves	2
1 tbsp	finely grated fresh root ginger	1 tbsp
6 tbsp	chicken bouillon (stock)	6 tbsp
1 tsp	confectioners' (icing) sugar	1 tsp
2 tbsp	Chinese light soy sauce	2 tbsp
1 tbsp	Chinese dark soy sauce	1 tbsp
1 tbsp	hoisin sauce	1 tbsp
	salt	
2 tsp	cornstarch (cornflour)	2 tsp

1. Wash the lettuces. Remove the thickest part of the stalk and cut each head into 4 pieces and slice the pieces into ½ in (1.25 cm) thick strips.
2. Heat the oil in a wok and stir fry the garlic and root ginger for 30 seconds.
3. Add the lettuce. Stir fry for 2 minutes.
4. Immediately add the bouillon (stock), sugar and soy sauces, the hoisin sauce and salt to taste. Stir well and simmer for 3 minutes over moderate heat.
5. Mix the cornstarch (cornflour) with 1 tbsp cold water.
6. Push the lettuce to one side of the wok, stir the cornstarch (cornflour) mixture into the liquid in the wok. Cook until the sauce thickens. Simmer for 2 minutes.
7. Stir the lettuce into the sauce and bring to the boil briefly.
8. Serve immediately in a warmed dish.

Braised cucumber

Tsjau jie gwa

Braised Zucchini (Courgettes)

	00.10	00.15

Serves 4 as side dish

American	Ingredients	Metric/Imperial
2	medium size zucchini (courgettes)	2
4 tbsp	groundnut oil	4 tbsp
1	coarsely chopped large onion	1
1	finely chopped garlic clove	1
1 tbsp	Chinese light soy sauce	1 tbsp
1 tbsp	oyster sauce	1 tbsp
2 tbsp	Chinese wine vinegar	2 tbsp
2 tsp	confectioners' (icing) sugar	2 tsp
	salt	
1 tsp	sesame oil	1 tsp
6 tbsp	boiling water	6 tbsp

1. Wash the zucchini (courgettes). Remove the ends. Cut obliquely into ½ in (1.25 cm) slices.
2. Heat the groundnut oil in a wok and stir fry the onion for 30 seconds
3. Add the garlic. Stir well then add the slices of zucchini (courgette). Stir well again and reduce the heat.
4. Add the soy sauce, oyster sauce, wine vinegar, sugar, salt to taste and the sesame oil.
5. Stir well and add 6 tbsp boiling water. Simmer until most of the liquid has evaporated. Turn the zucchini (courgettes) regularly.

Tsie txie hedoe

Braised Snow Peas (Mange-tout) with Corn and Tomatoes

	00.15	00.10

Serves 4 as side dish

American	Ingredients	Metric/Imperial
½ lb	snow peas (mange-tout)	225 g/8 oz
3	medium size skinned tomatoes	3
3-4 tbsp	groundnut oil	3-4 tbsp
2-3	chopped green shallots	2-3
1	finely chopped garlic clove	1
½ tsp	grated fresh root ginger	½ tsp
¾ cup	drained, cooked corn	125 g/4 oz
1 tbsp	Chinese light soy sauce	1 tbsp
1 tbsp	hoisin sauce	1 tbsp
1 tsp	confectioners' (icing) sugar	1 tsp
	salt	
1 tsp	sesame oil	1 tsp
6 tbsp	chicken bouillon (stock)	6 tbsp
1 tbsp	finely chopped chives	1 tbsp

1. Top and tail the snow peas (mange-tout).
2. Cut each tomato into 8 equal pieces. Remove the juice and the seed.
3. Heat the groundnut oil in a wok and add the green shallot, garlic and root ginger. Stir well.

4. Add the snow peas (mange-tout), stir fry for 1-2 minutes, then add the corn, soy sauce, hoisin sauce, sugar, salt to taste and sesame oil. Stir well.

5. Add 6 tbsp bouillon (stock), reduce the heat and simmer for 4 minutes, stirring occasionally, until most of the liquid has evaporated.

6. Carefully add the tomato pieces to the wok and warm through.

7. Transfer carefully into a warmed dish and sprinkle with some finely chopped chives.

Tsfau dong goe

Braised Mushrooms

	00.05 plus soaking time	00.15

American	Ingredients	Metric/Imperial
3 oz	large dried Chinese mushrooms	75 g/3 oz
3-4 tbsp	groundnut oil	3-4 tbsp
6	chopped green shallots	6
2 oz	peeled shrimp (prawns)	50 g/2 oz
2 tbsp	Chinese dark soy sauce	2 tbsp
2 tbsp	hoisin sauce	2 tbsp
1 tbsp	confectioners' (icing) sugar	1 tbsp
2 tsp	sesame oil	2 tsp

1. Place the dried mushrooms in a large bowl with warm water to just cover and leave to soak for 30 minutes. Remove the stalks from the caps and set aside. Squeeze as much liquid as possible out of the caps adding it to the soaking liquid.

2. Strain the liquid through a piece of wet muslin and measure out 1 cup (250 ml/8 fl oz).

3. Heat the groundnut oil in a wok and stir fry the green shallot together with the shrimp (prawns) until the shallot has gained some color.

4. Add the mushroom caps and stir fry for 4 minutes.

5. Add the strained liquid, soy sauce, hoisin sauce, sugar and sesame oil. Simmer over moderate heat until most of the liquid has evaporated.

6. Transfer into a warmed dish and serve.

Left to right: Braised zucchini (courgettes); Braised snow peas (mange-tout) with corn and tomatoes; Braised mushrooms

Joe mie dau doe
Braised Green Beans with Corn

	00.15	00.12
	Serves 4 as side dish	

American	Ingredients	Metric/Imperial
¾ lb	green beans	350 g/12 oz
4 tbsp	groundnut oil	4 tbsp
1	small coarsely chopped onion	1
1	very finely chopped garlic clove	1
1 tsp	finely grated root ginger	1 tsp
6 tbsp	water or bouillon (stock)	6 tbsp
1 tbsp	Chinese light soy sauce	1 tbsp
1½ tbsp	Chinese dark soy sauce	1½ tbsp
1 tbsp	hoisin sauce	1 tbsp
1 tsp	confectioners' (icing) sugar	1 tsp
	salt	
1 tsp	sesame oil	1 tsp
½ lb	cooked drained corn kernels	225 g/8 oz
2 tsp	cornstarch (cornflour)	2 tsp

1. Top and tail the green beans and cut into 1 in (2.5 cm) pieces.
2. Heat the groundnut oil in a wok and stir fry the onion for 30 seconds.
3. Add the garlic and root ginger. Stir for a few seconds then add the green beans and stir fry for 2 minutes.
4. Add the water or bouillon (stock), soy sauces, hoisin sauce, sugar, salt and sesame oil. Stir well, add the corn and simmer for 4 minutes.
5. Mix the cornstarch (cornflour) with 1 tbsp cold water.
6. Push the ingredients to one side of the wok and stir the cornstarch (cornflour) mixture into the liquid. Cook, until the sauce thickens. Simmer for 2 minutes.
7. Stir the ingredients into the sauce and boil briefly before serving.

Tsjau lie sjie
Braised Chestnuts

	00.05	00.15
	Serves 4 as side dish	

American	Ingredients	Metric/Imperial
2 tbsp	groundnut oil	2 tbsp
2	skinned garlic cloves	2
2	chopped green shallots	2
1 lb	canned cooked chestnuts	450 g/1 lb
¾ cup	hot chicken bouillon (stock)	200 ml/7 fl oz
3 tbsp	Chinese light soy sauce	3 tbsp
1 tbsp	Chinese dark soy sauce	1 tbsp
1 tbsp	oyster sauce	1 tbsp
1 tbsp	confectioners' (icing) sugar	1 tbsp
	salt	
2 tsp	sesame oil	2 tsp
1	very finely chopped red chili (optional)	1
	few drops chili sauce	

1. Heat the groundnut oil in a wok and stir fry the garlic cloves and the green shallot in this oil until golden brown. Remove from the pan.
2. Stir fry the chestnuts gently for 3 minutes.
3. Add the chicken bouillon (stock), soy sauces, oyster sauce, sugar and salt to taste. Simmer stirring occasionally, until most of the liquid has evaporated.
4. Stir in the sesame oil immediately before serving and sprinkle with some very finely chopped red chili, or stir in a few drops of chili sauce.

Tsjau zjie and goe
Mixed Braised Mushrooms

	00.15	00.18
	plus soaking time	

American	Ingredients	Metric/Imperial
1 oz	small dried Chinese mushrooms	25 g/1 oz
2 oz	large dried Chinese mushrooms	50 g/2 oz
¼ lb	fresh button mushrooms	125 g/4 oz
4 tbsp	groundnut oil	4 tbsp
4	chopped green shallots	4
2 tbsp	Chinese light soy sauce	2 tbsp
1 tbsp	oyster sauce	1 tbsp
1 tbsp	hoisin sauce	1 tbsp
2 tbsp	Chinese rice wine or sherry	2 tbsp
1 tsp	confectioners' (icing) sugar	1 tsp
1 tsp	sesame oil	1 tsp
1 tsp	cornstarch (cornflour)	1 tsp
4 tbsp	cooked peas	4 tbsp
4 tbsp	cooked corn	4 tbsp
	salt	
2	chopped scallions (spring onions)	2
1	skinned tomato	1

1. Place the dried Chinese mushrooms in separate bowls with warm water to just cover them. Soak the small mushrooms for 12 minutes, then chop roughly into pieces. Soak the large mushrooms for 30 minutes.
2. Wipe the button mushrooms and slice them finely. Remove the stalks from the caps of soaked mushrooms. Squeeze as much liquid as possible out of the caps and add to the soaking liquid. Cut the caps into slices. Strain all the liquid through a piece of wet muslin and measure out ¾ cup (200 ml/8 fl oz).
3. Heat the oil in a wok and stir fry the shallots for 2 minutes, add the soaked mushrooms and stir fry for 2 minutes.
4. Add the fresh mushrooms and stir fry for 3 minutes.
5. Add the strained soaking liquid, soy sauce, oyster sauce, hoisin sauce, rice wine or sherry, sugar and sesame oil. Simmer until reduced by half.
6. Mix the cornstarch (cornflour) with 1 tbsp cold water.
7. Push the mushrooms to one side of the wok and stir the cornstarch (cornflour) mixture into the liquid in the wok and cook until the sauce thickens. Simmer for 2 minutes.
8. Stir the mushrooms into the sauce and boil briefly.
9. Add the peas and corn and salt to taste.
10. Serve in a warmed dish, garnished with chopped scallion (spring onion) and a tomato 'flower'.

Left: Braised asparagus; Braised broccoli

Tsjau loe soen

Braised Asparagus

00.10   00.10

Serves 4 as side dish

American	Ingredients	Metric/Imperial
1 ½ lb	thick asparagus	700 g/1 ½ lb
4-5 tbsp	groundnut oil	4-5 tbsp
4	chopped green shallots	4
1 tsp	grated fresh root ginger	1 tsp
6 tbsp	chicken bouillon (stock)	6 tbsp
2 tbsp	Chinese light soy sauce	2 tbsp
1 tbsp	Chinese dark soy sauce	1 tbsp
1 tbsp	Chinese rice wine or sherry	1 tbsp
2 tbsp	confectioners' (icing) sugar	2 tbsp
2 tsp	sesame oil (optional)	2 tsp
1 tbsp	finely chopped chives	1 tbsp

1. Peel the asparagus thinly from the top toward the bottom. Cut slices 1-2 in (2.5-5 cm) long. Cut the thick stalks lengthwise into halves and then each half into 2 in (5 cm) pieces.
2. Heat the groundnut oil in a wok and stir fry the green shallot for 2 minutes.
3. Add the root ginger and stir thoroughly.
4. Add the asparagus and stir fry for 5 minutes.
5. Add the chicken bouillon (stock) and the soy sauces, rice wine or sherry and sugar. Simmer gently over moderate heat until the asparagus is tender the liquid should then have evaporated.
6. Stir the sesame oil into the dish.
7. Transfer the asparagus into a warmed dish.
8. Sprinkle with some finely chopped chives.

Tsjau jie jan

Braised Broccoli

00.10   00.15

Serves 4 as side dish

American	Ingredients	Metric/Imperial
1 lb	broccoli	450 g/1 lb
3 tbsp	groundnut oil	3 tbsp
1	medium size chopped onion	1
½	very finely chopped garlic clove	½
1 tsp	grated fresh root ginger	1 tsp
⅔ cup	chicken bouillon (stock)	150 ml/¼ pint
2 tbsp	Chinese light soy sauce	2 tbsp
1 tbsp	hoisin sauce	1 tbsp
2 tbsp	Chinese rice wine or sherry	2 tbsp
1 tsp	confectioners' (icing) sugar	1 tsp
	salt	
2 tsp	sesame oil	2 tsp

1. Clean the broccoli. Cut the stalks into ½ in (1.25 cm) pieces. Set the florets aside.
2. Heat the groundnut oil in a wok and stir fry the onion, garlic and root ginger for 30 seconds.
3. Add the pieces of broccoli stalk. Stir fry for 3 minutes.
4. Add the florets and continue frying for a further 2 minutes.
5. Add the chicken bouillon (stock), soy sauce, hoisin sauce, rice wine or sherry, sugar and salt. Simmer for 5 minutes.
6. Stir in the sesame oil immediately before serving.

Za cai

Mixed Vegetables (Peking)

⟍▽ 00.15   00.10 🍲

Serves 4 as side dish

American	Ingredients	Metric/Imperial
1	small head Chinese leaves	1
½ lb	cooked, drained corn kernels	225 g/8 oz
½ lb	fresh mushrooms	225 g/8 oz
4-5 tbsp	groundnut oil	4-5 tbsp
2	very finely chopped garlic cloves	2
½ lb	canned bamboo shoots drained, diced	225 g/8 oz
½ lb	canned water chestnuts drained and sliced	225 g/8 oz
1 tbsp	hoisin sauce	1 tbsp
1¼ cups	chicken bouillon (stock)	300 ml/½ pint
2 tbsp	Chinese light soy sauce	2 tbsp
½ tsp	confectioners' (icing) sugar	½ tsp
	salt	
	five spice powder	
2-3 tsp	cornstarch (cornflour)	2-3 tsp
1 tsp	sesame oil	1 tsp

1. Wash the head of Chinese leaves. Remove them thickest veins and the stalk. Cut them into finger width strips.
2. Wipe the mushrooms and trim the bottom of each stalk. Cut each mushroom into 4 pieces.
3. Heat the groundnut oil in a wok and stir fry the garlic for 30 seconds.
4. Add the mushrooms and the Chinese leaves. Stir fry for 2 minutes.
5. Add the corn, bamboo shoots and water chestnuts. Stir several times.
6. Add the hoisin sauce, bouillon (stock), soy sauce, sugar, salt to taste and a pinch of five spice powder. Bring to the boil, stirring constantly.
7. Mix the cornstarch (cornflour) with 1 tbsp cold water.
8. Push the ingredients to one side of the wok and stir the cornstarch (cornflour) mixture into the liquid. Cook, until the sauce thickens then simmer gently for 2 minutes.
9. Stir the ingredients into the sauce. Stir in the sesame oil and bring to the boil briefly again. Stir once more.
10. Transfer to a warmed dish and serve.

Left to right: Stuffed cucumbers;
Chinese leaves with shrimp (prawns)

Niang huanggua

Stuffed Cucumbers (Peking)

⟍▽ 00.20   00.20 🍲

Serves 4 as side dish

American	Ingredients	Metric/Imperial
¼ lb	fresh peeled shrimp (prawns)	125 g/4 oz
1 tbsp	Chinese rice wine or dry sherry	1 tbsp
1½ tbsp	Chinese light soy sauce	1½ tbsp
1 tbsp	shrimp or crab sauce	1 tbsp
2 tsp	grated fresh root ginger	2 tsp
4	very finely chopped green shallots or scallions (spring onions)	4
1 tbsp	cornstarch (cornflour)	1 tbsp
2 tbsp	sesame oil	2 tbsp
	salt	
¼ lb	ground (minced) pork	125 g/4 oz
2	medium size cucumbers	2
4-5 tbsp	groundnut oil	4-5 tbsp
	some pieces of cucumber	
¾ cup	chicken bouillon (stock)	200 ml/7 fl oz
2	skinned tomatoes	2

1. Chop the shrimp (prawns) extremely finely.
2. Mix the rice wine or sherry with the soy sauce, shrimp or crab sauce, root ginger, green shallots or scallions (spring onions) and cornstarch (cornflour).
3. Add the sesame oil, salt to taste and the ground (minced) pork. Knead well.
4. Wash the cucumbers, trim the ends and cut each cucumber into 6 equal pieces. Remove the seeds from each piece with an apple corer. Stuff the openings very firmly with the mince mixture.
5. Heat the oil in a wok and stir fry the stuffed cucumber pieces for 4 minutes until the stuffing is golden brown. Reduce the heat. Add the chicken bouillon (stock), cover the pan and simmer gently for 10 minutes. Remove the lid and simmer until most of the liquid has evaporated.

6. Serve in a warmed dish, garnished with large fans of cucumbers and tomatoes shaped into 'flowers'.

Cook's tip: replace some or all of the shrimp (prawns) with finely chopped white fish as a variation. Whiting fillets are ideal.

Baicai xiaren

Chinese Leaves with Shrimp (Prawns) (Peking)

00.10 — 00.05

Serves 4 as side dish

American	Ingredients	Metric/Imperial
1	*small head of Chinese leaves*	*1*
4-5 tbsp	*groundnut oil*	*4-5 tbsp*
1	*very finely chopped garlic clove*	*1*
5 tbsp	*chicken bouillon (stock)*	*5 tbsp*
2 tsp	*Chinese light soy sauce*	*2 tsp*
½ tsp	*shrimp sauce*	*½ tsp*
1 tbsp	*ginger syrup*	*1 tbsp*
¼ lb	*fresh peeled shrimp (prawns)*	*125 g/4 oz*

1. Wash the head of Chinese leaves, remove thick veins and cut into finger width strips.
2. Heat the oil in a wok and stir fry the garlic for 30 seconds.
3. Add the Chinese leaves and stir fry for 2 minutes.
4. Add the chicken bouillon (stock), soy sauce, shrimp sauce and ginger syrup. Bring to the boil. Stir well.
5. Stir in the shrimp (prawns) and serve immediately in a warmed dish.

Tiansuan baicai I

Sweet and Sour Cabbage (Peking)

00.10 — 00.10

plus drying time

American	Ingredients	Metric/Imperial
1 lb	*white or yellow cabbage*	*450 g/1 lb*
4 tbsp	*groundnut oil*	*4 tbsp*
2	*skinned garlic cloves*	*2*
1	*small dried red chili*	*1*
	salt	
2 tbsp	*mild Chinese vinegar or English malt vinegar*	*2 tbsp*
2 tbsp	*ginger syrup*	*2 tbsp*
1 tbsp	*hoisin sauce*	*1 tbsp*
2-3 tbsp	*chicken bouillon (stock)*	*2-3 tbsp*

1. Clean the cabbage. Remove any damaged outer leaves and a large part of the stalk. Cut the cabbage into long, very fine strips. Wash and drain well. Place the colander in a draughty place or use a lettuce centrifuge to dry the cabbage as much as possible.
2. Heat the oil in a wok and stir fry the garlic cloves and the dried red chili until the garlic is golden brown. Remove the garlic and the chili.
3. Stir fry the cabbage for 5 minutes.
4. Add all other ingredients. Stir well several times and bring to the boil. Serve immediately.

Tiansuan baicai II

Sweet and Sour Chinese Leaves (Peking)

00.10 — 00.10

Serves 4 as side dish

American	Ingredients	Metric/Imperial
1	*large head Chinese leaves*	*1*
5 tbsp	*groundnut oil*	*5 tbsp*
2	*skinned garlic cloves*	*2*
1	*small, seeded crushed red chili*	*1*
	salt	
2 tbsp	*rice vinegar or white wine vinegar*	*2 tbsp*
1 tbsp	*confectioners' (icing) sugar*	*1 tbsp*
2 tbsp	*ginger syrup*	*2 tbsp*
1 tbsp	*oyster sauce*	*1 tbsp*
2 tbsp	*chicken bouillon (stock)*	*2 tbsp*

1. Wash the Chinese leaves. Remove thick veins and cut off the stalk. Cut the leaves into finger width strips. Drain well in a colander (or use a lettuce centrifuge).
2. Heat the oil in a wok and stir fry the garlic clove until golden brown.
3. Remove the garlic clove and add the chili. Turn it over once and add the Chinese leaves. Stir fry for 4 minutes.
4. Add salt, vinegar, sugar, ginger syrup, oyster sauce and bouillon (stock). Stir well and bring to the boil.
5. Transfer immediately into a warmed dish and serve.

Tiansuan douya

Sweet and Sour Bean Sprouts (Peking)

	00.05		00.06
	plus drying time		

American	Ingredients	Metric/Imperial
¼ lb	bean sprouts	125 g/4 oz
4 tbsp	groundnut oil	4 tbsp
1	skinned garlic clove	1
1	small seeded crushed red chili	1
1 tsp	salt	1 tsp
2 tbsp	rice vinegar or white wine vinegar	2 tbsp
½ tbsp	confectioners' (icing) sugar	½ tbsp
1 tbsp	tomato ketchup	1 tbsp
½ tsp	grated fresh root ginger	½ tsp
4-5 tbsp	chicken bouillon (stock)	4-5 tbsp

1. Wash the bean sprouts several times in cold water. Remove as many seed cases as possible. Drain well in a colander. Place in a draughty place to dry the bean sprouts quickly.
2. Heat the oil in a wok and stir fry the garlic clove until golden brown. Remove from the oil.
3. Add the crushed red chili. Stir well and add the bean sprouts. Stir fry the bean sprouts for 30 seconds.
4. Add the salt, vinegar, sugar, tomato ketchup, root ginger and bouillon (stock). Stir well several times then leave to boil steadily for 1 minute.
5. Serve in a warmed dish.

Cook's tip: in Peking, after the bean sprouts have been transferred into a warmed dish, they are often sprinkled with some pieces of tender chicken or duck, tender beef, finely chopped fried or boiled chicken livers, freshly peeled shrimp (prawns) or pieces of shrimp (prawn). The meat or poultry is used when the main course is a fish dish, and crustaceans are used when the main course does not contain fish.

Tiansuan qincai

Sweet and Sour Celery (Peking)

	00.10		00.10
	Serves 4 as side dish		

American	Ingredients	Metric/Imperial
1	good head of celery	1
4 tbsp	groundnut oil	4 tbsp
1	skinned garlic clove	1
1	crushed dried red chili or	1
1 tsp	red pepper oil	1 tsp
	salt	
2 tbsp	rice vinegar or white wine vinegar	2 tbsp
1 tbsp	hoisin sauce	1 tbsp
2½ tbsp	confectioners' (icing) sugar	2½ tbsp
1 tbsp	ginger syrup	1 tbsp
3 tbsp	chicken bouillon (stock)	3 tbsp

1. Clean the celery. Remove the green leaves and trim the stalks. Cut the stalks into finger width strips.
2. Heat the oil in a wok and stir fry the skinned garlic clove until golden brown. Remove from the oil.
3. Add the crushed red chili or red pepper oil and stir well.
4. Immediately add the celery and stir fry for 4-5 minutes.
5. Add salt to taste and the vinegar, hoisin sauce, sugar, ginger syrup and bouillon (stock).
6. Stir well and boil steadily for 1-2 minutes.
7. Serve immediately in a warmed dish.

Tiansuan xierou xiancai

Sweet and Sour Vegetables with Crab (Peking)

	00.10		00.10
	Serves 4 as side dish		

American	Ingredients	Metric/Imperial
1	small head of Chinese leaves	1
1	medium size onion	1
3	green shallots or scallions (spring onions)	3
1	red bell pepper	1
¼ lb	crabmeat, thawed if frozen	125 g/4 oz
4-5 tbsp	groundnut oil	4-5 tbsp
1	skinned garlic clove	1
1	crushed dried red chili or	1
1 tsp	chili sauce or red pepper oil	1 tsp
	salt	
2 tbsp	rice vinegar or white wine vinegar	2 tbsp
½ tsp	finely chopped fresh root ginger	½ tsp
1 tbsp	Chinese light soy sauce	1 tbsp
1 tbsp	crab sauce	1 tbsp
1 tbsp	confectioners' (icing) sugar	1 tbsp
5 tbsp	chicken bouillon (stock)	5 tbsp

1. Clean the Chinese leaves. Remove any thick veins and the stalk. Cut the leaves into finger width strips.
2. Clean the onion and the green shallots or scallions (spring onions). Cut each onion into 8 equal pieces and separate the layers.
3. Wash, halve, seed and trim the bell pepper and cut the flesh into ½ inch (1.25 cm) strips.
4. Cut the crabmeat into small pieces and remove any pieces of shell.
5. Heat the oil in a wok and stir fry the skinned garlic clove until golden brown. Remove from the oil.
6. Add the crushed chili or chili sauce or red pepper oil.
7. Stir well and add the onion, the green shallot or scallion (spring onion) and the bell pepper. Stir fry for 2 minutes.
8. Add the Chinese leaves and stir fry for 3-4 minutes.
9. Add salt to taste, vinegar, root ginger, soy sauce, crab sauce, sugar and bouillon (stock). Stir well several times. Boil steadily for 1-2 minutes.
10. Stir in the crabmeat and serve immediately in a warmed dish.

Tiansuan xiaren xiancai

Sweet and Sour Vegetables with Shrimp (Prawns) (Peking)

 00.20   00.12

Serves 4 as side dish

American	Ingredients	Metric/Imperial
1	small cucumber	1
1	red bell pepper	1
2	sticks celery	2
2-3 oz	bean sprouts	50-75 g/2-3 oz
¼ lb	fresh peeled shrimps (prawns)	125 g/4 oz
4-5 tbsp	groundnut oil	4-5 tbsp
1	skinned garlic clove	1
1	crushed dried red chili or	1
1 tsp	chili sauce or red pepper oil	1 tsp
	salt	
2 tbsp	rice vinegar	2 tbsp
	or white wine vinegar	
1 tbsp	Chinese dark soy sauce	1 tbsp
1 tbsp	confectioners' (icing) sugar	1 tbsp
1 tsp	finely chopped fresh root ginger	1 tsp
5 tbsp	bouillon (stock)	5 tbsp

1. Wash the cucumber and remove the ends, cut into 3 pieces. Remove the seeds with an apple corer. Cut the pieces into ½ in (1.25 cm) slices.
2. Wash, halve, seed and trim the bell pepper and cut the flesh into strips ½ in (1.25 cm).
3. Clean the celery and cut into ½ in (1.25 cm) strips.
4. Wash the bean sprouts and remove as many seed cases as possible. Drain well.
5. Coarsely chop the shrimp (prawns) into small pieces.
6. Heat the oil in a wok and stir fry the skinned garlic clove until golden brown. Remove from the oil.
7. Add the crushed red chili or chili sauce or red pepper oil.
8. Stir well and add the celery and bell pepper. Stir fry for 3 minutes.

9. Add the cucumber and 1 minute later the bean sprouts. Stir fry for 2 minutes.
10. Add salt to taste and vinegar, soy sauce, sugar, root ginger and bouillon (stock). Stir well then boil steadily for 1 minute.
11. Stir in the shrimp (prawns) and serve immediately in a warmed dish.

Tiansuan jiucai

Sweet and Sour Leeks

00.10   00.08

Serves 4 as side dish

American	Ingredients	Metric/Imperial
¾ lb	medium size leeks	350 g/12 oz
4 tbsp	groundnut oil	4 tbsp
1	skinned garlic clove	1
1	small crushed red chili or	1
1 tsp	chili sauce	1 tsp
	salt	
2 tbsp	rice vinegar	2 tbsp
	or white wine vinegar	
1 tbsp	Chinese dark soy sauce	1 tbsp
1 tbsp	confectioners' (icing) sugar	1 tbsp
1 tbsp	ginger syrup	1 tbsp
4-5 tbsp	chicken bouillon (stock)	4-5 tbsp
1-2 tbsp	finely chopped coriander or celery leaves	1-2 tbsp

1. Clean the leeks. Remove any thick green leaves. Trim the roots and cut the white and light green-yellow parts into finger width rings.
2. Heat the oil in a wok and stir fry the skinned garlic clove until golden brown. Remove from the oil.
3. Add the crushed red chili or chili sauce, stir well and add the leek. Stir fry for 2-3 minutes.
4. Add salt, vinegar, soy sauce, sugar, ginger syrup and bouillon (stock). Stir well. Boil steadily for 1 minute.
5. Transfer immediately to a warmed dish and serve sprinkled with some finely chopped coriander or celery leaves.

Sweet and sour leeks

Sjie roe joe gwa

Stir Fried Zucchini (Courgettes) with Crab

	00.20 plus soaking time	00.15

American	Ingredients	Metric/Imperial
2	small zucchini (courgettes)	2
	juice of 1 lemon	
	salt	
	ground Szechwan pepper	
6	dried Chinese mushrooms	6
¼ lb	canned crabmeat	125 g/4 oz
2	medium size yellow or red bell peppers	2
1 (2 in)	piece fresh root ginger	1 (5 cm/2 in)
4-5 tbsp	groundnut oil	4-5 tbsp
2	medium size chopped onions	2
2	finely chopped garlic cloves	2
¾ cup	chicken bouillon (stock)	200 ml/7 fl oz
3 tbsp	Chinese rice wine or dry sherry	3 tbsp
2 tbsp	Chinese light soy sauce	2 tbsp
1 tbsp	hoisin sauce	1 tbsp
1 tbsp	crab sauce	1 tbsp
	five spice powder	
	freshly ground pepper	
2	chopped green shallots or scallions (spring onions)	2
2	medium size tomatoes cut into slices	2

1. Wash the zucchini (courgettes) and cut them into ¼-½ in (1-1.5 cm) slices. Cut these into 4 pieces. Sprinkle with the lemon juice to prevent the zucchini (courgettes) discoloring.
2. Sprinkle with salt and ground Szechwan pepper.
3. Place the Chinese mushrooms in a bowl with hot water to cover. Leave to stand for 30 minutes.
4. Strain the mushrooms. Remove the stalks. Gently squeeze more liquid out of the caps and reserve it. Cut the caps into 1 in (2.5 cm) strips.
5. Flake the crabmeat with a fork. Remove any pieces of shell and cut up large pieces.
6. Wash the bell peppers, trim, seed and cut them lengthwise then cut the flesh into squares.
7. Peel the root ginger and grate 2 tsp of this.
8. Heat the oil in a wok until hot and stir fry the onion, garlic and ginger for 30 seconds.
9. Add the bell pepper and stir fry for a further 2 minutes over a high heat.
10. Add the zucchini (courgettes) and stir fry for 2 minutes until the zucchini (courgettes) slightly change color.
11. Heat the bouillon (stock) with the Chinese rice wine or dry sherry and pour over the vegetable mixture.
12. Warm through and add the mushrooms and crabmeat.
13. Add the soy sauce, hoisin sauce, crab sauce, a pinch five spice powder, pepper and salt to taste. Partly cover the wok and simmer for 4 minutes.
14. Transfer to a warmed dish, sprinkle with the green shallot or scallion (spring onion).
15. Garnish with the tomato wedges and serve.

Roe jie bai tjai

Stir Fried Paksoi with Chicken and Pork

	00.30 Serves 4	00.20

American	Ingredients	Metric/Imperial
¾ lb	paksoi	350 g/12 oz
¼ lb	chicken breast fillets	125 g/4 oz
¼ lb	lean pork	125 g/4 oz
1 (2 in)	piece of fresh root ginger	1 (5 cm/2 in)
2	medium size red bell peppers	2
¼ lb	mushrooms	125 g/4 oz
5 tbsp	groundnut oil	5 tbsp
2	medium size chopped onions	2
2	finely chopped garlic cloves	2
2 tbsp	Chinese dark soy sauce	2 tbsp
1 tbsp	hoisin sauce	1 tbsp
1 tbsp	oyster sauce	1 tbsp
¾ cup	chicken bouillon (stock)	200 ml/7 fl oz
4 tbsp	Chinese rice wine or dry sherry	4 tbsp
1 tbsp	ginger syrup	1 tbsp
	five spice powder	
	pepper	
	salt	

1. Separate the paksoi and wash the leaves in plenty of cold water. Cut the stalks obliquely into pieces 1 in (2.5 cm) long and the leaves into strips ½ in (1.25 cm) wide.
2. Cut the chicken fillets into extremely thin slices and then into strips.
3. Cut the pork into ½ in (1.25 cm) cubes.
4. Peel the root ginger and grate 2 tbsp of this.
5. Wash, trim and seed the bell peppers. Halve and cut the flesh into thin strips or ½ in (1.25 cm) squares.
6. Wipe the mushrooms and trim the bottoms of the stalks. Cut the mushrooms into ½ in (1.25 cm) thick slices.
7. Heat the oil in a wok until hot.
8. Fry the onions and garlic for 30 seconds until golden yellow.
9. Add the chicken and pork and fry for 90 seconds until both meats change to a lighter color.
10. Add the root ginger, soy sauce, hoisin sauce and oyster sauce and stir fry for 1 minute.
11. Add the paksoi stalks and the bell pepper and fry for another 2 minutes.
12. Add the paksoi and the mushrooms. Fry for 1 minute.
13. Heat the bouillon (stock) with the rice wine or dry sherry and the ginger syrup.
14. Pour the bouillon (stock) over the contents of the wok.
15. Add a pinch of five spice powder and pepper and salt to taste. Stir again.
16. Cover with a lid and braise gently for 8 minutes.
17. Transfer to a warmed dish and serve immediately.

Douya xierou

Bean Sprouts with Crab (Peking)

◀━▷ 00.10   00.05 🥘
Serves 4 as side dish

American	Ingredients	Metric/Imperial
¼ lb	bean sprouts	125 g/4 oz
¼ lb	crabmeat, thawed if frozen	125 g/4 oz
4 tbsp	groundnut oil	4 tbsp
2 tbsp	rice vinegar or white wine vinegar	2 tbsp
1 tsp	confectioners' (icing) sugar	1 tsp
2 tsp	Chinese light soy sauce	2 tsp
½ tsp	Chinese dark soy sauce	½ tsp
1 tbsp	crab sauce	1 tbsp
	salt	

1. Wash the bean sprouts several times in plenty of cold water. Remove as many seed cases as possible. Drain well.
2. Cut the crabmeat into small pieces, removing any pieces of shell.
3. Heat the oil in a wok, add the bean sprouts and stir fry for 1 minute.
4. Add the rice vinegar or white wine vinegar, sugar, soy sauces, crab sauce and salt. Stir well several times.
5. Stir in the crabmeat and serve immediately in a warmed dish.

Tsing doe tsjau jie gan he doefoe

Stir Fried Green Beans with Chicken Liver and Soybean Curd (Tofu)

◀━▷ 00.30   00.20 🥘
Serves 4

American	Ingredients	Metric/Imperial
½ lb	young green beans or haricots verts	250 g/8 oz
¼ lb	canned bamboo shoots	125 g/4 oz
¼ lb	mushrooms	125 g/4 oz
1 ½	cakes soybean curd (tofu)	1 ½
5 tbsp	groundnut oil	5 tbsp
2	medium size chopped onions	2
2	finely chopped garlic cloves	2
¼ lb	chicken livers	125 g/4 oz
¾ cup	chicken bouillon (stock)	200 ml/7 fl oz
3 tbsp	Chinese rice wine or sherry	3 tbsp
2 tbsp	ginger syrup	2 tbsp
2 tbsp	Chinese light soy sauce	2 tbsp
1 tbsp	Chinese dark soy sauce	1 tbsp
1 ½ tbsp	oyster sauce	1 ½ tbsp
1-2 tbsp	finely chopped parsley or chives	1-2 tbsp

1. Top and tail the green beans and break them into 2 or 3 pieces.
2. Drain the bamboo shoots well and then cut them first into very thin slices and then into matchsticks.

3. Cut the soybean curd (tofu) into 1 in (2.5 cm) cubes.
4. Wipe the mushrooms, trim off the bottoms of the stalks and then cut them into ½ in (1.25 cm) slices.
5. Heat the oil in a wok and stir fry the onion and garlic for 30 seconds.
6. Add the chicken livers and stir fry for 1-1½ minutes until they change color.
7. Add the green beans and stir fry for 2 minutes over high heat.
8. Add the mushrooms and bamboo shoots and stir fry for 2 minutes.
9. Heat the bouillon (stock) with the rice wine or sherry and add to the contents of the wok.
10. Add the soybean curd (tofu), ginger syrup, soy sauces and oyster sauce and stir carefully. Partly cover and braise gently for 8 minutes until the beans are crisply tender.
11. Serve in a warmed dish and sprinkle with the finely chopped parsley or chives.

Sjiaren wan doe

Stir Fried Peas with Veal and Shrimp (Prawns)

◀━▷ 00.15   00.20 🥘
Serves 4

American	Ingredients	Metric/Imperial
4-5 tbsp	groundnut oil	4-5 tbsp
3	finely chopped green shallots or scallions (spring onions)	3
2	crushed garlic cloves	2
2	skinned, seeded, chopped tomatoes	2
½ lb	ground (minced) veal	225 g/8 oz
1 lb	shelled peas	450 g/1 lb
¼ lb	peeled shrimp (prawns)	125 g/4 oz
5 tbsp	chicken bouillon (stock)	5 tbsp
2 tbsp	ginger syrup	2 tbsp
2 tbsp	rice wine	2 tbsp
1 tbsp	hoisin sauce	1 tbsp
1 ½ tbsp	shrimp sauce	1 ½ tbsp
	black pepper	
	salt	
1-2 tbsp	finely chopped chives	1-2 tbsp

1. Heat the oil in a wok until hot. Stir fry the shallots or scallions (spring onions) and garlic for 30 seconds until golden yellow.
2. Add the tomato, fry for a further minute and add the meat. Separate and fry for 2 minutes over high heat.
3. Add the peas and fry for a further 2 minutes.
4. Add the shrimp (prawns) and stir fry for 1 minutes.
5. Heat the bouillon (stock) with the ginger syrup and the rice wine.
6. Pour the warm bouillon (stock) over the contents of the wok, add the hoisin sauce, shrimp sauce, pepper and salt to taste. Stir again, partly cover the wok and simmer for 8 minutes, until the liquid reduces slightly.
7. Transfer to a warmed dish and sprinkle with finely chopped chives.

Tiansuan huanggua
Sweet and Sour Cucumber (Peking)

00.10 Serves 4 as side dish   **00.10**

American	Ingredients	Metric/Imperial
1	large firm cucumber	1
5 tbsp	groundnut oil	5 tbsp
1	skinned garlic clove	1
1	crushed dried red chili or	1
1 tsp	red pepper oil	1 tsp
	salt	
2 tbsp	rice vinegar	2 tbsp
	or white wine vinegar	
1 tbsp	Chinese dark soy sauce	1 tbsp
1 tbsp	confectioners' (icing) sugar	1 tbsp
2 tbsp	ginger syrup	2 tbsp
4 tbsp	chicken bouillon (stock)	4 tbsp
1	chopped green shallot	1
	or scallion (spring onion)	

1. Wash the cucumber. Remove both ends. Cut into 4 pieces. Remove the seeds with an apple corer. Cut the pieces into ½ in (1.25 cm) slices.
2. Heat the oil in a wok and stir fry the skinned garlic clove until golden brown. Remove from the oil.
3. Add the crushed dried chili or pepper oil. Stir well and add the cucumber. Stir fry the cucumber for 3-4 minutes.
4. Add salt, vinegar, soy sauce, sugar, ginger syrup and bouillon (stock). Stir well and boil for 30 seconds.
5. Transfer immediately on to a warmed dish and serve sprinkled with the chopped green shallot or scallion (spring onion).

Cook's tip: sweet and sour cucumbers can be made into a main course if 1lb (450 g/1 lb) tender, diced chicken or pork is added just before serving. The dish can be served as soon as the meat has warmed through.

Xiezhe huanggua
Cucumber in Crab Sauce (Szechwan)

00.10 Serves 4 as side dish   **00.08**

American	Ingredients	Metric/Imperial
6 oz	crabmeat, thawed if frozen	175 g/6 oz
1	large cucumber	1
4 tbsp	groundnut oil	4 tbsp
2	very finely chopped garlic cloves	2
5 tbsp	chicken bouillon (stock)	5 tbsp
2 tbsp	shrimp or oyster sauce	2 tbsp
	salt	
1 tbsp	finely chopped coriander or parsley	1 tbsp
2	skinned tomatoes	2

1. Cut the crabmeat into small pieces.
2. Wash the cucumber and remove the ends. Cut lengthwise. Seed and cut each half lengthwise again and then cut these strips into 2in (5 cm) pieces.
3. Heat the oil in a wok and stir fry the garlic for 30 seconds.
4. Add the pieces of cucumber and stir fry for 2-3 minutes.
5. Add the bouillon (stock), shrimp or oyster sauce and some salt. Simmer until most of the liquid has evaporated.
6. Stir in the pieces of crabmeat and warm through.
7. Transfer to a warmed dish and sprinkle with coriander or parsley.
8. Garnish with one or more tomato flowers and serve.

Xiami huanggua
Cucumber in Shrimp Sauce (Szechwan)

00.10 plus soaking time   **00.10**

American	Ingredients	Metric/Imperial
2	small cucumbers or	2
4	large gherkins	4
3 tbsp	dried shrimp (prawns) or	3 tbsp
5 tbsp	peeled fresh shrimp (prawns)	5 tbsp
1 tsp	salt	1 tsp
4 tbsp	groundnut oil	4 tbsp
2	very finely chopped garlic cloves	2
2 tbsp	shrimp sauce (optional)	2 tbsp
1	chopped green shallot or scallion (spring onion)	1

1. Peel the cucumbers or gherkins. Cut them lengthwise, seed and cut the halves into ½ in (1.25 cm) slices.
2. Place the dried shrimp (prawns) in a bowl with boiling water to cover them generously. Soak for 15 minutes and leave to drain in a strainer. Strain the soaking liquid through a piece of wet muslin. Measure out 5 tbsp of the soaking liquid.
3. Dissolve the salt in the liquid while it is still warm.
4. Heat the oil in the wok, add the garlic and stir fry for 20 seconds.
5. Add the fresh or dried shrimp (prawns), stir well several times and add the cucumber or gherkins. Stir fry for 2-3 minutes.
6. Add the shrimp (prawn) liquid and shrimp sauce. Stir well again. Reduce the heat and partly cover the wok and simmer until most of the liquid has evaporated.
7. Serve immediately in a warmed dish, sprinkled with a little chopped green shallot or scallion (spring onion).

Cook's tip: if you use fresh shrimp (prawn) instead of the dried variety, you should first chop them extremely finely. Place in just over 5 tbsp warm water with a little salt. Leave to stand for 5 minutes. Strain the liquid through muslin and leave the shrimps (prawns) to drain well. Then follow the method in the previous recipe for dried shrimps (prawns).

6. Mix the cornstarch (cornflour) with 1 tbsp cold water and stir into the wok. Cook, until the sauce thickens. Cook gently for 1 minute.

7. Return the slices of eggplant (aubergine) to the wok, stir well several times and simmer for 2 minutes over a moderate heat. Serve immediately.

Sichuan tiansuan shicai

Sweet and Sour Vegetables (Szechwan)

		00.30	00.10	
		plus drying and pickling		

American	Ingredients	Metric/Imperial
1 ½ lb	carrots	700 g/1 ½ lb
3	large cucumbers	3
2	heads Chinese leaves	2
8 tbsp	coarse (sea) salt	8 tbsp
1-1 ½ tbsp	ground Szechwan pepper	1-1 ½ tbsp
2 tbsp	confectioners' (icing) sugar	2 tbsp
2 tsp	finely chopped root ginger	2 tsp
3 tbsp	rice vinegar or white wine vinegar	3 tbsp
2 tbsp	Chinese light soy sauce	2 tbsp
2 tbsp	Chinese dark soy sauce	2 tbsp
3-4	thinly sliced garlic cloves	3-4
5	red chilies cut into thin strips or	5
1-2 tsp	red pepper oil or chili sauce	1-2 tsp

1. Clean the carrots. Scrape if necessary and cut them obliquely into ½ inch (1.25 cm) slices.

2. Wash the cucumbers and remove the ends and cut both cucumbers obliquely into ½ inch (1.25 cm) slices.

3. Wash the Chinese leaves in cold water. Remove any thick veins and the stalks and cut into finger width strips.

4. Drain the vegetables well. Place each kind separately into a colander or strainer in a draughty place, so that the vegetables become totally dry before use.

5. Mix the salt and the pepper in a dry frying pan. Stir fry for 4 minutes.

6. Pour 3 quarts (3 litres/5 pints) boiling water into a well cleaned preserving jar.

7. Add the salt and pepper mixture, sugar, root ginger, vinegar, soy sauces, garlic and the red chilies, pepper oil or chili sauce. Stir until the salt and sugar have dissolved.

8. Leave the mixture to stand until it has cooled down to room temperature.

9. Fill the jar with the vegetables (if you wish have separate layers of the various kinds of vegetables).

10. Leave at least ½ in (1.25 cm) of liquid above the vegetables.

11. Seal the jar hermetically. Store in a dark, cool and dry place.

12. The vegetables can be eaten after 2 weeks. Do not keep them for longer than 2 months.

Cook's tip: the carrots, cucumbers and Chinese leaves can be replaced by any 3 of the following vegetables: celery cut into strips; unripe melon, seeded and diced; white cabbage, cut into strips; sour apples, diced; onions, halved and sliced; gherkins, sliced; fresh bamboo shoots, cut into strips; water chestnuts, cut into strips.

Fried eggplant (aubergine)

Chao qiezi

Fried Eggplant (Aubergine) (Szechwan)

		00.05	00.20	
		Serves 4 as side dish		

American	Ingredients	Metric/Imperial
1	large or 2 smaller eggplants (aubergines)	1
4 tbsp	groundnut oil	4 tbsp
2	very finely chopped garlic cloves	2
1 tbsp	finely grated root ginger	1 tbsp
1 tbsp	hoisin sauce	1 tbsp
1 tbsp	red pepper oil	1 tbsp
1 tbsp	rice vinegar or white wine vinegar	1 tbsp
2 tbsp	Chinese light soy sauce	2 tbsp
1 tbsp	tomato ketchup	1 tbsp
1 tbsp	confectioners' (icing) sugar	1 tbsp
	salt	
5-6 tbsp	chicken bouillon (stock)	5-6 tbsp
1 tsp	sesame oil	1 tsp
1 ½ tsp	cornstarch (cornflour)	1 ½ tsp

1. Wash the eggplants (aubergines). Remove the ends. Cut them obliquely into ½ in (1.25 cm) slices. Dry with kitchen paper.

2. Heat the oil in a wok until very hot.

3. Add the garlic and the root ginger, stir well and add the slices of eggplant (aubergine). Stir fry for 2-3 minutes over high heat.

4. Remove from the wok with a slotted spoon and drain on kitchen paper.

5. Add all other ingredients to the remaining oil, except the cornstarch (cornflour). Stir well and boil steadily for 1 minute.

1. Cut the bell peppers into strips, then into small squares.
2. Cut each onion into 8 segments and separate the layers.
3. Cut the pineapple slices into pieces.
4. Cut the chilies into very small slices.
5. Dry the meat with kitchen paper.
6. Heat the oil in a wok and stir fry the meat until lightly browned on all sides.
7. Add the onion and stir fry until transparent. Stir in the bell pepper, chili, pineapple, ginger and garlic and stir fry for 30 seconds.
8. Stir in the soy sauces, rice wine or sherry, vodka or gin, plum sauce, vinegar and sugar.
9. Add the bouillon (stock), bring to the boil and simmer for 5 minutes.
10. Mix the cornstarch (cornflour) 1 tbsp cold water. Push the meat and vegetables to one side of the wok and stir the cornstarch (cornflour) mixture into the liquid. Cook, stirring until the sauce thickens.
11. Add salt to taste and bring to the boil. Spoon the ingredients back into the sauce and simmer for 2-3 minutes.
12. Stir in the sesame oil and serve on a warmed dish.

Sweet and sour pork with bell pepper and pineapple

Po luo chu ziu

Sweet and Sour Pork with Bell Pepper and Pineapple

◢ 00.15
Serves 4

00.12 ⊟

American	Ingredients	Metric/Imperial
2	large, seeded red or green bell peppers	2
4	small onions	4
1	small fresh pineapple or 6 slices of canned pineapple well drained	1
2	seeded red chilies	2
1 lb	lean pork cut into ½ in (1.25 cm) cubes	450 g/1 lb
5 tbsp	groundnut oil	5 tbsp
2 tsp	finely grated fresh root ginger	2 tsp
2	crushed garlic cloves	2
2 tbsp	Chinese light soy sauce	2 tbsp
1 tbsp	Chinese dark soy sauce	1 tbsp
2 tbsp	Chinese rice wine or sherry	2 tbsp
1 tbsp	vodka or gin	1 tbsp
2 tbsp	Chinese plum sauce	2 tbsp
2-3 tbsp	white wine vinegar	2-3 tbsp
3 tbsp	sugar	3 tbsp
1¼ cups	hot chicken bouillon (stock)	300 ml/½ pint
2 tsp	cornstarch (cornflour)	2 tsp
	salt	
1-2 tbsp	sesame oil	1-2 tbsp

Huang gua huo dian

Fried Trout with Cucumber

◢ 00.15
plus soaking time

00.15 ⊟

American	Ingredients	Metric/Imperial
4-6	dried Chinese mushrooms	4-6
8	trout fillets	8
2 tbsp	lemon juice	2 tbsp
	salt	
1	onion	1
1	cucumber	1
4-5 tbsp	groundnut oil	4-5 tbsp
1	crushed garlic clove	1
2 tsp	coarsely grated fresh ginger	2 tsp
2 tbsp	Chinese light soy sauce	2 tbsp
1 tbsp	Chinese dark soy sauce	1 tbsp
3 tbsp	Chinese rice wine or sherry	3 tbsp
1½ tsp	sugar	1½ tsp
2 tbsp	white wine vinegar	2 tbsp
1 tsp	oyster sauce	1 tsp
1 tbsp	fish sauce	1 tbsp
¾ cup	fish bouillon (stock)	200 ml/7 fl oz
2 tsp	cornstarch (cornflour)	2 tsp
2 tsp	sesame oil	2 tsp
2-3	chopped shallots, scallions (spring onions) or leeks (white parts only)	2-3

1. Soak the dried mushrooms in boiling water to cover for about 30 minutes. Discard the stalks and cut the caps into thin strips.
2. Rinse the fish under cold running water and dry with kitchen paper.
3. Mix together the lemon juice, ½ tsp salt and stir until the salt has dissolved. Add the fish fillets and turn to coat with the mixture. Leave for 15 minutes.
4. Cut the onion into 8 segments and separate the layers.

5. Wash the cucumber and halve lengthwise. Remove the seeds. Cut each half into 3 long slices and each of these slices into 1½ in (4 cm) fingers.

6. Dry the fish again and cut each fillet into 3 pieces.

7. Heat the oil in a wok and carefully stir fry the fish in this for 3 minutes. Remove from the pan when cooked and keep warm.

8. Add the onion to the remaining oil and stir fry until transparent. Add the garlic and ginger. Stir well then add the cucumber, mushrooms, soy sauces, rice wine or sherry, sugar, vinegar, oyster and fish sauces, and the hot bouillon (stock).

9. Stir well, bring to the boil and simmer for 4-5 minutes.

10. Mix the cornstarch (cornflour) with 1 tbsp cold water. Push the fish and vegetables to one side of the wok and stir the cornstarch (cornflour) mixture into the sauce. Cook, stirring until the sauce thickens. Stir in the fish and vegetables and simmer for 1-2 minutes.

11. Stir in the sesame oil and the shallots or scallions (spring onions) or leeks and serve immediately on a warmed dish.

Je ziong chi pian

Chicken with Shrimp (Prawns) and Coconut

	00.10	00.10
	Serves 4	

American	Ingredients	Metric/Imperial
3-4 tbsp	groundnut oil	3-4 tbsp
2	chopped onions	2
2	finely chopped garlic cloves	2
1 tsp	finely chopped fresh root ginger	1 tsp
1 lb	boneless chicken	450 g/1 lb
4 tbsp	finely grated fresh coconut	4 tbsp
1¼ cups	hot chicken bouillon (stock)	300 ml/½ pint
2 tbsp	Chinese light soy sauce	2 tbsp
2 tbsp	Chinese rice wine or sherry	2 tbsp
2 tsp	sugar	2 tsp
1 tsp	hoisin sauce	1 tsp
3 oz	fresh peeled shrimp (prawns)	75 g/3 oz
2 tbsp	finely chopped shallot, scallion (spring onion) or leek (white part only)	2 tbsp
	pinch five spice powder	
⅓ tsp	ground Szechwan peppercorns	⅓ tsp
	salt	
2 tsp	sesame oil	2 tsp

1. Heat the oil in a wok and stir fry the onion until it looks transparent. Add the garlic and root ginger and cook gently for 2 minutes.

2. Slice the chicken finely and add it to the ingredients in the wok. Cook until the chicken is lightly browned on all sides.

3. Add the coconut and hot chicken bouillon (stock) and simmer for 4-5 minutes.

4. Add the soy sauce, rice wine or sherry, sugar, hoisin sauce, shrimp (prawns) shallot, scallion (spring onion) or leek, five spice powder, Szechwan peppercorns and salt to taste.

5. Stir well and bring to the boil.

6. Just before serving stir in the sesame oil.

7. Transfer to a warmed dish and serve immediately

Cook's tip: the addition of Szechwan pepper is always an indication that the dish will be very fiery. It gives this dish its individual flavor. If however it is too spicy, freshly ground black pepper may be used as a substitute.

Chicken with shrimp (prawns) and coconut

Stuffed melon

Du chi hong niang yu

Red Mullet with Black Beans

00.05 Serves 4 | 00.15

American	Ingredients	Metric/Imperial
4	small red mullet fillets	4
⅔ cup	groundnut oil	150 ml/¼ pint
4 tbsp	black beans	4 tbsp
2-3	crushed garlic cloves	2-3
1 tbsp	finely grated fresh root ginger	1 tbsp
2 tbsp	finely chopped shallot, scallion (spring onion) or leek (white part only)	2 tbsp
2 tbsp	Chinese light soy sauce	2 tbsp
3 tbsp	Chinese dark soy sauce	3 tbsp
	salt	
1 tsp	ground Szechwan peppercorns	1 tsp
2	skinned tomatoes cut into wedges	2
2	lemons cut into wedges	2

1. Rinse the fish under cold running water and dry with kitchen paper.
2. Heat all but 2 tbsp of the oil in a wok and fry the fish for about 6-8 minutes on each side, turning carefully. Remove from the pan and drain on kitchen paper.
3. Heat 2 tbsp oil in a clean wok and stir fry the black beans, garlic and ginger for 1 minute. Stir in the shallot, scallion (spring onion) or leek, the soy sauces and 3 tbsp water.
4. Bring to the boil and add salt and ground Szechwan pepper to taste.
5. Arrange the fish on a warmed serving dish and spoon over the sauce. Garnish with the tomato and lemon wedges and serve immediately.

Nia Zhu Shian Gua

Stuffed Melon

00.15 plus standing time | 00.30

American	Ingredients	Metric/Imperial
1	medium ripe melon	1
	salt	
2½ tbsp	groundnut oil	2½ tbsp
¼ lb	finely ground (minced) smoked bacon	125 g/4 oz
1 lb	lean ground (minced) beef	450 g/1 lb
2	coarsely chopped large onions	2
3	finely chopped garlic cloves	3
1½ tsp	finely grated fresh root ginger	1½ tsp
2 tbsp	Chinese light soy sauce	2 tbsp
3 tbsp	Chinese dark soy sauce	3 tbsp
3 tbsp	Chinese rice wine or dry sherry	3 tbsp
1 tbsp	sugar	1 tbsp
⅓ tsp	five spice powder	⅓ tsp
½-1 tsp	finely ground Szechwan peppercorns	½-1 tsp
1¼ cups	beef bouillon (stock)	300 ml/½ pint
1 tbsp	cornstarch (cornflour)	1 tbsp
2 tbsp	finely chopped coriander or parsley leaves	2 tbsp

1. Cut a thin slice off one end of the melon to make a steady base. Cut a lid off the other end and scoop out the seeds.
2. Remove most of the flesh, being careful not to damage the melon shell. Cut the flesh into ½ in (1.25 cm) cubes. Sprinkle with salt and leave to drain for 30 minutes.
3. Heat the oil in a wok and stir fry the bacon for 1 minute. Add the beef and stir fry until it crumbles and has changed color.
4. Add the onion, garlic and ginger, stir well and cook for a further 2 minutes.
5. Stir in the soy sauces, rice wine or sherry, sugar, five spice powder, Szechwan peppercorns and bouillon (stock). Bring to the boil.
6. Add the cubes of melon and simmer for 6-8 minutes.
7. Mix the cornstarch (cornflour) with 2 tbsp cold water. Stir into the contents of the wok and cook stirring, until the liquid thickens.
8. Stir in the chopped coriander or parsley and simmer for a further 3 minutes.
9. Pour into the empty melon shell and serve immediately. Serve any remaining filling in a warmed dish.

Chong pau yow yu

Squid with Scallions (Spring Onion)

◢▷ 00.15 _plus marinating_   00.10 ⌸

American	Ingredients	Metric/Imperial
1½ lb	cleaned squid cut into rings	700 g/1½ lb
3 tbsp	lemon or lime juice	3 tbsp
3 tbsp	Chinese rice wine or sherry	3 tbsp
½ tsp	sugar	½ tsp
2 tbsp	Chinese light soy sauce	2 tbsp
1-2 tbsp	Chinese dark soy sauce	1-2 tbsp
2 tbsp	cornstarch (cornflour)	2 tbsp
1½ oz	fresh root ginger	40 g/1½ oz
1	carrot	1
1	large onion	1
4 tbsp	groundnut oil	4 tbsp
5-10 tbsp	hot chicken or fish bouillon (stock)	5-10 tbsp
6	chopped shallots, scallions (spring onions) or leeks (white part only)	6
3 tbsp	Chinese rice wine or sherry	3 tbsp
1 tbsp	Chinese light soy sauce	1 tbsp
1 tbsp	Chinese dark soy sauce	1 tbsp
1 tsp	hoisin sauce	1 tsp
1 tbsp	sugar	1 tbsp
	salt	

1. Rinse the squid in cold water and dry carefully with kitchen paper.
2. Make the marinade by mixing together the lime or lemon juice, 3 tbsp rice wine or sherry, ½ tsp sugar, 2 tbsp Chinese light soy sauce, 1-2 tbsp Chinese dark soy sauce and the cornstarch (cornflour). Add the squid, stir well and leave to stand in a cool place for 1 hour, stirring occasionally.
3. Peel the ginger, slice thinly and cut into fine strips. Cut the carrot into julienne strips. Cut the onion into segments and slice thinly.
4. Heat the oil in a wok until very hot. Drain the squid, dry with kitchen paper and stir fry for 1 minute.
5. Add the ginger, carrot and onion. Stir fry until the onion looks transparent.
6. Add the hot bouillon (stock) and shallots, scallions (spring onions) or leeks, remaining rice wine or sherry, remaining soy sauces, hoisin sauce and sugar. Bring to the boil and simmer for 1 minute. Add salt to taste.
7. Transfer to a warmed dish and serve.

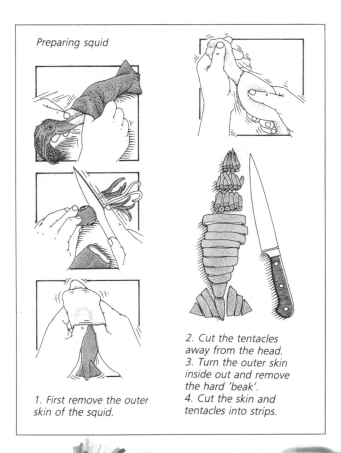

Preparing squid

1. First remove the outer skin of the squid.
2. Cut the tentacles away from the head.
3. Turn the outer skin inside out and remove the hard 'beak'.
4. Cut the skin and tentacles into strips.

Squid with scallions (spring onions)

Chian Suan yu
Fish in Sweet and Sour Sauce

00.15 **00.25**
plus soaking time and marinating

American	Ingredients	Metric/Imperial
6	large dried Chinese mushrooms	6
2	small, seeded red chilies	2
1½-2 tsp	finely grated fresh ginger	1½-2 tsp
1 tbsp	finely chopped onion	1 tbsp
1 tsp	salt	1 tsp
3 tbsp	Chinese rice wine or sherry	3 tbsp
½ tsp	sugar	½ tsp
1 tbsp	Chinese light soy sauce	1 tbsp
1	small cleaned cod	1
4 tbsp	cornstarch (cornflour)	4 tbsp
¾ cup	groundnut oil	200 ml/7 fl oz
4	chopped shallots, scallions (spring onions) or leeks (white part only)	4
⅔ cup	hot fish bouillon (stock)	125 ml/¼ pint
5 tbsp	white wine vinegar	5 tbsp
2 tbsp	Chinese light soy sauce	2 tbsp
½ tbsp	Chinese dark soy sauce	½ tbsp
2 tsp	hoisin sauce	2 tsp
5 tbsp	sugar	5 tbsp
	salt	
2 tsp	cornstarch (cornflour)	2 tsp
2 tsp	sesame oil	2 tsp
1 tbsp	coriander leaves or parsley	1 tbsp

1. Soak the dried mushrooms in boiling water to cover for 30 minutes. Drain them, discard the stalks and slice the caps.
2. Shred the chilies finely.
3. Make the marinade by mixing together the root ginger, onion, salt, rice wine or sherry, sugar and 1 tbsp Chinese light soy sauce.
4. Rinse the fish under cold running water and dry inside and out with kitchen paper. Put the fish in a dish and pour the marinade over, making sure that the fish is fully covered. Leave to stand for about 1 hour turning occasionally. Dry the fish with kitchen paper again.
5. Sprinkle 4 tbsp cornstarch (cornflour) over the fish and rub it in.
6. Heat the oil in a wok or large frying pan. Fry the fish for 5-6 minutes each side until golden brown. Remove the fish and keep warm, wrapped in aluminum foil.
7. Heat 1 tbsp oil in the wok and stir fry the sliced mushroom and chili for 30 seconds. Add the shallots, scallions (spring onions) or leeks and stir well.
8. Add the bouillon (stock) and the remaining ingredients except the fish, 2 tsp cornstarch (cornflour) and sesame oil. Simmer, stirring until the sugar has dissolved. Add salt to taste.
9. Mix the remaining cornstarch (cornflour) with 1 tbsp cold water and stir this mixture into the wok. Cook, stirring until the sauce thickens very slightly. Simmer for 2-3 minutes and stir in the sesame oil.
10. Put the fish on a warmed plate and spoon over the sauce.
11. Arrange the coriander leaves or parsley over the top and serve. Serve any remaining sauce separately.

MENU

Fish rolls with paksoi
Chicken fillets with ginger
Almond jelly and orange

Fish Rolls with Paksoi

00.10 **00.10**
Serves 4

American	Ingredients	Metric/Imperial
8	sole fillets	8
1 tbsp	cornstarch (cornflour)	1 tbsp
¼ lb	finely ground (minced) shrimp (prawns)	125 g/4 oz
¼ lb	shredded paksoi	125 g/4 oz
2	finely chopped scallions (spring onion), or leek	2
2 tbsp	Chinese rice wine or medium sherry	2 tbsp
1 tbsp	shrimp sauce	1 tbsp
	salt	
	pinch five spice powder	
1 tbsp	oil or soft butter	1 tbsp
1 tbsp	hoisin sauce	1 tbsp
1 tbsp	oyster sauce	1 tbsp
2-3 tbsp	Chinese rice wine or sherry	2-3 tbsp

1. Rinse the fish under cold running water. Dry with kitchen paper and place on a worktop or chopping board, skin side uppermost. Flatten them with the flat side of a large knife.
2. Sprinkle the cornstarch (cornflour over the shrimp (prawns) and stir. Add the paksoi, scallions (spring onion) or leek, rice wine or sherry, shrimp sauce, salt and five spice powder. Mix until smooth. Divide the mixture into 8 portions. Shape each into a ball the same size as the widest part of the flattened fish fillets.
3. Place one ball on each fillet and roll up round the ball. Secure with wooden cocktail picks.
4. Bring 2 quarts (2 litres) of salted water to the boil in a steamer. Brush the perforated part of the pan with oil or soft butter. Put the fish rolls upright on this part of the steamer. Cover the pan and steam for 8-10 minutes.
5. Make the sauce by mixing together the hoisin sauce, oyster sauce and 2-3 tbsp rice wine or sherry.
6. Transfer the steamed fish rolls to a warmed serving dish. Put a spoonful of the sauce over each roll and serve.

Chicken Fillets with Ginger

00.10 00.10

Serves 4

American	Ingredients	Metric/Imperial
1 lb	filleted chicken breasts	450 g/1 lb
2 tbsp	groundnut oil	2 tbsp
1	large finely chopped onion	1
2 tbsp	finely grated fresh fresh root ginger	2 tbsp
1	finely chopped garlic clove	1
⅔ cup	Chinese rice wine or sherry	150 ml/¼ pint
2 tsp	sugar	2 tsp
2 tbsp	honey	2 tbsp
2 tbsp	Chinese light soy sauce	2 tbsp
1 tbsp	Chinese dark soy sauce	1 tbsp
1 tbsp	ginger syrup	1 tbsp
1	chopped scallion (spring onion)	1

1. Dry the chicken with kitchen paper. Cut the chicken into very thin strips.
2. Heat the oil in a wok and stir fry the onions until transparent. Add the root ginger and garlic. Stir well.
3. Stir in the chicken, rice wine or sherry, sugar, honey, soy sauces and ginger syrup. Bring to the boil and cook until the liquid has reduced by half.
4. Transfer to a warmed serving dish, garnish with chopped scallion (spring onion) and serve.

Almond Jelly and Orange

00.10 01.00

plus soaking time

American	Ingredients	Metric/Imperial
1 cup	skimmed milk	250 ml/½ pint
⅔ envelope	unflavored gelatin	½ sachet
2 tbsp	sugar	2 tbsp
½ tsp	sweet almond essence	½ tsp
2	drops bitter almond essence	2
3 tbsp	Chinese rice wine or medium sherry	3 tbsp
2	large oranges	2
	few leaves mint (optional)	
	few small red fruits	

1. Bring the milk to the boil. Add the sugar and gelatin and stir until both have dissolved. Remove the pan from the heat.
2. Cool slightly, then stir in the two essences and rice or sherry. Transfer to a large, cold deep dish. Leave to set then chill for 1 hour.
3. Peel the oranges and remove the pith and membrane, divide into segments. Drain in a colander.
4. Cut the jelly, when cold, into pieces the same shape as the orange segments and arrange alternate slices of jelly and orange on individual plates.
5. Decorate with a mint leaf and small red fruit and serve.

INDONESIA

Nasi Putih
White Rice (Boiled)

	00.05		00.30
	Serves 4		

American	Ingredients	Metric/Imperial
1 cup	short grain rice	200 g/7 oz
1¼ cups	water	300 ml/½ pint
1 tsp	salt	1 tsp

1. Rinse the rice several times until the water runs clear. Drain in a colander or strainer.
2. Bring the water with the salt to the boil in a heavy-based saucepan. Add the rice all at one time. Stir well. Bring the water to the boil again. Stir again.
3. Cover the saucepan and reduce the heat. Cook the rice for 15-18 minutes. Do not remove the lid from the saucepan while the rice is cooking.
4. After cooking stir the rice well once with a large meat fork.
5. Allow it to steam dry and then serve on a warmed dish.

Nasi putih 11
White Rice (Steamed)

	00.05		00.35
	Serves 4		

American	Ingredients	Metric/Imperial
1 cup	short grain rice	200 g/7 oz
2¼ cups	water (to boil)	500 ml/18 fl oz
1 tsp	salt	1 tsp
2¼ cups	water (to steam)	500 ml/18 fl oz

1. Rinse the rice several times until the water runs clear.
2. Bring 2¼ cups (500 ml/18 fl oz) water and the salt to the boil in a saucepan and add the rice. Bring the water to the boil again, stirring. Cover the saucepan, reduce the heat and simmer for 8 minutes. Drain well.
3. Bring 2¼ cups (500 ml/18 fl oz) water to the boil in a steamer.
4. Place the rice in the upper section of the steamer. Bring the steamer to steam and cook the rice for 20-25 minutes. Turn once during cooking.
5. Serve the rice on a warmed dish.

Nasi kunyit
Rice with Turmeric

	00.05		00.35
	plus standing time		

American	Ingredients	Metric/Imperial
1 cup	glutinous rice	200 g/7 oz
1 tbsp	ground turmeric	1 tbsp
1	crushed garlic clove	1
1	finely crushed candle nut	1
¾ cup	thin coconut milk (see page 310)	200 ml/7 fl oz
1 tsp	salt	1 tsp
1	small squeezed lemon or lime	1

1. Rinse the rice several times until the water runs clear.
2. Put 2¼ cups (500 ml/18 fl oz) cold water in a saucepan and stir in the turmeric.

3. Add the garlic and the candle nut and stir well. Add the rice and leave to stand for 10-12 hours. Stir the rice occasionally. Drain well.
4. Bring ¾ cup (200 ml/7 fl oz) water to the boil in a saucepan. Add 5 tbsp thin coconut milk, salt and lemon or lime juice. Bring to the boil, stirring constantly.
5. Add the rice and stir until the liquid has come to the boil again. Cover the saucepan, reduce the heat and cook the rice for 20-22 minutes.
6. Add the remaining coconut milk a little at a time, stirring with a large meat fork. Leave the rice to stand for 2 minutes over very low heat then serve in a warmed dish.

Nasi uduk
Spiced Rice

	00.05		00.30
	Serves 4		

American	Ingredients	Metric/Imperial
1 cup	long grain rice	200 g/7 oz
1½ cups	thin coconut milk	300 ml/½ pint
1 tsp	salt	1 tsp
1	chopped onion	1
1	finely crushed garlic clove	1
1 tsp	ground cumin	1 tsp
1½ tsp	ground coriander	1½ tsp
½ tsp	trasi (shrimp (prawn) paste)	½ tsp
	kentjur (kenkur) (optional)	
	few blades lemon grass (sereh)	

1. Rinse the rice several times until the water runs clear. Drain in a colander or strainer.
2. Bring 4½ tbsp water to the boil in a heavy-based saucepan. Add all the ingredients, except the rice at one time and bring to the boil, stirring constantly.
3. Add the rice, stirring until the water comes to the boil again. Stir well once more. Cover the saucepan, reduce the heat and simmer gently for 18-20 minutes. Remove the lid from the saucepan. Stir the contents with a large meat fork. Remove the lemon grass and leave the rice to steam dry.
4. Serve the rice in a warmed dish.

Nasi kuning legkap
Yellow Spiced Rice

	00.05		00.25
	plus soaking time		

American	Ingredients	Metric/Imperial
1 cup	long grain rice	200 g/7 oz
2 tbsp	groundnut oil	2 tbsp
1	coarsely chopped onion	1
1	crushed garlic clove	1
1½ cups	thin coconut milk	350 ml/12 fl oz
1 tsp	salt	1
1½ tsp	ground turmeric	1½ tsp
2	salam leaves or 4 curry leaves	2
2	marbled eggs (see page 68)	2
1	cucumber	1
1	red chili	1
1	green chili	1

1. Rinse the rice several times until the water runs clear. Soak the rice for 30 minutes in cold water. Leave to drain for 30 minutes in a colander or strainer, stirring occasionally.

2. Heat the oil and stir fry the onion until transparent. Add the garlic. Stir again and add the rice. Stir for another 1-2 minutes until the rice begins to look transparent.

3. Add the remaining ingredients except the marbled eggs, cucumber and chilies. Bring to the boil, stirring well. Cover the saucepan, reduce the heat and cook the rice for 18-20 minutes. Remove the lid from the saucepan. Stir once with a large meat fork. Leave the rice to steam dry for a further 2-3 minutes.

4. Transfer the rice to a warmed dish. Garnish with the eggs cucumber and chilies and serve.

Cook's tip: in Indonesia a piece of banana leaf is placed over the rice to keep it warm. The Nasi kuning is usually served with three or more side dishes as it is regarded as a festive meal and so is often used in sacrifices.

Making chili flowers

1. Open the chili with a sharp knife and remove the seeds.
2. Hold by the stem and make fine incisions with the point of a knife.
3. Fan the strips out to form a flower.

Nasi kebuli

Spiced Rice with Fried Onions

➤▷   00.05   00.35 🍲
plus soaking time

American	Ingredients	Metric/Imperial
1 cup	long grain rice	200 g/7 oz
2 tbsp	groundnut oil	2 tbsp
2	large coarsely chopped onions	2
2	coarsely chopped garlic cloves	2
1¾ cups	chicken bouillon (stock)	350 ml/12 fl oz
1 tsp	ground root ginger	1 tsp
1 tsp	ground coriander	1 tsp
	pinch nutmeg	

1. Rinse the rice several times until the water runs clear. Soak the rice in plenty of cold water for 30 minutes.

2. Drain and dry the rice in a colander or strainer for 1 hour, giving it an occasional stir.

3. Heat the oil in a saucepan and stir fry the onion until lightly colored. Add the garlic and stir well a few times. Remove the onion and garlic from the saucepan with a skimmer. Drain over the saucepan and set aside.

4. Add the rice to the remaining oil in the pan and stir until the rice looks transparent. Add the boiling chicken bouillon (stock) and the remaining ingredients except the nutmeg and fried onions. Bring the mixture to the boil, stirring constantly.

5. Cover the saucepan and reduce the heat. Cook for 18-20 minutes.

6. Remove the lid from the pan and add half the fried onions and garlic. Sprinkle over a little nutmeg and stir with a large meat fork.

7. Transfer the rice to a warmed dish and distribute the remaining fried onion and garlic over it and serve immediately.

Left: Yellow spiced rice
Right: Spiced rice with fried onions

Nasi guri dan ayam
Spiced Rice in Coconut Milk with Chicken

00.10 Serves 4   **00.25**

American	Ingredients	Metric/Imperial
1 lb	boneless chicken breast	450 g/1 lb
1 tsp	ground root ginger	1 tsp
	pinch cayenne pepper	
	salt	
4	cloves	4
1	small peeled onion	1
1 cup	long grain rice	200 g/7 oz
2 tbsp	groundnut oil	2 tbsp
1¾ cups	thin coconut milk	400 ml/13 fl oz
1	salam leaf	1
2-4	skinned tomatoes (optional)	2-4

1. Dry the chicken with kitchen paper and cut into finger width strips.
2. Stir together the ground root ginger, cayenne pepper and a little salt and rub into the strips of chicken.
3. Push the cloves into the onion.
4. Rinse the rice several times until the water runs clear. Drain well in a strainer or colander and dry in a clean cloth.
5. Heat the oil in a wok. Stir fry the strips of chicken for 2 minutes. Add the rice and stir until the rice looks transparent.
6. Add the coconut milk, onion with cloves, salam leaf and 1 tsp of salt. Bring to the boil and reduce the heat. Stir well once more. Cover the wok and cook for 18-20 minutes until the rice is dry and tender.
7. Remove the onion and salam leaf and turn into a warmed dish. Stir lightly with a large fork and serve garnished with tomatoes.

Nasi goreng
Fried Rice

00.02 Serves 4   **00.10**

American	Ingredients	Metric/Imperial
2	large coarsely chopped onions	2
1	crushed garlic clove	1
1-2 tsp	sambal ulek or (see page 128)	1-2 tsp
½ tsp	sea salt (optional)	½ tsp
2½ tbsp	groundnut oil	2½ tbsp
½ lb	cooked, diced chicken, beef or pork plus fresh peeled shrimp (prawns) (optional)	225 g/8 oz
½ lb	cold cooked white rice	225 g/8 oz
1 tbsp	Indonesian salty soy sauce (ketyap benteng asin)	1 tbsp

1. Pound the onions, garlic and the sambal into a paste in a mortar or food processor. Add a little sea salt, if liked.
2. Heat the oil in a wok and gently fry the onion paste until golden red.
3. Add the diced meat. Stir together a few times and add the rice a little at a time, stirring constantly. Continue turning over until the rice is hot and partly fried.

4. Mix in the shrimp (prawns) if using and sprinkle the soy sauce over the dish. Stir well and serve in a warmed shallow dish.

Cook's tip: in Indonesia nasi goreng is eaten for breakfast. Leftovers from the previous evening's meal are nearly always worked into it. It is a dish which does not deny its Chinese origins, although the Chinese in Indonesia prepare there nasi goreng much more expansively, with more ingredients, and serve it as a main meal. It is usually served with fried egg or omelette cut into strips, and a few fried onions are often also scattered over it.

Lontong
Rice Cakes

00.05 plus cooling time   **00.55**

American	Ingredients	Metric/Imperial
1 cup	short grain rice	200 g/7 oz
2 oz	glutinous rice (ketan)	50 g/2 oz
1 tsp	salt	1 tsp

1. Rinse both types of rice several times until the water runs clear.
2. Bring 2¼ cups (500 ml/18 fl oz) water to the boil. Add the salt and the rice and bring back to the boil, stirring constantly.
3. Cover the saucepan, reduce the heat and cook for about 45 minutes until the rice is soft and fully cooked. Stir the rice several times during cooking.
4. Rinse a rectangular mould, such as a small baking tin in cold water. Pour the contents of the saucepan into it and smooth the surface with a spoon. Cool the lontong until completely cold, then cut it into small rectangular pieces and serve.

Cook's tip: many Indonesian families cook lontong in a mixture of equal parts thin coconut milk and water. Sometimes they add a little ground white pepper as well as the salt.

Sambal Ulek

00.10 makes 1 jar   **00.00**

American	Ingredients	Metric/Imperial
20	red chilies	20
2 tsp	sea salt	2 tsp

1. Rinse the chilies, trim the ends and chop into small pieces.
2. Place the chilies and salt in a mortar and grind to a paste.
3. Transfer to a small, clean jar. Seal and store in the refrigerator for up to 1 month.

Special Sambal

00.10   **00.00**

American	Ingredients	Metric/Imperial
20	red chilies	20
2 tsp	sea salt	2 tsp
1 tbsp	soft brown sugar	1 tbsp
6	ripe skinned tomatoes	6

1. Rinse the chilies and trim the ends.
2. Cut the chilies open and remove the seeds and pith. Simmer the flesh in water for 5 minutes. Pat dry with kitchen paper and chop finely.
3. Place in a mortar with the salt and sugar and grind to a fine paste.
4. Halve the tomatoes, remove the seeds and as much of the juice as possible. Finely grind the tomato flesh and mix with the paste.
5. Cover and store in the refrigerator for up to 2 days.

Cook's tip: in place of fresh tomatoes, add 2-3 tbsp tomato purée to the paste.

Sambal Serdadoe

◣	00.05	00.10

American	Ingredients	Metric/Imperial
20	red chilies	20
4	large onions	4
1	thick slice trasi	1
2 tsp	sea salt	2 tsp
2 tbsp	groundnut oil	2 tbsp

1. Rinse the chilies, trim the ends and chop into small pieces.
2. Chop the onions.

3. Wrap the trasi in aluminum foil and heat under a hot broiler (grill) or in a hot oven for 20-30 seconds. Put the trasi in a bowl and add 5 tbsp boiling water. Using a fork, crush the trasi finely and stir until dissolved.
4. Heat the oil in a wok and fry the chilies and onion until the onion is soft.
5. Add the trasi mixture. Cover the wok and leave to cook gently for 10 minutes.
6. Remove the lid and allow some of the liquid to evaporate to give a thick mass.

Sambal Trasi

◣	00.15	00.00
	makes 1 jar	

American	Ingredients	Metric/Imperial
20	red chilies	20
2 tsp	sea salt	2 tsp
1	slice trasi	1

1. Rinse the chilies, trim the ends and chop into small pieces.
2. Wrap the trasi in aluminum foil and place under a hot broiler (grill) for 20 seconds or put into a hot oven.
3. Crumble the trasi.
4. Put all the ingredients into a mortar and grind to a fine paste.
5. Transfer to a small, clean jar. Seal and store in the refrigerator for up to 1 month.

Sambal trasi

Sambal Kemiri

00.20   **00.00**

American	Ingredients	Metric/Imperial
20	red chilies	20
2	garlic cloves	2
10-12	candle nuts	10-12
2 tsp	sea salt	2 tsp

1. Rinse the chilies, trim the ends and chop into small pieces.
2. Chop the garlic cloves finely.
3. Roast the nuts until brown in a dry frying pan, under a moderately hot broiler (grill) or in a hot oven. Turn the nuts constantly so that they are evenly roasted.
4. Crush the warm nuts finely in a mortar and add the chilies, garlic and salt.
5. Work the mixture to a paste. If necessary, add 1-2 tsp water to soften.

Sambal Manis

00.10.
makes 1 jar
00.00

American	Ingredients	Metric/Imperial
20	red chilies	20
2 tsp	sea salt	2 tsp
2 tbsp	soft brown sugar	2 tbsp
1	egg size piece dried tamarind (asem)	1

1. Rinse the chilies, trim the ends and chop into small pieces.
2. Place all ingredients in a mortar and grind to a paste.
3. Remove as many of the tamarind pips as possible and any skin as it will spoil the texture.
4. Store in the refrigerator in a small, sealed jar for up to 1 month.

Sambal Djeroek

00.10
makes 1 jar
00.00

American	Ingredients	Metric/Imperial
20	red chilies	20
2 tsp	sea salt	2 tsp
	juice 1 large lemon or 2 limes	

1. Rinse the chilies, trim the ends and chop into small pieces.
2. Place in a mortar together with the salt and a little lemon or lime juice.
3. Grind the mixture to a fine paste, gradually adding the remaining lemon or lime juice.
4. Transfer to a small clean jar and store in a refrigerator for up to 1 month.

Sambal kemiri

Sambal goreng boontjes

Spiced Dish with French Beans

00.10
plus cooling time
00.20

American	Ingredients	Metric/Imperial
¾ lb	string beans	350 g/12 oz
2 tbsp	groundnut oil	2 tbsp
1	large chopped onion	1
1	crushed garlic clove	1
1 tsp	sambal ulek or sambal trasi (see page 128 or 129)	1 tsp
1 tsp	laos powder	1 tsp
1 tsp	soft brown sugar	1 tsp
1	blade lemon grass (sereh)	1
1	salam leaf	1
¾ cup	thin coconut milk	200 ml/7 fl oz
	salt	

1. String the beans if necessary. Trim the ends and cut into short lengths.
2. Heat the oil in a wok and stir fry the chopped onion until transparent. Add the garlic and stir a few times.
3. Add the beans and stir fry for 2 minutes.
4. Add the sambal ulek or sambal trasi, laos powder, sugar, lemon grass and salam leaf.
5. Stir well and pour in the coconut milk and 5 tbsp water. Leave to cook for 8-10 minutes. Remove the wok from the heat and leave to cool until just warm. Taste the beans after cooling and add salt to taste.
6. Remove the lemon grass and the salam leaf immediately before serving.

Cook's tip: add a handful of washed bean sprouts 2 minutes before the dish has finished cooking.

Sambal goreng kol
Spiced Dish with Cabbage

◖▱ 00.10   00.20 ⬤
Serves 4 as side dish

American	Ingredients	Metric/Imperial
2	large coarsely chopped onions	2
1	finely chopped garlic clove	1
1½ tsp	sambal trasi (see page 129)	1½ tsp
2 tbsp	groundnut oil	2 tbsp
¾ lb	white, green, or Savoy cabbage or Chinese leaves cut into narrow strips	350 g/12 oz
1 tsp	laos powder	1 tsp
1 tsp	soft brown sugar	1 tsp
1	blade lemon grass (sereh)	1
1	salam leaf	1
¾ cup	thin coconut milk	200 ml/7 fl oz
	salt	

1. Pound the onions, garlic and sambal trasi in a mortar or food processor to form a paste.
2. Heat the oil in a wok and stir fry the paste for 2 minutes.
3. Add the cabbage and stir fry until the cabbage is soft.
4. Add the laos, sugar, lemon grass, salam leaf and coconut milk. Bring to the boil.
5. Stir well a few times. Reduce the heat and simmer gently for 5 minutes.
6. Taste the sauce and add salt to taste.
7. Remove the lemon grass and salam leaf immediately before serving.

Sambal goreng tomat
Spiced Dish with Tomatoes

◖▱ 00.10   00.10 ⬤
plus cooling time

American	Ingredients	Metric/Imperial
6	large skinned tomatoes	6
2 tbsp	groundnut oil	2 tbsp
1	large chopped onion	1
1	crushed garlic clove	1
1 tsp	sambal ulek (see page 128)	1 tsp
1 tsp	laos powder	1 tsp
1 tbsp	soft brown sugar	1 tbsp
1 tsp	lemon juice	1 tsp
¾ cup	thin coconut milk	200 ml/7 fl oz

1. Cut each tomato into 6 and remove the seeds.
2. Heat the oil in a wok and stir fry the onion until transparent. Add the garlic. Stir well, then add the sambal ulek, laos powder, sugar and lemon juice.
3. Stir in the coconut milk and bring to the boil.
4. Add the pieces of tomato to the boiling liquid and after 1 minute remove the wok from the heat.
5. Leave the contents to cool until just warm before serving.

Cook's tip: to make the sambal goreng tomat more piquant, add a coarsely grated red chili at the same time as the tomatoes.

Sambal goreng tauge
Spiced Dish with Bean Sprouts

◖▱ 00.10   00.07 ⬤
plus cooling time

American	Ingredients	Metric/Imperial
6 oz	bean sprouts	175 g/6 oz
2 tbsp	groundnut oil	2 tbsp
2	large chopped onions	2
2	crushed garlic cloves	2
1 tsp	sambal ulek (see page 128)	1 tsp
1 tsp	sambal trasi (see page 129)	1 tsp
1 tbsp	soft brown sugar	1 tbsp
1	salam leaf	1
1¼ cups	thin coconut milk	300 ml/½ pint
5 tbsp	thick coconut milk	5 tbsp

1. Rinse the bean sprouts in cold water. Remove as many of the skins as possible. Drain well.
2. Heat the oil in a wok and stir fry the onion until transparent. Add the garlic and stir well.
3. Add the sambal ulek, sambal trasi, sugar, salam leaf and thin coconut milk. Bring to the boil and stir well.
4. Add the bean sprouts and stir in the thick coconut milk. Do not allow to come to the boil again.
5. Remove the salam leaf and serve hot or leave the dish to cool until just warm.

Sambal goreng atie ajam
Spiced Dish with Chicken Livers

◖▱ 00.10   00.12 ⬤
plus soaking time

American	Ingredients	Metric/Imperial
½ lb	chicken livers	225 g/8 oz
¾ cup	milk (optional)	200 ml/7 fl oz
3 tbsp	groundnut oil	3 tbsp
1	shredded onion	1
1	finely chopped garlic clove	1
2 tsp	sambal ulek (see page 128)	2 tsp
1 tsp	laos powder	1 tsp
2 tbsp	lemon juice	2 tbsp
1 tsp	soft brown sugar	1 tsp
1	blade lemon grass (sereh)	1
¾ cup	thin coconut milk	200 ml/¾ pint
	salt	

1. Rinse and trim the chicken livers. Soak the livers in milk for about 1 hour. Rinse the livers again in cold running water and dry with kitchen paper.
2. Heat the oil in a wok, add the onion and fry until transparent. Add the garlic and stir well.
3. Add the chicken livers and stir fry for 2 minutes, until the livers change color. Do not overcook.
4. Add the remaining ingredients except the salt.
5. Reduce the heat and simmer gently for 3-5 minutes.
6. Immediately before serving, remove the blade of lemon grass and add salt to taste.

Sambal goreng daging sapie
Spiced Dish with Beef

00.10 Serves 4 as side dish **01.45**

American	Ingredients	Metric/Imperial
¾ lb	lean beef	350 g/12 oz
3 tbsp	groundnut oil	3 tbsp
2	large shredded onions	2
2	finely chopped garlic cloves	2
2 tsp	sambal ulek (see page 128)	2 tsp
1 tsp	laos powder	1 tsp
3 tbsp	lemon juice	3 tbsp
1 tsp	soft brown sugar	1 tsp
1	salam leaf	1
1 cup	thin coconut milk	250 ml/8 fl oz
2 tbsp	thick coconut milk	2 tbsp
	salt	

1. Dry the meat with kitchen paper and cut into ¾ in (1.75 cm) cubes.
2. Heat the oil in a wok, add the onions and stir fry until transparent.
3. Add the garlic and stir well. Add the meat and stir fry until browned on all sides.
4. Add the sambal ulek, laos powder, lemon juice, sugar, salam leaf, and thin coconut milk. Bring to the boil, stirring and tossing continuously.
5. Reduce the heat and cover. Simmer gently for about 1½ hours until the meat is tender. Check from time to time and add a little water if necessary.
6. Add the thick coconut milk and salt to taste. Remove the salam leaf and serve.

Cook's tip: in Indonesia, just before serving, it is common for a little chopped coriander to be added to the dish.
Alternatively, just before removing the pan from the heat, add the diced flesh of 1 or 2 skinned tomatoes.

Left to right: Spiced dish with beef, Spiced dish with eggs, Spiced dish with soybean curd (tofu)

Sambal goreng telor
Spiced Dish with Eggs

00.10 Serves 4 as side dish **00.25**

American	Ingredients	Metric/Imperial
6	eggs	6
2 tbsp	groundnut oil	2 tbsp
1	large shredded onion	1
1	finely chopped garlic clove	1
1 tsp	sambal ulek or sambal trasi (see page 128 or 129)	1 tsp
1 tsp	laos powder	1 tsp
1 tsp	soft brown sugar	1 tsp
2	skinned, diced tomatoes	2
⅔ cup	thin coconut milk	150 ml/¼ pint
	lemon juice	
	salt	

1. Place the eggs in a pan of boiling water and boil for 10 minutes. Cool rapidly in cold water then remove the shells.
2. Heat the oil in a wok, add the onion and stir fry until it begins to change color.
3. Add the garlic, stir well, then add the sambal ulek or sambal trasi, laos powder, sugar, diced tomato and thin coconut milk. Bring to the boil, stirring continuously.
4. Reduce the heat and simmer gently until the diced tomato is very soft.

5. Add 5 tbsp water and bring to the boil, stirring vigorously. Put the eggs in the boiling liquid, reduce the heat and simmer for a few more minutes.

6. Add lemon juice and salt to taste. Halve the eggs. Arrange the egg halves on a warmed dish and pour sauce over.

Cook's tip: 1-2 tbsp of ketyap benteng manis (Indonesian sweet soy sauce) may be added to the sauce to taste to give the sauce a fuller flavor.

Sambal goreng tahoe

Spicy Dish with Soybean Curd (Tofu)

⊏▷ 00.10   00.25
plus standing time

American	Ingredients	Metric/Imperial
1 (2 in)	cube soybean curd (tofu)	1 (5 cm/2 in)
3 tbsp	lemon juice	3 tbsp
1 tsp	salt	1 tsp
2 tbsp	Indonesian sweet soy sauce (ketjap benteng manis)	2 tbsp
3 tbsp	groundnut oil	3 tbsp
1	large shredded onion	1
1	finely chopped garlic clove	1
2 tsp	sambal ulek or sambal trasi (see page 128 or 129)	2 tsp
1 tsp	laos powder	1 tsp
1	blade lemon grass (sereh)	1
⅔ cup	thin coconut milk	150 ml/¼ pint
	freshly ground pepper	

1. Cut the soybean curd (tofu) into ¾ in (1.75 cm) cubes.
2. Put the lemon juice in a bowl and add 3 tbsp water, salt and 1 tbsp sweet soy sauce. Stir until the salt dissolves.
3. Place the bean curd cubes in this marinade, and turn over carefully in the liquid to coat on all sides. Set aside for 1 hour, stirring from time to time. Drain in a strainer (sieve) or colander.
4. Heat the oil, add the soybean curd (tofu) cubes and stir fry until golden brown on all sides. Carefully remove them from the wok and drain again in a colander.
5. Add the onion to the remaining oil and stir fry until the onion begins to change color. Add the garlic, then stir in the sambal ulek or sambal trasi, laos powder, lemon grass and coconut milk. Bring to the boil, reduce the heat and simmer gently for 10 minutes.
6. Heat the soybean curd (tofu) cubes in the sauce.
7. Just before serving remove the blade of lemon grass, add the remaining soy sauce and sprinkle the dish with a little freshly ground pepper.

Bajem sajoer toemis

Spiced Spinach

⊏▷ 00.10   00.00
Serves 4 as side dish

American	Ingredients	Metric/Imperial
1½ lb	spinach	700 g/1½ lb
2 tbsp	groundnut oil	2 tbsp
1	large shredded onion	1
1	finely chopped garlic clove	1
1 tsp	sambal ulek (see page 128)	1 tsp
1 tsp	laos powder	1 tsp
1¼ cups	hot bouillon (stock)	300 ml/1½ pints
1-2 tsp	Indonesian sweet soy sauce (ketyap benteng manis)	1-2 tsp

1. Pick over the spinach and remove any thick stalks. Wash the spinach thoroughly and drain well.
2. Heat the oil in a wok, add the onion and stir fry the onion until it begins to change color.
3. Add the garlic. Stir well, then add the sambal ulek and the spinach.
4. Stir in the laos powder and the bouillon (stock) and bring to the boil.
5. Remove the wok from the heat and stir in soy sauce to taste.
6. Transfer to a warmed dish and serve.

Spiced vegetables

Sajoer lodeh
Spiced Vegetables

◢	00.20	00.20	🍲
	Serves 4 as side dish		

American	Ingredients	Metric/Imperial
½ lb	cauliflower or broccoli	225 g/8 oz
½ lb	French beans or haricots verts	225 g/8 oz
¼ lb	young carrots	125 g/4 oz
¼ lb	snow peas (mange-tout) (optional)	125 g/4 oz
2	peeled potatoes	2
3 tbsp	groundnut oil	3 tbsp
2	finely shredded onions	2
2	finely chopped garlic cloves	2
2 tsp	sambal ulek or sambal trasi (see page 128 or 129)	2 tsp
3	shelled, finely ground macadamia nuts	3
1½ tsp	laos powder	1½ tsp
1 tbsp	soft brown sugar	1 tbsp
1¼ cup	hot bouillon (stock)	300 ml/½ pint
1¼ cups	thin coconut milk	300 ml/½ pint
1	salam leaf	1
2 tbsp	lemon juice	2 tbsp
	salt (optional)	

1. Trim, wash and drain the vegetables thoroughly.
2. Divide the cauliflower or broccoli into small florets and cut the stalks into pieces.
3. Cut the beans into 1½ in (4 cm) pieces.
4. Cut the carrot into slices or strips.
5. Trim the snow peas (mange-tout).
6. Cut the potatoes into slices or strips.
7. Heat the oil in a wok, add the onion and stir fry until transparent.
8. Add the garlic and stir in the sambal ulek or sambal trasi and the finely ground nuts.
9. Add the various well-drained vegetables and stir fry for 1-2 minutes.
10. Add the laos, sugar, bouillon (stock), coconut milk and salam leaf. Bring to the boil then reduce the heat and cook

gently for 10-12 minutes. The vegetables should still be slightly undercooked.
11. Stir the lemon juice into the mixture and add salt to taste.
12. Transfer to a warmed dish and serve.

Bean Sajoer
Spiced French Beans

◢	00.15	00.15	🍲
	Serves 4 as side dish		

American	Ingredients	Metric/Imperial
¾ lb	French beans	350 g/12 oz
2 tbsp	groundnut oil	2 tbsp
1	large shredded onion	1
1	finely chopped garlic clove	1
½ tsp	sambal ulek (see page 128)	½ tsp
1¾ cups	bouillon (stock)	400 ml/14 fl oz
	salt	
	freshly ground black pepper	

1. Trim and string the beans if necessary. Cut into 1½ in (4 cm) lengths.
2. Heat the oil in a wok, add the shredded onion and stir fry until it begins to change color. Add the garlic and stir well.
3. Add the sambal ulek and the beans. Stir well and add the bouillon (stock). Cook gently for 8-10 minutes.

Spiced French beans

4. Add a little salt and/or freshly ground pepper to taste and serve immediately.

Cabbage sajoer toemis

Spiced Cabbage

	00.15	00.15
	Serves 4 as a side dish	

American	Ingredients	Metric/Imperial
½ lb	coarsely shredded white, green or Savoy cabbage	225 g/8 oz
2 tbsp	groundnut oil	2 tbsp
1	large shredded onion	1
1	finely chopped garlic clove	1
½ tsp	sambal ulek or sambal trasi (see page 128 or 129)	½ tsp
1 tsp	laos powder	1 tsp
¼ cups	bouillon (stock)	300 ml/½ pint
2	carrots, cut into very thin strips	2
1 tbsp	thinly sliced celery	1 tbsp

1. Rinse the cabbage and drain well in a colander.
2. Heat the oil in a wok, add the onion and stir fry until it begins to change color.
3. Add the garlic, stir well, then add the sambal ulek or sambal trasi and the cabbage. Stir continuously until the cabbage is just cooked.
4. Add the laos powder and bouillon (stock) and cook gently for 2-3 minutes.
5. Just before serving, stir in the strips of carrot.
6. Transfer to a warmed dish and sprinkle with the celery.

Sajoer asem

Spiced Vegetables with Beef

	00.20	02.45
	Serves 4 as side dish	

American	Ingredients	Metric/Imperial
¾ lb	knuckle of beef	350 g/12 oz
1	salam leaf	1
1	blade lemon grass (sereh)	1
1	blade mace	1
4	lightly crushed black peppercorns	4
	salt	
¼ lb	Chinese cabbage	125 g/4 oz
¼ lb	French beans or haricot verts	125 g/4 oz
1	red bell pepper	1
1	green bell pepper	1
2	thin leeks	2
1	large finely shredded onion	1
1	finely chopped garlic clove	1
1½ tsp	sambal ulek (see page 128)	1½ tsp
1 tsp	laos powder	1 tsp
2 tsp	soft brown sugar	2 tsp
2 tbsp	lemon juice	2 tbsp

1. Place the knuckle of beef in a saucepan with 1¾ cups (400 ml/⅔ pint) cold water. Bring to the boil. Carefully skim the surface of the bouillon (stock) once or twice.
2. Add the salam leaf, lemon grass, mace and peppercorns. Simmer gently, covered for 2-2½ hours.
3. Strain the bouillon (stock) and cut the meat into pieces. Set the meat aside. Season the bouillon (stock) with salt to taste.
4. Cut the cabbage into strips, and the beans into 1½ in (4 cm) pieces.
5. Trim, halve and seed the bell peppers. Cut the flesh into thin strips.
6. Cut the white and yellow part of the leeks into ½ in (1.25 cm) rings.
7. Mix the onion, garlic, sambal ulek, laos powder and sugar into the bouillon (stock). Bring to the boil. Add the beans, and 6 minutes later add the remaining vegetables and the meat.
8. Remove the pan from the heat, stir in the lemon juice and serve.

Cook's tip: a variety of vegetables can be used for this dish, such as: French beans, carrots and cabbage – French beans, eggplants (aubergines) and broccoli – Different types of cabbage and carrots – Dried pulses, boiled, with cabbage and red onions.

Sambal goreng ikan laoet dan oedang

Spiced Dish with Fish and Shrimp (Prawns)

	00.10	00.12
	plus standing time	

American	Ingredients	Metric/Imperial
½ lb	skinned, fillets mackerel or whiting	225 g/8 oz
	salt	
1 tbsp	lemon juice	1 tbsp
5 tbsp	groundnut oil	5 tbsp
1	large coarsely chopped onion	1
1	very finely chopped garlic clove	1
½ tsp	laos powder	½ tsp
½ tsp	ground root ginger	½ tsp
½ tsp	sambal trasi (see page 129)	½ tsp
3 tbsp	lemon juice	3 tbsp
¼ lb	fresh peeled shrimp (prawns)	125 g/4 oz

1. Rinse the fish under cold running water and dry with kitchen paper. Cut into 1 in (2.5 cm) cubes, or into thin strips 2 in (5 cm) in length.
2. Sprinkle the fish with a little salt and the lemon juice and set aside for 15 minutes.
3. Heat 3 tbsp groundnut oil in a wok. Dry the fish and fry, turning regularly, until golden brown on all sides.
4. Remove the fish from the wok, drain on kitchen paper and keep warm.
5. Remove the oil from the wok and wipe clean.
6. Heat the remaining oil in the pan and stir fry the onions until they begin to color.
7. Add the garlic, laos powder, ground ginger, sambal trasi and lemon juice and simmer for 2-3 minutes.
8. Return the fish to the wok. add the shrimp (prawns) and cook, stirring, for about 30 seconds. Do not overcook the shrimp (prawns).
9. Transfer to a warmed dish and serve immediately.

Left to right: Spiced chicken sambal, Spiced pork sambal

Sambal goreng ajam
Spiced Chicken Sambal

00.10   **00.10**
Serves 4 as side dish

American	Ingredients	Metric/Imperial
10 oz	boneless chicken breast	275 g/10 oz
3 tbsp	groundnut oil	3 tbsp
3	medium size roughly chopped onions	3
2	very finely chopped garlic cloves	2
1 tsp	sambal ulek (see page 128)	1 tsp
1 tsp	laos powder	1 tsp
1 tsp	ground root ginger	1 tsp
3 tbsp	lemon juice	3 tbsp
	salt	

1. Dry the chicken with kitchen paper and cut into ½ in (1.25 cm) cubes.
2. Heat the oil in a wok, add the onion and stir fry until transparent.
3. Add the garlic and stir well.
4. Add the pieces of chicken and stir fry until the chicken changes color.
5. Add the sambal ulek, salt, laos powder, ground root ginger, lemon juice and 3 tbsp water.
6. Stir well and simmer for 2-4 minutes.
7. Transfer to a warmed dish and serve.

Sambal goreng babi
Spiced Pork Sambal

00.15   **00.15**
Serves 4 as side dish

American	Ingredients	Metric/Imperial
10 oz	lean pork	275 g/10 oz
3 tbsp	groundnut oil	3 tbsp
2	large shredded onions	2
2	finely chopped garlic cloves	2
1	medium size leek cut into small strips	1
1-2 tsp	sambal ulek or sambal trasi (see page 128 or 129)	1-2 tsp
⅔ cup	bouillon (stock) (optional)	250 ml/¼ pint
2 tbsp	Indonesian sweet soy sauce (ketjap benteng manis)	2 tbsp
	salt	
	freshly ground pepper	

1. Dry the meat with kitchen paper and cut into finger width strips about 1½ in (4 cm) long.
2. Heat the oil in a wok, add the onions and fry until transparent. Add the garlic and stir well.
3. Add the meat and stir fry until the meat has changed color.
4. Add the strips of leek, sambal ulek or sambal trasi and the boiling bouillon (stock). Cover the wok and simmer for 6-8 minutes.
5. Add the soy sauce and add a little salt and pepper to taste and serve.

Sayur kari daging ayam
Chicken and Spiced Vegetables

⊳ 00.10   00.10 ⌂
Serves 4 as side dish

American	Ingredients	Metric/Imperial
1¼ cups	chicken bouillon (stock)	300 ml/½ pint
1¼ cups	thin coconut milk	300 ml/½ pint
½ tsp	sambal ulek (see page 128)	½ tsp
1 tsp	laos powder	1 tsp
1 tsp	ground turmeric	1 tsp
1 tsp	ground root ginger	1 tsp
1 tsp	ground coriander	1 tsp
	pinch ground cumin	
2 tsp	soft brown sugar	2 tsp
¾ lb	shredded white, green or Savoy cabbage	300 g/12 oz
½ lb	carrots, cut into thin strips	225 g/8 oz
2	large peeled potatoes cut into chips	2
½ lb	diced cooked chicken	225 g/8 oz
3 tbsp	lemon juice	3 tbsp
1-2 tsp	Indonesian sweet soy sauce (ketyap benteng manis)	1-2 tsp

1. Bring the bouillon (stock) to the boil with the coconut milk. Add the sambal ulek, laos powder, turmeric, ginger, coriander and cumin.
2. Stir in the sugar and add all the vegetables at the same time. Stir well and cook gently for 6-7 minutes.
3. Add the cooked chicken, bring back to the boil and remove the saucepan from the heat.
4. Add the lemon juice and soy sauce, stir well and serve in a warmed dish.

Special tomato sajoer asem
Spiced Tomatoes with Shrimp (Prawns)

⊳ 00.15   00.08 ⌂
Serves 4 as side dish

American	Ingredients	Metric/Imperial
1¾ cups	chicken bouillon (stock)	400 ml/14 fl oz
1	cake soybean curd (tofu) cut into small cubes	1
1½ lb	small unripe tomatoes	700 g/1½ lb
2	finely shredded onions	2
2	finely chopped garlic cloves	2
1½ tsp	sambal trasi (see page 129)	1½ tsp
1 tsp	laos powder	1 tsp
2 tsp	soft brown sugar	2 tsp
¼ lb	fresh peeled shrimp (prawns)	125 g/¼ lb

1. Bring the bouillon (stock) to the boil. Add the soybean curd (tofu). Reduce the heat, simmer for 3 minutes.
2. Wash the tomatoes and remove the stalks. Put the tomatoes into the bouillon (stock). Add the onions, garlic, sambal

trasi, laos powder and sugar. Stir well and remove as much tomato skin as possible.
3. As soon as the tomatoes have softened add the shrimp (prawns) and immediately remove the pan from the heat.
4. Transfer to a warmed dish and serve.

Sayur kari daging sapi
Beef and Spiced Vegetables

⊳ 00.30   02.15 ⌂
Serves 4 as side dish

American	Ingredients	Metric/Imperial
¾ lb	beef brisket	300 g/12 oz
1	unpeeled garlic clove	1
1	blade lemon grass (sereh)	1
1	salam leaf	1
1	blade mace	1
6	lightly bruised black peppercorns	6
½ lb	French beans or haricots verts	225 g/8 oz
½ lb	white, green or Savoy cabbage	225 g/8 oz
½ lb	young carrots	225 g/8 oz
2	large peeled potatoes	2
1¼ cups	thin coconut milk	300 ml/½ pint
1	large finely chopped onion	2
2	finely chopped garlic cloves	2
1 tsp	sambal ulek (see page 128)	1 tsp
1 tsp	laos powder	1 tsp
1 tsp	ground turmeric	1 tsp
1 tsp	ground root ginger	1 tsp
1 tsp	ground coriander	1 tsp
	pinch ground cumin	
2 tsp	soft brown sugar	2 tsp
2 tbsp	lemon juice	2 tbsp
1-2 tsp	Indonesian sweet soy sauce (ketyap benteng manis)	1-2 tsp
	few coarsely chopped coriander leaves (optional)	

1. Bring the meat to the boil in a saucepan with 2 cups (450 ml/¾ pint) cold water. Skim the surface carefully a few times.
2. Add the unpeeled garlic clove, lemon grass, salam leaf, mace and peppercorns. Simmer very gently for 2 hours (or longer). Strain the bouillon (stock) and put the meat to one side.
3. Clean and wash the vegetables. Cut the beans into 1½ in (4 cm) lengths. Coarsely shred the cabbage and cut the carrots and potatoes into fairly thick slices and then into strips.
4. Bring the bouillon (stock) to the boil with the coconut milk. Add the beans and simmer for 5 minutes.
5. Add the remaining vegetables and spices, except the lemon juice and soy sauce. Stir well and cook for 4-5 minutes.
6. Add the cooked meat and stir in the lemon juice and soy sauce immediately before serving. Remove salam leaf.
7. Serve in a warmed dish and sprinkle with chopped coriander leaves.

Cook's tip: in Indonesia a few finely pounded roasted candle nuts are sometimes added to the dish to give it a milder flavor.

Sweetcorn Soup

	00.05	00.15
	Serves 4	

American	Ingredients	Metric/Imperial
½ lb	canned sweetcorn	225 g/8 oz
1 quart	skimmed chicken bouillon (stock) sharply spiced	1 litre/1¾ pints
¼ lb	cooked chicken	125 g/4 oz
1½ tbsp	cornstarch (cornflour)	1½ tbsp
1 tbsp	Indonesian sweet soy sauce (ketyap benteng manis)	1 tbsp
1	large chopped onion	1
1	finely chopped garlic clove	1
2 tbsp	finely chopped coriander leaves or parsley	2 tbsp

1. Drain the sweet corn.
2. Bring the bouillon (stock) to the boil. Add the sweet corn and simmer gently for 3-4 minutes.
3. Cut the chicken into small pieces. Mix the cornstarch (cornflour) with 2 tbsp cold water and the soy sauce. Stir into the hot bouillon (stock) and add the onion and garlic. Simmer gently for a further 2-3 minutes.
4. Immediately before serving stir the coriander or parsley through the soup.
5. Serve the soup in warmed deep plates or bowls.

Soto ayam (I)

Main Course Soup with Chicken

	00.20	01.00
	Serves 4	

American	Ingredients	Metric/Imperial
1 (2¼ lb)	roasting chicken	1 (1 kg/2¼ lb)
	salt	
	coarsely ground black pepper	
6	sprigs roughly chopped coriander	6
1	large coarsely chopped onion	1
1 tbsp	finely grated fresh root ginger	1 tbsp
2	crushed garlic cloves	2
3 oz	rice vermicelli	75 g/3 oz
2-3 oz	bean sprouts	50-75 g/2-3 oz
2	finely chopped scallions (spring onions)	2
2	sliced hard-cooked (hard-boiled) eggs	2

1. Cut the chicken into 8 or more pieces. Put the pieces in a saucepan with boiling water to just cover. Bring to the boil and skim the surface carefully a few times.
2. Add a little salt (about 1½ tsp), pepper, coriander, onion, root ginger, and garlic. Bring to the boil again. Cover, reduce the heat and simmer gently for 30-40 minutes.
3. Remove the chicken pieces from the pan and leave to cool.
4. Strain the bouillon (stock) through a piece of wet muslin. Taste the bouillon (stock) and add a little salt. Skim off as much fat as possible.

5. Remove the skin and take the chicken meat off the bones. Cut the chicken meat into bite-size pieces.
6. Cook the rice vermicelli as directed on the packet.
7. Wash the bean sprouts in cold water and remove as many of the skins as possible. Drain the bean sprouts well in a colander. Pour 4-6 pints (2-3 litres) boiling water very slowly over them and drain again.
8. Bring the bouillon (stock) to the boil again. Add the chicken pieces and the rice vermicelli.
9. Put the bean sprouts in the bottom of a warmed soup tureen and pour on the soup. Sprinkle the scallions (spring onions) over the soup and float the slices of hard-cooked (hard-boiled) egg on top. Serve immediately.

Soto Madura

Main Course Soup with Chicken and Rice

	00.30	01.15
	Serves 4	

American	Ingredients	Metric/Imperial
1 (2¼ lb)	roasting chicken	1 (1 kg/2¼ lb)
4	large coarsely chopped onions	4
4	chopped garlic cloves	4
6	blades lemon grass (sereh)	6
	salt	
	freshly ground pepper	
3	finely pounded, roasted candle nuts	3
1 tsp	kencur (kenchur)	1 tsp
2 tsp	laos powder	2 tsp
2 tbsp	groundnut oil	2 tbsp
¾ cup	thin coconut milk	200 ml/7 fl oz
¼ lb	rice vermicelli	125 g/4 oz
3 oz	bean sprouts	75 g/3 oz
4	hard-cooked (hard-boiled) eggs	4
2	large, cooked, sliced potatoes	2
4 tbsp	fried onion	4 tbsp
1	lemon, quartered	1
½ lb	dry cooked rice	225 g/8 oz

1. Divide the chicken into 8 or more pieces. Put the pieces in a saucepan with water just to cover. Bring to the boil, skim the surface carefully a few times and add half of the onion, half of the garlic, lemon grass, 2 tsp of salt and a little pepper. Cover the pan and simmer gently for 30-40 minutes.
2. Pound the rest of the onion and garlic to a paste in a mortar or food processor. Add the finely pounded candle nuts, kencur, laos powder and a little salt.
3. Heat the oil in a large wok and stir fry the onion paste until it begins to change color. Remove the wok from the heat and leave to cool.
4. Remove the cooked chicken pieces from the bouillon (stock) and leave to cool. Strain the bouillon (stock) through a piece of wet muslin. Add the coconut milk to the bouillon (stock).
5. Cook the rice vermicelli as directed on the packet.
6. Wash the bean sprouts in cold water. Remove as many of the skins as possible. Drain in a colander then pour 4-6 pints (2-3 litres) boiling water over and drain again.
7. Take the chicken meat off the bones and remove the skin. Cut the chicken into bite-size pieces. Add the bouillon (stock)

to the contents of the wok. Stir well and bring to the boil. Simmer gently for 10 minutes.

8. Shell the eggs, cut them in four and place them on a small dish. Arrange the potatoes, rice vermicelli, chicken, bean sprouts, fried onions and lemon quarters on small dishes.

9. Serve the bouillon in a warmed tureen and hand the dishes of other ingredients separately.

10. Give each guest a large deep bowl into which he or she spoons some of the ingredients from the small dishes and then pour a little bouillon over. Serve the dry cooked rice separately.

Shrimp Bouillon

◼️▷	00.10 Serves 4	00.05 🍲

American	Ingredients	Metric/Imperial
1 quart	skimmed chicken bouillon (stock) sharply spiced	1 litre/1¾ pints
2 tbsp	finely chopped coriander leaves	2 tbsp
2	skinned tomatoes cut into thin strips	2
¼ lb	freshly peeled shrimp (prawns)	125 g/4 oz
½	crushed garlic clove	½
½ tsp	sugar	½ tsp
1 tbsp	lemon juice	1 tbsp
½ tbsp	sambal trasi (optional) (see page 129)	½ tbsp

1. Bring the bouillon (stock) to the boil.

2. Divide the coriander, strips of tomato and shrimp (prawns) between 4 warmed soup plates or bowls.

3. Mix the garlic with the sugar, lemon juice and sambal trasi (if used). Stir until the sugar dissolves. Stir the mixture through the boiling bouillon (stock) immediately before serving. Pour the bouillon into the plates or bowls and serve.

Crab Bouillon

◼️▷	00.15 Serves 4	00.10 🍲

American	Ingredients	Metric/Imperial
¼ lb	crabmeat, thawed if frozen	125 g/4 oz
1 quart	hot, skimmed chicken bouillon (stock) sharply spiced	1 litre/1¾ pints
2	skinned diced tomatoes	2
1 tbsp	chopped leek or scallion (spring onion)	1 tbsp
2	eggs	2
	salt	
	freshly ground pepper	
	pinch sambal ulek (see page 128)	
1 tbsp	groundnut oil	1 tbsp

1. Cut the crab into small pieces and cook in the hot bouillon (stock) for 4 minutes if raw.

2. Divide the diced tomato and the leek or scallion (spring onion) between four warmed soup plates or bowls.

3. Lightly beat the eggs. Add 1 tbsp of water, a little salt, pepper and a touch of sambal ulek.

4. Heat 1 tbsp of oil in a frying pan. Reduce the heat, pour the beaten egg mixture into the pan and fry a thin omelette. Allow the omelette to cool a little in the pan, roll it up quite tightly and set aside for a few minutes.

5. Cut the omelette into very thin strips. Pour the hot bouillon (stock) with pieces of crab into the plates or bowls and divide the omelette strips between them. Serve immediately.

Bouillon with Shrimp (Prawn) Balls

◼️▷	00.10 Serves 4	00.30 🍲

American	Ingredients	Metric/Imperial
1	red bell pepper	1
2	red chilies	2
1 quart	skimmed chicken bouillon (stock) moderately spiced	1 litre/1¾ pints
½ lb	fresh peeled shrimp (prawns)	225 g/8 oz
1½ tbsp	cornstarch (cornflour)	1½ tbsp
1	lightly beaten egg white	1
	salt	
	freshly ground pepper	
	pinch sambal trasi (see page 129)	

1. Trim, halve and seed the red bell pepper and chilies. Cut the flesh into small pieces.

2. Bring the bouillon (stock) to the boil. Add the bell pepper and chilies. Reduce the heat and simmer gently for 20 minutes. Strain the bouillon (stock) through a piece of wet muslin.

3. Chop the shrimp (prawns) very finely. Sprinkle with the cornstarch (cornflour) and knead well together.

4. Add the lightly beaten egg white, a little salt, pepper and a touch of sambal trasi. Knead together then chill for 10 minutes.

5. Using wetted hands, shape into small balls.

6. Bring the bouillon (stock) back to the boil. Add all the balls at the same time. Wait until the bouillon (stock) comes to the boil again then immediately reduce the heat.

7. Serve the soup as soon as the balls float to the surface of the liquid.

Bouillon with shrimp (prawn) balls

Pepesan ikan (I)

Foil Wrapped Fish

	00.20 plus standing time	00.30

American	Ingredients	Metric/Imperial
4	small, cleaned mackerel or fresh herrings heads removed	4
2 tbsp	lemon or lime juice	2 tbsp
½ tsp	salt	½ tsp
2	crushed garlic cloves	2
2 tsp	brown sugar	2 tsp
1 tsp	sambal ulek (see page 128)	1 tsp
2 tbsp	Indonesian salty soy sauce (ketyap benteng asin)	2 tbsp
½ tsp	ground root ginger	½ tsp
	fresh banana leaves or aluminum foil	
1 tbsp	groundnut oil	1 tbsp

1. Rinse the cleaned fish inside and out under cold running water. Dry with kitchen paper.
2. Pour the lemon or lime juice into a small bowl and stir in the salt, stirring until the salt has dissolved. Coat the fish with the mixture on the inside and outside and leave to stand for 15 minutes.
3. Mix the garlic with the sugar, sambal ulek, soy sauce and ground ginger. Lay out four pieces of banana leaf or aluminum foil and grease lightly with a little groundnut oil.
4. Heat the oven to 250°C/475°F/Gas Mark 9 or turn the broiler (grill) to the highest setting.
5. Dry the fish again on the inside and outside with kitchen paper, then coat with the soy sauce mixture. Place on the banana leaves or aluminum foil. Fold the leaves or foil into parcels and secure with cotton thread or wooden cocktail picks.
6. Place the parcels on the shelf in the middle of the hot oven or a rack 5 in (13 cm) below the hot broiler (grill). Turn the parcels over after about 10 minutes and cook for a further 10 minutes.
7. Serve the fish in the parcels accompanied by a dish of dry boiled rice and one or more small vegetable dishes.

Pepesan ikan (II)

Foil Wrapped Fish Fillets

	00.20 plus standing time	00.30

American	Ingredients	Metric/Imperial
1½ lb	cod fillet	700g/1½ lb
2 tbsp	lemon or lime juice	2 tbsp
½ tsp	salt	½ tsp
1-2 tbsp	groundnut oil	1-2 tbsp
1	large chopped onion	1
1	crushed garlic clove	1
1 tsp	sambal trasi (see page 129)	1 tsp
4 tbsp	thick coconut milk	4 tbsp
	fresh banana leaves or aluminum foil	

1. Divide the fish into 4 equal portions. Rinse the fish under cold running water and dry with kitchen paper.
2. Mix the salt with the lemon or lime juice. Stir until the salt

has dissolved. Coat the fish pieces with this mixture on all sides. Leave to stand for 15 minutes.
3. Heat 1 tbsp groundnut oil in a wok and stir fry the onion until it begins to change color.
4. Add the garlic and the sambal trasi. Stir well and add the coconut milk. Stir well again, transfer the mixture to a large, cold plate and allow to cool.
5. Heat the oven to 240°C/475°F/Gas Mark 9 or turn the broiler (grill) to the highest setting.
6. Lay out four pieces of banana leaf or aluminum foil and grease lightly. Dry the fish again with kitchen paper and coat with the coconut mixture.
7. Place the fish on the banana leaves or aluminum foil and divide the remainder of the coconut mixture between them.
8. Fold the leaves or foil into parcels and secure with cotton thread or wooden cocktail picks.
9. Place the parcels on the shelf in the middle of the hot oven or on the rack at a distance of about 5 in (13 cm) below the hot broiler (grill). Turn over after about 10 minutes and cook for a further 6-8 minutes, depending on the thickness of the fish.
10. Serve the fish in the parcels with a dish or dry boiled rice.

Pepesan ikan (III)

Foil Wrapped Sardines

	00.20 plus standing time	00.30

American	Ingredients	Metric/Imperial
12-16	cleaned fresh sardines or small herrings heads removed	12-16
2 tbsp	lemon or lime juice	2 tbsp
½ tsp	salt	½ tsp
6	candle nuts	6
1 tbsp	finely grated fresh root ginger	1 tbsp
1 tbsp	chopped onion	1 tbsp
1	crushed garlic clove	1
1 tsp	sambal ulek (see page 128)	1 tsp
1	trimmed, seeded red bell pepper cut into thin strips	1
4	medium size skinned tomatoes seeded, cut into thin strips	4
	fresh banana leaves or aluminum foil	
1 tbsp	groundnut oil	1 tbsp

1. Rinse the cleaned fish under cold running water and dry the inside and outside with kitchen paper.
2. Mix the lemon or lime juice with the salt and stir until the salt has dissolved. Coat the inside and outside of the fish with the mixture. Leave to stand for 15 minutes.
3. Roast the candle nuts for 5-8 minutes on a baking sheet in the middle of a hot oven. Shell them and pound them finely in a mortar.
4. Add 2 tbsp water, the root ginger, onion, garlic, and sambal ulek. Mix well to form a fairly smooth paste.
5. Add the strips of bell pepper and tomato and mix well.
6. Heat the oven to 250°C/475°F/Gas Mark 9 or turn the broiler (grill) to the highest setting.
7. Dry the pieces of fish again with kitchen paper. Lay out four pieces of banana leaf or aluminum foil and grease lightly with a little oil.
8. Place the fish on the banana leaves or aluminum foil (3 or 4 to a parcel). Divide the bell pepper and tomato mixture between the fish.

9. Secure the parcels with cotton thread or wooden cocktail picks. Place the parcels on the shelf in the middle of the hot oven or on the rack at a distance of about 5 in (13 cm) below the hot broiler (grill). Turn over after about 10 minutes and cook for a further 6-8 minutes.

10. Serve the fish in the parcels accompanied by dry boiled rice and a medium spiced sayur or similar.

Ikan bumbu santen

Fried Fish in Coconut Sauce

	00.10 plus standing time	00.20

American	Ingredients	Metric/Imperial
4	small, skinned filleted mackerel or red mullet	4
2 tbsp	lemon or lime juice	2 tbsp
½ tsp	salt	½ tsp
⅔ cup	groundnut oil	180 ml/¼ pint
2	large chopped onions	2
2	very finely chopped garlic cloves	2
1 tbsp	finely grated fresh root ginger	1 tbsp
1 tsp	sambal ulek or sambal trasi (see pages 128 or 129)	1 tsp
1 tsp	soft brown sugar	1 tsp
1 tbsp	Indonesian salty soy sauce (ketyap benteng asin)	1 tbsp
¾ cup	thin coconut milk	200 ml/7 fl oz
5 tbsp	thick coconut milk	5 tbsp
1	seeded, red chili	1

1. Rinse the fish under cold running water and dry with kitchen paper.

2. Mix the salt with the lemon or lime juice, stir until the salt has dissolved. Coat the fish with the mixture and leave to stand for 15 minutes.

3. Heat 2 tbsp oil in a wok and stir fry the onions until beginning to change color. Add the garlic and root ginger and stir well.

4. Add the sambal, sugar, soy sauce and thin coconut milk. Bring to the boil, stirring constantly. Reduce the heat and simmer gently for 5 minutes.

5. Heat the remainder of the oil in a a second wok or frying pan.

6. Dry the fillets again with kitchen paper. Quickly fry in the hot oil until golden brown on both sides. Drain for a moment on kitchen paper and arrange on a warmed serving dish.

7. Add the coconut milk to the hot sauce. Bring to boiling point again, stirring. Add a little salt to the sauce, if necessary then pour the boiling sauce over the fish and serve immediately, garnished with a red chili 'flower'.

Foil wrapped fish fillets

Ikan bumbu katyang
Fried Fish in Peanut Sauce

00.10 plus standing time   00.20

American	Ingredients	Metric/Imperial
1¼ lb	cod fillet	575 g/1¼ lb
3 tbsp	lemon or lime juice	3 tbsp
½ tsp	salt	½ tsp
1 tbsp	Indonesian salty soy sauce (ketyap benteng asin)	1 tbsp
1 tbsp	Indonesian sweet soy sauce (ketyap benteng manis)	1 tbsp
6 tbsp	thick coconut milk	6 tbsp
2 tbsp	peanut butter	2 tbsp
6 tbsp	groundnut oil	6 tbsp
1	large chopped onion	1
	freshly ground black pepper	
1 tbsp	finely chopped coriander leaves or parsley	1 tbsp
1	small, seeded red chili cut into thin strips	1

1. Cut the fish into four equal portions. Rinse the fish under cold running water and dry with kitchen paper.
2. Mix the salt with 2 tbsp lemon or lime juice and stir until the salt has dissolved. Coat the fish all over with the mixture. Leave to stand for 15 minutes.
3. Put the soy sauces, 1 tbsp lemon or lime juice, coconut milk and peanut butter into a small saucepan. Stir well and bring to the boil, stirring constantly until the sauce thickens. If the sauce is too thick, add 1 or more tbsp boiling water.
4. Heat the oil in a wok or frying pan and fry the onion until transparent.
5. Dry the fish again with kitchen paper and sprinkle with a little pepper. Fry in the hot oil until golden brown on all sides.
6. Remove as much oil as possible from the pan and pour in the hot sauce. Spoon the sauce over the fish and simmer very gently for 2-3 minutes.
7. Transfer the fish to warmed plates, pour the remaining sauce over the pieces of fish and sprinkle coriander leaves or parsley and strips of red chili on top. Serve immediately.

Gulai Padang (I)
Padang Braised Fish

00.10 plus standing time   00.20

American	Ingredients	Metric/Imperial
4	mackerel fillets	4
½ tsp	salt	½ tsp
4 tbsp	lemon or lime juice	4 tbsp
2 tbsp	groundnut oil	2 tbsp
2 large	chopped onions	2
2 tsp	sambal ulek (see page 128)	2 tsp
1 tsp	laos powder	1 tsp
2 tsp	ground turmeric	2 tsp
1 tsp	finely chopped basil	1 tsp
1	blade lemon grass	1
	salt	

Padang braised fish

1. Rinse the fish under cold running water and dry with kitchen paper. Cut each fish into 5 or 6 slices.
2. Mix the salt with 2 tbsp lemon or lime juice and stir until the salt has dissolved. Coat the slices of fish with the mixture. Leave to stand for 15 minutes.
3. Heat the oil in a wok and stir fry the onion until golden yellow. Add the sambal, laos, turmeric, 2 tbsp lemon or lime juice and basil. Stir well. Leave the mixture to cool, then pound it in a mortar or food processor to form a smooth paste.
4. Put the paste in a wide saucepan and add 1½ cups (350 ml/12 fl oz) boiling water. Bring slowly to the boil, stirring constantly. Boil gently for 5 minutes.
5. Add the blade of lemon grass and salt to taste and place the fish slices in the liquid. Cover the saucepan and simmer very gently for 12-15 minutes.
6. Serve the fish in the cooking liquid.

Gulai Padang II
Padang Braised Fish 11

00.15 plus standing time   00.20

American	Ingredients	Metric/Imperial
4	mackerel fillets	4
2 tbsp	lemon or lime juice	2 tbsp
½ tsp	salt	½ tsp
3 tbsp	groundnut oil	3 tbsp
3	large chopped onions	3
3	very finely chopped garlic cloves	3
2	red chilies	2
2	green chilies	2
2 tbsp	Indonesian sweet soy sauce (ketyap benteng manis)	2 tbsp
2 tsp	ground turmeric	2 tsp
1	blade lemon grass	1
	salt	

1. Rinse the fish under cold running water and dry with kitchen paper. Cut each fish into 5 or 6 slices.

2. Mix the lemon or lime juice with the salt. Stir until the salt has dissolved. Rub the slices of fish with the mixture. Leave to stand for at least 15 minutes.

3. Heat the oil in a wok and stir fry the onion until golden yellow. Add the garlic and stir fry for a further minute. Cool and pound to a smooth pulp in a mortar or food processor.

4. Rinse the chilies, trim, cut them in two lengthwise and seed. Cut the chilies into very thin strips.

5. Put the chili strips into a wide saucepan with the onion pulp, soy sauce, turmeric and lemon grass. Stir well and add 1½ cups (350 ml/12 fl oz) boiling water. Bring slowly to the boil, stirring constantly.

6. Salt lightly and add the slices of fish to the liquid. Bring back to the boil, cover the saucepan and simmer gently for 12-15 minutes.

7. Remove the slices of fish from the liquid with a skimmer and place them on a warmed dish.

8. Boil the braising liquid rapidly to ¾ of the original quantity. Remove the lemon grass.

9. Pour the liquid over the fish and serve hot.

Manado braised fish

Gulai Manado
Manado Braised Fish

American	Ingredients	Metric/Imperial
1 lb	turbot or cod fillets	450 g/1 lb
2 tbsp	lemon juice or lime juice	2 tbsp
½ tsp	salt	½ tsp
8	pete beans (bottled)	8
2 tbsp	groundnut oil	2 tbsp
2	chopped onions	2
1	very finely chopped garlic clove	1
1 tsp	sambal ulek (see page 128)	1 tsp
2	green chilies	2
1 tsp	laos powder	1 tsp
1 tsp	sugar	1 tsp
2	salam leaves	2
	salt	
¼ lb	fresh, peeled shrimp (prawns)	125 g/4 oz

1. Rinse the fish under cold running water. Dry with kitchen paper and cut into 1 in (2.5 cm) cubes.

2. Add the salt to the lemon or lime juice and stir until the salt has dissolved. Sprinkle over the fish cubes and turn over carefully. Leave to stand for 15 minutes.

3. Rinse the pete beans under cold running water. Cut into very thin strips.

4. Heat the oil and stir fry the onion until golden yellow. Add the garlic and fry for a further minute. Leave to cool then add the sambal and pound to a smooth pulp in a mortar or food processor.

5. Rinse the green chilies, trim and cut them into thin rings.

6. Put the onion pulp, pete beans, chilies, laos, sugar and salam leaves in a wide saucepan. Add 1¼ cups (300 ml/½ pint) boiling water and bring to the boil, stirring constantly.

7. Add salt to taste and add the cubes of fish to the liquid. Reduce the heat and simmer gently for 4-5 minutes.

8. Carefully stir in the shrimp (prawns) and serve immediately.

Ikan colo
Broiled (Grilled) Fish with Vegetables

American	Ingredients	Metric/Imperial
4	cleaned mackerel	4
2 tbsp	lemon juice	2 tbsp
½ tsp	salt	½ tsp
¼ lb	French beans or haricots verts	125 g/4 oz
1	small Chinese cabbage, iceberg lettuce or paksoi	1
1	medium size eggplant (aubergine)	1
3 tbsp	groundnut oil	3 tbsp
1	large chopped onion	1
1	finely chopped garlic clove	1
1 tsp	sambal ulek (see page 128)	1 tsp
3 tbsp	peanut butter	3 tbsp
¾ cup	thin coconut milk	200 ml/7 fl oz
2 tbsp	lemon or lime juice	2 tbsp

1. Rinse the mackerel under cold running water and dry with kitchen paper.

2. Dissolve the salt in the lemon juice and coat the fish inside and outside with the mixture. Leave to stand for 15 minutes.

3. Rinse the beans, trim and string them, if necessary. Cook for 4-5 minutes in salted boiling water. Drain and leave to cool.

4. Clean the Chinese leaves or iceberg lettuce. Shred the leaves finely. Place in a colander and very slowly pour several quarts/litres boiling water over. Drain and leave to cool.

5. Rinse the eggplant (aubergine). Trim the end and broil (grill) the eggplant (aubergine) under a hot broiler (grill) or over a barbecue until almost black. Peel and cut into thin slices.

6. Heat the oil in a wok and fry the onion until it begins to change color. Add the garlic and sambal ulek. Stir well a few times and add the peanut butter and coconut milk. Bring to the boil and stir in the lemon or lime juice. Leave the sauce to cool until just warm.

7. Dry the fish again with kitchen paper. Brush with a little oil and broil (grill) for 10-12 minutes under a hot broiler (grill) or over a barbecue until golden brown.

8. Place the fish in the center of a large platter. Arrange the vegetables around the fish and serve the sauce separately.

Ikan dan sayur
Fish with Vegetables

00.20 plus standing time   **00.15**

American	Ingredients	Metric/Imperial
4	mackerel or red mullet fillets	4
	salt	
2	peeled onions	2
4	red chilies	4
¼ lb	French beans or haricots verts	125 g/4 oz
¼ lb	canned bamboo shoots	125 g/4 oz
2	very finely chopped garlic cloves	2
1 tsp	finely grated fresh root ginger	1 tsp
2 tbsp	Indonesian salty soy sauce (ketyap benteng asin)	2 tbsp
4 tbsp	groundnut oil	4 tbsp
4	small skinned tomatoes cut into 'flowers'	4

1. Rinse the fish under cold running water and dry with kitchen paper. Sprinkle with a little salt and leave to stand for 15 minutes.
2. Chop one onion and cut the other into 8 segments. Loosen the layers of the onion segments.
3. Rinse the chilies, trim, halve and seed. Cut them into thin strips.
4. Trim the beans, string if necessary and cut into 1 in (2.5 cm) lengths.
5. Drain the bamboo shoots well and cut into thin strips.
6. Add the garlic, ginger and soy sauce to the chopped onion. Mix well together and pound into a smooth pulp in a mortar or food processor.
7. Heat the oil in a wok. Dry the fish again with kitchen paper and quickly fry the fillets on both sides until golden brown. Drain on kitchen paper.
8. Fry the onion pulp in the remaining oil until golden brown. Add the pieces of onion, chilies and beans. Stir fry for 2 minutes.
9. Add the bamboo shoot strips and 1 cup (250 ml/8 fl oz) boiling water. Stir well and bring to the boil. Reduce the heat and boil gently for 2 minutes.
10. Place the fried fillets on warmed plates and spoon over the hot sauce and vegetables. Garnish with tomato flowers and serve.

Left to right: Fish with vegetables,
Fish and shrimp (prawn) rissoles,
Surabaya cabbage rolls

Pergadel ikan dan udang

Fish and Shrimp (Prawn) Rissoles

00.20
plus cooling time

00.30

American	Ingredients	Metric/Imperial
1 lb	whiting fillets	450 g/1 lb
	salt	
1	scrubbed, sliced lemon	1
¼ lb	fresh peeled shrimp (prawns)	125 g/4 oz
1-2 tbsp	groundnut oil	1-2 tbsp
1	large chopped onion	1
1	crushed garlic clove	1
	freshly ground black pepper	
2	beaten eggs	2
4	large boiled, mashed potatoes	4
6-8 tbsp	breadcrumbs	6-8 tbsp
	oil for deep frying	

1. Rinse the fish under cold running water. Bring 2 cups (450 ml/¾ pint) water to the boil in a saucepan. Add ½ tsp salt and the lemon slices. Boil gently for 3 minutes.
2. Add the fish to the hot liquid and boil for 2 minutes.
3. Leave the fish to cool in the cooking liquid. Remove from the liquid and drain. Mash the fish finely with a fork and chop the shrimp (prawns) finely.
4. Heat 1 tbsp oil in a wok and stir fry the onion until it begins to change color. Add the garlic, a little pepper and salt and stir well. Remove the wok from the heat and add the cooked fish, shrimp (prawns) and half the egg. Stir in the mashed potato to make a coherent mass. Set aside until cold.
5. Shape 12 rissoles from the cold mixture. Dip them into the remaining beaten egg and roll them in the breadcrumbs.
6. Heat the remaining oil in a frying pan until very hot, fry the rissoles 3-4 at a time until golden brown and serve.

Ikan dan kol dari Surabaya

Surabaya Cabbage Rolls

00.20
plus standing and cooling time

00.35

American	Ingredients	Metric/Imperial
1 ¼ lb	cod fillet	575 g/1 ¼ lb
½ tsp	salt	½ tsp
2 tbsp	lemon or lime juice	2 tbsp
1	small white, green or savoy cabbage	1
4 tbsp	groundnut oil	4 tbsp
1	large chopped onion	1
1	finely chopped garlic clove	1
1 tsp	laos powder	1 tsp
2 tsp	sambal ulek (see page 128)	2 tsp
2 tsp	soft brown sugar	2 tsp
1	lightly beaten egg	1

1. Rinse the fish under cold running water and dry with kitchen paper. Chop the fish very finely.
2. Dissolve the salt in the lemon or lime juice and mix with the fish. Leave to stand for 30 minutes.
3. Take 12 good leaves from the cabbage. Remove the coarsest veins and boil the leaves for 5 minutes in plenty of salted water. Drain the leaves and set aside to cool. Shred ½ lb (225 g/8 oz) cabbage.
4. Heat 2 tbsp of oil in a wok and stir fry the onion until transparent. Add the garlic and shredded cabbage and stir fry for 3 minutes.
5. Add a little salt, the laos, sambal ulek and sugar. Stir well a few times.
6. Remove from the heat and add the fish and the lightly beaten egg. Stir well.
7. Preheat the oven to 200°C/400°/Gas Mark 6 and place a shelf a little below the middle of the oven.
8. Spread the drained cabbage leaves on a board or worktop. Divide the fish and cabbage mixture between the leaves, roll up and secure them with wooden cocktail picks.
9. Place the rolled up leaves side by side in an oiled ovenproof dish. Sprinkle a little oil on top and cover the dish with a lid or aluminum foil.
10. Bake for 20-25 minutes and serve.

Shrimp (prawns) and pineapple

Kari udang

Shrimp (Prawn) Curry

00.10 Serves 4   **00.12**

American	Ingredients	Metric/Imperial
1 lb	freshly peeled shrimp (prawns)	450 g/1 lb
	salt	
	freshly ground pepper	
1 tbsp	lemon or lime juice	1 tbsp
1 tbsp	groundnut oil	1 tbsp
1	chopped onion	1
1 tbsp	finely grated fresh root ginger	1 tbsp
1 tsp	ground turmeric	1 tsp
2 tsp	sambal trasi (see page 129)	2 tsp
6	roasted, finely ground candle nuts	6
1 tsp	soft brown sugar	1 tsp
1¼ cups	thin coconut milk	300 ml/½ pint
1 tbsp	finely chopped coriander leaves or parsley	1 tbsp

1. Sprinkle the shrimp (prawns) with a little salt, pepper and the lemon or lime juice. Leave to stand for 10 minutes. Turning carefully occasionally.
2. Heat the oil in a wok and stir fry the onion until beginning to change color. Add the root ginger, turmeric, sambal trasi, candle nuts and sugar. Stir for 1 minute.
3. Add the coconut milk, stir well and simmer gently for 3-4 minutes.
4. Add the shrimp (prawns), stir well and serve immediately in a warmed dish, sprinkled with coriander leaves or parsley.

Oedang pangang

Broiled (Grilled) Prawns

00.10 Serves 4   **00.15**

American	Ingredients	Metric/Imperial
8	king prawns, thawed if frozen	8
2-3 tbsp	groundnut oil	2-3 tbsp

1. Turn the broiler (grill) to the highest setting. Rinse the prawns under cold running water and dry with kitchen paper. Cut along the length of the underside and carefully remove the black thread. Cut off the legs but leave on the shell and tail. Brush all over with oil.
2. Brush the broiler (grill) rack with oil. Place the prawns on the rack and place about 4 in (10 cm) from the heat. Broil (grill) the prawns for 12-15 minutes, turning after 6-7 minutes, and brush with a little more oil.
3. Serve hot with a light sweet and sour sauce. (see page 147)
Cook's tip: the prawns can be cooked over a barbecue. If a few coconut shells are added to the barbecue wood, the dish will gain the authentic Indonesian aroma and a typically Indonesian flavor.

3. Heat the oil in a wok and stir fry the shrimp (prawns) for 2 minutes. Remove them from the pan and keep warm.
4. Add the garlic to the oil in the pan. Stir well a few times. Add the strips of bell pepper, pineapple cubes and sambal ulek. Stir fry for 1 minute.
5. Add the reserved pineapple juice and 1 cup (250 ml/8 fl oz) boiling water. Stir well and simmer gently for 3 minutes.
6. Add the soy sauce, sugar and lemon or lime juice. Stir well and add the shrimp (prawns).
7. Bring to the boil and serve immediately on a warmed dish, garnished with a few sprigs of coriander.

Light Sweet and Sour Sauce

	00.05	00.05
	Serves 4	

American	Ingredients	Metric/Imperial
1½ tbsp	tomato purée	1½ tbsp
1 tsp	sambal ulek (see page 128)	1 tsp
2 tbsp	lemon juice	2 tbsp
2 tbsp	Indonesian sweet soy sauce (ketyap benteng manis)	2 tbsp
2 tsp	soft brown sugar	2 tsp
2 tsp	cornstarch (cornflour)	2 tsp
1 tbsp	finely grated fresh root ginger (optional)	1 tbsp

1. Put ¾ cup (200 ml/7 fl oz) water in a pan and bring to the boil. Add the tomato purée, sambal ulek, lemon juice, soy sauce and sugar.
2. Mix the cornstarch (cornflour) with 2 tbsp water and stir into the sauce.
3. Cook, stirring until the sauce thickens.
4. Stir in the grated root ginger if liked and serve the sauce hot.

Udang nanas

Shrimp (Prawns) and Pineapple

	00.15	00.10
	Serves 4	

American	Ingredients	Metric/Imperial
1	small, slightly under-ripe pineapple	1
	salt	
1	red bell pepper	1
2 tbsp	groundnut oil	2 tbsp
1 lb	medium size, peeled cooked shrimp (prawns)	450 g/1 lb
4	very finely chopped garlic cloves	4
2 tsp	sambal ulek (see page 128)	2 tsp
1 tbsp	Indonesian salty soy sauce (ketyap benteng asin)	1 tbsp
2 tbsp	soft brown sugar	2 tbsp
2 tsp	lemon or lime juice	2 tsp
	few sprigs coriander (optional)	

1. Peel the pineapple and cut into four sections. Remove the hard core from each pieces. Cut the pieces into ½ in (1.25 cm) cubes. Reserve any juice. Sprinkle the pineapple cubes with a little salt.
2. Trim, halve and seed the bell pepper and cut the flesh into thin strips.

Binte biloehoeta

Shrimp (Prawns) with Corn and Tomato in Spicy Coconut Sauce

	00.15	00.20
	Serves 4	

American	Ingredients	Metric/Imperial
¾ lb	fresh peeled shrimp (prawns)	350 g/12 oz
	salt	
	freshly ground pepper	
1 (½ lb)	can cooked, drained corn	1 (225 g/8 oz)
1 tsp	soft brown sugar	1 tsp
4	large, skinned tomatoes cut into segments	4
2	dried chilies	2
1	sliced hard-cooked (hard-boiled) egg	1
3 oz	desiccated coconut	75 g/3 oz
2 tsp	Indonesian salty soy sauce (ketyap benteng asin) (optional)	2 tsp
1	squeezed lemon	1
4	finely sliced scallions (spring onions)	4

1. Season the shrimp (prawns) with a little salt and pepper. Stir and leave to stand for at least 10 minutes.
2. Bring 1¾ cups (400 ml/14 fl oz) water to the boil. Add ½ tsp salt and the corn, sugar and tomato. Cook gently for 3 minutes.
3. Crumble the dried chilies and together with the egg grind to a paste in a mortar. Add the paste to the contents of the pan.
4. Sprinkle with coconut, stirring continuously. Reduce the heat and simmer gently for 10 minutes. Try the sauce and add a little salt, pepper and soy sauce to taste.
5. Add the lemon juice and shrimp (prawns) and stir well. As soon as the shrimp (prawns) are heated through, transfer to a warmed dish and serve sprinkled with the scallions (spring onions.)

Paprika dan oedang (I)

Shrimp (Prawn) Stuffed Bell Peppers

00.15 plus standing time   **00.10**

American	Ingredients	Metric/Imperial
4	small red or green bell peppers	4
	salt	
¾ lb	fresh peeled shrimp (prawns)	350 g/12 oz
1	egg	1
2 tsp	cornstarch (cornflour)	2 tsp
½ cup	boiled rice	50 g/2 oz
	freshly ground pepper	
1	finely chopped garlic clove	1
1 tsp	sambal ulek (see page 128)	1 tsp
1 tsp	soft brown sugar	1 tsp
1 tsp	Indonesian salty soy sauce (ketyap benteng asin)	1 tsp
2-3 tbsp	groundnut oil	2-3 tbsp

1. Trim, halve lengthwise and seed the bell peppers.
2. Bring some lightly salted water to the boil. Remove from the heat, add the bell peppers and leave to soak for a few minutes. Drain in a colander and leave to cool.
3. Chop or grind (mince) the shrimp (prawns) very finely.
4. Lightly beat the egg and add the cornstarch (cornflour). Stir well. Add 1-2 tbsp water if necessary.
5. Add the rice to the finely chopped shrimp (prawns). Add salt, pepper, garlic, sambal, sugar, soy sauce and the egg mixture. Quickly work together with the wet fingers. Leave to stand in a cool place for a 15 minutes.
6. Set the oven to 220°F/425°C/Gas Mark 7.
7. Fill the bell peppers with the shrimp (prawn) mixture. Brush the filling and the outside of the bell peppers with oil.
8. Place the bell peppers on an oiled baking tray and bake for 10-12 minutes. Serve hot.

Perdekel Oedang Makasar

Steamed Ground (minced) Prawn Balls (Makasar)

00.20 plus standing time   **00.15**

American	Ingredients	Metric/Imperial
¼ lb	whiting or mackerel fillet	125 g/4 oz
¾ lb	peeled fresh shrimp (prawns)	350 g/12 oz
1	egg	1
1 tbsp	cornstarch (cornflour)	1 tbsp
¼ tsp	sambal trasi (see page 129)	¼ tsp
½ tbsp	lemon juice	½ tbsp
	salt	
	freshly ground pepper	
1 tsp	soft brown sugar	1 tsp
1 tbsp	groundnut or sesame oil	1 tbsp
8	salam leaves	8
1 tbsp	sea salt	1 tbsp

1. Rinse the fish under cold running water and dry with kitchen paper. Grind (mince) the fish and shrimp (prawns) very finely.
2. Lightly beat the egg and stir in the cornstarch (cornflour).
3. Mix the sambal with the lemon juice. Put the shrimp (prawn) and fish mixture in a bowl. Add the egg mixture and the sambal mixture and stir well. Add a little salt and pepper to taste, and the sugar. Set aside in a cool place for 15 minutes.
4. Form the mixture into 12 balls. Brush the perforated base of a steamer with the oil. Place the shrimp (prawn) balls on the base.
5. Bring 1¼ cups (300 ml/½ pint) water to the boil in a pan. Add the salam leaves and the sea salt to the water and boil gently for 5 minutes. Remove the salam leaves.
6. Place the steamer over the pan of boiling water, cover with the lid and steam the shrimp (prawn) balls for 10-12 minutes until cooked. Remove the salam leaves.
7. Serve the shrimp (prawn) balls hot or completely cold as a side dish.

Oedang bandung

Shrimps (Prawns) with Cauliflower

00.15 Serves 4   **00.20**

American	Ingredients	Metric/Imperial
¾ lb	fresh peeled shrimp (prawns)	350 g/12 oz
	salt	
	freshly ground pepper	
1½ tbsp	lemon juice	1½ tbsp
1½ tbsp	groundnut oil	1½ tbsp
1	large chopped onion	1
1 tsp	sambal ulek (see page 128)	1 tsp
	pinch soft brown sugar	
1	medium size cauliflower divided into small florets	1
2 tsp	cornstarch (cornflour)	2 tsp
4	chopped scallions (spring onions) or piece of leek	4
1 tbsp	finely chopped celery	1 tbsp

1. Sprinkle the shrimp (prawns) with a little salt, pepper and the lemon juice. Leave to stand for at least 10 minutes turning occasionally.
2. Heat the oil and fry the onion until transparent. Add the sambal ulek and sugar and stir.
3. Add the cauliflower florets, stir fry for 2 minutes then 1¼ cups (300 ml/½ pint) water and bring to the boil. Cook gently for 5 minutes.
4. Mix the cornstarch (cornflour) with 2 tbsp cold water and stir into the contents of the wok and bring back to the boil. Cook, stirring until the sauce has thickened slightly. Taste the sauce and add a little salt, if necessary.
5. Stir the scallion (spring onion) or leek and celery into the dish. Simmer gently for 1 minute. Add the shrimp (prawns), stir well and serve as soon as the shrimp (prawns) are heated through.

Ikan cuka dan nanas

Fish in Sour Sauce with Pineapple

⊳ 00.15   00.20 🍲
plus drying, cooling and marinating

American	Ingredients	Metric/Imperial
1½ lb	cod or mackerel fillets	700 g/1½ lb
8 tbsp	lemon or lime juice	8 tbsp
	salt	
6 tbsp	groundnut oil	6 tbsp
3 tbsp	coarsely grated fresh root ginger	3 tbsp
½ tsp	laos powder	½ tsp
2 tsp	sambal ulek (see page 128)	2 tsp
2	salam leaves	2
24	small peeled onions or shallots	24
½	peeled pineapple cut into strips	½
12	red chilies	12
2	chopped scallions (spring onions) (optional)	2

1. Rinse the fish under cold running water and dry with kitchen paper. Divide into 8-12 pieces of equal size and rub with a mixture of 1 tbsp lemon or lime juice and ½ tbsp salt. Leave the pieces of fish in a draughty place to dry for 15 minutes.
2. Heat the oil in a large frying pan and fry the pieces of fish a few at a time, until brown and fully cooked. Drain on kitchen paper.
3. Bring 2¼ cup (500 ml/18 fl oz) water to the boil in a saucepan. Add 1 tsp salt, the root ginger, laos, sambal ulek, salam leaves, onions or shallots, pineapple strips and the red chilies. Simmer gently for 10 minutes.
4. Remove the salam leaves, add the remaining lemon or lime juice and bring back to the boil. Remove the pan from the heat and leave to cool.
5. Put the pieces of fish in a dish and pour over the sauce. The fish should be just covered by the liquid. Cover the dish and chill for 12 hours.
6. Serve cold or reheat immediately before serving.

Toemis ikan dan oedang tjampoer djagoeng

Fish and Shrimp (Prawns) with Corn

⊳ 00.10   00.12 🍲
Serves 4

American	Ingredients	Metric/Imperial
¾ lb	mackerel fillets	350 g/12 oz
	salt	
¾ lb	cooked, drained sweetcorn	350 g/12 oz
2 tbsp	groundnut oil	2 tbsp
1	large chopped onion	1
2	very finely chopped garlic cloves	2
2 tsp	Java curry powder	2 tsp
1½ tsp	sambal ulek (see page 128)	1½ tsp
1	red bell pepper trimmed, seeded cut into thin strips	1
1	green bell pepper trimmed, seeded, cut into thin strips	1
6 oz	fresh peeled shrimp (prawns)	175 g/6 oz
1 tbsp	lemon or lime juice	1 tbsp
	few sprigs coriander	

1. Rinse the fish under cold running water and cut the fillets into finger-width strips.
2. Bring ¾ cup (200 ml/8 fl oz) water to the boil. Add ½ tsp salt and the corn and simmer for 5 minutes. Drain the corn well.
3. Heat the oil in a wok and stir fry the onion until transparent. Add the garlic and curry powder. Stir in the sambal ulek and strips of bell pepper.
4. Add ¾ cup (200 ml/7 fl oz) boiling water. Stir well and add the strips of fish. Simmer gently for 3 minutes.
5. Stir in the corn and shrimp (prawns) and heat through.
6. Add salt to taste and stir in the lemon or lime juice.
7. Transfer to a warmed serving dish and serve immediately garnished with coriander sprigs.

Fish and shrimp (prawns) with corn

Redang telor
Spiced Eggs (I)

00.10 Serves 4 as side dish   **00.15**

American	Ingredients	Metric/Imperial
4	shelled, hard-cooked (hard-boiled) eggs	4
1	finely chopped onion	1
1	crushed garlic clove	1
1 tsp	sambal ulek (see page 128)	1 tsp
½ tsp	laos powder	½ tsp
2	salam leaves	2
½ tsp	ground turmeric	½ tsp
½ tsp	ground ginger	½ tsp
1	blade lemon grass (sereh)	1
1 tsp	salt	1 tsp
1 tsp	soft brown sugar	1 tsp
¾ cup	coconut milk	200 ml/7 fl oz

1. Using a thick needle, pierce as many holes in the eggs as possible, so that the seasoning can penetrate deep inside.
2. Bring to the boil 5 tbsp water and add the onion, garlic, sambal, laos powder, salam leaves, turmeric, ground ginger, lemon grass, salt and sugar. Stir thoroughly and simmer gently for 5 minutes.
3. Mix in the coconut milk and place the eggs in the sauce. Cook until almost all the liquid has evaporated and the eggs are surrounded by a thick mixture.
4. Remove the blade of lemon grass and the salam leaves and serve the eggs and the sauce in a warmed dish.

Gulai telor bukittinggi
Poached Eggs with Green Chilies

00.05 Serves 4   **00.10**

American	Ingredients	Metric/Imperial
1¾ cups	thin coconut milk	400 ml/14 fl oz
1 tsp	sambal ulek (see page 128)	1 tsp
4	green chilies	4
1	large finely chopped onion	1
1 tsp	ground turmeric	1 tsp
	salt	
8	eggs	8
2	onions cut into rings fried until golden brown	2

1. Bring the coconut milk to the boil in a wok. Add the sambal ulek, stir and simmer gently for a few minutes.
2. Rinse the chilies, trim and slice them into rings. Stir the chili, onion and turmeric into the coconut milk, adding salt to taste.
3. Break the eggs on the side of the wok and carefully slide them them into the hot liquid. Reduce the heat and simmer very gently until the eggs are cooked.
4. Serve in a warmed dish garnished with fried onion rings if liked.

Telor dadar isis Djawa
Javanese Stuffed Omelette

00.25 Serves 4   **00.20**

American	Ingredients	Metric/Imperial
5	eggs	5
1¼ cups	thick coconut milk	300 ml/½ pint
	salt	
	freshly ground pepper	
1	large, finely chopped onion	1
2	crushed garlic cloves	2
2 tsp	ground coriander	2 tsp
1 tsp	soft brown sugar	1 tsp
1 tsp	ground cumin	1 tsp
½ tsp	laos powder	½ tsp
1 tsp	sambal ulek or sambal trasi (see page 128 or 129)	1 tsp
5 tbsp	sunflower oil or ghee	5 tbsp
½ lb	ground (minced) beef	225 g/8 oz
1 tbsp	lemon juice	1 tbsp
4 tbsp	sunflower, corn oil or ghee	4 tbsp
4	skinned tomatoes (optional)	4
½	cucumber (optional)	½

1. Lightly beat the eggs with 3 tbsp thick coconut milk and some salt and pepper. Leave to stand for 10 minutes, then beat briefly with a whisk.
2. Pound the onion, garlic, ground coriander, sugar, ground cumin, laos powder and sambal in a mortar or food processor to form a fairly smooth paste.
3. Heat 1 tbsp oil in a wok and fry the paste for 2 minutes, stirring continuously. Break up the ground (minced) meat and add to the wok. Stir fry for 10 minutes.
4. Stir in the remaining coconut milk and the lemon juice and simmer until most of the liquid has evaporated. Remove the wok from the heat.
5. In a frying pan heat 2 tbsp oil or ghee. Pour half the egg mixture into the pan. Reduce the heat, cover and fry the omelette until it has set on top. Turn the omelette over using the lid.
6. Immediately pile half the beef mixture on to the omelette, then slide the omelette on to a warmed dish. Fold the omelette in half, pressing the edges firmly together.
7. Prepare the second omelette in the same way and serve immediately.

Poached egg with green chilies

Hidden eggs

Telor bungkus
Hidden Eggs

	00.30 plus standing time	00.10

American	Ingredients	Metric/Imperial
¾ cup	oil for deep frying	200 ml/7 fl oz
4	hard-cooked (hard-boiled) eggs	4
1 lb	lean ground (minced) beef	450 g/1 lb
1	very finely shredded onion	1
1	crushed garlic clove	1
	salt	
1 tsp	soft brown sugar	1 tsp
	freshly ground pepper	
½ tsp	ground nutmeg	½ tsp
½ tsp	ground coriander	½ tsp
1	separated egg	1
4 tbsp	breadcrumbs	4 tbsp
2	skinned tomatoes	2
	gherkin or cucumber fans	

1. Heat the oil to 180°C/350°F.
2. Peel the eggs.
3. Mix together the ground (minced) beef, onion, garlic, salt, sugar, pepper, nutmeg and ground coriander and leave to stand for 10 minutes.
4. Mix the egg yolk with 2 tbsp water and stir in the breadcrumbs. Add this mixture to the mince and knead well. Divide into 4 portions.
5. Coat each hard-cooked (hard-boiled) egg with a layer of the beef mixture.
6. Beat the egg whites until slightly frothy. Roll the coated eggs in the egg white then fry in the hot oil until golden brown and crisp.
7. Lift them from the pan and drain on kitchen paper. Halve the eggs and arrange on a warmed plate with the round sides upward.
8. Garnish with slices of tomato and cucumber or gherkin fans.

Telor mata sapi bandung
Fried Eggs on a Bed of Green Vegetables

	00.15 Serves 4	00.15

American	Ingredients	Metric/Imperial
1¼ cups	groundnut oil or ghee	300 ml/½ pint
¼ lb	green beans or haricot vert 1 cut into 1 in (2.5 cm) lengths	25 g/4 oz
¼ lb	small, cleaned, sliced carrots	125 g/4 oz
¼ lb	broccoli, divided into florets stalks cut into small slices	125 g/4 oz
¼ lb	washed celery, cut into small pieces	125 g/4 oz
2	small onions, cut into segments layers separated	2
2	crushed garlic cloves	2
	salt	
	freshly ground pepper	
1 tsp	sambal ulek (see page 128)	1 tsp
⅔ cups	boiling bouillon (stock)	150 ml/¼ pint
¾ cup	thick coconut milk	200 ml/7 fl oz
1 tbsp	lemon juice	1 tbsp
8	eggs	8
4 tbsp	serendeng (from a jar)	4 tbsp

1. Heat 4 tbsp oil or ghee in a wok. Add the vegetables, onion and garlic and stir fry for 3 minutes.
2. Add salt and pepper to taste and the sambal ulek. Pour in the hot bouillon (stock) and simmer for 3 minutes.
3. Add the thick coconut milk and the lemon juice, stir well and simmer for further 2-3 minutes.
4. Fry the eggs in the remaining oil or ghee.
5. Divide the vegetables between warmed plates. Sprinkle them with the serendeng and top with the fried eggs. Serve immediately.

Omelette with crab and fresh herbs

Telor dadar kepiting dan bumbu kebun

Omelette with Crab and Fresh Herbs

00.10 Serves 4   **00.10**

American	Ingredients	Metric/Imperial
½ lb	crabmeat, thawed if frozen	225 g/8 oz
	salt	
	freshly ground pepper	
2 tbsp	very finely shredded coriander leaves or parsley	2 tbsp
5	eggs	5
1 tsp	soft brown sugar	1 tsp
½ tsp	ground root ginger	½ tsp
4 tbsp	sunflower, corn oil or ghee	4 tbsp
	few sprigs parsley	
2	skinned tomatoes	2

1. Pick over the crabmeat and cut into small pieces. Sprinkle with salt and pepper and add the fresh herbs. Stir well.
2. Lightly beat the eggs and mix in the salt, sugar, pepper, ground ginger and 3 tbsp water.
3. Heat 2 tbsp oil or ghee in a wok and pour in half the egg mixture. Spoon on half of the chopped crab and herb mixture and cook until the top of the omelette has set. Turn the omelette.
4. Turn off the heat and leave to stand for a few moments.
5. Make the second omelette in the same way.
6. Roll up the omelettes and cut them into diagonal 1 in (2.5 cm) strips.
7. Arrange on a warmed plate and serve immediately.

Telor dadar kentang

Small Omelettes with Potatoes

00.10 Serves 4   **00.15**

American	Ingredients	Metric/Imperial
1 lb	peeled potatoes	450 g/1 lb
4	eggs	4
1	very finely shredded onion	1
1	crushed garlic clove	1
1 tsp	sambal ulek (see page 128)	1 tsp
1 tsp	soft brown sugar	1 tsp
	salt	
	freshly ground black pepper	-
6 tbsp	sunflower, corn oil or ghee	6 tbsp
	tomato flowers and/or cucumber fans to garnish (optional)	

1. Grate the potatoes with a coarse grater. In a bowl, lightly beat the eggs and stir in the grated potato, onion, garlic and sambal ulek. Add the sugar and salt and pepper to taste.
2. In a large frying pan, heat 2 tbsp of oil or ghee. Scoop 4 small heaps of the egg mixture into the pan. The mixture will spread, so leave plenty of space. Cook over low heat with the pan covered until the omelettes have set on top, then turn and cook the second side until browned. Cook the remaining mixture in the same way to make a total of 12 omelettes.
3. Serve the omelettes on warmed plates.
4. Garnish with tomato flowers and/or cucumber fans (optional).

Ayam semur

Braised Chicken

00.15 plus standing time | 00.50

American	Ingredients	Metric/Imperial
1 (2 lb)	roasting chicken cut into 8 pieces	1 (900 g/2 lb)
2 tbsp	lemon juice	2 tbsp
	salt	
	freshly ground pepper	
3 tbsp	sunflower oil or ghee	3 tbsp
1	large chopped onion	1
1	finely chopped garlic clove	1
2 tbsp	Indonesian sweet soy sauce (ketyap benteng manis)	2 tbsp
1 tbsp	Indonesian salty soy sauce (ketyap benteng asin)	1 tbsp
1 tbsp	soft brown sugar	1 tbsp
1-2	red or green chilies	1-2

1. Dry the chicken pieces with kitchen paper.
2. Place the lemon juice in a bowl and add salt and pepper to taste. Add 1½ tbsp water. Stir until the salt has dissolved and coat the chicken on all sides with the mixture. Leave the chicken to stand for 1 hour, then dry with kitchen paper.
3. Heat the oil or ghee in a pan and fry the chicken until golden brown and crisp on all sides. Remove from the pan and keep hot.
4. Fry the onion in the pan until it begins to color. Add the garlic, stir and add ¾ cup (200 ml/7 fl oz) boiling water.
5. Add both types of soy sauce and the sugar and stir well. Return the chicken pieces to the pan and simmer for about 30 minutes with the pan half covered, until the meat is completely cooked. The sauce should reduce by about half. Do not allow to boil dry.
6. Serve the chicken in a warmed bowl, garnished with chili flowers.

Ayam semur II

Braised Chicken (II)

00.15 plus standing time | 00.50

American	Ingredients	Metric/Imperial
1 (2lb)	roasting chicken 1 cut into 8 pieces	(900 g/2 lb)
½ tsp	grated nutmeg	½ tsp
	salt	
2 tsp	soft brown sugar	2 tsp
	freshly ground pepper	
3 tbsp	groundnut or sunflower oil	3 tbsp
2	large chopped onions	2
2	finely chopped garlic cloves	2
2	cloves	2
2	seeded red chilies pounded to a paste	2
3 tbsp	Indonesian sweet soy sauce (ketyap benteng manis)	3 tbsp
½	cucumber	½

1. Dry the chicken pieces with kitchen paper.
2. Mix together the nutmeg, salt to taste, the brown sugar and pepper. Mix well and use to coat the chicken. Leave for at least 15 minutes.
3. Heat the oil or ghee in a wok and fry the chicken until brown and crisp. Remove from the pan and keep hot.
4. Add the onion to the pan and stir fry until beginning to change color. Add the garlic and stir until the onion starts to brown.
5. Add the cloves and chili paste. Stir well, then add ¾ cup (200 ml/7 fl oz) boiling water and the soy sauce.
6. Return the chicken pieces to the pan. Reduce the heat and simmer the chicken for about 30 minutes with the pan half-covered. Take care that the chicken does not boil dry. The liquid should reduce by about half.
7. Serve the chicken in a warmed dish garnished with the cucumber.

Braised chicken

Ajam berkuah jerik manis dan soya

Chicken Legs in Orange and Soy Sauce

⬛▷	00.15 Serves 4	00.25 🍲

American	Ingredients	Metric/Imperial
12	chicken drumsticks	12
	salt	
3 tbsp	groundnut oil	3 tbsp
1	large chopped onion	1
1	very finely chopped garlic clove	1
1 tsp	sambal ulek (see page 128)	1 tsp
5 tbsp	freshly squeezed, strained orange juice	5 tbsp
2 tbsp	lemon or lime juice	2 tbsp
4 tbsp	Indonesian sweet soy sauce (ketyap benteng manis)	4 tbsp
1 tbsp	soft brown sugar	1 tbsp
2 tsp	cornstarch (cornflour)	2 tsp

1. Dry the chicken with kitchen paper. Rub lightly with salt.
2. Heat the oil in a wok and stir fry the chicken for 8 minutes. Add the onion and stir fry until transparent.
3. Add the garlic and sambal ulek. Stir well, add the orange juice, lemon or lime juice, soy sauce and 5 tbsp boiling water.
4. Stir well, then dissolve the sugar in the sauce. Bring to the boil and simmer gently for 3 minutes.
5. Mix the cornstarch (cornflour) with 2 tbsp cold water. Push the chicken to one side of the wok and stir the cornstarch (cornflour) mixture into the liquid in the bottom of the pan. Cook, stirring until the sauce thickens lightly.
6. Stir the chicken through the sauce and simmer gently for 2 minutes. Try the sauce and add a little salt to taste.
7. Arrange the chicken drumsticks in a warmed dish and pour over the sauce.

Ayam pangang

Spiced Oven-Roast Chicken

⬛▷	00.10 plus standing time	00.45 🍲

American	Ingredients	Metric/Imperial
2 (1¾ lb)	roasting chickens, halved	2 (800 g/1¾ lb)
2 tbsp	Indonesian sweet soy sauce	2 tbsp
1 tbsp	Indonesian salty soy sauce	1 tbsp
2 tbsp	lemon juice	2 tbsp
1	finely chopped onion	1
2	crushed garlic cloves	2
2 tsp	sambal ulek (see page 128)	2 tsp
1 tsp	soft brown sugar	1 tsp
	freshly ground black pepper	
1¾ cups	chicken bouillon (stock)	400 ml/14 fl oz
5 tbsp	thick coconut milk	5 tbsp
1	sliced lemon	1
1-2	skinned tomatoes (optional)	1-2
1	sliced cucumber (optional)	1
	few gherkins (optional)	

1. Flatten the chicken halves with the side of a cleaver or a rolling pin.
2. Mix both types of soy sauce and add the lemon juice, onion, garlic and sambal. Stir well and add the soft brown sugar and a little salt and pepper.
3. Rub sauce over the chicken, leave to stand for 1 hour.
4. Bring the bouillon (stock) to the boil in a large pan; place the chicken in the bouillon (stock) and bring back to the boil. Reduce the heat and simmer for 10 minutes. Turn the chicken pieces over and spoon sauce over from time to time.
5. Heat the oven to 220°C/425°F/Gas Mark 7 and oil a baking sheet.
6. Remove the chicken from the sauce, dry with kitchen paper and place skin side upward on the baking sheet. Roast the chicken until well browned.
7. Meanwhile, allow the cooking liquid to boil until reduced to about 5 tbsp. Add 5 tbsp thick coconut milk and season with salt and pepper to taste.
8. Serve the chicken on warmed plates with the slices of lemon and serve the sauce separately in a warmed sauce boat. Garnish with the tomato, slices of cucumber or gherkins.

Ayam Petis 🍳

Chicken with Shrimp Sauce

⬛▷	00.10 Serves 4	00.50 🍲

American	Ingredients	Metric/Imperial
1 (2 lb)	roasting chicken cut into 8 pieces	1 (900 g/2 lb)
3 tbsp	groundnut or sunflower oil	3 tbsp
1	large onion cut into rings	1
3	finely chopped garlic cloves	3
1 tbsp	Chinese shrimp paste (petis)	1 tbsp
2 tsp	sambal trasi (see page 129)	2 tsp
½ tsp	ground turmeric	½ tsp
	salt	
	freshly ground pepper	
1¾ cups	thin coconut milk	400 ml/14 fl oz
1 tsp	soft brown sugar	1 tsp
2 tbsp	lemon juice	2 tbsp
¼ lb	peeled shrimp (prawns)	125 g/4 oz
1 tbsp	finely chopped coriander or parsley	1 tbsp

1. Dry the chicken pieces with kitchen paper.
2. Heat the oil in a wok and stir fry the onion until beginning to brown.
3. Add the garlic, petis, sambal, turmeric and a little salt and pepper. Stir well then add the chicken pieces.
4. Cook, stirring constantly and add the coconut milk. Bring to the boil, reduce the heat and simmer very gently for 30-35 minutes.
5. Remove chicken from the pan and keep warm. Boil the sauce until it thickens a little and then stir in the sugar and lemon juice.
6. Add the shrimp (prawns) to the sauce and cook until heated through.
7. Arrange the chicken on a shallow warmed dish. Pour the sauce over and sprinkle with finely chopped coriander leaves or parsley.

Chicken legs in orange and soy sauce

Ayam kacang (11)

Diced Chicken and Peanuts

00.10 Serves 4   **00.12**

American	Ingredients	Metric/Imperial
½ lb	shelled peanuts	225 g/8 oz
1 lb	boneless chicken breast	450 g/1 lb
	salt	
	freshly ground pepper	
2 tbsp	groundnut oil	2 tbsp
1	chopped onion	1
1 ½ tsp	sambal ulek	1 ½ tsp
1	chopped garlic clove	1
2 ½ tsp	Java curry powder	2 ½ tsp
2 tbsp	Indonesian sweet soy sauce (ketyap benteng manis)	2 tbsp
1 tbsp	Indonesian salty soy sauce (ketyap benteng asin)	1 tbsp
5 tbsp	chicken bouillon (stock)	5 tbsp
5 tbsp	thin coconut milk	5 tbsp
5 tbsp	thick coconut milk	5 tbsp
1	skinned tomato (optional)	1
	few sprigs coriander or parsley (optional)	

1. Roast the peanuts in a dry frying pan until they begin to color. Pour on to a large cold plate and leave to cool completely.
2. Dry the chicken with kitchen paper and cut it into ½ in (1.25 cm) cubes. Sprinkle with salt and pepper.
3. Heat the oil in a wok. Stir fry the chicken cubes for 2 minutes, then add the chopped onion. Stir until the onion looks transparent.
4. Add the sambal ulek, garlic and curry powder. Stir until the curry aroma is obvious.
5. Add both types of soy sauce, the bouillon (stock) and the thin coconut milk. Stir well and simmer for 3 minutes.
6. Stir in the thick coconut milk and bring to the boil. Immediately transfer to a warmed dish, sprinkle with the roast peanuts and serve garnished with a slice of skinned tomato and sprigs of coriander or parsley.

Ayam kacang (1)

Chicken Breasts with Peanuts

00.05 Serves 4   **00.35**

American	Ingredients	Metric/Imperial
½ lb	shelled unsalted peanuts	225 g/8 oz
2	skinned tomatoes	2
3 tbsp	groundnut oil	3 tbsp
1	finely chopped onion	1
1	finely chopped garlic clove	1
2 tbsp	Indonesian sweet soy sauce (ketyap benteng manis)	2 tbsp
1 tsp	soft brown sugar	1 tsp
2 tsp	sambal ulek or sambal trasi (see page 128 or 129)	2 tsp
1 tbsp	peanut butter	1 tbsp
4 tbsp	thin coconut milk	4 tbsp
4 (5 oz)	boneless chicken breasts	4 (150 g/5 oz)
	salt	
	freshly ground pepper	
	few sprigs coriander	

1. Heat a dry saucepan and roast the peanuts, stirring constantly, until they begin to change color. Spread them out on a cold plate and leave to cool completely.
2. Halve the tomatoes, remove juice. Cut into small pieces.
3. Heat 1 tbsp oil in a wok and stir fry the onion until it begins to look transparent. Add the garlic and stir well.
4. Add the pieces of tomato, soy sauce, sugar, sambal and ¾ cup (200 ml/7 fl oz) water. Bring to the boil, stirring constantly. Reduce the heat and simmer for 10 minutes.
5. Add the peanut butter and coconut milk and stir until a fairly stiff paste is formed. Keep hot.
6. Dry the chicken with kitchen paper and rub with a little salt and pepper.
7. Heat the remaining oil in a large saucepan and fry the chicken breasts for 8-10 minutes, until golden brown on both sides.
8. Arrange the chicken breasts on a warmed plate and spoon a little sauce beside them. Sprinkle the peanuts over the top and garnish with a few sprigs of coriander.

Ayam Bali

Chicken Balinese Style

00.15 Serves 4 — 00.45

American	Ingredients	Metric/Imperial
1 (2½ lb)	boiling chicken 1 cut into 8 pieces	(1.2 kg/2½ lb)
	salt	
5 tbsp	groundnut or sunflower oil	5 tbsp
1	chopped onions	1
2	crushed garlic cloves	2
1 tbsp	freshly grated root ginger	1 tbsp
2 tsp	sambal ulek (see page 128)	2 tsp
4	finely chopped candle nuts	4
2 tbsp	Indonesian sweet soy sauce (ketyap benteng manis)	2 tbsp
1 tbsp	soft brown sugar	1 tbsp
3 tbsp	lemon juice	3 tbsp
1¾ cups	thin coconut milk	400 ml/14 fl oz
2-3 tbsp	fried onion (optional)	2-3 tbsp

1. Dry the chicken pieces with kitchen paper and rub them with a little salt.
2. Heat 4 tbsp oil in a frying pan and fry the chicken until golden brown.
3. Mix the onion, garlic, ginger, sambal, candle nuts and soy sauce into a thin paste.
4. Remove the chicken pieces from the pan and drain on kitchen paper.
5. Heat 1 tbsp oil in a wok and stir fry the paste for 2 minutes. Add the sugar, lemon juice, a little salt and the coconut milk. Bring to the boil, stirring all the time.
6. Put the pieces of chicken into the sauce and simmer for 20-25 minutes, until tender. Turn the chicken pieces over regularly and keep pouring the sauce over. The sauce should reduce by about half during cooking.
7. Serve on warmed dish, sprinkled with fried onion if liked.

Ayam bumbu rujak

Chicken in Rujak Sauce

00.10 plus standing time — 00.45

American	Ingredients	Metric/Imperial
2¼ lb	chicken drumsticks	1 kg/2¼ lb
3 tbsp	lemon juice	3 tbsp
	salt	
1 tsp	soft brown sugar	1 tsp
2	finely crushed candle nuts	2
2 tsp	sambal ulek (see page 128)	2 tsp
4	crushed garlic cloves	4
1	chopped onion	1
4 tbsp	groundnut or sunflower oil	4 tbsp
1¾ cups	thin coconut milk	400 ml/14 fl oz
4	salam leaves	4
¾ cup	thick coconut milk	200 ml/7 fl oz

1. Dry the chicken drumsticks with kitchen paper.
2. Mix the lemon juice with 1½ tsp salt and the soft brown sugar. Stir until the salt and sugar have dissolved. Rub the chicken with this mixture and leave to stand for 1 hour.
3. Mix the candle nuts, sambal, garlic and onion to a smooth paste.
4. Heat the oil in a large wok and stir fry the chicken until brown on all sides. Remove from the wok and keep warm.
5. Remove all but 1 tbsp of the oil from the wok. Stir fry the paste in the remaining oil for 2 minutes. Add the thin coconut milk and bring to the boil, stirring continuously.
6. Add the salam leaves to the sauce, simmer for 1-2 minutes then return the chicken to the pan.
7. Simmer for 20-25 minutes until the sauce has reduced by about half and the chicken is tender. Remove the chicken pieces from the wok using a slotted spoon and arrange them in a warmed dish.
8. Add the thick coconut milk to the sauce and bring it rapidly to the boil. Add salt to taste, remove the salam leaves and pour the sauce over the drumsticks.

Cook's tip: Krupuk are savory wafers served as a side dish. Various types are available, either ready cooked or dried, which need to be fried.
To fry krupuk, heat some oil in a wok until it is hot enough to expand a piece of krupuk without it browning immediately. Place a piece of krupuk in the hot oil and, using 2 forks, gently stretch and flatten the wafer. Turn it over then remove from the pan and drain on kitchen paper. Serve fresh or store for a short time in an airtight container.

Kelinchi kerrie rambutan

Rabbit with Rambutans and Java Curry Sauce

00.10 Serves 4 — 00.45

American	Ingredients	Metric/Imperial
1 (2¼ lb)	rabbit	1 (1.2 kg/2¼ lb)
	salt	
10	slightly under-ripe rambutans	10
4 tbsp	groundnut oil	4 tbsp
1	large chopped onion	1
2	very finely chopped garlic cloves	2
2 tsp	Java curry powder	2 tsp
1 tsp	sambal ulek (see page 128)	1 tsp
1¼ cups	thick coconut milk	300 ml/½ pint
1 tbsp	Indonesian salty soy sauce (ketyap benteng asin)	1 tbsp
1-2 tsp	soft brown sugar	1-2 tsp
3 tbsp	lemon or lime juice	3 tbsp

1. Divide the rabbit into 12-16 pieces. Dry with kitchen paper and rub very lightly with a little salt.
2. Peel the rambutans and remove the pips. Cut the flesh into small pieces.
3. Heat the oil in a wok and stir fry the rabbit pieces until lightly browned on all sides.

Rabbit with rambutans and Java curry sauce

4. Remove all but 1 tbsp of oil. Add the chopped onion and continue stir frying until the onion appears transparent. Add the garlic, curry powder and sambal ulek. Stir well a few times.
5. Add 5 tbsp boiling water, stir well and add the coconut milk, soy sauce and sugar to taste. Simmer gently for 25-35 minutes.
6. Try the sauce and add a little salt and the lemon or lime juice to taste.
7. Serve in a warmed dish, topping with the pieces of rambutan at the last moment.

Kelinchi berkuah mango

Rabbit with Mango Sauce

■─▽   00.30   01.00 ⌂
Serves 4

American	Ingredients	Metric/Imperial
1 (2½ lb)	young rabbit	1 (1.25 kg/2½ lb)
3 tbsp	lemon or lime juice	3 tbsp
	salt	
1	large mango	1
1 tsp	sambal ulek (see page 128)	1 tsp
4 tbsp	Indonesian sweet soy sauce (ketyap benteng manis)	4 tbsp
1-2 tbsp	soft brown sugar	1-2 tbsp
4 tbsp	groundnut oil	4 tbsp
2	peeled garlic cloves	2
	few sprigs coriander (optional)	

1. Divide the rabbit into 12-16 pieces. Rub with lemon or lime juice and place in a draughty place to dry. Rub very lightly with a little salt.
2. Halve the mango, remove the stone and scoop the flesh out of the skin. Rub the flesh through a very fine strainer.
3. Put the fruit purée in a small saucepan with 5 tbsp water, the sambal ulek, soy sauce and sugar. Bring to the boil, stirring constantly. Simmer gently for another 2-3 minutes then keep the sauce warm.
4. Heat the oil in a wok and stir fry the garlic cloves until brown. Remove the garlic from the pan and fry the rabbit pieces in the hot oil until browned on all sides.
5. Remove as much oil as possible from the wok. Add the sauce to the remaining oil and bring to the boil, stirring constantly. Reduce the heat and simmer very gently for 25-35 minutes. Try the sauce and add a little salt to taste.
6. Serve in a warmed dish, garnished with a few sprigs of coriander.

Cook's tip: the rabbit dishes given here show the strong influence of both Chinese and Indian cuisine on the cooking of Indonesia. The use of fresh fruit and the stir frying indicate the Chinese influence, whilst the light curry flavor is borrowed from India. The Indonesians also make the best use of local fresh ingredients and add the authentic taste of Indonesia with the sambals, soy sauces and Java curry powder.

Nanas marak kerrie dan pinda

Pineapple and Peanut Curry

00.15 00.10
Serves 4 as side dish

American	Ingredients	Metric/Imperial
¼ lb	*shelled peanuts*	*125 g/4 oz*
2 tbsp	*desiccated coconut*	*2 tbsp*
1	*small slightly under-ripe pineapple*	*1*
1 tbsp	*groundnut oil*	*1 tbsp*
1	*medium size chopped onion*	*1*
1	*very finely chopped garlic clove*	*1*
2 tsp	*Java curry powder*	*2 tsp*
½ tsp	*sambal ulek (see page 128)*	*½ tsp*
1 cup	*thick coconut milk*	*250 ml/8 fl oz*
1 tsp	*salt*	*1 tsp*
2 tsp	*soft brown sugar*	*2 tsp*

1. Roast the peanuts in a dry frying pan until beginning to change color. Cool on a large plate. Pound half of the peanuts coarsely in a mortar.
2. Roast the coconut in exactly the same way and cool as soon as it has colored lightly.
3. Peel the pineapple and cut into four lengthwise. Remove the hard core from each piece and cut the pieces lengthwise again. Cut the strips into small cubes.
4. Heat the oil in a wok and stir fry the onion until transparent. Add the garlic, curry powder and sambal ulek. Stir well then add the pineapple cubes. Stir in the coconut milk, salt and sugar.
5. Turn the ingredients over a few times and simmer for 5 minutes over moderate heat.
6. Stir in the pounded peanuts immediately before serving.
7. Transfer to a warmed dish and serve topped with the remaining peanuts and the toasted coconut.

Pisang kerrie dengan klappa

Banana and Coconut Curry

00.10 00.10
Serves 4 as side dish

American	Ingredients	Metric/Imperial
4 tbsp	*desiccated coconut*	*4 tbsp*
1 tbsp	*groundnut oil*	*1 tbsp*
1	*medium size chopped onion*	*1*
1	*very finely chopped garlic clove*	*1*
2 tsp	*Java curry powder*	*2 tsp*
2 tsp	*sambal ulek (see page 128)*	*2 tsp*
4	*firm bananas*	*4*
1 cup	*thick coconut milk*	*250 ml/8 fl oz*
1 tsp	*salt*	*1 tsp*
2 tsp	*soft brown sugar*	*2 tsp*

1. Roast the desiccated coconut in a dry frying pan, turning over constantly until lightly colored. Pour on to a large plate to cool.
2. Heat the oil in a wok and stir fry the onion until transparent. Add the garlic, curry powder and sambal ulek.
Stir thoroughly.
3. Peel the bananas and cut into 1½ in (4 cm) pieces. Add to the wok and stir carefully. Add the coconut milk, salt and sugar, stir gently and simmer for 5 minutes.
5. Serve on a warmed dish, sprinkled with the roasted coconut.

Pacari

Pineapple and Coconut Milk Curry

⏱ 00.10	00.10 🍲
Serves 4 as side dish	

American	Ingredients	Metric/Imperial
1	small, slightly under-ripe pineapple	1
1 tbsp	groundnut oil	1 tbsp
1	medium size chopped onion	1
1	chopped garlic clove	1
1 (2 in)	stick cinnamon	1 (5 cm/2 in)
3	cloves	3
1 tsp	ground coriander	1 tsp
1 tsp	sambal ulek (see pages 128)	1 tsp
1 tsp	salt	1 tsp
¾ cup	thick coconut milk	200 ml/7 fl oz
2 tsp	soft brown sugar	2 tsp

1. Peel the pineapple and cut into four lengthwise. Remove the hard core from each piece and cut each piece lengthwise again. Cut the strips into small cubes.
2. Heat the oil in a wok and stir fry the onion until transparent.
3. Add the garlic, cinnamon, cloves, coriander and sambal ulek. Stir well then add the pineapple cubes. Stir in the salt, coconut milk and sugar.
4. Turn the ingredients over a few times and simmer very gently for 5 minutes over moderate heat.
5. Serve in a warmed dish.

Cook's tip: pineapple and coconut milk curry is an excellent side dish to serve with roast meat.

Goelai itik

Duck in Spiced Coconut Sauce

⏱ 00.10	01.00 🍲
Serves 4	

American	Ingredients	Metric/Imperial
1 (3½ lb)	duck	1 (1.5 kg/3½ lb)
	salt	
6 tbsp	groundnut oil	6 tbsp
2	large chopped onions	2
2	very finely chopped garlic cloves	2
1 tbsp	Java curry powder	1 tbsp
4 tsp	sambal ulek (see page 128)	4 tsp
2 tsp	ground root ginger	2 tsp
1 tsp	soft brown sugar	1 tsp
4 oz	desiccated coconut	125 g/4 oz
5	large onions cut into thin rings	5
2¼ cups	thin coconut milk	500 ml/18 fl oz
2¼ cups	thick coconut milk	500 ml/18 fl oz
1 tbsp	lemon or lime juice	1 tbsp
	red or green chilies	

1. Dry the duck inside and out with kitchen paper. Rub the inside of the duck with salt. Brush the duck skin with oil.
2. Roast the duck for up to 30 minutes until evenly browned, over the glowing charcoal in the barbecue or under a very hot broiler (grill). Turn regularly and brush with oil once or twice during roasting.
3. Allow the duck to cool a little, then cut into 16 equal pieces.
4. Stir fry the onion in 2 tbsp oil until beginning to gain color. Add the garlic and stir well. Add the curry powder, sambal ulek, ground ginger, 1 tsp salt, and the sugar.
5. Stir well, remove the wok from the heat and leave the mixture to cool.
6. Place the coconut in a bowl and sprinkle with 5 tbsp boiling water. Stir the coconut a few times.
7. Brush the duck on all sides with the mixture from the wok.
8. Heat the remaining oil in a wok and stir fry the onion rings until transparent. Add the thin coconut milk. Add the coconut and stir vigorously.
9. Place the pieces of duck into the sauce and simmer until the sauce is thick, stirring carefully ocassionally.
10. Add the thick coconut milk and the lemon or lime juice. Bring to the boil and add salt to taste.
11. Transfer to a warmed serving dish and garnish with chili flowers.

Left to right: Pineapple and peanut curry, Banana and coconut curry

Babi nanas
Pork and Pineapple

◀━▷ 00.20   00.25 🍲
Serves 4

American	Ingredients	Metric/Imperial
1 lb	lean pork steaks	450 g/1 lb
1	small, slightly under-ripe pineapple	1
1	green bell pepper	1
1	red bell pepper	1
2 tbsp	groundnut oil	2 tbsp
2	peeled garlic cloves	2
½ tsp	sambal ulek (see page 128)	½ tsp
	salt	
2 tbsp	Indonesian sweet soy sauce (ketyap benteng manis)	2 tbsp
2 tsp	cornstarch (cornflour)	2 tsp
2	chopped scallions (spring onions)	2

1. Dry the meat with kitchen paper and cut into finger width strips.

2. Peel the pineapple and cut into sections. Remove the hard core from each section and cut the flesh into strips, the same length and thickness as the strips of meat.

3. Trim, halve and seed the bell peppers and cut the flesh into strips which are thinner but the same length as the strips of meat.

4. Heat the oil in a wok and stir fry the garlic until brown.

5. Remove the garlic from the pan and stir fry the meat for 3 minutes.

6. Add the pineapple and the bell peppers. Stir fry for 3 minutes.

7. Add the sambal ulek and sprinkle on a little salt. Stir well and add 1 cup (250 ml/8 fl oz) boiling water.

8. Stir in the soy sauce and simmer for 3 minutes over moderate heat.

9. Mix the cornstarch (cornflour) with 2 tbsp cold water.

10. Push all the ingredients to one side of the wok and stir the cornstarch (cornflour) mixture through the liquid on the bottom of the pan. Cook, stirring until the sauce thickens.

11. Stir all the ingredients through the sauce and bring to the boil.

12. Serve in a warmed dish, sprinkled with chopped scallions (spring onions).

Left to right:
Pork and pineapple,
Pork with bell peppers and tomato
Pork with oranges

Babi paprika dan tomat

Pork with Bell Peppers and Tomatoes

◀━━▷ 00.10 00.20 🍲
Serves 4

American	Ingredients	Metric/Imperial
1 lb	lean pork steaks	450 g/1 lb
2	green bell peppers	2
6	large skinned tomatoes	6
2 tbsp	groundnut oil	2 tbsp
1	large chopped onion	1
1	very finely chopped garlic clove	1
1 tsp	sambal ulek (see page 128)	1 tsp
4 tbsp	Chinese tomato or barbecue sauce	4 tbsp
2 tbsp	Indonesian salty soy sauce (ketyap benteng asin)	2 tbsp
	drops of lemon or lime juice	
	pinch sugar	
	salt	
2	chopped scallions (spring onions) (optional)	2
1-2	red chilies (optional)	1-2

1. Dry the meat and cut it into ½ in (1.25 cm) cubes.
2. Trim, halve and seed the bell peppers and cut the flesh into ½ in (1.25 cm) squares.
3. Halve the tomatoes, remove the seeds and drain. Cut the flesh into ½ in (1.25 cm) squares.
4. Heat the oil in a wok and stir fry the meat until lightly browned. Add the chopped onion, stir fry until transparent.
5. Add the garlic, bell peppers and sambal ulek. Stir well a few times and add ¾ cup (200 ml/7 fl oz) boiling water, the tomato or barbecue sauce and the soy sauce.
6. Stir well and simmer for 5 minutes over moderate heat.
7. Spoon in the tomatoes and bring back to the boil.
8. Try the sauce and add lemon or lime juice, sugar and salt to taste.
9. Serve in a warmed dish, garnished with a little chopped scallion (spring onion) and one or more red chili flowers.

Lapis babi dengan jeruk manis

Pork and Oranges

◀━━▷ 00.15 00.30 🍲
Serves 4

American	Ingredients	Metric/Imperial
1 lb	lean pork steaks	450 g/1 lb
4 tbsp	lemon or lime juice	4 tbsp
	salt	
4	oranges	4
¾ cup	freshly squeezed, strained orange juice	200 ml/7 fl oz
2	green chilies	2
2 tbsp	groundnut oil	2 tbsp
1	large chopped onion	1
1	very finely chopped garlic clove	1
2 tbsp	Indonesian sweet soy sauce (ketyap benteng manis)	2 tbsp
2 tsp	cornstarch (cornflour)	2 tsp
1-2 tsp	soft brown sugar	1-2 tsp

1. Dry the meat with kitchen paper and cut into finger width strips. Sprinkle with 2 tbsp lemon or lime juice and leave in a draughty place to dry. Sprinkle the meat with a little salt.
2. Peel the oranges thickly so that the pith is also removed. Remove the flesh between the membranes and discard any pips. Reserve the juice.
4. Strain the reserved juice and add it, together with the remaining lemon or lime juice to the orange juice.
5. Rinse the chilies and remove the stalk and seeds. Cut the flesh into small pieces and finely pound the pieces in a mortar.
6. Heat the oil in a wok and stir fry the meat until golden brown.
7. Add the chopped onion and stir fry until transparent. Add the garlic and the green chilies.
8. Stir in the fruit juice and soy sauce. Stir well a few times and bring to the boil. Reduce the heat and simmer for 5 minutes.
9. Mix the cornstarch (cornflour) with 2 tbsp cold water. Push all the ingredients to one side of the wok and stir the cornstarch (cornflour) mixture through the liquid in the bottom of the pan. Cook, stirring until the sauce thickens.
10. Spoon the ingredients through the sauce and add the orange segments. Simmer gently for 2-3 minutes. Try the sauce and add sugar to taste.
11. Serve immediately in a warmed dish.

Gangsa
Beef with Red Chilies

00.10   **02.00**
Serves 4

American	Ingredients	Metric/Imperial
1 lb	lean braising beef	450 g/1 lb
4	red chilies	4
1 tsp	ground coriander seeds	1 tsp
½ tsp	ground cumin seeds	½ tsp
2	very finely chopped garlic cloves	2
½ tsp	ground root ginger	½ tsp
1 tsp	soft brown sugar	1 tsp
1 tsp	trasi	1 tsp
1 tsp	salt	1 tsp
2½ tbsp	groundnut oil	2½ tbsp
1 tbsp	lemon or lime juice	1 tbsp
2	chopped scallions (spring onions) (optional)	2
1-2	red or green chilies (optional)	1-2

1. In a saucepan bring 2½ cups (600 ml/1 pint) water to the boil. Add the meat, cover and leave to simmer for about 1½ hours, until the meat is tender.
2. Rinse the chilies, trim them and cut obliquely into thin rings.
3. Put the coriander, cumin, garlic, ground ginger, sugar, trasi and salt into a mortar or food processor and pound to a paste.
4. When the meat is tender, remove from the bouillon (stock) with a slotted spoon, drain and leave to cool.
5. Boil the bouillon (stock) until reduced to half the original quantity. Add the spice paste and the oil, stir well and continue to boil for 5 minutes.
6. Cut the meat into 1 in (2.5 cm) cubes and add to the sauce. Stir in the chili rings.
7. Reduce the heat and simmer until most of the liquid has evaporated.
8. Add the lemon or lime juice. Stir well and serve in a warmed dish, garnished with chopped scallions (spring onions) and one or more chili flowers.

Dendeng belado
Spiced Beef

00.15   **00.15**
plus standing time

American	Ingredients	Metric/Imperial
1 lb	lean beef	450 g/1 lb
	salt	
3 tbsp	lemon or lime juice	3 tbsp
6 tbsp	groundnut oil	6 tbsp
2	very finely chopped garlic cloves	2
3 tsp	sambal ulek (see page 128)	3 tsp
2	large chopped onions	2
	few coriander sprigs	
1	skinned tomato	1
	cucumber slices (optional)	

1. Cut the meat into ½ in (1.25 cm) slices. Cut into finger-width strips.
2. Dissolve ½ tsp salt in 2 tbsp lemon or lime juice and pour over the meat. Stir the meat well to coat it on all sides with the mixture.
3. Leave the meat to stand for 1 hour in a colander or strainer, stirring occasionally.
4. Dry the meat with kitchen paper.
5. Heat the oil in a wok and add the meat a few pieces at a time. Stir fry until the meat is brown and crisp. Remove from the wok with a slotted spoon, drain over the wok and keep warm.
6. In a mortar or food processor pound the garlic, sambal ulek and onions to a paste.
7. Stir fry the paste in the remaining oil until light brown. Add the remaining lemon or lime juice and the meat. Stir well and serve in a warmed dish, garnished with coriander sprigs and slices of tomato and or cucumber.

Dendeng belado dan katjang
Spiced Beef with Peanuts

00.20   **00.12**
plus standing time

American	Ingredients	Metric/Imperial
1 lb	lean beef	450 g/1 lb
	salt	
2 tbsp	lemon or lime juice	2 tbsp
4	very finely chopped garlic cloves	4
2	large chopped onions	2
2 tsp	sambal ulek (see page 128)	2 tsp
2 tbsp	peanut butter	2 tbsp
2 tbsp	desiccated coconut	2 tbsp
6 tbsp	groundnut oil	6 tbsp
6 oz	shelled, skinned peanuts	175 g/6 oz
	chili flowers (optional)	
	slices cucumber	

1. Cut the meat into ½ in (1.25 cm) slices and then into finger-width strips.
2. Dissolve ½ tsp salt in the lemon or lime juice.
3. Place the meat in a bowl and pour over the lemon or lime mixture. Stir, then leave to stand for 1 hour, stirring occasionally.
4. Dry the meat with kitchen paper.
5. Pound of the garlic, onions, sambal ulek and peanut butter to a paste in a food processor or mortar.
6. Place the coconut in a small bowl and sprinkle with 2 tbsp cold water. Stir well and leave to stand for 15 minutes, stirring occasionally.
7. Heat the oil in a wok and stir fry the meat until golden brown on all sides. Remove the meat from the wok and drain on kitchen paper.
8. Remove all but 1 tbsp oil from the wok. Heat this oil and stir fry the onion paste for 1 minute.
9. Stir in the coconut and add the peanuts and stir fry for 3 minutes.
10. Transfer the contents of the wok to a cold plate or dish and leave to cool completely. Immediately before serving, stir the meat into the onion paste.
11. Pour into a serving dish and garnish with chili flowers and slices of cucumber.

Ketoprak

Soybean Curd (Tofu) with Vegetables

◗▭◤ 00.20   00.15 ⊟
Serves 4

American	Ingredients	Metric/Imperial
1 (14 oz)	cake soybean curd (tofu)	1 (400 g/14 oz)
	salt	
5 tbsp	groundnut oil	5 tbsp
¼ lb	bean sprouts	125 g/4 oz
¼ lb	white or Chinese cabbage	125 g/4 oz
1	large skinnned tomato	1
½	cucumber	½
1	large finely chopped onion	1
2	crushed garlic cloves	2
1 tbsp	peanut butter	1 tbsp
1 tsp	sambal ulek (see page 128)	1 tsp
1 tsp	soft brown sugar	1 tsp
2 tbsp	Indonesian sweet soy sauce (ketyap benteng manis)	2 tbsp
1½ tbsp	lemon juice	1½ tbsp
1 tbsp	finely chopped celery	1 tbsp

1. Cut the soybean curd into ½ in (1.25 cm) cubes and season with salt.
2. Heat 3-4 tbsp oil in a wok and stir fry the soybean curd cubes until brown on all sides. Drain on kitchen paper.
3. Rinse the bean sprouts in cold water and remove as many seed cases as possible. Drain well then pour several quarts/litres boiling water very slowly over. Drain again.
4. Cut the cabbage into very narrow strips. Halve the tomato, remove the seeds and juice and cut the flesh into small strips.

Rinse the cucumber, trim and halve lengthwise and remove the seeds. Cut each half in half again and cut the pieces into small cubes.
5. Add the remaining oil to that in the wok and stir fry the onion until golden yellow. Add the garlic and stir in the peanut butter. Add the sambal ulek, sugar, soy sauce and lemon juice. Stir well until the mixture forms a fairly thick paste, adding 1-2 tbsp water if necessary.
6. Spoon the pieces of cucumber and the cabbage into the sauce and then a minute later, the bean sprouts and soybean curd. Stir in the tomato and celery and serve immediately.

Tahu goreng tepung

Fried Soybean Curd (Tofu)

◗▭◤ 00.10   00.10 ⊟
Serves 4

American	Ingredients	Metric/Imperial
4-5 tbsp	rice flour	4-5 tbsp
2	crushed garlic cloves	2
4	finely crushed candle nuts	4
½ tsp	ground turmeric	½ tsp
½ tsp	ground coriander seeds	½ tsp
	salt	
1 (14 oz)	cake soybean curd (tofu)	1 (400 g/14 oz)
¾ cup	groundnut oil	200 ml/7 fl oz

1. Mix the rice flour to a smooth cream with 6-7 tbsp cold water. Add the garlic, candle nuts, turmeric, coriander and a little salt. Stir well.
2. Cut the soybean curd into finger-width slices.
3. Heat the oil in a wok. Dip the slices of soybean curd into the batter and drain any excess back into the bowl. Fry 3-4 pieces at a time in the oil until golden brown.
4. Drain on kitchen paper and serve.

Soybean curd (tofu) with vegetables

Tahu goreng udang

Soybean Curd (Tofu) with Shrimp (Prawns) and Bean Sprouts

	00.10	00.10
	Serves 4	

American	Ingredients	Metric/Imperial
1 (14 oz)	cake soybean curd (tofu)	1 (400 g/14 oz)
	salt	
	freshly ground pepper	
	large pinch garlic powder	
4-5 tbsp	groundnut oil	4-5 tbsp
¼ lb	bean sprouts	125 g/4 oz
¼ lb	fresh peeled shrimp (small prawns)	125 g/4 oz
1 tsp	ground ginger	1 tsp
½ tsp	garlic powder	½ tsp
2 tbsp	Indonesian salty soy sauce (ketyap benteng asin)	2 tbsp
2 tbsp	finely chopped coriander or parsley	2 tbsp
1	red chili (optional)	1

1. Cut the soybean curd into ½ in (1.25 cm) cubes. Mix ½ tsp salt, slightly less pepper and a pinch garlic powder together in a bowl. Sprinkle this mixture over the soybean curd.
2. Heat 3-4 tbsp oil in a wok and stir fry the cubes of bean curd until golden brown. Drain on kitchen paper.
3. Rinse the bean sprouts in cold water and remove as many seed cases as possible. Drain well in a colander.
4. Heat 1 tbsp oil in a wok, add the shrimp (prawns) and sprinkle with the ground ginger and ½ tsp garlic powder. Stir well, then add the soy sauce, 1 tbsp water and the bean sprouts. Stir constantly until the bean sprouts are hot.
5. Add the cubes of fried soybean curd and the coriander or parsley and stir well.
6. Transfer to a warmed dish and serve immediately, garnished with a chili flower (optional).

Tahu goreng bawang

Soybean Curd (Tofu) with Onion

	00.05	00.15
	Serves 4	

American	Ingredients	Metric/Imperial
1 (14 oz)	cake soybean curd (tofu)	1 (400 g/14 oz)
1	large chopped onion	1
1 tbsp	lemon juice	1 tbsp
1 tsp	soft brown sugar	1 tsp
½ tsp	laos powder	½ tsp
	salt	
4-5 tbsp	groundnut oil	4-5 tbsp

1. Cut the soybean curd into ½ in (1.25 cm) slices.
2. Mix the onion with the lemon juice, sugar and laos powder into a paste.
3. Bring 1 cup (250 ml/9 fl oz) water to the boil. Stir in the paste and add a little salt.

Soybean curd (tofu) with shrimps (prawns) and beansprouts

4. Add the slices of soybean curd to the liquid and simmer until most of the liquid has evaporated.
5. Drain the soybean curd on kitchen paper.
6. Heat the oil in a wok and fry the soybean curd pieces over high heat until golden brown on both sides. Drain on kitchen paper and serve.

Tahu dadar

Soybean Curd (Tofu) with Egg Noodles

	00.05	00.10
	Serves 4	

American	Ingredients	Metric/Imperial
3 tbsp	Indonesian sweet soy sauce (ketyap benteng manis)	3 tbsp
1 tbsp	soft brown sugar	1 tbsp
1	crushed garlic clove	1
2 tsp	sambal ulek (see page 128)	2 tsp
1-1½ tbsp	lemon juice	1-1½ tbsp
	salt	
3	eggs	3
1 (8 oz)	cake soybean curd (tofu)	1 (225 g/8 oz)
3	small finely chopped scallions (spring onions) or a leek	3
	salt	
	freshly ground pepper	
2 tsp	oil	2 tsp
	few sprigs coriander or parsley	

1. Prepare the sauce. Bring 6 tbsp water to the boil in a small saucepan. Add the soy sauce, sugar and garlic. Stir well and simmer for a few minutes until reduced by about half. Remove the saucepan from the heat. Leave to cool slightly and stir in the sambal ulek, lemon juice and a small pinch of salt. Keep the sauce warm over very low heat.
2. Beat the eggs in a bowl. Crumble the soybean curd and mix the crumbs, scallions (spring onions) or leek and a little salt and pepper with the egg.
3. Heat 2 tsp oil in a heavy-based frying pan.
4. Reduce the heat and pour the egg and soybean curd mixture into the pan. Fry the omelette on both sides, turning it as soon as the upper side has set but still looks moist on top.
5. Turn the omelette out on to a warmed plate and fold it in half. Pour over the warm sauce and garnish with sprigs of coriander or parsley.

Tempe tante truus

Fermented Soybean Curd (Tempe) in Coconut Sauce

00.05 Serves 4   00.20

American	Ingredients	Metric/Imperial
1 (14 oz)	cake fermented soybean curd (tempe)	1 (400 g/14 oz)
	salt	
4 tbsp	creamed coconut (santen)	4 tbsp
1	large finely chopped onion	1
2	crushed garlic cloves	2
2 tsp	sambal ulek (see page 128)	2 tsp
1 tsp	soft brown sugar	1 tsp
½ tsp	laos powder	½ tsp
½ tsp	lemon grass powder	½ tsp
4	finely chopped candle nuts	4
2	salam leaves	2
1 tbsp	finely chopped chives (optional)	1 tbsp
1	red chili (optional)	1

1. Cut the tempe into 8 equal pieces.
2. Bring 1¼ cups (300 ml/½ pint) water to the boil. Add ¼ tsp salt and boil the tempe for 4 minutes. Place the tempe in a strainer or colander.
3. Dissolve the creamed coconut in the boiling water in the pan and bring slowly to the boil.
4. Pound the onion, garlic, sambal ulek, sugar, laos powder, lemon grass powder and the candle nuts in a mortar. Add this mixture and the salam leaves to the coconut mixture. Stir well and boil gently for a few minutes.
5. Add the pieces of tempe and boil gently until the mixture forms a thick sauce. Remove the salam leaves.
6. Serve on a warmed dish, garnished with finely chopped chives and a red chili flower.

Rempeyek kacang

Rempeyek with Peanuts

00.10 makes 10   00.20

American	Ingredients	Metric/Imperial
2 tbsp	creamed coconut (santen)	2 tbsp
2	crushed garlic cloves	2
½ tsp	ground coriander seeds	½ tsp
	pinch ground cumin seeds	
½ tsp	ground turmeric	½ tsp
	pinch ground ginger	
	salt	
3 oz	rice flour	75 g/3 oz
1 oz	cornstarch (cornflour)	25 g/1 oz
¼ lb	salted, shelled peanuts	125 g/4 oz
5 tbsp	groundnut oil	5 tbsp

1. Bring ⅔ cup (150 ml/¼ pint) water to the boil. Dissolve the creamed coconut (santen) in it and leave to cool. Add the garlic, coriander, cumin, turmeric, ginger and a little salt.
2. Put the rice flour and cornstarch (cornflour) in a bowl, mix well, then add the creamed coconut mixture. Stir well to form a smooth, liquid batter adding a little water if necessary. Stir in the peanuts.
3. Heat the oil in a frying pan and using a ladle, make 3 small heaps of peanut batter in the pan. This will spread in the pan. Cook until golden brown and crisp on both sides, then remove from the pan and cool on crumpled kitchen paper. Repeat with the remaining batter.
4. Store the rempeyek in a cooled, airtight container.

Rempeyek with peanuts

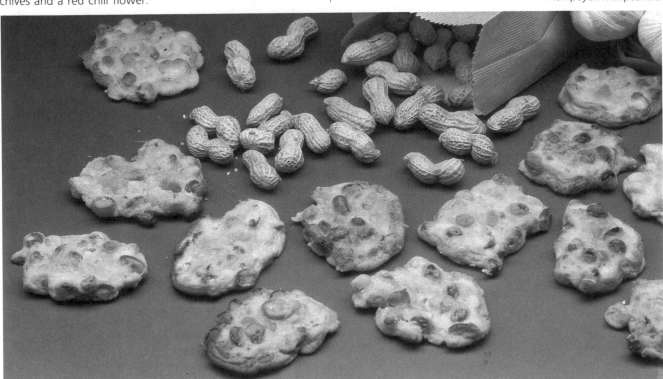

Steamed vegetables with coconut

Empal daging
Pressed Boiled Beef

	00.10	02.45
	plus cooling and pressing time	

American	Ingredients	Metric/Imperial
1	lemon	1
1	large chopped onion	1
1	finely chopped garlic clove	1
2 tbsp	soft brown sugar	2 tbsp
1 tbsp	Indonesian sweet soy sauce (ketyap benteng manis)	1 tbsp
1 tsp	ground coriander seeds	1 tsp
	pinch ground cumin seeds	
1	salam leaf	1
½ tsp	salt	½ tsp
1½ lb	very lean beefsteak	700 g/1½ lb
⅔ cup	groundnut oil	150 ml/¼ pint

1. Cut the lemon into 6 thin slices and discard the pips.
2. Pound the onion and garlic to a paste, using a food processor or mortar.
3. Bring 1 cup (250 ml/8 fl oz) water to the boil in a saucepan. Add the slices of lemon, the onion and garlic paste, sugar, soy sauce, coriander, cumin, salam leaf and salt. Stir well and bring back to the boil. Lay the meat flat in the pan.
4. Bring the water back to the boil, cover the pan and reduce the heat. Simmer for about 2 hours, adding more boiling water if necessary to keep the meat immersed in the liquid until about 30 minutes before it is cooked.
5. Remove the slices of lemon and the salam leaf and simmer for a further 30 minutes, uncovered, until the liquid has almost evaporated.
6. Put the meat on a chopping board and leave to cool a little. Place another chopping board or flat heavy object, such a saucepan full of water, on top of the meat and leave until completely cold.
7. Cut the meat into 8 equal pieces and replace the heavy object on top. Leave for at least 1 hour.
8. Heat the oil in a frying pan and cook half of the meat pieces until brown and crisp on both sides. Fry the remaining 4 pieces in the same way.
9. Leave the meat to cool and drain on a piece of kitchen paper and serve warm or cold as part of a larger meal or as a snack.

Urap
Steamed Vegetables with Coconut

	00.40	00.10
	Serves 4	

American	Ingredients	Metric/Imperial
¼ lb	French beans or haricots vert	125 g/4 oz
¼ lb	spinach	125 g/4 oz
¼ lb	bean sprouts	125 g/4 oz
¼ lb	white cabbage	125 g/4 oz
½	cucumber	½
1	small coconut	1
1	chopped onion	1
1	chopped garlic clove	1
1 tsp	sambal ulek (see page 128)	1 tsp
½ tsp	laos powder	½ tsp
	salt	
4	large lettuce leaves	4
4	lime leaves	4

1. Rinse the beans, trim and string them if necessary. Cut into 1 in (2.5 cm) lengths.
2. Pick over the spinach and rinse thoroughly. Drain and cut into strips, discarding any thick stalks.
3. Rinse the bean sprouts and remove as many seed cases as possible. Drain well.
4. Shred the cabbage.
5. Rinse the cucumber, trim and halve lengthwise. Remove the seeds and cut into strips, then into small cubes.
6. Mix the vegetables in a bowl. Cut the coconut open, reserving the liquid. Grate the coconut meat finely.
7. Pound the onion, garlic, sambal and laos in a mortar or food processor. Mix in the grated coconut, add some salt then stir the mixture into the vegetables.
8. Place 4 large washed and dried lettuce leaves on a work surface or board. Divide the vegetable mixture evenly between the leaves and place a lime leaf on top of each.
9. Fold the lettuce leaf around the vegetables as tightly as possible to form 4 small parcels. Brush the top section of a steamer with a little oil and place the parcels inside the pan.
10. Bring a generous quantity of water to the boil in the pan. Put the steamer on top, cover and steam the vegetables for 8-10 minutes and serve.

Kacang goreng
Fried Peanuts

	00.30	00.10
	plus cooling time	

American	Ingredients	Metric/Imperial
2¼ lb	raw peanuts in their shells	1 kg/2¼ lb
2 tbsp	groundnut oil	2 tbsp
2	peeled garlic cloves	2
	salt	

1. Shell the peanuts and remove the brown skins.
2. Heat the oil in a non-stick saucepan and fry the garlic cloves until golden brown. Discard the garlic cloves and add the peanuts to the pan. Stir fry the peanuts until golden yellow.
3. Roll the peanuts on a piece of kitchen paper to dry, then spread them out on a large cold plate.

4. Before the nuts are completely cold, sprinkle with a little salt and shake to distribute the salt evenly.

Cook's tip: a bowl of peanuts fried in this way can be placed on the table to accompany almost any Indonesian meal.

Pecel

Vegetables with Peanut Sauce

	00.15 plus cooling time	00.30

American	Ingredients	Metric/Imperial
½ lb	French beans	225 g/8 oz
½ lb	spinach	225 g/8 oz
2 oz	bean sprouts	50 g/2 oz
2 tbsp	groundnut oil	2 tbsp
2	chopped onions	2
1	finely chopped garlic clove	1
1 tsp	sambal ulek or sambal trasi (see page 128 or 129)	1 tsp
2 tsp	soft brown sugar	2 tsp
2 tsp	tamarind paste or 2 tbsp white vinegar	2 tsp
½ tsp	laos powder	½ tsp
4-5 tbsp	peanut butter	4-5 tbsp
2 tbsp	Indonesian sweet soy sauce (ketyap benteng manis) (optional)	2 tbsp

1. Rinse the French beans, trim and string if necessary. Cut the beans into 1 in (2.5 cm) lengths. Cook in boiling salted water for 5-6 minutes, drain and cool rapidly in cold water. Drain thoroughly.

2. Pick over the spinach, rinse very thoroughly then cook in boiling salted water for 2-3 minutes, stirring constantly. Drain thoroughly.

3. Rinse the bean sprouts in cold running water, removing as many seed cases as possible. Cook in boiling salted water for 30 seconds, then drain.

4. Heat the oil in a wok and stir fry the onions until transparent. Add the garlic and continue stirring until the onions are light brown. Add the sambal, sugar, tamarind paste or vinegar, laos powder and salt. Stir well and then add the peanut butter.

5. Stir in ¾ cup (200 ml/7 fl oz) boiling water and cook, stirring until the mixture forms a thick sauce. Add 2 tbsp soy sauce if liked and simmer for 1-2 minutes.

6. Put the cold vegetables in a dish and pour the hot sauce over. Serve immediately.

Cook's tip: to serve this dish as part of a complete vegetarian meal, stir in some fried cubes of soybean curd (tofu) and a few fried onions.

Vegetables with peanut sauce

Gado-gado

Vegetables with Egg and Peanut Sauce

◢◣ 00.25   00.30 🍲
Serves 4

American	Ingredients	Metric/Imperial
¼ lb	white or green cabbage	125 g/4 oz
	salt	
¼ lb	French beans or haricots vert	125 g/4 oz
¼ lb	bean sprouts	125 g/¼ lb
1	small cucumber	1
2-3	medium size boiled potatoes	2-3
	few lettuce leaves	
1 tbsp	groundnut oil	1 tbsp
2	finely chopped onions	2
3 tbsp	thick coconut milk	3 tbsp
6 tbsp	peanut butter	6 tbsp
1 tbsp	lemon juice or white vinegar	1 tbsp
½ tsp	garlic powder (optional)	½ tsp
1 tsp	sambal ulek (see page 128)	1 tsp
2 tsp	soft brown sugar	2 tsp
2 tsp	Indonesian sweet soy sauce (ketyap benteng manis)	2 tsp
	salt	
2	shelled hard-cooked (hard-boiled) eggs	2
1 tbsp	finely chopped coriander or parsley leaves	1 tbsp

1. Shred the cabbage finely and cook in lightly salted boiling water for 4-5 minutes. Drain well.
2. Rinse the beans, trim and string if necessary. Cut into 1½ in (4 cm) lengths. Cook in boiling salted water for 5-6 minutes. Drain, then cool rapidly in cold water. Drain well.
3. Rinse the bean sprouts in cold water and remove as many seed cases as possible. Drain well, then slowly pour over several quarts/litres boiling water. Drain thoroughly.
4. Rinse the cucumber, trim, halve lengthwise and remove the seeds. Cut each half into 3 long pieces, then into cubes.
5. Cut the potatoes into ¼ in (5 mm) slices.
6. Rinse and dry the lettuce leaves and shred them finely.
7. Heat the oil in a large frying pan and fry the onion until golden yellow.

Vegetables with egg and peanut sauce

Fried eggplant (aubergine) with cold sauce

8. Bring 1 cup (250 ml/8 fl oz) water to the boil in a small saucepan. Add the coconut milk and 1 tbsp fried onion, the peanut butter, lemon juice or vinegar, garlic powder, sambal, sugar, soy sauce and salt to taste. Bring back to the boil, stirring continuously.
9. Reduce the heat and stir until the sauce is thick. Simmer for 2-3 minutes.
10. Arrange the vegetables on a flat serving platter. Halve the eggs and place them on top of the vegetables. Pour over the sauce, sprinkle the remaining fried onion and the coriander or parsley over the top and serve.

Terong coloh-coloh agus

Fried Eggplant (Aubergine) with Cold Sauce

◢◣ 00.20   00.15 🍲
plus standing time

American	Ingredients	Metric/Imperial
1	large chopped onion	1
2-3	crushed garlic cloves	2-3
2 tsp	sambal ulek or sambal trasi (see page 128 or 129)	2 tsp
3 tbsp	Indonesian sweet soy sauce (ketyap benteng manis)	3 tbsp
2 tsp	soft brown sugar	2 tsp
1	long, thin eggplant (aubergine)	1
	salt	
2 tbsp	lemon juice	2 tbsp
4 tbsp	groundnut oil	4 tbsp
1	red chili	1

1. Pound the onion to a paste, in a food processor or mortar. Add the garlic, sambal, soy sauce and sugar. Mix vigorously for 1 minute. Leave the sauce to stand for at least 30 minutes, then rub it through a fine strainer (sieve).
2. Rinse the eggplant (aubergine) under cold running water. Trim the ends and cut the flesh into finger-width slices.
3. In a bowl, mix the lemon juice with ½ tsp salt. Brush over the eggplant (aubergine) slices and set aside for 15 minutes. Dry with kitchen paper.

4. Heat the oil in a wok and fry the slices of eggplant (aubergine), 6-8 at a time, until golden brown on both sides. Add more oil if necessary. Drain on kitchen paper.
5. Arrange the fried eggplant (aubergine) on a warmed dish and garnish with a red chili flower.
6. Serve the dipping sauce separately in individual bowls.

Kentang coloh-coloh
Fried Sweet Potatoes with Cold Sauce

00.15 plus standing time   00.35

American	Ingredients	Metric/Imperial
2	large chopped onions	2
2	garlic cloves	2
2 tsp	sambal ulek (see page 128)	2 tsp
4 tbsp	Indonesian salty soy sauce (ketyap benteng asin)	4 tbsp
2 tsp	soft brown sugar	2 tsp
4 tbsp	groundnut oil	4 tbsp
1 lb	sweet potatoes	450 g/1 lb
2 tbsp	lemon juice	2 tbsp
	salt	
1	red bell pepper (optional)	1
1	skinned tomato (optional)	1
1	sprig coriander or parsley (optional)	1

1. Pound the onion to a paste in a food processor or mortar. Add the garlic, sambal, soy sauce and soft brown sugar and mix vigorously for 1 minute. Leave the sauce to stand for at least 30 minutes then rub through a fine strainer (sieve) and stir in 1-2 tbsp cold water.
2. Brush the top section of a steamer with oil and place the sweet potatoes on it.
3. Bring some water to the boil in the pan, place the steamer on top, cover and cook for 15-18 minutes. Drain and leave to dry in a colander.
4. Put the lemon juice in a bowl and add ¼ tsp salt. Stir until the salt has dissolved. Peel and slice the sweet potatoes and sprinkle with the lemon and salt mixture. Leave for 3-4 minutes. Dry with kitchen paper.
5. Heat the oil and fry the sweet potatoes until golden brown and crisp. Drain on kitchen paper, then arrange on a warmed plate.
6. Spread a finely chopped red bell pepper over the top or garnish with a few slices of tomato and a sprig of coriander or parsley. Serve the dipping sauce in individual dishes.

Fried eggplant (aubergine) with cold sauce

Lalab kubis
Cabbage Salad

00.10 plus standing time   00.05

American	Ingredients	Metric/Imperial
1	small white cabbage	1
	salt	
1 tbsp	lemon juice	1 tbsp
1 tbsp	Indonesian salty soy sauce	1 tbsp
1 tsp	white sugar	1 tsp
1 tbsp	sambal ulek (see page 128)	1 tbsp
2	crushed garlic cloves	2
1 tbsp	groundnut oil	1 tbsp
1 tbsp	desiccated coconut (optional)	1 tbsp

1. Remove the outer leaves and the thickest part of the stalk from the cabbage. Select 12-16 leaves.
2. Bring a few quarts/litres of salted water to the boil in a large saucepan. Cook the cabbage leaves in the water for 3 minutes. Drain and cool thoroughly in a colander.
3. Dry the leaves with kitchen paper and remove the stalks.
4. Make a dressing by mixing together the lemon juice, soy sauce, sugar, sambal, garlic and groundnut oil. Brush each leaf with a thin layer of the dressing, then lay the leaves one on top of the other. Cover with a cloth and place a weight, such as a pan full of water, on top. Leave to stand for at least 30 minutes in a cool place.
5. Cut the leaves into finger-width strips. Place them in a serving dish and sprinkle with a tbsp of desiccated coconut.

Lalab buncis
Bean Salad

00.10 plus standing time   00.05

American	Ingredients	Metric/Imperial
½ lb	French beans or haricot verts	225 g/8 oz
	salt	
	zest of 1 lemon	
2 tbsp	lemon juice	2 tbsp
1½ tbsp	Indonesian sweet soy sauce (ketyap benteng manis)	1½ tbsp
1 tsp	white sugar	1 tsp
1½ tsp	sambal ulek (see page 128)	1½ tsp
	pinch garlic powder	
1½ tbsp	groundnut oil	1½ tbsp
2	skinned tomatoes	2
1 tbsp	finely chopped coriander, celery or parsley leaves	1 tbsp

1. Rinse the beans, trim and string if necessary. Cut to equal length.
2. Bring a few quarts/litres salted water to the boil in a saucepan. Add the lemon zest and the beans and boil for 4-5 minutes. Drain in a colander.
3. Make the dressing by mixing together the lemon juice, soy sauce, sugar, sambal, garlic powder and groundnut oil. Add the beans to the dressing while they are still warm and set aside in a cool place, until cold.
4. Arrange the beans in a dish. Slice the tomatoes, dip them in the remaining dressing and sprinkle with coriander, celery or parsley leaves. Arrange the tomatoes around the beans.

Left to right: Spinach salad, Pineapple salad

Lalab bayam

Spinach Salad

00.10 plus cooling time		00.02

American	Ingredients	Metric/Imperial
½ lb	spinach	225 g/8 oz
	salt	
1 tsp	sambal ulek (see page 128)	1 tsp
	pinch garlic powder	
1½ tbsp	lemon juice	1½ tbsp
1 tsp	white sugar	1 tsp
1	skinned tomato	1

1. Rinse the spinach very thoroughly and remove any thick stalks.
2. Bring a few pints/litres of salted water to the boil in a saucepan. Add the spinach, stir well and bring to the boil again. Immediately turn into a colander and drain thoroughly, pressing with a small plate or saucer to squeeze out as much liquid as possible.
3. Shred the cooked spinach.
4. Make the dressing by mixing together the sambal, garlic powder, lemon juice and sugar. Just before serving pour the dressing over the spinach and toss lightly.
5. Place the spinach in a bowl and garnish with a tomato flower.

Lalab ketimun

Cucumber Salad

00.10 Serves 4 as side dish		00.00

American	Ingredients	Metric/Imperial
1	large cucumber	1
1 tsp	sambal ulek (see page 128)	1 tsp
2 tbsp	lemon juice or vinegar	2 tbsp
	salt	
1-2 tbsp	chopped red onion	1-2 tbsp

1. Rinse the cucumber, trim and halve lengthwise. Remove the seeds and cut the two halves into 1½ in (4 cm) pieces. Leave the cucumber to drain in a cool place for 15 minutes.
2. Mix together the sambal ulek, lemon juice or vinegar and a little salt. Just before serving add the cucumber pieces and stir well.
3. Serve the salad, sprinkled with the chopped red onion.

Lalab cendawan

Mushroom Salad

00.15 Serves 4 as side dish		00.15

American	Ingredients	Metric/Imperial
1 lb	mushrooms	450 g/1 lb
	zest of 2 lemons	
	salt	
1½ tbsp	lemon juice	1½ tbsp
1½ tbsp	Indonesian sweet soy sauce (ketyap benteng manis)	1½ tbsp
1 tsp	soft brown sugar	1 tsp
1 tsp	sambal ulek (see page 128)	1 tsp
1 tbsp	chopped shallot or onion	1 tbsp
1	crushed garlic clove	1
2 tbsp	groundnut oil	2 tbsp
½	seeded red bell pepper	½
3-4 tbsp	canned, drained sweetcorn	3-4 tbsp
2 tbsp	finely chopped coriander leaves, celery or parsley	2 tbsp

1. Wipe the mushrooms and trim the stalks, cut into slices.
2. Bring a few quarts/litres of salted water to the boil in a saucepan. Add the lemon zest. Boil vigorously for 3 minutes, then add the mushrooms and bring back to the boil. Simmer for 3 minutes then drain the mushrooms in a colander.
3. Make the dressing by mixing together the lemon juice, soy sauce, soft brown sugar, sambal, shallot or onion, garlic and groundnut oil. Add the mushrooms to the dressing and leave to stand in a cool place for 15 minutes.
4. Cut the bell pepper into very small squares and place in a pan with a little cold water.

5. Bring to the boil then drain in a colander and leave to cool completely.

6. Mix the bell pepper with the drained sweetcorn and add to the mushrooms.

7. Serve the salad in a bowl, sprinkled with chopped coriander leaves, celery or parsley.

Lalab nenas muda
Pineapple Salad

◣ 00.15   00.00
plus standing time

American	Ingredients	Metric/Imperial
1	small unripe pineapple	1
	salt	
1 tsp	soft brown sugar	1 tsp
1 tbsp	lemon juice	1 tbsp
1 tbsp	Indonesian sweet soy sauce (ketyap benteng manis)	1 tbsp
1 tsp	sambal ulek (see page 128)	1 tsp
½	seeded red bell pepper	½
	few large lettuce leaves (optional)	
1 tbsp	finely chopped chives	1 tbsp

1. Peel the pineapple and remove any blemishes. Slice, remove the hard core and cut the fruit into cubes.

2. Sprinkle the pineapple with a little salt and place in a colander. Leave to drain in a cool place for at least 15 minutes.

3. Make the dressing by mixing together the soft brown sugar, lemon juice, soy sauce and sambal.

4. Cut the bell pepper into long thin slices.

5. Just before serving, place the pineapple cubes in the dressing. Place them on a dish lined with lettuce leaves, sprinkled with the chives and arrange the bell pepper on top.

Lalab tauge
Bean Sprout Salad

◣ 00.20   00.00
plus standing time

American	Ingredients	Metric/Imperial
¼ lb	bean sprouts	125g/4 oz
1 tbsp	Indonesian salty soy sauce (ketyap benteng asin)	1 tbsp
2 tbsp	lemon juice or vinegar	2 tbsp
3 tsp	sambal ulek (see page 128)	3 tsp
¼	cucumber or 1 large gherkin	¼
	radishes and chives to garnish	

1. Rinse the bean sprouts in cold water and remove as many seed cases as possible. Drain thoroughly. Pour a few pints/litres boiling water very slowly over the bean sprouts and leave to drain.

2. Make the dressing by mixing together the soy sauce, lemon juice or vinegar and sambals.

3. Rinse the cucumber, trim and halve lengthwise. Remove the seeds, then coarsely grate the cucumber or gherkin. Add the cucumber or gherkin to the dressing and set aside for 15 minutes, until the dressing is partly absorbed.

4. Just before serving, add the bean sprouts to the dressing and cucumber or gherkin. Stir well then transfer to a serving bowl. Garnish with radish flowers and chives.

Lalab bunga kol
Cauliflower Salad

◣ 00.10   00.05
plus cooling time

American	Ingredients	Metric/Imperial
1	small cauliflower	1
	salt	
1 ½ tbsp	lemon juice	1 ½ tbsp
½ tbsp	Indonesian sweet soy sauce (ketyap benteng manis)	½ tbsp
1 tsp	white sugar	1 tsp
1 tsp	sambal trasi (see page 129)	1 tsp

1. Rinse the cauliflower and cut into small florets.

2. Cook the cauliflower in boiling salted water for 4-5 minutes. Drain thoroughly and cool.

3. Make a dressing by mixing together the lemon juice, soy sauce, sugar and sambal. Just before serving pour the dressing over the cauliflower.

Lalab telor dan daging sapi
Beef and Egg Salad

◣ 00.15   00.20
plus cooling

American	Ingredients	Metric/Imperial
1	small Chinese cabbage or white cabbage	1
1 tbsp	groundnut oil	1 tbsp
1	chopped onion	1
1	finely chopped garlic clove	1
¼ lb	coarsely ground (minced) beef	125 g/4 oz
½	coarsely grated cucumber	½
2	skinned, diced tomatoes	2
	salt	
2	chopped onions	2
2	crushed garlic cloves	2
2 tsp	sambal ulek (see page 128)	2 tsp
2 tbsp	Indonesian sweet soy sauce (ketyap benteng manis)	2 tbsp
3 tbsp	lemon juice	3 tbsp
½ tsp	white sugar	½ tsp
1 tbsp	groundnut oil	1 tbsp
	few lettuce leaves	
2	hard-cooked (hard-boiled) eggs	2

1. Rinse the cabbage and shred it finely.

2. Heat 1 tbsp oil in a wok and stir fry 1 onion, until transparent. Add 1 garlic clove and the beef. Stir fry for 6-8 minutes until the beef is light brown and crumbles.

3. Stir in the cabbage and fry gently for 2-3 minutes.

4. Add the cucumber and diced tomato and season with a little salt. Stir once then remove from the heat and leave to cool.

5. Make the sauce by pounding 2 onions, 2 garlic cloves and the sambal into a paste. Add the soy sauce, lemon juice, sugar, oil and a little salt to taste. Just before serving, pour the sauce over the meat mixture.

6. Serve on a plate lined with lettuce leaves, topped with slices of hard-cooked (hard-boiled) egg.

Bami jawa (I)
Javanese Bami (I)

00.25 Serves 4   **00.15**

American	Ingredients	Metric/Imperial
¾ lb	egg noodles	350 g/12 oz
1½ lb	chicken legs	700 g/1½ lb
2 oz	bean sprouts	50 g/2 oz
4 tbsp	groundnut oil	4 tbsp
2	chopped onions	2
2	finely chopped garlic cloves	2
1	small chopped leek (white part only)	1
¼ lb	chopped white cabbage	125 g/4 oz
¼ lb	chopped French beans	125 g/4 oz
2-3 tsp	sambal ulek (see page 128)	2-3 tsp
2 tbsp	finely chopped coriander leaves or celery	2 tbsp
	pinch soft brown sugar	
	salt	
2 tbsp	Indonesian sweet soy sauce (ketyap benteng manis)	2 tbsp
1 tsp	lemon juice	1 tsp
½	cucumber	½
1	tomato	1
	chopped chives	

1. Cook the egg noodles according to the instructions on the packet.
2. Remove the chicken skin, cut the meat off the bone and shred it.
3. Rinse the bean sprouts in cold water and remove as many of the seed cases as possible. Drain in a colander.
4. Heat the oil in a wok and stir fry the onion until transparent. Add the garlic, stir well then add the chicken. Fry gently, stirring constantly, for 2 minutes.
5. Add the leek, cabbage and beans and stir fry gently for 3-4 minutes.
6. Add the sambal ulek and bean sprouts. Fry for a few seconds, then sprinkle with the coriander or celery, sugar and salt to taste.
7. Add the noodles a few at a time and heat through, stirring all the time. Add the soy sauce and lemon juice, stir once more then transfer to a warmed serving dish.
8. Serve garnished with lightly salted cucumber slices, tomato slices and chives.

Javanese Bami (I)

Bami jawa (II)
Javanese Bami (II)

00.25 Serves 4   **00.15**

American	Ingredients	Metric/Imperial
¾ lb	egg noodles	350 g/12 oz
¾ lb	skinned chicken legs	350 g/12 oz
4	sticks celery	4
¼ lb	mushrooms	¼ lb
3-4 tbsp	groundnut oil	3-4 tbsp
2	chopped onions	2
2	finely chopped garlic cloves	2
1	small chopped leek (white part only)	1
2 tsp	sambal ulek (see page 128)	2 tsp
¼ lb	fresh peeled small shrimp	125 g/4 oz
2 tbsp	finely chopped chives	2 tbsp
1-2	green and red chilies	1-2

1. Prepare the egg noodles according to the instructions.
2. Cut the meat off the chicken bones and shred it.
3. Rinse the celery and chop it very finely.
4. Wipe the mushrooms, trim the stalks and slice the caps.
5. Heat the oil in a wok and stir fry the onion until transparent. Add the garlic then the chicken. Stir fry for 2 minutes.
6. Add the mushrooms, leek and celery and continue to stir fry gently for 3-4 minutes.
7. Add the sambal, followed by the shrimp (prawns). Add the noodles a few at a time and stir fry gently until the noodles are hot.
8. Transfer to a warmed dish, sprinkle with chives and garnish with one or more chili flowers.

Bami jawa (III)
Javanese Bami (III)

00.15 Serves 4   **00.35**

American	Ingredients	Metric/Imperial
2	eggs	2
	salt	
	freshly ground pepper	
2 tbsp	finely chopped celery	2 tbsp
1 oz	butter or oil	1 oz
¾ lb	egg noodles	350 g/¾ lb
1	small red bell pepper	1
¼ lb	French beans	¼ lb
4 tbsp	groundnut oil	4 tbsp
2	chopped onions	2
2	finely chopped garlic cloves	2
¾ lb	coarsely ground (minced) beef or lamb	350 g/12 oz
½ lb	chopped Chinese cabbage or white cabbage	225 g/8 oz
2 tsp	sambal ulek (see page 128)	2 tsp
¼ lb	crabmeat, thawed if frozen	125 g/4 oz
2 tbsp	Indonesian sweet soy sauce (ketyap benteng manis)	2 tbsp
½	cucumber	½

Javanese Bami (II)

1. Beat the eggs, add salt and pepper to taste and 1 tbsp celery. Fry in a little oil to make a thin omelette. Roll up the omelette and cut into narrow strips.

2. Cook the egg noodles according to the instructions on the packet.

3. Rinse the bell pepper, trim, halve and seed. Dice the flesh very finely.

4. Rinse the beans, trim and string them if necessary. Cut into small pieces.

5. Heat the oil in a wok and stir fry the onions until transparent. Add the garlic and the meat. Reduce the heat and gently fry the meat for about 6 minutes until light brown and crumbled.

6. Add the beans, cabbage and bell pepper. Continue to fry for 3-4 minutes then add the sambal ulek and stir several times.

7. Sprinkle on 1 tbsp chopped celery and add the noodles gradually, followed by the crabmeat. Fry gently until the noodles are hot. Stir in the soy sauce.

8. Transfer to a warmed dish and garnish with a lattice of omelette strips and four small cucumber fans.

Ikan dan Mihun

Fish and Shrimp (Prawns) with Fried Rice Vermicelli

	00.10	00.20
	Serves 4	

American	Ingredients	Metric/Imperial
1 lb	sole, turbot or brill fillets	450 g/1 lb
9 tbsp	groundnut oil	9 tbsp
1	chopped onion	1
1	finely chopped garlic clove	1
2 tbsp	finely chopped celery	2 tbsp
2 tsp	sambal trasi (see page 129)	2 tsp
1 tbsp	Indonesian sweet soy sauce (ketyap benteng manis)	1 tbsp
	salt	
	freshly ground pepper	
2 tbsp	finely chopped chives	2 tbsp
¼ lb	fresh peeled shrimp (prawns)	125 g/4 oz
1 tsp	cornstarch (cornflour)	1 tsp
1	red chili	1
1	green chili	1
¾ lb	rice vermicelli	350 g/12 oz

1. Rinse the fish under cold running water, dry with kitchen paper and cut into small pieces.

2. Heat 3 tbsp oil in a wok and stir fry the onion until transparent. Add the garlic and the pieces of fish.

3. Sprinkle the celery over the dish and add the sambal trasi and ¾ cup (200 ml/7 fl oz) boiling water. Cook for 1 minute, then add the soy sauce and a little salt and pepper to taste. Stir in the chives, cover the pan and cook for another 4 minutes.

4. Add the shrimp (prawns). Mix the cornstarch (cornflour) with 1 tbsp cold water and stir into the contents of the wok. Cook, stirring until the sauce has thickened.

5. Cut off the chili stalks and cut the flesh into small rings.

6. Fry the rice vermicelli a few at a time in 6 tbsp oil, following the instructions on the packet. Drain and place in a warmed bowl. Put the fish mixture on top and garnish with an edging of red and green chili rings.

Daging sapi dan mihun

Beef with Fried Rice Vermicelli

	00.10	02.45
	Serves 4	

American	Ingredients	Metric/Imperial
1 lb	lean, cubed braising beef	450 g/1 lb
9 tbsp	groundnut oil	9 tbsp
2	chopped onions	2
4	finely chopped garlic cloves	4
2 tsp	sambal ulek (see page 128)	2 tsp
1 cup	hot beef bouillon (stock)	250 ml/8 fl oz
2-3 tbsp	Indonesian sweet soy sauce (ketyap benteng manis)	2-3 tbsp
1½ tsp	cornstarch (cornflour)	1½ tsp
2 tbsp	finely chopped chives	2 tbsp
2-3 oz	fresh peeled shrimp (prawns)	50-75 g/2-3 oz
	pinch ground ginger	
	salt	
	freshly ground pepper	
	pinch soft brown sugar	
¾ lb	rice vermicelli	350 g/12 oz
1	small cucumber	1
2	skinned, sliced tomatoes	2

1. Dry the meat with kitchen paper. Heat 3 tbsp oil in a wok and stir fry the onions until transparent.

2. Add the garlic and then the meat. Stir fry until brown. Add the sambal, stir well and add the hot bouillon (stock).

3. Cover the wok and simmer for 2-2½ hours until the meat is tender.

4. Add the soy sauce. Mix the cornstarch (cornflour) with 1½ tbsp cold water and stir into the contents of the wok. Cook gently for a few minutes then stir in the chives, shrimp (prawns), ground ginger, a little salt and pepper to taste, and the sugar.

5. Heat 6 tbsp oil in a second wok or large frying pan. Fry the rice vermicelli according to the instructions on the packet, a few at a time, until golden.

6. Drain the vermicelli and transfer to a warmed bowl. Spread the meat mixture over the noodles and garnish with cucumber fans and slices of tomato.

Bebek betutu Bali

Balinese Duck

00.30
Serves about 8

02.00

American	Ingredients	Metric/Imperial
1 (5½ lb)	duck	1 (2.5 kg/5½ lb)
4	red chilies	4
2 tbsp	groundnut oil	2 tbsp
3	large coarsely chopped onions	3
3	very finely chopped garlic cloves	3
2 tbsp	grated fresh root ginger	2 tbsp
12	finely grated candle nuts	2
1 tsp	cardamom seeds	1 tsp
1 tsp	ground turmeric	1 tsp
1 tsp	trasi	1 tsp
2 tsp	salt	2 tsp
2 tsp	soft brown sugar	2 tsp
1 tsp	ground black pepper	1 tsp
1 tbsp	groundnut oil	1 tbsp
	salt	
	freshly ground pepper	
	fresh banana leaves or aluminum foil	

1. Dry the duck inside and out with kitchen paper.
2. Rinse the chilies, trim, halve and seed them. Cut the flesh into small pieces.
3. Heat the oil in a wok and stir fry the onions until beginning to change color. Add the garlic and root ginger and fry very gently with the onions for 1 minute. Add the chilies, candle nuts, cardamom seeds, turmeric, trasi, salt, sugar and pepper. Stir well a few times then transfer the ingredients to a mortar or food processor and pound to a fine paste.
4. Set the oven to 200°C/400°F/Gas Mark 6.
5. Stuff the duck with the paste, reserving 1 tbsp. Sew up the cavity with thin string or strong cotton.
6. Mix the reserved paste with a little oil, some salt and freshly ground pepper. Rub the outside of the duck with the mixture.
7. Spread the fresh banana leaves or a large sheet of double folded aluminum foil on a work surface and carefully wrap the duck. Secure the banana leaves with wooden cocktail picks or string.
8. Place the duck in a roasting tin and put on a shelf a little below the middle of the oven. After 15 minutes reduce the oven heat to 180°C/350°F/Gas Mark 4. Roast for a further 1¾ hours.
9. Serve the duck in its wrapping and open the leaves or foil at the table and carve.

Left to right:
Balinese duck,
Chicken and shrimp (prawns),
Spiced Balinese chicken

Opor ajam dan udang
Balinese Chicken and Shrimp (Prawns)

◣━━━━◢ 00.15 plus standing time **00.15 ◔**

American	Ingredients	Metric/Imperial
1½ lb	boneless chicken breasts	700 g/1½ lb
1	large coarsely chopped onion	1
2	very finely chopped garlic cloves	2
1 tsp	ground root ginger	1 tsp
1 tsp	ground turmeric	1 tsp
2	roasted, finely pounded candle nuts	2
½ tsp	ground coriander	½ tsp
2 tsp	sambal ulek (see page 128)	2 tsp
½ tbsp	salt	½ tbsp
3 tbsp	sunflower or corn oil	3 tbsp
1¼ cups	thin coconut milk	300 ml/½ pint
1 tbsp	lemon or lime juice	1 tbsp
½ lb	fresh peeled shrimp (prawns)	225 g/8 oz
¾ cup	thick coconut milk	200 ml/7 fl oz
2 tbsp	finely chopped chives (optional)	2 tbsp

1. Dry the chicken with kitchen paper and cut into finger width strips.
2. In a mortar or food processor pound the onion, garlic, ground root ginger, turmeric, candle nuts, coriander, sambal ulek and ½ tsp salt to form a fine paste.

3. Heat 1 tbsp oil in a wok and stir fry the paste for 2 minutes. Remove the wok from the heat and leave to cool.
4. Rub the strips of chicken with the paste and leave to stand for 1 hour.
5. Heat 2 tbsp oil in a wok and very quickly stir fry the strips of chicken until golden brown.
6. Add the thin coconut milk and bring to the boil, stirring constantly. Simmer very gently for 5 minutes.
7. Stir in the lemon or lime juice and the shrimp (prawns). Stir well a few times and add the thick coconut milk.
8. Bring to the boil then immediately transfer to a warmed serving dish. Sprinkle with chopped chives and serve.

Ayam pangang Bali
Spiced Balinese Chicken

◣━━━━◢ 00.20 Serves 4 **00.45 ◔**

American	Ingredients	Metric/Imperial
2 (1¾ lb)	roasting chickens	2 (800 g/1¾ lb)
1	large chopped onion	1
2	very finely chopped garlic cloves	2
1 tbsp	grated fresh root ginger	1 tbsp
2 tsp	sambal ulek (see page 128)	2 tsp
4	roasted, finely pounded candle nuts	4
2 tbsp	Indonesian sweet soy sauce (ketyap benteng manis)	2 tbsp
6 tbsp	sunflower or corn oil	6 tbsp
2 tbsp	soft brown sugar	2 tbsp
2 tbsp	lemon or lime juice	2 tbsp
½ tsp	salt	½ tsp
1¼ cups	thin coconut milk	300 ml/½ pint

1. Halve the chickens and then flatten them.
2. Pound the onion, garlic, root ginger, sambal ulek, candle nuts and soy sauce to a fine paste in a mortar or food processor.
3. Heat 5 tbsp oil in a large frying pan. Dry the chickens with kitchen paper and fry until golden brown on both sides. Remove from the frying pan and drain on kitchen paper.
4. Heat 1 tbsp of oil in a wok and stir fry the paste for 3 minutes. Add the sugar, lemon or lime juice, salt and coconut milk. Bring to the boil, stirring constantly. Add the chicken to the sauce. Partly cover the wok, reduce the heat and simmer gently for 15-20 minutes.
5. Serve in a warmed dish.

Babi guling

Roast Suckling Pig

00.30 plus cooling time

02.30

American	Ingredients	Metric/Imperial
1 (10 lb)	small, cleaned suckling pig	1 (4.5 kg/10 lb)
¼ lb	fresh root ginger	125 g/4 oz
1 tbsp	ground turmeric	1 tbsp
1 tbsp	ground chili	1 tbsp
2 tbsp	salt	2 tbsp
1 tsp	soft brown sugar	1 tsp
½ tsp	grated nutmeg	½ tsp
2 tsp	trasi	2 tsp
1 tsp	lemon grass powder	1 tsp
8	cloves	8
2 tsp	black peppercorns	2 tsp
1 tbsp	lemon or lime juice	1 tbsp
5 tbsp	lard or sunflower seed oil	5 tbsp
2	coarsely chopped large onions	2
4	very finely chopped garlic cloves	4
2 tbsp	vegetable oil	2 tbsp
1 tsp	salt	1 tsp
½ tsp	finely ground black pepper	½ tsp

1. Dry the suckling pig, inside and the outside with kitchen paper.
2. Thinly peel the root ginger and chop or grate it very finely.
3. Put the ginger in a bowl with the turmeric, ground chili, salt, sugar, nutmeg and trasi. Add 1 tbsp water and mix well.
4. Add the lemon grass, cloves, peppercorns and lemon or lime juice. Work well together, using the fingers, if necessary.
5. Heat the lard or oil in a wok and stir fry the onions until beginning to change color. Add the garlic and stir well a few times. Add all the spices and seasonings, except 2 tbsp vegetable oil, 1 tsp salt and ½ tsp finely ground black pepper. Stir fry for 2-3 minutes.
6. Remove the wok from the heat and leave contents to cool until just warm.
7. Rub the suckling pig on the inside with a little salt and stuff the abdominal cavity with the contents of the wok. Sew up the opening with thin string or strong cotton. Rub the outside of the pig with a mixture of 2 tbsp oil, 1 tsp salt and ½ tsp finely ground black pepper.
8. Skewer the suckling pig on a spit and broil (grill) over the glowing charcoal of a barbecue or roast in a preheated oven (220°OC/425°F/Gas Mark 7) for 2-2½ hours. Turn the pig regularly so that it is evenly broiled (grilled) or roasted on all sides. Brush with oil several times during cooking. Test the meat wit a skewer. When the juices are completely clear the meat is fully cooked.
9. Before carving allow the meat to rest for 15 minutes.

Left to right: Balinese fried rice, Balinese omelette, Vegetable salad with peanut sauce

Nasi goreng Bali

Balinese Fried Rice

00.20 00.10

Serves 4

American	Ingredients	Metric/Imperial
4 tbsp	margarine	4 tbsp
2	coarsely chopped onions	2
½ lb	cooked ham cut into thin strips	225 g/8 oz
1	very finely chopped garlic clove	1
1 tbsp	sambal ulek (see page 128)	1 tbsp
4	chopped scallions (spring onions)	4
½ lb	cold dry boiled rice	225 g/8 oz
½ lb	fresh peeled shrimp (prawns)	225 g/8 oz
1 tbsp	Indonesian salty soy sauce (ketyap benteng asin)	1 tbsp
3-4	eggs (scrambled)	3-4
1-2	skinned tomatoes cut into segments (optional)	1-2
	few sprigs coriander (optional)	

1. Heat the margarine in a wok and stir fry the onions until beginning to change color. Add the strips of ham and the garlic. Stir well a few times.
2. Add the sambal ulek and the scallions (spring onions). Stir and add the cold dry boiled rice a little at a time. Continue stirring until the rice is hot.
3. Add the shrimp (prawns) and sprinkle on the soy sauce. Continue stirring until the shrimp (prawns) are hot.
4. Serve in a large warmed dish and sprinkle with the scrambled eggs. Garnish with slices of skinned tomato and sprigs of coriander.

Dadar Bali

Balinese Omelette

00.10 00.20

Serves 4

American	Ingredients	Metric/Imperial
2 tbsp	sunflower oil	2 tbsp
1	very finely chopped onion	1
¾ lb	coarsely ground (minced) lean chicken meat	50 g/12 oz
1 tsp	Java curry powder	1 tsp
½ tsp	sambal ulek (see page 128)	½ tsp
1 tbsp	Indonesian sweet soy sauce (ketjap benteng manis)	1 tbsp
2	skinned, diced tomatoes	2
1 tbsp	finely chopped coriander leaves or parsley	1 tbsp
8	eggs	8
1 tsp	soft brown sugar	1 tsp
	salt	
	freshly ground pepper	
2-3 tbsp	sunflower oil or margarine	2-3 tbsp

1. First prepeare the filling. Heat the oil and stir fry the onion until beginning to change color.
2. Add the chicken and the Java curry powder. Stir fry until the chicken has lost its original color.
3. Add the sambal ulek, stir well a few times and sprinkle the soy sauce over the mixture.
4. Stir in the diced tomato and the coriander or parsley. Keep the mixture warm over very low heat.
5. Lightly beat the eggs with 4-5 tbsp water and add the sugar and a little salt and pepper to taste.
6. Fry four omelettes in a very little oil or margarine.
7. Spoon the chicken mixture on to the omelettes and fold them over. Serve immediately on warmed plates.

Gado-gado Bali
Vegetable Salad with Peanut Sauce

▬▷ 00.30   **00.30 🍲**
Serves 4

American	Ingredients	Metric/Imperial
2 tbsp	sunflower oil	2 tbsp
1	chopped onion	1
1	chopped garlic clove	1
1 tsp	sambal ulek (see page 128)	1 tsp
1 tbsp	soft brown sugar	1 tbsp
1 tbsp	lemon or lime juice	1 tbsp
1 tbsp	Indonesian sweet soy sauce (ketyap benteng manis)	1 tbsp
	salt	
¼ lb	peanut butter	125 g/4 oz
2	roasted, finely pounded candle nuts	2
1 cup	thin coconut milk	250 ml/8 fl oz
½ lb	spinach	225 g/8 oz
4	young carrots cut into thin strips	4
1	thick slice fermented soybean curd (tempe)	1
1 tbsp	sunflower oil	1 tbsp
¼ lb	bean sprouts	125 g/4 oz
2	large boiled sliced potatoes	2
6 tbsp	cooked sweetcorn	6 tbsp
6 oz	trimmed, steamed French beans or haricots verts	175 g/6 oz
¼	sliced cucumber	¼
4	coarsely chopped scallions (spring onions)	4
2	hard-cooked (hard-boiled) sliced eggs	2
2	skinned tomatoes cut into segments	2

1. Heat the oil in a wok and fry the onion until beginning to change color. Add the garlic and stir fry briefly. Add the sambal ulek, sugar, lemon or lime juice, soy sauce and a little salt. Stir well together. Stir in the peanut butter and the finely pounded candle nuts and then the thin coconut milk. Bring to the boil, stirring constantly. Add a little water if the sauce appears too thick and simmer gently for a few minutes stirring constantly to prevent the sauce sticking to the bottom of the pan. Keep the sauce warm, but do not boil again.
2. Steam the spinach leaves for 2 minutes and drain.
3. Steam the carrots for 2 minutes and drain.
4. Dice the soybean curd (tempe) and quickly stir fry in 1 tbsp oil until golden brown on all sides. Drain on kitchen paper.
5. Rinse the bean sprouts in cold water and remove as many seed cases as possible. Drain in a colander then pour several pints/litres boiling water very slowly over them. Drain the bean sprouts again.
6. Arrange the vegetables, cucumber, scallions (spring onions), eggs and tomatoes on a large flat dish. Sprinkle the cubes of fried bean curd over the top and serve handing the sauce separately.

MENU

Vegetable soup
with soybean curd (tofu)
Spiced chicken with pineapple
Javanese pancakes

Vegetable Soup with Soybean Curd (Tofu)

▬▷ 00.10   **03.10 🍲**
Serves 4

American	Ingredients	Metric/Imperial
1 lb	lean beef	450 g/1 lb
1	onion	1
4	cloves	4
2	salam leaves	2
1	blade mace	1
2 tbsp	groundnut oil	2 tbsp
½ lb	chopped fresh vegetables	225 g/½ lb
2 tbsp	coarsely chopped coriander leaves	2 tbsp
2	cakes soybean curd (tofu)	2
	salt	
1 tbsp	finely chopped parsley	1 tbsp

1. Put the beef in a saucepan with 6¼ cups (1.5 litres/2½ pints) water and bring to the boil. Skim the surface carefully several times.
2. Prick the onion with the cloves and add it to the saucepan. Add the salam leaves and mace and simmer gently for 2½-3 hours until the liquid has reduced by half. Strain the broth through a piece of damp muslin and set aside.
3. Heat the oil in a wok. Stir fry the vegetables for 2 minutes. Add the coriander and pour on the broth.
4. Cut the soybean curd (tofu) into ½ in (1.25 cm) cubes and add them to the soup. Simmer for 10 minutes and add salt to taste.
5. Transfer to warmed bowls and sprinkle with parsley just before serving.

Spiced Chicken with Pineapple

▶ 00.05   00.15 🍲
Serves 4

American	Ingredients	Metric/Imperial
4 (1 ½ lb)	chicken breasts	4 (650 g/ 1 ½ lb)
	salt	
2	chopped onions	2
2	crushed garlic cloves	2
2 tsp	sambal ulek (see page 128)	2 tsp
3 tbsp	groundnut oil	3 tbsp
4-6	slices canned chopped pineapple	4-6
2 tbsp	Indonesian sweet soy sauce (ketyap benteng manis)	2 tbsp
2 tsp	cornstarch (cornflour)	2 tsp

1. Dry the chicken with kitchen paper. Cut the meat into 12 equal strips and sprinkle with a little salt.
2. Pound the onions, garlic, sambal and a little salt to a smooth paste, in a mortar or food processor.
3. Heat the oil in a wok and stir fry the onion paste for 2 minutes.
4. Add the chicken strips and stir fry for 6 minutes. Remove the chicken strips from the wok and keep warm on plates.
5. Add 1 cup (250 ml/8 fl oz) boiling water and the pineapple pieces to the wok. Bring to the boil briefly and stir well. Add the soy sauce.
6. Mix the cornstarch (cornflour) with 2 tbsp cold water and stir into the contents of the wok. Cook, stirring until the sauce thickens.
7. Spoon the pineapple sauce over the chicken on the plates and serve immediately with dry boiled rice.

Javanese Pancakes

▶ 00.05   00.15 🍲
plus standing time

American	Ingredients	Metric/Imperial
½ cup	all-purpose flour	75 g/3 oz
¾ cup	thin coconut milk	200 ml/7 fl oz
1	lightly beaten egg	1
	pinch salt	
	groundnut oil	
½ cup	desiccated coconut	50 g/2 oz
1 tsp	ground cinnamon	1 tsp
2 tbsp	soft brown sugar	2 tbsp
16	scoops vanilla ice cream (optional)	6

1. Mix together the flour, coconut milk, egg and salt, beating with a whisk until a smooth batter is formed.
2. Lightly oil a pancake pan or small frying pan and fry 8 pancakes from the batter. Keep the pancakes warm.
3. Mix together the coconut, cinnamon and brown sugar. Sprinkle with 4 tbsp hot water. Stir the mixture once, carefully and sprinkle with a further 2 tbsp hot water. Leave to stand for 5-10 minutes.
4. Divide the coconut mixture between the pancakes, spreading it smoothly. Roll up the pancakes and place on warmed plates.
5. Serve immediately with one or more scoops of vanilla ice cream.

Stuffed Melon

00.10 plus chilling time   **00.00**

American	Ingredients	Metric/Imperial
1	large scooped melon	1
2	peeled, oranges	2
1	peeled, diced mango	1
1	peeled, sliced banana	1
1 tbsp	lemon juice	1 tbsp
2 tbsp	superfine (caster) sugar	2 tbsp

1. Cut out the segments of orange flesh between the membranes and reserve the juice.
2. Mix the fruit together and put into the melon skin.
3. Mix the lemon juice with the superfine (caster) sugar and 1-2 tbsp reserved orange juice. Pour over the contents of the melon. Put the melon cap on top and chill the whole melon for 1 hour before serving.

Banana Rolls

00.10 Serves 4   **00.15**

American	Ingredients	Metric/Imperial
8	spring roll wrappers	8
4	bananas	4
2 tbsp	white sesame seeds	2 tbsp
3 tbsp	sugar	3 tbsp
	oil for deep frying	
¾ cup	hot thin coconut milk	200 ml/7 fl oz
½ cup	sugar	125 g/4 oz

1. Lay the spring roll wrappers out and place half a peeled banana on each. Sprinkle with sesame seeds and sugar. Roll up the wrappers and press the edges firmly together.
2. Fry the rolls in hot oil until golden brown and crisp.
3. Dissolve the sugar in the hot coconut milk.
4. Serve the sauce in individual bowls and dip the banana rolls in the sauce after each bite.

Nanas manis
Sweet Pineapple

00.10 plus standing time   **00.00**

American	Ingredients	Metric/Imperial
1	medium size pineapple	1
3 tbsp	soft brown sugar	3 tbsp
½ tsp	sambal ulek (see page 128)	½ tsp
4 tbsp	toasted, desiccated coconut	4 tbsp

1. Peel the pineapple and cut into ¾ in (1.75 cm) slices. Remove the hard core and cut the flesh into cubes.
2. Mix together 2 tbsp water, sugar and sambal ulek. Pour over the cubes of pineapple and leave to stand for 1 hour.
3. Roll the cubes of pineapple in the toasted coconut and serve immediately on cocktail picks.

MENU

Medan toast
Red pork with Bean Sprouts
Javanese pudding with mangoes

Medan Toast

00.05 Serves 4   **00.05**

American	Ingredients	Metric/Imperial
1 lb	cooked beef	450 g/1 lb
1 tbsp	groundnut oil	1 tbsp
1	chopped onion	1
1	crushed garlic clove	1
1 tsp	sambal ulek (see page 128)	1 tsp
1 tsp	Indonesian sweet soy sauce (ketyap benteng manis)	1 tsp
1 tbsp	finely chopped parsley	1 tbsp
4	slices white bread, toasted with the crusts removed	4

1. Shred the beef finely.
2. Heat the oil in a wok and fry the onion until golden. Add the garlic, sambal and soy sauce. Stir well.
3. Rub the contents of the wok through a strainer and return the purée to the wok. Stir in the shredded beef and stir fry for 2 minutes.
4. Sprinkle with chopped parsley and spread the mixture on to the slices of toast.
5. Serve immediately as an hors d'oeuvre.

Red Pork with Bean Sprouts

00.10 Serves 4   **01.45**

American	Ingredients	Metric/Imperial
1¼ lb	lean pork steaks cut into 1 in (2.5 cm) slices	550 g/1¼ lb
	salt	
	freshly ground pepper	
2 tbsp	groundnut oil	2 tbsp
2 oz	peeled, sliced fresh root ginger	50 g/2 oz
3 tbsp	Indonesian sweet soy sauce (ketyap benteng manis)	3 tbsp
3½ tbsp	dry sherry	3½ tbsp
2 tsp	cornstarch (cornflour)	2 tsp
¼ lb	bean sprouts	125 g/4 oz
2 tbsp	groundnut oil	2 tbsp
1 tsp	sambal ulek (see page 128)	1 tsp
2 tbsp	finely chopped coriander	2 tbsp
1 tbsp	Indonesian sweet soy sauce (ketyap benteng manis)	1 tbsp

1. Dry the meat with kitchen paper and sprinkle with salt and pepper.

2. Heat 2 tbsp oil in a wok and stir fry the meat until it changes color.

3. Bring enough water to the boil in a saucepan, to just cover the meat. Add the meat, root ginger, 3 tbsp soy sauce and the dry sherry. Bring to the boil slowly, reduce the heat and cover the pan. Simmer gently for 1½ hours.

4. Rinse the bean sprouts in cold water and remove as many of the seed cases as possible. Drain, pour over several pints/litres of boiling water and drain again.

5. Remove the meat from the pan. Strain the cooking liquid and bring back to the boil.

6. Mix the cornstarch (cornflour) with 2 tbsp cold water and stir into the cooking liquid. Bring to the boil, stirring and add salt and pepper to taste.

7. Place the meat in the sauce and braise gently for 3-4 minutes.

8. Heat the remaining groundnut oil in a wok and stir in the sambal. Add the bean sprouts and stir fry for 3 minutes. Sprinkle over the coriander and the remaining soy sauce.

9. Arrange the bean sprouts on warmed plates and divide the meat between them. Pour over the sauce and serve.

Cook's tip: the main dish in this menu shows the great influence of Chinese cuisine in Indonesia as Red Pork and Bean sprouts is also well known in China. The use of Indonesian soy sauce and sambal ulek, however give it a special flavor and distinguish it from its Chinese ancestor.

Javanese Pudding with Mangoes

	00.15 plus chilling time	00.15

American	Ingredients	Metric/Imperial
2 cups	thick coconut milk	500 ml/16 fl oz
4 tbsp	cornstarch (cornflour)	4 tbsp
2	eggs	2
4 tbsp	soft brown sugar	4 tbsp
2	small mangoes	2

1. Bring the coconut milk to the boil.

2. Mix the cornstarch (cornflour) with 6 tbsp cold water and stir into the boiling coconut milk. Cook, stirring until the mixture forms a thick sauce. Remove the pan from the heat.

3. Separate the eggs. Lightly beat the yolks in a bowl with 2 tbsp water. Stir the cooled pudding mixture into the egg yolks.

4. Place the saucepan over moderate heat and bring the mixture to the boil very briefly, stirring constantly.

5. Remove the pan from the heat immediately and stir in the sugar, stirring for 1 minute. Leave the mixture until just warm.

6. Beat the egg whites and fold as lightly as possible into the pudding mixture. Pour into a pudding mould brushed with egg white or oil. Leave to cool, chill for 3 hours until set.

7. Peel the mangoes and cut them through the center. Remove the stones and cut the flesh into cubes.

8. Turn the pudding out into a dish and arrange the mango cubes around it.

MENU

Calves liver in tamarind sauce
Spiced fish fillets
Spiced eggs
Steamed bananas in coconut sauce

Calves Liver in Tamarind Sauce

00.05 plus standing time | 00.10

American	Ingredients	Metric/Imperial
2 tbsp	*dried tamarind pulp*	*2 tbsp*
1	*chopped onion*	*1*
1	*finely chopped garlic clove*	*1*
2 tsp	*finely grated fresh root ginger*	*2 tsp*
1 tsp	*sambal ulek*	*1 tsp*
½ tsp	*ground turmeric*	*½ tsp*
1 tsp	*soft brown sugar*	*1 tsp*
	salt	
1 lb	*calves liver cut into ½ in (1.25 cm) slices*	*450 g/1 lb*
3 tbsp	*groundnut oil*	*3 tbsp*
4 tbsp	*thin coconut milk*	*4 tbsp*
2 tbsp	*thick coconut milk*	*2 tbsp*
4	*small green chilies*	*4*

1. Put the tamarind pulp into a bowl with 2 tbsp warm water and leave to stand for 20 minutes.
2. Squeeze the pulp, then strain the liquid through a piece of wet muslin and set aside.
3. Pound the onion, garlic, root ginger and sambal to a fine paste in a mortar or food processor. Add the turmeric, sugar and a little salt to the paste.
4. Dry the liver with kitchen paper and rub a little salt into the meat.
5. Heat the oil in a frying pan and fry the liver for 1 minute on each side. Remove from the pan and keep warm.
6. Add the onion paste to the remaining oil and stir fry for 2 minutes. Add the reserved tamarind liquid and the thin coconut milk. Cook gently, stirring until the liquid is reduced by half. Put the slices of liver into the sauce and simmer for 3-4 minutes.
7. Transfer the liver to warmed plates.
8. Stir the thick coconut milk into the sauce and bring to the boil, stirring constantly. Add a little salt to taste.
9. Spoon the sauce over the liver and serve garnished with green chili flowers.

Spiced Fish Fillets

00.20 Serves 4 as starter | 00.10

American	Ingredients	Metric/Imperial
4 (1 lb)	*sole fillets*	*4 (450 g/1 lb)*
	salt	
1	*chopped onion*	*1*
1	*finely chopped garlic clove*	*1*
1 tbsp	*Indonesian sweet soy sauce (ketyap benteng manis)*	*1 tbsp*
½ tsp	*ground cumin*	*½ tsp*
½ tsp	*sambal ulek or sambal trasi (see page 128 or 129)*	*½ tsp*
2	*roasted finely ground macadamia nuts*	*2*
4 tbsp	*thick coconut milk*	*4 tbsp*
1 tbsp	*groundnut oil*	*1 tbsp*
1 tbsp	*lemon or lime juice*	*1 tbsp*
1	*small lemon or lime cut into segments*	*1*

1. Rinse the fish in cold running water and dry with kitchen paper. Rub the fillets with a little salt.
2. Pound the onion and garlic to a paste in a mortar or food processor. Add the soy sauce, cumin, sambal and macadamia nuts and grind to a thick pulp.
3. Add the pulp to the coconut milk and stir vigorously.
4. Put the fillets into a bowl and pour the coconut mixture over. Turn the fish in the mixture to coat. Leave to stand in a cool place for 15 minutes.
5. Coat a broiler (grill) rack with oil.
6. Remove the fish from the coconut mixture and dry with kitchen paper. Broil (grill) the fillets until golden brown for about 6 minutes on both sides.
7. Strain the remaining coconut mixture and bring to the boil. Stir in the lemon or lime juice and add a little salt to taste.
8. Transfer the fish to warmed plates and spoon over a few tbsp hot sauce. Serve, garnished with one or more lemon or lime segments.

Spiced Eggs

⊳ 00.05 00.15 🍲

Serves 4

American	Ingredients	Metric/Imperial
4	large hard-cooked (hard-boiled) eggs	4
	groundnut oil (for frying)	
1 tbsp	groundnut oil	1 tbsp
1	chopped onion	1
1	finely chopped garlic clove	1
1 tsp	finely grated fresh root ginger	1 tsp
½ tsp	lemon grass powder	½ tsp
1 tbsp	lime or lemon juice	1 tbsp
½ tsp	ground turmeric	½ tsp
	salt	
	pinch soft brown sugar	

1. Shell the eggs and prick the surface carefully all over with a fork.
2. Heat the oil in a frying pan and fry the eggs until golden and drain them.
3. Heat 1 tbsp oil in a small wok and fry the onion until transparent. Add the garlic and root ginger and stir. Add the lemon grass powder, lime or lemon juice, turmeric, a little salt, sugar and 3 tbsp boiling water. Stir well and put the eggs into the sauce.
4. Simmer gently until almost all the sauce has evaporated, turning the eggs regularly.

5. Cut the eggs in half, arrange them on a dish with the cut sides uppermost and serve.

Steamed Bananas in Coconut Sauce

⊳ 00.02 00.15 🍲

Serves 4

American	Ingredients	Metric/Imperial
4	large bananas	4
4 tbsp	thick coconut milk	4 tbsp
2 tbsp	soft brown sugar	2 tbsp
	pinch turmeric	
	pinch salt	
1 tbsp	lime or lemon juice	1 tbsp

1. Put the unpeeled bananas on the perforated section of a steamer. Bring the water to the boil. Place the perforated section on top and cover the pan. Steam the bananas for 10-12 minutes.
2. Bring the coconut milk to the boil and stir in the sugar, turmeric and salt. Stir until the sugar has dissolved.
3. Remove the pan from the heat and stir in the lemon or lime juice.
4. Remove the bananas from the steamer. Remove two strips of skin from each banana and spoon a little sauce on to the flesh.
5. Serve the bananas on warmed plates with the remaining sauce served separately.

MALAYSIA

Nasi Goreng with Cauliflower and Cucumber

00.05 Serves 4   **00.15**

American	Ingredients	Metric/Imperial
2 cups	boiled rice	225 g/8 oz
1	small cauliflower	1
	salt	
1	small cucumber	1
2	eggs	2
	freshly ground pepper	
1 oz	butter	25 g/1 oz
2	tomatoes	2
2	green chilies	2
3 tbsp	groundnut or sunflower oil	3 tbsp
4	coarsely chopped red onions	4
2	crushed garlic cloves	2
¾ lb	chicken breast fillets cut into narrow strips	350 g/12 oz
2	seeded red chilies cut into narrow strips	2
½ lb	fresh peeled shrimp (prawns)	225 g/8 oz
	few sprigs of parsley	

1. Make sure that the rice is completely cold.

2. Divide the cauliflower into small florets and roughly slice the stalks. Put the cauliflower into a pan with plenty of boiling salted water. Boil for 5 minutes. Drain and cool in a colander.

3. Rinse and trim the cucumber and cut in half lengthwise. Remove the seeds from both halves. Cut lengthwise again and then into small pieces.

4. Lightly beat the eggs in a bowl. Add 1 tbsp water and a little salt and pepper to taste.

5. Heat the butter in a frying pan and put in the egg mixture. Stir and turn slowly until set. Remove the pan from the heat.

6. Cut each tomato and the green chilies into flowers.

7. Heat the oil in a wok and stir fry the onions until transparent. Add the garlic and chicken. Stir well, then add the red chilies. Stir fry for 2 minutes and then add the cauliflower, rice, cucumber and shrimp (prawns), a little at a time, stirring continuously. Add a little salt and pepper to taste. Spoon the scrambled eggs into the mixture as soon as everything is warmed through.

8. Transfer to a warmed, shallow serving dish. Garnish with the tomato and chili flowers and a few sprigs of parsley and serve immediately.

Cook's tip: serve Indonesian sweet and salty soy sauces (ketyap benteng manis and ketyep benteng asin) in small bowls and offer small bowls of sambal ulek (see pages 128) and possibly a dish or bottle of Chinese tomato sauce. Nasi goreng can be accompanied by prawn crackers freshly fried in oil.

Nasi Goreng with Pork and Celery

	00.05	00.15
	Serves 4	

American	Ingredients	Metric/Imperial
2 cups	boiled rice	225 g/8 oz
10 oz	streaky pork rashers	285 g/10 oz
	salt	
6-8	sticks celery	6-8
2	tomatoes	2
1	small cucumber	1
1	yellow bell pepper	1
2	eggs	2
	freshly ground pepper	
1 oz	butter	25 g/1 oz
4-5 tbsp	groundnut or sunflower oil	4-5 tbsp
6	coarsely chopped red onions	6
2	crushed garlic cloves	2
1 tbsp	sambal ulek (see page 128)	1 tbsp
¼ lb	thickly sliced boiled ham cut into small cubes	125 g/4 oz
½ lb	fresh peeled shrimp (prawns)	225 g/8 oz
	few sprigs of parsley	

1. Make sure that the rice is completely cold.
2. Put the pork in a pan with water to cover. Add a little salt, and cook the meat for 5-8 minutes. Remove the meat from the liquid. Drain, leave in a colander to dry until cold. Cut the meat into slices, then into narrow strips.
3. Cut the celery into narrow strips.
4. Roughly slice the tomatoes.
5. Rinse and trim the cucumber. Slice to the same thickness as the sliced tomatoes. Sprinkle the cucumber slices with a little salt and drain in a colander.
6. Rinse, trim and seed the bell pepper. Cut the flesh into very narrow strips.
7. Scramble the eggs as described in the previous recipe.
8. Heat the oil in a wok and stir fry the onions until transparent. Add the garlic and strips of pork and stir fry for 3 minutes. Add the strips of celery and sambal ulek and sprinkle with a little salt. Stir fry for 2 minutes, then add the rice, ham, shrimp (prawns) and scrambled eggs a little at a time, stirring continuously.
9. As soon as the rice and shrimp (prawns) are warmed through, transfer to a large warmed serving dish.
10. Garnish with overlapping slices of tomato and cucumber, strips of yellow pepper and sprigs of parsley.

Left to right: Nasi goreng with cauliflower and cucumber, Nasi goreng with pork and celery, Nasi goreng with chicken and mushrooms

Nasi Goreng with Chicken and Mushrooms

	00.05	00.15
	plus soaking time	

American	Ingredients	Metric/Imperial
2 cups	boiled rice	225 g/8 oz
4-6	large dried Chinese mushrooms	4-6
½ lb	fresh button mushrooms	225 g/8 oz
3 tbsp	groundnut or sunflower oil	3 tbsp
4	coarsely chopped red onions	4
2	crushed garlic cloves	2
2	seeded green chilies cut into very narrow strips	2
1	seeded red chili cut into very narrow strips	1
2	sticks celery or paksoi cut into narrow strips	2
	salt	
	freshly ground pepper	
8	small roasted chicken drumsticks	8
4	chopped scallions (spring onions)	4
2 tbsp	cooked peas	2 tbsp
2	skinned tomatoes cut into narrow strips	2
2	hard-cooked (hard boiled) eggs cut into segments	2

1. Make sure that the rice is totally cold.
2. Put the dried mushrooms in a bowl with boiling water to cover. Leave to soak for 30 minutes. Discard the stalks and cut the caps into strips. Drain the strips in a colander.
3. Wipe the fresh mushrooms with a damp cloth or kitchen paper. Slice off the bottom of the stalks. Leave small mushrooms whole. Cut the large ones into segments.
4. Heat the oil in a wok and stir fry the onions until transparent. Add the garlic and Chinese and fresh mushrooms. Stir fry

for 3 minutes. Add the chilies and stir fry for 3 minutes. Add the celery and sprinkle with salt and pepper.
5. Stir well, then add the rice, a little at a time.
6. When the rice has warmed through, transfer to a warmed dish.
7. Arrange the roast chicken drumsticks at one side. Sprinkle with the chopped scallions (spring onions), peas and pieces of tomato. Garnish with the hard-cooked (hard-boiled) egg segments.

Nasi lemak
Spiced Rice

	00.05	00.35
	Serves 4	

American	Ingredients	Metric/Imperial
1½ cups	long grain rice	350 g/12 oz
1½ tbsp	ghee	1½ tbsp
1	thinly sliced red onion	1
3	lightly crushed cardamom pods	3
3	garlic cloves	3
1 (2 in)	stick cinnamon	1 (5 cm/2 in)
2½ cups	boiling bouillon (stock)	600 ml/1 pint
	salt	

1. Pick over the rice. Rinse in several changes of water until the rinsing water runs clear. Drain in a colander.
2. Heat the ghee and fry the onion over moderate heat until slightly transparent.
3. Add the cardamom pods, garlic and cinnamon.
4. Stir well, then add the dried rice. Continue stirring until the rice is transparent and shiny.
5. Pour on the boiling bouillon (stock) and add a little salt to taste. Stir well, cover the pan and reduce the heat. Cook for 20-25 minutes then turn off the heat. Leave the pan to stand, covered over the cooling heat source for 5 minutes.
6. Just before serving, stir the rice with a large meat fork and remove the cardamom pods, garlic and cinnamon.

Spiced rice

Ketoepat
Pressed Rice

American	Ingredients	Metric/Imperial
1 ½ cups	round grain rice	350 g/12 oz
1 tsp	salt	1 tsp

1. Pick over the rice. Rinse in several changes of water until the rinsing water runs clear.
2. Put the rice in a pan with 3¼ cups (750 ml/1¼ pints) boiling salted water. Bring back to the boil, cover the pan, reduce the heat and cook for 40 minutes until the rice is tender and sticky and the liquid has been absorbed.
3. Brush a shallow baking tin with oil. Put the rice in and press down with the palm of the hand. Put a wooden board or tray on top. Place a weight on top and leave for 3 hours or until cold. Then chill in the weighted tin for 3 hours.
4. Turn the rice out on to a dish and cut into small squares, strips or triangles.

Nasi koening
Yellow Rice

American	Ingredients	Metric/Imperial
1 ½ cups	round grain glutinous rice	350 g/12 oz
1 tsp	salt	1 tsp
1 tsp	ground turmeric	1 tsp
1	curry leaf (daun salam)	1
	pinch garlic salt	
	pinch dried onion	
5 tbsp	thin coconut milk	5 tbsp
2	lightly fried onions, cut into rings, or 3 chopped scallions (spring onions) (optional)	2

1. Pick over the rice and rinse in several changes of water until the rinsing water runs clear.
2. Put the rice in a pan with 2¼ cups (500 ml/18 fl oz) boiling water. Add the salt, ground turmeric, curry leaf, garlic salt and dried onion. Bring back to the boil, stirring continuously. Cover the pan and simmer for 10 minutes. Stir the rice with a large meat fork and add the coconut milk. Stir well. Cover the pan and simmer for 10 minutes. Remove the curry leaf.
3. Transfer the rice to a warmed dish and garnish with fried onion rings or chopped scallions (spring onions).

Cook's tip: yellow rice is best served with sea fish fried in oil or broiled (grilled), or with dishes incorporating shrimp (prawns), freshly fried in oil.

Mie siam kering
Fried Rice Noodles

American	Ingredients	Metric/Imperial
¾ lb	rice noodles	350 g/12 oz
2	Chinese sausages (lap tsjong) cut into slices	2
¼ lb	bean sprouts	125 g/4 oz
4 tbsp	groundnut or sunflower oil	4 tbsp
2	chopped red onions	2
2	crushed garlic cloves	2
½ lb	roast pork cut into strips	225 g/8 oz
2 tsp	sambal ulek (see page 128)	2 tsp
½ lb	fresh peeled shrimp (prawns)	225 g/8 oz
2 tbsp	Indonesian sweet soy sauce (ketyap benteng manis)	2 tbsp
2 tbsp	Indonesian salty soy sauce (ketyap benteng asin)	2 tbsp
1 tbsp	Chinese oyster sauce	1 tbsp
2	lightly beaten eggs	2
	salt	
	freshly ground pepper	
4	chopped scallions (spring onions) or 1 piece yellow leek	4
2	skinned tomatoes cut into flowers	2
	few sprigs of parsley	

1. Prepare the rice noodles according to the instructions on the packet. Drain well. Rinse in cold running water and cut the noodles into 4 in (10 cm) pieces.
2. Steam the sausages for 10 minutes in a steaming pan or basket. Cut into very thin slices.
3. Rinse the bean sprouts in several changes of cold water. Remove as many of the seed cases as possible. Drain well.
4. Heat 3 tbsp oil in a wok and fry the onions until beginning to color. Add the garlic, stir well and add the pork and sambal ulek. Stir fry for 3 minutes and add the bean sprouts and shrimp (prawns). Stir well, turn off heat.
5. Heat 1 tbsp oil in a second (larger) wok and add the two soy sauces. Stir well and add the drained rice noodles. Stir continuously until the noodles are warmed through. Sprinkle over the oyster sauce and stir. Add the contents of the other wok. Stir well until everything is warmed through.
6. Sprinkle the lightly beaten egg over the top and then sprinkle with a little salt and pepper and stir carefully.
7. Transfer to a warmed dish and sprinkle with chopped scallion (spring onion) or leek, and garnish the dish with tomato flowers and sprigs of parsley.

Ikan goreng taotjo
Fried Fish with Soy Sauce

00.05 plus standing time   **00.15**

American	Ingredients	Metric/Imperial
4 (1½ lb)	cod fillets	4 (675 g/1½ lb)
2 tbsp	lemon juice	2 tbsp
	salt	
⅔ cup	groundnut oil	150 ml/¼ pint
2	coarsely chopped onions	2
1	crushed garlic clove	1
2 tsp	grated fresh root ginger	2 tsp
1 tbsp	soybean paste (taotjo)	1 tbsp
1 tsp	sambal ulek (see page 128)	1 tsp
2 tbsp	Indonesian salty soy sauce (ketyap benteng asin)	2 tbsp
1 tbsp	Indonesian sweet soy sauce (ketyap benteng manis)	1 tbsp
1 tbsp	finely chopped coriander	1 tbsp
4	skinned tomatoes cut into flowers	4

Fried fish with soy sauce

1. Rinse the fish under cold running water. Dry with kitchen paper and sprinkle with lemon juice. Leave to stand for 15 minutes. Dry and rub a little salt into the skin.
2. Heat the oil in a wok and fry the fish quickly until brown on both sides. Remove from the wok with a slotted spoon. Drain over the pan, then on kitchen paper.
3. Remove all but 2 tbsp oil from the wok and stir fry the onions in the remaining oil until beginning to change color. Add the garlic, root ginger and soybean paste.
4. Stir well and add the sambal and soy sauces. Stir, then add ¾ cup boiling water, stirring continuously. Cook gently. Add the fish to the sauce and warm through.
5. Serve the fish with the sauce in a warmed shallow dish. sprinkled with coriander and garnished with tomato flowers.

Cook's tip: serve accompanied by boiled rice and prawn crackers.

Ikan kelapa
Fish in a Jacket with Coconut

00.05 plus standing time   **00.18**

American	Ingredients	Metric/Imperial
1½ lb	cod fillets	675 g/1½ lb
3 oz	desiccated coconut	75 g/3 oz
1	crushed garlic clove	1
1 tbsp	finely grated fresh root ginger	1 tbsp
1 tbsp	mild curry powder	1 tbsp
1 tsp	salt	1 tsp
2 tsp	lemon juice	2 tsp
2 tbsp	coriander or coarsely chopped celery	2 tbsp
1 tbsp	sesame or groundnut oil	1 tbsp

1. Rinse the fish under cold running water. Dry with kitchen paper and divide into four equal pieces.
2. Put the coconut into a bowl with ⅔ cup (150 ml/¼ pint) boiling water. Stir well. Leave to stand for 5 minutes.
3. Purée the coconut, garlic, root ginger, curry powder, salt, lemon juice and half of the coriander or celery in a food processor. Add 1-2 tbsp boiling water, if necessary.
4. Brush four sheets of aluminum foil with sesame oil.
5. Spoon 1 tbsp of the coconut mixture on to each sheet. Spread over the sheet and place the fish on top. Put the rest of the mixture on top of the fish. Spread as evenly as possible. Fold the aluminum foil around the pieces of fish and leave the parcels to stand for 15 minutes.
6. Steam the fish for 15-18 minutes, until tender in a steaming pan or basket.
7. Open the packets at the top and sprinkle the contents with the rest of the coriander or celery leaves.
8. Serve in their jackets.

Goelai ikan kelapa
Braised Fish in Coconut Sauce

	00.08 plus standing time	00.15

American	Ingredients	Metric/Imperial
1½ lb	firm white fish fillets	675 g/1½ lb
3 tbsp	lemon juice	3 tbsp
2 oz	desiccated coconut	50 g/2 oz
2	chopped onions	2
2	chopped garlic cloves	2
1 cup	thin coconut milk	250 ml/8 fl oz
1 tsp	sambal ulek (see page 128)	1 tsp
1 tsp	ground turmeric	1 tsp
1 tsp	garam masala	1 tsp
	salt	
4	chopped scallions (spring onions) or 1 piece pale yellow leek	4

1. Rinse the fish under cold running water. Dry with kitchen paper and cut into 2½ in (3 cm) pieces. Sprinkle the pieces with lemon juice and leave to stand for 15 minutes.
2. Place the coconut in a bowl with 5 tbsp boiling water. Leave to stand for 15 minutes.
3. Purée the coconut, onion, garlic, 3 tbsp thin coconut milk, sambal, ground turmeric and garam masala in a food processor. Add a little salt and the remaining thin coconut milk. Process again until the mixture is quite thin. Add 2-4 tbsp of water if necessary.
4. Bring the mixture to the boil in a pan.
5. Transfer half of the sauce into a warmed shallow dish. Place the pieces of fish in this, then spoon the rest of the sauce over the fish.
6. Cover the dish with aluminum foil or a lid and place the dish in the center of a preheated oven 220°C/425°F/Gas Mark 7 and bake for 8-10 minutes.
7. Serve the fish immediately, sprinkled with a little chopped scallion (spring onion) or leek.

Cook's tip: serve accompanied with spiced rice or arrange pieces of Ketupat around the dish.

Atjar ikan kota kinabaloe
Fish in Piquant Sweet and Sour Sauce

	00.10 plus standing time	00.35

American	Ingredients	Metric/Imperial
1½ lb	mackerel fillets	675 g/1½ lb
2 tbsp	lemon juice	2 tbsp
	salt	
1	head of Chinese cabbage or paksoi	1
4 tbsp	groundnut oil	4 tbsp
2	large chopped onions	2
2	crushed garlic cloves	2
2 tsp	sambal ulek (see page 128)	2 tsp
2 tsp	sugar	2 tsp
2 tbsp	mild vinegar	2 tbsp
2 tsp	cornstarch (cornflour)	2 tsp
2½ tbsp	Indonesian salty soy sauce (ketyap benteng asin)	2½ tbsp

1. Rinse the mackerel fillets under cold running water and dry with kitchen paper. Cut into 2 in (5 cm) pieces.
2. Coat with lemon juice in which a little salt is dissolved. Leave to stand for 15 minutes.
3. Rinse the Chinese cabbage or paksoi. Drain and cut into ½ in (1.25 cm) wide strips.
4. Bring a generous quantity of water to the boil in a pan. Add a little salt and add the cabbage or paksoi. Cook gently for 4 minutes. Drain in a colander and rinse with cold water until the cabbage or paksoi is cold.
5. Heat 3 tbsp oil in a wok.
6. Dry the pieces of fish with kitchen paper and quickly fry them in the hot oil until brown on all sides. Remove from the oil with a slotted spoon, drain over the wok and then on kitchen paper.
7. Remove all but 2 tbsp oil from the wok and stir fry the onions in the remaining oil until transparent. Add the garlic and stir well.
8. Stir in the sambal and add ¾ cup (200 ml/7 fl oz) boiling water.
9. Stir well and add the sugar and vinegar and cook, stirring for 2-3 minutes.
10. Mix the cornstarch (cornflour) with 2 tbsp cold water and stir into the contents of the wok. Cook, stirring until the sauce thickens.
11. Add the soy sauce and salt to taste.
12. Stir the sauce and add the pieces of fish. Simmer gently over very moderate heat until the fish is warmed through.
13. Heat 1 tbsp oil in a second wok (or frying pan).
14. Stir fry the cabbage or paksoi until warmed through.
15. Arrange the cabbage or paksoi on 4 warmed plates. Spoon the pieces of fish and sauce on top and serve.

Sweet and sour fish

Atjar ikan

Sweet and Sour Fish

◣▭▷	00.06	00.12	⌒
	plus standing time		

American	Ingredients	Metric/Imperial
1½ lb	tuna fillets	675 g/1½ lb
2 tbsp	lemon juice	2 tbsp
	salt	
1	finely chopped small red onion	1
1	finely chopped garlic clove	1
1 tbsp	fresh grated root ginger	1 tbsp
2	macadamia nuts	2
1½ tsp	sambal ulek or sambal trasi (see pages 128/129)	1½ tsp
3 tbsp	groundnut oil	3 tbsp
1 tbsp	sesame oil	1 tbsp
3 tbsp	mild vinegar	3 tbsp
3 tbsp	finely chopped coriander or parsley	3 tbsp
4	skinned, diced tomatoes	4

1. Rinse the fish under cold running water. Dry with kitchen paper and cut first into 1 in (2.5 cm) thick slices, then into strips 1 in (2.5 cm) wide.
2. Coat the strips of fish with a mixture of lemon juice and salt. Leave to stand for 15 minutes.
3. Purée the onion, garlic, root ginger, nuts, sambal and 1 tbsp groundnut oil in a food processor.
4. Heat the remaining groundnut oil and sesame oil in a wok.
5. Dry the strips of fish with kitchen paper and quickly fry in the hot oil until brown on all sides. Remove with a slotted spoon. Drain over the wok then on kitchen paper.
6. Remove all but 2 tbsp oil from the wok. Add the onion paste and stir fry for 2 minutes.
7. Add ¾ cup (200 ml/7 fl oz) boiling water. Stir well and cook vigorously for 2 minutes.
8. Stir the vinegar into the sauce and add salt to taste.
9. Stir well and lay the strips of fried fish in the sauce. Leave to warm through.
10. Divide the fish and sauce between 4 warmed plates and sprinkle with coriander or parsley and garnish with diced tomato.

Cook's tip: in Malaysia, this dish is accompanied by a vegetable dish e.g. Sajoer masak lemak, prawn crackers, and boiled rice.

Sambal goreng ikan

Fried Fish Sambal

◣▭▷	00.05	00.15	⌒
	Serves 4		

American	Ingredients	Metric/Imperial
1¾ lb	fresh cleaned sardines	800 g/1¾ lb
	salt	
4 tbsp	flour	4 tbsp
¾ cup	groundnut oil	200 ml/7 fl oz
2	chopped onions	2
2	finely chopped garlic cloves	2
4	blades lemon grass (sereh)	4
1 tbsp	sambal ulek or sambal trasi (see page 128/129)	1 tbsp
4 tbsp	lemon or lime juice	4 tbsp
2	curry leaves	2

1. Rinse the fish inside and out under cold running water. The heads may be removed or left. Dry the fish with kitchen paper.
2. Stir a little salt into the flour and roll the fish in it until thinly coated on all sides. Shake off the surplus.
3. Heat the oil in a wok and fry the fish, 3-4 at a time, turning continuously, until golden brown on all sides and tender. Remove from the oil with a slotted spoon. Drain over the wok and then on kitchen paper.
4. Remove all but 2 tbsp oil, from the wok and fry the onions in the remaining oil until golden brown. Add the garlic, lemon grass and sambal, stir well.
5. Add ¾ cup (200 ml/7 fl oz) boiling water, the lemon or lime juice and curry leaves. Bring to the boil and cook until the liquid is reduced to a quarter. Remove the curry leaves.
6. Add the fish, turn carefully and serve in a warmed dish.

Cook's tip: serve accompanied by boiled rice and a cucumber and tomato salad.

Goelai ajam reboeng

Braised Chicken with Bamboo Shoots

	00.07	00.50
	Serves 4	

American	Ingredients	Metric/Imperial
2¼ lb	chicken pieces	1 kg/2¼ lb
1½ tsp	ground turmeric	1½ tsp
	salt	
4 tbsp	groundnut oil	4 tbsp
2	onions	2
2 tsp	sambal trasi (see page 129)	2 tsp
1 tsp	sugar	1 tsp
1¾ cups	thin coconut milk	400 ml/14 fl oz
1¼ cups	thick coconut milk	300 ml/½ pint
2	curry leaves	2
1 (9 oz)	can bamboo shoots, drained	1 (250 g/9 oz)
2	chopped scallions (spring onions)	2
2	skinned tomatoes (optional)	2

1. Dry the chicken pieces with kitchen paper. Rub a mixture of ground turmeric and a little salt into the skin.
2. Heat the oil in a wok and stir fry the onions until transparent.
3. Add the chicken pieces and stir fry until golden brown.
4. Slide the chicken pieces to one side of the wok and add the sambal and sugar. Stir well, then add the thin and thick coconut milk. Stir well and add a little salt to taste. Bring to the boil, stirring then reduce the heat. Bring the chicken pieces back into the sauce and add the curry leaves. Cook very gently for 30-35 minutes until the oil is beginning to separate from the thickened sauce.
5. Cut the bamboo shoots into narrow strips and add them to the wok and warm through. Remove the curry leaves.
6. Serve the mixture on a warmed dish sprinkled with chopped scallions (spring onions) and garnished with tomato flowers.

Braised chicken with bamboo shoots

Kari ajam kelapa

Braised Chicken in Coconut Sauce

00.05 plus standing time

00.30

American	Ingredients	Metric/Imperial
2¼ lb	chicken pieces	1 kg/2¼ lb
4 oz	desiccated coconut	125 g/4 oz
1¾ cups	thick coconut milk	400 ml/14 fl oz
2	chopped onions	2
2	finely chopped garlic cloves	2
1 tsp	sambal trasi (see page 129)	1 tsp
1 tsp	sambal ulek (see page 128)	1 tsp
1 tbsp	mild curry powder	1 tbsp
1 tbsp	lemon or lime juice	1 tbsp
4 tbsp	groundnut oil	4 tbsp
	salt	
1 tsp	sugar	1 tsp
2	curry leaves	2
	finely chopped coriander or parsley	

1. Dry the chicken pieces with kitchen paper.
2. Heat a dry non-stick frying pan and dry roast the desiccated coconut over very moderate heat until very lightly colored, shaking and stirring continuously. Spread out the coconut on a large cold plate and leave to cool until completely cold.
3. Pour ¾ cup (200 ml/7 fl oz) of thick coconut milk into a bowl and stir in the cold coconut.
4. Purée the onions, garlic, sambals, curry powder, lemon or lime juice, 1 tbsp oil and 2 tbsp water in a food processor.
5. Heat the remaining oil in a wok and stir fry the paste for 2-3 minutes. Add the coconut mixture and the remaining coconut milk and stir well. Add salt and sugar to taste.
6. Put the chicken pieces and curry leaves into the sauce. Bring to the boil, reduce the heat and cover the wok. Cook the chicken pieces for 20-25 minutes, until tender. Remove the curry leaves.
7. Serve on a warmed dish, sprinkled with finely chopped coriander or parsley.

Left to right: Braised chicken in coconut sauce, Spiced chicken in coconut sauce, Chicken in spiced coconut sauce

Ajam rendang

Spiced Chicken in Coconut Sauce

▬▷   00.05   00.38 🥘
　　　Serves 4

American	Ingredients	Metric/Imperial
2 ¼ lb	chicken pieces	1 kg/2 ¼ lb
2	coarsely chopped onions	2
2	finely chopped garlic cloves	2
1 tbsp	finely grated fresh root ginger	1 tbsp
1 tbsp	sambal ulek (see page 128)	1 tbsp
1 tsp	laos powder	1 tsp
1 tsp	ground turmeric	1 tsp
	salt	
1 tsp	sugar	1 tsp
	freshly ground black pepper	
2 ¼ cups	thin coconut milk	500 ml/18 fl oz
5 tbsp	thick coconut milk	5 tbsp
	finely chopped coriander	

1. Dry the chicken pieces with kitchen paper.
2. Purée the onions, garlic, root ginger, sambal ulek, laos powder and ground turmeric in a food processor.
3. Add 1 tsp salt, 1 tsp sugar and a pinch of finely ground black pepper to the paste.
4. Stir in the thin coconut milk. Bring to the boil, stirring continuously, over a moderate heat.
5. Put the chicken pieces in the sauce and simmer for 30-35 minutes until almost all of the liquid has evaporated.
6. Just before serving, stir in the thick coconut milk and warm through.
7. Transfer to a warmed serving dish, sprinkle with a little finely chopped fresh coriander and serve.

Ajam kelapa

Chicken in Spiced Coconut Sauce

▬▷   00.05   00.37 🥘
　　　Serves 4

American	Ingredients	Metric/Imperial
2 ¼ lb	chicken pieces	1 kg/2 ¼ lb
1 ½ tbsp	finely grated fresh root ginger	1 ½ tbsp
2	medium size chopped onions	2
2	crushed garlic cloves	2
1 tbsp	sambal ulek (see page 128)	1 tbsp
1 ½ tsp	ground turmeric	1 ½ tsp
	salt	
4 tbsp	groundnut oil	4 tbsp
2 ¼ cups	thick coconut milk	500 ml/18 fl oz
1 tsp	sugar	1 tsp
2	curry leaves	2
1	chopped scallion (spring onion) (optional)	1

1. Dry the chicken pieces with kitchen paper.
2. Purée the root ginger, onions, garlic, sambal ulek and 2 tbsp water in a food processor or mortar.
3. Rub the ground turmeric mixed with a little salt into the chicken pieces.
4. Heat the oil in a wok and stir fry the paste for 2 minutes over moderate heat.
5. Add the chicken pieces and stir fry for 10 minutes, until the chicken pieces are golden brown.
6. Add the thick coconut milk, sugar and curry leaves. Stir well. Add a little salt to taste, then partly cover the wok and simmer for 20-25 minutes. Remove the curry leaves.
7. Serve in a warmed dish sprinkled with chopped scallion (spring onion).

Gulai ayam (I)

Chicken and Curry Sauce (I)

00.05 Serves 4   **01.30**

American	Ingredients	Metric/Imperial
1 (3 lb)	boiling chicken	1 (1.5 kg/3 lb)
2½ cups	thin coconut milk	600 ml/1 pint
1	chopped onion	1
2	chopped garlic cloves	2
1 tsp	sambal ulek (see page 128)	1 tsp
½ tbsp	mild curry powder	½ tbsp
	salt	
2	curry leaves (daun salam)	2
3 tbsp	ghee or margarine	3 tbsp
	freshly ground pepper	
2 tbsp	lemon or lime juice	2 tbsp

1. Put the cleaned boiling chicken in a suitable saucepan with thin coconut milk to ¾ cover the bird.

2. Put the onion, garlic, sambal ulek, curry and a little salt in a bowl. Add 5 tbsp luke warm water and stir well.

3. Add the mixture and the curry leaves (daun salam) to the coconut milk in the saucepan. Bring slowly to the boil. Boil vigorously for 15 minutes, turn the bird over, reduce the heat and cover the saucepan. Simmer gently for 1 hour. Turn the bird over after 30 minutes and baste with the braising liquid occasionally. Remove the chicken from the saucepan and drain for a second over the saucepan. Dry the chicken with kitchen paper.

4. Strain the braising liquid and boil gently over moderate heat until reduced to a thick sauce.

5. Heat the ghee or margarine in a wok and quickly fry the chicken until golden brown on all sides.

6. Season the sauce with a little salt and freshly ground pepper to taste. Stir in the lemon or lime juice. Place the chicken in the sauce. Pour a little sauce over it and simmer for 2-3 minutes. Remove the curry leaves.

7. Transfer to a warmed dish. Divide into pieces at the table and serve.

Cook's tip: serve with a separate dish of dry boiled rice or ketupat and a cucumber and yogurt salad, for example. A salad of mixed tropical fruit goes well with this dish.

Gulai ayam (II)

Chicken with Curry Sauce (II)

00.10 Serves 4   **00.45**

American	Ingredients	Metric/Imperial
¾ cup	chicken bouillon (stock)	200 ml/7 fl oz
¾ cup	thin coconut milk	200 ml/7 fl oz
1 tsp	sambal ulek (see page 128)	1 tsp
1 tbsp	mild curry powder	1 tbsp
1	chopped onion	1
1	finely chopped garlic clove	1
	salt	
1 (2¼ lb)	roasting chicken	1 (1 kg/2¼ lb)
3 tbsp	ghee or margarine	3 tbsp
5 tbsp	thick coconut milk	5 tbsp
2 tbsp	lemon or lime juice	2 tbsp
1	lemon or lime in segments	1

1. Bring the bouillon (stock) and thin coconut milk to the boil in a saucepan large enough to hold the chicken.

2. Add the sambal ulek, curry powder, onion, garlic and a little salt. Stir well and put the chicken in the liquid so that the chicken is ¾ covered. Add a little bouillon (stock), if necessary. Simmer for 35 minutes. Turn the chicken carefully after 20 minutes.

3. Remove the chicken from the pan, drain over the pan for a second and dry it completely with kitchen paper.

4. Heat the ghee or margarine in a wok and fry the chicken golden brown on all sides.

5. Reduce the cooking liquid to a fairly thick sauce. Stir in the thick coconut milk. Simmer the sauce for 2 minutes. Try the sauce and add a little more salt to taste and stir in the lemon or lime juice.

6. Warm the chicken through in the sauce and transfer it to a warmed dish and pour the sauce over.

7. Serve, garnished with lemon or lime segments.

Gulai ayam Cameron

Chicken with Chicken Livers and Fresh Fruit

	00.10 plus soaking time	00.10

American	Ingredients	Metric/Imperial
1 lb	chicken breast fillets	450 g/1 lb
1 tsp	ground turmeric	1 tsp
½ lb	chicken livers	225 g/8 oz
2¼ cups	milk	500 ml/18 fl oz
3 tbsp	desiccated coconut	3 tbsp
3	oranges	3
3	slices canned pineapple	3
12	canned lychees	12
3 tbsp	groundnut oil or ghee	3 tbsp
1	chopped onion	1
1	finely chopped garlic clove	1
1 tsp	sambal ulek (see page 128)	1 tsp
2 tsp	mild curry powder	2 tsp
2 tsp	finely grated fresh root ginger	2 tsp
	salt	
	freshly ground pepper	
¾ cup	thin coconut milk	200 ml/7 fl oz
¾ cup	thick coconut milk	200 ml/7 fl oz
2 tbsp	Indonesian sweet soy sauce	2 tbsp
	a few orange segments or pineapple pieces (optional)	

1. Dry the chicken meat with kitchen paper and cut it into 2 in × ½ in (5 cm × 1.25 cm) strips. Rub the strips of chicken with the ground turmeric.

2. Rinse the chicken livers under cold running water. Halve the livers and place them in the milk for 30 minutes.

3. Heat a frying pan and roast the coconut, shaking the pan until the coconut is golden brown. Spread the coconut out on a cold plate to cool.

4. Peel the oranges, removing the pith. Cut the segments between the membranes. Reserve the juice. Cut the pineapple into small pieces. If lychees are fresh, peel very thinly and remove the stones.

5. Carefully rinse the soaked chicken livers under cold running water to remove all traces of milk. Dry them with kitchen paper.

6. Heat the oil in a wok and stir fry the onion until transparent.

7. Stir in the garlic. Add the sambal ulek and curry powder. Stir well and add the strips of chicken meat and the chicken livers. Stir fry for 3 minutes.

8. Add the root ginger and a little salt and pepper. Stir well and add the thin and thick coconut milk, soy sauce and reserved orange juice. Stir well.

9. Bring to the boil, reduce the heat and simmer for 2 minutes. Add the fruit, stir well and transfer to a warmed dish as soon as the fruit has warmed through.

10. Sprinkle on the roasted coconut and garnish with a few segments of orange or pieces of pineapple.

Left to right: Chicken and curry sauce, Vegetable curry, Chicken and curry sauce (11)

Semoeir ati boekit besi

Spiced Chicken Livers

�▶ 00.05   00.12 🍲
plus soaking time

American	Ingredients	Metric/Imperial
1 lb	chicken livers	450 g/1 lb
3¼ cups	milk (optional)	750 ml/1¼ pints
3 tbsp	groundnut oil or ghee	3 tbsp
1	small thinly sliced onion	1
1	finely chopped garlic clove	1
1 tsp	fresh grated root ginger	1 tsp
1 tsp	sugar	1 tsp
2 tsp	curry powder	2 tsp
	salt	
3 tbsp	Indonesian sweet soy sauce (ketyap benteng manis)	3 tbsp
1	chopped scallion (spring onion) or 1 piece leek (optional)	1
2	skinned tomatoes (optional)	2

1. Rinse the livers in cold running water. Trim and cut in half. Soak in milk for 30 minutes to remove the bitter aftertaste. Rinse under cold running water once more to remove all traces of milk. Dry each piece of liver with kitchen paper.
2. Heat the oil or ghee in a wok and stir fry the onion slices until beginning to color. Add the garlic, root ginger, sugar and curry powder.
3. Stir in the livers and fry over high heat for 2 minutes, turning continuously. Sprinkle with a little salt to taste.
4. Stir in the soy sauce and add ⅔ cup (150 ml/¼ pint) boiling water. Stir well then simmer gently over low heat.
5. Serve immediately on a warmed dish, garnished with chopped scallion (spring onion) or leek and slices or segments of tomato.

Sayur masak lemak

Vegetable Curry

▣▶ 00.05   00.20 🍲
Serves 4 as side dish

American	Ingredients	Metric/Imperial
1	small, washed Chinese cabbage	1
1¼ cups	thin coconut milk	300 ml/½ pint
1	chopped onion	1
1	finely chopped garlic clove	1
1 tsp	sambal ulek or sambal trasi (see page 128/129)	1 tsp
1 tsp	mild curry powder	1 tsp
1 tsp	ground turmeric	1 tsp
¼ lb	peeled and diced potatoes	125 g/4 oz
	salt	
1 tbsp	Indonesian sweet soy sauce (ketyap benteng manis)	1 tbsp
1-2 tsp	lemon or lime juice	1-2 tsp
2	large skinned diced tomatoes	2

1. Shred the Chinese cabbage into ¼ in (5 mm) strips.
2. Bring the coconut milk to the boil in a saucepan with 5 tbsp water and the onion, garlic, sambal ulek or sambal trasi, curry powder and turmeric.
3. Stir well, add the diced potato and simmer for 10 minutes.

Add the Chinese cabbage and stir well and simmer for 5 minutes or until the potatoes are cooked.
4. Add a little salt to taste and stir in the soy sauce and the lemon or lime juice.
5. Serve on a warmed dish garnished with diced tomato.

Sayur masak lemak dan boontjes

Vegetable Curry (II)

▣▶ 00.05   00.15 🍲
Serves 4 as side dish

American	Ingredients	Metric/Imperial
½ lb	French beans or haricots verts	225 g/8 oz
½ lb	white cabbage	225 g/8 oz
3 oz	bean sprouts	75 g/3 oz
1¼ cups	thin coconut milk	300 ml/½ pint
1	chopped onion	1
1	finely chopped garlic clove	1
1 tsp	sambal ulek (see page 128)	1 tsp
1 tsp	mild curry powder	1 tsp
1 tsp	ground turmeric	1 tsp
	salt	
1-2 tsp	lemon or lime juice	1-2 tsp

1. Rinse the beans or haricots verts, trim and string them if necessary. Cut them into 2 in (5 cm) pieces.
2. Shred the white cabbage into small pieces.
3. Rinse the bean sprouts in plenty of cold water. Remove as many of the seed cases as possible.
4. Add 5 tbsp water to the coconut milk, bring to the boil.
5. Add the onion, garlic, sambal ulek, curry powder and turmeric. Stir well and add the beans. Cook gently for 6-8 minutes and stir in the cabbage. Simmer for 2 minutes and add the bean sprouts and salt to taste. Stir well and bring back to the boil.
6. Stir in the lemon or lime juice. Stir well once more and serve immediately on a warmed dish.

Atykar kuning

Vegetables in Sweet and Sour Sauce

▣▶ 00.10   00.15 🍲
Serves 4 as side dish

American	Ingredients	Metric/Imperial
6	young carrots	6
¼ lb	French beans or haricots verts	125 g/4 oz
¼ lb	cauliflower or broccoli florets	125 g/4 oz
1	small cucumber	1
3	red chilies	3
2	green chilies	2
2 tbsp	groundnut oil	2 tbsp
2	halved garlic cloves	2
2 oz	sliced fresh root ginger	50 g/2 oz
1 tsp	ground turmeric	1 tsp
1 tsp	mild curry powder	1 tsp
⅔ cup	white vinegar	150 ml/¼ pint
1 tbsp	sugar	1 tbsp
	salt	

Fried cauliflower

1. Scrape the carrot and cut it into thin strips.
2. Rinse the beans, trim and and string them, if necessary. Cut them into 2 in (5 cm) pieces.
3. Divide the cauliflower into florets.
4. Rinse the cucumber under cold running water. Halve it lengthwise and remove the seeds. Cut the halves into ¼ in (5 mm) slices.
5. Rinse, trim and seed the chilies and cut them into very thin strips.
6. Heat the oil in a wok and stir fry the garlic cloves and slices of root ginger until the garlic is light brown. Remove the garlic and root ginger from the wok with a skimmer. Drain over the wok.
7. Add the turmeric and curry powder to the hot oil. Stir rapidly and add ¾ cup (200 ml/7 fl oz) boiling water, the vinegar, sugar and a little salt. Stir well and boil briskly for 1 minute, then add the beans. Simmer for 3 minutes, add the strips of carrot, cauliflower or broccoli and the chili. Stir well and simmer for 5 minutes.
8. Add the pieces of cucumber and bring back to the boil, stirring and turning over constantly. Boil briskly for exactly 1 minute.
9. Transfer the vegetables to a cold dish or glass bowl. Leave to cool. Cover and chill for at least 2 hours.

Cook's tip: Atyar kuning should always be served cold in the cooking liquid. It tastes particularly good with roast pork, chicken or other poultry, but also with fried fish.

Sambal goreng kol

Fried Cauliflower

00.05 00.10
Serves 4 as side dish

American	Ingredients	Metric/Imperial
1	small cleaned cauliflower divided into florets	1
3 tbsp	groundnut oil	3 tbsp
2	chopped onions	2
2 tsp	sambal ulek (see page 128)	2 tsp
2	finely chopped garlic cloves	2
5 tbsp	chicken bouillon (stock)	5 tbsp
	salt	
1	chopped scallion (spring onion) or piece of leek (optional)	1

1. Rinse the cauliflower florets and drain well in a colander.
2. Heat the oil in a wok and fry the onions until transparent.
3. Add the sambal ulek and garlić.
4. Stir well and add the cauliflower. Stir continuously for 2 minutes. Reduce the heat and add the boiling hot bouillon (stock) and a little salt. Cover the wok and simmer for 5- 7 minutes. Remove the lid and leave to boil cook until almost all of the liquid has evaporated.
5. Serve the dish sprinkled with a little chopped scallion (spring onion) or leek to garnish.

Cook's tip: Sambal goreng kol can quickly be transformed from a side dish to a main course by adding ½ lb (225 g/8 oz) fresh peeled shrimp (prawns) immediately before serving. The dish may be served as soon as the shrimp (prawns) are hot. If adding shrimp (prawns), replace the sambal ulek with sambal trasi and sprinkle some Indonesian sweet soy sauce over the dish before serving.

Taukwa dan atyar

Soybean Curd (Tofu) with Mixed Vegetables

00.10 Serves 4 as side dish **00.15**

American	Ingredients	Metric/Imperial
2	cakes soybean curd (tofu)	2
	salt	
½ lb	French beans or haricots verts cut into ¼ in (5 mm) pieces	225 g/8 oz
6	young carrots cut into thin strips	6
½ lb	broccoli florets	225 g/8 oz
2	seeded red bell peppers cut into strips	2
2	seeded green chilies cut into very thin strips	2
¼ lb	bean sprouts	125 g/4 oz
3 tbsp	groundnut oil	3 tbsp
2	halved garlic cloves	2
1	chopped onion	1
1 tsp	sambal ulek or sambal trasi (see page 128/129)	1 tsp
1½ tbsp	Indonesian sweet soy sauce (ketyap benteng manis)	1½ tbsp

1. Cut the soybean curd (tofu) into ½ in (1.25 cm) slices and then into 2 in (5 cm) strips.
2. Bring a generous quantity of salted water to the boil.
3. Add the beans, followed 2-3 minutes later by the strips of carrot, broccoli florets, bell peppers and chilies. Boil for 4-5 minutes. Drain well in a colander.
4. Rinse the bean sprouts in plenty of cold water. Remove as many seed cases as possible. Drain in a colander.
5. Heat the oil in a wok and stir fry the garlic cloves until brown. Remove them from the oil with a skimmer and drain them over the wok.
6. Add the onion and stir in the sambal. Add the strips of soybean curd (tofu) and stir well.
7. Sprinkle on the soy sauce and immediately add the cooked vegetables.
8. Add a little salt to taste and the bean sprouts. Continue turning over very carefully until warmed through.
9. Serve as hot as possible in a warmed dish.

Cook's tip: accompany with a separate dish of Chinese egg noodles or rice vermicelli which have first been boiled and then fried in a little oil.

Soybean curd (tofu) with mixed vegetables

Taukwa dan tauge

Soybean Curd (Tofu) with Bean Sprouts

◣▬▬▷ 00.05   00.10 ⊑

Serves 4 as side dish

American	Ingredients	Metric/Imperial
2	cakes soybean curd (tofu)	2
¼ lb	French beans or haricots verts	125 g/4 oz
	salt	
½ lb	bean sprouts	225 g/8 oz
2 tbsp	groundnut oil	2 tbsp
2	finely chopped garlic cloves	2
½ tsp	sambal ulek (see page 128)	½ tsp
1 tbsp	Indonesian sweet soy sauce (ketyap benteng manis)	1 tbsp

1. Cut the soybean curd (tofu) into ½ in (1.25 cm) cubes.
2. Rinse the beans or haricot verts, trim and string them if necessary. Cut them into 1 in (2.5 cm) pieces. Boil them in plenty of salted water for 5 minutes and drain in a colander.
3. Rinse the bean sprouts in plenty of cold water. Remove as many of the seed cases as possible. Drain in a colander.
4. Heat the oil in a wok and add the garlic. Stir well and add the sambal ulek.
5. Stir well again and immediately add the diced soybean curd (tofu). Stir well a few times.
6. Sprinkle on the soy sauce and add the beans and bean sprouts and a little salt to taste. Continue turning over until the vegetables have warmed through.
7. Serve as hot as possible in a warmed serving dish.

Gulai kambing

Lamb or Mutton Curry

◣▬▬▷ 00.06   02.35 ⊑

Serves 4

American	Ingredients	Metric/Imperial
1¼ lb	lean lamb or mutton cut into cubes	550 g/1¼ lb
4 tbsp	desiccated coconut	4 tbsp
2	squeezed lemons or limes	2
2	coarsely chopped onions	2
2	crushed garlic cloves	2
1 tbsp	fresh grated root ginger	1 tbsp
1 tbsp	mild curry powder	1 tbsp
4	small dried chilies	4
1 tsp	grated lemon or lime peel	1 tsp
3 tbsp	groundnut oil	3 tbsp
4	skinned, diced ripe tomatoes	4
1¼ cups	thin coconut milk	300 ml/½ pint
5 tbsp	thick coconut milk	5 tbsp
	salt	

1. Dry the pieces of meat with kitchen paper.
2. Heat a small frying pan and roast the coconut shaking it constantly, until golden brown. Spread out the coconut on a large cold plate to cool.
3. Purée the lemon or lime juice, onions, garlic, root ginger, curry powder, crumbled dried chilies and the lemon or lime peel in a food processor.
4. Add the cooled coconut and process for 30 seconds.
5. Heat the oil in a wok and add the paste. Stir fry for 3 minutes over moderate heat.
6. Add the cubes of meat and stir fry for 5 minutes.
7. Add the pieces of tomato, thin coconut milk and 5 tbsp water. Stir well, bring to the boil and reduce the heat. Cover the wok and simmer for 1 hour (lamb) or 2½ hours mutton) until the meat is cooked. Stir occasionally and add more water if necessary.
8. Stir in the thick coconut milk after the meat is cooked and most of the liquid has evaporated. Add salt to taste.
9. Serve as hot as possible in a warmed dish.

Shami kebab

Lamb Rissoles with Lentils

◣▬▬▷ 00.05   01.10 ⊑

Serves 4 as side dish

American	Ingredients	Metric/Imperial
¼ lb	red lentils	125 g/4 oz
½ lb	fine ground (minced) lean lamb	225 g/8 oz
2	chopped onions	2
2 tsp	mild curry powder	2 tsp
	salt	
1	egg	1
2 tsp	cornstarch (cornflour)	2 tsp
¾ cup	sunflower seed oil	200 ml/7 fl oz

1. Pick over the lentils, rinse and put them in a saucepan with the meat. Add 1¼ cups (300 ml/½ pint) boiling water. Bring slowly to the boil.
2. Add the onion, curry powder and a little salt and simmer for 50 minutes, until the lentils are cooked. Cook, stirring constantly, until almost all of the cooking liquid has evaporated.
3. Lightly beat the egg and add 1 tbsp water and the cornstarch (cornflour). Stir the mixture into the contents of the saucepan and remove from the heat.
4. Leave to cool then shape into 6-9 small, flat cakes.
5. Heat the oil in a wok and fry the cakes, 3 at a time, until brown on both sides. Drain on kitchen paper and serve hot.

Soto ayam pedas

Highly Spiced Main Course Chicken Soup

◢▽ 00.10   01.10 ⊂▭
       Serves 4

American	Ingredients	Metric/Imperial
1 (2¼ lb)	roasting chicken	1 (1 kg/2¼ lb)
	salt	
12	lightly bruised black peppercorns	12
6	sprigs leaf celery	6
2	large coarsely chopped onions	2
1 tbsp	groundnut oil	1 tbsp
2	curry leaves (daun salam)	2
3	finely chopped garlic cloves	3
2 tsp	sambal ulek (see page 128)	2 tsp
1 tsp	grated fresh root ginger	1 tsp
¼ lb	Chinese rice vermicelli	125 g/4 oz
2	sliced, hard-cooked (hard-boiled) eggs	2
6	chopped scallions (spring onions)	6

1. Divide the chicken into 8 pieces. Put the pieces in a suitable saucepan with boiling water just to cover. Add a little salt and bring back to the boil. Carefully skim the surface a few times with a skimmer.
2. Add the peppercorns, leaf celery and half of the onions. Reduce the heat and cook the chicken pieces for 30-40 minutes. Leave the chicken to cool in the liquid until lukewarm. Remove from the liquid. Remove the skin and bones and cut the chicken meat into strips.
3. Strain the bouillon (stock) through a piece of muslin and bring back to the boil.
4. Heat the oil in a wok and stir fry the remaining onions until golden yellow.
5. Add the curry leaves, garlic and sambal. Stir well and add the root ginger. Stir well and pour on the hot bouillon (stock). Reduce the heat and simmer for 5-8 minutes.

6. Cook the rice vermicelli as directed on the packet. Rinse under cold water and drain. Cut it into 3 in (7.5 cm) pieces. Add to the bouillon (stock) with the chicken meat. Bring the bouillon (stock) just to the boil.
7. Remove the curry leaves and serve the soup in a large warmed tureen. Put the slices of egg in the soup and sprinkle with the scallion (spring onion).

Cook's tip: in Malaysia, soto ayam is always accompanied by a small dish of potato crisps or emping melinje. The crisps or emping should be sprinkled over the soup by the guests.

Sayur udang bayam 👨‍🍳

Main Course Soup with Shrimp (Prawns) and Spinach

◢▽ 00.10   00.25 ⊂▭
       Serves 4

American	Ingredients	Metric/Imperial
1 lb	large shrimp (prawns) thawed if frozen	450 g/1 lb
	salt	
3 tbsp	groundnut oil	3 tbsp
½ lb	spinach	225 g/½ lb
1	chopped onion	1
1 tsp	sambal ulek (see page 128)	1 tsp
1	garlic clove	1
½ tsp	mild curry powder	½ tsp
2¼ cups	thin coconut milk	500 ml/18 fl oz
5 tbsp	thick coconut milk	5 tbsp
3	chopped scallions (spring onions) or a piece of leek	3

1. Peel the shrimp (prawns) and remove the black thread. Rinse them under cold running water and dry with kitchen paper. Set aside the peelings.

2. Heat 1 tbsp oil in a wok and stir fry the shrimp (prawn) peelings for 3 minutes. Add 2¼ cups (500 ml/18 fl oz) boiling water and 1 tsp salt. Simmer until the liquid is reduced by half. Strain the shrimp (prawn) bouillon (stock) through a piece of wet muslin and set aside.

3. Rinse the spinach and remove any thick stems. Cut the spinach into coarse pieces.

4. Heat the remaining oil in a wok and add the onion, sambal ulek, garlic and curry powder. Stir well and add the spinach and shrimp (prawn) bouillon (stock). Add a little salt to taste. Cook for 2 minutes, then add the thin coconut milk. Stir well. Reduce the heat and simmer for 5 minutes.

5. Chop the shrimp (prawns) into small pieces and add them to the wok. Stir in the thick coconut milk.

6. Stir the soup a few times and simmer for 2 minutes. Add a little salt to taste.

7. Serve the soup in a large warmed tureen or in cups, bowls or plates. Sprinkle on the chopped scallion (spring onion) or leek immediately before serving.

Cook's tip: the soup is even more nutritious when 4-5 tbsp cooked rice are added at the same time as the shrimp (prawns).

Sothi
Coconut Sauce/Soup

▱ 00.02   00.09 ▱
Serves 4 as side dish

American	Ingredients	Metric/Imperial
¾ cup	chicken bouillon (stock)	200 ml/7 fl oz
2	thinly sliced onions	2
1 tsp	mild curry powder	1 tsp
1 tsp	sambal ulek (see page 128)	1 tsp
2 tsp	dried shrimp (prawns)	2 tsp
1¼ cups	thick coconut milk	300 ml/½ pint
	salt	
2 tsp	lemon or lime juice	2 tsp

1. Bring the chicken bouillon (stock) to the boil and add the onions, curry powder, sambal ulek and dried shrimp (prawns). Stir well and boil briskly for 5 minutes.

2. Stir in the thick coconut milk. Cook, stirring until the sauce thickens.

3. Add a little salt to taste and stir in the lemon or lime juice immediately before serving.

4. Serve the sauce as hot as possible.

Left to right: Highly spiced main course chicken soup, Main course soup with shrimp (prawns) and spinach, Coconut sauce/soup

Malay beef sates

Satay daging Malaya
Malay Beef Sates

◣	00.07	00.08 ⌣
	plus marinating	

American	Ingredients	Metric/Imperial
1 ½ lb	tender rib of beef, trimmed with fat	675 g/1 ½ lb
2 tsp	ground turmeric	2 tsp
1 tsp	curry powder	1 tsp
1 tsp	ground cumin	1 tsp
1 tsp	sambal ulek (see page 128)	1 tsp
1 tsp	grated lemon zest	1 tsp
1 tsp	salt	1 tsp
1 tbsp	soft brown sugar	1 tbsp
4 tbsp	thick coconut milk	4 tbsp

1. Dry the meat with kitchen paper and cut it into 1 in (2.5 cm) cubes.
2. Put all other ingredients in a bowl and stir well until the salt and sugar have dissolved.
3. Add the cubes of beef and turn the ingredients over a few times to ensure that the meat is coated with the spicy mixture. Leave to stand for at least 1 hour, turning over every 15 minutes.
4. Soak 12 wooden sate sticks in water to ensure that they do not catch fire under the broiler (grill). Thread 4-5 cubes of meat on to each stick. Grill (broil) the sates over the barbecue or under a very hot, broiler (grill) for 6-8 minutes. Turn regularly during cooking so that the meat is cooked for an equal length of time on all sides.

5. Serve the sates on a warmed dish and accompany with piquant peanut sauce.
Cook's tip: the Malaysians like to serve Ketupat with sate.

Saus katyang Malaya
Malay Peanut Sauce

◣	00.03	00.06 ⌣
	for 12 sates	

American	Ingredients	Metric/Imperial
3 tbsp	coconut oil	3 tbsp
6	small dried chilies	6
2	chopped onions	2
4-6	finely chopped garlic cloves	4-6
1 tsp	sambal trasi (see page 129)	1 tsp
1 ¼ cups	thin coconut milk	300 ml/½ pint
4 tbsp	peanut butter	4 tbsp
2 tbsp	Indonesian sweet soy sauce (ketyap benteng manis)	2 tbsp
2 tbsp	lemon juice	2 tbsp
	salt	

1. Heat the oil and add the crumbled chilies, onions and garlic. Stir well and add the sambal trasi.
2. Stir in the coconut milk. Bring to the boil, stirring constantly. Cook, stirring for 2 minutes.
3. Add the peanut butter and soy sauce and continue stirring until very thick and quite smooth. Stir in the lemon juice and add a little salt to taste.
4. Serve the sauce in one or more warmed bowls.

Roti jala

Crispy Pancakes

⊐ 00.10   00.25

makes 12 pancakes

American	Ingredients	Metric/Imperial
½ cup	flour	125 g/4 oz
1	pinch salt	1
2	eggs	2
2¼ cups	thin coconut milk	500 ml/18 fl oz
5 tbsp	ghee	5 tbsp

1. Sieve the flour and the salt in a bowl. Make a well in the center.

2. Lightly beat the eggs in a bowl and slowly add the coconut milk, beating constantly with a small whisk.

3. Pour one third of the mixture into the well in the flour. Stir well and add another third of the egg mixture. Stir until the batter is completely smooth. Add the rest of the egg mixture and 2 tbsp ghee. Beat briskly with a small whisk.

4. Heat 2 tsp ghee in a heavy-based frying pan. Spoon enough batter into the pan to form a very thin layer on the bottom. Constantly shake the frying pan to prevent the pancake sticking. Turn the pancake over as soon as the top has set. Fry over very high heat until crisp on one side. Lift the pancake a few times.

5. Fry 11 more pancakes using no more than ¾ tsp ghee for frying.

6. Serve from the pan as the pancakes lose their crispness if kept warm.

Sambal kelapa

Coconut Sambal

⊐ 00.10   00.00

Serves 4 as side dish

American	Ingredients	Metric/Imperial
3 oz	desiccated coconut	75 g/3 oz
½ tsp	salt	½ tsp
1 tsp	sambal trasi (see page 129)	1 tsp
1	finely chopped small onion	1
2 tbsp	lemon or lime juice	2 tbsp

1. Put the coconut in a bowl and sprinkle 2 tbsp boiling water over. Leave to stand for a minute, then stir with a fork. Leave to stand for 5 minutes.

2. Mix together the salt, sambal trasi, onion and lemon or lime juice.

3. Stir the mixture into the coconut with a fork.

4. Serve sambal kelapa in a bowl or in individual bowls.

Crispy pancakes

Gula Malaya
Sago Pudding

	00.05	00.10
	plus chilling time	

American	Ingredients	Metric/Imperial
⅔ cup	soft brown sugar	125 g/4 oz
	pinch mild curry powder	
	pinch ground cinnamon	
	pinch ground root ginger	
¾ cup	sago	125 g/4 oz
¾ cup	thick coconut milk	200 ml/7 fl oz

1. Dissolve the sugar in 5 tbsp boiling water. Strain the syrup if the sugar is not completely pure.
2. Bring 1¾ cups (400 ml/⅔ pint) water to the boil in a small saucepan. Add the curry powder, cinnamon and root ginger and stir in the sago. Cook, stirring until the mixture is stiff.
3. Add the sugar syrup and thick coconut milk, stirring constantly. Simmer for 2-3 minutes.
4. Pour the mixture into 1 large or 4 small moulds which have been rinsed in cold water. Leave the pudding to set. Chill until completely set.

Cook's tip: in Malaysia the sago puddings are usually served with a sauce made by mixing 5 tbsp fruit juice with ⅔ cup (125 g/4 oz) soft brown sugar made up to a syrup.

Serikaya dengan
Agar-agar Jelly

	00.00	00.15
	plus soaking and chilling time	

American	Ingredients	Metric/Imperial
1 (¼ oz)	piece agar-agar	1 (8 g/¼ oz)
	pinch mild curry powder	
	pinch ground root ginger	
2 tsp	ground cinnamon	2 tsp
1 ⅓ cups	brown candy sugar	225 g/8 oz
¾ cup	thick coconut milk	200 ml/7 fl oz

1. Loosen the agar-agar threads. Put them in a bowl and pour ¾ cup (200 ml/7 fl oz) warm water over. Soak for at least 6 hours.
2. Put in a saucepan and add 1 cup (250 ml/8 fl oz) cold water. Bring to the boil, stirring constantly. Reduce the heat and simmer gently, stirring occasionally until the agar-agar has completely dissolved.
3. Add the curry powder, root ginger and cinnamon. Dissolve the sugar in ⅔ cup (150 ml/¼ pint) boiling water, stirring constantly. Strain the syrup if the sugar is not completely pure.
4. Stir the sugar syrup into the pudding mixture and add the coconut milk, stirring for 2 minutes.
5. Pour into a mould which has been rinsed with cold water. Leave to cool.
6. Chill the jelly for at least 2 hours until completely set.

Cook's tip: turn the pudding out on to a dish and surround it with fresh tropical fruit or segments of tinned mandarin. 6-8 tbsp very finely chopped canned pineapple pieces may be stirred into the boiling pudding mixture. Skinned orange segments cut into small pieces are also very suitable for adding to the pudding mixture.

MENU

Crab salad
Curry with chicken livers
Stuffed mango

Crab Salad

	00.05	00.05
	Serves 4	

American	Ingredients	Metric/Imperial
½ lb	cooked crabmeat	225 g/8 oz
3 oz	bean sprouts	75 g/3 oz
1	small cucumber	1
	salt	
4	skinned tomatoes	4
1 tbsp	lemon or lime juice	1 tbsp
1 tsp	sambal ulek (see page 128)	1 tsp
3 tbsp	groundnut oil	3 tbsp
1 tsp	sesame oil	1 tsp
4	washed lettuce leaves	4

1. Pick over the crabmeat, removing any pieces of shell and cut the crabmeat into small pieces.
2. Rinse the bean sprouts in plenty of cold water and remove as many seed cases as possible. Pour over several quarts/litres of cold water and drain in a colander.
3. Rinse the cucumber, trim and halve it lengthwise and remove the seeds. Cut the halves lengthwise again and then into small pieces. Sprinkle with a little salt and leave to drain in a colander.
4. Halve the tomatoes, remove the seeds and cut the flesh into thin strips.
5. Dissolve 1 tsp salt in the lemon or lime juice, stirring continuously. Add the sambal and groundnut and sesame oils. Stir well.
6. Put the crabmeat, bean sprouts and cucumber in a bowl and stir carefully. Sprinkle the tomato strips over and pour the dressing over the salad.
7. Lay one lettuce leaf on each plate, divide the salad between the plates and serve.

Curry with Chicken Livers

	00.06	00.10
	plus standing time	

American	Ingredients	Metric/Imperial
1 lb	chicken livers	450 g/1 lb
2¼ cups	milk	500 ml/18 fl oz
2	chopped onions	2
1	crushed garlic clove	1
½ tsp	ground turmeric	½ tsp
	salt	
1 tsp	soft brown sugar	1 tsp
2 tsp	sambal ulek	2 tsp
1 tbsp	fresh ground root ginger	1 tbsp
1 tbsp	lemon or lime juice	1 tbsp
3 tbsp	groundnut oil	3 tbsp
2	curry leaves (daun salam)	2
1 tbsp	mild curry powder	1 tbsp
1 cup	thin coconut milk	250 ml/8 fl oz
1	dried red chili	1

1. Rinse the chicken livers under cold running water and trim if necessary. Halve the livers and place them in the milk. Leave to stand for 30 minutes. Remove the livers and rinse again to remove all traces of milk. Dry with kitchen paper.
2. Purée the onions, garlic, turmeric, a little salt, the sugar, sambal ulek, root ginger and lemon or lime juice in a food processor.
3. Heat the oil in a wok and stir fry the onion paste until golden brown. Add the chicken livers and curry leaves and stir fry until the chicken livers begin to color. Stir in the curry powder. Stir well and simmer for 1½ minutes.

4. Stir in the coconut milk and add a little salt to taste. Bring to the boil, stirring constantly. Reduce the heat and cook, stirring for 2-3 minutes. Remove the curry leaves.
5. Transfer to a warmed dish and serve garnished with a red chili 'flower'.

Stuffed Mango

	00.10	00.00
	plus chilling time	

American	Ingredients	Metric/Imperial
2	medium size mangoes	2
4 tbsp	thin coconut milk	4 tbsp
2 tbsp	thick coconut milk	2 tbsp
2 tbsp	soft brown sugar	2 tbsp
1 tbsp	lemon or lime juice	1 tbsp

1. Rinse the mangoes well and halve them. Remove the stones carefully and discard. Scoop out the flesh carefully and set aside the shells. Chop the flesh into ½ in (1.25 cm) pieces.
2. Put the mango pieces in a bowl and stir in the thin and thick coconut milk.
3. Stir the sugar into the lemon or lime juice, stirring until the sugar has dissolved. Pour into the mango and coconut mixture. Stir well.
4. Put the mango mixture back into the shells and chill for 1-2 hours before serving.

THE
PHILIPPINES

Paksiw

Braised Fish with Vegetables

	OO.15 plus soaking time	OO.15

American	Ingredients	Metric/Imperial
1 tbsp	dried shrimps (prawns) (ebi)	1 tbsp
1	cucumber	1
1	small eggplant (aubergine)	1
1	small head of paksoi or endive	1
2	green chilies	2
1	red chili	1
1½ lb	cod fillets	675 g/1½ lb
1½ tbsp	coarsely grated fresh root ginger	1½ tbsp
	salt	
4 tbsp	spiced vinegar, lemon or lime juice	4 tbsp
1 cup	fish bouillon (stock)	250 ml/8 fl oz
4	skinned tomatoes, cut into segments	4
	freshly ground pepper	

1. Put the shrimp (prawns) in a bowl with 4 tbsp warm water. Soak until the liquid is completely cold. Strain and set the shrimps (prawns) aside. Reserve the liquid.
2. Wash, trim and halve the cucumber. Scoop out the seeds and cut the cucumber into finger-width pieces.
3. Peel the eggplant (aubergine) and cut the flesh into ½ in (1.25 cm) cubes.
4. Wash the paksoi or endive and cut into strips.
5. Rinse, trim and seed the chilies. Cut the flesh into very narrow strips.
6. Place the strips of paksoi or endive in the bottom of a shallow pan. Put the eggplant (aubergine) on top and arrange the pieces of cucumber over these. Scatter half the strips of chili on top.
7. Rinse the fish under cold running water. Cut into thick slices and place on the bed of vegetables.
8. Scatter the shrimps (prawns), root ginger, remaining strips of chili and a little salt over the fish.
9. Add the strained shrimp (prawn) liquid, vinegar and bouillon (stock) and bring to the boil slowly. Cover the pan. Reduce the heat and simmer gently for 12-15 minutes. Transfer carefully into a warmed dish so that the vegetables are at the bottom and the fish at the top.
10. Garnish with tomato segments and sprinkle with a little salt and pepper and serve with boiled rice.

Cook's tip: any 2, but preferably 3 different varieties of vegetable or fruit can be used for this dish. They should be made up of a firm variety such as cucumber, zucchini (courgette) or broccoli, a softer kind which disintegrates during cooking, such as eggplant (aubergine) flesh, ripe tomatoes or sharp melon and a tough leaf vegetable e.g. paksoi or endive.

Braised fish with vegetables

Adobo (I)

Adobo with Shrimp (Prawns)

	OO.10 plus soaking time	OO.10

American	Ingredients	Metric/Imperial
1 lb	fresh peeled shrimp (prawns)	450 g/1 lb
2 tbsp	dried shrimps (prawns) (ebi)	2 tbsp
¼ cup	butter	50 g/2 oz
4	sliced garlic cloves	4
½ cup	sifted flour	30 g/1 oz
1	crumbled bay leaf	1
3 tbsp	spiced vinegar, lemon or lime juice	3 tbsp
	salt	
	freshly ground pepper	
2 tbsp	coarsely chopped coriander or parsley	2 tbsp

1. Put the dried shrimp (prawns) in a bowl with 1 cup (250 ml/8 fl oz) warm water. Leave to stand until the liquid is completely cold. Strain and set aside the shrimp (prawns) and the liquid.
2. Heat the butter in a wok and stir fry the garlic for 1 minute.
3. Add the flour and stir well until the mixture forms a smooth paste.
4. Add the shrimp (prawns) soaking liquid and the bay leaf and vinegar, or lemon and lime juice. Cook gently for 5 minutes then strain the sauce through a fine strainer (sieve).
5. Bring back to the boil and add a little salt and pepper to taste.
6. Stir in the fresh and soaked shrimp (prawns) and the coriander or parsley. Simmer until the shrimp (prawns) are warmed through.
7. Serve in a warmed dish.
Cook's tip: serve accompanied by boiled rice. 1-2 tsp light soy sauce (Japanese or Chinese) can be added to the sauce.

Adobo (II)
Fish Adobo

00.10 plus standing time   **00.10**

American	Ingredients	Metric/Imperial
1½ lb	plaice fillets	675 g/1½ lb
1 tbsp	Chinese or Japanese light soy sauce	1 tbsp
2 tbsp	lemon or lime juice	2 tbsp
2 tbsp	groundnut oil	2 tbsp
2	large coarsely chopped onions	2
6	finely chopped garlic cloves	6
4 oz	cooked peas, French beans or haricot verts cut into small pieces	125 g/4 oz
2 tsp	sifted flour	2 tsp
1	large skinned ripe tomato cut into pieces	1
¾ cup	fish bouillon (stock)	200 ml/7 fl oz
	salt	
	freshly ground pepper	
2	sliced tomatoes (optional)	2

1. Rinse the fish under cold running water and dry with kitchen paper. Cut the fish into finger width strips.
2. Mix together the soy sauce and lemon or lime juice.
3. Place the strips of fish in the soy sauce mixture and turn carefully until coated on all sides. Leave to stand for one hour and turn over carefully every 15 minutes.
4. Heat the oil in a wok and stir fry the onion until transparent.
5. Add the garlic and fry gently for 1 minute.
6. Add the peas or pieces of French bean or haricot verts. Sprinkle with the flour and stir well.
7. Add the pieces of tomato and the fish bouillon (stock) and cook, stirring until the sauce has thickened.
8. Add a little salt and pepper and stir the fish into the sauce. Simmer for 3-4 minutes until the tomato has disintegrated.
9. Serve in a warmed dish garnished with a few unskinned sliced tomatoes (optional).

Adobo (III)
Adobo with Chicken

00.10 Serves 4   **00.35**

American	Ingredients	Metric/Imperial
1 (2¼ lb)	roasting chicken	1 (1 kg/2¼ lb)
1 tsp	salt	1 tsp
1 tsp	ground black pepper	1 tsp
½ tsp	ground paprika	½ tsp
2	bay leaves	2
12	finely chopped garlic cloves	12
⅔ cup	spiced vinegar, lemon or lime juice	150 ml/¼ pint
3 tbsp	oil or butter	3 tbsp
3-4	skinned, quartered tomatoes	3-4
	a few sprigs of coriander or parsley	

1. Divide the chicken into 12-16 small portions.
2. Mix together the salt, pepper and paprika.
3. Dry the chicken pieces with kitchen paper and stir into the salt mixture.
4. Put into a pan and place the bay leaves between the pieces of chicken and sprinkle with garlic.
5. Add the vinegar or lemon or lime juice and ⅔ cup (150 ml/¼ pint) water and slowly bring to the boil.
6. Reduce the heat and simmer, turning occasionally, until the chicken is tender and the liquid in the pan has been reduced to 5 tbsp.
7. Remove the chicken pieces from the pan, drain and dry them with kitchen paper. Keep the cooking liquid warm.
8. Heat the oil or butter in a frying pan, increase the heat and quickly fry the cooked chicken pieces until golden brown on all sides.
9. Serve the chicken pieces on warmed dishes. Spoon 1 or more tbsp of the remaining cooking liquid over the chicken and garnish with tomato quarters and sprigs of coriander or parsley.
Cook's tip: serve Adobo with Chicken as a main course, accompanied by boiled rice and a little bowl of light soy sauce (Chinese or Japanese).

Adobo with chicken

Pipi-an (I)

Chicken with Pork in Peanut Sauce

	00.15	00.45
	Serves 4	

American	Ingredients	Metric/Imperial
1 lb	chicken drumsticks	450 g/1 lb
¾ lb	lean pork	350 g/12 oz
1	red chili	1
	salt	
	freshly ground pepper	
2 tbsp	groundnut oil	2 tbsp
1 tsp	annatto seeds	1 tsp
1	large chopped onion	1
2	finely chopped garlic cloves	2
3 oz	lean diced bacon	75 g/3 oz
6 tbsp	coarse peanut butter	6 tbsp
2-3 tsp	light soy sauce (optional)	2-3 tsp
2	skinned tomatoes, cut into segments	2
1	bunch of coriander or parsley	1

1. Skin and bone the chicken drumsticks. Cut the chicken into small pieces.
2. Cut the pork into small pieces and put both meats into a small pan.
3. Rinse, trim and seed the chili, cut the flesh into small pieces and grind finely in a mortar.
4. Add to the meat with ½ tsp salt, ½ tsp pepper and 1 cup (250 ml/8 fl oz) water and gently bring to the boil. Stir well, reduce the heat and simmer for 30-35 minutes. Add a few tbsp water if necessary.
5. Heat the oil in a wok and stir fry the annatto seeds, the oil should turn orange. Remove the seeds as soon as they start to pop.
6. Add the onion and stir fry until transparent. Add the garlic and stir fry, until the onion is golden.
7. Stir in the diced bacon and fry over high heat for 1 minute.
8. Stir in the peanut butter. Pour in the cooking liquid from the meat and cook, stirring until the sauce has thickened. Add a little more stock or water if necessary (the sauce should be quite thick).
9. Season with a little more salt and/or pepper and light soy sauce if liked. Warm the meat in the sauce.
10. Transfer the meat and sauce into a warm dish and serve, garnished with tomato segments and a few sprigs of coriander or parsley.

Left to right: Chicken with pork in peanut sauce
Chicken with ham and peanut sauce
Pork with shrimp (prawns) in peanut sauce

Pipi-an (II)

Chicken with Ham in Peanut Sauce

▭◸ 00.10
Serves 4
00.45 🍲

American	Ingredients	Metric/Imperial
1¼ lb	chicken pieces	550 g/1¼ lb
¾ lb	raw ham	350 g/12 oz
1	red chili	1
	salt	
	freshly ground pepper	
2 tbsp	groundnut oil	2 tbsp
1 tsp	annatto seeds	1 tsp
1	large chopped onion	1
2	finely chopped garlic cloves	2
6 tbsp	peanut butter	6 tbsp
1-2 tsp	light soy sauce (Chinese or Japanese)	1-2 tsp
1 tbsp	finely chopped coriander or parsley	1 tbsp
1	skinned, sliced tomato	1
1	small red bell pepper	1

1. Skin and bone the chicken pieces. Cut the chicken meat into small pieces.
2. Cut the ham into ¼ in (5 mm) pieces.
3. Rinse, trim and seed the chili. Cut the flesh into small pieces, and grind finely in a mortar.
4. Put the chicken meat and ham in a pan with the chili, a little salt and pepper and 1 cup (250 ml/8 fl oz) water. Bring slowly to the boil, reduce the heat and simmer for 30-35 minutes.
5. Heat the oil in a wok and fry the annatto seeds until they pop. Remove them from the oil.
6. Add the onion and stir fry until transparent. Add the garlic and gently stir fry until the onion is golden brown.
7. Stir in the peanut butter and add the cooking liquid from the meat. Add a little more water if necessary and cook, stirring until the sauce is thick.
8. Stir the meat into the sauce, and warm through.
9. Season to taste with a little more salt, pepper and 1-2 tsp soy sauce (Chinese or Japanese) (optional).
10. Transfer to a warmed dish, sprinkle with coriander or parsley and garnish with tomato slices or very finely diced red bell pepper.

Pipi-an (III)

Pork with Shrimp (Prawns) in Peanut Sauce

▭◸ 00.10
Serves 4
00.45 🍲

American	Ingredients	Metric/Imperial
1 lb	lean pork	450 g/1 lb
1	red chili	1
	salt	
	freshly ground pepper	
2 tbsp	groundnut oil	2 tbsp
1 tbsp	annatto seeds	1 tbsp
1	large chopped onion	1
2	finely chopped garlic cloves	2
6 tbsp	peanut butter	6 tbsp
1-2 tsp	light soy sauce (Chinese or Japanese) (optional)	1-2 tsp
¼ lb	fresh peeled shrimp (prawns)	125 g/4 oz
2	chopped scallions (spring onions) shallots or a piece of leek.	2
1	red chili (optional)	1

1. Dry the meat and cut into ½ in (1.25 cm) cubes.
2. Rinse, trim and seed the chili. Cut into small pieces and grind finely in a mortar.
3. Put the meat in a pan with the chili, salt and freshly ground pepper and 1 cup (250 ml/8 fl oz) water. Bring slowly to the boil, reduce the heat and simmer for 30-35 minutes.
4. Heat the oil in a wok and fry the annatto seeds until they pop. Remove from the oil.
5. Add the onion and stir fry until transparent. Add the garlic and stir fry until the onion is golden brown.
6. Stir in the peanut butter and add the meat cooking liquid. Cook, stirring until the sauce has thickened. Add a little more water if necessary.
7. Season the sauce to taste with a little salt and pepper and stir in 1-2 tsp soy sauce (optional).
8. Add the meat and shrimp (prawns) to the sauce. Stir well and warm through.
9. Stir in half the chopped scallions (spring onions), shallots or leek.
10. Transfer to a warmed serving dish and sprinkle with the remaining scallions (spring onions), shallots or leek.
11. Serve garnished with a red chili "flower".

Spare Ribs

	00.05	01.10
	plus drying time	

American	Ingredients	Metric/Imperial
4 lb	spare ribs	2 kg/4 lb
1	large quartered onion	1
3	skinned garlic cloves	3
2 tbsp	Indonesian sweet soy sauce (ketyap benteng manis)	2 tbsp
1 tbsp	Indonesian salty soy sauce (ketyap benteng asin)	1 tbsp
½ tsp	salt	½ tsp
½ tsp	coarsely ground black pepper	½ tsp
4 tbsp	groundnut oil	4 tbsp
7 tbsp	soft brown sugar	7 tbsp
1 tsp	salt	1 tsp
4 tbsp	Indonesian sweet soy sauce (ketyap benteng manis)	4 tbsp
1	large finely chopped onion	1
1	finely chopped garlic clove	1
1 tbsp	finely grated fresh root ginger	1 tbsp

1. Separate the ribs.
2. Put the ribs in a pan and add the quartered onion, 3 garlic cloves, 1 tbsp sweet and 1 tbsp salty soy sauce, salt and pepper. Add boiling water just to cover. Cover the pan, bring to the boil and cook for 40-50 minutes over moderate heat.
3. Remove the ribs from the pan, drain and leave to dry completely in a large colander. Dry with kitchen paper if necessary.
4. Mix together the oil, 1 tbsp soy sauce and 3 tbsp sugar. Stir until the sugar has dissolved.
5. Brush the spare ribs on all sides with this mixture. Leave them to stand and coat again.

6. Place the spare ribs on a baking sheet, moistened with a little water, and place in a preheated oven, 250°C/475°F/Gas Mark 9.
7. Bake the spare ribs for 12-15 minutes, until dark brown and crisp on all sides.
8. Put 4 tbsp sugar, 1 tsp salt, 1 tbsp sweet soy sauce, 1 chopped onion, 1 chopped garlic clove and 1 tbsp root ginger in a pan. Cook gently for 5 minutes until the sauce is syrupy.
9. Serve the spare ribs on warmed plates.
10. Offer the sauce separately in individual bowls and pour over the spare ribs.

Mechado

Braised Beef

	00.10	01.40
	Serves 4	

American	Ingredients	Metric/Imperial
4	large coarsely chopped onions	4
2	finely chopped garlic cloves	2
4	large skinned diced tomatoes	4
2 lb	braising beef	900 g/2 lb
2	fresh ground red chilies	2
1	bay leaf	1
1 (1 in)	piece of lemon or lime peel	1 (2.5 cm/1 in)
4 tbsp	spiced vinegar, lemon or lime juice	4 tbsp
	salt	
8-12	large peeled and quartered potatoes	8-12
2 tbsp	groundnut oil, butter or lard	2 tbsp
4 tbsp	chopped scallion (spring onion), shallot or leek (optional)	4 tbsp

1. Spread the onions over the base of a heavy-based pan. Scatter the garlic and pieces of tomato over the top.
2. Lay the meat on top and add the chilies, bay leaf, lemon or lime peel, vinegar or lemon or lime juice, salt and boiling water to cover generously. Bring to the boil, cover the pan, reduce the heat and cook very gently for at least 1¼ hours. Add more water if necessary.
3. Add the potatoes and cook for 20 minutes.
4. Remove the meat from the pan. Dry with kitchen paper and leave to cool slightly.
5. Heat the oil, butter or lard in a frying pan and fry the meat quickly until golden brown on all sides. Cut into ¼ in (5 mm) slices.
6. Arrange the slices of meat on warmed plates.
7. Reheat the sauce with the potatoes. Remove the bay leaf and the piece of lemon or lime peel.
8. Spoon the sauce with the potatoes on to the plates next to the meat, or arrange the meat in a crown in the center of the plate and spoon the sauce with the potatoes round it.
9. Sprinkle a little chopped scallion (spring onion), shallot or leek over the sauce and potatoes and serve.

Left: Braised beef

Almondigas (I)
Meat Balls in Bouillon (Stock)

00.07 Serves 4   **00.15**

American	Ingredients	Metric/Imperial
1 lb	ground (minced) pork or ground (minced) pork and ground (minced) beef or lamb	450 g/1 lb
1	lightly beaten egg	1
2-3 tbsp	breadcrumbs	2-3 tbsp
	salt	
	freshly ground pepper	
2	finely chopped garlic cloves	2
1 tbsp	flour (optional)	1 tbsp
2 tbsp	groundnut oil	2 tbsp
2	ripe skinned diced tomatoes	2
1¼ cups	bouillon (stock)	300 ml/½ pint
2 tbsp	dark soy sauce (Chinese or Japanese)	2 tbsp
2	finely chopped scallions (spring onions), shallots or leek	2

1. Mix the ground (minced) meat with the egg, breadcrumbs, salt, pepper and half of the garlic. Shape into balls, the size of walnuts. Roll in a little flour (optional).
2. Heat the oil in a wok and stir fry the balls quickly, a few at a time, until browned on all sides.
3. Add the remaining garlic and the tomatoes. Stir well and cook very gently over moderate heat until the tomato disintegrates.
4. Add the bouillon (stock) and soy sauce and simmer for 10 minutes turning the meatballs occasionally.
5. Sample the sauce and add a little salt and pepper to taste.
6. Transfer the meatballs to a warmed dish, and just before serving sprinkle with the chopped scallion (spring onion), shallots or leek.

Left: Meat balls in bouillon (stock)
Right: Meat balls with shrimp (prawns)

Almondigas (II)
Meat Balls with Shrimp (Prawns)

00.10 plus standing time   **00.25**

American	Ingredients	Metric/Imperial
2 tbsp	dried shrimp (prawns) (ebi)	2 tbsp
½ lb	fresh peeled shrimp (prawns)	225 g/8 oz
¾ lb	ground (minced) pork	350 g/12 oz
½ tbsp	cornstarch (cornflour)	½ tbsp
1	finely chopped scallion (spring onion)	1
2	finely chopped garlic cloves	2
1	small finely chopped onion or shallot	1
	salt	
	freshly ground pepper	
2 tbsp	groundnut oil	2 tbsp
2 tbsp	light soy sauce (Chinese or Japanese)	2 tbsp
1	skinned tomato (optional)	1
	few sprigs of coriander or parsley (optional)	

1. Put the dried shrimp (prawns) in a bowl with 1 cup (250 ml/8 fl oz) hot water. Stir well and leave to stand until the liquid is completely cold. Strain through a fine strainer or piece of wet muslin. Set aside the shrimp (prawns) and the liquid.
2. Grind the fresh shrimp (prawns). Mix with the ground (minced) pork in a bowl.
3. Mix the cornstarch (cornflour) with 2 tbsp cold water. Stir into the ground (minced) meat and shrimp (prawn) mixture. Add the scallion (spring onion), garlic, onion or shallot and a little salt and pepper. Stir well, then leave to stand for 15 minutes in a cool place.
4. Shape into egg-size balls. Flatten them slightly.
5. Heat the oil in a wok and fry the balls a few at a time, until brown on all sides.
6. Add the soaked shrimp (prawns) and their liquid and the soy sauce. Bring to the boil, reduce the heat and cook very gently for 10-15 minutes.
7. Serve the meatballs with the sauce in a warmed dish, garnished with tomato segments and a sprig of coriander or parsley (optional).

Meat balls with liver

Almondigas (III)

Meat Balls with Liver

▬▷ 00.07 Serves 4   **00.30 ⌂**

American	Ingredients	Metric/Imperial
5 oz	pig's liver	150 g/5 oz
2	large boiled potatoes	2
¾ lb	ground (minced) pork	350 g/12 oz
	salt	
	freshly ground pepper	
1	crushed garlic clove	1
1	finely chopped scallion (spring onion), shallot or piece of leek	1
1 tbsp	flour (optional)	1 tbsp
2 tbsp	groundnut oil	2 tbsp
1	large or 2 smaller finely chopped onions	1
2	skinned, diced tomatoes	2
1¼ cups	bouillon (stock)	300 ml/½ pint
1	red chili (optional)	1

1. Finely grind the pig's liver in a food processor.
2. Mash the potatoes until smooth.
3. In a bowl, mix the mashed potato, pork and liver.
4. Add the salt, pepper, garlic and scallion (spring onion), shallot or leek. Mix well (with wettened fingers). Shape into walnut-size balls. Roll in a little flour, if liked.
5. Heat the oil in a wok and fry the balls a few at a time until brown on all sides.
6. Add the onion and stir fry until lightly colored. Add the tomato, reduce the heat and cook very gently for 2-3 minutes until the tomato disintegrates.
7. Add the bouillon (stock) and cook gently for 10 minutes.
8. Remove the meatballs from the liquid and put into a warm dish.
9. Increase the heat and bring the liquid to the boil until reduced to a thick mixture. Spoon the mixture over the meatballs
10. Garnish with a red chili flower (optional) and serve.

Spring Rolls

▬▷ 00.15 Serves 8   **00.25 ⌂**

American	Ingredients	Metric/Imperial
8	spring roll wrappers	8
8	good lettuce leaves	8
2 tbsp	groundnut oil	2 tbsp
1	small chopped onion	1
1	finely chopped garlic clove	1
¼ lb	French beans or haricot verts cut into 1 in (2.5 cm) pieces	125 g/4 oz
2	peeled and coarsely grated potatoes	2
¼ lb	shredded white cabbage	125 g/4 oz
2	very finely chopped scallions (spring onions), shallot or leek	2
1 tbsp	finely chopped coriander or parsley	1 tbsp
2	small scraped and coarsely grated carrots	2
1 tbsp	light soy sauce (Chinese or Japanese)	1 tbsp
	salt	
	freshly ground pepper	
4 tbsp	Indonesian sweet soy sauce (ketyap benteng manis)	4 tbsp
3 tbsp	soft brown sugar	3 tbsp
2	crushed garlic cloves	2
4 tbsp	vegetable bouillon (stock)	4 tbsp
½ tsp	cornstarch (cornflour)	½ tsp
1 tsp	sambal ulek (see page 128)	1 tsp
	oil for frying	

1. Thaw spring roll wrappers if frozen, interleaving them between cloths.
2. Wash the lettuce leaves. Remove the thickest part of the stalks. Dry thoroughly.
3. Heat the oil in a wok and stir fry the onion until transparent.
4. Add the garlic, French beans or haricots verts and grated potatoes. Stir fry for 2 minutes.
5. Add the cabbage, scallions (spring onions), coriander or parsley and carrots.
6. Stir well and add the light soy sauce, 2 tbsp water and a little salt and pepper.
7. Stir well and bring to the boil. Reduce the heat and cook gently until almost all the liquid has evaporated. Transfer to a dish and allow to cool slightly.
8. Make the sauce by slowly bringing to the boil the Indonesian soy sauce, sugar, a little salt and pepper, 2 crushed garlic cloves and the vegetable bouillon (stock). Dissolve the sugar in the sauce, stirring continuously. Cook gently for 2-3 minutes.
9. Mix the cornstarch (cornflour) with 1 tbsp cold water. Stir into the sauce and cook, stirring until the sauce has thickened. Simmer for 2-3 minutes.
10. Add 1 tsp sambal ulek to the sauce, if liked.
11. Lay the lettuce leaves on the spring roll wrappers. Spoon some of the filling on to each lettuce leaf. Moisten the edges of the spring roll wrappers with water. Fold the wrappers round the filling.
12. Heat the oil in a wok and fry the spring rolls 2-3 at a time until golden brown.

13. Remove the spring rolls from the pan, drain on kitchen paper and serve.

Cook's tip: in the Philippines spring roll wrappers are made from a batter which for 8-10 spring rolls, consists of: 1 cup (160 g/6 oz) flour, ½ cup (50 g/2 oz) rice flour, 1 tbsp cornstarch (cornflour), 1 lightly beaten egg, a pinch of salt and 1 tbsp groundnut oil. Add enough water, stirring continuously, to give a flowing, relatively thin batter. Leave the batter to stand in a cool place, then beat and fry in a square frying pan until the spring roll wrapppers are golden.

Morcon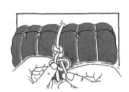

Braised Rolled Beef

� ▷ 00. 15   02.20 🍲
Serves 4

American	Ingredients	Metric/Imperial
1 (1½ lb)	piece rolled beef	1 (675 g/1½ lb)
2	crushed garlic cloves	2
1 tsp	sambal ulek (see page 128)	1 tsp
	salt	
	freshly ground pepper	
3 tbsp	groundnut oil	3 tbsp
1¾ cups	beef bouillon (stock)	400 ml/14 fl oz
3	medium size onions, cut into segments	3
2 tbsp	light soy sauce (Chinese or Japanese	2 tbsp
1	small cucumber	1
2 tbsp	spiced vinegar, lemon or lime juice	2 tbsp
½ tsp	cornstarch (cornflour)	½ tsp
1	chopped scallion (spring onion)	1
1	skinned, diced tomato	1
1	sprig coriander or parsley (optional)	1

1. Ask the butcher not to tie up the roll. Dry the meat with kitchen paper.
2. In a bowl, mix the garlic, sambal ulek and a little salt and pepper.

3. Coat the meat with this mixture on one side. Roll up the meat and tie with a piece of thick cotton thread or kitchen string.
4. Heat the oil in a large wok and quickly fry the roll until brown on all sides. Reduce the heat and add the bouillon (stock). Bring to the boil, add the onion segments and soy sauce. Cover the pan and simmer for 1½-2 hours.
5. Rinse, trim and halve the cucumber and scoop out the seeds. Cut the cucumber into finger-width pieces.
6. Remove the cooked meat from the pan. Add the cucumber and vinegar, lemon or lime juice. Increase the heat and cook vigorously for 4 minutes to reduce the liquid by half.
7. Mix the cornstarch (cornflour) with 1 tbsp cold water. Stir into the liquid in the pan. Cook, stirring until the sauce thickens. Cook for a further 2-3 minutes. Add a little salt and pepper to taste.
8. Remove the thread or string from the roll. Cut the meat into ½ in (1.25 cm) slices. Arrange them overlapping, on a dish.
9. Spoon over the sauce with the pieces of cucumber, so that the pieces of cucumber in the sauce are next to the meat, and sprinkle on the scallion (spring onion) and diced tomato and serve garnished with a sprig of coriander or parsley.

Cook's tip: in place of cucumber, zucchini (courgettes) or fresh mushrooms (button or flat) can be used in the sauce.

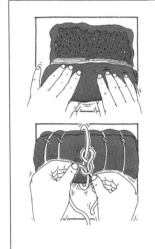

Rolling beef
1. Spread the paste over the beef and roll up.
2. Tie four single strings across the roll.
3. Tie an additional piece in the center of the roll, and pull tight to secure.

Braised rolled beef

Kari kari
Braised Beef with Vegetables

00.10 Serves 4   **02.35**

American	Ingredients	Metric/Imperial
2¼ lb	oxtail, chopped into small pieces	1 kg/2¼ lb
1 lb	lean beef, cut into 1 in (2.5 cm) cubes	450 g/1 lb
	salt	
2	bay leaves	2
3 tbsp	groundnut oil	3 tbsp
2	large coarsely chopped onions	2
3	finely chopped garlic cloves	3
½ lb	French beans or haricot verts, cut into 1 in (2.5 cm) pieces	225 g/8 oz
1 cup	boiled rice	125 g/4 oz
2 oz	shelled, skinned peanuts	50 g/2 oz
2	coarsely chopped scallions (spring onions), shallots or pieces of leek,	2
	freshly ground pepper	
1 tbsp	finely chopped coriander or parsley	1 tbsp
1	tomato or red chili (optional)	1

1. Put the oxtail into a pan with the meat. Sprinkle on 1 tsp salt and add the bay leaves.
2. Add 1½ quarts (1.5 litres/2¾ pints) boiling water and quickly bring to the boil. Reduce the heat and cook very gently for 2 hours. Remove the pieces of oxtail and the beef from the pan. Leave to go cold.
3. Take the meat off the oxtail bones. Dry the oxtail meat and the beef cubes as much as possible.
4. Strain the bouillon (stock). Bring to the boil over moderate heat and reduce to 1¾ cups (400 ml/14 fl oz).
5. Heat 1 tbsp oil in a wok and stir fry the onion until transparent. Add the garlic and continue stirring until the onion begins to change color.
6. Stir in the French beans or haricot verts and the rice. Pour in the bouillon (stock) and simmer for 20 minutes.
7. Roast the peanuts in a dry frying pan, turning continuously, until beginning to change color. Remove from the pan and spread on a large, cold plate and leave until completely cold.
8. Stir the scallions (spring onions), shallots or leek into the mixture in the pan. Add salt and pepper to taste.
9. Transfer to a warm dish, sprinkle coriander or parsley over the cold roasted peanuts and decorate with a tomato or red chili flower.

Cook's tip: there are many different versions of kari kari. Other varieties of vegetable such as pieces of eggplant (aubergine), broccoli or cauliflower florets, slices of celery, sliced zucchini (courgette), sliced carrot and very small onions or shallots can be added. The sauce can be thickened with a little cornstarch (cornflour) and sometimes the roasted peanuts are finely ground with a pestle and mortar (or in a food processor), and stirred into the sauce, again thickening it slightly. Alternatively 1-2 tbsp peanut butter can be stirred into the sauce.

Pancit guisado
Fried Noodles with Meat and Vegetables

00.10 Serves 4   **00.15**

American	Ingredients	Metric/Imperial
½ lb	Chinese egg noodles	225 g/8 oz
2-3 tbsp	groundnut oil	2-3 tbsp
½ lb	chicken drumsticks cut into small pieces	225 g/8 oz
½ lb	coarsely ground (minced) pork	225 g/8 oz
¼ lb	coarsely ground (minced) beef	125 g/4 oz
½ lb	shredded white or Chinese cabbage	225 g/8 oz
¼ lb	fresh coarsely chopped peeled shrimp (prawns)	125 g/4 oz
2 tbsp	light soy sauce (Chinese or Japanese)	2 tbsp
	salt	
	freshly ground pepper	
1 tbsp	fried onions	1 tbsp
1 tbsp	finely chopped coriander or parsley	1 tbsp
1	skinned tomato	1

1. Prepare the noodles according to the instructions on the packet. Rinse with enough cold water to cool the noodles completely. Leave to dry, stirring from time to time. Add 1-2 tsp oil to the water in which the noodles are cooked to prevent them sticking.
2. Heat the remaining oil in a wok and stir fry the chicken, pork and beef for 3 minutes.
3. Stir in the cabbage and 2 minutes later add the shrimp (prawns), soy sauce and a little salt and pepper.
4. Stir well, then add the noodles a little at a time.
5. Stir continuously and transfer to a warm dish as soon as the noodles are warmed through.
6. Serve garnished with fried onions, herbs and tomato segments.

Cook's tip: with Pancit guisado, individual bowls of salty soy sauce should be served and the dish can be garnished with hard-cooked (hard-boiled) eggs, cut into segments.

Gulaman
Fruits in Jelly

00.15 plus setting time   **00.10**

American	Ingredients	Metric/Imperial
2	bananas	2
2 tsp	lemon juice	2 tsp
1	orange	1
1	mango	1
2	slices of pineapple	2
5 tbsp	skimmed milk	5 tbsp
4 tbsp	sugar	4 tbsp
½ oz	gelatin	15 g/½ oz

Fried noodles with meat and vegetables

1. Peel the bananas. Cut into slices and sprinkle with lemon juice to prevent discoloring.

2. Peel the orange, removing the white pith. Cut the segments away from their skins. Remove the pips, and cut the segments in half. Collect any juice. Strain, and add to the milk.

3. Cut the mango in half, remove the stone, scoop the flesh out of the skins and dice.

4. Cut the pineapple into small pieces.

5. Mix the fruits together in a bowl.

6. Add water to the milk and fruit juice to make up to 1 ¼ cups (300 ml/½ pint) Bring to the boil. Dissolve the sugar in this liquid, stirring continuously.

7. Remove the pan from the heat, and add the gelatin to the liquid, stir well until the gelatin has dissolved.

8. Pour a quarter of the mixture into the bottom of a smooth blancmange mould, rinsed out with water.

9. Put the mould in the refrigerator for a few minutes so that the jelly begins to set.

10. Arrange the fruits over the jelly and pour on the remainder of the jelly. Leave to cool, then put the mould into the refrigerator to allow the jelly to set completely.

11. Just before serving the fruits in jelly, turn out on to a large cold dish, rinsed with water.

Sapin sapin

Yam Cake

	00.10 plus cooling time	00.50

American	Ingredients	Metric/Imperial
¼ lb	yams or sweet potato	125 g/4 oz
1 cup	rice flour	125 g/4 oz
2 tbsp	cornstarch (cornflour)	2 tbsp
2	lightly beaten eggs	2
2 ½ cups	thin coconut milk	600 ml/1 pint
1 ⅓ cups	soft brown sugar	225 g/8 oz
4 tbsp	grated desiccated coconut	4 tbsp
1 tbsp	butter	1 tbsp

1. Cook the sweet potatoes in their jackets for 15-20 minutes, in plenty of water until tender. Drain, leave to dry and cool slightly in a colander.

2. Mix the rice flour with the cornstarch (cornflour) in a bowl and beat in the eggs, coconut milk and sugar until the sugar is dissolved.

3. Roast the coconut in a dry non-stick frying pan until golden. Spread out on a cold plate and leave to cool.

4. Peel the potatoes and quickly purée them.

5. Add the purée to the rice flour mixture. Stir vigorously.

6. Put the mixture into a cake tin, lightly greased with a little butter. Place the tin in a steamer and cover with a clean cloth. Bring a generous quantity of water to the boil in the pan, and steam the cake for 30 minutes, until cooked. Leave the cake to cool in the tin.

7. Turn the cake out on to a plate. Sprinkle with coconut, and press into the cake firmly. Leave until completely cold. Slice the cake into fingers and serve.

MENU

Vegetable soup with shrimp (prawns)
Steak Manila
Bananas in jelly

Vegetable Soup with Shrimp (Prawns)

◀━▽   00.06
Serves 4   00.12 🍲

American	Ingredients	Metric/Imperial
¾ lb	Chinese cabbage	350 g/12 oz
1	green chili	1
1	red bell pepper	1
2 tbsp	groundnut oil	2 tbsp
1	large coarsely chopped onion	1
1	finely chopped garlic clove	1
3 tbsp	lemon or lime juice	3 tbsp
4	large skinned tomatoes cut into narrow strips	4
½ lb	fresh peeled shrimp (prawns)	225 g/8 oz
	salt	
	freshly ground pepper	
1 tbsp	Chinese light soy sauce (optional)	1 tbsp

1. Rinse the cabbage and cut into very thin strips.
2. Rinse, trim and seed the chili.
3. Rinse, trim and seed the bell pepper.
4. Heat the oil in a wok and stir fry the onion until transparent.
5. Add the garlic and stir until the onion is beginning to color.
6. Add the cabbage and stir fry for 3 minutes. Add 3¼ cups (750 ml/1¼ pints) boiling water and the lemon or lime juice and bring to the boil. Boil vigorously for 2 minutes.
7. Add the tomatoes, chili and bell pepper. Reduce the heat and simmer for 3-4 minutes.
8. Stir in the shrimp (prawns) and season to taste. Stir in 1 tbsp Chinese soy sauce if liked.

Steak Manila

◀━▽   00.05
plus marinating   00.20 🍲

American	Ingredients	Metric/Imperial
4 (¼ lb)	rump steaks	4 (125 g/4 oz)
	salt	
	freshly ground pepper	
2 tbsp	lime or lemon juice	2 tbsp
4 tbsp	Chinese light soy sauce	4 tbsp
2 tbsp	sugar	2 tbsp
3	large chopped onions	3
2	crushed garlic cloves	2
½ tbsp	oil	½ tbsp

1. Dry the meat with kitchen paper and rub in a little salt and pepper.
2. Mix together the lime or lemon juice, soy sauce and sugar. Stir until the sugar has dissolved.
3. Put the steaks into the marinade and leave to stand for 1 hour, turning the meat in the marinade every 15 minutes. Remove the meat from the marinade and dry it.
4. Add the onion and garlic to the rest of the marinade and bring to the boil. Add 5 tbsp boiling water and simmer gently for 10 minutes to evaporate some of the liquid.
5. Transfer to a strainer (sieve) and rub the solid ingredients through. Bring the remaining sauce back to the boil.
6. Brush the steaks with oil and broil (grill) them over the barbecue or under a hot broiler (grill) for 6-8 minutes, until browned on both sides.
7. Transfer the steaks to warmed plates and spoon the hot sauce over.

Cook's tip: serve with boiled rice, into which has been stirred chopped scallions (spring onions) and 1 tsp grated orange or lemon peel.

Bananas in Jelly

⏱ 00.10
plus chilling time

00.10 🍲

American	Ingredients	Metric/Imperial
4	bananas	4
2 tbsp	strained lemon or lime juice	2 tbsp
2	slices canned, drained pineapple	2
1	small mango	1
4 tbsp	sugar	4 tbsp
½ oz	gelatin	15 g/½ oz
5 tbsp	Chinese rice wine or dry sherry	5 tbsp
	few mint leaves	

1. Peel the bananas and cut them obliquely into ½ in (1.25 cm) slices. Sprinkle with lemon or lime juice to prevent discoloring.

2. Finely chop the pineapple slices.

3. Peel and stone the mango and dice the flesh.

4. Bring ¾ cup (200 ml/7 fl oz) water to the boil. Stir in the sugar until it has dissolved. Remove the pan from the heat and stir in the gelatin until it has dissolved.

5. Add a further ¾ cup (200 ml/7 fl oz) water and the rice wine or sherry. Stir well and leave the mixture to stand until just beginning to set.

6. Put ⅓ of the mixture into a small mould, rinsed with cold water. Chill this until the jelly is set. Spread the pineapple and mango over the surface of the jelly.

7. Spoon ½ the remaining jelly over the fruits and return the mould to the refrigerator until set.

8. Arrange the slices of banana, overlapping on top of the second layer of set jelly and pour the remaining jelly over the top, just to cover. Chill for at least 2 hours until the jelly is completely cold and set.

9. Turn the jelly out on to a plate and cut into 12 slices. Place 3 slices on each plate and garnish with mint leaves.

Philippino Spring Rolls

00.10
plus standing time

00.15

American	Ingredients	Metric/Imperial
4	sheets spring roll dough	4
2 oz	shelled, skinned, unroasted peanuts	50 g/2 oz
½ lb	very finely chopped chicken breast fillet	225 g/8 oz
½ lb	very finely chopped cooked ham	225 g/8 oz
	salt	
	freshly ground pepper	
1 tbsp	cornstarch (cornflour)	1 tbsp
1	beaten egg	1
½ tsp	sambal ulek (see page 128)	½ tsp
4	chopped scallions (spring onions)	4
	oil for deep frying	

1. Thaw frozen spring roll dough completely. Cut each sheet into 4 squares.
2. Heat a non-stick frying pan and dry roast the peanuts until beginning to color. Spread them out on a large cold plate to cool. Grind to crumbs in a mortar.
3. Mix together the chicken, ham, peanuts, salt and pepper.
4. Stir the cornstarch (cornflour) into the lightly beaten egg and add the sambal. Stir this mixture into the chopped meat and stir well. Leave to stand for 1 hour in a cool place. Shape the mixture into 16 small rolls. Roll these in the chopped scallions (spring onions) and place one on each piece of spring roll dough.
5. Moisten the edges of the spring roll dough, fold round the filling and press together firmly.
6. Heat the oil and fry the spring rolls 3-4 at a time until golden brown and crisp. Drain then serve immediately on warmed dishes.

Sauce for Spring Rolls

00.02
Serves 4

00.03

American	Ingredients	Metric/Imperial
5 tbsp	Indonesian sweet soy sauce (ketyap benteng manis)	5 tbsp
5 tbsp	chicken bouillon (stock)	5 tbsp
	pinch garlic salt	
2 tbsp	soft brown sugar	2 tbsp
2 tbsp	Chinese tomato or barbecue sauce	2 tbsp
1 tbsp	cornstarch (cornflour)	1 tbsp
	salt	

MENU

Philippino spring rolls
Roast chicken legs
Papaya salad
Coconut milk shake

1. Bring the soy sauce and chicken bouillon (stock) to the boil. Add the garlic salt, sugar and tomato or barbecue sauce. Stir well and simmer for 2 minutes.
2. Mix the cornstarch (cornflour) with 3 tbsp cold water. Stir into the sauce and cook, stirring until the sauce thickens slightly. Add salt to taste. Serve in individual bowls.

Roast Chicken Legs

00.10
plus standing time

00.20

American	Ingredients	Metric/Imperial
1 tbsp	lemon juice	1 tbsp
1 tbsp	Chinese light soy sauce	1 tbsp
½ tsp	sambal ulek (see page 128)	½ tsp
1 tbsp	groundnut oil	1 tbsp
8	small chicken legs	8
4 tbsp	peanut butter	4 tbsp
¾ cup	chicken bouillon (stock)	200 ml/7 fl oz
1 tbsp	Chinese light soy sauce	1 tbsp
½ tsp	sambal ulek (see page 128)	½ tsp
1 tbsp	soft brown sugar	1 tbsp
	salt	

1. Mix the lemon juice, 1 tbsp soy sauce, ½ tsp sambal ulek and the groundnut oil together in a bowl.
2. Dry the chicken legs with kitchen paper. Rub them with the mixture and leave to stand for 1 hour.
3. Roast the chicken legs, turning occasionally, in a moderate oven, (180°C/350°F/Gas Mark 4) for 12-15 minutes or until golden brown all over.
4. Bring the peanut butter, bouillon (stock), remaining soy sauce and sambal, sugar and salt to the boil, stirring continuously. Add more water if necessary.
5. Transfer the chicken legs to warmed plates, spoon over the sauce and serve.

Papaya Salad

◢▷	00.10 plus chilling time	00.00 ⌸

American	Ingredients	Metric/Imperial
1	medium size firm papaya	1
2	slightly sour apples	2
2	sticks celery	2
2	canned pineapple slices	2
2 tbsp	groundnut oil	2 tbsp
1 tsp	sesame oil	1 tsp
2 tbsp	lemon juice	2 tbsp
1 tsp	Indonesian sweet soy sauce (ketyap benteng manis)	1 tsp
½ tsp	sambal ulek (see page 128)	½ tsp

1. Peel, halve and seed the papaya. Cut the flesh into thin strips.
2. Peel and core the apples and cut the flesh into thin strips.
3. Cut the celery into thin strips.
4. Cut the pineapple into thin strips.
5. Mix the fruit and vegetable together and chill.
6. Mix together the groundnut and sesame oils, lemon juice, soy sauce and sambal. Pour this dressing over the salad just before serving.

Coconut Milk Shake

◢▷	00.05 Serves 4	00.15 ⌸

American	Ingredients	Metric/Imperial
¾ cup	thin coconut milk	200 ml/7 fl oz
4 tbsp	sugar	4 tbsp
2 sachets	vanilla sugar	2 sachets
1 (2 in)	cinnamon stick	1 (5 cm/2 in)
¾ cup	thick coconut milk	200 ml/ 7 fl oz
	crushed ice	

1. Bring the thin coconut milk to the boil. Dissolve the sugar and the vanilla sugar in it, stirring continuously.
2. Reduce the heat, add the cinnamon stick and simmer for 10 minutes over very moderate heat. Leave to cool. Remove the cinnamon stick.
3. Add the thick coconut milk and stir vigorously. Add 6-8 tbsp crushed ice and beat thoroughly.
4. Pour the milk shake into tall glasses and serve.

THAILAND

Nam pla (I)
Thai Fish Sauce

00.10 plus standing time   **00.00**

American	Ingredients	Metric/Imperial
1 lb	salted anchovy fillets	450 g/1 lb
5 tbsp	soft brown sugar	5 tbsp
5 tbsp	Chinese light soy sauce	5 tbsp
1 tbsp	sea salt	1 tbsp
2 tsp	coarsely ground black pepper	2 tsp
6	small, crumbled, dried red chilies	6
4	chopped garlic cloves	4
1 tsp	ground coriander	1 tsp
¾ cup	fish bouillon (stock)	200 ml/7 fl oz

1. Cut the anchovy fillets into small pieces.
2. Using a food processor, purée the anchovy pieces with all other ingredients to a smooth paste.
3. Put the paste into a clean, airtight jar and leave to stand in the refrigerator for 2 weeks.
4. Strain the contents of the jar, and put the sauce into a clean bottle.
5. Store the fish sauce for up to a month in the refrigerator.

Left to right: Lightly spiced fish in sweet and sour sauce
Spiced fish in sweet and sour sauce
Fried fish in sweet and sour ginger sauce

Nam pla (II)
Sittwe Thai Fish Sauce

00.10 plus standing time   **00.00**

American	Ingredients	Metric/Imperial
3 oz	dried shrimp (prawns)	75 g/3 oz
½ lb	salted anchovy fillets	225 g/8 oz
2 tbsp	soft brown sugar	2 tbsp
2-3 tbsp	Chinese light soy sauce	2-3 tbsp
½ tsp	ground coriander	½ tsp
4 tsp	sea salt	4 tsp
2	crushed garlic cloves	2

1. Put the dried shrimp (prawns) into a bowl and pour on ¾ cup (200 ml/7 fl oz) warm water. Leave to stand until the water is completely cold.
2. Cut the anchovy fillets into small pieces.
3. Using a food processor, purée the anchovy pieces, shrimp (prawns) and their soaking liquid and all other ingredients. Add a little more salt if necessary.
4. Put the paste into a clean, airtight jar and leave to stand in the refrigerator for 2 weeks.
5. Strain the contents of the jar and put the sauce into a clean bottle. Seal tightly.
6. Store the sauce for in the refrigerator for 5 to 6 days, after which the flavor begins to deteriorate.

Pla priou wan (1)

Lightly Spiced Fish in Sweet and Sour Sauce

00.10 plus standing time   **00.20**

American	Ingredients	Metric/Imperial
1 lb	pike fillets	450 g/1 lb
	salt	
	freshly ground black pepper	
1	small cucumber	1
3 tsp	soft brown sugar	3 tsp
3 tsp	lime or lemon juice	3 tsp
2-3	pineapple slices (canned if necessary)	2-3
2 tbsp	cornstarch (cornflour)	2 tbsp
8-9 tbsp	groundnut oil	8-9 tbsp
1	large chopped onion	1
1	finely chopped garlic clove	1
1	small green chili cut into thin strips	1
1 tbsp	finely grated fresh root ginger	1 tbsp
¾ cup	fish bouillon (stock)	200 ml/7 fl oz
4 tsp	Thai fish sauce	4 tsp
1 tbsp	finely chopped coriander or parsley	1 tbsp
1	small lime or lemon, cut into segments	1

1. Rinse the fish under cold running water. Dry with kitchen paper and cut into finger width slices. Rub a mixture of 2 parts salt and 1 part ground black pepper into the skin. Leave to stand for 10 minutes.
2. Rinse and trim and halve the cucumber and scoop out the seeds. Cut the cucumber into ½ in (1.25 cm) strips.
3. Dissolve the sugar in the lime or lemon juice.
4. Cut the pineapple into small pieces.
5. Coat the fish slices with the cornstarch (cornflour).
6. Heat the oil in a large frying pan and quickly fry the slices of fish until brown on all sides. Remove them from the pan and keep warm.
7. Fry the onion in the remaining oil until transparent.
8. Stir in the garlic, green chili and root ginger.
9. Add the cucumber strips and pineapple pieces and stir well.
10. Bring the bouillon (stock) to the boil and pour over the contents of the pan.
11. Add the sugar solution, fish sauce and a little salt and simmer for 3-4 minutes.
12. Add the fish. Remove from the heat as soon as the pieces of fish have heated through.
13. Put the slices of fish on to warmed plates and spoon the sauce with the cucumber and pineapple around the fish.
14. Sprinkle a little finely chopped coriander or parsley over the top and garnish with lime or lemon segments.

Pla priou wan (II)

Spiced Fish in Sweet and Sour Sauce (II)

00.10 plus standing time   **00.20**

American	Ingredients	Metric/Imperial
1 lb	tuna, thawed if frozen	450 g/1 lb
	salt	
	freshly ground black pepper	
¼ lb	French beans or haricots verts	125 g/4 oz
3 tbsp	soft brown sugar	3 tbsp
3 tbsp	lemon or lime juice	3 tbsp
2 tbsp	cornstarch (cornflour)	2 tbsp
8-9 tbsp	groundnut oil	8-9 tbsp
1	large chopped onion	1
1	finely chopped garlic clove	1
1	small green chili, cut into thin strips	1
1½ tsp	finely grated fresh root ginger	1½ tsp
3	large, skinned, diced tomatoes	3
1	pineapple slice (canned if necessary) cut into pieces	1
¾ cup	fish bouillon (stock)	200 ml/7 fl oz
1½ tsp	Thai fish sauce	1½ tsp
1 tbsp	finely chopped coriander or parsley	1 tbsp
1	small lime or lemon, cut into segments	1
4	small green chilies (optional)	4

1. Rinse the fish under cold running water and dry with kitchen paper. Cut the fish into ½ in (1.25 cm) slices. Rub a mixture of 2 parts salt and 1 part ground black pepper into the skin. Leave to stand for 10 minutes.
2. Rinse, trim and string the French beans or haricots verts and cut into ½ in (1.25 cm) pieces.
3. Bring ⅔ cup (1.5 litres/¼ pint) water to the boil in a pan. Add a little salt and cook the beans for 4 minutes. Drain in a colander and rinse with cold water until completely cold.
4. Dissolve the sugar in the lime or lemon juice.
5. Coat the fish slices with the cornstarch (cornflour).
6. Heat the oil in a large frying pan and quickly fry the slices of fish until brown. Remove from the pan and keep warm.
7. Stir fry the onion in the remaining oil until transparent.
8. Add the garlic, chili and root ginger.
9. Stir well, add the beans, tomato and pineapple pieces.
10. Bring the bouillon (stock) to the boil and stir into the contents of the pan. Stir well and simmer for 2 minutes.
11. Add the fish sauce and sugar mixture. Put the slices of fish on top, and remove the pan from the heat as soon as the fish is warmed through.
12. Transfer the fish slices to warmed plates and spoon the French beans, tomato and pineapple sauce around the fish.
13. Sprinkle with coriander or parsley, and garnish with lime or lemon segments and small green chili flowers (optional).

Pla priou wan khing

Fried Fish in Sweet and Sour Ginger Sauce

00.10 Serves 4   **00.20**

American	Ingredients	Metric/Imperial
3 tbsp	white vinegar	3 tbsp
1	piece fresh root ginger cut into thin strips	1
4 tbsp	soft brown sugar	4 tbsp
2-3	red chilies	2-3
6	scallions (spring onions) or shallots	6
1½ tbsp	groundnut oil	1½ tbsp
2 tsp	cornstarch (cornflour)	2 tsp
	salt	
1 tsp	Thai fish sauce	1 tsp
2 tsp	sesame oil (optional)	2 tsp
1½ lb	sole fillets	700 g/1½ lb
4 tsp	lime or lemon juice	4 tsp
2 tbsp	groundnut oil	2 tbsp
2½ tbsp	cornstarch (cornflour)	2½ tbsp
	oil for frying	
½	cucumber	½

1. Bring ¾ cup (200 ml/7 fl oz) water to the boil in a pan. Add the vinegar, root ginger and sugar. Stir, until the sugar dissolves. Simmer over a moderate heat until half the liquid has evaporated.
2. Rinse and trim the chilies and grind to a paste.
3. Cut the scallions (spring onions) or shallots into ½ in (1.25 cm) pieces.
4. Heat 1½ tbsp oil in a small frying pan. Add the chili paste and the scallions (spring onions) and stir fry for 2 minutes. Add to the vinegar mixture.
5. Mix 2½ tsp cornstarch (cornflour) with 2 tbsp cold water. Stir this mixture into the sauce and cook, stirring until the sauce thickens. Simmer gently for 3 minutes. Add a little salt to taste and the fish sauce.
6. Keep the sauce warm in a bain marie, and just before serving, stir in 2 tsp sesame oil.
7. Rinse the fish under cold running water and dry with kitchen paper. Rub the skins with a mixture of a little salt and lemon or lime juice. Leave to stand for 10 minutes, then coat with a little oil and roll in the remaining cornstarch (cornflour).
8. Heat the oil until very hot and quickly fry the fish, 3-4 at a time until golden brown on all sides.
9. Put the fish on to warmed plates. Pour on the sauce, and garnish with large cucumber fans sprinkled with a little salt.

Steamed 'yellow' fish fillets

Pla nerng leung
Steamed "Yellow" Fish Fillets

	00.06	00.15
	plus standing time	

American	Ingredients	Metric/Imperial
1 lb	cod fillets	450 g/1 lb
	salt	
1	small crumbled dried chili	1
1	medium size chopped onion	1
2-3	finely chopped garlic cloves	2-3
1 tsp	ground coriander	1 tsp
1 tsp	ground turmeric	1 tsp
½ tsp	finely ground black pepper	½ tsp
1 tbsp	Thai fish sauce	1 tbsp
4 tbsp	thick coconut milk	4 tbsp
1	lightly beaten egg	1
5 tbsp	cornstarch (cornflour)	5 tbsp
1 tbsp	sesame oil	1 tbsp

1. Rinse the fish under cold running water and dry with kitchen paper. Cut obliquely into strips ½ in (1.25 cm) thick and up to 3 in (9 cm) long. Rub with a little salt and leave to stand for 10 minutes.
2. Grind the crumbled chili, onion, garlic, coriander and turmeric, pepper and fish sauce to a smooth paste in a food processor.
3. Mix the paste with the coconut milk and lightly beaten egg. Coat the fish with the mixture, then roll in the cornstarch (cornflour).
4. Brush the top part of a steamer with oil and put the fish on top. Bring a few quarts/litres water to the boil in the pan. Put the perforated part of the pan on top. Cover and steam for 12-14 minutes.
5. Serve the strips of fish on warmed dishes with boiled rice and place a small bowl at the side of each plate, with a sauce made by mixing together 1 part Thai fish sauce, 1 part Chinese light soy sauce and 1 part water.

Koong nam ketig
Shrimp (Prawns) in White Sauce

	00.15	00.20
	Serves 4	

American	Ingredients	Metric/Imperial
6-8	large shrimp (prawns) thawed if frozen	6-8
2 tbsp	oil	2 tbsp
1	chopped onion	1
1	chopped garlic clove	1
1	small, finely crushed chili	1
1 tsp	sugar	1 tsp
	salt	
	freshly ground pepper	
5 tbsp	thin coconut milk	5 tbsp
5 tbsp	thick coconut milk	5 tbsp
1½ tbsp	lime or lemon juice	1½ tbsp
1 tbsp	finely chopped coriander or parsley	1 tbsp

1. Prepare the shrimp (prawns) as directed in the recipe for shrimp (prawns) in golden sauce.
2. Heat the oil in a wok and stir fry the onion until transparent.
3. Stir in the garlic and chili.
4. Add the sugar, a little salt and pepper and the thin coconut milk. Stir well. Simmer gently for 6-8 minutes and add the thick coconut milk and lime or lemon juice. Stir well and bring back to the boil.
5. Heat the shrimp (prawns) in the sauce for 1-1½ minutes.
6. Transfer to a warmed dish and serve sprinkled with a little finely chopped coriander or parsley.

Koong sai tong

Shrimp (Prawns) in Golden Sauce

	00.15	00.25
	Serves 4	

American	Ingredients	Metric/Imperial
6-8	large shrimp (prawns) thawed if frozen	6-8
	salt	
2½ tbsp	oil	2½ tbsp
1	chopped onion	1
4	finely chopped garlic cloves	4
2	finely crushed red chilies	2
6	large, skinned, diced ripe tomatoes	6
2 tbsp	tomato purée	2 tbsp
1 tbsp	dried ground shrimp (prawns)	1 tbsp
1 tbsp	finely grated fresh root ginger	1 tbsp
1 tbsp	soft brown sugar	1 tbsp
	pepper	
2 tbsp	lime or lemon juice	2 tbsp
	a few sprigs of fresh coriander or parsley	

1. Rinse the shrimp (prawns) under cold running water and dry with kitchen paper.
2. Bring to the boil several quarts/litres of water with 1 tbsp salt per litre added. Add the shrimp (prawns) and cook for 3 minutes. Leave to cool in the liquid. Peel and cut the tails down the center lengthwise. Remove the black thread.
3. Heat the oil in a wok and stir fry the onion until transparent.
4. Add the garlic, chilies and tomato. Stir well and simmer gently until the tomato disintegrates.
5. Stir in the tomato purée, dried shrimp (prawns), root ginger, sugar and a little salt and pepper.
6. Pour in ⅔ cup (150 ml/¼ pint) boiling water and stir well. Simmer for 10 minutes.
7. Add the lime or lemon juice and heat the shrimp (prawns) in the sauce for a minute.
8. Serve in a warmed dish and garnish with the sprigs of parsley or coriander.

Riou wan koong

Shrimp (Prawns) with Cucumber in Tomato Sauce

	00.15	00.10
	Serves 4	

American	Ingredients	Metric/Imperial
1	large cucumber	1
2 tbsp	oil	2 tbsp
1	chopped onion	1
1	finely chopped garlic clove	1
2	finely crushed red chilies or 3 tbsp sambal ulek (see page 128)	2
4	large, skinned, diced ripe tomatoes	4
1 tsp	ground red chili	1 tsp
1½ tsp	sugar	1½ tsp
1 tbsp	Thai fish sauce	1 tbsp
1 tbsp	lime or lemon juice	1 tbsp
	salt	
1 lb	fresh peeled shrimp (prawns)	450 g/1 lb
1 tbsp	finely chopped coriander or parsley	1 tbsp

1. Rinse and trim the cucumber. Halve lengthwise and scoop out the seeds. Cut the halves in half lengthwise again, then into 1 in (2.5 cm) pieces.
2. Heat the oil in a wok and stir fry the onion until transparent.
3. Add the garlic and chilies or sambal ulek. Stir well and add the cucumber, tomato, ground red chili and 5 tbsp boiling water. Stir well and simmer for 3-5 minutes until the pieces of tomato disintegrate.
4. Add the sugar, fish sauce, lime or lemon juice and a little salt to taste. Stir well.
5. Heat the shrimp (prawns) in the sauce for 1½ minutes.
6. Transfer to a warmed dish and serve sprinkled with finely chopped coriander or parsley.

Shrimp (prawns) with cucumber in tomato sauce

Radhed ruchi

Shrimp (Prawn) Balls with Meat and Mushrooms

■━━━▷ 00.10
plus standing time

00.25 🍲

American	Ingredients	Metric/Imperial
¼ lb	cod fillets	125 g/4 oz
¾ lb	fresh peeled shrimp (prawns)	350 g/12 oz
1	egg white	1
	salt	
1 tsp	Thai fish sauce	1 tsp
3 tbsp	cornstarch (cornflour)	3 tbsp
½ lb	lean pork	225 g/8 oz
¼ lb	chicken breast fillets	125 g/4 oz
½ lb	small mushrooms	225 g/8 oz
3 tbsp	oil	3 tbsp
1	chopped onion	1
1	chopped garlic clove	1
4	chopped scallions (spring onions) or green shallots	4
2 tbsp	Thai fish sauce	2 tbsp
2 tbsp	cornstarch (cornflour)	2 tbsp
2 tbsp	finely chopped coriander or parsley	2 tbsp

1. Rinse the fish under cold running water and dry with kitchen paper.
2. Finely chop the fish and shrimp (prawns).
3. Lightly beat the egg white and add to the shrimp (prawn) and fish mixture with a little salt, 1 tsp fish sauce and 1 tbsp cornstarch (cornflour). Knead together with the fingers and leave to stand for 15 minutes.
4. Shape the mixture into walnut size balls and coat with the remaining cornstarch (cornflour).
5. Bring several quarts/litres water to the boil in a pan. Add the shrimp (prawn) balls and bring back to the boil. Cook until the balls float to the surface. Boil for 2 minutes then remove with a slotted spoon. Drain on kitchen paper, and keep warm.
6. Dry the pork and chicken with kitchen paper and cut the meat into ½ in (1.25 cm) cubes and sprinkle with salt.
7. Wipe the mushrooms with a damp cloth or a piece of kitchen paper and trim.
8. Heat the oil in a wok and stir fry the onion until transparent.
9. Add the garlic, stir well, add the meat and stir fry for 3-4 minutes.
10. Add 2 tbsp fish sauce, ¾ cup (200 ml/¼ pint) water and the mushrooms. Simmer for 3-4 minutes.
11. Add the scallions (spring onions) or shallots and a little salt.
12. Mix the remaining cornstarch (cornflour) with 2 tbsp cold water. Stir into the contents of the wok and cook, stirring until the sauce has thickened. Simmer gently for a 2-3 minutes.
13. Transfer to warmed plates, arrange the warm shrimp (prawn) balls round the outside and serve garnished with coriander or parsley.

Broiled (grilled) fish rolls

Tod nam pla

Broiled (Grilled) Fish Rolls

■━━━▷ 00.15
plus chilling time

00.40 🍲

American	Ingredients	Metric/Imperial
¾ lb	ground (minced) pork	350 g/12 oz
½ lb	finely shredded crabmeat	225 g/8 oz
1	crushed garlic clove	1
2 tbsp	finely chopped coriander	2 tbsp
1	large coarsely chopped onion	1
2 tbsp	finely ground roasted peanuts or peanut butter	2 tbsp
1 tsp	red spiced paste	1 tsp
	salt	
2 tbsp	Thai fish sauce	2 tbsp
2-3 tbsp	thick coconut sauce	2-3 tbsp
	sea salt	
	oil	

1. Mix all the ingredients together well, cover and chill for 30 minutes.
2. Shape the mixture into thin rolls, 2-3 in (5-6 cm) long, and 1 in (2.5 cm) in diameter. Wrap each roll in a piece of greaseproof paper.
3. Bring a generous quantity of water to the boil in a steamer. Add 1 tablespoon of sea salt per litre of water. Brush the perforated part of the pan with oil.
4. Place the rolls in the pan. Cover the pan and steam for 20 -25 minutes. Leave to cool completely in the pan.
5. Just before serving, remove the greaseproof paper and broil (grill) the cold fish rolls until golden brown.

Yam hoy mangpoo
Spiced Mussels

◣▽   00.15   00.10 🍲
Serves 4

American	Ingredients	Metric/Imperial
6-8 lb	mussels	3-4 kg/6-8 lb
8	finely chopped scallions (spring onions) or shallots	8
4	finely chopped garlic cloves	4
1 tbsp	grated root ginger	1 tbsp
10	small dried red chilies	10
6 tbsp	Thai fish sauce	6 tbsp
3 tbsp	sugar	3 tbsp
¾ cup	lemon juice	200 ml/7 fl oz
2 tbsp	oil	2 tbsp
	few blades fresh lemon grass	
2	poeroet leaves (daoen poeroet)	2
	salt	
2 tbsp	cornstarch (cornflour)	2 tbsp
	few sprigs of coriander or parsley	

1. Rinse the mussels in cold running water. Pick over and clean them. Remove any that are open or that feel heavy. Remove the mussels from the shells, put them into a colander and drain reserving the liquid.
2. Grind the scallions (spring onions) or shallots, garlic, root ginger, chilies, fish sauce, sugar and lemon juice to a paste in a food processor.
3. Heat the oil in a wok and stir fry the paste for 1 minute.

4. Add the lemon grass, poeroet leaves, reserved mussel liquid and ⅔ cup (150 ml/¼ pint) boiling water. Stir well, add a little salt to taste and bring to the boil.
5. Mix the cornstarch (cornflour) with 2 tbsp cold water. Stir into the contents of the wok. Cook, stirring until the sauce thickens. Simmer gently for 3 minutes.
6. Add the mussels and cook stirring for 5 minutes, until tender.
7. Divide the mussels and sauce between four warmed plates. Sprinkle with coriander or parsley and serve.

Hoy mangpoo ob mor din
Boiled Mussels

◣▽   00.10   00.20 🍲
Serves 4

American	Ingredients	Metric/Imperial
8 lb	mussels	4 kg/8 lb
	zest of 1 lemon	
	salt	
6	coarsely chopped green chilies	6
6	coarsely chopped scallions (spring onions) or shallots	6
5 tbsp	lemon or lime juice	5 tbsp

1. Rinse the mussels in cold running water. Remove any that are open or feel heavy.

2. Cut the lemon zest into small pieces.

3. Bring 1¼ cups (300 ml/½ pint) water to the boil in a large deep pan. Add 1 tbsp salt.

4. Put one third of the mussels into the pan. Sprinkle on half the lemon zest, half the chilies and half the scallions (spring onions) or shallots.

5. Add the remainder of the mussels, and sprinkle with the remaining lemon zest, chilies and scallions (spring onions) or shallots. Sprinkle with 1 tbsp salt and pour over the lime or lemon juice. Cover the pan and bring to the boil. Shake the pan during cooking.

6. Remove the pan from the heat as soon as all of the shells have opened.

7. Transfer the mussels into large warmed dishes. Serve immediately.

Pad ped kai hoy mangpoo

Fried Chicken with Mussels

00.10 Serves 4   **00.15**

American	Ingredients	Metric/Imperial
1 lb	chicken breast fillets	450 g/1 lb
1 lb	mussels	450 g/1 lb
	salt	
3 tbsp	oil	3 tbsp
2	large chopped onions	2
4	finely chopped garlic cloves	4
1 tbsp	Chinese light soy sauce	1 tbsp
2	finely chopped red chilies	2
2 tsp	soft brown sugar	2 tsp
2 tbsp	lime or lemon juice	2 tbsp
3 tbsp	Thai fish sauce	3 tbsp
1½ tsp	cornstarch (cornflour)	1½ tsp
1 tbsp	finely chopped coriander or parsley	1 tbsp

1. Dry the chicken with kitchen paper and cut into small cubes.

2. Rinse the mussels in cold running water. Pick over to clean and remove any that are open or heavy.

3. Bring 1¼ cups (300 ml/½ pint) water to the boil in a deep pan. Add 1 tbsp salt. Put the mussels in the pan bring back to the boil and cover. Leave the mussels to cook, shaking the pan during cooking. Remove the pan from the heat as soon as the shells have opened. Take the mussels out of their shells.

4. Heat the oil in a large wok and stir fry the onions until transparent.

5. Add the garlic, soy sauce and red chilies and stir well.

6. Add the diced chicken and mussels and fry for 2 minutes, turning occasionally.

7. Dissolve the sugar in the lime or lemon juice.

8. Add the fish sauce, sugar solution, a little salt and ⅔ cup (150 ml/¼ pint) boiling water. Cook, stirring for 5 minutes. Slide all the ingredients to one side of the wok.

9. Mix the cornstarch (cornflour) with 2 tbsp cold water. Stir into the liquid in the wok and cook, stirring until the sauce has thickened.

10. Bring the ingredients back into the sauce and cook gently for 2 minutes.

11. Transfer on to warmed plates. Sprinkle with a little finely chopped coriander or parsley and serve.

*Left to right: Spiced mussels
Boiled mussels
Fried chicken with mussels*

Braised chicken in spicy sauce

Pratak Iohm

Crab Rolls

◤ 00.15   00.20 ⌥
Serves 4

American	Ingredients	Metric/Imperial
¾ lb	crabmeat, thawed if frozen	350 g/12 oz
½ lb	lean pork	225 g/8 oz
6	dried Chinese mushrooms	6
2 tbsp	oil	2 tbsp
1	small chopped onion	1
2	finely chopped garlic cloves	2
½ tsp	ground red chili	½ tsp
	salt	
2 tsp	Thai fish sauce	2 tsp
1	lightly beaten egg	1
2 tsp	ground coriander	2 tsp
2 tbsp	cornstarch (cornflour)	2 tbsp
12	wonton wrappers	12
	oil for frying	

1. Pick over the crabmeat and remove any pieces of shell. Grind (mince) the crabmeat finely.

2. Grind (mince) the pork finely.
3. Put the mushrooms into a bowl with warm water to cover. Leave to soak for 20 minutes. Discard the stalks and chop the caps finely. Strain the soaking liquid through a piece of wet muslin and reserve.
4. Heat the oil in a wok and stir fry the onion until transparent.
5. Stir in the garlic and add the pork and mushrooms, stir continuously until the meat changes color.
6. Stir in the ground red chili and add 2 tbsp of the mushroom soaking liquid, a little salt, and the fish sauce.
Stir well and leave the mixture to cool slightly.
7. Mix the cooled mixture with the lightly beaten egg, coriander, cornstarch (cornflour) and crabmeat. Leave to go cold.
8. Lay out the 12 wonton wrappers. Shape the crabmeat and meat mixture into rolls a little thinner than the wrappers. Place the rolls on the wrappers. Brush the uncovered edges of each wrapper with water. Fold the wrappers round the fillings to cover the filling well, press the edges to close.
9. Heat the oil and fry the rolls 3-4 at a time until golden brown. Drain on kitchen paper and serve on warmed plates.

Cook's tip: serve accompanied by a sauce, in individual bowls made by mixing 3 tbsp fish sauce with 1 grated garlic clove, a little finely ground chili, the juice of 1 lime or lemon, and 1 tsp sugar.

Kai pad ped

Braised Chicken in Spicy Sauce

00.05 plus standing time — 00.50

American	Ingredients	Metric/Imperial
2 (1 lb)	halved roasting chickens	2 (450 g/1 lb)
3	crushed garlic cloves	3
	salt	
	freshly ground black pepper	
¾ cup	thick coconut milk	200 ml/7 fl oz
1 tbsp	garam masala	1 tbsp
½ tsp	ground coriander	½ tsp
½ tsp	ground cumin	½ tsp
½ tsp	ground turmeric	½ tsp
4	finely ground red chilies	4
2 tbsp	peanut butter	2 tbsp
2 tbsp	lime or lemon juice	2 tbsp

1. Dry the chicken with kitchen paper.
2. Mix together the crushed garlic, salt and pepper. Rub the mixture into the skin of the chicken and leave to stand for 10 minutes.
3. Put the chicken into a heavy-based pan with the thick coconut milk and enough water to cover. Bring to the boil, reduce the heat and simmer for 45 minutes or until the chicken is tender. Remove the chicken from the pan and keep warm.
4. Add the garam masala, coriander, cumin, turmeric, a little salt and the ground red chili to the coconut milk mixture. Bring to the boil, stirring continuously. Cook gently for 2-3 minutes.
5. Add the peanut butter and cook, stirring until the sauce thickens.
6. Return the chicken to the sauce and warm through. Transfer the chicken to warmed plates.
7. Stir the lime or lemon juice into the sauce, pour over the chicken and serve.

Kaeng khieu kai wan

Chicken in Green Spiced Sauce

00.05 Serves 4 — 00.50

American	Ingredients	Metric/Imperial
¾ cup	thin coconut milk	200 ml/7 fl oz
2 (1 lb)	roasting chickens cut into pieces	2 (450 g/1 lb)
3	crushed garlic cloves	3
	salt	
	freshly ground pepper	
2 tbsp	green spice paste	2 tbsp
1 tbsp	grated lime or lemon zest	1 tbsp
2	finely chopped green chilies	2
¾ cup	thick coconut milk	200 ml/7 fl oz
2 tsp	sugar	2 tsp
4 tbsp	finely chopped coriander or parsley	4 tbsp

1. Bring the thin coconut milk to the boil.
2. Dry the chicken with kitchen paper.
3. Mix together the garlic, salt and pepper and rub the mixture into the skin of the chicken. Put the chicken into the boiling coconut milk. Reduce the heat and simmer for 45 minutes or until the chicken is tender. Remove the chicken pieces from the pan and transfer to warmed plates.
4. Add the green spice paste, lime or lemon zest, chilies, thick coconut milk, sugar and herbs to the remaining coconut milk. Bring to the boil, stirring continuously and add a little salt to taste.
5. Spoon the sauce over the pieces of chicken and serve.

Kaeng keong

Green Spiced Paste

00.05 makes 1 small jar — 00.00

American	Ingredients	Metric/Imperial
4 tbsp	fresh green peppercorns	4 tbsp
4	large chopped onions	4
8	finely chopped garlic cloves	8
1 tsp	grated lime or lemon zest	1 tsp
3 tsp	salt	3 tsp
2 tsp	lemon grass powder	2 tsp
6 tbsp	finely chopped fresh coriander	6 tbsp
10	chopped green chilies	10
½ tsp	ground turmeric	½ tsp
1 tbsp	ground cumin	1 tbsp
1 tbsp	laos powder	1 tbsp
1 tbsp	sesame oil	1 tbsp

1. Using a food processor, purée all the ingredients until completely smooth.
2. Put the paste into a clean jar. Seal tightly and store in the refrigerator for 4 days.

Kaeng daeng

Red Spiced Paste

00.05 makes 1 small jar — 00.00

American	Ingredients	Metric/Imperial
6	large, ground fresh red chilies	6
4	large chopped onions	4
8	finely chopped garlic cloves	8
1 tsp	grated lemon or lime zest	1 tsp
3 tsp	salt	3 tsp
2 tsp	lemon grass powder	2 tsp
6 tbsp	finely chopped coriander	6 tbsp
10	chopped green chilies	10
½ tsp	ground turmeric	½ tsp
1 tbsp	ground cumin	1 tbsp
1 tbsp	laos powder	1 tbsp
1 tbsp	sesame oil	1 tbsp

1. Using a food processor, purée all the ingredients to a completely smooth paste.
2. Transfer to a clean jar, seal tightly and store in a refrigerator for up to 4 days.

MENU

Chicken balls with scallions
(spring onions)
Fried mussels with bell peppers
Sweet nut soup

Chicken Balls with Scallions (Spring Onions)

⬛▷ 00.00.
plus chilling time

00.00 🍲

American	Ingredients	Metric/Imperial
3 tbsp	groundnut oil	3 tbsp
¾ lb	diced chicken breast fillets	350 g/12 oz
1	small chopped onion or shallot	1
½	finely chopped garlic clove	½
1 tbsp	finely chopped celery	1 tbsp
1	egg	1
1 tbsp	Chinese dark soy sauce	1 tbsp
1 tbsp	Chinese rice wine or dry sherry	1 tbsp
	salt	
6	scallions (spring onions)	6
¼ lb	rice vermicelli	125 g/4 oz
1 tbsp	Chinese light soy sauce	1 tbsp

1. Heat the oil in a wok and stir fry the chicken for 3 minutes. Remove from the wok with a slotted spoon and drain over the wok. Put the chicken on a large cold plate to cool.
2. Fry the onion or shallot in the remaining oil until transparent.
3. Add the garlic and celery, stir, then remove with a slotted spoon. Drain well.
4. Grind (mince) the chicken and onion mixture finely in a food processor.
5. Lightly beat the egg and add to the chicken and onion mixture. Add the dark soy sauce, rice wine or sherry and a little salt. Stir well then leave to chill for 30 minutes. Shape the mixture into walnut size balls.
6. Rinse the scallions (spring onions) and cut into 1 in (2.5 cm) lengths.
7. Prepare the rice vermicelli according to the instructions on the packet. Drain well.

8. Heat the remaining oil in the wok and fry the chicken balls a few at a time until golden brown. Remove from the wok with a slotted spoon and keep warm.
9. Fry the scallions (spring onions) in the remaining oil and add the rice vermicelli. Stir well and sprinkle with a little light soy sauce.
10. Divide the rice vermicelli and scallions (spring onions) between 4 warmed dishes and lay the chicken balls on top.

Fried Mussels with Bell Peppers

⬛▷ 00.05
Serves 4

00.15 🍲

American	Ingredients	Metric/Imperial
2	red bell peppers	2
2	green bell peppers	2
1½ lb	cooked, shelled mussels	700 g/1½ lb
3 tbsp	groundnut oil	3 tbsp
1	large chopped onion	1
1	finely chopped garlic clove	1
3 tbsp	Chinese light soy sauce	3 tbsp
3 tbsp	Chinese rice wine or dry sherry	3 tbsp
2 tsp	cornstarch (cornflour)	2 tsp
	salt	
1 tbsp	finely chopped celery or chives (optional)	1 tbsp

1. Rinse, trim and seed the bell peppers and cut the flesh into thin strips.
2. Drain the cooked mussels well.
3. Heat the oil in a wok and stir fry the onion until transparent. Add the garlic and stir in the strips of bell pepper.

4. Add the mussels and stir fry over low heat until the mussels are warmed through. Slide the mixture to one side of the wok.

5. Add the soy sauce, rice wine or dry sherry and 5 tbsp boiling water.

6. Mix the cornstarch (cornflour) with 2 tbsp cold water. Stir into the wok and cook, stirring until the sauce thickens.

7. Stir the mussels and bell pepper back into the sauce and add a little salt to taste. Cook, gently for 3-4 minutes.

8. Transfer to warmed dishes and serve garnished with finely chopped celery or chives.

1. Heat both oils in a wok and stir fry the hazelnuts and walnuts for 2-3 minutes.

2. Stir in the flaked almonds and sugar, stirring until the sugar begins to change color. Immediately remove the wok from the heat. Turn the mixture on to a large cold plate and leave to cool.

3. Mix the cornstarch (cornflour) with 3 tbsp cold water.

4. Add 3¼ cups (750 ml/1¼ pints) water to the wok and stir. Bring the water to the boil and add the nuts.

5. Stir in the cornstarch (cornflour) mixture. Cook, stirring until the soup thickens slightly. Simmer for 2 minutes.

6. Stir in the cream and serve the soup into warmed bowls.

Sweet Nut Soup

	00.10	00.10
	Serves 4	

American	Ingredients	Metric/Imperial
3 tbsp	groundnut oil	3 tbsp
1 tsp	sesame oil	1 tsp
¼ lb	shelled, peeled hazelnuts	125 g/4 oz
2 oz	shelled, peeled walnuts	50 g/2 oz
2 oz	flaked almonds	50 g/2 oz
6 tbsp	sugar	6 tbsp
1 tbsp	cornstarch (cornflour)	1 tbsp
5 tbsp	light (single) cream	5 tbsp

Cook's tip: the nuts can be chopped before frying. Stir fry them for 1½ minutes in 1½ tbsp hot groundnut oil before adding the almonds and sugar. Then continue as directed above.

MENU

Shrimp (prawn) soup
Fried fish with ginger sauce
Cucumber salad
Sweet banana rice

Shrimp (Prawn) Soup

▬▷ 00.03   00.10 🍲
Serves 4

American	Ingredients	Metric/Imperial
12	finely chopped sprigs coriander	12
6	finely chopped sprigs parsley	6
1	large coarsely chopped onion	1
1	finely chopped garlic clove	1
1 tbsp	groundnut oil	1 tbsp
8	chopped scallions (spring onions)	8
2 tbsp	Thai fish sauce	2 tbsp
½ tbsp	sugar	½ tbsp
	salt	
½ tbsp	Chinese light soy sauce	½ tbsp
½ lb	fresh peeled shrimp (prawns)	225 g/8 oz
2	lightly beaten eggs	2

1. Grind the herbs, onion and garlic to a fine paste in a food processor.
2. Heat the oil in a wok and stir fry the paste for 2 minutes. Add 2½ cups (600 ml/1 pint) boiling water, bring back to the boil, reduce the heat and simmer for 5 minutes.
3. Add the scallions (spring onions), fish sauce, sugar, a little salt, the soy sauce and shrimp (prawns). Bring to the boil, stirring continuously.
4. Add the lightly beaten eggs and stir well. Remove the pan from the heat, immediately and pour the soup into warmed bowls and serve.

Fried Fish with Ginger Sauce

▬▷ 00.10   00.25 🍲
Serves 4

American	Ingredients	Metric/Imperial
2 (½ lb)	cleaned cod	2 (225 g/8 oz)
1 tsp	salt	1 tsp
6 tbsp	lime or lemon juice	6 tbsp
6 tbsp	soft brown sugar	6 tbsp
6 tbsp	fish bouillon (stock)	6 tbsp
2 tbsp	Chinese light soy sauce	2 tbsp
1 tbsp	Thai fish sauce	1 tbsp
4 tbsp	finely grated fresh root ginger	4 tbsp
2 tsp	cornstarch (cornflour)	2 tsp
¼ tsp	ground black pepper	¼ tsp
2 tbsp	sifted flour	2 tbsp
¾ cup	oil	200 ml/7 fl oz
4	chopped scallions (spring onions)	4
2	tomatoes (optional)	2

1. Rinse the fish inside and out under cold running water and dry with kitchen paper. Sprinkle a little salt inside and out.
2. Put the lime or lemon juice, sugar, fish bouillon, soy sauce, fish sauce, root ginger and a little salt in a saucepan and bring to the boil. Simmer gently for 5 minutes.
3. Mix the cornstarch (cornflour) with 2 tbsp cold water. Stir into the contents of the pan and cook stirring for 2-3 minutes.
4. Mix a little salt and pepper into the sifted flour.

5. Dry the inside of the fish again with kitchen paper. Make 3-4 oblique incisions on each side of the fish. Roll the fish in the flour mixture.

6. Heat the oil in a frying pan and fry the fish for 12-15 minutes over moderate heat until golden brown on all sides. Drain on kitchen paper.

7. Arrange the fish on a large warmed dish. Spoon the hot sauce over the fish and sprinkle with chopped scallions (spring onion). Serve garnished with one or more tomato flowers.

Cucumber Salad

	00.05 plus standing time	00.00

American	Ingredients	Metric/Imperial
1	cucumber	1
	salt	
1	small chopped onion	1
1	crushed garlic clove	1
1 tsp	sambal ulek (see page 128)	1 tsp
2 tsp	Thai fish sauce	2 tsp
2 tbsp	lime or lemon juice	2 tbsp
2 tbsp	oil	2 tbsp

1. Rinse and trim the cucumber. Coarsely grate the flesh and sprinkle with 1 tsp salt. Stir well and leave to drain for 20 minutes.

2. Put the onion, garlic, sambal ulek, fish sauce, lime or lemon juice, oil and a little salt in a bowl and mix well.

3. Put the cucumber into individual dishes, spoon over a few tsp of the dressing and toss the salad. Serve the cucumber salad chilled.

Sweet Banana Rice

	00.10 plus chilling time	00.45

American	Ingredients	Metric/Imperial
½ cup	cracked rice	125 g/4 oz
2	bananas	2
1	lightly beaten egg	1
5 tbsp	soft brown sugar	5 tbsp
2 tsp	lime or lemon juice	2 tsp
2 tbsp	thick coconut milk	2 tbsp

1. Rinse the rice in several changes of cold water until the water runs clear. Put the rice into a saucepan with 1¼ cups (300 ml/½ pint) water. Bring to the boil slowly, cover the pan and simmer for 40 minutes until tender.

2. Peel the bananas and mash the flesh.

3. Add the egg, sugar, lime or lemon juice and the coconut milk. Stir continuously, until the mixture is smooth.

4. Add the mixture to the cooked rice and stir for 2 minutes. Leave to cool until cold. Shape the rice mixture into 12 equal size balls. Flatten the balls and chill for 1 hour before serving.

VIETNAM

Pho

Beef Soup with Rice Vermicelli and Vegetables

00.05 Serves 4

06.00

American	Ingredients	Metric/Imperial
2 lb	beef bones	1 kg/2 lb
14 oz	shin beef or braising steak	400 g/14 oz
2	onions, cut into rings	2
1 tbsp	coarsely grated fresh root ginger	1 tbsp
1 (2 in)	cinnamon stick	1 (5 cm/2 in)
12	crushed black peppercorns	12
¼ lb	rice vermicelli (mihoen)	125 g/4 oz
¼ lb	bean sprouts	125 g/4 oz
6	scallions (spring onions)	6
4	tomatoes	4
4	sticks celery	4
2	red chilies	2
2	green chilies	2
	salt	
½ lb	lean roasting beef or rump steak	225 g/8 oz
	Vietnamese fish sauce (Nuoc mam)	
1-2	lemons or limes cut into segments	1-2

1. Put the bones into a deep saucepan together with the shin beef or braising steak, onions, root ginger, cinnamon and crushed peppercorns.
2. Pour over at least 2 quarts (2 litres/3½ pints) water to cover ingredients completely. Bring to the boil and skim the surface several times. Cover with a lid, reduce the heat and simmer very gently for 6 hours.
3. Strain the bouillon (stock) through a piece of wet muslin. Leave the bouillon (stock) to cool and remove any fat.
4. Prepare the rice vermicelli as indicated on the packet. Drain thoroughly.
5. Rinse the bean sprouts in plenty of cold water and remove as many seed cases as possible. Drain well.

6. Cut the scallions (spring onions) into ¾ in (1.75 cm) pieces.
7. Skin the tomatoes and cut them into pieces. Remove the juice and the seeds.
8. Cut the celery sticks into thin strips.
9. Wash the chilies, trim and cut them into thin rings.
10. Place the groups of vegetables on a serving dish.
11. Bring the bouillon (stock) to the boil again and add salt to taste.
12. Reheat the rice vermicelli and transfer to a large warmed bowl.
13. Cut the beef into ¼ in (4 mm) slices and then into thin strips. Put into a serving dish.
14. Place the dishes with vegetables, warm rice vermicelli and meat on the table. Add one or more small bowls of Vietnamese fish sauce (Nuoc mam), one or more small bowls of red and green chilies cut into thin rings, and a bowl of lemon or lime segments. Place a deep, warmed bowl with the boiling bouillon (stock) on to a food warmer.

Cook's tip: each guest receives a warmed soup bowl into which he spoons 1 tbsp rice vermicelli, 1-2 tbsp of different vegetables and 1 tbsp meat. Then he pours some bouillon (stock) over it. Vietnamese fish sauce (Nuoc mam) and lemon or lime segments can be added to taste.

Com chien

Vietnamese Style Fried Rice

00.05 plus drying time

00.35

American	Ingredients	Metric/Imperial
1 cup	long grain rice	225 g/8 oz
3 tbsp	groundnut oil	3 tbsp
	few drops Vietnamese fish sauce (Nuoc mam)	

1. Wash the rice in cold water until the water runs clear. Drain the rice for 1½ hours in a draughty place.
2. Heat the oil in a pan and add the rice a little at a time. Stir fry the rice for 12-15 minutes until golden yellow.

Beef soup with rice vermicelli and vegetables

3. Add enough boiling water to just cover the rice. Boil with the pan covered with a lid until the rice is tender (approximately 20 minutes). Remove the lid. Stir the rice well several times with a large fork and leave to steam until completely dry.

4. Sprinkle with a few drops of fish sauce and stir well.

Ca chien sot ca
Fried Fish in Tomato Sauce

00.10 plus standing time   00.15

American	Ingredients	Metric/Imperial
1¼ lb	mackerel fillets	575 g/1¼ lb
	salt	
2	garlic cloves	2
2	small onions or shallots	2
4	skinned ripe tomatoes	4
4 tbsp	groundnut oil	4 tbsp
2 tbsp	Vietnamese fish sauce (Nuoc mam)	2 tbsp
1 tbsp	sugar	1 tbsp
	freshly ground pepper	

1. Rinse the fish fillets under cold running water. Dry with kitchen paper and rub with a little salt. Leave to stand for 15 minutes.

2. Cut the garlic and onions or shallots into paper thin slices.

3. Halve the tomatoes, remove the juice and the seeds. Chop the flesh very finely.

4. Heat the oil in a large frying pan and fry the fish until tender and golden brown on both sides. Remove from the pan and keep warm.

5. Remove all but 1 tbsp of the oil from the pan.

6. Add the onions and stir fry until lightly browned.

7. Add the garlic and fry with the onion for 1 minute, stirring continuously.

8. Add the tomatoes and the fish sauce, sugar, a little salt and some freshly ground pepper. Stir well and simmer for 1-2 minutes.

9. Arrange the fish on a warmed dish and spoon over the sauce.

Ca kho to
Steamed Cod

00.10 Serves 4   00.20

American	Ingredients	Metric/Imperial
1¼ lb	cod fillets	575 g/1¼ lb
2 tbsp	Vietnamese fish sauce (Nuoc mam)	2 tbsp
1 tbsp	sugar	1 tbsp
	salt	
	freshly ground pepper	
3 tbsp	groundnut oil	3 tbsp
2	large chopped onions	2
3	finely chopped garlic cloves	3
2 tbsp	soft brown sugar	2 tbsp
4	chopped scallions (spring onions)	4

1. Rinse the fish under cold running water. Dry with kitchen paper and divide the fish into 4 equal portions.

2. Mix the fish sauce and sugar in a small bowl and add a little salt and freshly ground pepper. Keep stirring until the sugar and salt have dissolved.

3. Brush the fish pieces with this mixture on all sides.

4. Heat 1 tbsp oil in a wok and stir fry the onion until lightly colored.

5. Add the garlic and stir several times. Push everything to one side of the wok and add the remaining oil.

6. Fry the fish pieces until golden brown on both sides.

7. Spoon the onions and garlic on to the fish.

8. Sprinkle with the brown sugar and add ⅔ cup (150 ml/¼ pint) boiling water. Cover the wok and simmer for 8-10 minutes. Serve in a warmed dish sprinkled with chopped scallions (spring onions).

Cook's tip: the dish can be enriched by adding several kinds of vegetables at the same time as the garlic. Carrots cut into thin strips, celery, cucumber and a few strips of tomato, for example. The quantity of fish sauce can be reduced to 1 tbsp, in which case a little extra salt should be added.

Ca hap (I)
Steamed Fish (I)

00.15 plus soaking time   00.25

American	Ingredients	Metric/Imperial
1 lb	mackerel fillets	450 g/1 lb
6	dried Chinese mushrooms	6
3 oz	rice vermicelli (mihoen)	75 g/3 oz
2	young carrots	2
3	slices peeled, fresh root ginger	3
1 tbsp	groundnut oil	1 tbsp
	salt	
¼ lb	lean pork	125 g/4 oz
1 tbsp	Vietnamese fish sauce (Nuoc mam)	1 tbsp
6 tbsp	thin coconut milk	6 tbsp
2 tbsp	chopped scallions (spring onions)	2 tbsp

1. Rinse the fish under running cold water.

2. Place the mushrooms in a bowl with enough boiling water to cover them generously and soak for 30 minutes. Discard the stalks and cut the caps into thin strips.

3. Prepare the rice vermicelli as indicated on the packet. Drain well and cut into small pieces.

4. Cut the carrots and the root ginger slices into extremely fine strips.

5. Brush a bowl with some oil and place the fish fillets into it. Sprinkle with a little salt.

6. Add the rice vermicelli, mushrooms, carrots, root ginger and pork.

7. Mix together the fish sauce and the coconut milk and spread evenly over the contents of the bowl.

8. Sprinkle with the scallions (spring onions). Place the bowl in the top part of a steamer. Cover with a lid and steam for about 20 minutes.

Ca hap (II)
Steamed Fish (II)

00.10 plus standing time   **00.45**

American	Ingredients	Metric/Imperial
1 lb	mackerel fillets	450 g/1 lb
	salt	
2 tbsp	groundnut oil	2 tbsp
¾ cup	washed and throughly drained long grain rice	175 g/6 oz
1	small sliced cucumber	1
3	young sliced carrots	3
1 tbsp	coarsely grated fresh root ginger	1 tbsp
2	sticks celery cut into thin strips	2
1 tbsp	Vietnamese fish sauce (Nuoc mam)	1 tbsp
2 tbsp	chopped scallions (spring onions)	2 tbsp
3 oz	fresh, peeled shrimp (prawns) (optional)	75 g/3 oz

1. Rinse the fish under cold running water. Dry with kitchen paper. Cut into finger width strips. Sprinkle with a little salt and leave to stand for 10 minutes.
2. Heat the oil in a pan and add the rice a little at a time stirring continuously. Fry the rice for about 10 minutes or until golden yellow in color.
3. Add enough boiling water to just cover the rice.
4. Brush a dish with some oil and arrange the cucumber and carrot slices in the dish.
5. Mix the fish, grated root ginger and celery strips into the rice. Sprinkle with salt.

6. Add the fish sauce. Stir well and put on top of the cucumber and carrot. Cover the dish with a piece of aluminum foil and place the dish in the top part of a steamer.
7. Cover the pan with a lid and steam for 25 minutes or until tender.
8. Just before serving sprinkle with the scallions (spring onions) and the shrimp (prawns).

Ca rut zuong du Lo
Filled Fish

00.20 Serves 4   **00.40**

American	Ingredients	Metric/Imperial
2	large cleaned mackerel	2
	salt	
	freshly ground pepper	
½ lb	ground (minced) pork	225 g/8 oz
1	chopped onion	1
2	chopped garlic cloves	2
1	egg white	1
2 tbsp	groundnut oil	2 tbsp
2	hard-cooked (hard-boiled) eggs cut into pieces	2
2	skinned tomatoes cut into pieces	2
2	limes, cut into pieces	2
	sprigs parsley	

1. Set the oven to 200°C/400°F/Gas mark 6. Rinse the fish inside and out, under cold running water. Carefully remove the bones (the fishmonger may do this for you). Dry the fish inside and out with kitchen paper.

Left: Fried fish in sweet and sour sauce
Right: Steamed fish

2. Sprinkle the inside with some salt and pepper.
3. Mix the pork with the onion, garlic and egg white and add salt and pepper to taste.
4. Fill each fish with this mixture and tie with strong thread to close the openings. Dry the outside again with kitchen paper and brush with a little oil.
5. Place the fish on an oiled rack. Put the rack in the center of the preheated oven for about 10 minutes then reduce the heat to 180°C/350°F/Gas mark 4, brush the fish with oil and cook for a further 25 minutes.
6. Remove the threads from the fish. Place the filled fish on a flat dish and garnish with pieces of egg, tomato, lime and sprigs of parsley.

Ca lan bot chien sot chua ngot

Fried Fish in Sweet and Sour Sauce

	00. 15	00. 15
	Serves 4	

American	Ingredients	Metric/Imperial
1 ¼ lb	whiting fillets	575 g/1 ¼ lb
3 tsp	cornstarch (cornflour)	3 tsp
	salt	
	pepper	
8 tbsp	groundnut oil	8 tbsp
1	coarsely choppped onion	1
1	finely chopped garlic clove	1
2	grated carrots	2
2	skinned tomatoes cut into small pieces	2
1 tbsp	Vietnamese fish sauce (Nuoc mam)	1 tbsp
2 tbsp	sugar	2 tbsp
1 tbsp	lemon or lime juice	1 tbsp

1. Rinse the fish fillets under cold running water. Dry with kitchen paper.
2. Place the cornstarch (cornflour) into a bowl with some salt and pepper and stir in 6-8 tbsp cold water. Keep stirring until smooth.
3. Heat the oil in a wok.
4. Dip the fish fillets in the cornstarch (cornflour) mixture and fry in the hot oil for about 6 minutes until golden brown on both sides. Drain on kitchen paper and keep warm.
5. Remove all but 2 tbsp oil from the pan and stir fry the onion until lightly colored.
6. Add the garlic and stir well.
7. Add the carrots, tomatoes, fish sauce, sugar and 6 tbsp water. Stir thoroughly and simmer gently for 3 minutes.
8. Stir in the lemon or lime juice and salt to taste. Cook, stirring for 2 minutes.
9. Place the fillets on warmed plates and spoon over the sauce.

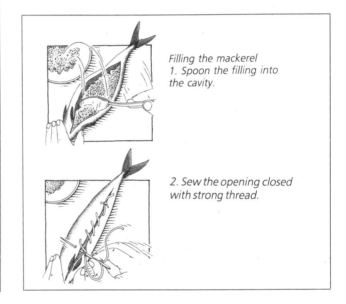

Filling the mackerel
1. Spoon the filling into the cavity.

2. Sew the opening closed with strong thread.

Crab with rice vermicelli

Cua xao bun tau
Crab with Rice Vermicelli

00.15 Serves 4   **00.10**

American	Ingredients	Metric/Imperial
¾ lb	crabmeat, thawed if frozen	350 g/12 oz
6 oz	rice vermicelli (mihoen)	175 g/6 oz
2 tbsp	groundnut oil	2 tbsp
1	large chopped onion	1
1	finely chopped garlic clove	1
1 tbsp	Vietnamese fish sauce (Nuoc mam)	1 tbsp
	salt	
	freshly ground pepper	
	lettuce leaves	
1	skinned tomato cut into segments	1
2	hard-cooked (hard-boiled) eggs cut into segments	2
4	chopped scallions (spring onions)	4

1. Pick over the crabmeat and cut into small pieces.
2. Prepare the rice vermicelli as directed on the packet. Drain well.
3. Heat the oil and stir fry the onion until beginning to color.
4. Add the garlic and stir several times.
5. Add the crab pieces. Fry for 2 minutes over moderate heat and stir well.
6. Add 3 tbsp boiling water, the fish sauce and salt and pepper to taste. Stir again.
7. Cover a flat serving dish with the lettuce leaves and cover with the rice vermicelli. Spoon over the crab mixture. Garnish with tomato and egg segments and sprinkle with the scallions (spring onions).

Cook's tip: shrimp (prawns) can be used to replace ¼ of the crabmeat, stirring them into the mixture just before serving.

Tom rin
Shrimp (Prawns) in Fish Sauce

00.05 Serves 4   **00.10**

American	Ingredients	Metric/Imperial
1 tbsp	groundnut oil	1 tbsp
1	large chopped onion	1
1	chopped garlic clove	1
3 tbsp	Vietnamese fish sauce (Nuoc mam)	3 tbsp
2 tbsp	soft brown sugar	2 tbsp
	salt	
	freshly ground pepper	
¾ lb	fresh peeled shrimp (prawns)	300 g/12 oz
2	skinned tomatoes cut into pieces	2
2	coarsely chopped scallions (spring onions)	2

1. Heat the oil in a wok.
2. Stir fry the onion until beginning to gain color.
3. Add the garlic and stir well.
4. Add 5 tbsp boiling water, the fish sauce, sugar and a little salt and freshly ground pepper to taste. Mix well and boil steadily for 2 minutes.
5. Add the shrimp (prawns) and keep stirring until thoroughly heated. Transfer to a warmed dish.
6. Arrange the tomato pieces round the dish and sprinkle with the scallions (spring onions).

Thit ga kho gung
Braised Chicken with Ginger

➤ 00.10 00.20 🍲
plus standing time

American	Ingredients	Metric/Imperial
1½ lb	chicken breast fillets	700 g/1½ lb
2 oz	finely grated fresh root ginger	50 g/2 oz
1 tbsp	sugar	1 tbsp
3 tbsp	Vietnamese fish sauce (Nuoc mam)	3 tbsp
	freshly ground pepper	
2 tbsp	groundnut oil	2 tbsp
4	garlic cloves	4
2 tbsp	soft brown sugar	2 tbsp

1. Dry the chicken with kitchen paper and cut into 2 in x 1½ in (5 cm×3 cm) strips.
2. Put the chicken in a bowl with the root ginger, sugar, fish sauce and some pepper. Stir well and leave to stand for 30 minutes.
3. Heat the oil in a wok and stir fry the garlic until golden brown. Remove from the oil.
4. Add the chicken mixture to the oil and stir well several times. Reduce the heat. Cover the wok with a lid and simmer for 10 minutes.
5. Add the sugar, stir well then place the lid back on the wok and simmer very gently for a further 5 minutes.
6. Serve in a warmed dish.

Ga hap ca
Steamed Chicken with Tomato

➤ 00.15 00.25 🍲
Serves 4

American	Ingredients	Metric/Imperial
1¼ lb	chicken breast fillets	575 g/1¼ lb
4	ripe, skinned tomatoes cut into cubes	4
3	scallions (spring onions)	3
1 tbsp	coarsely grated fresh root ginger	1 tbsp
2 tbsp	Vietnamese fish sauce (Nuoc mam)	2 tbsp
½ tsp	salt	½ tsp
1 tsp	sugar	1 tsp
½ tsp	coarsely ground black pepper	½ tsp
2 tbsp	sesame oil	2 tbsp
1	tomato (optional)	1
1 tbsp	finely chopped coriander leaves or parsley (optional)	1 tbsp

1. Dry the chicken with kitchen paper and cut into finger width strips.
2. Put the chicken strips in a bowl with the remaining ingredients. Stir, then put the bowl in the top part of a steamer. Cover the pan and steam for 20-25 minutes.
3. Garnish with a tomato 'flower' and sprinkle with some finely chopped coriander leaves or parsley.

Steamed chicken with tomato

Nam dong co tiem ga

Steamed Chicken with Mushrooms

00.15 plus soaking time | 00.40

American	Ingredients	Metric/Imperial
8	*large dried Chinese mushrooms*	8
1 tbsp	*coarsely grated fresh root ginger*	1 tbsp
4	*coarsely chopped scallions (spring onions)*	4
	salt	
	freshly ground pepper	
2 tbsp	*Vietnamese fish sauce (Nuoc mam)*	2 tbsp
1 tbsp	*sesame oil*	1 tbsp
16-20	*chicken portions, preferably drumsticks*	16-20
½ lb	*rice vermicelli (mihoen)*	225 g/8 oz

1. Put the mushrooms in a bowl with enough boiling water to just cover. Leave to soak for 30 minutes. Discard the stalks and cut the caps into thin strips.
2. Put the mushroom pieces in a bowl and add the root ginger, scallions (spring onions), a little salt, some pepper, fish sauce and the sesame oil. Stir well.
3. Put the chicken portions in a bowl which has been brushed with some sesame oil.
4. Spread the mushroom mixture over the chicken. Place the bowl in the top part of a steamer. Cover the pan with a lid and steam for 30-40 minutes.
5. Prepare the rice vermicelli as directed on the packet. Drain well.
6. Serve the chicken on a shallow dish and serve the rice vermicelli separately.

Canh ga bi dao

Chicken Soup with Pumpkin

00.10 Serves 4 | 02.20

American	Ingredients	Metric/Imperial
1¼ lb	*chicken bones*	575 g/1¼ lb
6	*chopped scallions (spring onions)*	6
	salt	
1 lb	*pumpkin*	450 g/1 lb
1 tbsp	*Vietnamese fish sauce (Nuoc mam)*	1 tbsp
	freshly ground pepper	

1. Bring 1¼ quarts (1.25 litres/2¼ pints) water to the boil.
2. Add the chicken bones, scallions (spring onions) and a little salt. Carefully skim the surface with a slotted spoon several times. Simmer for 2 hours with a lid on the pan.
3. Remove the skin from the piece of pumpkin and cut the flesh into ¾ in (1.75 cm) cubes.
4. Strain the bouillon (stock) through a piece of wet muslin. Bring the bouillon (stock) back to the boil.
5. Add any pieces of chicken meat (optional).
6. Stir in the pumpkin cubes, fish sauce and a little pepper. Simmer the soup for 2-3 minutes and serve in warmed bowls.

Cahn Cham

Fish Soup with Red Chilies and Vegetables

00.15 Serves 4 | 00.40

American	Ingredients	Metric/Imperial
2 tbsp	*groundnut oil*	2 tbsp
¾ lb	*fish bones and other fish trimmings*	350 g/12 oz
1	*large coarsely chopped onion*	1
1	*medium size leek cut into rings*	1
2	*crushed, dried red chilies*	2
	salt	
1	*head Chinese leaves or paksoi cut into thin strips*	1
1	*large carrot, cut into thin strips*	1
1 lb	*firm fish fillets*	450 g/1 lb
1 cup	*boiled rice*	125 g/4 oz
2	*fresh seeded red chilies cut into very thin strips*	2
3-4 tbsp	*Vietnamese fish sauce (Nuoc mam)*	3-4 tbsp

1. Heat the oil in a deep pan.
2. Rinse the fish bones and trimmings thoroughly under cold running water. Drain and add to the pan. Fry gently for 3 minutes, stirring continuously.
3. Add the onion, leek and the dried red chilies and stir well.
4. Add 2 quarts (2 litres/3½ pints) boiling water and bring to the boil. Carefully skim the surface several times, reduce the heat and simmer gently for 20 minutes. Strain the bouillon (stock) through a piece of muslin. Bring the bouillon (stock) to the boil again in a clean pan.
5. Add a little salt, the strips of Chinese leaves or paksoi and carrot strips and boil for 5 minutes.
6. Rinse the fish under cold running water and cut into thin strips. Add them to the bouillon (stock) and simmer for 3-4 minutes.
7. Add the rice, fresh red chilies and the fish sauce. Stir well and simmer for a further 3-4 minutes then serve the soup in warmed bowls.

Cahn bun tau
Fish Soup with Rice Vermicelli

	00.15 plus standing time		00.15	

American	Ingredients	Metric/Imperial
¾ lb	whiting fillets	350 g/12 oz
1 tbsp	finely grated fresh root ginger	1 tbsp
1 tsp	salt	1 tsp
	freshly ground pepper	
2 tbsp	Vietnamese fish sauce (Nuoc mam)	2 tbsp
2 oz	rice vermicelli (mihoen)	50 g/2 oz
2 tbsp	groundnut oil	2 tbsp
1	chopped large onion	1
2	finely chopped garlic cloves	2
1 tsp	ground turmeric	1 tsp
1 tsp	grated lemon or lime zest	1 tsp
3	chopped scallions (spring onions)	3

1. Rinse the fish under cold running water and dry with kitchen paper. Cut into ½ in (1.25 cm) cubes and place these in a bowl with the root ginger, a little salt, some pepper and the fish sauce. Stir and leave to stand for 15 minutes.
2. Prepare the rice vermicelli as directed on the packet. Drain well and cut into 3 in (8 cm) lengths.
3. Heat the oil in a wok and stir fry the onion until beginning to color.
4. Add the garlic and stir well. Sprinkle with the turmeric and add 1¼ quarts (1.25 litres/2¼ pints) boiling water. Stir thoroughly and bring to the boil.
5. Add the fish mixture then stir in the grated lemon or lime zest. Cook, stirring for 3 minutes.
6. Add the vermicelli and the scallions (spring onions) and serve in warmed bowls.

Cahn dau hu
Shrimp (Prawn) and Soybean Curd (Tofu) Soup

	00.10 Serves 4		00.20	

American	Ingredients	Metric/Imperial
2 quarts	fish bouillon (stock)	2 litres/3½ pints
1	small cake soybean curd (tofu)	1
6	large skinned tomatoes	6
1 cup	boiled rice	125 g/4 oz
3 tbsp	Vietnamese fish sauce (Nuoc mam)	3 tbsp
½ lb	fresh peeled shrimp (prawns)	225 g/8 oz
2 tbsp	finely chopped coriander leaves	2 tbsp

1. Bring the bouillon (stock) to the boil.
2. Cut the soybean curd (tofu) into thin strips.
3. Halve the tomatoes. Remove the seeds and the juice and cut the flesh into thin strips.

4. Add the soybean curd (tofu) and the tomato strips to the boiling bouillon (stock). Reduce the heat and simmer gently, stirring continuously, until the tomatoes and the most of the soybean curd (tofu) have disintegrated.
5. Add the rice and the fish sauce. Simmer gently for 3-4 minutes.
6. Stir in the shrimp (prawns) just before serving and allow the shrimp (prawns) to warm through. Do not allow the soup to boil.
7. Stir in the coriander leaves and serve.

Cahn tom vo vien
Fish Soup with Shrimp (Prawn) Balls

	00.15 Serves 4		00.35	

American	Ingredients	Metric/Imperial
¾ lb	fresh peeled shrimp (prawns)	350 g/12 oz
¼ lb	ground (minced) pork	125 g/4 oz
1	beaten egg	1
1½ tbsp	cornstarch (cornflour)	1½ tbsp
5 tbsp	Vietnamese fish sauce (Nuoc mam)	5 tbsp
	salt	
	pinch sugar	
3 tbsp	groundnut oil	3 tbsp
6	peeled garlic cloves	6
2 quarts	fish bouillon (stock)	2 litres/3½ pints
1 tbsp	lemon or lime juice	1 tbsp
1 tsp	sugar	1 tsp
1 cup	boiled rice	125 g/4 oz
6	very finely chopped scallions (spring onions)	6

1. Finely chop the shrimp (prawns). Mix in the ground (minced) pork, 2-3 tbsp beaten egg, cornstarch (cornflour), 1 tbsp fish sauce, a little salt and a pinch of sugar. Shape into small balls.
2. Heat the oil in a wok and quickly fry the balls a few at a time until golden brown all over. Drain on kitchen paper.
3. Bring the bouillon (stock) to the boil. Add the garlic cloves and simmer for 20 minutes. Remove the garlic.
4. Taste the bouillon (stock) and add some salt if necessary.
5. Stir in the lemon or lime juice, 1 tsp sugar and the remaining fish sauce.
6. Add the rice, bring to the boil and simmer gently for a few minutes.
7. Add the shrimp balls and scallions (spring onions) and cook, until the shrimp balls are warmed through.
8. Serve in warmed bowls.

Bo xao mang

Beef with Bamboo Shoots

	00.15	00.08
	Serves 4	

American	Ingredients	Metric/Imperial
1 lb	lean fillet or rump steak	450 g/1 lb
½ lb	canned, drained bamboo shoots	225 g/8 oz
4 tbsp	groundnut oil	4 tbsp
6	chopped scallions (spring onions)	6
1 tbsp	Vietnamese fish sauce (Nuoc mam)	1 tbsp
	salt	
1	finely chopped garlic clove	1
4 tbsp	lightly dry roasted sesame seeds	4 tbsp
1	skinned tomato	1

1. Dry the meat with kitchen paper and cut it into thin slices.
2. Cut the bamboo shoots into strips.
3. Heat the oil in a wok and fry the meat slices in the oil for no longer than 1 minute. Keep turning them over during frying. Remove the meat from the wok with a slotted spoon and keep warm.
4. Stir fry the bamboo shoots and the scallions (spring onions) for 2 minutes.
5. Add the fish sauce, 3 tbsp boiling water, a pinch of salt and the garlic. Boil steadily for a few seconds then add the meat slices. Stir well.
6. Stir in half the sesame seeds. Transfer to a warmed dish and sprinkle with the remaining sesame seeds. Garnish the dish with a tomato 'flower'.

Thit heo kho kho

Pork in Sweet Sauce

	00.10	00.15
	Serves 4	

American	Ingredients	Metric/Imperial
1 ¼ lb	lean pork	575 g/1 ¼ lb
2 tbsp	groundnut oil	2 tbsp
4	chopped scallions (spring onions)	4
	freshly ground pepper	
	salt	
1 tbsp	sugar	1 tbsp
3 tbsp	Vietnamese fish sauce (Nuoc mam)	3 tbsp
	celery or coriander leaves	

1. Dry the meat with kitchen paper and cut into ¾ in (1.75 cm) cubes.
2. Heat the oil in a wok and stir fry the meat cubes until brown on all sides.
3. Add the scallions (spring onions), some pepper, a little salt and the sugar. Stir well.
4. Stir in enough boiling water to just cover the meat.
5. Add the fish sauce, bring to the boil and simmer gently over moderate heat until all but about 5 tbsp of the liquid has evaporated. Serve in a warmed dish and garnish with celery or coriander leaves.

Cook's tip: as the taste of the fish sauce is quite strong in this sauce, the stated quantity of fish sauce may be reduced by half if preferred. The Vietnamese often stir a handful of washed bean sprouts into this dish just before serving.

Left to right: Beef with bamboo shoots
Pork in sweet sauce
Vietnamese sate

Nem nuong

Vietnamese Sate

	00.20 plus soaking time	00.10

American	Ingredients	Metric/Imperial
1 ¼ lb	slightly fatty pork	575 g/1 ¼ lb
2	crushed garlic cloves	2
½ tsp	salt	½ tsp
½ tsp	coarsely ground black pepper	½ tsp
½ tsp	soft brown sugar	½ tsp
2 tbsp	Vietnamese rice wine or dry sherry	2 tbsp
1 tbsp	groundnut oil	1 tbsp
¼ lb	rice vermicelli (mihoen)	125 g/4 oz
1	head lettuce	1
	few drops Vietnamese fish sauce (Nuoc mam)	
2 tbsp	finely chopped coriander leaves	2 tbsp

1. Dry the meat with kitchen paper and cut into ½ in (1.25 cm) cubes.
2. Mix together the garlic, salt, pepper, sugar, rice wine or sherry and oil. Stir until the salt and sugar dissolve.
3. Stir the meat into the sauce ensuring that it is completely covered. Leave to stand for at least 30 minutes.
4. Soak 16 bamboo skewers in cold water for 20 minutes.
5. Thread the meat cubes on to the skewers.
6. Prepare the rice vermicelli as directed on the packet, drain thoroughly. Put the rice vermicelli in a large bowl.
7. Clean the lettuce, wash the leaves and then dry them as well as possible. Place the lettuce leaves in a bowl.
8. Broil (grill) the sate for 8-12 minutes over the glowing charcoal of the barbecue or under a preheated hot broiler (grill). Turn the sticks regularly so that the meat is cooked evenly.
9. Serve the sate on a warmed platter, accompanied by bowls of rice vermicelli and lettuce leaves and individual bowls of fish sauce and chopped coriander or parsley.
Cook's tip: each guest should take a lettuce leaf, spoon a little rice vermicelli on top and then add one sate, a spoonful of fish sauce and sprinkle it with a little coriander or parsley. Then they should fold the lettuce leaf round and remove the stick from the sate and eat from the hand.

Dui heo kho noi dat

Braised Pork

	00.10 plus standing time	01.15

American	Ingredients	Metric/Imperial
1 ½ lb	pork, in one piece, preferably with a little fat	700 g/1 ½ lb
4	crushed garlic cloves	4
1 tsp	salt	1 tsp
½ tsp	coarsely ground black pepper	½ tsp
2 tbsp	Vietnamese fish sauce (Nuoc mam)	2 tbsp
2 tbsp	groundnut oil	2 tbsp

1. Dry the meat dry with kitchen paper. Cut a diamond pattern into the fat of the meat with the point of a sharp knife.
2. In a bowl, mix the garlic, salt, pepper and fish sauce. Keep stirring until the salt has dissolved. Rub this mixture into the meat. Leave to stand for 30 minutes.
3. Heat the oil in a wok and fry the meat until brown on all sides.
4. Place the meat in a close fitting pan and pour over enough boiling water to just cover. Cover the pan with a lid and simmer the meat for 1 hour. Add extra boiling water to keep the meat covered with liquid.
5. Remove the lid after 45 minutes and leave the meat to simmer gently until almost all of the liquid has evaporated.
6. Leave the meat to cool then slice thinly and arrange on a serving dish. Serve as part of a buffet.

MENU

Stuffed grapefruit
Boiled pork in coconut sauce
Fried chinese leaves and egg
Soybean curd (tofu) in syrup

Stuffed Grapefruit

00.15   00.00
Serves 4

American	Ingredients	Metric/Imperial
2	large grapefruit	2
2 oz	bean sprouts	50 g/2 oz
1 tbsp	lemon juice	1 tbsp
1 tsp	sugar	1 tsp
	salt	
1	small red chili	1
1	sprig parsley	1
2-3	blades fresh lemon grass	2-3
½ lb	fresh peeled shrimp (prawns)	225 g/8 oz

1. Halve the grapefruits and remove the segments between the membranes. Remove the pith from the skins.
2. Rinse the bean sprouts in plenty of cold water and remove as many seed cases as possible. Put the bean sprouts in a colander and pour over several quarts/litres of boiling water. Drain thoroughly and leave to cool.
3. Put the bean sprouts in a bowl and sprinkle with the lemon juice, sugar and a little salt. Stir well.
4. Divide the bean sprouts between the hollowed out grapefruits and top with the grapefruit segments.
5. Rinse, trim, halve and seed the red chili. Cut the flesh into small pieces.
6. Chop the sprig of parsley and the lemon grass very finely and stir into the chili pieces.
7. Stir the chili mixture into the shrimp (prawns) and fill the grapefruits to the top with the mixture.

Boiled Pork in Coconut Sauce

00.05   01.40
Serves 4

American	Ingredients	Metric/Imperial
1 lb	streaky pork in one piece	450 g/1 lb
¾ cup	thin coconut milk	200 ml/7 fl oz
	salt	
4 tbsp	Vietnamese fish sauce (Nuoc mam)	4 tbsp
4 tbsp	sugar	4 tbsp
	freshly ground pepper	
1 tbsp	finely chopped coriander leaves or parsley	1 tbsp

1. Put the pork in a pan with enough boiling water to just cover. Bring to the boil. Carefully skim the surface several times.
2. Add the coconut milk, a little salt, the fish sauce and sugar. Cover the pan with a lid and simmer gently over low heat for 1½ hours. Remove the pork from the pan and keep warm.
3. Simmer the liquid in the pan until all but ¾ cup (200 ml/ 7 fl oz) has evaporated and add a little pepper to taste.
4. Slice the meat and arrange it on a warmed serving dish. Pour the sauce over and sprinkle with coriander or parsley.
5. Serve a dish of dry boiled rice or boiled noodles fried in a little oil separately.

Fried Chinese Leaves and Egg

■▭◹ 00.08   00.10 🍲
Serves 4

American	Ingredients	Metric/Imperial
1	small head Chinese leaves or paksoi	1
1	egg	1
1 tsp	Vietnamese fish sauce (Nuoc mam)	1 tsp
2 tbsp	groundnut oil	2 tbsp
1	garlic clove	1
	salt	
	freshly ground pepper	

1. Wash the Chinese leaves or paksoi thoroughly, drain well, dry as far as possible and shred the leaves finely.
2. Lightly beat the egg and stir in the fish sauce.
3. Heat the oil in a wok and fry the garlic clove until beginning to color. Remove the garlic from the wok.
4. Add the Chinese leaves or paksoi and stir fry for 3 minutes.
5. Make a well in the center of the shredded Chinese leaves or paksoi and pour in the egg mixture. Sprinkle with a little salt and pepper, and stir the leaves into the egg starting in the center.
6. Serve immediately on a warmed dish.

Soybean Curd (Tofu) in Syrup

■▭◹ 00.05   00.15 🍲
Serves 4

American	Ingredients	Metric/Imperial
1 (½ lb)	cake soybean curd (tofu)	1 (225 g/ 8 oz)
½ cup	soft brown sugar	115 g/4 oz
1 tsp	finely grated fresh root ginger	1 tsp
2 tbsp	sesame oil	2 tbsp
1	squeezed lime	1

1. Cut the soybean curd (tofu) into ½ in (1.25 cm) cubes.
2. Bring ⅔ cup (150 ml/¼ pint) water to the boil in a small saucepan. Add the sugar and stir until it dissolves.
3. Add the root ginger and simmer very gently for 10 minutes.
4. Heat the oil in a wok and stir fry the cubes of soybean curd (tofu) for 3 minutes. Drain well and transfer to a deep warmed dish.
5. Stir the lime juice through the sugar syrup and immediately pour the mixture over the soybean curd (tofu) cubes.
6. Serve the dish as hot as possible with fresh peaches or apricots.

KOREA

Song i bahb
Rice with Mushrooms

	00.15	00.30
	Serves 4	

American	Ingredients	Metric/Imperial
½ lb	wiped, trimmed mushrooms	225 g/8 oz
½ lb	lean beef	225 g/8 oz
2 tbsp	groundnut oil or lard	2 tbsp
2	chopped onions	2
1 cup	long grain rice	225 g/8 oz
	salt	
	freshly ground pepper	
2 tbsp	Chinese light soy sauce	2 tbsp
2 tbsp	lightly roasted sesame seeds	2 tbsp

1. Slice the mushrooms and cut into thin strips.
2. Dry the meat with kitchen paper. Cut into ¼ in (5 mm) slices and then into strips.
3. Heat the oil or lard in a deep pan. Stir fry the onions, mushrooms and meat for 3 minutes.
4. Add the rice and stir continuously for 2 minutes. Add 2 cups (500 ml/16 fl oz) boiling water, a little salt, freshly ground pepper and the soy sauce. Stir several times. Bring to the boil then reduce the heat. Cover the pan with a lid and simmer for 20 minutes. Remove the lid just before serving. Stir with a fork and transfer into a warmed dish.
5. Sprinkle with sesame seeds and serve.

Bokum bahb
Fried Rice with Chicken and Mushrooms

	00.10	00.10
	plus soaking time	

American	Ingredients	Metric/Imperial
6	large dried Chinese mushrooms	6
4 tbsp	groundnut oil	4 tbsp
1	chopped onion	1
1 tbsp	finely chopped celery	1 tbsp
¾ lb	roast chicken cut into small pieces	350 g/12 oz
2 cups	boiled long grain rice	225 g/8 oz
2	chopped scallions (spring onions)	2
1 tbsp	Chinese light soy sauce	1 tbsp
	salt	
2 tsp	sesame oil	2 tsp
	piece of cucumber (optional)	
2	gherkins (optional)	2

1. Put the mushrooms in a bowl with boiling water to cover. Soak for 20 minutes. Discard the stalks. Squeeze the mushroom caps thoroughly and cut into thin strips.
2. Heat the oil in a wok and stir fry the onion and mushrooms for 2 minutes.
3. Add the celery and chicken pieces. Stir several times.
4. Add the rice gradually, continuing to stir.
5. Stir in the scallions (spring onions), and stir until all the ingredients are heated through. Sprinkle with soy sauce, add salt and sesame oil to taste and stir.

6. Transfer to a warmed dish and serve garnished with cucumber and gherkin fans.

Tomi gun
Fried Fish with Sesame Seeds

	00.15	00.10
	Serves 4	

American	Ingredients	Metric/Imperial
1 ½ lb	mackerel or whiting fillets	675 g/1 ½ lb
	salt	
	freshly ground pepper	
3 tbsp	flour	3 tbsp
1 tbsp	cornstarch (cornflour)	1 tbsp
2	eggs	2
	oil for frying	
12	lettuce leaves	12
1	onion, cut into rings	1
½	cucumber, cut into oblique slices	½
2 tbsp	lightly roasted sesame seeds	2 tbsp

1. Rinse the fish under cold running water. Dry with kitchen paper and divide into 12 equal pieces.
2. Rub the fish pieces with salt and pepper.
3. Mix the flour and cornstarch (cornflour) in a bowl. Add the eggs, stir well into a smooth batter.
4. Dip the fish pieces into the batter and fry 3 at a time until golden brown. Drain on kitchen paper.
5. Place the lettuce leaves on a cold dish. Put a few onion rings and pieces of cucumber on each lettuce leaf. Sprinkle with a little salt and pepper. Place the fish pieces on top and sprinkle with some roasted sesame seeds.

John saengsun
Fried Fish in Light Sour Soy Sauce

	00.15	00.10
	plus standing time	

American	Ingredients	Metric/Imperial
1 ½ lb	white fish fillets	675 g/1 ½ lb
2 tbsp	lemon or lime juice	2 tbsp
	salt	
	freshly ground pepper	
4 tbsp	sifted flour	4 tbsp
	groundnut oil	
2	beaten eggs	2
2 tbsp	sugar	2 tbsp
1 ½ cups	white vinegar	350 ml/12 fl oz
4 ½ tbsp	Chinese light soy sauce	4 ½ tbsp
2 tsp	ground ginger	2 tsp
1 tbsp	finely chopped pine kernels	1 tbsp
4	scallions (spring onions) or green shallots (optional)	4

1. Rinse the fish under cold running water and dry on kitchen paper. Cut it into 8-12 equal pieces.

2. Rub the lemon or lime juice over the fish on all sides and leave to stand for 10 minutes. Dry them again on kitchen paper. Rub the pieces with equal parts of salt and freshly ground pepper.

3. Roll them in the flour and shake off any excess.

4. Heat the oil until very hot.

5. Just before frying dip the fish pieces into the beaten egg. Drain, then slide them into the hot oil, 4-5 pieces at a time. Fry for about 5 minutes until all fish pieces are golden brown all over.

6. Bring 2 tbsp water to the boil. Dissolve the sugar in the boiling water and add the vinegar. Stir well.

7. Remove the pan from the heat and add the remaining ingredients. Stir the sauce vigorously. Spoon the lukewarm sauce on to warmed plates and place the pieces of fish in the center.

8. Garnish with long thin strips of scallions (spring onions) or green shallots and serve.

Gun saengsun
Broiled (Grilled) Fish

00. 10 00. 15
Serves 4

American	Ingredients	Metric/Imperial
4	small, cleaned mackerel	4
3 tbsp	Chinese light soy sauce	3 tbsp
2 tbsp	sesame oil	2 tbsp
1 tbsp	finely chopped fresh root ginger	1 tbsp
1	crushed garlic clove	1
	red chilies (optional)	

1. Rinse the fish thoroughly under cold running water. Dry inside and out, with kitchen paper.

2. In a bowl mix the soy sauce, sesame oil, root ginger and garlic. Brush the fish inside and out with the sauce. Place the fish on a greased rack, under a very hot broiler (grill)

or over the glowing charcoal in the barbecue. Broil (grill) the fish for 6-7 minutes each side until golden brown and tender. Baste regularly with the remaining sauce.

3. Serve the fish on a warmed dish garnished with red chili flowers.

Bokum bahb
Fried Rice with Shrimp (Prawns) and Pork

00. 15   00. 15
Serves 4

American	Ingredients	Metric/Imperial
4 tbsp	groundnut oil	4 tbsp
2	coarsely chopped onions	2
½ lb	coarsely shredded roast pork	225 g/8 oz
½	trimmed green bell pepper cut into small pieces	½
2 cups	boiled long grain rice	225 g/8 oz
½ lb	freshly peeled shrimp (prawns)	225 g/8 oz
1 tbsp	Chinese light soy sauce	1 tbsp
	salt	
2 tsp	sesame oil	2 tsp
3-4	young carrots, cut into very thin strips	3-4

1. Heat the oil in a wok, add the onions and stir fry until transparent.

2. Add the pork and bell pepper and stir fry for 2 minutes.

3. Gradually add the rice, stirring continuously.

4. Add the shrimp (prawns) stirring, until everything is heated thoroughly.

5. Sprinkle with soy sauce and a little salt to taste.

6. Add the sesame oil and stir well.

7. Transfer to a warmed dish, garnish with thin carrot strips and serve.

Broiled (grilled) fish

Bokum bahb

Fried Rice with Crab and Pork

	00.10	00.10
	Serves 4	

American	Ingredients	Metric/Imperial
4 tsp	groundnut oil	4 tsp
1	skinned garlic clove	1
1 tsp	finely grated fresh root ginger	1 tsp
¼ lb	crabmeat, thawed if frozen cut into pieces	125 g/4 oz
½ lb	coarsely shredded roast pork	225 g/½ lb
2 cups	boiled long grain rice	225 g/8 oz
2 tbsp	shredded leek or scallion (spring onion)	2 tbsp
	salt	
1 tbsp	Chinese light soy sauce	1 tbsp
2 tsp	sesame oil	2 tsp
	few celery leaves (optional)	
2	skinned tomatoes (optional)	2
1	piece cucumber (optional)	1

1. Heat the groundnut oil in a wok. Stir fry the garlic until golden brown. Remove from the wok
2. Add the root ginger, crabmeat and pork. Stir thoroughly.
3. Add the rice and leek or scallions (spring onions) gradually, stirring until everything is thoroughly heated.
4. Add salt to taste and sprinkle with soy sauce.
5. Stir in the sesame oil and transfer to a warmed serving dish.
6. Garnish with celery leaves, tomato flowers, or with cucumber fans.

Tuigim saengsun

Fried Fish

	00.15	00.15
	plus standing time	

American	Ingredients	Metric/Imperial
1½ lb	white fish fillets	675 g/1½ lb
2 tbsp	Chinese light soy sauce	2 tbsp
	salt	
	freshly ground pepper	
2	chopped scallions (spring onions)	2
4 tbsp	groundnut oil	4 tbsp
2	large, skinned tomatoes	2
12	lettuce leaves	12
1	onion, cut into rings	1

1. Rinse the fish under cold running water. Dry with kitchen paper and cut into 12 equal pieces.
2. In a bowl, mix the soy sauce with a little salt and pepper and the scallions (spring onions). Add the fish pieces and stir until all the fish is coated in a thin layer of marinade. Leave to stand for at least 15 minutes. Dry the fish on kitchen paper.
3. Heat the oil in a wok and fry all the fish pieces until golden brown all over.
4. Cut each tomato into 6 slices. Place the lettuce leaves on a cold dish. Put some onion rings and tomato slices on each leaf. Sprinkle with salt and pepper and place the fried fish on top. Serve immediately.

Cook's tip: The Koreans nearly always serve small individual bowls with Chinese tomato sauce and Chinese light soy sauce.

Left: Fried rice with crab and pork
Right: Fried rice with shrimp (prawns) and pork

Fried chicken with mushrooms

Chai-yuk san-cha
Vegetable Salad with Pork

▬▷ 00.15   00.00 ⊟
Serves 4

American	Ingredients	Metric/Imperial
½ lb	cooked pork, cut into thin strips	225 g/8 oz
2	sticks celery, cut into thin strips	2
2	carrots, cut into thin strips	2
2 tbsp	cooked peas	2 tbsp
1	ripe eating pear, cut into thin strips	1
1	slightly sour apple, cut into thin strips	1
1 tbsp	Chinese light soy sauce	1 tbsp
1 tsp	finely grated fresh root ginger	1 tsp
1	garlic clove	1
1	chopped scallion (spring onion)	1
1 tbsp	vinegar	1 tbsp
1 tsp	sugar	1 tsp
1 tsp	sesame oil	1 tsp

1. Mix the pork, celery, carrots, peas, pear and apple together in a bowl.
2. Make the sauce by mixing together the soy sauce, root ginger, garlic, scallion (spring onion) vinegar, sugar and sesame oil in a second bowl, stirring until the sugar has dissolved.
3. Carefully pour the sauce over the salad. Do not toss the salad but try to distribute the sauce evenly.
4. Serve on small plates.

Dak Busut jim
Fried Chicken with Mushrooms

▬▷ 00.15   00.25 ⊟
Serves 4

American	Ingredients	Metric/Imperial
1 ½ lb	boneless chicken cut into 1 in (2.5 cm) cubes	675 g/1 ½ lb
	salt	
2 tbsp	Chinese light soy sauce	2 tbsp
1 tbsp	sesame oil	1 tbsp
1 tbsp	red chili oil	1 tbsp
2 tbsp	groundnut oil	2 tbsp
1	cleaned onion cut into 8 segments	1
1 lb	wiped button mushrooms	450 g/1 lb
4	coarsely chopped scallions (spring onions) or a piece of leek	4
1-2 tbsp	lightly roasted sesame seeds (optional)	1-2 tbsp

1. Dry the chicken pieces with kitchen paper and rub the pieces with a little salt.
2. In a bowl, stir together the soy sauce, sesame oil and red chili oil.
3. Put the chicken pieces in the bowl with the marinade and stir until each piece is coated with the marinade. Leave to stand for 30 minutes, then stir again.
4. Heat the groundnut oil in a wok. Stir fry the onion until transparent. Add the chicken pieces and fry them, stirring continuously until golden brown.
5. Add the mushrooms and the scallions (spring onions) or leek. Stir well and add ¾ cup (200 ml/7 fl oz) boiling water. Simmer until almost all the liquid has evaporated.
6. Serve in a warmed dish, sprinkled with 1-2 tbsp sesame seeds.

Tak pok-kum
Braised Chicken with Mushrooms

	00.15	00.25
	Serves 4	

American	Ingredients	Metric/Imperial
1	small roasting chicken	1
½ lb	wiped, trimmed, sliced mushrooms	225 g/8 oz
4½ tbsp	Chinese light soy sauce	4½ tbsp
4	chopped scallions (spring onions) green shallots or a thin leek	4
3	crushed garlic cloves	3
2 tbsp	sugar	2 tbsp
	salt	
	freshly ground pepper	
2 tsp	sesame oil (optional)	2 tsp
	chopped green chilies (optional)	

1. Divide the chicken into 8 pieces. Then cut each piece into 1 in (2.5 cm) cubes. Put them into a pan with boiling, salted water to cover. Bring to the boil, skim the surface, several times. Reduce the heat and simmer for 10 minutes.
2. Bring the soy sauce to the boil in a pan, with the scallions (spring onions), green shallots or leek and the garlic, sugar and a little freshly ground pepper, stirring continuously.
3. Add the cubes of cooked chicken and the mushroom slices. Stir well. Strain the cooking liquid from the chicken through a piece of wet muslin and add enough of this to the chicken cubes to just cover them. Bring to the boil and simmer until just over half the liquid has evaporated and the chicken cubes are tender.
4. Stir in the sesame oil and transfer to a warmed dish.
5. Serve garnished with chopped green chilies.

Cook's tip: Serve boiled rice separately with chopped vegetables (scallions (spring onions), carrots and/or beans) added just before serving. Use 2 tbsp chopped vegetables per head.

Tak jim
Chicken with Vegetables

	00.15	00.20
	plus soaking time	

American	Ingredients	Metric/Imperial
6	large dried Chinese mushrooms	6
12	gingko nuts	12
1½ lb	boneless chicken cut into 1 in (2 cm) cubes	675 g/1½ lb
1 tbsp	Chinese light soy sauce	1 tbsp
1 tsp	ground red pepper	1 tsp
	salt	
3-4	washed celery sticks cut into thin strips	3-4
6	finely chopped scallions (spring onions)	6
1 tsp	sesame oil	1 tsp

1. Put the mushrooms in a bowl with boiling water to cover. Leave to soak for 30 minutes.
2. Broil (grill) the gingko nuts under a hot broiler (grill) until the skins peel off easily. Crush the nuts with a pestle and mortar or in a coffee mill.
3. Discard the stalks from the soaked mushrooms. Cut the caps into thin strips. Strain the soaking liquid through a piece of wet muslin.
4. Dry the chicken pieces with kitchen paper. Place in a saucepan.
5. Add the soy sauce, red pepper a little salt and ⅔ cup (150 ml/¼ pint) boiling water. Bring quickly to the boil. Reduce the heat and cover the pan with a lid and simmer for 10 minutes.
6. Add the mushrooms, crushed gingko nuts, celery and scallions (spring onions).
7. Add a further ⅔ cup (150 ml/¼ pint) boiling water, stir well. Cover and simmer for 10 minutes.
8. Stir in the sesame oil and serve immediately.

Cook's tip: in Korea this dish is sprinkled with thin strips of green chilies just before serving. As a garnish you can use green chilies in the shape of flowers.

Cogi busut bokum
Beef with Mushrooms

	00.10	00.15
	plus standing time	

American	Ingredients	Metric/Imperial
1 lb	fillet of beef	450 g/1 lb
1	garlic clove	1
1 tsp	finely grated root ginger	1 tsp
2 tsp	Chinese light soy sauce	2 tsp
1 tsp	sesame oil	1 tsp
	salt	
2 tbsp	groundnut oil or sunflower oil	2 tbsp
½ lb	wiped, trimmed, sliced mushrooms	225 g/8 oz
¾ cup	beef bouillon (stock)	200 ml/7 fl oz
2 tsp	cornstarch (cornflour)	2 tsp
1 tsp	finely chopped celery	1 tsp
2	skinned tomatoes cut into thin strips	2

1. Dry the meat with kitchen paper and cut into ¼ in (5 mm) slices and then into strips.
2. In a small bowl, mix the garlic, root ginger, soy sauce and sesame oil. Add the meat strips. Sprinkle with a little salt and stir well. Leave to stand for at least 15 minutes.
3. Heat the oil in a wok and add all the meat at the same time. Stir-fry for 2 minutes.
4. Add the mushrooms and stir well.
5. Add the bouillon (stock) as soon as the mushrooms have gained color. Stir well and simmer briefly.
6. Mix the cornstarch (cornflour) with 2 tbsp cold water. Push all the ingredients in the wok to one side.
7. Stir the cornstarch (cornflour) mixture into the liquid in the wok. Cook, stirring until the sauce has thickened slightly.
8. Stir in the celery and then push the ingredients back to the center of the wok. Stir well again.
9. Transfer to a warmed dish and top with the tomato strips.

Gogi bokum
Fried Beef

00.15 plus standing time | **00.25**

American	Ingredients	Metric/Imperial
1 lb	fillet of beef	450 g/1 lb
1 tbsp	sesame oil	1 tbsp
	salt	
	freshly ground pepper	
2	chopped scallions (spring onions) or piece of leek	2
1	finely chopped garlic clove	1
½ tsp	sugar	½ tsp
1 tbsp	Chinese light soy sauce	1 tbsp
5 tbsp	groundnut oil or sunflower oil	5 tbsp
16-20	lettuce leaves	16-20

1. Dry the meat with kitchen paper. Cut it into ⅛ in (3 mm) slices.
2. Brush a flat dish with sesame oil. Sprinkle with salt and pepper. Place the meat slices, overlapping on to the dish.
3. Put the remaining sesame oil into a small bowl. Add the scallions (spring onions) or leek, sugar and soy sauce. Stir until the sugar has dissolved. Coat the meat slices with this mixture. Leave to stand for 4 hours at room temperature.
4. Heat the oil in a wok and stir fry the garlic until golden brown and then remove it.
5. Fry the meat, 6-8 meat slices at a time, for 2 minutes each side until brown on both sides.
6. Place the lettuce leaves on a cold dish. Place a slice of meat on to each lettuce leaf and serve immediately.

Cook's tip: serve boiled rice separately with a sauce prepared by mixing equal parts of dry sherry or Chinese rice wine, with Chinese light soy sauce and Chinese barbecue sauce with sugar to taste.

Yukkar jang kuk
Braised Beef

00.10 Serves 4 | **02.00**

American	Ingredients	Metric/Imperial
1½ lb	lean braising beef	675 g/1½ lb
	salt	
	freshly ground pepper	
½ cup	rice vermicelli (mihoen)	125 g/4 oz
1 lb	scallions (spring onions) cut into 1 in (2.5 cm) strips	450 g/1 lb
1 tsp	sugar	1 tsp
1 tsp	red chili oil	1 tsp
2 tbsp	groundnut oil or sunflower oil	2 tbsp
2	beaten eggs	2

1. Put the meat in a large saucepan with boiling water to cover. Add a little salt and pepper. Bring to the boil. Skim the surface several times. Reduce the heat, cover and simmer for 1½ hours. Allow to cool then shred the cold meat finely. Leave the meat in the braising liquid.
2. Prepare the vermicelli as directed on the packet. Rinse the vermicelli under cold running water and drain.
3. Reheat the meat. Add the scallions (spring onions), sugar and chili oil to the shredded meat and the braising liquid. Stir well until the sugar has dissolved and the mixture is heated through.
4. Heat the oil in a wok and stir fry the vermicelli, until it is hot and has gained some color. Stir the vermicelli into the meat mixture.
5. Pour the eggs over the mixture. Stir lightly then remove the pan from the heat.
6. Serve immediately.

Braised beef

Bulgogi
Korean Barbecue

◢ 00.10
plus standing time

00.05 🍲

American	Ingredients	Metric/Imperial
1¼ lb	entrecôte beef	550 g/1¼ lb
2 tbsp	Chinese dark soy sauce	2 tbsp
2 tbsp	Chinese light soy sauce	2 tbsp
1	very finely chopped scallion (spring onion)	1
2	crushed garlic cloves	2
1 tsp	freshly grated root ginger	1 tsp
	freshly ground pepper	
1 tsp	sesame oil	1 tsp
	celery leaves (optional)	
2 tsp	groundnut oil or sunflower oil	2 tsp

1. Dry the meat with kitchen paper. Cut into ¼ in (5 mm) slices and then into 2×1 in (5×2.5 cm) slices.
2. Mix together the soy sauces, scallion (spring onion), garlic, root ginger, pepper and sesame oil.
3. Stir the meat into the mixture and leave to stand for 15 minutes. Place the marinaded meat slices on to a dish. Add some celery leaves if liked.
4. Brush a griddle with groundnut oil. Heat the griddle and fry the meat for 1 minute on each side.
5. Transfer to a warmed dish and serve immediately.

Cook's tip: serve boiled rice, sesame sauce, cucumber salad and bean sprout salad separately.

Oyi namulh
Cucumber Salad

◢ 00.10
plus standing time

00.00 🍲

American	Ingredients	Metric/Imperial
2	cucumbers	2
2 tsp	salt	2 tsp
2 tbsp	herb vinegar	2 tbsp
2 tsp	sugar	2 tsp
1 tbsp	red chili oil	1 tbsp
1	crushed garlic clove	1
2	very finely chopped scallions (spring onions)	2

1. Rinse the cucumbers under cold running water. Remove the ends and grate the cucumbers as coarsely as possible over a bowl.
2. Add 4½ tbsp cold water and the salt. Stir well. Leave to stand for 30 minutes. Transfer the cucumber into a strainer and chill.
3. In a bowl, mix the herb vinegar, sugar, red chili oil, garlic and scallions (spring onions). Just before serving add this mixture to the well drained, ice cold cucumber.
4. Serve the salad in individual bowls.

Cook's tip: sesame seed sauce can be varied by adding 1 tbsp of ginger syrup to the sauce.

Kong namulh
Bean Sprout Salad

◢ 00.10
Serves 4

00.00 🍲

American	Ingredients	Metric/Imperial
4 oz	bean sprouts	125 g/4 oz
2 tbsp	herb vinegar	2 tbsp
1 tsp	sugar	1 tsp
1 tsp	red chili oil	1 tsp
2 tsp	Chinese light soy sauce	2 tsp

1. Wash the bean sprouts in plenty of water. Remove as many seed cases as possible. Drain in a colander then slowly pour a few pints/litres of boiling water over the bean sprouts. Drain the bean sprouts well. Place the colander in a draughty place to dry the bean sprouts quickly or roll them over a cloth or a piece of kitchen paper to dry.
2. Mix the herb vinegar with the sugar, red chili oil and soy sauce, stirring until the sugar has dissolved. Add the bean sprouts and stir well.
3. Arrange the salad in individual bowls and serve.

Cho kanjang
Sesame Seed Sauce

◢ 00.00
Serves 4

00.05 🍲

American	Ingredients	Metric/Imperial
3 oz	sesame seeds	75 g/3 oz
1½ tbsp	sugar	1½ tbsp
3 tbsp	lemon juice or herb vinegar	3 tbsp
3 tbsp	Chinese light soy sauce	3 tbsp
1-2	garlic cloves	1-2
2	very finely chopped scallions (spring onions)	2

1. Roast the sesame seed for 3-4 minutes in a dry frying pan. Allow the seeds to cool on a large cold plate and then crush them.
2. Add all the other ingredients and stir until the sugar has dissolved. Serve the sauce in individual bowls.

Nabuk kimgi
Salted Giant Radish

◢ 00.10
makes 1 large jar

00.10 🍲

American	Ingredients	Metric/Imperial
2¼ lb	giant radish (Daikon)	1 kg/2¼ lb
1	chopped onion	1
6	crushed garlic cloves	6
1 tsp	finely grated fresh root ginger	1 tsp
2 tsp	ground chili	2 tsp
3 tbsp	salt	3 tbsp

1. Peel the giant radishes and cut into ¼ in (5 mm) slices, then strips and then into tiny cubes.
2. Place the radish in a pan and add all remaining ingredients. Stir well.

Left to right: Thin pancakes, Korean firepot, Salted giant radish

3. Add 4½ tbsp boiling water and bring to boiling point. Remove the pan from the heat. Transfer into a carefully cleaned storage jar.

4. Seal, label and store the jar in a cool, dry, dark place for at least 2 weeks when they will be fairly sharp.

Cook's tip: in Korea they would be left for at least 2-3 months.

Shin sullro

Korean Fire Pot

	00.15	00.08
	Serves 4	

American	Ingredients	Metric/Imperial
1 lb	beef fillet	450 g/1 lb
1 lb	calf or lamb's liver	450 g/1 lb
½ lb	chicken breast fillet	225 g/8 oz
½ lb	lean, ground (minced) beef	225 g/8 oz
1	small chopped onion	1
	garlic clove	1
1	beaten egg	1
1 tsp	salt	1 tsp
	freshly ground pepper	
1 tsp	Chinese light soy sauce	1 tsp
6	scallions (spring onions) cut into thin strips	6
¼ lb	wiped, sliced mushrooms	125 g/4 oz
1 cup	shelled, skinned hazelnuts or ginko nuts	125 g/4 oz
1 oz	pine kernels	25 g/1 oz
9 cups	skimmed beef bouillon (stock)	2 litres/3 ½ pints

1. Dry the beef and the liver with kitchen paper and cut both into ⅛ in (3 mm) slices.

2. Cut the chicken into finger width strips, 2 in (5 cm) long.

3. Mix the ground (minced) beef with the onion, garlic, beaten egg, a little salt and pepper and the soy suace
Shape the mixture into balls about the size of a walnut.

4. Line a pot with the beef, liver and chicken, keeping the meats separate. Place the mince balls on to the bottom of the pot.

5. Sprinkle the scallions (spring onions), celery, carrots, mushrooms, nuts and pine kernels over the meats.

7. Pour the hot bouillon (stock) over just before serving and if possible cook at table for 7-8 minutes.

Cook's tip: the guests should serve themselves, by choosing the ingredient from the pot and serving it with chopsticks or a small serving spoon.

Bindae duk

Thin Korean Pancakes

	00.01	00.30
	plus soaking time	

American	Ingredients	Metric/Imperial
½ cup	chick-peas	125 g/4 oz
2 tbsp	cornstarch (cornflour)	2 tbsp
2	beaten eggs	2
¼ lb	ground (minced) pork	125 g/4 oz
1	chopped onion	1
1	crushed garlic clove	1
	salt	
	freshly ground pepper	
	few shredded cabbage leaves	
1 oz	washed, finely chopped bean sprouts	25 g/1 oz
3 tbsp	groundnut oil or sunflower oil	3 tbsp

1. Soak the chick-peas for 6-8 hours in plenty of cold water and drain.

2. Put the chick-peas and cornstarch (cornflour) with 6 tbsp cold water in a food processor and purée.

3. Add the eggs, ground (minced) pork, onion, garlic and salt and pepper. Process for 30 seconds, then remove.

4. Stir the shredded cabbage leaves and bean sprouts into the paste.

5. Heat 1 tbsp of oil in a frying pan and fry 3 pancakes over moderate heat for 4 minutes each side until golden brown. Heat the remaining oil and repeat until all the batter is used.

Baichu saing kim gi
Pickled Chinese Leaves

00.10 plus standing time   **00.00**

American	Ingredients	Metric/Imperial
1	large head Chinese leaves washed, cut into thin strips	1
1 tbsp	salt	1 tbsp
4 oz	very finely chopped raw oysters or mussels	125 g/4 oz
1	peeled, coarsely grated green apple	1
4 oz	washed, chopped watercress	125 g/4 oz
1 tbsp	red chili oil	1 tbsp
1 tbsp	finely grated fresh root ginger	1 tbsp
1 tbsp	sesame oil	1 tbsp
2 tbsp	Chinese light soy suace	2 tbsp
2 tbsp	herb vinegar	2 tbsp
1 tbsp	sugar	1 tbsp

1. Put the Chinese leaves into a large bowl and sprinkle with salt. Add all the other ingredients and stir well. Leave to stand for 3 hours. Drain the leaves thoroughly. Stir well.
2. Transfer into a carefully cleaned jar. Press down firmly.
3. Seal, label and store the jar in a refrigerator for 3-4 days. The pickle will not keep for more than 1 week.

Put kim gi
Salted Green Vegetables

00.10 plus standing time   **00.00**

American	Ingredients	Metric/Imperial
2¼ lb	spinach or endive	1 kg/2¼ lb
3 tbsp	salt	3 tbsp
2	coarsely chopped onions	2
6	garlic cloves	6
1 tsp	finely grated root ginger	1 tsp
2 tbsp	finely grated red bell pepper	2 tbsp
2 tbsp	sugar	2 tbsp

1. Wash the spinach or endive carefully. Remove stalks and hard membranes. Dry thoroughly in a salad spinner and cut into thin strips. Sprinkle with salt and stir well.
2. Add the onions, garlic cloves root ginger and bell pepper. Leave to stand for 6 hours, stirring carefully every hour. Rinse and drain the vegetables very thoroughly.
3. Add 4½ tbsp boiling water and the sugar and stir well. Transfer into a large carefully cleaned jar.
4. Seal, label and store in the refrigerator for 3-4 days. The pickle cannot be kept for longer than 1 week.

Cook's tip: Korean pickles do not keep for very long. Although the flavor of home-made is preferable to store-bought, unless a great deal of Korean cooking is planned, perhaps for a party, the pickles available from stores stocking far Eastern ingredients (see glossary) will do perfectly well.

MENU

Cold cucumber soup
Stuffed eggplant (aubergine)
Rice pudding with red beans

Cold Cucumber Soup

00.20 plus chilling time   **00.05**

American	Ingredients	Metric/Imperial
2	medium size cucumbers	2
2 tsp	salt	2 tsp
2 tbsp	Chinese light soy sauce	2 tbsp
1 tbsp	white vinegar	1 tbsp
1 tbsp	sugar	1 tbsp
1 tsp	red pepper oil	1 tsp
4	finely chopped scallions (spring onions) or shallots	4
3 tbsp	white sesame seeds	3 tbsp
3¼ cups	skimmed, ice cold chicken bouillon (stock)	750 ml/1¼ pints
1 tsp	sesame oil	1 tsp

1. Clean and trim the cucumbers. Halve lengthwise and seed. Grate the cucumber coarsely. Sprinkle with 1 tsp salt, stir well and leave to drain in a strainer (sieve) for 15-20 minutes.
2. In a bowl, mix together the soy sauce, vinegar, sugar, red pepper oil and scallions (spring onions) or shallots. Stir until the salt and sugar have dissolved.
3. Stir in the cucumber, cover and chill for 1 hour.
4. Heat a dry frying pan and roast the sesame seeds until they begin to change color. Spread them on a large cold plate and leave to go cold. Pour the seeds on to a piece of kitchen paper, cover with another pieces and crush them by rolling them with a rolling pin.
5. Add the chicken bouillon (stock), sesame oil and sesame seeds to the cucumber mixture. Stir well.
6. Serve the soup immediately in individual bowls.

5. In a steamer, bring some water to the boil. Brush the perforated part of the steamer with oil to coat. Place the stuffed eggplants (aubergines) on this part and set it on the steamer. Cover and steam for 10 minutes.
6. Serve immediately on a warmed dish.

Cook's tip: serve accompanied by noodles which have been first boiled and then fried in a little oil and mixed with a little finely grated white radish.

Stuffed Eggplant (Aubergine)

	00.06	00.20
	plus standing time	

American	Ingredients	Metric/Imperial
4	small eggplants (aubergines)	4
	salt	
2 tbsp	groundnut oil	2 tbsp
1	large chopped onion	1
1	finely crushed garlic clove	1
1 lb	lean ground (minced) beef	450 g/1 lb
2 tbsp	Chinese dark soy sauce	2 tbsp
	freshly ground black pepper	
2 tsp	sugar	2 tsp
2 tbsp	cornstarch (cornflour)	2 tbsp
2 tbsp	Chinese light soy sauce	2 tbsp

1. Clean and trim the eggplants (aubergines). Halve lengthwise, scoop the flesh out of the skins and chop it finely and sprinkle with a little salt, stir well and drain for 15 minutes. Sprinkle the scooped out skins with salt, and turn them upside down. Leave for 15 minutes.
2. Heat the oil in a wok and fry the onion until transparent.
3. Add the garlic, stir and add the beef, stirring constantly until the beef crumbles. Add the dark soy sauce, a little salt, freshly ground black pepper and sugar. Stir well and add 4 tbsp boiling water. Simmer for 3 minutes.
4. Mix the cornstarch (cornflour) with the light soy sauce and 2 tbsp cold water. Stir vigorously into the meat mixture, then mix in the finely chopped eggplant (aubergine) flesh. Remove the wok from the heat and fill the eggplant (aubergine) skins with the meat mixture.

Rice Pudding with Red Beans

	00.05	00.55
	plus chilling time	

American	Ingredients	Metric/Imperial
½ cup	small red beans	125 g/4 oz
½ cup	cracked rice	125 g/4 oz
3 tbsp	rice flour	3 tbsp
4 tbsp	sugar	4 tbsp
	few small fresh fruits	

1. Rinse the beans several times in cold water and leave to drain.
2. Rinse the rice until the rinsing water is clear and drain.
3. Bring 2 cups (450 ml/¼ pint) water to the boil. Add the beans and cook gently over moderate heat for 45 minutes.
4. Add the rice and continue cooking until a mash is obtained. Remove from the heat and rub the mixture through a very fine strainer (sieve). Sift the rice flour over the mixture and add the sugar. Stir well and return to the heat. Bring the mixture back to the boil, stirring, until stiff.
5. Rinse 4 moulds or cups with cold water and transfer the mixture to these. Leave to cool, then chill for 2 hours.
6. Turn the puddings out on to small plates, decorate with a few small fresh fruits and serve.

MENU

Spinach soup
Chicken and bell peppers
Grapefruit with ginger

Spinach Soup

	00.05	00.20
	Serves 4	

American	Ingredients	Metric/Imperial
¼ lb	rump steak	125 g/4 oz
2	chopped scallions (spring onions)	2
1	finely chopped garlic clove	1
1 tbsp	sesame seeds	1 tbsp
	salt	
½ lb	spinach	225 g/8 oz
1 tbsp	dark soy sauce	1 tbsp

1. Dry the meat with kitchen paper. Cut it into thin slices, then into strips, then into pieces.
2. Heat a wok, then dry fry the meat, scallions (spring onions), garlic and sesame seeds for 1 minute, stirring constantly. Add 3¼ cups (750 ml/1¼ pints) water and stir well. Bring to the boil. Reduce the the heat and simmer for 10 minutes.
3. Wash the spinach and cut into narrow strips.
4. Add a little salt to the soup.
5. Stir in the strips of spinach and bring to the boil.
6. Add the soy sauce and remove the wok from the heat.
7. Serve the soup in warmed dishes.

Chicken and Bell Peppers

	00.10	00.15
	Serves 4	

American	Ingredients	Metric/Imperial
1¼ lb	chicken fillet	550 g/1¼ lb
2	green bell peppers	2
1	red bell pepper	1
2 tbsp	groundnut oil	2 tbsp
1	large chopped onion	1
2	finely chopped garlic cloves	2
	salt	
2 tbsp	light soy sauce	2
2 tbsp	cornstarch (cornflour)	2 tbsp
4	scallions (spring onions)	4

1. Dry the chicken with kitchen paper. Cut into thin slices, then into strips.
2. Wash, trim, halve and seed the bell peppers. Cut the flesh into very narrow strips.
3. Heat the oil in a wok. Add the chicken strips and stir fry for 2 minutes.
4. Add the onion, garlic and strips of bell pepper. Stir well, then simmer over moderate heat for a further 3-4 minutes, stirring constantly. Add 1 cup (250 ml/8 fl oz) boiling water. Add salt to taste and the soy sauce and cook for 1 minute. Push all ingredients to one side of the wok.
5. Mix the cornstarch (cornflour) with 2 tbsp cold water and stir into the liquid in the wok. Cook, stirring until the sauce thickens. Bring the ingredients back into the center of the wok and cook for a further 3-4 minutes.
6. Transfer to a warmed serving dish and serve garnished with scallion (spring onion).

Grapefruit with Ginger

⏲ 00.10
Serves 4

00.15 🍲

American	Ingredients	Metric/Imperial
1 (3½ oz)	piece fresh root ginger	1 (100 g/3½ oz)
¾ cup	sugar	170 g/6 oz
2	grapefruits	2

1. Peel the root ginger thinly and cut into slices, then into narrow strips.

2. Bring ⅓ pint (200 ml/7 fl oz) water to the boil and add the strips of root ginger. Simmer gently for 5 minutes. Strain the water from the pan and add a further ⅓ pint (200 ml/7 fl oz) boiling water. Simmer for a further 5 minutes, add the sugar and stir constantly until the sugar has dissolved. Reduce the heat and simmer until the liquid has evaporated, leaving a thick syrup. Leave to go cold.

3. Remove as many strips of ginger as possible from the syrup and reserve them.

4. Halve the grapefruits, remove the segments and drain them well in a colander. Remove the pith from the peel carefully. Divide the grapefruit segments between the empty grapefruit shells, sprinkle with the strips of root ginger and serve.

SINGAPORE

Country captain

Spicy Chicken with Onions

00. 10   00. 40
plus standing time

American	Ingredients	Metric/Imperial
1 (2½ lb)	roasting chicken	1 (1.2 kg/2½ lb)
2	crushed garlic cloves	2
1 tsp	coarse sea salt	1 tsp
½ tsp	freshly ground black pepper	½ tsp
½ tsp	ground turmeric	½ tsp
4 tbsp	ghee or groundnut oil	4 tbsp
4	large onions	4
2	chilies	2
1	chopped scallion (spring onion) or leek	1

1. Cut the chicken into eight pieces. Dry with kitchen paper.
2. Place the garlic, salt, pepper and turmeric in a mortar or food processor. Grind to a smooth paste. Add 1 tsp ghee or oil to the paste if necessary.
3. Coat the pieces of chicken with the paste on all sides. Leave to stand for 15 minutes.
4. Peel the onions and cut them into very thin slices, then separate into rings.
5. Rinse the chilies, trim the ends, open the chilies and remove the seeds and pith. Cut the flesh into extremely thin strips.
6. Heat the ghee or oil in a frying pan or wok with a lid. Stir fry half the onion rings until golden brown. Remove from the pan with a slotted spoon. Drain over the pan, then set aside. Fry the remaining onion rings until transparent.
7. Add the strips of chili and stir well.
8. Add the chicken and cook until golden brown all over.

Spicy chicken with onions

9. Pour on 1 cup (250 ml/8 fl oz) boiling water. Cover the pan and reduce the heat. Cook the chicken very gently for 20-25 minutes until tender. Stir occasionally and add extra water if too much liquid evaporates. Remove the chicken pieces from the pan when cooked. Place on a warm dish.
10. Add the reserved onions to the contents of the pan. Bring quickly to the boil and boil until most of the liquid in the pan

Singapore croquettes and Crispy fried chicken

has evaporated. Pour as evenly as possible over the chicken pieces.

11. Sprinkle with a little chopped scallion (spring onion) or leek.

Singapore chicken

Crispy Fried Chicken

00.10 plus drying time **00.45**

American	Ingredients	Metric/Imperial
1 (2½ lb)	roasting chicken	1 (1.2 kg/2½ lb)
2 tsp	salt	2 tsp
2½ tsp	five spice powder	2½ tsp
1 tsp	cayenne pepper	1 tsp
2 tsp	ground cinnamon	2 tsp
4 tbsp	honey	4 tbsp
1 tbsp	lemon juice	1 tbsp
3 quarts	oil for frying	3 litres/5¼ pints
1	large sliced lemon or 2 limes	1

1. Pat the chicken dry inside and out with kitchen paper.

2. Mix 1 tsp of salt with ½ tsp of five spice powder. Rub this mixture over the chicken and sprinkle a little into the cavity.

3. Bring 3 quarts (3 litres/5¼ pints) water to the boil in a deep pan. Add the remaining five spice powder, cayenne pepper, cinnamon and ½ tsp of salt. Stir well.

4. Place the chicken in the liquid. Reduce the heat and leave the chicken to cook gently for 20 minutes. Remove the chicken from the pan and drain in a colander.

5. Bring 1 quart (1 litre/1¾ pints) water to the boil in a small pan. Add the honey and lemon juice, stirring continuously until the honey has dissolved.

6. Slowly pour the boiling liquid over the chicken. Place the chicken on a rack and leave in a draughty place to dry quickly. When completely dry, tie the legs and wings against the breast (see drawings).

7. Heat the oil in a large pan until very hot. Reduce the heat slightly.

8. Lower the chicken carefully into the oil and fry for about 15 minutes, until golden brown.

9. Divide the chicken into pieces and slice the breast meat. Arrange the pieces and slices on a warmed plate, as far as possible in the shape of the whole chicken.

10. Garnish with slices of lemon or lime and serve.

Singapore croquettes

Singapore Croquettes

00.15 **00.40** makes 16 croquettes

American	Ingredients	Metric/Imperial
2	green chilies	2
2-3 tbsp	groundnut oil	2-3 tbsp
2	large chopped onions	2
1	finely chopped garlic clove	1
½ tsp	grated fresh root ginger	½ tsp
2 tsp	ground coriander seeds	2 tsp
1 tsp	ground cumin	1 tsp
1 tsp	salt	1 tsp
½ tsp	freshly ground black pepper	½ tsp
2 tbsp	finely chopped coriander leaves or parsley	2 tbsp
6	chopped scallions (spring onions)	6
1 lb	finely ground (minced) lean beef	450 g/1 lb
2 lb	boiled, mashed potatoes	1 kg/2 lb
2	lightly beaten eggs	2
	lightly toasted white breadcrumbs	
	oil for frying	

1. Rinse the chilies, trim the ends, halve and remove the seeds and pith. Chop the chilies very finely.

2. Heat the oil in a wok and stir fry the chopped onion until transparent.

3. Add the garlic, root ginger and chilies. Stir well.

4. Add the coriander seeds, cumin, salt, pepper, coriander leaves or parsley, scallions (spring onions) and finely ground (minced) beef. Cook, stirring continuously until the meat changes color and the mixture crumbles. Leave to cool.

5. Mix the mixture with the mashed potato. Shape into 16 (or more) croquettes.

6. Coat with the lightly beaten egg and roll in the breadcrumbs.

7. Heat the oil until very hot and fry the croquettes 4 at a time until golden brown. Remove from the oil and drain on kitchen paper. Serve the croquettes as hot as possible.

Cook's tip: any finely ground (minced) meat or chicken can be substituted for the beef used in the croquettes.

Tying Crispy fried chicken

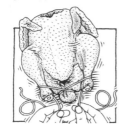

1. Take a piece of string under the parson's nose, cross over and round the wings.

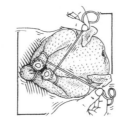

2. Bring the string under the wings and cross over again.

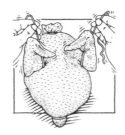

3. Turn the chicken over and bring the string up the body.

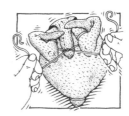

4. Tie the flap over the body.

Main course soup with pork or chicken and crab balls

Bak wan kepiting

Main Course Soup with Pork or Chicken and Crab Balls

00.15 Serves 4 — 00.20

American	Ingredients	Metric/Imperial
1 lb	*pork or chicken fillet*	*450 g/1 lb*
10 oz	*crabmeat, thawed if frozen*	*300 g/10 oz*
5 oz	*canned bamboo shoots*	*150 g/5 oz*
4	*scallions (spring onions) or piece of leek*	*4*
2	*young carrots*	*2*
1 tbsp	*groundnut oil*	*1 tbsp*
1	*medium size chopped onion*	*1*
1 tsp	*salt*	*1 tsp*
½ tsp	*freshly ground black pepper*	*½ tsp*
	pinch sereh powder (lemon grass)	
1	*lightly beaten egg*	*1*
1½ quarts	*chicken bouillon (stock)*	*1.5 litres/2¾ pints*
2 tbsp	*finely chopped coriander leaves or parsley*	*2 tbsp*

1. Grind (mince) the meat finely. Pick over and discard any gristle.
2. Finely grind (mince) the crabmeat. Pick over and discard any pieces of shell.
3. Finely chop the bamboo shoots, scallions (spring onions) or leek and the carrots.
4. Heat the oil in a wok. Add the chopped onion and stir fry until golden brown.
5. Mix the meat and crabmeat with the bamboo shoots, scallion (spring onion) or leek, carrots and fried onion.
6. Add the salt, pepper and sereh powder and stir.
7. Add the lightly beaten egg and combine into a stiff mixture. With wet hands shape into walnut size balls.
8. Bring the bouillon (stock) to boiling point in a shallow pan. Put the balls into the bouillon (stock). Reduce the heat and cook very gently for about 20 minutes. Transfer the soup and balls into warmed, deep dishes.
9. Serve, sprinkled with finely chopped coriander leaves or finely chopped parsley.

Cook's tip: in Singapore a few tsp Chinese light soy sauce is often added to the soup before serving. This gives it a more highly seasoned flavor.

Laksa

Fish Soup with Rice Vermicelli

00.20 makes 8 bowls — 00.40

American	Ingredients	Metric/Imperial
6-7	*large shrimp (prawns) thawed, if frozen*	*6-7*
4 oz	*crabmeat, thawed if frozen*	*125 g/4 oz*
1 lb	*cod or mackerel fillets*	*450 g/1 lb*
8	*scallions (spring onions) or piece of leek*	*8*
1 tsp	*salt*	*1 tsp*
	freshly ground black pepper	
1	*lightly beaten egg*	*1*
¼ lb	*rice vermicelli*	*125 g/4 oz*
¼ lb	*bean sprouts*	*125 g/4 oz*
3 tbsp	*groundnut oil*	*3 tbsp*
2	*thinly sliced onions*	*2*
1	*finely chopped garlic clove*	*1*
1 tsp	*grated lemon zest*	*1 tsp*
½ tsp	*trasi (dried shrimp paste)*	*½ tsp*
1 tsp	*laos powder*	*1 tsp*
1 tsp	*ground turmeric*	*1 tsp*
2 tsp	*ground coriander seeds*	*2 tsp*
1 quart	*thin coconut milk*	*1 litre/1¼ pints*
½	*coarsely grated cucumber*	*½*
½ tsp	*sugar*	*½ tsp*
	salt	
1	*finely chopped parsley sprig*	*1*

1. Cook the shrimp (prawns) in water, kept just at boiling point, for 5 minutes. Rinse in cold running water, and peel.
2. Pick over the crabmeat and remove any pieces of shell.
3. Rinse the fish fillets in cold running water and finely grind with the shrimp (prawns) and crabmeat.
4. Chop half the scallions (spring onions) or leek. Add to the fish mixture. Add the salt and pepper.
5. Add the lightly beaten egg and stir well. Shape the mixture into four balls.
6. Bring 1 quart (1 litre/1¼ pints) water to the boil in a pan. Place the fish balls in the liquid. Reduce the heat and simmer for 20 minutes. Remove from the liquid and drain in a strainer (sieve) or colander. Reserve the cooking liquid.
7. Cut the remaining scallions (spring onions) or leek into small pieces.
8. Prepare the rice vermicelli according to the instructions on the packet (instructions vary from one manufacturer to another).
9. Rinse the bean sprouts in cold water. Remove as many of the seed cases as possible. Place the bean sprouts in a colander and rinse with several quarts/litres of boiling water. Drain well.
10. Heat the oil in a large wok and stir fry the onion until it begins to change color. Add the garlic and stir well.
11. Add the lemon zest and trasi shrimp paste. Stir well once again and add the laos powder, turmeric and coriander.
12. Add the coconut milk and 1¼ cups (300 ml/½ pints) of the reserved liquid, stir well and cook gently for 10-12 minutes. Add sugar and a little more salt to taste and stir regularly to prevent the coconut milk from curdling.
13. Serve half the rice vermicelli into large warm deep dishes.

14. Put half the bean sprouts and half the cucumber on top, sprinkle with some of the scallion (spring onion) or leek.

15. Cut the balls into ⅛ in (3 mm) slices. Serve half the slices into the dishes, then pour the soup on top, repeat until all the ingredients are used.

16. Sprinkle with finely chopped parsley and serve.

Hokkien mee

Main Course Soup with Pork and Noodles

00.15 makes 8 bowls **00.10**

American	Ingredients	Metric/Imperial
½ lb	thick noodles	225 g/8 oz
¼ lb	rice vermicelli	125 g/4 oz
¼ lb	bean sprouts	125 g/4 oz
¼ lb	spinach leaves	125 g/4 oz
1 (¾ lb)	piece cooked pork	1 (350 g/¾ lb)
½ cup	fresh pork fat	115 g/4 oz
3 tbsp	groundnut oil	3 tbsp
4	dried chilies	4
3	large chopped onions	3
1½ quarts	chicken bouillon (stock)	1.5 litres/2¾ pints
	salt	
1-2 tbsp	Chinese light soy sauce	1-2 tbsp
¾ lb	peeled cooked fresh shrimp (prawns)	350 g/12 oz

1. Prepare the noodles and vermicelli according to the instructions on the packet. Drain well.

2. Wash the bean sprouts in cold water and remove as many seed cases as possible. Drain the bean sprouts in a colander, then slowly pour over 3 quarts (3 litres/5¼ pints) boiling water and drain again.

3. Wash the spinach and remove all stalks. Place the leaves in a colander and slowly pour over 3 quarts (3 litres/5¼ pints) boiling water. Drain well, and cut the leaves into narrow strips.

4. Cut the cooked pork into thin strips.

5. Dice the fresh pork fat.

6. Heat the oil in a wok and fry the diced pork fat. Remove the crackling with a slotted spoon. Drain and set aside.

7. Soak the dried chilies in a little warm water. Dry with kitchen paper and chop into small pieces.

8. Stir fry the onions until golden brown in the mixture of oil and fat left in the wok.

9. Add the chili and fry for 30 seconds.

10. Add the noodles and vermicelli and quickly brown the mixture, stirring continuously.

11. Bring the bouillon (stock) to the boil adding salt and soy sauce to taste.

12. Divide half the noodle mixture into four bowls. Top with the other ingredients and pour stock over to cover about ⅓ of the noodles. Sprinkle with a little reserved crackling and serve.

Fish soup with rice vermicelli

Mah mee

Main Course Soup with Noodles

◀▬▭	00.10	00.20 ⌾
	Serves 4	

American	Ingredients	Metric/Imperial
½ lb	crabmeat, thawed if frozen	225 g/8 oz
1 (½ lb)	piece streaky bacon	1 (225 g/8 oz)
½ lb	fine noodles	225 g/8 oz
5 oz	bean sprouts	150 g/5 oz
1 tbsp	sesame oil	1 tbsp
1	crushed garlic clove	1
½ tsp	finely grated fresh root ginger	½ tsp
1½ quarts	chicken bouillon (stock)	1.5 litres/2¾ pints
1 tsp	five spice powder	1 tsp
	salt	
½ lb	fresh cooked peeled shrimp (prawns)	225 g/8 oz
8	scallions (spring onions) or 1 large piece leek cut into pieces	8
1	scrubbed coarsely grated cucumber	1

1. Pick over the crabmeat and remove any pieces of shell then cut the crabmeat into very small pieces.
2. Broil (grill) the bacon over the barbecue or under a hot broiler (grill), for 10-15 minutes until cooked and brown all over. Leave the meat to cool, then cut into narrow strips.
3. Prepare the noodles according to the instructions on the packet. Cut the noodles into 2 in (5 cm) pieces.
4. Rinse the bean sprouts in cold water and remove as many seed cases as possible. Drain the bean sprouts in a colander

then slowly pour over 3 quarts (3 litres/5¼ pints) boiling water. Drain well again.
5. Heat the oil in a wok. Add the garlic and root ginger and stir fry for 30 seconds.
6. Add the bouillon (stock). Cook gently for a few minutes.
7. Add the noodle strips, the strips of meat and the bean sprouts.
8. Stir in the five spice powder and a little salt to taste.
9. Just before serving add the shrimp (prawns) and crabmeat. Bring to the boil.
10. Serve the soup in a large tureen, with the scallion (spring onion) or leek and cucumber in separate dishes.

Nasi lemak

Rice in Coconut Milk

◀▬▭	00.10	00.50 ⌾
	plus soaking time	

American	Ingredients	Metric/Imperial
1½ cups	long grain rice	350 g/12 oz
¾ cup	thin coconut milk	200 ml/7 fl oz
1-2 tsp	salt	1-2 tsp

1. Rinse the rice in cold water until the water runs clear then soak overnight. Drain in a colander. Steam the rice for 30 minutes in a rice steamer stirring carefully after 15 minutes.
2. Heat the coconut milk and salt to just below boiling point, stirring continuously. Do not allow the coconut milk to boil.
3. Add the steamed rice. Stir well and leave the pan to stand uncovered for 25-30 minutes over very moderate heat, until all the coconut milk has been absorbed by the rice. Just before serving, stir carefully.

Cook's tip: just before serving the rice, sprinkle on or stir in, 1-2 tbsp of finely chopped scallion (spring onion), leek or celery leaves.

Main course soup with noodles

Singapore sate
Singapore Sate

American	Ingredients	Metric/Imperial
1¼ lb	lean beef	550 g/1¼ lb
1	piece lemon zest	1
2	medium size chopped onions	2
1	finely chopped garlic clove	1
1 tbsp	Chinese light soy sauce	1 tbsp
2 tbsp	groundnut oil	2 tbsp
1 tsp	ground cumin	1 tsp
1 tsp	ground turmeric	1 tsp
1 tsp	salt	1 tsp
3 tbsp	finely ground roasted peanuts	3 tbsp

1. Dry the beef with kitchen paper and cut into cubes.
2. In a food processor, blend the lemon zest, onions, garlic, soy sauce, oil, cumin, turmeric and salt to a purée. Add the finely ground peanuts.
3. Coat the meat in the mixture. Leave to stand for 1-2 hours in a cool place. Turn at intervals.
4. Soak wooden sate sticks in cold water for 20 minutes.
5. Skewer the meat on the sticks and broil (grill) the sates evenly over a barbecue or under a hot broiler (grill), until brown all over. Turn the sates several times during cooking and serve.

Singapore sate sauce (I)
Singapore Sate Sauce (I)

American	Ingredients	Metric/Imperial
1 tbsp	tamarind	1 tbsp
1	piece lemon zest or 1 blade lemon grass (sereh)	1
1	coarsely chopped large onion	1
2-3	finely chopped garlic cloves	2-3
2 tsp	trasi (dried shrimp paste)	2 tsp
2 cups	finely crushed roasted peanuts	225 g/8 oz
4 tbsp	groundnut oil	4 tbsp
1 tsp	cayenne pepper	1 tsp
1½ tsp	laos powder	1½ tsp
2 tbsp	soft brown sugar	2 tbsp
½ tsp	salt	½ tsp

1. Place the tamarind in a bowl with 1 cup (250 ml/8 fl oz) boiling water. Stir well and leave to stand for 15 minutes. Stir again and strain off the liquid.
2. In a food processor or blender, blend the lemon zest or lemon grass with the onion, garlic, shrimp paste, peanuts and 2 tbsp of oil to a smooth paste.
3. Heat the remaining oil in a wok and stir fry the paste for 2 minutes.
4. Add the tamarind liquid, cayenne pepper, laos powder, sugar and salt. Stir well.
5. Dilute the sauce slightly with a little water and simmer gently for a further 10 minutes stirring continuously to prevent sticking. The sauce may be prepared in advance and reheated before serving.

Singapore sate sauce (II)
Singapore Sate Sauce (II)

American	Ingredients	Metric/Imperial
2 tbsp	groundnut oil	2 tbsp
1	large very finely chopped onion	1
2	finely chopped garlic cloves	2
1 tsp	trasi (dried shrimp paste)	1 tsp
1 tsp	cayenne pepper	1 tsp
½ tsp	laos powder	½ tsp
6 tbsp	Chinese dark soy sauce	6 tbsp
3 tbsp	soft brown sugar	3 tbsp
1 tbsp	lemon or lime juice	1 tbsp

1. Heat the oil in a wok and stir fry the onion until it begins to change color.
2. Add the garlic and stir well.
3. Add all the remaining ingredients plus 4 tbsp boiling water. Stir well and simmer gently over very moderate heat for 5 minutes. Strain the sauce, if necessary. Allow approximately 1 tbsp sauce per piece of sate.

Filling spring rolls

1. Lay out the wrapper and place filling in the center folding the edges from the sides to the middle.

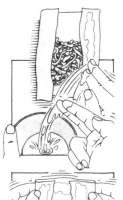

2. Brush the edges with a little of the cornstarch (cornflour) solution.

3. Fold the bottom edge of the wrapper in to the middle and brush the edge with a little cornstarch (cornflour) solution.

4. Fold the top edge to the bottom to complete the parcel.

Spring rolls
Spring Rolls

00.10 plus soaking time   **00.25**

American	Ingredients	Metric/Imperial
1	packet 24 frozen spring roll wrappers	1
6	dried Chinese mushrooms	6
2 tbsp	groundnut oil	2 tbsp
2 tbsp	sesame oil	2 tbsp
1	finely chopped garlic clove	1
½ tsp	finely grated fresh root ginger	½ tsp
¾ lb	lean pork cut into narrow strips or diced	350 g/12 oz
1 lb	coarsely shredded Chinese cabbage	450 g/1 lb
5 oz	giant radish	150 g/5 oz
8	finely chopped, canned water chestnuts	8
9 oz	finely chopped, canned bamboo shoots	250 g/9 oz
5 oz	washed bean sprouts	150 g/5 oz
12	finely sliced scallions (spring onions)	2
2 tbsp	Chinese light soy sauce	2 tbsp
1 tbsp	oyster sauce (optional)	1 tbsp
2 tbsp	cornstarch (cornflour)	2 tbsp
½ lb	fresh peeled shrimp (prawns)	225 g/8 oz
	oil for frying	

1. Leave the frozen wrappers to thaw, carefully following the instructions on the packet.
2. Put the mushrooms in a bowl with boiling water to cover and soak for 30 minutes. Remove the stalks and cut or chop the caps into small pieces.
3. Heat the groundnut and sesame oils in a large wok. Add the garlic and root ginger and stir fry for 30 seconds.
4. Add the meat and stir fry until the meat changes color.
5. Immediately add the vegetables, soy sauce, oyster sauce if using and 2 tbsp of water. Stir well and slide the contents of the wok to one side.
6. Mix 1½ tbsp cornstarch (cornflour) with 3 tbsp cold water. Stir into the liquid in the wok. Cook, stirring until the sauce thickens. Add a little salt to taste. Stir the contents of the wok once more. Remove the wok from the heat.
7. Leave to cool then stir in the shrimp (prawns).
8. Lay out the wrappers on a work surface or board.
9. Mix the remaining cornflour with 2 tbsp cold water.
10. Place 2-3 heaped spoonfuls of filling on each wrapper. Roll up the wrappers and fold tightly.
11. Brush the edges of the wrappers with the cornstarch (cornflour) solution and press together firmly. Leave the spring rolls to stand for 5-10 minutes.
12. Heat the oil until very hot and fry the spring rolls 3 at a time until golden brown on the outside. Serve the spring rolls as hot as possible.

Cook's tip: spring rolls are accompanied by a sauce made by mixing 2 parts Chinese dark soy sauce with 5 parts Chinese light soy sauce. They can also, however, be served with sweet Indonisian soy sauce (ketyap benteng manis).

Filled Chinese pancakes form a complete meal which should be served at the table as follows: Arrange one or more hot plates on the table to take the various hot dishes. Lay out the cold accompaniments and the bowl of lettuce. The guests now help themselves. They should begin by taking a pancake on to a warmed plate. Then a lettuce leaf should be laid on top and 2 or more tbsp of the filling. One or more of the accompaniments may be added to the filling to taste. A little Indonesian sweet soy sauce may be sprinkled on to the filling, and the pancakes should then be rolled up and eaten. A bottle or jug of soy sauce, should be placed on the table with one or more dishes of sambal oelek and possibly a little five spice salt (3 parts of salt mixed with 1 part five spice powder).

Poh pia
Chinese Pancakes

00.10 plus standing time   **00.20**

American	Ingredients	Metric/Imperial
3 tbsp	groundnut oil or ghee	3 tbsp
2 cups	sifted flour	225 g/8 oz
	good pinch of salt	
4	beaten eggs	4

1. Add 4 tbsp cold water to the oil or ghee.
2. Sift the flour and salt together into a basin. Make a well in the flour and pour in the egg mixture. Stir thoroughly, working outwards from the center until a smooth batter is formed.
3. Add a further 1-2 tbsp of water if necessary. Leave the batter to stand for 30 minutes then stir well.
4. Fry 24 pancakes in a small non-stick frying pan or pancake pan over very moderate heat until the pancakes are cooked on both sides but barely change color. Keep the pancakes warm by placing them between two warmed bowls placed in a pan of water, kept just at boiling point.

Left to right: Chinese pancakes, Chinese pancake filling, Spring rolls

Poh pia

Chinese Pancake Filling

00.05 makes 24 — 00.10

American	Ingredients	Metric/Imperial
½ lb	fresh soybean curd (tofu)	225 g/8 oz
3 tbsp	groundnut oil	3 tbsp
1 tbsp	sesame oil	1 tbsp
1 lb	roast streaky pork cut into narrow strips	450 g/1 lb
4	finely chopped garlic cloves	4
4 tbsp	finely crushed, canned salt black beans	4 tbsp
1½ lb	canned, drained bamboo shoots cut into thin strips	700 g/1½ lb
½ lb	fresh peeled shrimp (prawns)	225 g/½ lb
	pinch salt (optional)	

1. Dice the soybean curd (tofu).
2. Heat the two kinds of oil in a wok. Add the soybean curd (tofu) and stir fry until golden brown on all sides. Remove from the wok with a slotted spoon. Drain over the pan and keep warm.
3. Stir fry the strips of pork in the remaining oil until the meat begins to brown.
4. Add the garlic and salt black beans. Stir well.
5. Add the bamboo shoots and stir fry to heat through.
6. Stir in the shrimp (prawns) and add salt to taste.
7. Stir in the reserved soybean curd (tofu), just before serving with the pancakes.

Poh pia

Chinese Pancake Garnish

00.10 — 00.20

American	Ingredients	Metric/Imperial
1	lettuce	1
½ lb	cooked crabmeat or lobster thawed if frozen	225 g/½ lb
1-2	cucumbers	1-2
	salt	
	fresh bean sprouts	200 g/
6-8	Chinese sausages (lap tajong)	6-8
4	eggs	4
	salt	
	freshly ground pepper	
1 tbsp	sesame oil	1 tbsp
8	crushed garlic cloves	8
2 tbsp	Indonesian sweet soy sauce (ketyap benteng manis)	2 tbsp
1	bunch watercress, coriander leaves or parsley	1

1. Rinse the lettuce in cold water and dry as well as possible.
2. Pick over the crabmeat or lobster and remove any pieces of shell. Cut into small pieces.
3. Peel the cucumbers and halve lengthwise. Seed with a spoon and cut the cucumber halves into narrow strips. Sprinkle the cucumber strips with a little salt and drain in a colander.
4. Rinse the bean sprouts in cold water. Remove as many skins as possible. Drain the bean sprouts in a colander and slowly pour over 3 quarts (3 litres/5¼ pints) boiling water. Drain again.
5. Steam the sausages in a steamer for 10-14 minutes. Cut the sausages into slices and remove the skin if possible.
6. Lightly beat the eggs in a basin. Add 2 tbsp water and a little salt and pepper to taste. Divide into four and fry four thin omelettes. Roll up the omelettes then cut into thin strips.
7. Heat the sesame oil in a small wok. Add the garlic and fry for 30 seconds. Remove the wok from the heat and stir in 2 tbsp Indonesian sweet soy sauce.
8. Rinse the green leaves of the watercress, coriander or parsley then dry. Put all garnish ingredients into large and small bowls or dishes.

Toffee Apples

Toffee apples

00.10 plus standing time

00.30

American	Ingredients	Metric/Imperial
2	large firm apples	2
1	squeezed lemon	1
1¼ cups	sifted flour	150 g/5 oz
	pinch salt	
1	lightly beaten egg with 3 tbsp water	1
1¼ cups	sugar	300 g/10 oz
1 tbsp	black sesame seeds	1 tbsp
	oil for frying	

1. Peel and core the apples and cut each into 8 equal segments. Sprinkle each segment with the lemon juice and leave to stand for at least 10 minutes.
2. Make a batter by mixing the flour and salt into a bowl. Make a well in the center and add the lightly beaten eggs with the water. Stir, working from the center to a smooth batter which runs from the spoon in a thick ribbon. Add another 1-2 tbsp water if necessary. Beat the batter vigorously and leave to stand for 30 minutes. Beat vigorously once more.
3. Make the caramel by dissolving the sugar in ½ cup (100 ml/4 fl oz) water then bringing to the boil. Boil rapidly stirring continuously until the mixture is just beginning to change color. Remove the pan from the heat and stir the sesame seeds into the sugar solution.
4. Heat the oil until very hot.
5. Have ready a large basin of ice cold water, containing a few ice cubes, in which to immerse the toffee apples.
6. Spear the apple segments on a large fork and dip them in the batter. Allow any surplus batter to run off. Fry the segments in the hot oil, 4-5 at a time, until golden brown. Remove from the oil with a slotted spoon. Drain over the oil, then dip them immediately in the sugar mixture and immerse them in the ice cold water. Leave in the water for 30-40 seconds. Drain on kitchen paper, and serve as quickly as possible.

Toffee Apples

MENU

Shang palace soup
Beet with onions and Chinese leaves
Singapore trifle

Shang Palace Soup

00.15 plus standing time

00.15

American	Ingredients	Metric/Imperial
¼ lb	chicken fillets	125 g/4 oz
	salt	
	freshly ground pepper	
1½ tbsp	groundnut oil	1½ tbsp
5½ oz	cooked crabmeat	150 g/5½ oz
2 oz	bean sprouts	50 g/2 oz
3⅔ cups	chicken bouillon (stock)	800 ml/28 fl oz
3	chopped scallions (spring onions)	3

1. Dry the chicken with kitchen paper. Mix the salt and pepper togther and rub the mixture lightly over the chicken.
2. Heat the oil in a small frying pan and fry the chicken over medium heat until golden yellow on both sides, but not completely cooked. Remove from the pan, drain and leave to cool on kitchen paper. Cut the chicken diagonally into 8-12 very thin slices.
3. Pick over the crabmeat, remove any pieces of shell and cut the crab into small pieces.
4. Rinse the bean sprouts in cold water. Remove as many of the seed cases as possible and drain the bean sprouts in a colander.
5. Arrange the chicken slices overlapping on warmed plates and arrange the crab pieces alongside.
6. Bring the bouillon (stock) to the boil.
7. Add the bean sprouts, bring back to the boil and boil vigorously for 2 minutes.
8. Pour the bouillon (stock) with the bean sprouts over the plates with the chicken and crab, sprinkle with the scallions (spring onions) and serve.

Cook's tip: serve with a separate dish of dry boiled rice or noodles which have been boiled and then fried in a little oil. Spread the noodles over a large warmed plate and arrange the beef with onions and Chinese leaves over the top as evenly as possible.

Beef with Onions and Chinese Leaves

◣▷ 00.10   00.15 🍲
Serves 4

American	Ingredients	Metric/Imperial
1 lb	fillet of beef	450 g/1 lb
2 tbsp	groundnut oil	2 tbsp
½ lb	peeled, washed small onions	225 g/8 oz
½ lb	thinly shredded Chinese leaves	225 g/8 oz
3 tbsp	Indonesian sweet soy sauce	3 tbsp
½ tsp	sambal ulek (see page 128)	½ tsp
⅔ cup	beef bouillon (stock)	150 ml/¼ pint
1½ tsp	cornstarch (cornflour)	1½ tsp
	few coriander sprigs	
1	skinned tomato cut into segments	1

1. Dry the meat with kitchen paper. Cut it diagonally into thin slices and then into thin strips.
2. Heat the oil in a wok and stir fry the strips of beef until brown. Remove from the wok with a skimmer and keep warm.
3. Stir fry the onions for 3 minutes in the remaining oil.
4. Add the shredded Chinese leaves and stir fry for a further 2 minutes.
5. Add the soy sauce and sambal ulek and the beef bouillon (stock). Bring to the boil, reduce the heat and simmer for 3 minutes. Push the ingredients to one side of the wok.
6. Mix the cornstarch (cornflour) with 1½ tbsp cold water. Stir into the liquid in the wok. Cook, stirring until the sauce thickens. Bring the ingredients back into the middle of the

wok. Stir well a few times and add the meat.
7. Thoroughly heat the contents of the pan, stirring constantly.
8. Serve on to warmed plates and garnish with coriander sprigs and tomato segments.

Singapore Trifle

◣▷ 00.10   00.10 🍲
plus cooling time

American	Ingredients	Metric/Imperial
⅓ cup	sugar	75 g/3 oz
1 cup	peeled, skinned peanuts	150 g/5½ oz
	butter	
4	thick slices plain cake	4
2 tbsp	strawberry jam	2 tbsp
2 tbsp	rum	2 tbsp
2¼ cups	vanilla custard	550 ml/18 fl oz
4	mandarin oranges	4

1. Bring 3 tbsp water to the boil in a small, heavy-based saucepan. Dissolve the sugar in the boiling water, stirring constantly. Allow to boil slowly until the sugar mixture begins to turn light brown. Remove the pan from the heat.
2. Stir the peanuts through the sugar and then turn on to a large, cold plate which has been lightly greased with butter. Leave to cool then chop it into very small pieces.
3. Spread the slices of cake with a thick layer of jam and cut into small cubes. Divide between 4 glasses or bowls.
4. Sprinkle the cake cubes with rum and spoon some vanilla custard into each glass or bowl.
5. Peel the mandarins, divide them into segments and remove the pith and any pips. Divide the segments between the glasses, sprinkle with caramelised peanuts and serve.

Sri Lanka

Ceylon curry
Ceylon Curry

00.07 Serves 4		00.15

American	Ingredients	Metric/Imperial
1 (4 in)	cinnamon stick	1 (8 cm/4 in)
3	cardamom pods	3
½ lb	coriander seeds	225 g/8 oz
¼ lb	fennel seeds	125 g/4 oz
1 tbsp	fenugreek seeds	1 tbsp
1 tbsp	cloves	1 tbsp
8	curry leaves	8
1 tbsp	black peppercorns	1 tbsp
¼ cup	lightly roasted rice ground to a powder (optional)	50 g/2 oz

1. Pound the cinnamon stick into small pieces.
2. Remove the seeds from the cardamom pods.
3. Roast all the ingredients separately in a dry frying pan until they turn brown. Combine all the ingredients, including the ground rice, if used, and grind to a fine powder. An electric coffee mill is excellent for this purpose.

Ceylon curry
Ceylon Curry (Mild)

00.07 Serves 4		00.15

American	Ingredients	Metric/Imperial
1 (2 in)	cinnamon stick	1 (5 cm/2 in)
3	cardamom pods	3
½ lb	coriander seeds	225 g/8 oz
2 oz	fennel seeds	50 g/2 oz
1 tbsp	fenugreek seeds	1 tbsp
1 tbsp	cloves	1 tbsp
8	curry leaves	8
1 tsp	black peppercorns	1 tsp
¼ cup	lightly roasted rice ground to a powder	50 g/2 oz

1. Pound the cinnamon stick into small pieces.
2. Remove the seeds from the cardamom pods.
3. Roast all the ingredients separately in a dry frying pan until they turn brown. Combine all the ingredients, including the ground rice and grind to a fine powder. An electric coffee mill is excellent for this purpose.

Cook's tip: because mild Ceylon curry contains ground roasted rice, it may also be used as a light thickening for sauces. As an alternative add the same quantity of cornstarch (cornflour) to the spice mixture instead of the ground roasted rice. This will not be an authentic Sri Lankan mixture but it is ideal when used as a thickening.

Abbe
Ceylon Mustard

00.05 plus standing time		00.00

American	Ingredients	Metric/Imperial
5 oz	black or dark brown mustard seeds	150 g/5 oz
1¾ cups	spiced vinegar	400 ml/14 fl oz
1 tsp	salt	1 tsp
2 tsp	soft brown sugar	2 tsp

1. Put the mustard seeds in a glass jar and pour on sufficient vinegar to cover well. Leave to stand for at least 48 hours. Pour into a food processor.
2. Add salt and sugar. Process until the mixture forms an almost smooth paste. Put the mustard in a carefully cleaned glass jar, sealed by an airtight lid. Provided it is kept in a dark, cool, dry place the mustard can be stored for a few months.

Cook's tip: in Sri Lanka there are many variations on the above recipe. A range of different flavors can be obtained by adding finely pounded garlic, finely pounded fresh root ginger, the blanched and finely chopped flesh of red and/or green chilies, ground black pepper and Ceylon curry.

Bedhapu wambotu sambol
Eggplant (Aubergine) Sambol

00.10 plus standing time		00.10

American	Ingredients	Metric/Imperial
2	medium size eggplants (aubergines)	2
2 tbsp	salt	2 tbsp
4-5 tbsp	groundnut oil	4-5 tbsp
3	dried red chilies	3
2	large chopped onions	2
1 tbsp	lemon juice	1 tbsp
1 tbsp	salt	1 tbsp
	pinch sugar	

1. Rinse and trim the eggplants (aubergines) and slice thinly. Put them in a strainer or colander and sprinkle with approximately 2 tsp salt. Leave to stand for 1 hour turning the slices occasionally. Dry the eggplant (aubergine) with kitchen paper.
2. Heat the oil in a wok and stir fry the eggplant (aubergine) slices until soft and golden brown all over.
3. Remove the seeds from the chilies and crumble. Add the chilies and the onions and stir fry until the onions begin to brown.
4. Add the lemon juice, the salt and a pinch of sugar. Stir well and remove the pan from the heat. Leave to stand for 10 minutes. Pour off as much of the oil as possible.
5. Rub the mixture through a coarse strainer (sieve) and put the sambol in a clean, airtight jar.

Cook's tip: in Sri Lanka they usually add a few tbsp of thick coconut milk to this sambol immediately before serving. Allow 1 tbsp of coconut milk to 2 tbsp of sambol. An 'enriched' sambol of this kind tastes particulary good with shellfish dishes.

Mung eta sambol
Bean Sprout Sambol

	00.10	00.00
	Serves 4	

American	Ingredients	Metric/Imperial
3 oz	fresh bean sprouts	75 g/3 oz
4	green chilies	4
1	medium size onion	1
3 tbsp	fresh, grated coconut	3 tbsp
1 tsp	salt	1 tsp
2 tbsp	lemon juice	2 tbsp

1. Rinse the bean sprouts in plenty of cold water and remove as many of the seed cases as possible. Drain well.
2. Rinse the chilies, remove the ends, halve and seed: Cut or chop the flesh very finely.
3. Chop the onion.
4. Mix the chilies, onion, coconut, salt and lemon juice as lightly as possible in a bowl.
5. Add the well drained bean sprouts immediately before serving. Stir well and serve the sambol in individual bowls.

Eggplant (aubergine) sambol

Cook's tip: 1 or 2 of the chilies may be replaced with one finely chopped small bell pepper. The green bell pepper gives the sambol a much milder flavor. Another variation is to double the quantity of bean sprouts, which again gives a much milder flavor.

Kuni sambol
Sambol with Small Shrimps

	00.10	00.00
	Serves 4	

American	Ingredients	Metric/Imperial
¼ lb	freshly peeled shrimp (prawns)	125 g/4 oz
2	red chilies	2
1	finely chopped medium size onion	1
1 tsp	fenugreek seeds	1 tsp
1 tbsp	lemon juice	1 tbsp
1 tsp	salt	1 tsp
4 oz	grated coconut	125 g/4 oz

1. Pick over the shrimp (prawns), rinse in cold water and drain.
2. Rinse the chilies, remove the ends, halve and seed and cut or chop the flesh very finely.
3. Put the onion, chili, fenugreek seed, lemon juice, salt and coconut in a bowl. Stir well and add 4 tbsp lukewarm water. Stir well.
4. Stir in the shrimp (prawns) immediately before serving.

Bedhapu luna sambol

Fried Onion Sambol

00.06 00.15
plus standing time

American	Ingredients	Metric/Imperial
5 tbsp	groundnut oil	5 tbsp
3-4	large chopped onions	3-4
6-8	small dried red chilies	6-8
2 tbsp	dried fish or shrimp powder	2 tbsp
2 tbsp	salt	2 tbsp
1 tsp	sugar	1 tsp
2 tbsp	lemon juice	2 tbsp

1. Heat the oil in a wok and fry the onions until transparent.
2. Crumble the chilies and add these to the onions. Stir well.
3. Add the powdered dried fish or shrimp (prawns) and stir fry until the onions are golden brown.
4. Add the salt and sugar and stir well.
5. Add the lemon juice. Stir well a few more times and remove the pan from the heat. Stand for 10 minutes and then pour off as much oil as possible from the pan. Put the onion mixture in a clean, airtight jar.

Lunu miris sambol

Onion Sambol

00.05 00.00
Serves 4

American	Ingredients	Metric/Imperial
10	small dried red chilies	10
1 tbsp	finely pounded dried Maldive fish or Indonesian ikan bilis or Indian Bombay duck	1 tbsp
1	chopped small onion	1
2 tbsp	lemon juice	2 tbsp
½ tsp	salt	½ tsp
½ tsp	brown sugar	½ tsp

1. Crumble the chilies and put them into a food processor.
2. Add the finely pounded fish, onion, lemon juice, salt and brown sugar. Process until a smooth paste is obtained.

Cook's tip: to obtain a rather less sharp sambol remove the seeds from the chilies. Instead of the finely pounded fish finely crushed dried shrimp (prawns) may be used. The paste then has a flavor similar to that of the Malaysian bladyan or the Indonesian trasi.

Fried onion sambol

Left to right: Cucumber sambol, Roasted coconut sambol

Pol sambol
Coconut sambol

	00.10 Serves 4	00.00

American	Ingredients	Metric/Imperial
1 tsp	salt	1 tsp
½ tsp	ground red chili	½ tsp
2 tsp	mild ground paprika	2 tsp
2 tsp	powdered dried fish or shrimp (prawns)	2 tsp
2 tbsp	lemon juice	2 tbsp
1	medium size chopped onion	1
¼ lb	fresh grated coconut	125 g/4 oz

1. Stir together salt, chili and paprika in a bowl.
2. Add the powdered dried fish or shrimp (prawns) and stir well.
3. Sprinkle on the lemon juice.
4. Add the onion and stir well once more. Add 2 tbsp boiling water and stir well again.
5. Mix in the grated fresh coconut immediately before serving.

Kalupol sambol
Roasted Coconut Sambol

	00.05 Serves 4	00.10

American	Ingredients	Metric/Imperial
1 tsp	groundnut oil	1 tsp
¼ lb	fresh grated coconut	125 g/4 oz
2	medium size chopped onions	2
1 tsp	salt	1 tsp
2 tbsp	powdered dried fish or shrimp (prawns)	2 tbsp
3 tbsp	lemon juice	3 tbsp

1. Heat the oil in a wok and stir fry the fresh coconut until golden brown. Spoon on to a large plate and spread out to cool quickly.
2. Pour the remaining ingredients into a food processor and process until reduced to a smooth paste.
3. Add 2-3 tbsp of cold water and mix in the coconut immediately before serving.

Cook's tip: it is not essential to stir fry the coconut in a wok until it is brown. It may be roasted in a dry non-stick frying pan.

Pipinja sambol
Cucumber sambol

	00.15 plus standing and chilling time	00.00

American	Ingredients	Metric/Imperial
2	medium size cucumbers	2
2 tsp	salt	2 tsp
5 tbsp	thick coconut milk	5 tbsp
1	seeded, finely chopped red chili	1
1	seeded, finely chopped green chili	1
1	finely chopped small onion	1
2 tbsp	lemon juice	2 tbsp

1. Rinse the cucumbers under running water. Halve lengthwise and remove the seeds with a spoon. Grate the halves very coarsely. Put the grated cucumber in a bowl. Sprinkle on the salt. Stir, then drain well in a strainer or colander for at least 1 hour. Squeeze out as much liquid as possible.
2. Stir the thick coconut milk, chilies, onion and lemon juice together in a bowl.
3. Stir in the grated cucumber. Cover the bowl and chill for at least 30 minutes. Serve in individual bowls or small dishes.

Malu kari
Simple Fish Curry

⏱ 00.10 Serves 4   00.30 🍲

American	Ingredients	Metric/Imperial
1¾ lb	sliced cod	800 g/1¾ lb
½ tsp	black pepper	½ tsp
1 tsp	salt	1 tsp
1 tsp	ground turmeric	1 tsp
⅔ cup	groundnut oil	150 ml/¼ pint
2	large chopped onions	2
1	crushed garlic clove	1
½ tsp	fenugreek seeds	½ tsp
1 tbsp	coarsely grated fresh root ginger	1 tbsp
1-1½ tsp	Ceylon curry (see page 282)	1-1½ tsp
4 tbsp	mild vinegar or	4 tbsp
6 tbsp	tamarind juice	6 tbsp
1¾ cups	thin coconut milk	400 ml/14 fl oz

1. Rinse the cod slices under cold running water. Dry with kitchen paper.
2. Mix the pepper, salt and turmeric together in a bowl.
3. Rub the mixture into the slices of fish.
4. Heat 4 tbsp of oil in a large frying pan and fry the cod slices very quickly for 6 minutes until golden brown on both sides.
5. Heat 2 tbsp of oil in a wok and stir fry the onion until transparent.
6. Add the garlic, fenugreek seeds, root ginger and Ceylon curry. Stir fry until the onion has turned golden brown.
7. Add the vinegar or tamarind juice and the coconut milk. Bring to the boil and stir well.
8. Put in the cod slices and simmer very gently for a further 8 minutes. Serve on warmed plates.

Cook's tip: accompany the curry with separate dishes of dry boiled or dry steamed rice. In Sri Lanka it is nearly always served with one or two sambols. It goes particularly well with shrimp (prawn) or cucumber sambol.

Left to right: Simple fish curry,
Fish curry with tomatoes

Thakkali malu
Fish Curry and Tomatoes

◀▽   00.10   00.35 🍲
Serves 4

American	Ingredients	Metric/Imperial
1½ lb	cod fillets	700 g/1½ lb
1 tsp	ground turmeric	1 tsp
1 tsp	salt	1 tsp
½ tsp	black pepper	½ tsp
5 tbsp	groundnut oil	5 tbsp
1	large chopped onion	1
2	very finely chopped garlic cloves	2
2 tbsp	coarsely grated fresh root ginger	2 tbsp
4	large, ripe, skinned tomatoes cut into pieces	4
2-3 tsp	Ceylon curry (see page 282)	2-3 tsp
1 tsp	ground red chili	1 tsp
4 tbsp	mild vinegar or	4 tbsp
6 tbsp	tamarind juice	6 tbsp
1¾ cups	thin coconut milk	400 ml/14 fl oz
	few sprigs dillweed or coriander	

1. Rinse the fish under cold running water. Dry with kitchen paper and cut into 8-12 equal pieces.
2. Mix the turmeric, salt and black pepper together in a bowl. Rub the mixture into the pieces of fish.
3. Heat 3 tbsp of oil in a large frying pan and quickly fry the pieces of fish until golden brown on all sides. Remove from the pan, drain on kitchen paper and keep warm.
4. Heat the remainder of the oil in a wok and stir fry the onion until beginnning to color.
5. Add the garlic and root ginger and stir well.
6. Add the pieces of tomato and stir fry gently for 5-8 minutes until mixture thickens.
7. Add the Ceylon curry, chili, vinegar or tamarind juice and coconut milk. Continue stirring until the mixture comes to the boil. Reduce the heat. Taste the sauce. Add a little salt to taste.

8. Put the pieces of fish in the sauce and simmer gently for 3-5 minutes. Serve the dish on four warmed plates garnished with a little dillweed or coriander.

Malu 'Minah'
Spiced Fish in a Parcel

◀▽   00.10   00.22 🍲
plus standing time

American	Ingredients	Metric/Imperial
4	small cleaned mackerel	4
2 tbsp	lemon juice	2 tbsp
1 tsp	salt	1 tsp
1 tsp	ground turmeric	1 tsp
	pinch black pepper	
1	large chopped onion	1
1-2	coarsely chopped garlic cloves	1-2
1½ tsp	Ceylon curry (see page 282)	1½ tsp
1 tsp	ground red chili	1 tsp
1 tbsp	groundnut oil	1 tbsp

1. Rinse the fish on the inside and outside under cold running water. Dry with kitchen paper.
2. Mix the lemon juice with salt, turmeric and pepper.
3. Use a sharp knife to make deep incisions in the skin of the fish at ¾ in (1.75 cm) intervals. Rub the fish with the lemon juice mixture. Leave to stand for 15 minutes.
4. Put the onion, garlic, curry, chili and 1 tbsp of water in a food processor. Process until the ingredients form a fine paste.
5. Brush 4 sheets of aluminum foil with a little oil. Rub the fish with the onion paste and put them on the sheets of foil. Fold the foil loosely round them.
6. Put the parcels on the rack of a broiler (grill) pan or on the middle shelf of a hot (240°C/475°F/ Gas Mark 9) oven and cook for 20 minutes, turning the parcels over after 10 minutes.
7. Open the parcels and cook for a further 2 minutes. Serve immediately, still in the foil packets.

Cook's tip: accompany with a few sambols and dry boiled rice, served separately.

Malu bola
Deep Fried Fish Balls

00.25 Serves 4   **00.15**

American	Ingredients	Metric/Imperial
1 lb	mackerel fillets	450 g/1 lb
1 ½ lb	peeled, boiled cold potatoes	700 g/1 ½ lb
1 tbsp	groundnut oil	1 tbsp
1	large chopped onion	1
2	lightly beaten eggs	2
6 tbsp	breadcrumbs	6 tbsp
1 tsp	salt	1 tsp
	pinch black pepper	
1 tsp	Ceylon curry (see page 282)	1 tsp
1 tbsp	finely chopped dillweed	1 tbsp
1	seeded, finely chopped red chili	1
1	seeded, finely chopped green chili	1
8 tbsp	lightly toasted breadcrumbs	8 tbsp
	groundnut oil for deep frying	

1. Rinse the fish under cold running water. Dry with kitchen paper. Chop the fish into small pieces or grind (mince) finely. Put the chopped or ground (minced) fish on a piece of muslin, fold the muslin round the fish and squeeze out as much liquid as possible.
2. Mash the boiled potatoes very finely. Add the fish and mix.
3. Heat 1 tbsp of oil in a wok and stir fry the onion until beginning to color. Leave the onion to cool and add it, together with the eggs, 6 tbsp breadcrumbs, salt, pepper, curry, dillweed and chilies, to the fish and potato mixture. Work together well with the fingers. Shape the mixture into walnut-sized balls. Roll them through the toasted bread-crumbs. Press the breadcrumbs into the mixture.
4. Fry the fish balls a few at a time until golden brown.

Cook's tip: accompany the deep fried fish balls with a few sambols (see page 283-284), dry boiled rice and a salad.

Kaku luwo
Crab Curry

00.05 Serves 4   **00.45**

American	Ingredients	Metric/Imperial
2 tbsp	groundnut oil	2 tbsp
3	chopped onions	3
3-4	very finely chopped garlic cloves	3-4
1 tbps	grated fresh root ginger	1 tbsp
½ tsp	fenugreek seeds	½ tsp
1 (1 in)	cinnamon stick	1 (2.5 cm/1 in)
1 tsp	ground turmeric	1 tsp
½ tsp	ground red chili	½ tsp
1 ½ tsp	salt	1 ½ tsp
4 tbsp	desiccated coconut	4 tbsp
2 ¼ cups	thin coconut milk	500 ml/18 fl oz
2 tbsp	lemon juice	2 tbsp
1 ½ lb	crabmeat, thawed if frozen	700 g/1 ½ lb
½ tsp	Ceylon curry (see page 282)	½ tsp

1. Heat the oil in a wok and stir fry the onions until transparent.
2. Add the garlic, root ginger, fenugreek, cinnamon, turmeric, chili, salt and coconut and stir well.
3. Add the coconut milk and lemon juice. Bring to the boil then reduce the heat. Cover the wok and simmer gently for 30 minutes. Strain the sauce into a saucepan and bring back to the boil.
4. Cut the crabmeat into 1 in (2.5 cm) pieces. Add to the hot sauce and cook for 10-12 minutes (fresh crab), 4-5 minutes (frozen crab).
5. Add the Ceylon curry and stir well. Transfer to deep warmed plates and serve.

Cook's tip: accompany with dry boiled rice served in individual bowls. In Sri Lanka a curry of this kind is always served in combination with one or more sambols (see pages 283-284).

Isso thel dhala
Fried Shrimp (Prawns) in Tomato Sauce

00.15 Serves 4   **00.40**

American	Ingredients	Metric/Imperial
1 ¼ lb	large peeled shrimp (prawns) thawed if frozen	575 g/1 ¼ lb
3 tbsp	groundnut oil	3 tbsp
3	large chopped onions	3
1	very finely chopped garlic clove	1
½ tsp	ground red chili	½ tsp
1 tbsp	ground paprika	1 tbsp
	pinch ground turmeric	
1 tbsp	dried shrimp or fish powder (optional)	1 tbsp
5 tbsp	tomato purée	5 tbsp
2 tsp	sugar	2 tsp
4	skinned tomatoes cut into segments	4
1-2	seeded green chilies cut into very thin strips	1-2
6-8	slices white bread with the crusts removed, cut into strips and fried in hot oil	6-8

1. Dry the shrimp (prawns) with kitchen paper.
2. Heat 2 tbsp of oil in a wok and stir fry the onions until beginning to color.
3. Add the garlic and stir well.
4. Add the chili, paprika, turmeric and fish or shrimp powder. Stir well a few times.
5. Add the tomato purée and sugar. Pour on 1 ¼ cups (300 ml/½ pint) boiling water and stir thoroughly. Reduce the heat, cover and simmer gently for 30 minutes.
6. Cut each shrimp (prawn) tail into 3-4 pieces.
7. Heat the remainder of the oil in a wok or frying pan and stir fry the shrimp (prawns) for 5-6 minutes until cooked. (Chopped frozen shrimp (prawns) for 3 minutes). Stir the fried shrimp (prawns) through the sauce and serve on warmed plates.
8. Garnish with tomato segments and strips of chili. Serve the fried bread separately.

Kaku luwo omlet

Crab Omelette

▟ 00.15
Serves 4

00.10 ⌁

American	Ingredients	Metric/Imperial
½ lb	crabmeat, thawed if frozen	225 g/8 oz
1 tbsp	lemon juice	1 tbsp
	salt	
	freshly ground pepper	
6	lightly beaten eggs	6
2 tbsp	ghee or butter	2 tbsp
3	coarsely chopped scallions (spring onions)	3
1	small, seeded red chili cut into very thin strips	1
1 tbsp	finely chopped dillweed	1 tbsp
½ tbsp	groundnut oil	½ tbsp

1. Cut the crabmeat into 1 in (2.5 cm) pieces and sprinkle with lemon juice.
2. Add salt and pepper to the lightly beaten eggs.
3. Heat the ghee or butter in a frying pan and stir fry the scallions (spring onions) for 1 minute.
4. Add the strips of red chili and fry with the onion for a few seconds. Reduce the heat and add the beaten egg.
5. Immediately sprinkle the dillweed over the egg. Cover the pan with a lid and cook the egg mixture until it has set on top, but still appears moist on top.
6. Stir fry the pieces of crab in a little groundnut oil for 5 minutes (raw crab) 2 minutes (frozen crab).
7. Distribute the fried crab evenly over the omelette.
8. Slide the omelette on to a warmed plate and fold it over.

Alu kehel curry

Banana Curry

▟ 00.05
Serves 4

00.25 ⌁

American	Ingredients	Metric/Imperial
6	green bananas	6
1 tsp	salt	1 tsp
1 tsp	ground turmeric	1 tsp
4 tbsp	groundnut oil	4 tbsp
1¼ cups	thin coconut milk	300 ml/½ pint
1	small chopped onion	1
¾ tsp	salt	¾ tsp
1 tsp	Ceylon curry (see page 282)	1 tsp
1 (2 in)	cinnamon stick (optional)	1 (5 cm/2 in)
5 tbsp	thick coconut milk	5 tbsp

1. Peel the bananas and cut obliquely into ¼ in (5 mm) slices.
2. Mix together 1 tsp salt and ground turmeric and rub into the slices of banana.
3. Heat the oil and stir fry the banana slices until golden brown on both sides.
4. Bring the coconut milk to the boil in a small saucepan.
5. Add the onion and simmer gently for 10 minutes.
6. Add ¾ tsp salt, curry and the cinnamon stick if using. Stir well.
7. Add the thick coconut milk and stir well again.
8. Add the slices of banana to the sauce and simmer very gently for 5-8 minutes.
9. Remove the cinnamon stick and serve the curry in warmed individual dishes or bowls.

Cook's tip: the banana curry may be 'enriched' by adding the diced flesh of 1 ripe mango immediately before serving. Similar side dishes to the banana curry can be made in the same manner with zucchini (courgettes), eggplants (aubergines) and cucumbers. Cut all of these into ¼ in (5 mm) slices after they have been scrubbed or peeled. Sprinkle the slices with a little salt and let them drain for at least 30 minutes. Dry with kitchen paper and rub with a mixture of 3 parts ground turmeric to 1 part salt. Then treat in exactly the same way as indicated in the recipe for banana curry.

Crab curry

Vegetables in coconut sauce

Elolu kiri hodhi

Vegetables in Coconut Milk Sauce

	00.15	00.15
	Serves 4	

American	Ingredients	Metric/Imperial
1	trimmed, seeded red bell pepper cut into thin strips	1
1	trimmed, seeded green bell pepper , cut into thin strips	1
½ lb	haricots verts or thin string beans, cut into 1 in (2.5 cm) pieces	225 g/8 oz
1	small cauliflower, divided into small sprigs, or	1
¾ lb	broccoli, divided into sprigs stalks cut into ½ in (1.25 cm) slices	350 g/12 oz
2	seeded red chilies cut into very thin strips	2
1	large onion, cut into 8 segments and the layers loosened	1
⅔ cup	thin coconut milk	150 ml/¼ pint
1 tsp	ground turmeric	1 tsp
1 tbsp	lemon juice	1 tbsp
2 tsp	salt	2 tsp
½ tsp	Ceylon curry (see page 282)	½ tsp
⅔ cup	thick coconut milk	150 ml/¼ pint

1. Put all the vegetables in a saucepan.
2. Add the red chilies and onion. Stir well together.
3. Add the thin coconut milk and stir in the ground turmeric.
4. Bring quickly to the boil and boil gently for 8-10 minutes.
5. Add the lemon juice, salt, curry and the thick coconut milk. Stir well and bring to the boil.
6. Serve immediately in a large warmed bowl.

Watakka curry

Pumpkin Curry

	00.10	00.15
	Serves 4	

American	Ingredients	Metric/Imperial
1 ¼ lb	peeled pumpkin cut into cubes	575 g/1 ¼ lb
1	chopped onion	1
1	crushed garlic clove	1
2	seeded red chilies cut into very thin strips	2
1 ¼ cups	thin coconut milk	300 ml/½ pint
1 tsp	salt	1 tsp
1 ½ tsp	Ceylon curry (see page 282)	1 ½ tsp
5 tbsp	thick coconut milk	5 tbsp
1 tsp	finely ground black mustard seeds	1 tsp

1. Put the cubes of pumpkin in a saucepan.
2. Add the onion, garlic, red chilies and thin coconut milk. Bring slowly to the boil. Simmer gently for up to 8 minutes with the lid on the saucepan until the pumpkin is tender.
3. Add the salt, curry and thick coconut milk. Bring to the boil again.

4. Sprinkle on the mustard seeds and stir carefully a few times. Transfer the curry to a large warmed dish.
Cook's tip: unripe melon, peaches, pears and apples can be prepared in the same way to create delicious side dishes.

Aam Chatni

Mango Chutney

□◁──▷ 00.10
plus standing time
00.00 🍲

American	Ingredients	Metric/Imperial
1 lb	ripe mango	450 g/1 lb
2	green chilies	2
1½ tsp	salt	1½ tsp
3 tsp	sugar	3 tsp
2 tbsp	finely chopped mint leaves	2 tbsp

1. Peel the mango, halve it and cut the stone out of the flesh. Chop the flesh very finely.
2. Rinse the chilies, trim, seed and cut them lengthwise. Chop the flesh very finely. Mix in the chopped mango.
3. Add the salt, sugar and mint leaves. Leave the mixture to stand for 15 minutes. Rub the mixture through a very fine strainer (sieve) or purée in a blender or food processor.

Tamatar chatni

Tomato Chutney

□◁──▷ 00.10
plus standing time
00.00 🍲

American	Ingredients	Metric/Imperial
4	large ripe, skinned tomatoes	4
2 tsp	sambal ulek (see page 128)	2 tsp
1 tsp	finely grated fresh root ginger	1 tsp
1 tsp	salt	1 tsp
½ tsp	ground black pepper	½ tsp
2 tbsp	lemon juice	2 tbsp
2 tbsp	finely chopped coriander or parsley leaves	2 tbsp

1. Halve the tomatoes. Remove the seeds and the liquid. Chop the flesh very finely.
2. Mix the tomatoes with the sambal ulek.
3. Add the remaining ingredients. Leave to stand for 15 minutes then rub the chutney through a fine strainer (sieve) or purée in a blender or food processor.

Tamatar chatni (II)

Tomato Chutney (II)

□◁──▷ 00.15
plus standing time
00.00 🍲

American	Ingredients	Metric/Imperial
4	large, ripe, skinned tomatoes	4
1	green chili	1
2	chopped scallions (spring onions)	2
1 tsp	finely grated fresh root ginger	1 tsp
¾ tsp	salt	¾ tsp
½ tsp	sugar	½ tsp
	small pinch ground black pepper	
1 tbsp	lemon juice	1 tbsp
1 tsp	finely chopped coriander leaves or parsley	1 tsp

1. Halve the tomatoes. Remove the seeds and the liquid. Chop the flesh very finely.
2. Rinse, trim and seed the chili. Chop the flesh very finely.
3. Put all the ingredients in a bowl and stir well. Leave to stand for 15 minutes then rub through a fine strainer (sieve) or purée in a blender or food processor.

Cook's tip: like all the other Sri Lankan chutneys, the tomato chutney tastes best when it is fresh, but if kept it in a well sealed jar it can be stored in the refrigerator for a few days. The flavor then begins to be lost.

Pumpkin curry

MENU

Fish balls in curry sauce
Braised beef in coconut sauce
Leek with chilies
Coconut blancmange

Fish Balls in Curry Sauce

00. 15 Serves 4   00.25

American	Ingredients	Metric/Imperial
1 lb	cod fillets	450 g/1 lb
¼ lb	fresh peeled shrimp (prawns)	125 g/4 oz
	salt	
	freshly ground pepper	
1	lightly beaten egg	1
2 tbsp	flour	2 tbsp
2 tbsp	white bread crumbs	2 tbsp
1 tbsp	groundnut oil	1 tbsp
1	large chopped onion	1
2 tbsp	curry powder	2 tbsp
2	finely chopped garlic cloves	2
2 tbsp	desiccated coconut	2 tbsp
	oil for frying	

1. Rinse the fish under cold running water. Dry with kitchen paper and cut into pieces. Grind (mince) the fish finely.
2. Mix the fish with the shrimp (prawns) and add salt, pepper and 1 tbsp lightly beaten egg. Work together well with the fingers and shape the mixture into walnut sized balls.
3. Mix the flour and breadcrumbs together.
4. Dip the fish balls in the remaining beaten egg, then roll them in the flour and breadcrumb mixture.
5. Heat 1 tbsp groundnut oil in a wok and fry the onion until beginning to color. Add the curry powder and garlic and fry gently for 1 minute. Stir in the desiccated coconut and immediately add ⅓ pint (200 ml/7 fl oz) boiling water. Cook, stirring for about 10 minutes until the sauce thickens. Keep warm.
6. Heat the oil until very hot and fry the fish balls a few at a time until golden brown. Drain well.
7. Arrange the fish balls on a warmed dish and spoon the hot sauce over.

Braised Beef in Coconut Sauce

00.05 Serves 4   02.10

American	Ingredients	Metric/Imperial
2 cups	thin coconut milk	450 ml/¾ pint
2	medium size chopped onions	2
2	crushed garlic cloves	2
1 tbsp	finely grated fresh root ginger	1 tbsp
1 tsp	ground turmeric	1 tsp
½ tsp	fenugreek seeds	½ tsp
2 tbsp	lemon juice	2 tbsp
	salt	
	freshly ground pepper	
1 lb	lean beef, in one piece	450 g/1 lb
½	sliced cucumber (optional)	½

1. Bring the coconut milk to the boil. Add all other ingredients except the meat and cucumber. Stir well, add the meat and bring back to the boil.
2. Cover the pan, reduce the heat and cook for 2 hours until the meat is tender.
3. Remove the meat from the pan and slice thinly. Arrange the slices on a warmed dish and keep warm.
4. Bring the sauce to the boil again and simmer until approximately ¾ of the original quantity remains. Spoon the sauce over the meat.
5. Serve garnished with slices of cucumber.

Leek with Chilies

00.05 Serves 4 — 00.06

American	Ingredients	Metric/Imperial
2	red chilies	2
4 tbsp	groundnut oil	4 tbsp
4	medium size leeks cut into rings	4
2 tbsp	crushed dried fish (Ikan bilis or bombay duck)	2 tbsp
	salt	

1. Rinse the chilies, trim, seed and slice very thinly.
2. Heat the oil in a large pan and fry the leeks for 2 minutes.
3. Add the chilies and fry for 3 minutes.
4. Add the dried fish and ⅓ pint (200 ml/7 fl oz) boiling water. Stir well and simmer gently for 3 minutes.
5. Add a little salt to taste and serve on a warmed dish.

Watalappan

Coconut Blancmange

00.20 Serves 4 — 00.00

American	Ingredients	Metric/Imperial
2	eggs	2
3	egg yolks	3
1 tbsp	superfine (caster) sugar	1 tbsp
1 cup	heavy (double) cream	250 ml/8 fl oz
⅓ pint	thick coconut milk	200 ml/7 fl oz
½ tsp	ground cinnamon	½ tsp
	pinch ground cardamom	
	pinch ground mace	
1 cup	palm sugar	225 g/8 oz

1. Beat the eggs, egg yolks and superfine (caster) sugar together until creamy.
2. In a bain marie bring the cream and coconut milk to the boil. Immediately pour the mixture slowly into the eggs in a thin stream, stirring in the cinnamon, cardamom and mace.
3. Reheat the mixture carefully, stirring until it thickens. Do not heat for too long or the mixture will curdle.
4. Pour the mixture into a mould or moulds and leave to set.
5. Put the palm sugar into a pan over low heat, with ⅓ pint (200 ml/7 fl oz) water. Dissolve the sugar in the water stirring continuously. Strain the liquid, return to the pan and boil rapidly until the liquid is syrupy.
6. Pour the syrup over the blancmange just before serving.

BURMA

Ohn htaminh (I)
Rice Boiled in Coconut Milk

	00.05	00.20	
	Serves 4		

American	Ingredients	Metric/Imperial
2 cups	long grain rice	450 g/1 lb
2 cups	thin coconut milk	450 ml/¾ pint
1-1½ tsp	salt	1-1½ tsp

1. Rinse the rice in several changes of cold water until the water runs clear. Put the wet rice into a pan.
2. Add the coconut milk and salt. Slowly bring to the boil, stirring continuously. Cover the pan. Reduce the heat and cook for 20 minutes. Do not remove the lid from the pan during the cooking time. When cooked, stir well and remove the lid. Leave the rice in the pan for a few minutes for any remaining liquid to evaporate.

Ohn htaminh (II)
Rice Boiled in Coconut Milk (II)

	00.10	00.25	
	Serves 4		

American	Ingredients	Metric/Imperial
1 cup	long grain rice	225 g/8 oz
2 cups	thin coconut milk	450 ml/¾ pint
1 tsp	salt	1 tsp
1	small red chili plus ½ tsp sea salt or	1
2 tsp	sambal ulek (see page 128)	2 tsp
1½ tbsp	groundnut oil	1½ tbsp
1	finely chopped onion	1
1	crushed garlic clove	1

1. Cook the rice as directed in Rice boiled in coconut milk (1).
2. Add 1 tsp of salt.
3. Rinse and trim the chili and grind to a fine paste with the sea salt in a mortar or food processor.
4. Heat the oil in a wok and stir fry the onion until golden.
5. Add the garlic and a few seconds later the red pepper paste or sambal ulek. Stir well and fry until soft. Rub through a fine strainer (sieve) until smooth.
6. Add the mixture to the rice when the rice is cooked and the pan lid can be removed. Stir the rice with a large fork to distribute the spice mixture evenly. Leave the rice to steam dry for a few minutes.

Cook's tip: serve this spiced rice with dishes and side dishes that are only lightly spiced, but in which the same flavorings are used as for the rice.

See htaminh
Rice Dish with Sesame Seeds

	00.10	00.50	
	plus drying and cooling time		

American	Ingredients	Metric/Imperial
½ cup	long grain rice	125 g/4 oz
½ cup	glutinous rice	125 g/4 oz
4 tbsp	groundnut oil	4 tbsp
2	large coarsely chopped onions	2
1 tsp	ground turmeric	1 tsp
	salt	
6 tbsp	sesame seeds	6 tbsp

1. Rinse the two kinds of rice separately in plenty of cold water until the rinsing water runs clear. Drain in a colander, in a draughty place to dry the rice quickly.
2. Heat the oil in a pan and stir fry the onions until golden brown.
3. Stir in the turmeric. Remove half of the onions from the pan with a slotted spoon. Set aside.
4. Add the rice a little at a time to the remaining onions, stirring and turning continuously until every grain is glazed with oil.
5. Add 2 cups (450 ml/¾ pint) boiling water and a little salt. Bring back to the boil, stirring continuously. Cover the pan, reduce the heat and simmer for 35-40 minutes.
6. Heat a dry frying pan, and roast the sesame seeds until they pop, shaking the pan continuously. Leave to go cold on a large cold plate.
7. Transfer the rice to a warmed dish. Top with the reserved fried onions and sprinkle with sesame seeds.

Kyasan
Rice Vermicelli

	00.00	00.10	
	Serves 4		

American	Ingredients	Metric/Imperial
½ lb	rice vermicelli or noodles	225 g/8 oz

1. Prepare the rice vermicelli exactly as directed on the packet.

Cook's tip: a number of other ingredients are always served with the cooked rice vermicelli, which is placed in the center of a large warmed dish. These are generally limited to three or four, such as: – chopped scallions (spring onions) – finely chopped coriander leaves – paste made from chilies, finely ground with salt. (This could be replaced with sambal ulek – (see page 128) – lemon segments – coarsely chopped garlic clove, possibly lightly fried in oil – bean sprouts, rinsed and drained well.)

Kauekswe kyau
Fried Noodles with Chicken and Vegetables

00.10 plus soaking time **00.20**

American	Ingredients	Metric/Imperial
6	large dried Chinese mushrooms	6
½ lb	Chinese egg noodles	225 g/8 oz
2 tbsp	sesame oil	2 tbsp
1 lb	chicken breast fillets	450 g/1 lb
3-4	chicken livers	3-4
6 tbsp	groundnut oil	6 tbsp
2	large coarsely chopped onions	2
2 tbsp	soy sauce	2 tbsp
½ lb	shredded Chinese leaves	225 g/8 oz
½ lb	coarsely chopped white, green or savoy cabbage	225 g/8 oz
3	finely chopped garlic cloves	3
2	sticks thinly sliced blanched celery	2
6	chopped scallions (spring onions) or 1 leek	6
4	eggs	4
	salt	
	freshly ground pepper	

1. Put the dried mushrooms in a bowl with boiling water to cover. Leave to soak for 30 minutes. Discard the stalks and slice the caps thinly. Drain well.
2. Prepare the noodles as instructed on the packet. Drain, then sprinkle with sesame oil. Turn the noodles a few times to ensure that all of the noodles are covered with the oil.
3. Dry the chicken and chicken livers with kitchen paper. Cut the chicken into narrow strips and the livers into small cubes.
4. Heat 4 tbsp of oil in a wok and stir fry the onions until golden.
5. Stir in the pieces of chicken. Add the chicken liver and stir fry until the chicken has changed color.
6. Stir in the soy sauce and add all the vegetables, the garlic and mushrooms. Stir fry gently for 3 minutes. Transfer to a warmed dish and keep hot.
7. Lightly beat the eggs with a little salt, pepper and 2 tbsp water.
8. Heat 1 tbsp of oil in a wok, add the eggs and stir fry until scrambled and quite dry. Leave to cool on a large cold plate.
9. Heat a further tbsp of oil in a wok and stir fry the noodles for 3-4 minutes. Spread the noodles on a large shallow warmed dish.
10. Spoon over the meat and vegetable mixture and top with the scrambled eggs.

Cook's tip: this dish can be served warm or cold. It is almost always accompanied by a little bowl of finely ground red and/or green chilies.

Fried noodles with chicken and vegetables

Htaminh lethoke

Burmese Meal with Rice and Side Dishes

◣ 00.15	00.30 ⌂
Serves 4	

American	Ingredients	Metric/Imperial
1 cup	long grain rice	225 g/8 oz
1 tsp	salt	1 tsp
2 tsp	finely ground red chilies or sambal ulek	2 tsp
3 oz	cooked vermicelli	75 g/3 oz
2 oz	cooked Chinese egg noodles	50 g/2 oz
3-4	large, unpeeled boiled potatoes	3-4
¼ lb	bean sprouts	125 g/4 oz
4	eggs	4
	salt	
	freshly ground pepper	
1 ½ tbsp	groundnut oil	1 ½ tbsp
8	large coarsely chopped onions	8
4 tbsp	groundnut oil	4 tbsp
8	finely chopped garlic cloves	8
2 oz	dried shrimp (prawns)	50 g/2 oz
1 cup	chick-pea flour (besan)	100 g/4 oz
4 tbsp	finely ground red chilies or sambal ulek	4 tbsp
5 tbsp	Burmese fish sauce (ngan pya ye)	5 tbsp
	juice of 2 lemons	

1. Rinse the rice in plenty of cold water until the rinsing water runs clear. Put the rice into a pan with 1½ cups (350 ml/12 fl oz) cold water. Add 1 tsp salt, bring the water to the boil, reduce the heat and simmer for 20 minutes.

2. Stir in 2 tsp finely ground red chilies or sambal ulek with a large (meat) fork, and leave to steam dry for 2-3 minutes. Keep warm.

3. Cook the rice vermicelli and egg noodles according to the instructions on the packet and keep warm.

4. Skin the boiled potatoes, cut into slices and keep warm.

5. Rinse the bean sprouts under cold running water and remove as many seed cases as possible. Drain in a colander. Pour a few quarts/litres boiling water over the bean sprouts and drain once more.

6. Arrange the rice in the middle of a large, shallow warmed dish.

7. Arrange the rice vermicelli, the egg noodles, the slices of boiled potato and the bean sprouts around the outside.

8. Place the side dishes in small bowls around the dish.

Side dishes:

1. Lightly beat the eggs in a bowl. Add a little salt, pepper and 2 tbsp of water.

2. Heat ½ tbsp oil in a wok and pour in the egg mixture and stir continuously until dry scrambled. Transfer the scrambled eggs into one or more small bowls.

3. Place half the chopped onions in a colander. Slowly pour over 2 quarts/litres boiling water. Drain well and transfer into a small bowl.

4. Heat 4 tbsp of oil in a wok and stir fry the remaining onions until beginning to color.

5. Add half the garlic and fry gently for 1 minute. Spoon into a strainer (sieve). Drain for 2 minutes and put into a small bowl.

6. Place the remaining garlic in a bowl.

7. Place the dried shrimp (prawns), chick-pea flour, 4 tbsp finely ground red chilies or sambal ulek, fish sauce and lemon juice into small bowls.

8. Put the large dish with the rice and accompaniments in the center of the table. Arrange the bowls around it and each guest serves himself by taking some rice or one of the other ingredients from the large dish and mixing it with one of the ingredients from the bowls.

Burmese meal with rice and side dishes

Panthe kaukswe

Chicken in Coconut Sauce with Egg Noodles

OO.15
Serves 4

OO.35

American	Ingredients	Metric/Imperial
2 lb	chicken breast fillets	900 g/2 lb
2	chopped garlic cloves	2
2	medium size chopped onions	2
1 tbsp	grated fresh root ginger	1 tbsp
½ tsp	shrimp (prawn) paste (ngapi)	½ tsp
2 tbsp	groundnut oil	2 tbsp
	salt	
2¼ cups	thick coconut milk	500 ml/18 fl oz
2 tbsp	chick-pea flour (besan)	2 tbsp
½ lb	egg noodles (approx 8 nests)	225 g/8 oz
2 tbsp	sesame oil	2 tbsp
8	chopped scallions (spring onions) or 1 leek	8
4 tbsp	finely chopped coriander leaves	4 tbsp
1	lemon, cut into segments	1
3 oz	washed, drained bean sprouts	75 g/3 oz

1. Dry the chicken with kitchen paper and cut into 1 in (2.5 cm) cubes.
2. Purée the garlic, onions, root ginger and shrimp (prawn) paste and 1 tbsp of oil in a food processor or mortar.
3. Heat the remaining groundnut oil in a wok and stir fry the paste until beginning to darken.
4. Add the chicken and salt to taste, and fry gently for 2 minutes.
5. Add the coconut milk and ¾ cup (200 ml/7 fl oz) boiling water. Stir well.
6. Mix the chick-pea flour with 3 tbsp cold water and stir into the contents of the wok. Reduce the heat and cook very gently for 5-7 minutes. Add salt to taste.
7. Prepare the egg noodles according to the instructions on the packet. Drain well and sprinkle with a little sesame oil.
8. Warm the noodles over very low heat in a wok, stirring continuously. Transfer to a warmed dish and sprinkle with scallions (spring onions) or leek.
9. Transfer the chicken and sauce to a warmed dish.
10. Place the dishes on the table and arrange some small bowls containing coriander leaves, lemon segments and bean sprouts around them.

Cook's tip: accompany this dish with a rolled omelette (made from 3-4 eggs) if liked.

Nga tha lauk paung
Soused Fish

00. 10   06.00
Serves 4

American	Ingredients	Metric/Imperial
4	cleaned mackerel or herring	4
1	large thinly sliced onion	1
3	finely grated garlic cloves	3
1 tbsp	coarsely grated fresh root ginger	1 tbsp
12	lightly crushed black peppercorns	12
2	trimmed, seeded green chilies	2
	salt	
2 quarts	white vinegar	2 litres/3 ½ pints

1. Rinse the fish inside and out, their heads, tails and fins removed, under cold running water. Dry with kitchen paper.
2. Heat the oven to 150°C/300°F/Gas Mark 2.
3. Place the fish in an ovenproof dish large enough to lay them side by side. Arrange the onion slices over the fish.
4. Sprinkle with the garlic, root ginger and peppercorns.
5. Place halved chilies between the fish and sprinkle on a little salt.
6. Add vinegar to cover.
7. Place the dish just below the center of the oven and reduce the heat to 120°C/250°F/Gas Mark ½. Cook for about 6 hours. Add extra vinegar if necessary.
8. Serve the fish in the dish and accompany with boiled rice.

Chicken in coconut sauce with egg noodles

Fish in a parcel

Pazoon kyaw
Broiled (Grilled) Spiced Prawns

	00.05 Serves 4	00.10

American	Ingredients	Metric/Imperial
16-20	large prawns (scampi or Chinese king prawns)	16-20
1 tsp	salt	1 tsp
1½ tsp	ground paprika	1½ tsp
1 tsp	ground turmeric	1 tsp
½ tsp	ground chili	½ tsp
½ tsp	ground root ginger	½ tsp
3 tbsp	groundnut oil	3 tbsp
½ tsp	sesame oil	½ tsp
1	head lettuce	1

1. Mix together the salt, paprika, turmeric, chili and ginger.
2. Add the groundnut and sesame oils and stir well.
3. Coat the prawns in the seasoned oil.
4. Thread the peeled prawns on to a metal skewer or sate sticks that have first been soaked in water for 30 minutes (this prevents them from burning when broiling (grilling) the prawns). Cook the prawns for 7-10 minutes, under a hot broiler (grill) or over a barbecue, turning occasionally.
5. Serve the prawns on a bed of lettuce leaves or finely chopped iceberg lettuce.

Cook's tip: the spiced prawns are equally delicious fried in hot vegetable oil.

Nga baungh doke
Fish in a Parcel

	00.10 Serves 4	00.20

American	Ingredients	Metric/Imperial
2 lb	cod fillets	900 g/2 lb
	salt	
	freshly ground pepper	
2	large chopped onions	2
2	chopped garlic cloves	2
	pinch ground turmeric	
1 tbsp	fresh grated root ginger	1 tbsp
2 tbsp	thick coconut milk	2 tbsp
1 tbsp	ground rice	1 tbsp
2 tbsp	sesame oil	2 tbsp
8	leaves of Chinese mustard cabbage	8

1. Rinse the fish under cold running water and dry with kitchen paper. Divide into 8 equal pieces and sprinkle with a little salt and pepper.
2. Purée half the onions, the garlic, turmeric, root ginger, coconut milk, ground rice and sesame oil in a food processor or mortar.
3. Lay out 8 pieces of aluminum foil on the work surface and spread with the paste. Lay the fish on top.
4. Trim the cabbage leaves and lay the leaves on top of the fish.
5. Scatter the remaining onions over and wrap the foil loosely round the fish.

6. Place the fish parcels in a large steaming pan and steam the fish for 15-20 minutes.
7. Serve the fish in the parcels.

Cook's tip: serve accompanied with boiled rice, or egg noodles that have been boiled and then fried.

Nga see bayan
Fish Curry with Special Sauce

	00.10	00.15	
	plus standing time		

American	Ingredients	Metric/Imperial
2 lb	cod fillets	900 g/2 lb
2 tbsp	Burmese fish sauce (ngan pya ye) or Vietnamese fish sauce (nuoc mam)	2 tbsp
2 tbsp	groundnut oil	2 tbsp
2	large chopped onions	2
1	finely shredded garlic clove	1
1 tsp	fresh grated root ginger	1 tsp
1	piece lemon zest	1
	salt	
1 tsp	ground turmeric	1 tsp
2	trimmed, seeded, shredded green chilies	2

1. Rinse the fish under cold running water and dry with kitchen paper. Cut into 1 in (2.5 cm) cubes.
2. Place the cubes in a dish and sprinkle with the fish sauce, turning the cubes in the sauce several times. Leave to stand for 15 minutes.
3. Heat the oil in a wok and stir fry the onions until golden brown.
4. Add the garlic and root ginger, lemon zest, a little salt, the ground turmeric and finely shredded chilies. Stir well. Place the mixture in a strainer (sieve) and rub the solid ingredients through. Return the mixture to the wok and reheat.
5. Add the cubes of fish and stir fry in the mixture until cooked.

Cook's tip: to serve fish curry with a variation of the sauce.
1. Add 1¼ cups (300 ml/½ pint) thin coconut milk directly after reheating the mixture. Bring the sauce to the boil, stirring continuously.
2. Add the cubes of fish. Cook the cubes of fish, stirring continuously and carefully.
3. Add 5 tbsp of thick coconut milk and carefully stir once more. Serve as soon as the sauce has come to the boil. In place of fish sauce, the Burmese also use fish pastes which they eat in small portions with boiled rice and sweet and sour vegetables.

Ngapi htaung
Shrimp (Prawn) Paste

	00.05	00.10	
	Serves 4		

American	Ingredients	Metric/Imperial
2 tbsp	shrimp (prawn) paste (ngapi)	2 tbsp
2	medium size onions	2
2-4	garlic cloves	2-4
2-3 tbsp	dried shrimp (prawns)	2-3 tbsp
2 tbsp	lemon juice	2 tbsp
2 tsp	sesame oil	2 tsp
2 tsp	ground paprika	2 tsp
½ tsp	salt	½ tsp

1. Place the shrimp (prawn) paste on a 10 in (25 cm) square piece of aluminum foil. Fold the foil loosely but carefully to form a parcel (double over the seams). Cook the parcel for approximately 2 minutes on either side under a hot broiler (grill).
2. Peel and chop the onions and garlic and parcel them up in the same way in another piece of aluminum foil.
3. Broil (grill) the onion and garlic mixture put it with the shrimp (prawn) paste, dried shrimp (prawns), lemon juice, sesame oil, paprika and salt to taste in a food processor or mortar and purée.

Ngan pya ye chet
Cold Fish Sauce with Garlic

	00.05	00.02	
	Serves 4		

American	Ingredients	Metric/Imperial
2	medium size onions	2
5-6	garlic cloves	5-6
3	shallots or scallions (spring onions)	3
1 tbsp	groundnut oil	1 tbsp
⅔ cup	fish sauce (ngan pa ye)	150 ml/¼ pint
	chopped zest of ⅓ of a lemon	
½ tsp	ground paprika	½ tsp
	salt	

1. Peel and finely shred the onions and garlic cloves.
2. Peel and chop the shallots or scallions (spring onions).
3. Heat the oil in a pan and fry the onion and garlic for 10 seconds over high heat.
4. Add the fish sauce and gradually bring to the boil, stirring continuously. Remove the pan from the heat.
5. Add the lemon zest, paprika and salt, to taste. Stir well and leave the contents of the pan to cool. Place in a container and chill until just before serving.

Wethani kyet
Curry with Pork

	00.06	00.55
	plus standing time	

American	Ingredients	Metric/Imperial
1½ lb	lean pork or ham	675 g/1½ lb
2	chopped onions	2
2	chopped garlic cloves	2
2 tbsp	fresh grated root ginger	2 tbsp
	salt	
2 tsp	vinegar or lemon juice	2 tsp
1	finely ground red chili or 1 tsp sambal ulek	1
2 tbsp	sesame oil	2 tbsp
2 tbsp	groundnut oil	2 tbsp
1 tsp	ground turmeric	1 tsp

1. Dry the meat with kitchen paper and cut into 1 in (2.5 cm) cubes.
2. Purée the onions, garlic, root ginger, a little salt, vinegar or lemon juice, chili or sambal ulek and 1 tsp sesame oil in a food processor. Spoon the purée into a strainer (sieve) and express as much liquid as possible.
3. Sprinkle the meat with the liquid. Leave the meat to stand for 30 minutes, turning occasionally.
4. Add the remaining sesame oil and the groundnut oil to the paste and bring to the boil. Simmer for 20 minutes.
5. Add the meat and cook, stirring continuously, until it changes color.
6. Add the ground turmeric and 4 tbsp of water. Reduce the heat and simmer for 30 minutes.
7. Add 1-2 tbsp of water if necessary. Serve in a warmed dish.

Cook's tip: in most curry dishes, red onions taste very much better. They have a fuller flavor than white onions. To achieve the sharp and sweet flavor so popular in many Asian countries, in place of the 1-2 tbsp of water added at the end of the cooking time, add 2-3 tbsp of ginger syrup.

Curry with Pork

Serve this curry with an accompaniment of boiled rice, boiled egg noodles or transparent noodles. The noodles should be prepared following the instructions on the packet.

Ame hnat
Beef Curry

	00.10	03.40
	Serves 4	

American	Ingredients	Metric/Imperial
1½ lb	lean braising beef	675 g/1½ lb
4 tbsp	groundnut oil	4 tbsp
2	large coarsely chopped onions	2
2	crushed garlic cloves	2
2 tbsp	fresh grated root ginger	2 tbsp
1	small lemon or lime	1
	salt	
	freshly ground pepper	

1. Dry the meat with kitchen paper and cut into ½ in (1.25 cm) cubes.
2. Heat the oil in a wok and stir fry the meat until lightly browned on all sides.
3. Add the onions, garlic and root ginger and stir fry until the onions appear transparent.
4. Add ¾ cup (200 ml/7 fl oz) boiling water. Stir well.
5. Add the lemon or lime.
6. Sprinkle with a little salt and pepper and stir well.
Reduce the heat, cover the wok and simmer very gently for 3½ hours until the meat is cooked. Add 1-3 tbsp boiling water from time to time if necessary. Most of the liquid should have evaporated at the end of the cooking time. Serve in a warmed dish.

Cook's tip: in Burma a little fried onion is often scattered over the dish just before serving. It is generally accompanied by boiled rice and a vegetable dish.

Ametha net aloo
Curry with Beef and Potatoes

	00.10	02.40
	Serves 4	

American	Ingredients	Metric/Imperial
1½ lb	lean braising beef	675 g/1½ lb
5 tbsp	groundnut oil	5 tbsp
1	large coarsely chopped onion	1
2	crushed garlic cloves	2
1 tbsp	fresh grated root ginger	1 tbsp
1 tsp	ground turmeric	1 tsp
½ tsp	cayenne pepper	½ tsp
½ tsp	ground cumin	½ tsp
½ tsp	ground coriander seeds	½ tsp
	salt	
1 lb	peeled potatoes	450 g/1 lb
1-2	red chilies (optional)	1-2

1. Dry the meat with kitchen paper and cut into ½ in (1.25 cm) cubes.
2. Heat the oil in a wok and stir fry the onion until transparent.
3. Add the garlic and root ginger and stir fry for 1 minute.
4. Add the ground turmeric, cayenne pepper, cumin, ground coriander seeds and a little salt. Stir well.
5. Stir in the meat and 2¼ cups (500 ml/18 fl oz) boiling water. Bring to the boil, cover the wok and reduce the heat. Simmer gently for 2½ hours.
6. Cut the potatoes into ½ in (1.25 cm) cubes.
7. Stir into the meat mixture and simmer gently until the meat and potatoes are cooked.
8. Serve on a warmed dish, garnished with one or more red chili 'flowers.'

Ametha net swephayone

Beef Curry with Pumpkin

| ◢ | 00.10 Serves 4 | 02.20 | |

American	Ingredients	Metric/Imperial
1½ lb	lean braising beef	675 g/1½ lb
1¼ lb	peeled pumpkin	550 g/1¼ lb
5 tbsp	groundnut oil	5 tbsp
1	large coarsely chopped onion	1
2	crushed garlic cloves	2
1 tbsp	fresh grated root ginger	1 tbsp
1 tsp	ground turmeric	1 tsp
½ tsp	cayenne pepper	½ tsp
	salt	
	little finely chopped scallion (spring onion) (optional)	

1. Dry the meat with kitchen paper and cut into ½ in (1.25 cm) cubes.
2. Cut the flesh of the pumpkin into ½ in (1.25 cm) cubes.
3. Heat the oil in a wok and stir fry the onion until transparent.
4. Add the garlic and root ginger and stir fry for 1 minute.
5. Stir in the ground turmeric, cayenne pepper and a little salt and stir fry for 1 minute.
6. Add the meat and 1¼ cups (300 ml/½ pint) boiling water. Stir well. Cover the wok and simmer for 2 hours until the meat is cooked. Add a few tbsp of boiling water from time to time, to maintain the quantity of liquid.
7. Stir the cubes of pumpkin into the dish as soon as the meat is cooked and simmer gently for 2-3 minutes.
8. Serve on a warmed dish, sprinkled with a little chopped scallion (spring onion) (optional).

Cook's tip: this curry dish can be accompanied by boiled rice. As the curry is served with a sauce, a vegetable dish need not be served.

Sanwin makin

Semolina Tart

| ◢ | 00.06 Serves 4 | 00.55 | |

American	Ingredients	Metric/Imperial
2½ cups	thick coconut milk	600 ml/1 pint
¾ cup	coarsely ground semolina	125 g/4 oz
½ cup	sugar	125 g/4 oz
	pinch salt	
3	separated eggs	3
	butter	
3 tbsp	sesame seeds	3 tbsp

1. Bring the coconut milk to the boil.
2. Sprinkle on the semolina and stir until the mixture thickens.
3. Stir in the sugar, salt and egg yolks. Remove the pan from the heat.
4. Whisk the egg whites until stiff and fold into the cooled semolina mixture as lightly as possible. Turn into a round pie dish, lightly greased with butter. Smooth the surface.
5. Heat the oven to 160°C/350°F/Gas Mark 4.
6. Sprinkle the mixture with sesame seeds. Place the dish on the center shelf of the preheated oven. Bake the tart for 40-45 minutes, until golden brown. Leave the tart in the dish to cool.
7. Serve the cold tart cut into fingers.

Kyauk kiau

Burmese Coconut Pudding

| ◢ | 00.10 | 00.15 | |
| | | plus standing and cooling time | |

American	Ingredients	Metric/Imperial
1 (1 oz)	stick agar-agar	1 (25 g/1 oz)
3½ oz	creamed coconut (santen)	100 g/3½ oz
1 cup	sugar	225 g/8 oz

1. Place the agar-agar in a large bowl with water to cover. Leave to soak for 2-3 hours. Remove the agar-agar.
2. Measure out ⅔ cup (150 ml/¼) pint cold water. Take 10 tbsp of this water and bring to the boil in a pan with ¼ crumbled creamed coconut. Stir until the coconut has melted. Remove the pan from the heat and leave to stand.
3. Add the remaining creamed coconut to a second pan with the soaked agar-agar and the sugar.
4. Bring the remainder of the measured quantity of water to the boil in a third pan, then add to the pan with the agar-agar, sugar and creamed coconut and simmer gently on a low heat until the mixture is smooth and creamy. Continue stirring to prevent any lumps from forming and the mixture from catching on the bottom of the pan. Pour the hot mixture into a square glass or earthenware dish, rinsed with water. Allow the mixture to cool a little until tepid.
5. Pour the creamed coconut dissolved in water on to the mixture. Leave to set in a cool place (not the refrigerator) for approximately 1½ hours, until the mixture is sufficiently stiff to be cut with a knife into 2 in (5 cm) cubes or diamond shapes.
6. Place the coconut pudding on an attractive dish and, if liked, decorate with a candied fruit.

Moh let saung
Chilled Coconut Drink

American	Ingredients	Metric/Imperial
4 tbsp	tapioca (sago)	4 tbsp
3 tbsp	soft brown sugar	3 tbsp
2¼ cups	thick coconut milk	500 ml/18 fl oz
	ice cubes	

00.00 plus chilling time   **00.15**

1. Bring 2¼ cups (500 ml/18 fl oz) water to the boil.
2. Add the tapioca and stir continuously until the mixture has thickened slightly.
3. Dissolve the sugar in this mixture, stirring continuously. Leave the mixture to go cold.
4. Whisk in the coconut milk. Chill for 1 hour and whisk again. Pour into tall glasses and add a few cubes of ice.

Cook's tip: this coconut drink acquires a rather special flavor if a few tbsp of dark rum are added.

Kyauk kyaw
Iced Burmese Drink

00.05 plus setting time   **00.15**

American	Ingredients	Metric/Imperial
2¼ cups	water	500 ml/18 fl oz
8 tbsp	soft brown sugar	8 tbsp
	powdered jelly	
3-4	drops rose or almond essence	3-4
	thin coconut milk	
	ice cold water	

1. Pour the water into a heavy-based pan and bring to the boil.
2. Add the sugar and stir until dissolved. Remove the pan from the heat and leave the contents to cool.
3. Add 3-4 drops rose or almond essence and quickly stir through the sugar solution.
4. Mix the powdered jelly according to the instructions on the packet (use, for example, quince powder available from the delicatessen) and leave to set. Press the jelly through a wide-meshed strainer (sieve) into a pan of ice cold water, so that the threads of jelly solidify immediately.
5. Fill a tall glass with 2 tsp syrup, a few tbsp of jelly threads, coconut milk and ice cold water. Serve with a long spoon or drinks stirrer.

Cook's tip: there are many striking vegetable colors available from Chinese and Indian shops. You can color the syrup with these for a party. There are also many different flavors of essence and it is well worth trying some of them out. There are also all kinds of jelly-type granules and threads in a wide range of colors. These are cooked as above and then swell in size.

MENU

Roast shrimp (prawns)
Pork curry with onions
Mixed vegetables in sour sauce
Cold fruit soup

Roast Shrimp (Prawns)

00.02 Serves 4   **00.06**

American	Ingredients	Metric/Imperial
12	large shrimp (prawns) thawed if frozen	12
3 tbsp	groundnut oil	3 tbsp
1 tbsp	sesame oil	1 tbsp
1 tsp	salt	1 tsp
1 tsp	ground turmeric	1 tsp
1 tsp	cayenne pepper	1 tsp

1. Peel the shrimp (prawns), cut them lengthwise and remove the black thread. Rinse and dry with kitchen paper.
2. Mix the two kinds of oil together and add the salt, turmeric and cayenne pepper. Stir well until the salt has dissolved.
3. Coat the shrimp (prawns) in the spiced oil and thread them on to skewers or sate sticks which have been soaked in water.
4. Roast the shrimp (prawns) under a hot broiler (grill) or over a barbecue for 5-6 minutes, brushing with the oil if necessary.
5. Serve immediately.

Cook's tip: the shrimp (prawns) are delicious served with a sauce made of equal parts Indonesian sweet soy sauce, rice wine or dry sherry and ginger syrup.

Pork Curry with Onions

00.05 Serves 4   **00.55**

American	Ingredients	Metric/Imperial
2	large chopped onions	2
4	chopped garlic cloves	4
1 tsp	fresh grated root ginger	1 tsp
2 tbsp	groundnut oil	2 tbsp
1 lb	lean diced pork	450 g/1 lb
1 tbsp	curry powder	1 tbsp
2 tbsp	lemon juice	2 tbsp
1 tbsp	Burmese fish sauce (ngam pya ya)	1 tbsp
1	skinned tomato	1

1. Purée the onion, garlic and root ginger in a food processor.
2. Heat the oil in a wok and stir fry the paste for 5 minutes.
3. Add the pork and stir fry for 5 minutes.
4. Stir in the curry powder and 1 cup (250 ml/8 fl oz) boiling water. Stir well, reduce the heat cover the pan and simmer for 45 minutes.
5. Add the lemon juice and fish sauce and stir well.
6. Transfer to a warmed dish and garnish with a tomato flower.

Mixed Vegetables in Sour Sauce

00.05 Serves 4		00.10

American	Ingredients	Metric/Imperial
½ lb	haricots verts	225 g/8 oz
¼ lb	young carrots	125 g/4 oz
¼ lb	broccoli	125 g/4 oz
1	small head Chinese leaves or paksoi	1
2 tbsp	sesame oil	2 tbsp
1	coarsely chopped onion	1
1	crushed garlic clove	1
2 tbsp	vinegar	2 tbsp
	salt	

1. Cut the haricot verts and carrots into 2 in (5 cm) lengths.
2. Cut the broccoli into small rosettes and the stalks into ½ in (1.25 cm) lengths.

3. Cut the Chinese leaves or paksoi into thin strips.
4. Put all the vegetables into a deep pan with 3 quarts (3 litres/5 pints) boiling water and bring to the boil. Boil for 3 minutes, then drain well in a colander.
5. Heat the oil in a wok and stir fry the onion until golden yellow. Add the garlic, stir well and add the vegetables. Continue stirring until the vegetables are warmed through.
6. Sprinkle with the vinegar and a little salt. Stir well.
7. Transfer to a warmed dish and serve.

Cold Fruit Soup

00.15 Serves 4		00.00

American	Ingredients	Metric/Imperial
1	large ripe mango	1
2 tbsp	coarsely grated fresh coconut	2 tbsp
2 tbsp	sugar	2 tbsp
2 tbsp	lemon or lime juice	2 tbsp
4-8	small red fruits (optional)	4-8

1. Halve and stone the mango. Remove the skin and rub the flesh through a fine strainer.
2. Add the coconut and sugar. Stir well then make up to 2¼ cups (500 ml/18 fl oz) with ice cold water. Stir in the lemon or lime juice.
3. Transfer to small individual serving dishes and garnish with small red fruits.

Cook's tip: this soup can be made with any fresh soft fleshed fruits, such as papaya, melon, avocado or guava. Always use fresh coconut but adjust the quantities of sugar and or lemon or lime juice according to the sweetness of the fruit.

INDIA
AND
PAKISTAN

Garam Masala

	00.15 plus cooling time		00.00

American	Ingredients	Metric/Imperial
4 tbsp	coriander seeds	4 tbsp
2 tbsp	cumin seeds	2 tbsp
2 tbsp	black peppercorns	2 tbsp
2 tsp	cardamom seeds	2 tsp
3 (3 in)	cinnamon sticks	3 (8 cm/3 in)
1 tsp	cloves	1 tsp
1	whole nutmeg	1

1. Heat one or more frying pans and use to dry roast each ingredient (except the nutmeg) separately. Shake the pan to keep the seeds and spices moving. As soon as they start to release their aroma, transfer to a plate and leave to cool.
2. Finely grind the seeds and spices in a coffee mill or with a pestle and mortar.
3. Grate the nutmeg and stir into the spice mixture.
4. Store the garam masala in an airtight jar in a cool, dark place for up to a year.

Panir

Fresh Milk Cheese

	00.05 plus draining time		00.05

American	Ingredients	Metric/Imperial
5 quarts	fresh milk	5 litres/9 pints
1 tsp	salt	1 tsp
⅔ cup	strained lemon or lime juice or white vinegar	150 ml/¼ pint

1. Bring the milk to the boil. Add the salt and lemon or lime juice or vinegar just as the milk begins to boil up in the pan.
2. Bring back to the boil then remove from the heat. Stir until the milk curdles and separates into curds and whey.
3. Line a colander with a wet piece of muslin. Pour the curdled milk into the cloth and leave to drain for 30 minutes.
4. Lift the corners of the cloth with one hand and press out as much liquid as possible with the other. Tie the cloth tightly around the cheese.
5. Put a plate on top of the cheese in the colander and put weights on top. Leave for 2-3 hours before using the cheese.

Coconut Milk

	00.03		00.00

American	Ingredients	Metric/Imperial
2 cups	desiccated coconut	175 g/7 oz
5 cups	boiling water	1.2 litres/2 pints

1. For 1½ cups (350 ml/12 fl oz) thick coconut milk, put the desiccated coconut in a blender or food processor. Add 2½ cups (600 ml/1 pint) boiling water and process for 30 seconds.
2. Strain through a strainer (sieve) lined with a piece of muslin.

3. Leave until the coconut is cool enough to handle then squeeze out as much liquid as possible.
4. To make 2 cups (500 ml/16 fl oz) thin coconut milk, return the same coconut to the blender or food processor and process with a further 2½ cups (600 ml/1 pint) boiling water.
5. Strain and squeeze out as much liquid as possible.

Cook's tip: canned and dried coconut milk are available from many stores stocking Indian and South East Asian ingredients.

Namkin chawal

Perfect Cooked Rice

	00.10		00.30
	plus soaking and drying time		

American	Ingredients	Metric/Imperial
1 cup	long grain rice	225 g/8 oz
1 tbsp	ghee	1 tbsp
½ tsp	salt	½ tsp

1. Rinse the rice very thoroughly in cold water then leave to soak for 30 minutes in cold water to cover.
2. Drain the rice then leave to dry for 30 minutes.
3. Heat the ghee in a large pan. Add the rice and cook gently, stirring for about 2 minutes, until the rice looks opaque.
4. Add 1½ cups (350 ml/12 fl oz) boiling water and the salt. Bring to the boil, cover the pan and simmer for 20-25 minutes.
5. Remove the lid, stir the rice and leave to steam for 2 minutes.
6. Fluff up the rice with a fork and serve.

Left: Spiced rice with lentils
Right: Spiced rice with peas

Khitchri
Spiced Rice with Lentils

01.00 Serves 4   **00.30**

American	Ingredients	Metric/Imperial
¾ cup	long grain rice	175 g/6 oz
¾ cup	red lentils	175 g/6 oz
1 tbsp	ghee or groundnut oil	1 tbsp
2	chopped onions	2
1½ tsp	salt	1½ tsp
1½ tsp	garam masala	1½ tsp

1. Rinse the rice thoroughly in cold water. Leave to soak in cold water for 30 minutes. Drain for 30 minutes.
2. Pick over the lentils and wash them in plenty of cold water. Drain thoroughly.
3. Heat the ghee or groundnut oil in a large, heavy-based saucepan.
4. Add the chopped onion and stir fry until transparent.
5. Remove half the onion from the saucepan and set aside.
6. Add the rice and stir constantly for about three minutes until the rice looks transparent.
7. Add the lentils and 1¼ cups (300 ml/½ pint) boiling water, salt and garam masala. Stir and bring quickly to the boil.
8. Stir again then cover and simmer over a low heat for 25 minutes.
9. Turn into a warmed dish and serve sprinkled with the reserved onions.

Mattar pilau
Spiced Rice with Peas

01.00 Serves 4   **00.30**

American	Ingredients	Metric/Imperial
1 cup	long grain rice	225 g/8 oz
1 tbsp	ghee or groundnut oil	1 tbsp
4	cloves	4
1	cinnamon stick	1
2	cardamom pods	2
1 tsp	cumin seeds	1 tsp
½ tsp	ground turmeric	½ tsp
½ lb	shelled peas	225 g/8 oz
1½ tsp	salt	1½ tsp

1. Rinse the rice thoroughly in cold water. Leave to soak in cold water for 30 minutes. Drain for 30 minutes.
2. Heat the ghee or groundnut oil in a large heavy-based saucepan.
3. Add the cloves, cinnamon, cardamom pods and cumin seeds. Stir fry for 2 minutes and add the ground turmeric.
4. Stir in the rice and peas and add 1¼ cups (300 ml/½ pint) boiling water and the salt. Stir, bring quickly to the boil.
5. Cover and simmer over low heat for 25 minutes.
6. Just before serving, stir the rice and peas with a large fork and remove the cloves, cinnamon stick and cardamom pods.

Sabzi pilau
Spiced Rice with Vegetables

01.00 Serves 4   **00.40**

American	Ingredients	Metric/Imperial
1 cup	long grain rice	225 g/8 oz
¼ lb	french beans	125 g/4 oz
1	small red bell pepper	1
1	potato	1
2 tbsp	ghee or groundnut oil	2 tbsp
2	large chopped onions	2
2	finely chopped garlic cloves	2
1 tsp	garam masala	1 tsp
1 tsp	salt	1 tsp
½ cup	shelled peas	125 g/4 oz

1. Rinse the rice thoroughly in cold water. Leave to soak in cold water for 30 minutes. Drain for 30 minutes.
2. Trim the beans, string if necessary and cut into 1 in (2.5 cm) pieces.
3. Halve the bell pepper and remove the seeds and pith. Cut the flesh into 1 in (2.5 cm) strips.
4. Peel and slice the potato. Cut the slices into strips, 1 in (2.5 cm) long.
5. Heat the ghee, add the chopped onion and cook until it gains color.
6. Add the garlic and the rice. Stir for 2 minutes, until the rice looks transparent.
7. Add 1¼ cups (300 ml/½ pint) boiling water, the garam masala and salt. Stir well, and bring to the boil.
8. Cover and simmer over a low heat for 10 minutes.
9. Add the peas and cook for a further 20-25 minutes.
10. Remove the lid and leave for 5 minutes for the steam to escape.
11. Turn into a warmed dish and serve.

Khumbi pilau
Spiced Rice with Morilles

01.00 Serves 4   **00.35**

American	Ingredients	Metric/Imperial
1 cup	long grain rice	225 g/8 oz
2 tbsp	dried morilles	2 tbsp
2 tbsp	ghee or groundnut oil	2 tbsp
1	large shredded onion	1
1	finely chopped garlic clove	1
½ tsp	grated fresh root ginger	½ tsp
1 tsp	salt	1 tsp
¼ tsp	garam masala	¼ tsp
2 tbsp	finely chopped coriander	2 tbsp

1. Rinse the rice thoroughly in cold water. Leave to soak in cold water for 30 minutes. Drain for 30 minutes.
2. Wash the morilles in several changes of cold water. Place them in a bowl and pour over enough boiling water to cover. Leave to soak for 30 minutes.

3. Strain the mushroom soaking liquid through muslin or a coffee filter and make it up to 1¼ cups (300 ml/½ pint) with water. Bring the liquid to the boil.
4. Cut the morilles into thick strips.
5. Heat the ghee or oil in a large heavy-based saucepan.
6. Add the onion and fry until it begins to change color.
7. Add the garlic and root ginger. Stir well.
8. Stir in the rice for 2 minutes until it begins to look transparent.
9. Add the morilles and the liquid, a little salt, and the garam masala. Bring quickly to the boil then stir well.
Cover and simmer over low heat for 25 minutes.
10. Remove the lid and leave for 5 minutes to allow the steam to escape.
11. Transfer to a warmed dish.
12. Sprinkle with coriander and serve.

Parsi pilau
Spiced Saffron Rice with Raisins and Almonds

01.00 Serves 4   **00.30**

American	Ingredients	Metric/Imperial
1 cup	long grain rice	225 g/8 oz
½ tsp	saffron threads	½ tsp
2 tbsp	ghee	2 tbsp
4	crushed cardamom pods	4
1 (2 in)	cinnamon stick	1 (2in/5 cm)
4	cloves	4
12	black peppercorns	12
1 tbsp	grated orange rind	1 tbsp
1 tsp	salt	1 tsp
2 tbsp	raisins	2 tbsp
2 tbsp	blanched almonds	2 tbsp
2 tbsp	blanched pistachio nuts	2 tbsp

1. Rinse the rice thoroughly in cold water. Leave to soak in cold water for 30 minutes. Drain for 30 minutes.
2. Soak the saffron threads in 2 tbsp hot water for 10 minutes.
3. Heat the ghee, in a large heavy-based saucepan.
4. Stir fry the cardamom pods, cinnamon, cloves and peppercorns in the ghee for 2 minutes.
5. Stir in the rice then add 1¼ cup (300 ml/½ pint) boiling water, the saffron and soaking liquid, orange rind and salt. Stir well and bring quickly to the boil.
6. Cover and simmer for about 20 minutes on a low heat. Sprinkle the raisins over the top. Simmer for 5 minutes.
7. Transfer to a warmed dish, sprinkle with the almonds and pistachio nuts, and serve.

Kima mattar pilau

Spiced Rice with Ground (Minced) Meat and Peas

01.00   00.40
Serves 4

American	Ingredients	Metric/Imperial
1 cup	long grain rice	225 g/8 oz
2 tbsp	ghee or groundnut oil	2 tbsp
1	medium size sliced onion	1
½ tsp	cumin seeds	½ tsp
1	garlic clove	1
½ tsp	grated root ginger	½ tsp
4	cloves	4
12 oz	ground (minced) lamb or beef	350 g/12 oz
7 oz	shelled peas	7 oz
2 tsp	salt	2 tsp
1	pinch garam masala	1

1. Rinse the rice thoroughly in cold water. Leave to soak in cold water for 30 minutes. Drain for 30 minutes.
2. Heat the ghee in a large saucepan, add the onion and fry gently until transparent.
3. Add the rice, cumin seeds, garlic, ginger and cloves.
4. Stir in the ground (minced) meat and cook, stirring continuously, until the meat crumbles and has changed color.
5. Add the peas and ¾ cup (200 ml/7 fl oz) boiling water. Cook for 5 minutes, then add a further ½ cup (125 ml /4 fl oz) boiling water, the salt and garam masala. Stir well, cover the pan and simmer gently for 20 minutes.
6. Serve immediately in a warmed dish.

Spiced saffron rice with raisins and almonds

Spiced rice with shrimp (prawns)

Jhinga pilau

Spiced Rice with Shrimp (Prawns)

01.00   00.30
Serves 4

American	Ingredients	Metric/Imperial
12	large uncooked shrimp (prawns) thawed if frozen	12
1 cup	long grain rice	225 g/8 oz
4 tbsp	ghee or groundnut oil	4 tbsp
1	large chopped onion	1
2	finely chopped garlic cloves	2
½ tbsp	grated root ginger	½ tbsp
4	lightly crushed cardamom pods	4
1 (2 in)	cinnamon stick	1 (5 cm/2 in)
1 tsp	garam masala	1 tsp
2	cored and seeded red bell peppers	2
1 tsp	salt	1 tsp
1	sliced cucumber	1
1 tsp	finely chopped coriander leaves	1 tsp

1. Peel the shrimp (prawns), cut open the backs and remove and discard the black thread. Cut the shrimp (prawns) into ¾ in (1.75 cm) pieces.
2. Rinse the rice thoroughly in cold water. Leave to soak for 30 minutes. Drain for 30 minutes.
3. Heat the ghee or groundnut oil in a large pan. Add the onion and fry gently until transparent.
4. Add the shrimp (prawns) and cook, stirring continuously, until they begin to change color. Remove from the pan and set aside.
5. Add the garlic and ginger to the remaining ghee.
6. Stir in the cardamom pods and cinnamon.
7. Add the rice, garam masala, red bell peppers and salt. Stir well and pour in 1¼ cups (300 ml/½ pint) boiling water. Bring quickly to the boil, cover and simmer for 25 minutes.
8. Remove the bell peppers, cardamom pods and cinnamon. Stir in the shrimp (prawns).
9. Transfer to a warmed dish, arrange the cucumber slices round the edge and sprinkle the coriander over. Serve immediately.

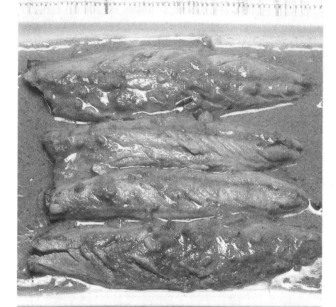

Fish in coconut milk

Machchi moli
Fish in Coconut Milk

00.15 Serves 4   **00.20**

American	Ingredients	Metric/Imperial
18 oz	mackerel fillets	500 g/18 oz
1 tsp	salt	1 tsp
½ tsp	ground turmeric	½ tsp
1 tsp	ghee or groundnut oil	1 tsp
1	small chopped onion	1
1	very finely chopped garlic clove	1
1 tsp	grated fresh root ginger	1 tsp
1 tbsp	curry powder	1 tbsp
2 cups	thin coconut milk	450 ml/¾ pint
1 cup	thick coconut milk	250 ml/8 fl oz
2	squeezed limes	2

1. Rinse the mackerel fillets under cold running water. Pat dry with kitchen paper. Rub with a mixture of salt and ground turmeric. Leave to stand for 10 minutes.
2. Heat the ghee, add the onion and fry gently until it looks transparent.
3. Add the garlic, root ginger and curry powder and fry gently for 2 minutes.
4. Stir in the thin coconut milk and bring slowly to simmering point, stirring constantly. Do not allow to boil.
5. Add the fish fillets and poach for 8-10 minutes.
6. Remove the fish from the pan and transfer to a warmed serving plate.
7. Add the thick coconut milk to the pan and bring almost to boiling point. Remove from the heat and stir in the lime juice.
8. Spoon the sauce over the dish and serve immediately.

Machchi ki kari
Simple Fish Curry

00.15 Serves 4   **00.20**

American	Ingredients	Metric/Imperial
1 ½ lb	firm white fish fillets	700 g/1 ½ lb
	salt	
2 tbsp	ghee or groundnut oil	2 tbsp
1	medium size onion	1
1 tbsp	curry paste	1 tbsp
1	very finely chopped garlic clove	1
1 tbsp	finely grated fresh root ginger	1 tbsp
1¾ cup	coconut milk	400 ml/¾ pint
	lemon juice to taste	
	parsley to garnish	

1. Rinse the fish under cold running water. Pat dry with kitchen paper. Cut into 1in (2.5 cm) strips. Rub with salt and leave to stand for 10 minutes.
2. Heat the ghee or oil and stir fry the onion until it begins to change color.
3. Add the curry paste, garlic and root ginger. Stir well and fry lightly.
4. Add the coconut milk and bring almost to boiling point, stirring.
5. Place the fish strips in the pan, reduce the heat and poach for 7 minutes.
6. Remove the pan from the heat and add salt and lemon juice to taste.
7. Transfer to a warmed serving dish, garnish with parsley and serve immediately.

Pastrani machchi
Fish in Foil

00.25 Serves 4   **00.15**

American	Ingredients	Metric/Imperial
18 oz	cod fillet, cut into 4 pieces	500 g/18 oz
2 tsp	salt	2 tsp
1	lemon	1
2	large coarsely chopped onions	2
1 tsp	grated root ginger	1 tsp
2	chopped garlic cloves	2
1	cored, seeded and sliced green bell pepper	1
1	seeded, chopped green chili	1
4 tbsp	finely chopped coriander	4 tbsp
1 tsp	cumin seeds	1 tsp
½ tsp	fenugreek seeds	½ tsp
½ cup	desiccated coconut	½ cup
2 tbsp	ghee or groundnut oil	2 tbsp
1 tsp	garam masala	1 tsp

1. Rinse the fish under cold running water. Pat dry with kitchen paper. Rub with salt and leave to stand for 10 minutes.
2. Remove the lemon zest with a potato peeler and cut into very thin strips. Peel the white pith from the lemon and cut into segments between the membranes. Catch any juice.

3. Using a blender or food processor, make a fine paste from the lemon juice and flesh, onions, root ginger, garlic, bell pepper, green chili, coriander, cumin seeds and fenugreek seeds. Mix the paste with the desiccated coconut.

4. Heat the ghee or oil and gently stir fry the paste for about 3 minutes. Remove from the heat and add a little salt and the garam masala.

5. Preheat the oven to 425°F/220°C, Gas Mark 7.

6. Grease 4 pieces of aluminum foil with a little ghee or oil. Place a fillet of fish on each piece and coat the fish on one side with the fried coconut mixture. Fold over the foil to make sealed packets and place on a baking sheet.

7. Bake for 12-15 minutes depending on the thickness of the fish fillets.

8. Serve the fish in the foil packets.

Khatti wali machchi kari
Sweet and Sour Fish Curry

00.30 Serves 4   **00.15**

American	Ingredients	Metric/Imperial
1½ lb	firm white fish fillets	700 g/1½ lb
1½ tsp	salt	1½ tsp
1 tbsp	tamarind pulp	1 tbsp
1	large chopped onion	1
2	very finely chopped garlic cloves	2
1 tsp	grated fresh root ginger	1 tsp
1 tsp	ground coriander	1 tsp
2 tsp	ground cumin	2 tsp
1 tsp	ground fenugreek	1 tsp
1 tsp	paprika pepper	1 tsp
2 tbsp	ghee or groundnut oil	2 tbsp
1 tbsp	lemon juice	1 tbsp
1 tbsp	chopped coriander leaves	1 tbsp
	sprigs coriander leaves	
4	tomato 'flowers'	4

1. Rinse the fish under cold running water. Pat dry with kitchen paper. Cut into 1 in (2.5 cm) strips. Rub with a little salt and leave to stand for 10 minutes.

2. Place the tamarind pulp into a bowl and pour over 1½ quarts (1.4 litres/2½ pints) boiling water. Leave to stand for 5 minutes. Pour into a strainer (sieve) and rub through as much of the pulp as possible.

3. Place the onion, garlic, root ginger and 2 tbsp of the tamarind juice into a blender or food processor. Process to a smooth purée then add the ground spices and mix well.

4. Heat the ghee or oil in a heavy-based saucepan. Stir fry the purée for 1 minute.

5. Add the remaining tamarind juice, lemon juice and salt. Bring to the boil, stirring constantly and add 1 cup (250 ml/8 fl oz) boiling water.

6. Add the strips of fish, reduce the heat and cook gently for 8 minutes.

7. Transfer the fish to a warmed serving dish, sprinkle with chopped coriander and garnish with sprigs of coriander and tomato flowers.

Machchi tamatar ki kari
Fish Curry with Tomatoes

00.10   **00.20**
Serves 4

American	Ingredients	Metric/Imperial
4 (6 oz)	cod cutlets	4 (6 oz/175 g)
1 tsp	salt	1 tsp
2 tbsp	ghee or groundnut oil	2 tbsp
1	medium size chopped onion	1
2	very finely chopped garlic cloves	2
2 tbsp	finely chopped coriander	2 tbsp
1 tsp	ground cumin	1 tsp
1 tsp	ground turmeric	1 tsp
½ tsp	paprika pepper	½ tsp
3	large, ripe, skinned diced tomatoes	3
1 tsp	garam masala	1 tsp
	lemon juice to taste	

1. Rinse the cod cutlets under cold running water. Pat dry with kitchen paper. Rub lightly with a little salt. Leave to stand for 10 minutes.

2. Heat the ghee or oil and stir fry the onion until it begins to change color.

3. Add the garlic and then the coriander, cumin, turmeric, paprika and tomato.

4. Cook, stirring until the tomato has softened and formed a sauce. Add the garam masala.

5. Place the cod cutlets in the sauce and spoon some over them. Cover the pan and cook gently over a low heat for 10 minutes.

6. Transfer the fish to a warmed serving dish, add the lemon juice to the sauce to taste.

Pour the sauce over the fish and serve immediately.

Sweet and sour fish curry

Tali machchi

Fried fish

00.10 Serves 4 00.10

American	Ingredients	Metric/Imperial
1 ½ lb	small haddock or cod fillets	700 g/1 ½ lb
3 tbsp	sifted flour	3 tbsp
3 tbsp	chick-pea flour (besan)	3 tbsp
1 tsp	salt	1 tsp
1 tsp	garam masala	1 tsp
½ tsp	ground turmeric	½ tsp
1	lightly beaten egg	1
6-7 tbsp	groundnut oil	6-7 tbsp
	lemon slices and parsley to garnish	

1. Rinse the fish under cold running water. Dry with kitchen paper.
2. Mix the flour, chick-pea flour (besan), salt, garam masala and ground turmeric. Place in a plastic bag.
3. Dip the fish fillets into the beaten egg. Place them in the bag of flour mixture. Shake to coat.
4. Heat the oil and fry the pieces of fish for 8-12 minutes until golden brown on both sides. Drain on kitchen paper.
5. Serve on a warmed dish, garnished with lemon and parsley.

Tali machchi 11

Fried Fish

00.30 Serves 4 00.10

American	Ingredients	Metric/Imperial
4	small, cleaned mackerel	4
2	very finely chopped garlic cloves	2
1 tsp	sea salt	1 tsp
1 tsp	grated fresh root ginger	1 tsp
½ tsp	ground turmeric	½ tsp
½ tsp	ground black pepper	½ tsp
1 ½ tsp	ground chili (optional)	1 ½ tsp
1	squeezed lemon	1
5 tbsp	groundnut oil	5 tbsp
1	small, seeded red bell pepper flesh cut into strips	1
	fresh coriander or parsley leaves, to garnish	

1. Rinse the fish under cold running water. Dry with kitchen paper.
2. Place the garlic, sea salt, root ginger, turmeric, pepper, chili and 2 tbsp of lemon juice, into a food processor. Process until smooth, add more juice if needed.
3. Rub the mixture over the fish, inside and out. Leave to stand for 20 minutes.
4. Heat the oil and fry the fish for 10-12 minutes, turning once.
5. Place the fish on a warmed dish and arrange the strips of pepper on top.
6. Serve garnished with coriander or parsley leaves.

Machchi kebab
Broiled (Grilled) Fish Kebabs

00.40 Serves 4   **00.08**

American	Ingredients	Metric/Imperial
1 lb	firm white fish fillets	700 g/1½ lb
2 tsp	grated fresh root ginger	2 tsp
3	finely chopped garlic cloves	3
1 tsp	salt	1 tsp
4 tsp	ground coriander	4 tsp
1 tsp	garam masala	1 tsp
½ tsp	ground chili	½ tsp
3 tbsp	lemon juice	3 tbsp
2 tbsp	groundnut oil	2 tbsp
1 cup	yogurt	250 ml/8 fl oz
3 tbsp	sifted flour	3 tbsp

1. Rinse the fish under cold running water. Dry with kitchen paper. Cut into 1 in (2.5 cm) cubes.
2. Mix the root ginger, garlic, salt, coriander, garam masala, chili, lemon juice, oil and yogurt.
3. Place the fish cubes in the marinade, turn to coat with the mixture. Leave to stand for 30 minutes. Toss in flour.
4. Grease 4-6 skewers and divide the fish between them.
5. Preheat the broiler (grill) or barbecue. Arrange the kebabs on the broiler (grill) rack and broil (grill) for 6-8 minutes, turning regularly.
6. Place the skewers with the kebabs on 4 warmed plates.

Jhinga bhajia
Shrimp (Prawn) Fritters

00.30 Serves 4   **00.10**

American	Ingredients	Metric/Imperial
¾ lb	cooked peeled shrimp (prawns)	350 g/12 oz
1 tbsp	groundnut oil	1 tbsp
1	very finely chopped onion	1
1	very finely chopped garlic clove	1
½ tsp	salt	½ tsp
1 tsp	grated fresh root ginger	1 tsp
2 tbsp	finely chopped coriander leaves	2 tbsp
	freshly ground pepper	
1 tsp	ground cumin	1 tsp
½ tsp	garam masala	½ tsp
4 tbsp	sifted flour	4 tbsp
3 tbsp	chick-pea flour (besan)	3 tbsp
8-10 tbsp	groundnut oil	8-10 tbsp

1. Finely chop or grind (mince) the shrimp (prawns).
2. Heat 1 tbsp groundnut oil and stir fry the onion until it begins to brown.
3. Add the garlic, salt, root ginger, coriander leaves, a little pepper, cumin and garam masala. Stir well, remove the pan from the heat.
4. Spread the mixture on a plate to cool.
5. When the spice mixture is cool, mix it with the shrimp (prawns). Add 1 tbsp flour and stir well.
6. Mix the remaining flour with the chick-pea flour (besan).
7. Shape the shrimp (prawn) mixture into balls the size of walnuts. Roll the balls in the flour mixture.
8. Heat the remaining oil in a wok. Quickly fry the shrimp (prawn) balls a few at a time, until they are golden on all sides. Drain on kitchen paper and fry the remaining balls.
9. Serve immediately.

Left to right: Fried fish
Grilled fish kebabs
Fried fish 11

Goan spiced mussels

Thisra

Goan Spiced Mussels

	00.30	00.15
	Serves 8-10 as an hors d'oeuvre	

American	Ingredients	Metric/Imperial
3 quarts	fresh, cleaned, sorted mussels	2 kg/4 lb
1 tbsp	grated root ginger	1 tbsp
6	chopped garlic cloves	6
4 tbsp	ghee or groundnut oil	4 tbsp
3	large chopped onions	3
1	very finely chopped seeded, red chili	1
½ tsp	ground turmeric	½ tsp
2 tsp	ground cumin	2 tsp
1	small finely grated coconut	1
	salt	

1. Carefully check the mussels, discarding any heavy ones which may be filled with sand or clay and any which are partly open.
2. Purée the root ginger and garlic in a food processor.
3. Heat the ghee or oil in a wok and stir fry the onions until transparent.
4. Add the ginger and garlic mixture and stir in the chili, turmeric and cumin. Add the fresh coconut and 2 cups (450 ml/¾ pint) water.
5. Bring to the boil, stirring and turning over constantly. Simmer gently for 5 minutes.
6. Transfer the contents of the wok to a large saucepan. Bring to the boil again and add the mussels. Cover the pan and shake the sauce and the mussels together. Bring quickly to the boil. Cook the mussels until all shells open.
7. After a few minutes shake the whole contents of the saucepan again, transfer to a warmed dish and serve.

Jhinga moli

Shrimp (Prawns) in Coconut Milk

	00.15	00.25
	Serves 4	

American	Ingredients	Metric/Imperial
1 lb	shrimp (prawns) thawed if frozen	450 g/1 lb
1 tbsp	groundnut oil	1 tbsp
2	thinly sliced large onions	2
3	very finely chopped garlic cloves	3
2	seeded red or green chilies cut into very thin strips	2
1 tsp	ground turmeric	1 tsp
8	curry leaves (optional)	8
1 tbsp	grated fresh root ginger	1 tbsp
2½ cups	coconut milk	600 ml/1 pint
1 tsp	salt	1 tsp
1 tbsp	lemon juice	1 tbsp

1. Heat the oil and stir fry the onion until transparent.
2. Add the garlic, chilies, turmeric, curry leaves and root ginger and fry for 30 seconds.
3. Stir in the coconut milk and bring slowly to the boil. Immediately reduce the heat and simmer gently for 10 minutes. Add salt to taste.
4. Add the shrimp (prawns) to the sauce and simmer for 6-8 minutes for raw shrimp (prawns) 2-3 minutes for cooked.
5. Remove from the heat, stir in the lemon juice and serve.

Left to right:
Shrimps (prawns) in coconut milk
Shrimp (prawn) curry
Shrimp (prawn) with zucchini
and tomatoes

Jhinga kari

Shrimp (Prawn) Curry

00.15 Serves 4   **00.25**

American	Ingredients	Metric/Imperial
1 lb	peeled shrimp (prawns) thawed if frozen	450 g/1 lb
2 tbsp	desiccated coconut	2 tbsp
1 tbsp	rice flour	1 tbsp
2¼ cups	coconut milk	500 ml/18 fl oz
2 tbsp	ghee	2 tbsp
12	curry leaves	12
2	large chopped onions	2
6	finely chopped garlic cloves	6
1 tbsp	grated root ginger	1 tbsp
2 tsp	garam masala	2 tsp
1 tsp	ground chili	1 tsp
1 tbsp	ground paprika	1 tbsp
1 tsp	salt	1 tsp
1 tbsp	lemon juice	1 tbsp

1. Heat a dry, heavy-based saucepan. Stir fry the coconut and rice flour until they gain a very light color. Remove the pan from the heat and stir in 8 tbsp of coconut milk.
2. Heat the ghee and stir fry the curry leaves for 1 minute.
3. Stir in the onion, garlic, root ginger and garam masala, chili, paprika and salt.
4. Immediately add the coconut and rice flour mixture. Stir well, add the remainder of the coconut milk. Simmer very gently for 10 minutes.
5. Stir in shrimp (prawns) and simmer for 6-8 minutes for raw and 2-3 minutes for cooked shrimp (prawns). Remove the pan from the heat and add salt to taste.
6. Remove the curry leaves, stir in the lemon juice and serve.

Jhinga aur ghya

Shrimp (Prawns) with Zucchini (Courgettes) and Tomatoes

00.25 plus standing time   **00.15**

American	Ingredients	Metric/Imperial
1 lb	zucchini (courgettes)	450 g/1 lb
	salt	
2¼ lb	tomatoes	1 kg/2¼ lb
5 tbsp	ghee	5 tbsp
1	very finely chopped garlic clove	1
1	seeded green chili, flesh cut into thin strips	1
2 tbsp	finely chopped coriander or parsley	2 tbsp
1 tsp	ground turmeric	1 tsp
1 tsp	ground cumin	1 tsp
1 tsp	finely grated root ginger	1 tsp
	freshly ground black pepper	
18 oz	peeled, fresh, cooked shrimp (prawns)	500 g/18 oz
4	small tomatoes in wedges	4

1. Wash the zucchini (courgettes). Remove the ends and cut into thin slices and then into thin strips. Place the strips in a strainer or colander and sprinkle over a little salt. Leave to stand for 1 hour.
2. Skin, halve and seed the tomatoes. Cut the flesh into very small pieces.
3. Heat the ghee and stir fry the garlic in it for 30 seconds. Add the chili, coriander or parsley, turmeric, cumin powder and root ginger.
4. Add the tomato and stir until it is cooked and softens.
5. Stir in the zucchini (courgette) strips and simmer very gently for 5 minutes. Add pepper and salt to taste.
6. Heat the shrimp (prawns) in the sauce. Remove the pan from the heat.
7. Serve on 4 warmed plates garnished with small wedges of tomato.

Shahjahani murghi

Chicken Shahjahani

00.15 Serves 4   **01.00**

American	Ingredients	Metric/Imperial
8	chicken quarters or drumsticks	8
1 tsp	salt	1 tsp
	freshly ground pepper	
1 ½ tbsp	grated fresh root ginger	1 ½ tbsp
3	coarsely chopped garlic cloves	3
½ cup	blanched almonds	75 g/2 ½ oz
4 tbsp	groundnut oil	4 tbsp
3	cardamom pods	3
1 (1 ½ in)	cinnamon stick	1 (4 cm/1 ½ in)
1	bay leaf	1
3	cloves	3
1	large chopped onion	1
1 tsp	ground cumin	1 tsp
4 tbsp	Greek-style yogurt (at room temperature)	4 tbsp
1 ¼ cups	light (single) cream (at room temperature)	300 ml/ ½ pint
2 tbsp	raisins	2 tbsp
	pinch garam masala	

1. Skin the chicken pieces and dry with kitchen paper. Season with salt and pepper.
2. Mix the ginger, garlic, 3 tbsp almonds, 1 tbsp oil and 2 tbsp water to a smooth paste in a food processor.
3. Heat the remaining oil and fry the pieces of chicken until golden brown on all sides. Remove from the pan, allow any oil to drain back. Keep hot.
4. Stir fry the cardamom pods, cinnamon, bay leaf and cloves for a few seconds. Add the onion and stir fry until golden yellow.
5. Add the almond paste, cumin and a little freshly ground pepper. Stir well, then mix in the yogurt, 1 tbsp at a time, until thick.
6. Gradually stir in the cream, add salt to taste and finally, just as the sauce is coming to the boil, add the chicken.
7. Reduce the heat, cover the pan and simmer very gently for 25-30 minutes.
8. Wash the raisins and after 10 minutes of the cooking time, add them to the sauce.
9. Roast the remaining almonds in a dry frying pan until they begin to change color, then leave to cool on a cold plate.
10. Remove the pan with the chicken from the heat, add the garam masala and stir a few times.
11. Transfer the contents of the pan to a hot serving dish and sprinkle the toasted almonds over. Serve as hot as possible.

Chicken shahjahani
with yogurt and cucumber
and tomato salad (see page 326)

Masala murghi
Grilled Chicken

00.15 plus marinating   00.20

American	Ingredients	Metric/Imperial
8	small chicken quarters or drumsticks	8
3 tbsp	garam masala	3 tbsp
2	crushed garlic cloves	2
1 tbsp	grated root ginger	1 tbsp
1 tsp	paprika	1 tsp
1 tsp	salt	1 tsp
1 tbsp	rice flour	1 tbsp
1 tbsp	sesame oil	1 tbsp
1 tbsp	lemon juice	1 tbsp

1. Dry the chicken with kitchen paper. Make 4 small, deep incisions in each piece.
2. In a bowl, mix the garam masala, garlic, ginger, paprika, salt and rice flour. Add 2 tbsp boiling water, stirring constantly. Add the sesame oil and lemon juice. Stir until thick and evenly mixed, then add the chicken pieces and turn them to coat with the mixture. Cover and chill for 12 hours.
3. Preheat the broiler (grill) until hot and cook for 15-20 minutes, turning once. Serve very hot.

Murgh masalam
Spicy Stuffed Chicken

00.20 plus soaking time   01.30

American	Ingredients	Metric/Imperial
1 (2½ lb)	roasting chicken	1 (1.2 kg/2½ lb)
½ tsp	saffron threads	½ tsp
½ tsp	ground black pepper	½ tsp
½ tsp	ground turmeric	½ tsp
½ tsp	ground cumin	½ tsp
	pinch ground cloves	
	pinch ground cinnamon	
	pinch ground nutmeg	
2	crushed garlic cloves	2
2 tbsp	Greek-style yogurt	2 tbsp
1½ tsp	salt	1½ tsp
⅓ cup	long grain rice	75 g/3 oz
4 tbsp	shelled peas	4 tbsp
6 tbsp	ghee or groundnut oil	6
3	thinly sliced onions	3
¾ cup	chicken bouillon (stock)	250 ml/7 fl oz
3	skinned, finely chopped ripe tomatoes	3
2 tbsp	Greek-style yogurt	2 tbsp
	few coriander leaves	

1. Dry the chicken with kitchen paper.
2. Soak the saffron threads in 2 tbsp boiling water for 10 minutes. Add the pepper, turmeric, cumin, cloves, cinnamon, nutmeg, garlic, yogurt and salt. Stir until smooth and spread half over the chicken.
3. Wash the rice thoroughly then leave to soak in cold water to cover for 30 minutes.
4. Put the rice and peas in a pan with ⅔ cup (150 ml/¼ pint) boiling water. Boil for 10 minutes.
5. Drain well and stir in the remaining spice paste. Stuff the chicken with this mixture and sew up the opening. Leave to stand for about 30 minutes.
6. Heat the ghee or oil and fry the onions, stirring constantly, until beginning to change color. Remove from the pan with a slotted spoon, drain over the pan and keep hot.
7. Fry the chicken in the remaining ghee or oil until golden brown. Add the onions and bouillon (stock), cover the pan, reduce the heat and simmer for about 40 minutes, until tender. Turn the chicken occasionally.
8. Remove the lid and boil rapidly until the liquid is reduced to an almost syrupy sauce.
9. Remove the chicken from the pan and put it on a warm serving dish. Add chopped tomatoes, yogurt and a pinch of salt to the sauce and bring to the boil. Stir until thick.
10. Pour the sauce over the chicken and sprinkle coriander leaves over. Serve immediately.

Murghi do piaz
Chicken Dopiaza

| | 00.10 plus standing time | 01.00 |

American	Ingredients	Metric/Imperial
2 (2 lb)	small roasting chickens	2 (900 g/2 lb)
1½ tsp	salt	1½ tsp
3 tbsp	lemon juice	3 tbsp
6 tbsp	ghee	6 tbsp
6	cloves	6
1	cardamom pod	1
1 (1 in)	cinnamon stick	1 (2.5 cm/1 in)
12	black peppercorns	12
1 tbsp	grated root ginger	1 tbsp
1 tsp	ground turmeric	1 tsp
1 tsp	ground chili	1 tsp
4	large coarsely chopped onions	4
3	crushed garlic cloves	3
1¼ cups	Greek-style yogurt	300 ml/½ pint
1 tsp	garam masala	1 tsp
4	large, peeled, sliced tomatoes	4
	few coriander leaves	
1	large coarsley chopped onion (lightly fried)	1

1. Cut each chicken into 8 pieces and dry with kitchen paper. Add the salt to the lemon juice and stir until the salt has dissolved. Rub the chicken with the mixture and leave to stand for about 30 minutes.
2. Heat the ghee and add the cloves, cardamom, cinnamon and peppercorns. Stir fry lightly for about 30 seconds.
3. Add the chicken pieces and fry until golden yellow on all sides. Remove from the pan and keep hot.
4. Add the ginger, turmeric, chili and onions to the pan. Stir until the onions look transparent then add the garlic and continue stir frying until the onions are brown.
5. Reduce the heat and gradually stir in the yogurt. Simmer until a thick sauce is obtained. Stir in 1 cup (250 ml/9 fl oz) boiling water.
6. Add the chicken pieces and simmer gently for 30 minutes.
7. Just before serving, sprinkle on the garam masala and stir carefully. Garnish with tomato slices and sprigs of coriander and top with the fried onion.

Chicken dopiaza

Dahl murghi
Tomato and Yogurt Chicken

| | 00.15 Serves 4 | 00.50 |

American	Ingredients	Metric/Imperial
2 (2 lb)	roasting chickens	2 (900 g/2 lb)
3	large chopped onions	3
2	finely chopped garlic cloves	2
2 tsp	grated root ginger	2 tsp
	fresh coriander leaves	
5 tbsp	ghee	5 tbsp
1 tsp	ground turmeric	1 tsp
1 tsp	garam masala	1 tsp
1 tsp	ground chili	1 tsp
⅔ cup	Greek-style yogurt	150 ml/¼ pint
6	ripe, skinned, chopped tomatoes	6
	few coriander leaves	

1. Divide each chicken into 8 pieces. Remove the skin, dry the pieces with kitchen paper and season with a little salt.
2. Purée the onion, garlic, ginger and coriander leaves in a food processor.
3. Heat the ghee and fry the chicken pieces until golden yellow on all sides. Remove from the pan and keep hot.
4. Fry the onion mixture in the remaining ghee for 1 minute. Add the turmeric, garam masala, and chili. Stir well then stir in the yogurt 1 tbsp at a time. Bring almost to boiling point.
5. Add the tomatoes and cook stirring, until very soft and the mixture is thick. Add 6 tbsp boiling water, stir well and add the chicken, spooning the sauce over to coat.
6. Cover the pan and cook very slowly over low heat for 20-25 minutes, until tender. Turn the chicken occasionally and add a little more boiling water if too much liquid boils away.
7. Serve the chicken and the sauce on a warmed dish and sprinkle coriander over the top.

Murghi vindaloo
Chicken Vindaloo

⊟ 00.20 00.45
plus standing time

American	Ingredients	Metric/Imperial
2 (2 lb)	roasting chickens	2 (900 g/2 lb)
4 tsp	ground turmeric	4 tsp
2 tbsp	ground chili	2 tbsp
2 tsp	ground cumin seeds	2 tsp
2-3 tsp	salt	2-3 tsp
¾ cup	wine vinegar	200 ml/7 fl oz
4	chopped bay leaves	4
5 tbsp	ghee	5 tbsp
1	large, coarsely chopped onion	1
8	crushed garlic cloves	8
2	ground red or green fresh chilies with seeds	2
1 tbsp	grated root ginger	1 tbsp
½ tsp	cardamom seeds	½ tsp
2	skinned, chopped tomatoes	2
1 tbsp	dark brown sugar	1 tbsp
2 tbsp	grated fresh coconut (optional)	2 tbsp
	coriander leaves (optional)	

1. Cut each chicken into 8 pieces and dry thoroughly with kitchen paper. Make several incisions with the point of a knife to help the spices to penetrate the meat.
2. Mix the turmeric, chili, cumin and half the salt with enough vinegar to form a thick paste. Rub into the chicken pieces and leave to stand for about 30 minutes.
3. Put the chicken pieces in a bowl with the bay leaves and the remaining vinegar. Add enough water to cover the chicken and leave to stand in a cool place for about 4 hours.
4. Heat the ghee in a large frying pan and fry the chopped onion. Add the garlic, chilies, ginger and cardamom seeds. Fry over a medium heat until light brown.
5. Remove the chicken from the marinade and drain. Add the chicken to the pan and fry over medium heat for 10 minutes until golden brown. Add a little more ghee if necessary.
6. Add the tomatoes, brown sugar and the marinade. Reduce the heat and simmer for about 25 minutes until the chicken is tender and the liquid has thickened to a thick sauce.
7. Add salt to taste and serve sprinkled with grated coconut and coriander leaves.

Cook's tip: Vindaloo dishes originated in south west India, especially Goa. They are always very hot and made with vinegar. They have a slightly sour taste which goes very well with meat. In Goa vindaloos are normally based on pork, but as pork is less popular in other parts of the sub-continent it has been adapted for use with duck and chicken. The above recipe offers a simple method of creating vindaloo which is usually very elaborate. In some Asian stores vindaloo paste can be bought. If used, rub it into the chicken pieces, and omit the ginger, chili and cumin from the ingredients above.

Chicken tandoori

Tandoori murgh
Chicken Tandoori

⊟ 00.15 01.30
Serves 4

American	Ingredients	Metric/Imperial
1 (3½ lb)	large-roasting chicken	1 (1.5kg/3½ lb)
4	seeded, roughly chopped red bell peppers	4
1 tsp	ground turmeric	1 tsp
2 tsp	coriander seeds	2 tsp
2 tsp	garam masala	2 tsp
6	crushed garlic cloves	6
1	chopped onion	1
1½ tbsp	grated root ginger	1½ tbsp
2 tbsp	salt	2 tbsp
4 tbsp	lemon juice	4 tbsp
5 tbsp	ghee	5 tbsp
1½ tsp	saffron threads	1½ tsp
4	sliced lemons	4
1	large onion, cut into rings	1

1. Remove the skin from the chicken. Dry it inside and out with kitchen paper.
2. Place the chopped bell pepper, turmeric, coriander, garam masala, garlic, onion and ginger, salt and lemon juice in a food processor and purée to form a smooth paste.
3. Place the chicken in a steamer and steam for exactly 10 minutes. Leave to drain and dry with kitchen paper.
4. Rub the spice paste over the chicken, both inside and out. Leave to stand for 10-15 minutes.
5. Preheat the oven to 240°C/475°F/Gas Mark 9.
6. Heat the ghee in a deep saucepan. Sprinkle the saffron over the ghee and stir slowly. Put the chicken into the pan and fry gently until golden brown on all sides.
7. Put the spice mixture and the chicken into an ovenproof dish with a well fitting lid and cook in the oven for 35-45 minutes.
8. Serve immediately, with lemon slices and onion rings.

Makhani murgh

Chicken Tandoori in Tomato and Butter Sauce

◼▷◻ 00.00   00.35 ◻
Serves 4

American	Ingredients	Metric/Imperial
1	tandoori chicken (see page 323)	1
1½ lb	skinned, seeded and finely chopped ripe tomatoes	700 g/1½ lb
1 tbsp	finely grated root ginger	1 tbsp
1 cup	light (single) cream	250 ml/8 fl oz
1 tsp	garam masala	1 tsp
1 tsp	salt	1 tsp
1 tsp	sugar	1 tsp
2	green chilies	2
1 tbsp	finely chopped coriander	1 tbsp
2 tbsp	lemon juice	2 tbsp
1 tsp	dry roasted cumin seeds	1 tsp
4 tbsp	ghee	4 tbsp
¼ cup	chilled butter	50 g/2 oz

1. Put the tomatoes in a saucepan with ¾ cup (200 ml/7 fl oz) water. Bring very slowly to the boil, stirring constantly then cook until thick.
2. Add the ginger and cream and simmer very gently for 15 minutes.
3. Add the garam masala, salt, sugar, whole chilies, coriander, lemon juice and cumin seeds. Stir well and simmer for a few minutes.
4. When the chicken is ready to serve, heat the ghee, add the tomato mixture and stir well. Bring quickly to the boil, remove from the heat and beat in the chilled butter, a little at a time.
5. Pour the sauce over the chicken and serve immediately.

Mootay moli

Eggs in Coconut Sauce

◼▷◻ 00.15   00.15 ◻
Serves 4

American	Ingredients	Metric/Imperial
8	freshly hard-cooked (hard-boiled), shelled eggs	8
3 tbsp	ghee or groundnut oil	3 tbsp
2	thinly sliced onions	2
2	finely chopped garlic cloves	2
1 tbsp	finely grated root ginger	1 tbsp
2	seeded, chopped, green chilies	2
2 tsp	mild curry powder	2 tsp
¾ cup	thin coconut milk	200 ml/7 fl oz
¾ cup	thick coconut milk	200 ml/7 fl oz
1 tsp	salt	1 tsp
1 tbsp	finely chopped parsley (optional)	1 tbsp

1. Heat the oil or ghee and fry the onion, stirring constantly, until transparent. Add the garlic, ginger and chilies. Stir well a few times then stir in the curry powder. Fry for 30 seconds then add the thin coconut milk and bring almost to boiling point, stirring constantly.
2. Stir in the thick coconut milk and the salt. Put the eggs into the sauce and simmer very gently for 5 minutes.
3. Serve immediately, sprinkled with parsley.

Parsi omlat

Parsi Vegetable Omelette

◼▷◻ 00.20   00.20 ◻
plus standing and cooling time

American	Ingredients	Metric/Imperial
1 lb	small, trimmed zucchini (courgettes)	450 g/1 lb
1 tsp	salt	1 tsp
5 tbsp	groundnut oil or ghee	5 tbsp
2	chopped onions	2
3	large, peeled, thinly sliced potatoes	3
2	seeded, finely chopped green chilies	2
3	large, peeled, diced tomatoes	3
1 tsp	ground cumin seeds	1 tsp
	freshly ground pepper	
8	large, beaten eggs	8
3 tbsp	finely chopped coriander leaves	3 tbsp

1. Coarsely grate the the zucchini (courgettes) and put in a strainer (sieve). Season with a little salt and leave to drain for 30-45 minutes, tossing occasionally.

2. Heat half of the oil or ghee in a large deep saucepan and fry the chopped onions for 30 seconds, stirring constantly. Add the potato and chili and fry very gently for 5 minutes, stirring carefully.

3. Add the grated zucchini (courgettes), tomatoes, cumin and a little freshly ground black pepper. Stir well and remove the pan from the heat.

4. Transfer the vegetables to a large, cold plate and allow to cool completely.

5. Mix the vegetable mixture with the eggs, add salt to taste and the coriander.

6. Wipe the saucepan with kitchen paper then heat the remaining oil or ghee and add the eggs and vegetables. Cover the saucepan and cook over very low heat until the top of the mixture has solidified but still looks moist.

7. Turn the omelette over by placing a large plate over the top of the pan and then turning the pan upside down. Slide the omelette back into the pan and fry for a further 3-4 minutes.

8. Remove from the heat and carefully slide the omelette on to a warmed plate. Serve immediately.

Left to right:
Eggs in coconut sauce
Parsi, vegetable omelette
Egg curry

Anda kari

Egg Curry

▬▭ 00.10		00.20 🍲
Serves 4		

American	Ingredients	Metric/Imperial
8	freshly hard-cooked (hard-boiled) eggs	8
2 tbsp	ghee	2 tbsp
2	chopped onions	2
2	finely chopped garlic cloves	2
1 tbsp	grated root ginger	1 tbsp
2 tsp	ground coriander seeds	2 tsp
2 tsp	ground cumin seeds	2 tsp
1 tsp	ground turmeric	1 tsp
	pinch ground chili	
4	skinned, diced tomatoes	4
1 tsp	salt	1 tsp
1½ tsp	garam masala	1½ tsp

1. Shell and halve the eggs, lengthwise.

2. Heat the ghee and fry the chopped onions until transparent. Add the garlic and ginger, stir well and fry until the onions are golden yellow in color.

3. Add the coriander, cumin, turmeric and chili. Stir in the tomato. Reduce the heat and simmer gently for 5 minutes until the tomato is very soft.

4. Add a little salt and ⅔ cup (150 ml/¼ pint) boiling water. Continue to cook, stirring occasionally until the mixture is thick and even.

5. Stir in the garam masala then pour the sauce into a warmed, shallow serving dish. Arrange the eggs, yolks upward, in the sauce and serve immediately.

Anda vindaloo

Eggs Vindaloo

00.10 Serves 4   **00.15**

American	Ingredients	Metric/Imperial
4	crushed garlic cloves	4
1 tbsp	finely grated root ginger	1 tbsp
1 tsp	ground chili	1 tsp
1 tsp	ground cumin seeds	1 tsp
1½ tsp	salt	1½ tsp
1 tbsp	dark brown sugar	1 tbsp
2 tbsp	wine vinegar	2 tbsp
3 tbsp	groundnut oil	3 tbsp
1 (1½ in)	cinnamon stick	1 (3 cm/1½ in)
3	large, chopped onions	3
2 tsp	paprika pepper	2 tsp
3	skinned, finely chopped, ripe tomatoes	3
8	eggs	8
	pinch garam masala	

1. In a bowl mix the garlic, ginger, chili, cumin, salt, sugar and vinegar. Stir until the salt and sugar dissolve.
2. Heat the oil and fry the cinnamon for 10 seconds. Add the onion and fry, stirring constantly, until just beginning to change color.
3. Add the paprika, stir well then add the spice and vinegar mixture and the tomatoes. Stir well, add ¾ cup (200 ml/7 fl oz) boiling water and simmer very gently for 8 minutes.
4. Hard-cook (hard-boil) and shell the eggs and cut in half lengthwise.
5. Stir the garam masala into the sauce and remove the cinnamon stick.
6. Pour the sauce into a warmed serving dish and add the eggs, yolks upward. Serve immediately.

Eggs vindaloo

Piaz kachumbar

Onion Salad

00.30 plus standing time   **00.00**

American	Ingredients	Metric/Imperial
3	medium size onions sliced into very thin rings	3
1½ tsp	salt	1½ tsp
2 tbsp	dark brown sugar	2 tbsp
3 tbsp	lemon juice	3 tbsp
3	skinned, thinly sliced, ripe tomatoes	3
1 tbsp	coarsely grated root ginger	1 tbsp
1	seeded, very finely chopped green chili	1
1	seeded, very finely chopped small red bell pepper	1
1	seeded, very finely chopped small green bell pepper	1
2 tbsp	finely chopped coriander	2 tbsp

1. Place the onion rings in a colander and sprinkle with the salt. Shake well, then leave to stand for about 1 hour.
2. Place the onions in a bowl.
3. Mix together the sugar and the lemon juice. Stir until the sugar dissolves. Add 1 tbsp water and slowly pour over the onions.
4. Stir carefully, then add the remaining ingredients. Mix carefully, cover and chill for 30 minutes.
5. Toss the salad just before serving.

Tamatar salad

Tomato Salad

00.20 plus chilling time   **00.00**

American	Ingredients	Metric/Imperial
6	large, skinned, sliced ripe tomatoes	6
6	small scallions (spring onions)	6
1 tbsp	coarsely grated root ginger	1 tbsp
2 tbsp	finely chopped coriander, mint leaves or parsley	2 tbsp
3 tbsp	lemon juice	3 tbsp
1 tbsp	sugar	1 tbsp
½ tsp	salt	½ tsp
	freshly ground pepper	
	pinch ground chili	

1. Arrange the tomato slices in overlapping circles in a round serving dish.
2. Chop the scallions (spring onions) and place half in the middle of the dish.
3. Sprinkle the remainder over the tomatoes, followed by the ginger and the chopped coriander leaves, mint or parsley.
4. Mix together the lemon juice, sugar and salt. Stir in the freshly ground pepper and the chili. Pour the dressing over the tomatoes, cover the salad and chill for about 30 minutes before serving.

Onion salad

Gajar ka salat
Carrot Salad

⏱ 00.20 plus standing time	🍲 00.00

American	Ingredients	Metric/Imperial
1 lb	young, scraped carrots	450 g/1 lb
½ tsp	salt	½ tsp
1 tbsp	ghee or groundnut oil	1 tbsp
1 tbsp	black mustard seeds	1 tbsp
1 tbsp	lemon juice	1 tbsp
1 tsp	sugar	1 tsp

1. Grate the carrots coarsely or cut into julienne strips. Sprinkle with salt, shake them well and leave to stand in a colander for 1 hour.
2. Heat the ghee or oil and fry the mustard seeds until they begin to jump in the pan. Cool the seeds on a large, cold plate.
3. Mix the lemon juice and the sugar and stir until the sugar has dissolved.
4. Just before serving, pour the dressing over the carrots and toss lightly. Sprinkle the mustard seeds over the top and serve.

Khira raita
Yogurt and Cucumber

⏱ 00.10 plus draining time	🍲 00.00

American	Ingredients	Metric/Imperial
1	large cucumber	1
1½ tsp	salt	1½ tsp
⅔ cup	Greek-style yogurt	150 ml/¼ pint
1	crushed garlic clove	1
½ tsp	grated root ginger	½ tsp
½ tbsp	lemon or tamarind juice	½ tbsp

1. Coarsely grate the cucumber, season with salt and leave to drain for 1 hour in a colander.
2. Mix together the yogurt, garlic, ginger and lemon or tamarind juice.
3. Just before serving, pour the yogurt over the cucumber, stir lightly and serve.

Baingan raita
Yogurt and Eggplant (Aubergine)

⏱ 00.25 Serve 4	🍲 00.30

American	Ingredients	Metric/Imperial
2	medium size eggplants (aubergines)	2
½ tsp	salt	½ tsp
1	large, seeded, finely chopped, green chili	1
1 tbsp	grated root ginger	1 tbsp
1½ tbsp	ghee	1½ tbsp
3	crushed garlic cloves	3
¼ tsp	ground cumin seeds	¼ tsp
½ tsp	ground turmeric	½ tsp
2½ cups	Greek-style yogurt	600 ml/1 pint

1. Slice the eggplants (aubergines) thinly and season with a little salt.
2. Mix together the chili and ginger and rub over the eggplants (aubergines). Leave them to stand for 15 minutes.
3. Heat the ghee in a frying pan and fry the eggplant (aubergine) slices, a few at a time, until brown.
4. Mix the garlic, cumin and turmeric into the yogurt. Stir the eggplant (aubergine) slices into the spiced yogurt whilst still hot then chill the raita until required.

Siem ka bhujia
Braised Spiced Beans

	00.15	00.15
	Serves 4	

American	Ingredients	Metric/Imperial
1 ¼ lb	French beans	575 g/1 ¼ lb
3	large, ripe, skinned tomatoes	3
1 tbsp	ghee	1 tbsp
1	chopped onion	1
½ tsp	grated root ginger	½ tsp
1 tsp	ground turmeric	1 tsp
1 tsp	garam masala	1 tsp
	salt	
	few drops lemon or lime juice	

1. Trim the beans and cut them into 1 in (2.5 cm) pieces.
2. Halve the tomatoes, seed and cut into small pieces.
3. Heat the ghee and stir fry the onion until transparent. Stir in the root ginger. Fry for 30 seconds and add the turmeric and garam masala. Stir well.
4. Add the pieces of tomato. Stir well and add the beans, a little salt and 4 tbsp of water. Bring to the boil. Partially cover the saucepan, reduce the heat and simmer for 8 10 minutes, stirring occasionally. Remove the lid from the pan a few minutes before the beans have finished cooking to allow all the water to evaporate. Do not overcook.
5. Just before serving, stir in a few drops of lemon or lime juice and transfer to a warmed dish.

Dahl
Lentil Purée

	00.10	01.00
	plus soaking time	

American	Ingredients	Metric/Imperial
1 ¼ cups	lentils	250 g/9 oz
1 ½ tbsp	ghee	1 ½ tbsp
1	large chopped onion	1
2	very finely chopped garlic cloves	2
2 tsp	finely grated root ginger	2 tsp
1 pinch	ground turmeric	1
½ tsp	garam masala	½ tsp
	salt	

1. Pick over the lentils then wash them and put them in a large bowl with enough cold water to cover. Stir well a few times and then remove all those which float to the surface. Leave to soak for 2-3 hours then drain thoroughly.
2. Heat the ghee and stir fry the onion until transparent. Add the garlic and the root ginger. Stir well a few times and fry for another minute. Add the ground turmeric and stir well.
3. Add the lentils, stir well and pour on 2¼ cups (500 ml/18 fl oz) boiling water. Bring to the boil again, stirring constantly. Reduce the heat and simmer for 30-35 minutes, until soft.
4. Add the garam masala and a little salt. Stir well and simmer for a little longer until the lentils disintegrate and form a coarse purée. Stir thoroughly then serve the purée in a warmed dish.

Braised spiced vegetables

Gobi fugath
Fried Cabbage

	00.10	00.14
	Serves 4	

American	Ingredients	Metric/Imperial
1	small white cabbage	1
3 tbsp	ghee	3 tbsp
1	large chopped onion	1
1	seeded, finely chopped red chili	1
1	seeded, finely chopped green chili	1
2	finely chopped garlic cloves	2
1 tsp	grated root ginger	1 tsp
1 tsp	ground turmeric	1 tsp
	salt	
2 tbsp	desiccated coconut	2 tbsp

1. Remove any damaged outside leaves from the cabbage. Cut in half and remove the greater part of the stalk from both halves. Cut the cabbage into finger-width strips.
2. Heat the ghee and stir fry the onion until transparent. Add the chilies and the garlic. Stir fry with the onion for 30 seconds, add the root ginger, followed by the ground turmeric. Stir well.
3. Add the cabbage a little at a time. Stir well after adding each portion. When it has all been added, fry gently for 10-12 minutes over a moderate heat. Do not overcook.
4. Just before serving sprinkle the cabbage with a little salt. Stir well and transfer to a warmed dish.
5. Sprinkle the coconut on top and serve.

Dhingri kari
Mushroom Curry

	00.10	00.10
	Serves 4	

American	Ingredients	Metric/Imperial
1½ lb	mushrooms (cultivated) chanterelles or morilles	700 g/1½ lb
3 tbsp	ghee	3 tbsp
1	very finely chopped garlic clove	1
1	small chopped onion	1
2 tsp	ground root ginger	2 tsp
2 tsp	curry powder	2 tsp
	salt	
⅔ cup	thick coconut milk	150 ml/¼ pint
	few drops of lemon or lime juice	
6	chopped scallions (spring onions)	6

1. Wipe the mushrooms. Trim the stalks and cut any large ones into quarters.
2. Heat the ghee and add the garlic, onion, ground root ginger and curry powder. Stir well and immediately add the mushrooms. Stir fry for 3-4 minutes over a moderate heat, cover the pan and braise the mushrooms for 3-4 minutes.
3. Add a little salt and the coconut milk. Stir well and bring to the boil. Immediately remove the pan from the heat. Stir well. Sprinkle with a little lemon or lime juice.
4. Transfer to a warmed dish and serve sprinkled with chopped scallions (spring onion).

Bhindi kari
Okra Curry

	00.10	00.20
	Serves 4	

American	Ingredients	Metric/Imperial
1¼ lb	okra	575 g/1¼ lb
2 tbsp	ghee	2 tbsp
1	onion, cut into thin rings	1
1	thinly sliced garlic clove	1
1 tsp	grated root ginger	1 tsp
1 tsp	ground turmeric	1 tsp
1 tsp	curry powder	1 tsp
1¼ cups	thick coconut milk	300 ml/½ pint
	salt	

1. Wash the okra, remove the stalks and cut into small pieces.
2. Heat the ghee and stir fry the onion rings until they begin to change color. Add the garlic, then the root ginger, ground turmeric and curry powder. Stir well and add the okra. Fry gently for 2-3 minutes.
3. Add the coconut milk and a little salt. Stir thoroughly, cover the pan and simmer gently for 8-10 minutes over a very moderate heat until the okra is soft. Serve immediately.

Trazi khumbi alu mattar kari
Mushroom, Potato and Pea Curry

	00.10	00.30
	Serves 4	

American	Ingredients	Metric/Imperial
1 lb	button mushrooms	450 g/1 lb
1½ lb	small, scraped new potatoes	700 g/1½ lb
2 tbsp	ghee	2 tbsp
1	chopped onion	1
2 tsp	grated root ginger	2 tsp
1	very finely chopped garlic clove	1
1 tsp	ground turmeric	1 tsp
2 tbsp	finely chopped coriander leaves	2 tbsp
8 oz	green peas, fresh or frozen	225 g/8 oz
	salt	
1 tsp	garam masala	1 tsp

1. Wipe the mushrooms. Trim the stalks. Cut any large mushrooms and potatoes into quarters.
2. Heat the ghee and stir fry the onion until transparent. Add the root ginger, garlic, ground turmeric and coriander leaves. Stir well.
3. Add the mushrooms, potatoes and peas and stir. Add ⅔ cup (150 ml/¼ pint) boiling water and cook for 20 minutes over a moderate heat. Do not stir, but shake the pan occasionally.
4. Sprinkle on a little salt and add the garam masala. Stir carefully once or twice. Simmer for a few minutes longer. Most of the liquid should have evaporated by the time the dish has finished cooking.
5. Serve on a warmed dish.

Mushroom, potato and pea curry

Chapatis
Flat Bread

	00.30 plus resting time	00.40

American	Ingredients	Metric/Imperial
4 cups + 4 tbsp	wholewheat flour	500 g/18 oz
2 tsp	salt	2 tsp
2 tbsp	ghee	2 tbsp

1. Reserve 2 tbsp of the flour for use later for rolling out the dough. Mix the remainder of the flour with the salt. Sprinkle the ghee on top, then add 1 cup (250 ml/8 fl oz) water. Stir the ingredients quickly together to make a firm dough. Knead the dough for at least 10 minutes.
2. Shape the dough into a ball and let it rest for at least 1 hour, covered with a damp cloth.
3. Divide the dough into small balls the size of walnuts. On a floured surface, roll out the balls into very thin rounds, looking like pancakes.
4. Heat a heavy-based frying pan and fry the dough rounds one at a time for 1-1½ minutes on each side. Press them against the bottom of the pan with a wooden spatula or spoon during frying to prevent them curling up and to allow air bubbles to form making them light and crisp.

Left to right:
Stuffed chapatis with lentils and spinach
Naan, Chapatis

Dal chapati
Lentil and Spinach Chapatis

	01.00 plus resting time	00.30

American	Ingredients	Metric/Imperial
4 cups + 4 tbsp	wholewheat flour	500g/18 oz
2 tsp	salt	2 tsp
2 tbsp	ghee	2 tbsp
1 cup	red lentils	250 g/9 oz
1 lb	spinach	450 g/1 lb
2 tbsp	ghee	2 tbsp
1	chopped onion	1
1	very finely chopped garlic clove	1
1 tsp	ground cumin	1 tsp
½ tsp	garam masala	½ tsp
	salt	
	few drops of lemon or lime juice (optional)	

1. Make the dough for the chapatis as directed in the previous recipe. Prepare the filling while the dough is resting.

2. Pick over the lentils. Rinse them well and place them in a large saucepan, with 1 cup (250 ml/8 fl oz) water. Bring to the boil and simmer for 15 minutes.

3. Pick over the spinach and rinse it thoroughly in plenty of cold water. Drain it well.

4. Place the spinach in the pan with the cooked lentils. Bring back to the boil, stir the contents of the pan thoroughly. Continue cooking for about 15 minutes until the lentils are soft.

5. Drain in a fine strainer. Rub the lentils and spinach through the strainer or purée in a food processor.

6. Heat the ghee in a wok or large frying pan and fry the onion until transparent.

7. Add the garlic, cumin, garam masala, a little salt (about ¾ tsp) and a few drops of lemon or lime juice. Stir thoroughly, remove the pan from the heat and add the purée. Stir thoroughly, then leave the mixture to cool.

8. Divide the dough for the chapatis into 12 equal pieces. Shape them into balls. Roll them through a little flour and then press them flat with the fingers to form rounds 4 in (10 cm) in diameter. Spoon a portion of the filling exactly in the center of each round. Fold the dough round the filling and seal firmly with the fingers. The filling must be completely covered. Use a rolling pin to roll out the chapatis on a floured surface to form pancakes 6 in (15 cm) in diameter.

9. Fry the chapatis for 1½-2 minutes on each side in a dry, hot frying pan.

Naan I

Naan Bread

01.00   00.12

makes 8 individual loaves

American	Ingredients	Metric/Imperial
1½ packages	active dried yeast	1 sachet
1 tsp	sugar	1 tsp
4 cups + 4 tbsp	white all-purpose (plain) flour	500 g/18 oz
1½ tsp	salt	1½ tsp
½ cup	yogurt	125 ml/4 fl oz
1	lightly beaten egg	1
5 tbsp	melted ghee	5 tbsp
2 tbsp	poppy seeds and/or sesame seeds	2 tbsp

1. Put the yeast in a small bowl with 5 tbsp warm water and the sugar. Stir, then leave to stand for about 5 minutes until frothy.

2. Sift the flour with the salt into a large bowl. Make a well in the center.

3. Mix together the yeast mixture, yogurt and egg and pour into the flour. Stirring from the middle and gradually adding 5 tbsp warm water, mix to a smooth batter.

4. Stir in the ghee. As soon as the ghee has been absorbed into the dough knead it by hand for 15 to 20 minutes until it is supple and elastic. Alternatively mix in a food processor or electric food mixer.

5. Shape the dough into a ball, put into a large bowl, cover with a damp cloth and leave to rise for about 1 hour in a warm place. The dough should double in volume.

6. Divide the ball into 8 pieces. Knead lightly and shape into balls. Flatten the balls and pull them into ovals, making one end wider than the other to form a pear shape.

7. Place the loaves on a baking sheet, cover with a damp cloth and leave to rise for 15 minutes.

8. Preheat the oven to 450°F (230°C) Gas Mark 8. Just before baking, brush the loaves with ghee and sprinkle with poppy or sesame seeds.

9. Bake for 10-12 minutes, until golden brown.

Chapatis
In India, the dough for chapatis is left to stand for 7-9 hours, rather than 1 hour. This gives an even lighter texture and allows more air bubbles to form.

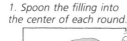

1. Spoon the filling into the center of each round.

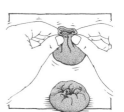

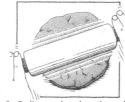

2. Fold the dough around the filling, like a little purse.

3. Roll out the dough to form 6 in (15 cm) pancakes.

Paratha

Ghee bread

	00.40 plus resting time		01.00

American	Ingredients	Metric/Imperial
2 cups + 2 tbsp	wholewheat flour	250 g/9 oz
2 cups + 2 tbsp	white all-purpose (plain) flour	250 g/9oz
2 tsp	salt	2 tsp
8 tbsp	ghee, or melted butter to serve	8 tbsp

1. Sift the flours and salt together in a bowl.
2. Add 2 tbsp of ghee and stir well. Add about 1 cup (200 ml/ 8 fl oz) cold water a little at a time, stirring to form a firm dough. Knead the dough for about 10 minutes until it no longer clings to the sides of the bowl. Shape the dough into a ball and let it rest for 1 hour in a cool place, covered with a damp cloth.
3. Divide the dough into 12 pieces. Roll the pieces into balls, then roll them out on a floured surface to form rounds ¼ in (5 mm) thick.
4. Brush each round with warm ghee. Spread the ghee with the fingers over the whole surface of the dough. Make an incision with scissors from the edge to the center of each round.
5. Roll the dough into a cone, flatten and press the edges together to seal. Roll out each piece again on a floured surface. The thinner it is rolled the lighter and crisper it will be.
6. Heat a large frying pan and brush lightly with ghee.
7. Fry each paratha for 2-3 minutes on each side. Lift regularly during cooking to prevent sticking.
8. Serve hot, brushed with a little ghee or butter.

Cook's tip: a variation is parathas with ajawan or cumin, for which add 2 tbsp ajawan or cumin seeds to the flour before mixing the dough. Continue as for the previous recipe.

Phool gobi paratha

Cauliflower Parathas

	00.40 plus resting time		00.45

American	Ingredients	Metric/Imperial
2 cups + 2 tbsp	wholewheat flour	250 g/9 oz
2 cups + 2 tbsp	white all-purpose (plain) flour	250 g/9 oz
1 ½ tsp	salt	1 ½ tsp
8 tbsp	ghee	8 tbsp
½ lb	cauliflower florets	225 g/8 oz
2 tsp	finely grated root ginger	2 tsp
½ tsp	garam masala	½ tsp
	salt	

1. Make the dough exactly as directed in the recipe for parathas. Cover with a damp cloth and leave to rest in a cool place for 1 hour.
2. Meanwhile, make the filling. Chop the cauliflower very finely, preferably in the food processor. Add the ginger and garam masala plus a little salt to taste.
3. Divide the dough into 8 pieces. Shape into balls between the hands, then roll the balls out on a floured board to form rounds 4 in (10 cm) in diameter.
4. Brush the rounds with a little melted ghee and place about 1 tbsp of the filling in the center of each. Fold the dough around the filling and then roll it out again, without pressing too hard, to form 6 in (15 cm) rounds.
5. Brush a frying pan with ghee and fry the parathas for 2-4 minutes each side, until golden yellow.

Cook's tip: for Spinach parathas, instead of cauliflower, make a purée of 10 oz (275 g) spinach. Drain well, squeezing out any excess moisture. Purée 4 tbsp cooked lentils or chick peas and 1 tbsp fried onion. Mix together the purées and season to taste with lemon juice and salt. Proceed as in the previous recipe.

Cauliflower parathas

Muli ke paratha

Radish Parathas

00.40 plus resting time **00.45**

American	Ingredients	Metric/Imperial
4 cups + 4 tbsp	white all-purpose (plain) flour	500 g/18 oz
1½ tsp	salt	1½ tsp
8 tbsp	ghee	8 tbsp
¾ lb	giant white radish (daikon)	300 g/12 oz
2 tsp	salt	2 tsp
1	seeded, finely chopped green chili	1
1 tsp	ground cumin	1 tsp
½ tsp	garam masala	½ tsp
2 tsp	finely chopped coriander leaves	2 tsp

1. Make the dough as directed in the paratha recipe. Prepare the filling while the dough is resting.

2. Scrape the radish under cold running water then grate finely. Mix the salt with the radish and spoon it into a nylon strainer. Leave to stand for 20 minutes to drain. Squeeze to remove excess moisture.

3. Mix the chopped chili with the grated radish. Stir in the ground cumin, garam masala and coriander.

4. Continue as directed in the recipe for Cauliflower parathas.

Poori

Fried Bread Cakes

00.40 plus resting time **00.50**

American	Ingredients	Metric/Imperial
4 cups + 4 tbsp	wholewheat flour	500 g/18 oz
2 tsp	salt	2 tsp
2 tbsp	ghee	2 tbsp
2 cups	groundnut oil	450 ml/¾ pint

1. Reserve 2 tbsp of the flour for rolling out. Mix the remaining flour with the salt. Sprinkle the ghee on top then add 1 cup (250 ml/8 fl oz) warm water. Mix together to make a firm dough then knead for at least 10 minutes.

2. Shape the dough into a ball and leave to rest for at least 1 hour, covered with a damp cloth.

3. Shape the dough into 24 small balls. On a floured surface roll out the balls to form rounds 4 in (10 cm) in diameter.

4. Heat the oil in a wok or deep frying pan. The oil should be about 1½ in (4 cm) deep.

5. Fry one or two pooris at a time for 1 minute on each side, spooning hot oil over the top to help them to puff up.

6. Drain briefly on kitchen paper and serve immediately.

Cook's tip: Kachori or Stuffed pooris are deep fried stuffed chapatis. The composition and the method of making stuffed pooris is exactly the same as that of stuffed chapatis. In making the fillings for the pooris, however, even more care should be taken to ensure that they contain as little moisture as possible, so that they do not spit when they are fried.

Palak poori

Spinach Pooris

00.40 plus resting time **00.50**

American	Ingredients	Metric/Imperial
7 oz	finely chopped spinach frozen if necessary	200 g/7 oz
3 cups	wholewheat flour	350 g/12 oz
2 tsp	salt	2 tsp
2 tsp	finely grated root ginger	2 tsp
1-2 tsp	ghee	1-2 tsp
2 cups	groundnut oil	450 ml/¾ pint

1. Completely thaw frozen spinach. Put the spinach in a strainer (sieve) and press out as much of the moisture as possible with a saucer.

2. Put the spinach in a bowl. Sift the flour and salt over it and add the root ginger and ghee. Mix well together, then knead to make a firm but supple dough. Add a little extra sifted flour, if necessary.

3. Shape the dough into a ball and leave to rest in a cool place for about 1 hour covered with a damp cloth.

4. Divide the dough into 24 small balls. Roll the balls out into rounds about ¼ in (5 mm) thick.

5. Heat the oil in a deep frying pan or wok. The oil should be about 1½ in (4 cm) deep. Deep fry the pooris one or two at a time in the hot oil for 1 minute on each side, spooning hot oil over the top to help them to puff up.

6. Drain briefly on kitchen paper and serve immediately.

Aloo Poori

Potato Pooris

00.40 plus resting time **00.50**

American	Ingredients	Metric/Imperial
½ lb	scrubbed potatoes	250 g/8 oz
2¾ cups	white all-purpose (plain) flour	300 g/11 oz
2 tsp	salt	2 tsp
2 tsp	ghee	2 tsp
2 cups	groundnut oil	450 ml/¾ pint

1. Boil the potatoes for 20 to 25 minutes in plenty of water then drain and dry them. Leave to cool, then peel the potatoes and rub them through a fine strainer (sieve).

2. Put the potatoes in a bowl, with the flour, salt, ghee and about 5 tbsp of hot water. Quickly knead the ingredients into a firm, but supple dough. Shape the dough into a ball and leave it in a cool place for about 1 hour, covered with a damp cloth.

3. Divide the dough into 24 small balls. Roll them out on a floured surface into rounds ¼ in (5 mm) thick.

4. Heat the oil in a deep frying pan or wok. The oil should be about 1½ in (4 cm) deep.

5. Deep fry one or two pooris at a time for 1 minute on each side, spooning hot oil over them to help to puff them up.

6. Drain briefly on kitchen paper and serve immediately.

Singaras

Potato Singaras

00.35
plus resting time

01.00

American	Ingredients	Metric/Imperial
4 cups + 4 tbsp	wholewheat flour	500 g/18 oz
1 tsp	salt	1 tsp
3 tbsp	ghee	3 tbsp
1 lb	potatoes	450 g/1 lb
1 tbsp	ghee	1 tbsp
1	large chopped onion	1
2	very finely chopped garlic cloves	2
2 tsp	curry powder	2 tsp
	salt	
1 tbsp	lemon or lime juice	1 tbsp
2 tbsp.	finely chopped coriander leaves	2 tbsp
	groundnut oil for frying	

1. Prepare the dough as directed in the recipe for samosas.
2. Scrub the potatoes under cold running water. Place them in a pan with boiling water to cover. Boil for exactly 15 minutes, then rinse in a colander under cold running water until cold. Peel the potatoes and cut into small cubes.
3. Heat the ghee and stir fry the chopped onion until transparent.
4. Add the remaining ingredients, except the coriander. Stir well several times and remove the pan from the heat.
5. Stir the potato pieces and the coriander into the spice mixture and leave to cool.
6. Continue as in the recipe for samosas.

Samosas
Meat Samosas

00.35
plus resting time

01.00

American	Ingredients	Metric/Imperial
4 cups + 4 tbsp	flour	500 g/1 lb
1 tsp	salt	1 tsp
5 tbsp	ghee or groundnut oil	5 tbsp
1	large, very finely chopped onion	1
2	very finely chopped garlic cloves	2
2 tsp	finely grated root ginger	2 tsp
2 tsp	curry powder	2 tsp
	salt	
2 tbsp	lemon or lime juice	2 tbsp
14 oz	ground (minced) lean lamb or beef	400 g/14 oz
2 tbsp	finely chopped coriander leaves or mint leaves	2 tbsp
	groundnut oil for frying	

1. Sieve the flour with the salt into a bowl. Make a well in the center and add ⅔ cup (150 ml/¼ pint) boiling water and 3 tbsp ghee. Stir from the center outward and add 1 or more tbsp boiling water if the mixture is too dry. Knead for about 10 minutes until the mixture forms a flexible and elastic dough. Alternatively use a food processor or electric mixer. Shape the dough into a ball and leave it to stand for at least 1 hour, covered with a damp cloth.

Potato singaras

2. Heat the remaining ghee and stir-fry the onion until transparent.

3. Add the garlic, ginger and curry powder. Stir in about ¾ tsp salt and the lemon or lime juice. Stir well and then add the ground (minced) meat. Cook, stirring constantly until the meat changes color and separates into crumbs.

4. Add ⅔ cup (150 ml/¼ pint) boiling water (or lamb or beef stock). Stir well, then cover the pan and simmer for 15 minutes over moderate heat.

5. Remove the lid and simmer until most of the liquid in the pan has evaporated. Remove from the heat and leave to cool.

6. Stir in the coriander or mint leaves.

7. Divide the dough into 8 pieces, shape into balls. On a floured surface roll out into rectangles 9×3 in (23×7.5 cm), ⅛ in (3mm) thick. Cut each piece into 3 squares.

8. Place 2-3 tsp of the filling in the center of each square. Make the dough around the filling wet with a small brush and water. Fold the squares diagonally across the filling to make triangles. Press the edges firmly together to seal. Place the samosas on to a damp cloth and cover them with another damp cloth. Leave them to rest for 15 minutes.

9. Heat the oil and fry 2-3 samosas at a time until golden brown, turning them once or twice during frying.

10. Drain the samosas briefly on kitchen paper and serve.

Samosas
In India, one or more chutneys are served with samosas. Each person taking a small spoonful of each, as a complimentary flavor to the samosa.

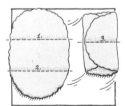

1. Roll out the balls of dough into rectangles.

2.Cut each rectangle into 3 more or less equal squares.

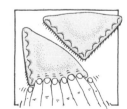

3. Divide the filling between the squares and fold them diagonally.

Namkin dahl
Savory Fried Pulses

	00.20 plus soaking time	00.20

American	Ingredients	Metric/Imperial
1 cup	chick-peas, lentils, split peas or other dried pulses	225 g/8 oz
⅔ cup	skimmed milk	150 ml/pint
	groundnut oil for frying	
	pinch salt	
½ tsp	ground chili	½ tsp
	pinch garam masala	

1. Pick over the pulses. Rinse them thoroughly in cold water. Pour the milk into a bowl and add 1 cup (250 ml/9 fl oz) water. Stir in the pulses and leave to soak for 8-12 hours, (3 hours for lentils, 1 hour for red lentils).

2. Drain well in a colander then dry them by rolling in a dry cloth or a piece of kitchen paper.

3. Heat the oil and fry the pulses 4-5 tbsp at a time for 2 to 3 minutes. Be careful as the oil may spray. Remove from the oil with a slotted spoon, drain briefly above the pan then spread out on a piece of kitchen paper. Do not fry the pulses for too long, as this makes them very hard and bitter. Leave to cool.

4. Mix the salt, chili and garam masala and sprinkle over the fried pulses. Shake to distribute the spice mixture.

Kele ke chips
Banana Chips

	00.10 Serves 4-8	00.10

American	Ingredients	Metric/Imperial
4	green, unripe bananas	4
	groundnut oil for frying	
1 tsp	fine sea salt	1 tsp
½ tsp	ground chili	½ tsp
½ tsp	amchur (ground dried mangoes)	½ tsp
	pinch garam masala	

1. Peel the bananas and cut obliquely into slices ⅛ in (3 mm) thick.

2. Heat the oil. Fry 8-12 slices at a time in the hot oil, ensuring that the slices do not stick together. Turn a few times during frying so that they brown evenly.

3. Remove from the oil with a slotted spoon and spread on kitchen paper to drain and cool.

4. Mix the salt, chili, amchur and garam masala in a small bowl.

5. Place all of the fried banana slices in a bowl. Sprinkle with the spice mixture and shake a few times.

Samosas Kerala
Vegetable Samosas

◣▷ 00.35   00.40 ◥
plus resting time

American	Ingredients	Metric/Imperial
4 cups + 4 tbsp	flour	500 g/18 oz
1 tsp	salt	1 tsp
3 tbsp	ghee or groundnut oil	3 tbsp
2 tbsp	ghee	2 tbsp
2	large chopped onions	2
2	very finely chopped garlic cloves	2
2 tsp	garam masala	2 tsp
5 oz	very finely chopped spinach	150 g/5 oz
7	chopped carrots	7
4 tbsp	shelled peas frozen if necessary	4 tbsp
	salt	
1 cups	boiled rice	125 g/4 oz
1	beaten egg	1
	groundnut oil for frying	

1. Prepare the dough as directed for samosas.
2. Heat the ghee and stir fry the onions until transparent. Add the garlic and garam masala and stir well. Add the spinach, carrots and peas. Add 5 tbsp boiling water and stir. Cover the pan and simmer for 5 minutes over a moderate heat.
3. Remove the lid and simmer until almost all of the liquid has evaporated. Stir occasionally. Add a little salt to taste, remove the pan from the heat and leave to cool. Stir in the rice and egg.
4. Divide the dough in half and shape into 2 rolls each with a diameter of 2 in (5 cm). Cut each into 12 thin slices.

5. On a floured surface, roll out each slice until it has a diameter of 5 in (13 cm). Place a spoonful of the filling on to each round. Brush the dough around the filling with water and fold the dough across the filling to form semi-circles. Curve into crescent shapes and press the edges firmly to seal.
6. Put the crescents on a damp cloth, cover with another damp cloth and leave to rest for 15 minutes.
7. Heat the oil and fry the singaras 2-3 at a time until golden brown, turning during cooking to brown evenly. Drain briefly on kitchen paper and serve immediately.

Pakoras
Fried Snacks

◣▷ 00.30   00.30 ◥

American	Ingredients	Metric/Imperial
1 cup	chick-pea flour (besan)	125 g/4 oz
½ cup	wheat flour	75 g/2 oz
1 tsp	salt	1 tsp
½ tsp	ground chili	½ tsp
½ tsp	garam masala	½ tsp
1 tbsp	finely chopped coriander leaves	1 tbsp
18 oz	bite-size pieces of vegetable eg potato, cauliflower, broccoli, bell pepper, eggplant (aubergine), zucchini (courgette), mushroom	500 g/18 oz
2	eggs	2
6 oz	chicken fillets	175 g/6 oz
2 tbsp	lemon or lime juice or vinegar	2 tbsp
	groundnut oil for frying	

Fried snacks

Vegetable samosas

1. Sift both flours into a bowl. Add the salt, chili, garam masala and coriander leaves and gradually stir in ⅔ cup (150 ml/¼ pint) cold water, using a whisk. The batter should be of the consistency of thin cream. Leave to stand for 30 minutes.
2. Prepare the vegetables as follows.
Potatoes: Peel and cut into slices ½ in (1 cm) thick. Rinse in a colander. Dry with kitchen paper before frying.
Cauliflower and broccoli: Use only the florets. Divide them into small pieces 2 in (5 cm) long, trimming off the stalks.
Bell Peppers: Remove the stalks, seeds and the pith. Cut the flesh into finger-width strips.
Eggplant (aubergine): Choose small firm fruits. Trim them, cut into slices ½ in (1 cm) thick. Soak in cold water with a little added lemon juice or vinegar. Dry with kitchen paper just before dipping them in the batter.
Zucchini (courgette): Select small zucchini (courgette). Trim the ends and cut obliquely into slices ½ in (1 cm thick. Soak in cold water with a little added vinegar or lemon juice. Dry with kitchen paper before using.
Mushrooms: Choose button mushrooms. Wipe them clean with kitchen paper. Trim the stalks.
3. Hard-cook (hard-boil), cool, shell and quarter the eggs.
4. Dry the chicken fillets with kitchen paper. Cut into finger-width strips. Sprinkle with a little lemon or lime juice. Marinate for 30 minutes, then dry with kitchen paper just before dipping them into batter.
5. Heat the oil. Whisk the batter. Dip 6-8 pieces of the same ingredient into the batter and carefully add them to the oil. Fry for 3-5 minutes until golden brown, turning several times during cooking to brown evenly on all sides.
6. Drain on kitchen paper and serve as hot as possible.

Masala Kaju badam

Spiced Fried Nuts

	00.00 plus cooling time	00.20

American	Ingredients	Metric/Imperial
⅔ cup	groundnut oil	150 ml/¼ pint
3 tbsp	sesame oil or mustard seed oil	3 tbsp
1 cup	shelled cashew nuts	125 g/4 oz
1 cup	blanched almonds	125 g/4 oz
2 cups	shelled, skinned peanuts	250 g/8 oz
1 tsp	garam masala	1 tsp
1 tsp	ground chili	1 tsp
	salt	

1. Heat both the oils in a wok or large frying pan. Add ⅓ of the nuts and stir fry until golden brown. Remove from the oil with a skimmer and drain on kitchen paper. Roll the nuts over the kitchen paper to remove most of the oil.
2. Fry the remaining nuts in 2 batches and drain. Put all the fried nuts in a large bowl.
3. Mix together the garam masala, chili and a little salt (about ½ tsp). Sprinkle this mixture over the nuts and shake well a few times.
4. Allow the nuts to become completely cold. Serve freshly cooked.

Cook's tip: if the spiced fried nuts are to be stored, do not add the salt to the spice mixture, as this softens the nuts. Store the spiced fried nuts in an airtight container and sprinkle with a little salt immediately before serving.

Tamatar ki chutney

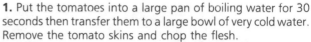

Tomato Chutney

00.10 makes 1 large jar 00.50

American	Ingredients	Metric/Imperial
1 ¼ lb	ripe tomatoes	575 g/1 ¼ lb
9 oz	sugar	250 g/9 oz
2	crushed garlic cloves	2
2	bay leaves	2
⅔ cup	herb vinegar	150 ml/¼ pint
2-3 tbsp	raisins	2-3 tbsp
1-2 tbsp	flaked almonds	1-2 tbsp
1 tsp	caraway seed	1 tsp
½ tsp	ground chili	½ tsp
1 tsp	salt	1 tsp

1. Put the tomatoes into a large pan of boiling water for 30 seconds then transfer them to a large bowl of very cold water. Remove the tomato skins and chop the flesh.
2. In a large pan bring ¾ cup (200 ml/7 fl oz) water to the boil. Add the sugar and tomato.
3. Bring back to the boil and add remaining ingredients. Reduce the heat and simmer for 45 minutes, stirring frequently.
4. Remove the pan from the heat and discard the bayleaves.
5. Transfer the hot chutney to 1 large or 2 small jars.
6. Seal, label and store in a cool, dry, dark place for up to 4 weeks.

Tomato Chutney with Coconut

00.20 makes 1 large jar 01.00

American	Ingredients	Metric/Imperial
½ cup	desiccated coconut	75 g/3 oz
1 lb	skinned, roughly chopped tomatoes	450 g/1 lb
1 cup	sugar	225 g/8 oz
⅔ cup	herb vinegar	150 ml/¼ pint
6 tbsp	raisins	6 tbsp
½ tsp	ground chili	½ tsp
1 tsp	ground cumin	1 tsp
1 tsp	salt	1 tsp
2	bay leaves	2
4	cloves	4

1. Place the coconut in a bowl and slowly add 5 tbsp boiling water. Stir lightly, then leave to stand for 15 minutes.
2. Bring ¾ cup (200 ml/7 floz) water to the boil in a large pan. Add all the ingredients, stir well and bring to the boil.
3. Reduce the heat and simmer gently for 40-50 minutes. Stir occasionally.
4. Remove from the heat. Discard the bay leaves and the cloves. Transfer the hot chutney to 1 large or 2 small jars. Seal, label and store in a cool, dry, dark place for up to 4 weeks.

Tomato Chutney with Green Chilies

	00.10	01.20
	makes 1 large jar	

American	Ingredients	Metric/Imperial
1 1b	skinned, roughly chopped tomatoes	450 g/1 lb
6-8	green chilies	6-8
1 cup	sugar	225 g/8 oz
2	crushed garlic cloves	2
1	large chopped onion	1
⅔ cup	herb vinegar	150 ml/¼ pint
3 tbsp	raisins	3 tbsp
3 tbsp	flaked almonds	3 tbsp
4	cloves	4
2	bay leaves	2
½ tsp	ground chili	½ tsp
1 tsp	salt	1 tsp

Left to right: Tomato chutney with bell peppers, Tomato chutney with coconut, Tomato chutney with green chilies

1. Bring ¾ cup (200 ml/7 fl oz) water to the boil in a large pan. Add the tomato, bring to the boil and simmer for 15 minutes.
2. Pour the tomato into a fine strainer and rub through as much as possible, using a wooden spoon.
3. Wash the chilies, remove the ends, seeds and pith. Chop the flesh finely.
4. Add the chili and the remaining ingredients to the tomato purée.
5. Simmer gently for 40 minutes, stirring ocasionally. Discard the bay leaves and cloves.
6. Transfer the hot chutney to 1 large or 2 small jars. Seal, label and store in a cool, dark, dry place for up to 4 weeks.

Tomato Chutney with Bell Peppers

	00.15	01.00
	makes 1 large jar	

American	Ingredients	Metric/Imperial
18 oz	skinned, ripe tomatoes	500 g/18 oz
9 oz	soft brown sugar	250 g/9 oz
2	red bell peppers	2
2	crushed garlic cloves	2
1	large chopped onion	1
⅔ cup	herb vinegar	150 ml/¼ pint
2	bay leaves	2
2-3 tbsp	raisins	2-3 tbsp
2-3 tbsp	flaked almonds or finely chopped walnuts	2-3 tbsp
4	cloves	4
½ tsp	ground chili	½ tsp
1 tsp	salt	1 tsp

1. Roughly chop the tomatoes.
2. Bring ¾ cup (200 ml/7 fl oz) water to the boil in a large pan and dissolve the sugar in it. Add the tomatoes and bring to the boil then reduce the heat and simmer for 10 minutes.
3. Wash the bell peppers, remove the stalks, seeds and pith. Cut the bell peppers into small pieces.
4. Add the peppers and the remaining ingredients to the tomatoes. Stir well, reduce the heat and simmer gently for 40 minutes.
5. Remove the pan from the heat and discard the bay leaves and the cloves.
6. Transfer the hot chutney into 1 large or 2 small jars. Seal and store in a cool, dark, dry place for up to 4 weeks. Keep for at least 3 days before use to allow the flavor to develop.

Plum Chutney

00.15   01.00

makes 1 large jar

American	Ingredients	Metric/Imperial
1 ½ lb	firm, ripe plums	700 g/1 ½ lb
½ lb	cooking apples	225 g/½ lb
½ lb	unripe tomatoes	225 g/½ lb
1 ⅓ cups	raw cane sugar	225 g/½ lb
2 tbsp	corn (golden) syrup	2 tbsp
1	chopped onion	1
4 tbsp	raisins	4 tbsp
⅔ cup	cider vinegar	150 ml/¼ pint
2	crushed garlic cloves	2
1 tbsp	finely grated fresh root ginger	1 tbsp
½ tsp	garam masala	½ tsp
1 tsp	salt	1 tsp

1. Wash the plums. Remove the skins and the stones.
2. Cut the apples into quarters and remove the cores. Cut into small pieces.
3. Skin the tomatoes. Cut into small pieces and remove seed.
4. Bring ¾ cup (200 ml/7 fl oz) water to the boil in a pan. Stir in the sugar and syrup and all other ingredients.
5. Stir well and bring to the boil. Reduce the heat and simmer gently for 45-55 minutes, until thick.
6. Transfer the hot chutney to 1 large or 2 small jars. Seal, label and store in a cool, dry, dark place for up to 4 weeks.

Mango Chutney

00.10   00.50

makes 1 large jar

American	Ingredients	Metric/Imperial
1 ½ lbs	lightly unripe mangoes	700 g/1 ½ lb
1 cup	sugar	225 g/8 oz
1	chopped onion	1
4 tbsp	raisins	4 tbsp
1	crushed garlic clove	1
1 tsp	salt	1 tsp
1 tsp	ground ginger	1 tsp
½ tsp	garam masala	½ tsp
⅔ cup	herb vinegar	150 ml/¼ pint

1. Peel the mangoes, remove the stones and cut the flesh into small pieces.
2. Bring ⅔ cup (150 ml/¼ pint) water to the boil in a large pan. Add the pieces of mango and all other ingredients. Stir well and bring to the boil.
3. Reduce the heat and simmer for 40-45 minutes until thick.
4. Transfer the hot chutney to 1 large or 2 small jars. Seal label and store in a cool, dark, dry place for up to 4 months.

Nariyal ki chutney
Coconut Chutney

00.30   00.02

American	Ingredients	Metric/Imperial
1	small coconut	1
1	seeded and finely chopped green chili	1
½ tsp	salt	½ tsp
½ cup	Greek-style yogurt	125 ml/4 fl oz
1 tbsp	sesame oil	1 tbsp
2 tsp	mustard seeds	2 tsp
2	bay leaves	2

1. Crack the coconut, discard the liquid and place the coconut pieces in a hot oven for 5 minutes.
2. Cool the coconut and remove the flesh. Peel off the brown skin then chop or grate the coconut extremely finely.
3. Mix with the chili and salt, then stir in the yogurt.
4. Heat the sesame oil and add the mustard seeds and bay leaves. Stir until the seeds begin to jump. Remove the bay leaves and sprinkle mustard seeds over the chutney. Serve immediately.

Tomato and Green Mango Chutney

00.15   01.20

makes 1 large jar

American	Ingredients	Metric/Imperial
1	large unripe (green) mango	1
1 ¼ lb	skinned ripe tomatoes	575 g/1 ¼ lb
1 ⅓ cups	soft brown sugar	225 g/8 oz
⅔ cup	tamarind liquid	150 ml/¼ pint
1	large chopped onion	1
1	crushed garlic clove	1
2	bay leaves	2
1 tsp	garam masala	1 tsp
1 tsp	salt	1 tsp

1. Peel the mango and remove the stone. Cut the flesh into small pieces or grate it on a coarse grater.
2. Cut the tomatoes into pieces and remove the seed.
3. Bring ¾ cup (200 ml/7 fl oz) water to the boil in a large pan. Add the sugar, tomatoes, and the mango.
4. Bring to the boil, then simmer gently for 10 minutes.
5. Add the remaining ingredients and bring to the boil. Reduce the heat and simmer for about 1 hour, until the mango can be crushed with a wooden spoon against the side of the pan.
6. Remove the bay leaves and transfer the hot chutney to 1 large or 2 small jars. Seal, label and store in a cool, dark, dry place for up to 4 weeks.

Rhubarb and Date Chutney

00.15 makes 1 large jar **00.45**

American	Ingredients	Metric/Imperial
1 lb	young rhubarb	450 g/1 lb
½ lb	fresh dates	225 g/8 oz
1 cup	sugar	225 g/8 oz
⅔ cup	herb vinegar	150 ml/¼ pint
1 tsp	mustard seeds	1 tsp
1 tsp	garam masala	1 tsp
1 tsp	ground root ginger	1 tsp
1 tsp	salt	1 tsp

1. Rinse the rhubarb and cut into small pieces.
2. Stone the dates and chop into small pieces.
3. Bring ¾ cup (200 ml/8 fl oz) water to the boil in a pan. Dissolve the sugar in it, stirring constantly. Add the rhubarb, dates and other ingredients. Stir well and bring to the boil again. Simmer for 45 minutes, stirring occasionally, until a fairly stiff consistency is obtained.
4. Transfer the hot chutney to 1 large or 2 small jars. Seal, label and store in a cool, dark, dry place for 2-3 months.

Apple Chutney with Apricots

00.15 makes 1 large jar **00.40**

American	Ingredients	Metric/Imperial
1½ lb	green, slightly unripe apples	700 g/1½ lb
6	large, dried, stoned apricots	6
1⅓ cups	soft brown sugar	225 g/8 oz
⅔ cup	cider vinegar	150 ml/¼ pint
1 (2 in)	cinnamon stick	1 (2 in/5 cm)
4	cloves	4
1	bay leaf	1
1 tsp	salt	1 tsp
½ tsp	ground chili	½ tsp

1. Peel the apples, quarter and core then cut into small pieces.
2. Rinse the apricots under running cold water then cut into extremely thin strips.
3. Bring to the boil ¾ cup (200 ml/8 fl oz) water in a pan. Dissolve the sugar in it stirring constantly. Add the apple, apricots and other ingredients. Bring to the boil, then reduce the heat and simmer for 30-40 minutes.
4. Remove the cinnamon stick, cloves and the bay leaf.
5. Transfer the hot chutney to 1 large or 2 small jars. Seal, label and store in a cool, dark, dry place for up to 4 weeks.

Apple Relish with Cucumber

00.20 makes 1 large jar **00.15**

American	Ingredients	Metric/Imperial
1 lb	sour green cooking apples	450 g/1 lb
1	large green cucumber	1
3	crushed dried chilies	3
1	chopped onion	1
1½ cups	sugar	350 g/12 oz
⅔ cup	cider vinegar	150 ml/¼ pint
1 tsp	salt	1 tsp
½ tsp	curry powder	½ tsp
2	bay leaves	2

1. Cut the apples into quarters. Remove the cores, then cut the quarters into strips of 3×¼ in (4 cm×5 cm).
2. Halve the cucumber lengthwise. Remove the seeds and trim the ends. Cut into 3×¼ in (4 cm×5 cm).
3. Place the strips of apple and cucumber, the crushed chilies and the chopped onion in a pan. Stir well.
4. Place ½ cup (100 ml/ 4 fl oz) water into another pan and add the remaining ingredients. Bring to the boil, stirring until the sugar and salt have dissolved. Simmer for 5 minutes then pour over the strips of apple and cucumber.
5. Stir, then bring slowly to the boil. Simmer for 3 minutes then remove from the heat and remove the bay leaves.
6. Transfer the hot chutney to 1 large or 2 small jars. Seal, label and store in a cool, dark, dry place for up to 8 weeks. Keep for 1 week before use.

Piaz sambal
Onion Sambal

00.10 **01.00**

American	Ingredients	Metric/Imperial
2	coarsely chopped onions	2
2 tbsp	tamarind liquid (asem)	2 tbsp
	lemon or lime juice	
1 tsp	ground chili	1 tsp
½ tsp	salt	½ tsp
pinch	sugar (optional)	

1. Place all the ingredients in a bowl and mix well.
2. Cover and chill for 1 hour.
3. Stir the sambal well before serving.

Channa dahl

Chick-pea Purée

▬▷ 00.10   01.20 🍲
Serves 4

American	Ingredients	Metric/Imperial
1 ½ cups	chick-peas or split dried peas	200 g/7 oz
1	large chopped onion	1
2 tbsp	thick coconut milk	2 tbsp
½ tsp	ground turmeric	½ tsp
½ tsp	ground chili	½ tsp
	salt	
½ tsp	garam masala	½ tsp
1 tbsp	groundnut oil	1 tbsp
½ tsp	mustard seeds	½ tsp
½ tsp	cumin seeds	½ tsp

1. Pick over the chick-peas, then rinse thoroughly.
2. Bring 2½ cups (600 ml/1 pint) water to the boil. Add the chick-peas and bring back to the boil. Boil rapidly for 5 minutes.
3. Add the onion, coconut milk, turmeric and chili. Stir well. Cover the pan, reduce the heat and cook gently for about 1 hour, until the peas are tender and most of the liquid has been absorbed. Add the garam masala and salt to taste. Stir well.
4. Heat the oil in a frying pan and add the mustard and cumin seeds. Cook until the seeds burst, being careful not to burn them.
5. Add the seeds to the peas and stir well. Cook gently for 5 minutes before serving.

Mung

Spiced Mung Beans

▬▷ 00.10   01.45 🍲
plus soaking time

American	Ingredients	Metric/Imperial
¾ lb	mung beans	350 g/12 oz
2	onions	2
2 tbsp	thick coconut milk	2 tbsp
2	chopped green chilies	2
½ tsp	ground turmeric	½ tsp
½ tsp	ground chili	½ tsp
1 tbsp	groundnut oil	1 tbsp
½ tsp	ground mustard seeds	½ tsp
	pinch hing (asafetida) (optional)	
	salt	
2	peeled tomatoes cut into segments	2

1. Pick over the beans and remove any husks or stones etc. Wash carefully in several changes of cold water. Soak for 6 hours (or longer) in plenty of cold water. Drain and put into a pan.
2. Add the onions, coconut milk, chilies, ground turmeric and ground chili.
3. Heat the oil in a frying pan and add mustard seeds and hing (if used). Cook until the seeds burst then add to the beans.
4. Add 1½ cups (350 ml/12 fl oz) water. Bring slowly to the boil, cover the pan and cook gently for 1½ hours.
5. As this should be quite a dry dish, remove the lid from the pan 15 minutes before the end of the cooking time to allow as much liquid as possible to evaporate, if necessary. Add salt to taste.
6. Serve in a warmed dish, garnished with the tomato segments.

Urad dahl
Spiced Black Beans

00.10 plus soaking time   **00.50**

American	Ingredients	Metric/Imperial
2½ cups	urad dahl (black beans)	350 g/12 oz
½ tsp	ground turmeric	½ tsp
½ tsp	ground chili	½ tsp
	salt	
¼ cup	ghee	40 g/1½ oz
1	chopped onion	1
	few sprigs of coriander	

1. Pick over the beans then rinse throughly. Soak in water to cover for 30 minutes.
2. In a large pan bring 3½ cups (900 ml/1½ pints) water to the boil. Add the beans and boil for 5 minutes.
3. Add the ground turmeric and chili. Cover the pan, reduce the heat and simmer for about 30 minutes, until the beans are almost tender.
4. Heat the ghee and fry the onion until it is golden brown.
5. Add the onions to the beans and salt to taste, stir well and cook until the beans are tender.
6. Garnish with sprigs of coriander and serve.

Left to right: Spiced mung beans, Spiced black beans, Spiced red lentils

Masur dahl
Spiced Red Lentils

00.10 plus soaking time   **00.30**

American	Ingredients	Metric/Imperial
1½ cups	red lentils	350 g/12 oz
1 cup	ghee	225 g/8 oz
2	crushed garlic cloves	2
½ tsp	ground turmeric	½ tsp
1 tsp	ground chili	1 tsp
1 tsp	finely grated root ginger	1 tsp
3	medium size onions	3
	few sprigs of coriander (optional)	

1. Pick over the lentils then rinse thoroughly. Soak in cold water to cover for 1 hour 30 minutes. Drain well and dry.
2. Heat 1 tbsp ghee in a pan. Add the lentils, garlic, turmeric, chili and root ginger. Stir fry gently for 3 minutes.
3. Add boiling water to just cover the lentils. Cover the pan and cook gently for about 20 minutes.
4. Cut each onion into 8 or 10 pieces, separate the layers. Heat the remaining ghee in a frying pan and fry the onions until golden brown.
5. Transfer the beans to a warmed dish and top with the fried onions. Garnish with a few sprigs of coriander and serve.

Hussaini siech kebabs
Grilled Lamb Kebabs

00.15 plus marinating   **00.15**

American	Ingredients	Metric/Imperial
1 lb	lean lamb	450 g/1 lb
2 tsp	finely grated root ginger	2 tsp
4	crushed garlic cloves	4
3-4	seeded red chilies, cut into small pieces	3-4
½ tsp	ground cumin	½ tsp
1 tbsp	finely chopped coriander	1 tbsp
1 tbsp	ghee	1 tbsp
16	peeled shallots or small onions	16
	salt	
	coriander sprigs	
½ cup	blanched almonds	75 g/3 oz
1¼ cups	thin coconut milk	300 ml/½ pint
2 tbsp	ghee	2 tbsp
½ tsp	ground cardamom seeds	½ tsp
	freshly ground black pepper	

1. Cut the meat into 1 in (2.5 cm) cubes.
2. In a food processor, blender or pestle and mortar, grind the root ginger, garlic, chilies, cumin, coriander and 1 tbsp ghee to a fine paste.
3. Rub the meat with the paste then leave to stand for at least 1 hour.
4. Meanwhile, make the sauce. Toast the almonds in a dry frying pan until lightly colored. Cool, then grind finely.
5. Bring the coconut milk to the boil. Add the almonds, 2 tbsp ghee and a little salt. Simmer gently to make a thickened sauce.
6. Stir in the cardamom seeds and black pepper to taste. Keep the sauce hot.
7. Skewer the meat cubes and shallots on skewers.
8. Broil (grill) the kebabs under a moderately hot broiler (grill) for 8 minutes, turning regularly during cooking. After cooking, salt the meat.
9. Serve the kebabs with a little sauce spooned over and garnish with coriander sprigs. Serve the remaining sauce separately.

Tikka kebab
Grilled Beef Kebabs

00.20 plus marinating   **00.10**

American	Ingredients	Metric/Imperial
1 lb	rump steak	450 g/1 lb
1	seeded, green bell pepper	1
¼ lb	wiped, trimmed, button mushrooms	125 g/4 oz
8	cherry tomatoes	8
12	peeled shallots or small onions	12
4 tbsp	lemon or lime juice	4 tbsp
1 tsp	ground chili	1 tsp
2 tbsp	groundnut oil	2 tbsp
	salt	

1. Cut the meat into 1 in (2.5 cm) cubes.
2. Cut the bell pepper into 1 in (2.5 cm) squares.
3. Mix the lemon or lime juice and chili together. Add the meat, bell peppers, mushrooms, shallots and tomatoes. Stir well and leave to stand in a cool place for 2-3 hours.
4. Divide the ingredients between four large skewers. Pat the kebabs dry with kitchen paper then brush with a little oil.
5. Broil (grill) the kebabs under a hot broiler (grill), for 5-6 minutes, turning regularly and basting with oil.
Sprinkle a little salt over the kebabs and serve on warmed plates.

Grilled lamb kebabs, Grilled beef kebabs

Tandoori murgh tangeen
Grilled Chicken Drumsticks

00.15 Serves 4   **00.20**

American	Ingredients	Metric/Imperial
12-16	chicken drumsticks	12-16
1 tsp	ground chili	1 tsp
½ tsp	ground cumin	½ tsp
½ tsp	garlic salt	½ tsp
½ tsp	ground ginger	½ tsp
½ tsp	ground coriander	½ tsp
1½ tsp	salt	1½ tsp
4 tbsp	groundnut oil	4 tbsp
2 tbsp	lemon or lime juice	2 tbsp
3	large onions cut into rings	3
½ tsp	garam masala	½ tsp
2	skinned tomatoes cut into pieces	2
4	lemons or limes cut into pieces	4

1. Dry the drumsticks with kitchen paper. Mix together the chili, cumin, garlic salt, ginger and coriander (tandoori masala) and the salt and rub into the skins.
2. Thread the chicken legs on to skewers, then brush with oil.
3. Broil (grill) the drumsticks for about 15 minutes, under a hot broiler (grill) until tender and red brown. Turn and brush with oil regularly.
4. Immediately after grilling, sprinkle with lemon or lime juice.
5. Heat 1½ tbsp oil in a wok and stir fry the onion rings until golden.
6. Sprinkle the onions with a little salt and the garam masala.
7. Serve the chicken on a bed of fried onions, garnished with tomato pieces. Serve the lemon or lime pieces separately.

Shakambhari ghoramghor
Vegetable Soup

◤ 00.10   00.15 🥘
Serves 4

American	Ingredients	Metric/Imperial
4 tbsp	ghee	4 tbsp
2	large coarsely chopped onions	2
2	crushed garlic cloves	2
1	large carrot cut into narrow strips	1
2	sticks celery, cut into strips	2
11 cup	shredded white cabbage	150 g/6 oz
8	skinned, diced tomatoes	8
1 tsp	finely ground black pepper	1 tsp
1 tsp	ground turmeric	1 tsp
	salt	
1-2 tbsp	finely chopped coriander	1-2 tbsp

1. Heat the ghee in a large pan. Fry the onions until transparent. Add the garlic and cook until the onion turns golden.
2. Add all vegetables at the same time with 1½ quarts (1.5 litres/2¾ pints) boiling water. Stir well and cook gently for 10-12 minutes.
3. Add the pepper, ground turmeric and a little salt to taste. Stir well and sprinkle with herbs. Serve.

Mung dahl soup
Mung Bean Soup

◤ 00.10   01.00 🥘
Serves 4

American	Ingredients	Metric/Imperial
1 cup	mung beans or split peas	225 g/8 oz
1 tsp	ground turmeric	1 tsp
2 tbsp	ghee	2 tbsp
2	large coarsely chopped onions	2
½ tsp	garam masala	½ tsp
4	large, skinned, roughly chopped tomatoes	4
2	sticks celery, cut into narrow strips	2
½ tsp	finely ground black pepper	½ tsp
	salt	
1-2 tbsp	finely chopped coriander	1-2 tbsp
2 tsp	lime or lemon juice	2 tsp

1. Pick over the beans then rinse them thoroughly.
2. Put the mung beans in a pan with 1 quart (1 litre/1¾ pints) cold water. Bring slowly to the boil and cook gently for 10 minutes.
3. Carefully skim the surface then add the ground turmeric. Stir well and cook for about 30 minutes, until tender.
4. Heat the ghee and fry the onions, stirring until golden. Stir in the garam masala and add the tomatoes, celery, pepper and a little salt. Stir well and continue cooking for 8-10 minutes.
5. Serve the soup in warmed bowls sprinkled with the herbs and the lime or lemon juice.
6. Serve the fried onions separately to be added to the soup to taste.

Left: Vegetable soup Right: Mung bean soup

Bhari phulgobi

Spiced Cauliflower

00.10 Serves 4 00.15

American	Ingredients	Metric/Imperial
1	large, trimmed cauliflower divided into florets	1
4 tbsp	groundnut oil	4 tbsp
2 tsp	fennel seeds	2 tsp
2 tsp	black mustard seeds	2 tsp
4	finely chopped garlic cloves	4
½ tsp	ground turmeric	½ tsp
	freshly ground black pepper	
	salt	

1. Rinse the cauliflower florets and drain well.
2. Heat the oil then add all the seeds. Stir well and add the garlic as soon as the seeds begin to burst. Stir fry the garlic until golden brown.
3. Add the cauliflower and sprinkle with ground turmeric, pepper and a little salt. Stir fry for 3-5 minutes.
4. Add 5 tbsp boiling water, bring to the boil and cook for 4-5 minutes, until the florets are tender. The liquid should all evaporate. Add more if necessary.
5. Transfer to warm dish and serve immediately.

Rasedaar khumbi

Spiced Mushrooms

00.10 Serves 4 00.15

American	Ingredients	Metric/Imperial
1 tbsp	coarsely grated fresh root ginger	1 tbsp
3	coarsely chopped garlic cloves	3
3	ripe, skinned, diced tomatoes	3
3 tbsp	groundnut oil	3 tbsp
2	cardamom pods	2
1 tsp	cumin seeds	1 tsp
1½ tsp	coriander seeds	½ tsp
1 lb	trimmed, wiped, button mushrooms	450 g/1 lb
	freshly ground black pepper	
	salt	
½ tsp	garam masala	½ tsp
1-2 tbsp	finely chopped coriander	1-2 tbsp

1. In the food processor, make a fine paste from the root ginger, garlic and tomatoes.
2. Heat the oil, then add the cardamom pods, cumin and coriander seeds. Cook until the seeds burst, then add the garlic, ginger and tomato paste. Fry gently for 1 minute, stirring continuously.

Left to right: Spiced cauliflower, Spiced mushrooms, Carrots with potatoes and onions.

3. Add the mushrooms and ⅔ cup (150 ml/¼ pint) boiling water. Bring to the boil stirring, then reduce the heat and leave to cook gently for 8-10 minutes. At least half the liquid in the pan should evaporate.

4. Season with pepper and salt. Just before serving, add the garam masala. Transfer to a warmed dish and sprinkle with coriander.

Gajar mattar

Carrots with Potatoes and Onions

◢	00.20 Serves 4	00.30

American	Ingredients	Metric/Imperial
¾ lb	scrubbed potatoes	350 g/12 oz
3 tbsp	groundnut or mustard oil	3 tbsp
2	small, crumbled dried red chilies	2
1 tsp	cumin seeds	1 tsp
½ tsp	black mustard seeds	½ tsp
3-4	large, peeled onions halved and sliced	3-4
½ lb	scraped, young carrots cut into ¾ in (1.75 cm) lengths	225 g/8 oz
¾ cup	shelled peas	125 g/4 oz
	salt	
1 tsp	sugar	1 tsp
	sprigs of coriander or parsley	

1. Boil the potatoes for 15 minutes. Drain and cool slightly. Peel them and cut into ¾ in (1.75 cm) cubes.

2. Heat the oil. Add the chilies and seeds. Fry until the seeds burst then add the onion and fry, stirring, until transparent.

3. Add the carrot, stir well and add the peas. Cover the pan, and cook very gently for 5 minutes.

4. Remove the lid from the pan, stir in the diced potatoes and fry gently for a further 3-5 minutes.

5. Sprinkle with a little salt and the sugar and mix well.

6. Transfer to a warmed serving dish and serve garnished with a few sprigs of coriander or parsley.

Alu badam

Potatoes with Almonds

◢	00.10 Serves 4	00.25

American	Ingredients	Metric/Imperial
1¼ lb	small, washed, scraped new potatoes	575 g/1¼ lb
	oil for frying	
½ cup	flaked almonds	75 g/3 oz
1 tsp	garam masala	1 tsp
	salt	

1. Dry the potatoes with kitchen paper. Heat the oil in a large frying pan and fry the potatoes for 10 minutes. Remove from the pan and leave to drain and cool.

2. Roast the almonds in a dry frying pan, shaking continuously until they gain color. Remove from the pan, spread them out and leave until completely cold.

3. Reheat the oil. When it is very hot fry the potatoes for 3-4 minutes, until golden brown. Drain on kitchen paper. Transfer to a serving dish and sprinkle with the almonds, garam masala and a little salt and serve.

Arbi piaz

Sweet Potato with Onions

00.10
Serves 4
00.50

American	Ingredients	Metric/Imperial
1½ lb	washed, sweet potatoes	700 g/1½ lb
3 tbsp	ghee	3 tbsp
1 tsp	mustard seeds	1 tsp
1 tsp	cumin seeds	1 tsp
3	large, coarsely chopped or sliced onions	3
½ tsp	ground chili	½ tsp
1 tsp	garam masala	1 tsp
1 tsp	amchur (powdered mango) (optional)	1 tsp

1. Put the unpeeled sweet potatoes into a pan of boiling water and cook for 15-20 minutes, until tender. Drain and leave to cool in a colander.
2. Heat the ghee and add the mustard and cumin seeds. As soon as they begin to burst, add the onions and fry, stirring until golden brown.
3. Stir in the chili and garam masala and simmer gently for a few minutes.
4. Meanwhile, peel and slice the sweet potatoes. Add to the onions, sprinkle with amchur and cook on maximum heat until the liquid has evaporated from the pan, and the slices of sweet potato are crisp on the outside. Serve on a warm dish.

Bathua ki dahl

Pulses with Spinach

00.15
plus soaking time
00.45

American	Ingredients	Metric/Imperial
1 cup	black beans (urad dahl)	225 g/8 oz
1¼ lb	spinach	575 g/1¼ lb
	salt	
2 tsp	ghee	2 tsp
1 tsp	cumin seeds	1 tsp
1	crushed garlic clove	1
2	skinned tomatoes cut into pieces	2

1. Pick over the beans, rinse thoroughly, then soak in cold water to cover for 1 hour.
2. Meanwhile, wash the spinach thoroughly and drain well. Remove any thick stalks and chop the spinach coarsely.
3. Drain the beans and put into a pan with the spinach and 1 cup (150 ml/¼ pint) water. Bring to the boil, cover, reduce the heat and cook gently for 30-35 minutes, stirring occasionally.
4. A few minutes before the end of the cooking time, remove the lid from the pan and allow as much of the liquid as possible to evaporate. Salt lightly.
5. Heat the ghee in a small pan. Add the cumin seeds and cook until the seeds begin to burst. Stir in the crushed garlic and pour over the beans and spinach. Mix well, transfer to a warmed serving dish and garnish with the tomato pieces.

Alu tariwale

Potatoes with Tomatoes

00.10
Serves 4
00.45

American	Ingredients	Metric/Imperial
1¼ lb	washed potatoes	575 g/1¼ lb
3 tbsp	ghee	3 tbsp
1 tsp	cumin seeds	1 tsp
1 tsp	mustard seeds	1 tsp
½ tsp	ground coriander seeds	½ tsp
½ tsp	ground turmeric	½ tsp
½ tsp	ground chili	½ tsp
5	large, ripe, skinned tomatoes cut into pieces	5
2	chopped small onions (optional)	2

1. Cook the unpeeled potatoes for 15-20 minutes in boiling water until tender.
2. Drain the potatoes, cool slightly, then peel and slice them.
3. Heat the ghee and add the cumin and mustard seeds. Cook until the seeds burst then add the coriander, turmeric and chili. Stir well then add the tomatoes and salt to taste.
4. Cook, stirring until the tomatoes are very soft. Stir vigorously and add 5 tbsp boiling water.
5. Add the potato and simmer gently until most of the liquid has evaporated.
6. Sprinkle with chopped onion and serve in a warmed dish.

Palak alu

Spinach and Potatoes

00.20
Serves 4
00.35

American	Ingredients	Metric/Imperial
1¾ lb	leaf spinach	800 g/1¾ lb
1 lb	scrubbed potatoes	450 g/1 lb
6 tbsp	groundnut or mustard oil	6 tbsp
2	dried, crumbled red chilies	2
1 tbsp	black mustard seeds	1 tbsp
1 tbsp	finely grated fresh root ginger	1 tbsp
	salt	
	freshly ground pepper	
4 tbsp	Greek-style yogurt	4 tbsp

1. Wash the spinach very thoroughly. Drain well and remove any thick stalks. Chop the spinach coarsely.
2. Boil the potatoes for 15 minutes. Drain and leave to cool. Remove the skins from the potatoes and cut them into ½ in (1 cm) cubes.
3. Heat 3 tbsp of oil in a pan, and add the chilies and the mustard seeds. Cook until the seeds burst.
4. Add the potatoes and fry, stirring and turning regularly until golden brown on all sides. Drain the potatoes on kitchen paper.
5. In another pan, heat 3 tbsp of oil. Fry the root ginger for 1 minute then add the spinach. Stir fry for 2 minutes. Sprinkle with a little salt, and a little coarsely ground black pepper.
6. Stir in the yogurt and add the fried diced potato. Mix well and heat the potatoes through. Serve immediately.

Lobhia
Black-eyed Beans in Spicy Sauce

	00.10	02.00
	plus soaking time	

American	Ingredients	Metric/Imperial
1 cup	black-eyed beans	225 g/8 oz
4	large, coarsely chopped onions	4
1½ tbsp	coarsely grated fresh root ginger	1½ tbsp
1	small, seeded, chopped green chili	1
2-3	finely chopped garlic cloves	3
2 tbsp	ghee or groundnut oil	2 tbsp
1 tsp	cumin seeds	1 tsp
½ tsp	ground chili	½ tsp
½ tsp	ground coriander seeds	½ tsp
½ tsp	ground turmeric	½ tsp
	salt	
5 tbsp	Greek-style yogurt	5 tbsp
2 tbsp	finely chopped coriander leaves	2 tbsp
2-3	red chilies	2-3

1. Pick over the beans, rinse thoroughly then leave to soak in water to cover for 3-4 hours.
2. In a food processor, make a fine paste of the onions, root ginger, garlic and green chili.
3. Heat the ghee or oil and add the cumin seeds and cook until the seeds begin to burst. Add the paste and fry for 5-7 minutes, stirring constantly.
4. Add the ground chili, coriander, turmeric and a little salt. Stir in the yogurt, 1 tbsp at a time.

5. Fry gently until the ghee or oil begins to separate out from the mixture.
6. Stir in the beans, and add 1 quart (1 litre/1¾ pints) water. Bring to the boil. Cover the pan, reduce the heat and cook gently for 1 hour.
7. Remove the lid and leave to cook gently for a further 25 minutes, to allow as much liquid as possible to evaporate.
8. Transfer to a warm serving dish and sprinkle with coriander.

Guda

	00.10	00.15
	Serves 4	

American	Ingredients	Metric/Imperial
2 tbsp	groundnut oil	2 tbsp
2	large, roughly chopped onions	2
4	skinned tomatoes cut into pieces	4
	salt	
2	trimmed, sliced, medium size zucchini (courgettes)	2
1½ tsp	garam masala	1½ tsp
1-2 tsp	finely chopped coriander or parsley	1-2 tsp

1. Heat the oil, and stir fry the onions until golden. Add the tomatoes and cook until very soft.
2. Add a little salt, then add the slices of zucchini (courgette). Turn several times and cook gently for 5-7 minutes until tender.
3. Stir in the garam masala, transfer to a serving dish and sprinkle with a little finely chopped coriander or parsley.

Guda

Barfi badam

Almond Cream Sweetmeat

	00.05 plus cooling time	01.00	

American	Ingredients	Metric/Imperial
1 cup	blanched almonds	150 g/5 oz
1 ¼ cups	milk	300 ml/½ pint
½ cup	sugar	125 g/4 oz
½ cup	ghee	125 g/4 oz
	almonds to decorate	

1. Pulverize the blanched almonds in a blender.
2. Boil the milk in a large saucepan until reduced and very thick. Stir constantly.
3. Add the sugar and boil for 10 minutes over low heat.
4. Stir in the pulverized almonds and the ghee. Continue to cook until the mixture sticks together and comes away from the sides of the pan.
5. Turn into a buttered loaf tin, smooth the top and cool slightly.
6. Before the barfi is firm, cut into fingers and top each piece with an almond. Leave to cool completely.

Kulfi

Almond ice

	00.05 plus cooling time and freezing	00.30	

American	Ingredients	Metric/Imperial
4 tbsp	rice flour	4 tbsp
3 ¼ cups	milk	750 ml/1 ¼ pints
½ cup	sugar	75 g/3 oz
½ cup	blanched almonds	125 g/4 oz
⅔ cup	heavy (double) cream	150 ml/¼ pint
2 tsp	rosewater	2 tsp

Almond Ice

1. Mix the rice flour with ⅔ cup (150 ml/¼ pint) milk.
2. Bring the remaining milk to the boil. Remove from the heat and add the rice flour mixture.
3. Return to the heat and simmer, stirring often, for 15 minutes. Leave to cool.
4. Add the sugar and stir until dissolved.
5. Put the almonds in a plastic bag and crush with a rolling pin.
6. Stir the cream, almonds and rosewater into the cooled milk mixture and pour into shallow freezer trays.
7. Freeze until just beginning to set, then turn out of the trays and beat until smooth. Repeat.
8. Freeze until firm then serve out in small squares or scoops.

Almond cream sweetheart

Barfi 11

Almond Cream with Semolina

	00.05	01.00
	plus cooling time	

American	Ingredients	Metric/Imperial
½ cup	ghee	125 g/4 oz
¾ cup	light (single) cream	200 ml/8 fl oz
4½ cups	milk	1 litre/1¾ pints
½ cup	sugar	125 g/4 oz
3 tbsp	semolina	3 tbsp
3 tbsp	ground almonds	3 tbsp
	few drops almond essence	
1½ tsp	ground cardamom seeds	1½ tsp

1. Melt ¼ cup (75 g/2 oz) ghee in a pan. Stir in the cream and bring slowly to the boil. Add the milk and bring back to the boil, stirring constantly.
2. Add the sugar and boil for 10 minutes over low heat, stirring.
3. Melt the remaining ghee and stir in to the milk mixture.
4. Stir in the semolina and ground almonds. Continue to cook until the mixture sticks together and comes away from the sides of the pan.
5. Stir in the almond essence and turn into a buttered loaf tin, smooth the top and cool slightly.
6. Before the barfi is firm, cut into fingers and sprinkle with the ground cardamom seeds. Leave to cool completely.

Firni

Rice Blancmange

	00.00	00.10
	plus cooling time	

American	Ingredients	Metric/Imperial
3 oz	rice flour	75 g/3 oz
1 quart	milk	1 litre/1¾ pints
⅓ cup	sugar	75 g/3 oz
1 tsp	rosewater	1 tsp
¼ cup	blanched almonds or pistachios	40 g/1½ oz
4	mint leaves	4
	few small red fruits	

1. Mix the rice flour to a smooth cream with a little cold milk.
2. Bring the remaining milk to the boil with the sugar, stirring until the sugar dissolves.
3. Remove from the heat and stir in the rice mixture.
4. Bring to the boil again and cook, stirring, for 3 minutes.
5. Stir in the rosewater and nuts. Pour into individual serving dishes and cool.
6. Serve warm or chilled, topped with sprigs of mint and red fruits.

Almond cream with semolina

Gulab jaman
Rosewater Sweetmeats

	00.15	00.15
	makes 16	

American	Ingredients	Metric/Imperial
6 tbsp	flour	6 tbsp
½ tsp	baking powder	½ tsp
1 cup	full cream milk powder	125 g/4 oz
	milk	
1½ oz	butter	30 g/1½ oz
5 tbsp	ghee	5 tbsp
1 cup	sugar	225 g/8 oz
1 tbsp	rosewater	1 tbsp

1. Sift the flour, baking powder and milk powder into a bowl. Rub in the butter, then add enough milk to give a firm elastic dough.
2. Cut the dough into 16 portions and shape each piece into a ball.
3. Heat the ghee in a large frying pan and gently fry the balls until brown on all sides. Drain on kitchen paper.
4. Meanwhile dissolve the sugar in 1 cup (250 ml/8 fl oz) water and boil for 3 minutes. Add the rosewater.
5. Put the fried sweetmeats into the syrup, allow to cool, then chill slightly. The balls will absorb the syrup and become soft and spongy.

Rasgullas
Cream Cheese Balls in Syrup

	00.20	01.00
	plus resting and cooling time	

American	Ingredients	Metric/Imperial
1 quart	milk	1 litre/1¾ pints
3 tbsp	lemon or lime juice	3 tbsp
½ cup	semolina	50 g/2 oz
1½ cups	sugar	350 g/12 oz
2 tbsp	rosewater	2 tbsp

1. Put the milk in a large pan and bring to the boil.
2. Remove from the heat, add the lemon or lime juice and stir once.
3. Leave to stand for 5 minutes, after which the milk should have curdled. If not, reheat and add a little more lemon or lime juice.
4. Pour into a colander lined with muslin, drain for 30 minutes then place a plate on top and press out as much liquid as possible.
5. Turn the curd out on to the work surface and knead in the semolina until the cheese is smooth and feels oily. Shape into 16 balls.
6. Dissolve the sugar in 3¼ cups (600 ml/1 pint) water, bring to the boil and simmer for 5 minutes.
7. Reserve half of the syrup and add the cheese balls and 1½ tbsp rosewater to the remainder.
8. Bring to the boil, cover and simmer for 40-50 minutes, adding a little extra syrup if necessary.
9. Cool slightly and add the remaining rosewater to the syrup. Serve warm or at room temperature, but do not chill.

MENU
Lamb cutlets 'Kashmiri'
Eggplant (aubergine) in
Yogurt sauce
Carrot halva

Lamb Cutlets 'Kashmiri'

	00.10	01.00
	Serves 4	

American	Ingredients	Metric/Imperial
1¼ cups	skimmed milk	300 ml/½ pint
1 tsp	salt	1 tsp
8	crushed cardamom pods	8
8	crushed black peppercorns	8
8	cloves	8
1 (2 in)	cinnamon stick	1 (5 cm/2 in)
8	lamb cutlets	
1 cup	chick-pea flour (besan)	125 g/4 oz
1 tsp	ground coriander	1 tsp
½ tsp	salt	½ tsp
	pinch ground chili	
1 tbsp	ghee	1 tbsp
	groundnut oil for frying	
	sprigs watercress (optional)	

1. Bring the milk and ¾ cup (200 ml/8 fl oz) water or lamb bouillon (stock) to the boil in a pan. Add the salt, cardamom pods, peppercorns, cloves and cinnamon. Boil for 5 minutes then add the cutlets.
2. Cover and simmer gently for 20 minutes. Remove the lid and continue cooking for about 10 minutes, until more than half of the liquid left in the pan has evaporated.
3. Remove the cutlets from the pan, and leave to cool slightly. Dry with kitchen paper.
4. Prepare the batter by sifting the chick-pea flour (besan) together with the coriander, salt and ground chili. Add the ghee and ⅔ cup (150 ml/¼ pint) strained cooking liquid. Continue stirring with a wooden spoon until the batter is smooth and quite thick.
5. Leave the batter to stand for 30 minutes then stir well.
6. Heat the oil until very hot.
7. Dip the cutlets in the batter, then quickly fry them 2-3 at a time in the hot oil, until crisp and golden brown. Drain on kitchen paper.
8. Arrange the lamb cutlets on a warmed dish and surround them with generous sprigs of watercress.

Eggplant (Aubergine) in Yogurt Sauce

⊿ 00.10 Serves 4   00.40 ⌣

American	Ingredients	Metric/Imperial
2	medium-size eggplants (aubergines)	2
3 tbsp	ghee or groundnut oil	3 tbsp
2	large chopped onions	2
2	finely chopped garlic cloves	2
1 tbsp	grated fresh root ginger	1 tbsp
1 tsp	ground coriander	1 tsp
½ tsp	ground turmeric	½ tsp
½ tsp	ground chili	½ tsp
1 tsp	salt	1 tsp
1 tsp	sugar	1 tsp
1 cup	Greek-style yogurt	250 ml/8 fl oz

1. Preheat the oven to 260°C/500°F/Gas Mark 9.
2. Put the eggplants (aubergines) on a baking tray and bake for about 12 minutes, until the outsides are completely black.
3. Leave to cool then remove the blackened skin and stalk. Cut the flesh into small pieces.
4. Heat the ghee or groundnut oil and fry the onions until they begin to change color. Add the garlic and root ginger. Stir well.
5. Add the coriander, turmeric, ground chili, salt, sugar and 4 tbsp water. Stir well and reduce the heat. Simmer gently for 3 minutes.
6. Mix in the finely chopped eggplant (aubergine). Cover the pan and braise gently for 5 minutes.
7. Remove the lid and mix in the yogurt, a little at a time. Serve as soon as the mixture is heated through.

Gajjar halva

Carrot Halva

⊿ 00.05 plus cooling time   01.00 ⌣

American	Ingredients	Metric/Imperial
¾ lb	young carrots	350 g/12 oz
4 tbsp	ghee	4 tbsp
4 tbsp	sugar	4 tbsp
1 tsp	ground cinnamon	1 tsp
3 tbsp	skimmed milk	3 tbsp
3 tbsp	whipped cream	3 tbsp
	butter	

1. Peel and finely grate the carrots.
2. Heat the ghee in a pan and add the carrots. Add 2 tbsp water and bring to the boil. Stir well. Cover the pan and simmer until the carrots are quite tender.
3. Add the sugar, cinnamon, skimmed milk and whipped cream. Continue stirring until the mixture has dried out a little and comes away from the base of the pan.
4. Transfer the mixture to a buttered square dish. Smooth the top with a wet palette or pancake knife and leave to cool.
5. Cover and chill for at least 3 hours.
6. Turn out on to a flat plate and cut into 12 equal sized pieces.

Cook's tip: variations include adding a little grated root ginger or a pinch of ground cardamom seeds after boiling the carrots

JAPAN

'Sushi' are small Japanese snacks which almost always consist of spiced rice with fish. These snacks are very popular. They are served as an hors d'oeuvre, but are also eaten between meals and may be served with other small courses as a complete lunch.

Dashi
Fish Bouillon (Stock)

00.05 plus standing time   **00.10**

American	Ingredients	Metric/Imperial
1 (½ in)	cube dried seaweed (kombu)	1 (1.25 cm/½ in)
3 tbsp	shredded dried bonito (katsuobushi)	3 tbsp

1. Bring 1½ quarts (1.5 litres/2¾ pints) water to the boil.
2. Rinse the kombu under cold running water and add to the boiling water. Cook, stirring continuously for 3 minutes.
3. Remove the kombu and add the shredded bonito. Bring back to the boil, stirring continuously. Remove the pan from the heat and leave to stand for 5 minutes (the bonito will sink to the bottom of the pan). Strain the bouillon (stock) through a piece of wet muslin.

Cook's tip: if the ingredients for dashi are unavailable chicken bouillon (stock), prepared in the Japanese manner can be used as an alternative, although this cannot always take the place of dashi. Where this is so, it is indicated in the recipe.

Fish bouillon (stock)

Keiniku no sueu
Chicken Bouillon (Stock)

00.05 plus standing time   **01.40**

American	Ingredients	Metric/Imperial
1¼ lb	chicken pieces	550 g/1¼ lb
¾ lb	chicken bones	350 g/12 oz
4	slices fresh root ginger	4
1	coarsely chopped leek	1

1. Bring the chicken pieces and bones to the boil in a pan with 1½ quarts (1.5 litres/2¾ pints) water. Carefully skim the surface several times.
2. Add the root ginger and leek. Reduce the heat, cover the pan and simmer gently for 1-1½ hours. Remove the pan from the heat and leave to stand for 15 minutes. Strain the bouillon (stock) through wet muslin. Leave to cool completely. Skim the fat from the bouillon (stock). The bouillon (stock) must be completely clear so if necessary strain a second time.

Sushi
Spiced Rice

00.05 plus standing time   **00.30**

American	Ingredients	Metric/Imperial
2 cups	short grain rice	450 g/1 lb
1 (2 in)	cube dried seaweed (kombu)	1 (5 cm/2 in)
4 tbsp	rice vinegar	4 tbsp
3 tbsp	superfine (caster) sugar	3 tbsp
2 tsp	salt	2 tsp
2 tbsp	mirin, sake or dry sherry	2 tbsp

1. Rinse the rice in several changes of water until the rinsing water runs clear. Leave to soak for 20 minutes in plenty of cold water. Drain in a colander and leave for 30 minutes.
2. Bring 2½ cups (600 ml/1 pint) water to the boil. Add the rice. Add the kombu and bring to the boil again. Cover the pan and simmer for 15-18 minutes.
3. Put the rice vinegar, sugar, salt and mirin, sake or dry sherry in a bowl and stir until the salt and sugar dissolve.
4. Remove the pan of rice from the heat. Leave to stand, covered for 10 minutes.
5. Remove the kombu from the pan and transfer the rice to a large bowl. Stir the rice lightly with a large fork.
6. Immediately pour on the dressing and stir. Leave the rice to cool until it can be moulded into balls.

Nigiri-sushi

Raw Fish with Rice

◥▷	00.10	00.00 ⌸
	plus sushi and chilling time	

American	Ingredients	Metric/Imperial
1 lb	very fresh salmon or tuna	450 g/1 lb
	spiced rice (see page 356)	
2 tbsp	sushi dressing (see page 356)	2 tbsp
2 tsp	wasabi powder	2 tsp
1	thin leek	1

Raw fish with rice

1. Cut the fish diagonally into 24 equal, thin rectangular slices and lay them on a large dish. Cover with aluminum foil and chill for 30 minutes.
2. Add 2 tbsp of water to the sushi dressing and add to the sushi to moisten it.
3. Allowing 2 full tbsp rice for each ball, shape 24 equal size balls from the rice mixture.
4. Put the slices of chilled fish on a board or worktop.
5. Mix the wasabi powder with 1 tbsp ice cold water, stirring until it thickens, then spread a little on the upper side of each slice of fish.
6. Put one rice ball in the middle of each slice and wrap the fish round it.
7. Arrange the Nigiri-sushi closely together on a large dish and garnish with ribbons made from strips of leek.

Cook's tip: if preferred Japanese pickles, strips of roasted seaweed, celery or parsley may be used to garnish.

Inari-sushi (I)
Aburage with Rice (I)

◀▽ **00.05** *plus sushi*   **00.05** 🍲

American	Ingredients	Metric/Imperial
12	sheets fried soybean curd (aburage)	12
3 tbsp	mirin, sake or dry sherry	3 tbsp
3 tbsp	Japanese soy sauce	3 tbsp
3 tbsp	dashi	3 tbsp
2-3 tbsp	light sesame seeds	2-3 tbsp
	spiced rice (see sushi page 356)	
	coriander or parsley leaves	

1. Bring plenty of water to the boil in a large pan. Add the aburage for exactly 30 seconds. Remove the sheets with a skimmer and lay them out on a board or worktop. Leave to cool. Cut each sheet into two rectangular pieces.
2. Mix the mirin, sake or dry sherry with the soy sauce and dashi. Sprinkle the aburage with a little of this mixture.
3. Heat a dry frying pan and dry roast the sesame seeds until they begin to jump. Stir into the spiced rice.
4. Put 2 tbsp rice on to each piece aburage and roll up.

5. Arrange the rolls closely together on a large dish and garnish with a coriander or parsley leaf on each.
Cook's tip: if preferred fold finely crumbled scrambled egg into the rice instead of sesame seeds. Alternatively coriander leaves or celery, raw fish, mushrooms or peeled shrimps (prawns), all finely chopped, can be added.

Inari-sushi (II)
Aburage with Rice (II)

◀▽ **00.05** *plus sushi and chilling time*   **00.05** 🍲

American	Ingredients	Metric/Imperial
2 oz	crabmeat or lobster, thawed if frozen	50g/2 oz
	few drops lemon or lime juice	
12	sheets fried soybean curd (aburage)	12
3 tbsp	mirin, sake or dry sherry	3 tbsp
3 tbsp	Japanese soy sauce	3 tbsp
3 tbsp	dashi	3 tbsp
	spiced rice (see sushi page 356)	

Aburage with rice (II)

1. Pick over the crabmeat or lobster and cut into small pieces. Sprinkle with lemon or lime juice, cover and chill for 30 minutes.
2. Bring plenty of water to the boil and add the aburage for exactly 30 seconds. Remove with a skimmer and lay the sheets out on a board or worktop to cool. Cut each sheet into 2 rectangular pieces.
3. Mix together the mirin, sake or dry sherry, soy sauce and dashi. Sprinkle a little of the mixture over the aburage.
4. Fold the crabmeat or lobster into the spiced rice. Spoon onto the aburage and roll up.
5. Arrange closely together on a large dish and serve.

Inari-sushi (III)

Aburage with Rice (III)

00.10   00.05
plus sushi and chilling time

American	Ingredients	Metric/Imperial
2 oz	cooked chicken	50 g/2 oz
1 tbsp	tomato purée	1 tbsp
½ tsp	ground root ginger	½ tsp
	spiced rice (see sushi page 356)	
12	sheets fried soybean curd (aburage)	12
3 tbsp	mirin, sake or dry sherry	3 tbsp
3 tbsp	Japanese soy sauce	3 tbsp
3 tbsp	dashi	3 tbsp
½ lb	fresh peeled shrimp (prawns)	225 g/8 oz

1. Chop, mince or grind the chicken very finely.
2. Add the tomato purée and ground ginger and rub the mixture through a very fine strainer (sieve).
3. Add the mixture to the rice, cover and chill for 30 minutes. Stir the rice very thoroughly so that all the grains are evenly colored. Cover again and chill for another 30 minutes.
4. Bring plenty of water to the boil in a large pan. Add the aburage for exactly 30 seconds. Remove with a skimmer and lay out on a board or worktop to cool. Cut each sheet into two rectangular pieces.
5. Stir together the mirin, sake or dry sherry, soy sauce and dashi. Sprinkle the aburage with a little of the mixture.
6. Spoon 2 tbsp rice on to each piece of aburage and roll them up. Cut each roll into 2-3 pieces and arrange them on a dish with the fillings turned upward. Top each with a freshly peeled shrimp (prawn).

Inari-suchi (IV)

Aburage with Rice (IV)

00.05   00.05
plus sushi and standing time

American	Ingredients	Metric/Imperial
3 tbsp	chicken bouillon (stock) (see page 356)	3 tbsp
2 oz	finely chopped, wiped mushrooms	50 g/2 oz
3 tbsp	mirin, sake or dry sherry	3 tbsp
3 tbsp	Japanese soy sauce	3 tbsp
	spiced rice (see sushi page 356)	
12	sheets fried soybean curd (aburage)	12
	slices mushroom	

1. Bring the chicken bouillon (stock) to the boil.
2. Add the mushrooms and simmer for 2 minutes, stirring constantly.
3. Remove the pan from the heat and add the mirin, sake or dry sherry and the soy sauce. Stir well and leave to cool.
4. Stir into the rice and leave to stand for 30 minutes.
5. Bring plenty of water to the boil in a large pan. Add the aburage for exactly 30 seconds. Remove with a skimmer and lay out on a board or worktop to cool. Cut each sheet into 2 rectangular pieces.
6. Spoon 2 tbsp rice mixture on to each piece aburage. Roll up, cut the rolls into 2-3 pieces and arrange on a serving plate with the filling upward. Garnish with mushroom slices.

Norimaki-sushi (I)

Spiced Rice in Seaweed (I)

00.20   00.30
plus sushi, soaking and standing time

American	Ingredients	Metric/Imperial
	spiced rice (see page 356)	
4	dried Japanese mushrooms	4
2 tbsp	Japanese soy sauce	2 tbsp
1 tbsp	sugar	1 tbsp
3	eggs	3
	salt	
2 tbsp	groundnut or sunflower oil	2 tbsp
1	small green cucumber	1
¼ lb	fresh mackerel fillet	125 g/4 oz
6	leaves dried seaweed (nori)	6
	few sprigs leaf celery	

1. Cook the spiced rice and leave to cool.
2. Rinse the mushrooms under cold running water and put in a bowl with hot water to cover. Leave to soak for 30 minutes. Strain the liquid through a piece of wet muslin and set aside. Discard the mushroom stalks from the mushrooms and cut the caps into very thin strips.
3. In a small pan bring ⅔ cup (150 ml/¼ pint) of the mushroom soaking liquid to the boil, with the soy sauce and sugar. Add the mushroom strips and simmer for 10 minutes. Leave to cool.
4. Beat the eggs lightly with 2 tbsp water and a little salt.
5. Heat the oil in a rectangular Japanese omelette pan and fry two very thin omelettes. Leave to cool then roll up quite tightly and cut into very thin strips.
6. Rinse and trim the cucumber. Cut in half lengthwise, seed and cut the flesh into very thin strips.
7. Rinse the fish under cold running water and dry with kitchen paper. Cut the fish into slices and then into very thin strips.
8. Broil (grill) the nori leaves under a fairly hot broiler (grill) until crisp. Place a nori leaf on to a bamboo mat or linen napkin.
9. Spoon 4-5 tbsp spiced rice on to each leaf. Make a channel in the rice and place some strips of mushroom, cucumber, fish and omelette in it. Carefully press the rice on to the filling then roll the mat or napkin tightly. Press firmly and leave to stand for 10 minutes. Remove the mat or napkin and cut each roll into 5-6 even size pieces. Arrange on a dish and garnish with celery leaves.

Norimaki-sushi (II)

Spiced Rice in Seaweed (II)

00.20 plus sushi and standing time   **00.30**

American	Ingredients	Metric/Imperial
¼ lb	fresh peeled shrimp (prawns)	125 g/4 oz
2 tbsp	tomato ketchup	2 tbsp
	salt	
	spiced rice (see page 356)	
2 tbsp	Japanese light soy sauce	2 tbsp
1 tbsp	sugar	1 tbsp
3	eggs	3
2 tbsp	groundnut or sunflower oil	2 tbsp
6	leaves dried seaweed (nori)	6
	strips cucumber	
	few sprigs leaf celery	

1. Chop the shrimp (prawns) very finely.
2. Mix with the tomato ketchup and add a pinch of salt. Rub the mixture through a very fine strainer (sieve).
3. Cook the spiced rice and leave to cool.
4. Put the soy sauce in a bowl and stir in the sugar. Moisten the sushi with the mixture.
5. Lightly beat the eggs with 2 tbsp water.
6. Heat the oil in a rectangular Japanese omelette pan and fry two very thin omelettes. Roll up quite tightly and cut into thin strips.
7. Toast the nori leaves until crisp and place on a bamboo mat or linen napkin.
8. Spoon 4-5 tbsp rice on to each leaf. Make a channel in the rice and fill with shrimp (prawn) paste, strips of cucumber and omelette. Carefully press the rice on to the filling then roll the mat or napkin tightly. Press firmly and leave to stand for 10 minutes. Remove the mat or napkin and cut each roll into 5-6 even size pieces. Arrange the rolls on a serving dish and garnish with celery leaves.
Cook's tip: if preferred garnish each roll with a shrimp (prawn) or piece of tomato.

Norimaki-sushi (III)

Spiced Rice in Seaweed (III)

00.20 plus sushi and standing time   **00.30**

American	Ingredients	Metric/Imperial
¼ lb	smoked eel	125 g/4 oz
1 tbsp	lemon or lime juice	1 tbsp
3 tbsp	Japanese light soy sauce	3 tbsp
	spiced rice (see page 356)	
1 tbsp	sugar	1 tbsp
3	eggs	3
	salt	
2 tbsp	groundnut or sunflower oil	2 tbsp
6	leaves dried seaweed (nori)	6
1	small green cucumber cut into strips	1
1	chopped scallion (spring onion)	1

1. Chop the smoked eel very finely.
2. Add the lemon or lime juice and 1 tbsp of soy sauce and mix well. Rub the mixture through a very fine strainer (sieve), cover and chill for 30 minutes. Spoon the chilled mixture on to a piece of muslin and express as much moisture as possible.
3. Cook the spiced rice and leave to cool.
4. Stir 2 tbsp soy sauce and the sugar together. Moisten the spiced rice with the mixture.
5. Lightly beat the eggs with 2 tbsp water and a little salt.
6. Heat the oil in a rectangular Japanese omelette pan and fry two very thin omelettes. Leave to cool then roll tightly and cut into thin strips.
7. Toast the nori leaves until crisp and place on a bamboo mat or linen napkin.
8. Spoon 4-5 tbsp rice on to each leaf. Make a channel in the rice and fill with the eel mixture, strips of cucumber and omelette. Carefully press the rice on to the filling then roll the mat or napkin tightly. Press firmly and leave to stand for 10 minutes. Remove the mat or napkin and cut the rolls into 5-6 even size pieces. Arrange the rolls on a dish and garnish with chopped scallion (spring onion).
Cook's tip: there are numerous other ingredients which may be used for the preparation of Norimaki-sushi. for example: scrambled egg with mushrooms, ham, lightly fried onion, herbs, raw fish, cooked fish, raw vegetables (carrots, turnips, radish, black radish, potatoes.) All ingredients should be finely chopped.

Spiced rice in seaweed

Spiced rice with fish, crab and vegetables in omelett

Fukusa-sushi

Spiced Rice with Fish, Crab and Vegetables in Omelette

	00.20	00.30
	plus sushi and standing time	

American	Ingredients	Metric/Imperial
	spiced rice (see page 356)	
4	Japanese dried mushrooms	4
2 tbsp	Japanese soy sauce	2 tbsp
1 tbsp	sugar	1 tbsp
¼ lb	cooked crabmeat, thawed if frozen	125 g/4 oz
¼ lb	fresh filleted salmon or mackerel cut into very thin strips	125 g/4 oz
4	canned, drained bamboo shoots cut into very small pieces	4
4 tbsp	cooked peas	4 tbsp
6	eggs	6
	salt	
½ tbsp	groundnut oil	½ tbsp

1. Cook the spiced rice and leave to cool.
2. Rinse the mushrooms under cold running water. Put them in a bowl with boiling water to cover and leave to soak for 30 minutes. Strain the liquid through a piece of wet muslin and set aside. Discard the mushroom stalks and cut the caps into very thin strips.
3. In a small pan bring ⅔ cup (150 ml/¼ pint) of the mushroom soaking liquid to the boil with the soy sauce and sugar. Add the mushroom strips and simmer for 10 minutes. Leave to cool.
4. Pick over the crabmeat and cut into small pieces.
5. Drain the mushroom strips well, when cooled.
6. Mix the spiced rice with the mushroom strips, crabmeat, fish, bamboo shoots and peas.
7. Place all the ingredients in a rectangular container. Cover with a board which exactly fits the contents of the container and place a weight on top of that, to press the rice and the other ingredients together as tightly as possible.
8. Beat the eggs, 3 tbsp of water and a pinch of salt lightly together in a bowl.
9. Heat the oil in a rectangular Japanese omelette pan and fry 8 very thin omelettes. Leave the omelettes to go cold and put them on bamboo mats or linen napkins.
10. Divide the rice equally between the omelettes. Roll up the omelettes and then the bamboo mat or linen napkin very tightly. Press firmly and leave to stand for 10 minutes. Remove the mat or napkin and cut each roll into 4-5 equal size pieces. Arrange the rolls on a dish and garnish with strips of nori if liked.

Cook's tip: as every Japanese is free to create sushi according to his own taste, a selection of variations follow. Each is based on a particular kind of fish, most of which are sold in the West.

Fish for Sushi

Maguro – tuna with spiced rice. The tuna is nearly always cut into thin slices, in which the rice is rolled. The rolls are cut into 1 inch pieces after being tightly compressed.

Hiro maguro – fine tuna variety – with very lightly spiced rice. The tuna, which is cut into thin slices, has a very fine flavor, which is why the rice used with it is only very lightly spiced or not spiced at all. Many Japanese steam the rice over a very lightly spiced fish bouillon (stock).

Hamachi – a young variety of mackerel. The flesh of this fish is golden in color. The fish is cut into very thin slices and rolled up with lightly spiced rice. Sometimes the fish used is not raw but very lightly smoked.

Katsuo bonito – occurs in three varieties and is a member of the tuna family. This fish is difficult to freeze. In Japan the arrival of the bonito in the coastal waters heralds the spring. It is cut into slices and rolled up with spiced rice. The rolls are cut into pieces. The garnishing usually consists of a spring flower or some spring greenery.

Kohada – herring family – usually lightly salted like a sardine and cut into pieces.

Saba – mackerel – is very popular in Japan. It should be used as fresh as possible. The mackerel is usually very lightly salted with the skin and served cut up into pieces.

Sake – salmon – is cut into thin slices and rolled up with lightly spiced rice. It is occasionally lightly smoked and salted and served in thick slices without rice. The combination of salmon with lightly spiced rice and orange is especially popular in Japan.

Tai – bream – is particularly tasty. It can be cut into very thin slices and served in the shape of a flower.

Hirame – halibut – is nearly always cut wafer thin and served in the shape of a flower.

Suzuki – a kind of sea bream – can be cut wafer thin and is then served in the shape of a large flower under the name of Suzuki usu zukiri. It is always served with a soy sauce which has been 'enriched' with lemon juice.

Unagi – fresh water eel – is always skinned and filleted. After being cut into pieces and fried in hot oil, the cold eel is served as sushi with lightly spiced rice.

A selection of sushi, including nigiri sushi, (far right) Aburage with chicken,

Anago – sea eel – is skinned and filleted and then boiled and mixed in small pieces with sushi rice, the rice is usually rolled in very thin slices of cucumber or worked into hollowed out cucumber.

Tako – octopus – is always boiled before being cut into thin slices. It is usually rolled up with lightly spiced rice. Ika – squid – is always boiled before being cut into slices. It is filled with well spiced rice, compressed into rolls and served cut into pieces.

Awabi – abalone – this shellfish is always poached first and then cut into thin slices filled with spiced rice, rolled up and cut into pieces.

Kani – crab or lobster – is always cooked. The legs can be cut into pieces and served as they are. The meat is usually cut into small pieces and worked into spiced rice.

Ebi – large shrimp (prawn) – are particularly popular in Japan. The boiled and then peeled tails are very decorative and are nearly always served with sushi.

Ama ebi – large shrimp (prawn) – are served raw. In Japan they are regarded as a particularly fine delicacy and they form an indispensible part of a sushi.

and raw fish and squid to decorate. Far right: Japanese omelette with sushi.

Ikura – salmon roe – is very often included in sushi in Japan. It is an ideal sushi garnish.

Tokiki – flying fish roe – deep orange coloured roe. The eggs are smaller than those of the salmon, also used as a garnish.

Kazunoko – roe of fish of the herring family – is very popular in Japan. It is lightly pressed and then marinaded in sake with soy sauce, which gives it a golden color. In Japan a jug or bowl of soy sauce is always served seperately with sushi. People also like to serve it with gari, thin slices of root ginger flavored with rice vinegar and wasabi sauce. Wasabi powder is a finely grated green horse radish. It is made with water and has a very sharp flavor. Wasabi powder is also made up with water into a thick paste, from which are made balls the size of maize grains to be served with the dishes or used as a garnish.

Gohan
Dry Boiled Rice

	00.05	00.28
	plus standing time	

American	Ingredients	Metric/Imperial
1 cup	short grain rice	225 g/8 oz

1. Rinse the rice in cold water until the water runs clean. Leave to soak for 5 minutes in cold water to cover. Drain in a colander for 30 minutes.

2. Put the rice in a saucepan with 1¼ cups (300 ml/½ pint) cold water. Bring slowly to the boil then boil rapidly for 1 minute.

3. Cover the pan, reduce the heat and simmer for 20-25 minutes until the rice is tender and almost dry. Do not remove the lid or stir the rice during this time.

4. Remove the pan from the heat and leave to stand, covered, for a further 10 minutes. Lightly stir the rice with a large fork and serve in warmed bowls.

Rice balls

Onigiri
Rice Balls

	00.10	00.05
	plus dry boiled rice	

American	Ingredients	Metric/Imperial
2 cups	dry boiled short grain rice	225 g/8 oz
4 tbsp	black sesame seeds (gomasio) or dried seaweed (nori)	4 tbsp
¼ lb	raw seafish fillets (salmon, tuna, mackerel) or smoked seafish fillets	125 g/4 oz

1. Prepare the rice as in the previous rice.

2. Toast the sesame seeds very lightly in a dry frying pan. Cool on a large plate then pound to a powder in a mortar. Broil (grill) the seaweed until black. Crumble, then pound to a powder in a mortar.

3. Rinse the fish and dry with kitchen paper. Cut into very thin strips. (Do not rinse smoked fish before cutting into strips).

4. Cool the boiled rice then shape into 1 in (5 cm) balls. (It is easier to shape the balls with wet hands).

5. Make a hollow in each ball with a finger and push a couple of strips of fish into the hole. Seal the hole and reshape the ball.

6. Roll the balls through the sesame seeds or seaweed powder. Serve either warm or cold.

Cook's tip: a domburi is an earthenware dish in which rice meals are served. Such dishes are often used in Japan and they come in many sizes.

Fried soybean curd (aburage) domburi

Kitsume domburi
Fried Soybean Curd (Aburage) Domburi

▬▭▷ 00.05 00.15 🥘
Serves 4

American	Ingredients	Metric/Imperial
1 cup	dry boiled short grain rice	225 g/8 oz
3	sheets dried and fried soybean curd (aburage)	3
1¼ cups	dashi or chicken bouillon (stock) (see page 356)	300 ml/½ pint
4 tbsp	Japanese light soy sauce	4 tbsp
2 tbsp	Japanese dark soy sauce	2 tbsp
4 tbsp	mirin, sake or dry sherry with 1 tsp sugar	4 tbsp
1 tsp	sugar	1 tsp
6	scallions (spring onions) cut into thin rings	6

1. Prepare the rice (see page 364).
2. Put the sheets of soybean curd (aburage) in a pan of boiling water for 30 seconds, remove and drain thoroughly. Cut into thin strips 3 in (7.5 cm) long.
3. Bring the chicken bouillon (stock) to the·boil.
4. Add the soy sauces, mirin, sake or sherry with sugar and sugar. Bring back to the boil, stirring constantly.
5. Add the strips of soybean curd (aburage), reduce the heat and simmer for 10 minutes.
6. Add the scallions (spring onions), stir then remove the pan from the heat.
7. Spoon the hot rice into a warmed domburi or small casserole. Pour the hot stock, strips of soybean curd (aburage) and scallions (spring onions) evenly over the rice and serve immediately.

Ojako domburi
Domburi for the Family

▬▭▷ 00.15 00.10 🥘
Serves 4

American	Ingredients	Metric/Imperial
1 cup	dry boiled short grain rice	225 g/8 oz
10 oz	chicken breast fillets	275 g/10 oz
1¾ cups	chicken bouillon (stock) (see page 356)	400 ml/14 fl oz
2 tbsp	mirin, sake or dry sherry with 1 tsp sugar	2 tbsp
2 tbsp	Japanese soy sauce	2 tbsp
4	eggs	4
	salt	
6	scallions (spring onions)	6

1. Prepare the rice (see page 364).
2. Dry the chicken with kitchen paper, cut into thin slices and then into very thin strips or small cubes.
3. Bring the chicken bouillon (stock) to the boil.
4. Add the mirin, sake or dry sherry with sugar, soy sauce and chicken. Bring back to the boil, cover and simmer for 4 minutes.
5. Lightly beat the eggs. Add salt to taste.
6. Cut the scallions (spring onions) into very thin strips.
7. Stir the eggs and half of the scallions (spring onions) through the hot chicken bouillon (stock). Remove from the heat and leave to stand for 5 minutes. Stir well.
8. Spoon the rice into a warmed domburi, or small casserole, and spread the egg mixture evenly over the top.
9. Sprinkle the remaining scallions (spring onions) on top. Serve immediately.

Jakitori domburi
Chicken Domburi

	00.15	00.20
	plus marinating	

American	Ingredients	Metric/Imperial
1 cup	dry boiled short grain rice	225 g/8 oz
1 (2 lb)	roasting chicken divided into pieces	1 (900 g/2 lb)
6 tbsp	mirin, sake or dry sherry with 1 tsp white sugar	6 tbsp
6 tbsp	Japanese soy sauce	6 tbsp
2	crushed garlic cloves	2
1-2 tsp	grated fresh root ginger	1-2 tsp
5-6 tbsp	groundnut or sunflower oil	5-6 tbsp
1 cup	chicken bouillon (stock)	250 ml/8 fl oz
1-2 tsp	sugar	1-2 tsp
2	scallions (spring onions), cut into thin strips	2

1. Prepare the rice (see page 364).
2. Remove the skin and bones from the chicken pieces.
3. Mix together the mirin, sake or sherry with sugar, soy sauce, garlic and ginger.
4. Pour the marinade over the chicken pieces and marinate for 1 hour. Turn the chicken pieces occasionally so that they are marinated on all sides.
5. Remove the chicken pieces and dry with kitchen paper. Strain the remaining marinade.
6. Heat the oil in a wok and fry the chicken pieces, a few at a time until golden brown on all sides. Remove the pieces and cut into slices.
7. Bring the chicken bouillon (stock) to the boil.
8. Spoon the hot rice into a warmed domburi or small casserole. Arrange the chicken slices on top.
9. Stir the remaining marinade into the boiling stock.
10. Add the sugar and pour over the chicken and rice.
11. Sprinkle the strips of scallions (spring onions) on top and serve immediately.

Zarusoba
Cold Buckwheat Noodles

	00.05	00.10
	Serves 4	

American	Ingredients	Metric/Imperial
½ lb	buckwheat noodles (soba)	225 g/8 oz
1	leaf dried seaweed (nori)	1
1 tbsp	grated fresh root ginger	1 tbsp
2 tbsp	chopped scallions (spring onions)	2 tbsp
2 tbsp	Japanese dark soy sauce	2 tbsp
2 tbsp	mirin, sake or dry sherry with 1 tsp sugar	2 tbsp
	pinch salt	

1. Bring a large pan of water to the boil.
2. Add the buckwheat noodles (soba), followed by a dash of cold water. Bring back to the boil and cook for 3-4 minutes. Drain and rinse under cold running water. Drain well.
3. Toast the dried seaweed (nori) briefly under a hot broiler (grill).

4. Spoon the drained buckwheat noodles (soba) on to a dish and crumble the nori on top.
5. Mix the ginger and scallions (spring onions) in a small bowl. Spoon a little on to each plate.
6. Mix together the soy sauce, mirin, sake or dry sherry with sugar and salt to taste. Bring to the boil and pour into bowls.
Cook's tip: cook the buckwheat noodles (soba) according to the instructions on the packet. Different brands may have different instructions to those given in the recipe.

Tori gohan
Chicken and Mushrooms on Rice

	00.15	00.15
	Serves 4	

American	Ingredients	Metric/Imperial
1 cup	dry cooked short grain rice	225 g/8 oz
1 lb	chicken breast fillets	450 g/1 lb
	salt	
	freshly ground pepper	
3 tbsp	sifted flour	3 tbsp
4 tbsp	dry white breadcrumbs	4 tbsp
	oil for deep frying	
¾ lb	mushrooms	350 g/12 oz
3 tbsp	corn or sunflower oil	3 tbsp
1 tbsp	chopped onion	1 tbsp
4	scallions (spring onions) or shallots, cut into thin rings	4
1 tbsp	grated fresh root ginger	1 tbsp
¾ cup	chicken bouillon (stock) (see page 356)	200 ml/7 fl oz
3 tbsp	Japanese light soy sauce	3 tbsp
¼ lb	cooked peas	125 g/4 oz
2	lightly beaten eggs with a pinch salt	2

1. Prepare the rice (see page 364) and keep warm.
2. Cut each chicken breast, diagonally into two thin slices. Dry with kitchen paper and rub with a little salt and pepper.
3. Toss in a little flour, shake off the excess.
4. Draw the slices of chicken through the 1 lightly beaten egg and roll in the breadcrumbs. Press on the breadcrumbs and chill for a few minutes.
5. Heat the oil in a deep frying pan and fry the chicken until golden brown. Keep warm.
6. Wipe the mushrooms with a damp cloth or kitchen paper, trim and cut into very thin slices.
7. Heat the oil, add the mushrooms and stir fry for 2-3 minutes.
8. Sprinkle on the chopped onion and stir well.
9. Add the scallions (spring onions) or shallots and root ginger. Fry for 1 minute.
10. Add the chicken bouillon (stock) and soy sauce. Stir well, bring to the boil and add the peas.
11. Fry a thin omelette in a rectangular Japanese omelette pan or round frying pan. Roll up the omelette and cut into very thin strips.
12. Divide the rice between 4 warmed bowls.
13. Cut the chicken into thin strips and arrange on one side of the rice. Spoon the peas and mushrooms on the other half. Arrange the strips of omelette over the peas and mushrooms.

Chestnut Rice

00.10
plus standing time

00.35

American	Ingredients	Metric/Imperial
3½ oz	chestnuts (preferably Japanese)	100 g/3½ oz
1 cup	short grain rice	225 g/8 oz
2 tbsp	Japanese light soy sauce	2 tbsp
2 tbsp	mirin or medium dry sherry with 2 tsp sugar	2 tbsp
	salt	

1. Place the chestnuts in a strainer or colander and rinse under cold running water. Drain and chop into small pieces.
2. Rinse the rice in cold water until the water runs clear. Leave to soak for 5 minutes in cold water to cover. Drain in a colander for 30 minutes.
3. Put the rice and the chestnut pieces in a saucepan with 1¼ cups (300 ml/½ pint) cold water. Bring slowly to the boil then boil rapidly for 1 minute.
4. Cover the pan, reduce the heat and simmer for 20-25 minutes until the rice is tender and almost dry. Do not remove the lid or stir the rice during this time.
5. Remove the pan from the heat and leave to stand, covered, for a further 10 minutes. Lightly stir in a mixture of the soy sauce, mirin or sherry with sugar and a little salt, with a large meat fork.
6. Serve the rice in individual warmed bowls as an accompaniment to pork dishes.

Rice with Green Herbs

00.10
plus standing time

00.35

American	Ingredients	Metric/Imperial
1 cup	short grain rice	225 g/8 oz
½ lb	spinach leaves	225 g/8 oz
2 tbsp	ghee	2 tbsp
2 tbsp	finely chopped parsley or fresh coriander	2 tbsp
1 tbsp	finely chopped chives	1 tbsp
1 tsp	finely chopped celery	1 tsp

1. Rinse the rice in cold water until the water runs clear. Leave to soak for 5 minutes in cold water to cover. Drain in a colander for 30 minutes.
2. Line a saucepan with the spinach leaves to color the rice.
3. Put the rice in the pan with 1¼ cups (300 ml/½ pint) cold water. Bring slowly to the boil then boil rapidly for 1 minute.
4. Cover the pan, reduce the heat and simmer for 20-25 minutes until the rice is tender and almost dry. Do not remove the lid or stir the rice during this time.
5. Remove the pan from the heat and leave to stand, covered, for a further 10 minutes. Lightly stir in the ghee, parsley or coriander, chopped chives and celery with a large fork and serve in warmed bowls.
Cook's tip: rice with green herbs is delicious as an accompaniment to Broiled (Grilled) Salmon with Teriyaki Sauce.

Chicken and mushrooms on rice

Tonkatsu gohan
Rice and Pork

⏲ 00.15   Serves 4   00.15 🍲

American	Ingredients	Metric/Imperial
1 cup	short grain rice	225 g/8 oz
¾ lb	loin of pork, cut into 4 slices	350 g/12 oz
	salt	
	fresh ground pepper	
3 tbsp	sifted flour	3 tbsp
1	lightly beaten egg	1
4 tbsp	dry white breadcrumbs	4 tbsp
	oil for deep frying	
2	small onions	2
2-3 tbsp	groundnut or sunflower oil	2-3 tbsp
¾ cup	dashi (see page 356)	200 ml/7 fl oz
2 tbsp	mirin, sake or dry sherry with 1 tsp sugar	2 tbsp
2 tbsp	Japanese dark soy sauce	2 tbsp
1 tbsp	Japanese light soy sauce	1 tbsp
4	scallions (spring onions) cut into thin rings	4
6	lightly beaten eggs	6

1. Prepare the rice (see page 364) and keep it warm.
2. Dry the meat with kitchen paper and rub it with a little salt and pepper.
3. Toss the meat in a little flour, shake off the excess.
4. Draw the slices of pork through the egg and roll in the breadcrumbs. Press the breadcrumbs on to the meat. Chill until required.
5. Heat the oil in a deep frying pan. Add the pork and fry for 7-8 minutes. Remove from the pan and drain on kitchen paper. Keep warm.
6. Peel the onions and cut each into 8 segments. Loosen the layers.
7. Heat the oil and stir fry the onions until beginning to change color.
8. Add the dashi, mirin, sake or dry sherry with sugar, soy sauces and scallions (spring onions). Bring to the boil and stir well.
9. Add the lightly beaten eggs. Stir well and remove the pan from the heat.
10. Cut the pork into thin strips.
11. Spoon the hot rice into individual bowls. On one half arrange the strips of fried pork and spoon the onion and egg mixture on to the other half. Serve immediately.

Left to right: Chicken and egg domburi,
Rice and pork, Chicken , shrimp (prawn) and egg domburi

Oboro domburi
Chicken and Egg Domburi

⏲ 00.05   Serves 4   00.13 🍲

American	Ingredients	Metric/Imperial
1 cup	dry boiled short grain rice	225 g/8 oz
10 oz	chicken breast fillets	275 g/10 oz
1¼ cups	dashi or chicken bouillon (stock) (see page 356)	300 ml/½ pint
4 tbsp	Japanese dark soy sauce	4 tbsp
2 tbsp	Japanese light soy sauce	2 tbsp
4 tbsp	mirin, sake or dry sherry with 1 tsp sugar	4 tbsp
2 tsp	sugar	2 tsp
6	Japanese onions or scallions (spring onions), cut into thin rings	6
4	eggs	4

1. Prepare the rice (see page 364).
2. Cut the chicken breasts into thin strips or cubes.
3. Bring the chicken bouillon (stock) to the boil.
4. Add the soy sauces, mirin, sake or sherry with sugar and sugar. Bring back to the boil, stirring constantly.
5. Add the chicken, reduce the heat and simmer for 5 minutes.
6. Stir in the Japanese onions or scallions (spring onions) and leave to stand for 1 minute.
7. Lightly stir the eggs in a bowl, just enough to break them up. Add the eggs to the pan and leave to stand for a further 2 minutes. Carefully stir once.
8. Spoon the hot rice into individual bowls and divide the mixture from the pan between the bowls. Serve immediately.

Soboro domburi

Chicken, Shrimp (Prawn) and Egg Domburi

00.15 Serves 4   **00.20**

American	Ingredients	Metric/Imperial
1 cup	dry cooked short grain rice	225 g/8 oz
½ lb	chicken breast fillets	225 g/8 oz
1 tbsp	Japanese dark soy sauce	1 tbsp
3 tbsp	mirin, sake or dry sherry with 1 tsp sugar	3 tbsp
1 tsp	sugar	1 tsp
1 tsp	very finely grated fresh root ginger	1 tsp
3 tbsp	mirin, sake or dry sherry with 1 tsp sugar	3 tbsp
½ tsp	salt	½ tsp
½ lb	freshly peeled shrimp (prawns)	225 g/8 oz
4	eggs	4
½ tsp	salt	½ tsp
1 tbsp	Japanese light soy sauce	1 tbsp
1 tbsp	mirin, sake or dry sherry with 1 tsp sugar	1 tbsp
⅔ cup	dashi or chicken bouillon (stock) (see page 356)	200 ml/7 fl oz
4 tbsp	Japanese dark soy sauce	4 tbsp
1 tsp	sugar	1 tsp
2 tbsp	chopped scallions (spring onions) or shallot	2 tbsp

1. Prepare the rice (see page 364).
2. Prepare the chicken mixture. Cut the chicken breasts into very small cubes.
3. Bring 1 tbsp dark soy sauce, 3 tbsp mirin, sake or sherry with sugar to the boil in a small saucepan.
4. Add the root ginger and the diced chicken. Cook for 4 minutes over moderate heat, stirring constantly. Keep warm.
5. Prepare the shrimp (prawn) mixture. Bring 3 tbsp mirin, sake or dry sherry with sugar and 1 tsp sugar to the boil with the salt.
6. Add the shrimp (prawns). Stir carefully then pour into a strainer. Cover to keep shrimp (prawns) warm.
7. Prepare the egg mixture. Lightly beat the eggs.
8. Add salt, 2 tbsp water, 1 tbsp light soy sauce and the remaining mirin, sake or sherry with sugar. Scramble the eggs in a small saucepan.
9. Heat the dashi or chicken bouillon (stock) in a small saucepan.
10. Add the remaining soy sauce and sugar.
11. Spoon the rice into a warmed domburi or small casserole. Pour on the hot bouillon (stock), then spoon on the cubes of chicken, shrimp (prawns) and scrambled egg.
12. Immediately before serving sprinkle on the scallions (spring onions) or shallots.

Cook's tip: in Japan, soboro domburi is often served in the lacquered lunch boxes. A layer of rice is first spooned into the box and the chicken, shrimps (prawns) and egg arranged attractively on top.

Asuparagasugohan

Rice with Chicken and Asparagus

◣▷　00.10
plus standing time

00.30

American	Ingredients	Metric/Imperial
¾ lb	chicken breast fillets	350 g/12 oz
	salt	
12	green asparagus spears	12
1 quart	skimmed dashi or chicken bouillon (stock) (see page 356)	1 litre/1¾ pints
2 tbsp	Japanese light soy sauce	2 tbsp
1 tbsp	Japanese dark soy sauce	1 tbsp
2 tbsp	mirin, sake or dry sherry with ½ tbsp sugar	2 tbsp
1 tbsp	finely grated fresh root ginger	1 tbsp
1¼ cups	short grain rice, rinsed and dried	250-275 g/9-10 oz
2	finely chopped Japanese stem onions or scallions (spring onions) or 2 tbsp finely chopped chives	2

1. Dry the chicken with kitchen paper and cut into ¾ in (1.75 cm) cubes. Sprinkle with a little salt and leave to stand for 15 minutes.
2. Trim and thinly peel the asparagus. Cut into 1 in (2.5 cm) lengths, cutting any thick pieces down the middle.
3. In a pan bring the dashi or chicken bouillon (stock) to the boil.
4. Add the soy sauces, mirin, sake or sherry with sugar, root ginger and salt to taste. Stir well and bring back to the boil.
5. Slowly sprinkle in the rice so that the liquid continues to boil. Boil vigorously for 1-2 minutes. Reduce the heat, cover the pan and simmer for 10 minutes until almost all the liquid has been absorbed.
6. Arrange the pieces of chicken and asparagus on the rice. Replace the lid and simmer for a further 10-12 minutes. Remove from the heat and leave, covered, for 5 minutes. Stir with a large fork. Serve in warmed bowls, sprinkled with finely chopped Japanese stem onion, scallions (spring onions) or finely chopped chives.

Cook's tip: replace the chicken and asparagus with one of the following combinations, cutting the ingredients into pieces of equal size.
¾ lb (350 g/12 oz) lean pork and 4 sliced celery sticks.
¾ lb (350 g/12 oz) lean pork and 6 oz (175 g/6 oz) broccoli (the florets divided into pieces, the stalks sliced).

¾ lb (350 g/12 oz) veal and ½ lb (225 g/8 oz) fresh mushrooms.
¾ lb (350 g/12 oz) veal and ¼ lb (125 g/4 oz) fresh young maize grains or peas.
¾ lb (350 g/12 oz) lamb and ½ lb (225⅝ oz) green beans, cut into 1½ in (4 cm) lengths.
¾ lb (350 g/12 oz) lean duck meat (breast fillets) and 12 scallions (spring onions), cut into 1½ in (4 cm) lengths.
¾ lb (350 g/12 oz) boiled ham (thick slices, diced) and ¼ lb (125 g/4 oz) peas.

Shiitakegohan

Rice with Shiitake (Japanese Mushrooms) and Chicken

◣▷　00.10
plus soaking time

00.40

American	Ingredients	Metric/Imperial
6	large fresh or dried Japanese mushrooms (shiitake)	6
½ lb	chicken breast fillets	225 g/8 oz
	salt	
¼ lb	raw or boiled ham, in a thick slice	125 g/4 oz
1 quart	skimmed dashi or chicken bouillon (stock) (see page 356)	1 litre/1¾ pints
3 tbsp	Japanese light soy sauce	3 tbsp
2 tbsp	Japanese dark soy sauce	2 tbsp
2 tbsp	mirin, sake or dry sherry with ½ tbsp sugar	2 tbsp
1¼ cups	short grain rice, rinsed and dried	275 g/10 oz
1	Japanese stem onion or scallion (spring onion)	1

1. Rinse fresh mushrooms for a few seconds in cold running water or wipe with a damp cloth. Soak dried Japanese mushroom (shiitake) in warm water for 30 minutes then remove and discard the stems. Broil (grill) the caps over a barbecue or under a hot broiler (grill), turning regularly, for up to 5 minutes. Cut into strips.

2. Dry the chicken with kitchen paper, cut into pieces and sprinkle lightly with salt.

3. Cut the ham into pieces.

4. In a pan bring the dashi or chicken bouillon (stock) to the boil. Add the soy sauces, mirin, sake or sherry with sugar, and salt to taste.

5. Add the mushrooms, stir well and bring back to the boil.

6. Slowly sprinkle in the rice so that the liquid continues to boil. Stir well and boil vigorously for 1-2 minutes. Cover the pan, reduce the heat and simmer for 10 minutes, until almost all the liquid is absorbed.

7. Add the chicken and ham, replace the lid and simmer for a further 12-15 minutes. Remove from the heat and leave, covered, for a further 5 minutes. Stir with a large fork and serve in warmed bowls, sprinkled with finely chopped Japanese onion or scallion (spring onion).

Takenokagohan

Rice with Bamboo Shoots and Chicken

	00.15 Serves 4	00.40

American	Ingredients	Metric/Imperial
10 oz	chicken breast fillets	275 g/10 oz
	salt	
9 oz	canned bamboo shoots	250 g/9 oz
3½ cups	skimmed chicken bouillon (stock) (see page 356)	900 ml/1 ½ pints
3 tbsp	Japanese light soy sauce	3 tbsp
2 tbsp	mirin, sake or dry sherry with ½ tbsp sugar	2 tbsp
1¼ cups	short grain rice, rinsed and dried	275 g/10 oz
1	sheet toasted, crumbled dried seaweed (nori)	1

1. Dry the chicken with kitchen paper and cut into ¾ in (1.75 cm) cubes. Sprinkle with a little salt.

2. Drain the bamboo shoots; cut lengthwise into ¾ in (1.75 cm) strips, then dice.

3. In a pan bring the bouillon (stock) to the boil. Add the soy sauce, mirin, sake or sherry with sugar and salt to taste.

4. Add the bamboo shoots. Stir well and bring back to the boil.

5. Slowly sprinkle the rice in so that the liquid continues to boil. Cook vigorously for 1 minute then cover the pan and reduce the heat. Simmer for 10 minutes.

6. Add the chicken and simmer for a further 12-15 minutes, until almost all the liquid has been absorbed. Remove from the heat and leave to stand, covered, for a further 5 minutes. Stir with a large fork, spoon into warmed bowls and serve, garnished with the crumbled seaweed (nori).

Cook's tip: with the composite rice dishes serve a sauce made by mixing 6 tbsp dashi or chicken bouillon (stock) with 3 tbsp Japanese dark soy sauce, 2 tbsp Japanese light soy sauce and 2 tbsp mirin, sake or sherry, ½ tbsp sugar and ½ tsp red chili oil. Serve the sauce in small individual bowls.

Left to right: Rice with chicken and asparagus, Rice with shiitake (Japanese mushrooms) and chicken, Rice with bamboo shoots and chicken

Ingengohan
Rice with Chicken and Beans

00.15 Serves 4 **00.40**

American	Ingredients	Metric/Imperial
½ lb	young green beans or French beans	225 g/8 oz
½ lb	chicken breast fillets	225 g/8 oz
	salt	
3½ cups	skimmed chicken bouillon (stock) (see page 356)	900 ml/1 ½ pints
4 tbsp	Japanese light soy sauce	4 tbsp
2-3 tbsp	Japanese dark soy sauce	2-3 tbsp
2 ½ tbsp	mirin, sake or dry sherry with ½ tbsp sugar	2 ½ tbsp
1 ¼ cups	short grain rice, rinsed and dried	275 g/10 oz
3	finely chopped Japanese stem onions or scallions (spring onions)	3

1. Wash and trim the green beans or French beans, stringing if necessary. Cut into 1½ in (4 cm) lengths.
2. Dry the chicken with kitchen paper and cut into ½ in x 1½ in (1.25 cm×4 cm) strips. Sprinkle with a little salt.
3. In a pan bring the chicken bouillon (stock) to the boil. Add the soy sauces, mirin, sake or sherry with sugar and salt to taste.
4. Slowly sprinkle in the rice so that the liquid continues to simmer. Boil rapidly for 1 minute. Cover the pan, reduce the heat and simmer for 15 minutes until almost all the liquid is absorbed.
5. Add the green beans and chicken, bring back to the boil, cover the pan and cook for a further 15-17 minutes.
6. Sprinkle with the Japanese onion or scallions (spring onions). Replace the lid and after ½ minute remove from the heat and leave to stand for 5 minutes. Stir with a large fork and serve immediately in warmed bowls.

Torimeshi
Rice with Chicken and Mushrooms

00.15 Serves 4 **00.30**

American	Ingredients	Metric/Imperial
½ lb	chicken breast fillets	225 g/8 oz
	salt	
½ lb	small fresh mushrooms	225 g/8 oz
1	Japanese stem onion or medium size leek	1
3½ cups	skimmed chicken bouillon (stock) (see page 356)	900 ml/1 ½ pints
3 tbsp	Japanese light soy sauce	3 tbsp
2 tbsp	mirin, sake or dry sherry with ½ tbsp sugar	2 tbsp
10 oz	short grain rice, rinsed and dried	275 g/10 oz

1. Dry the chicken with kitchen paper, cut into ¾ in (1.75 cm) cubes and sprinkle with a little salt.
2. Wipe the mushrooms clean with a damp cloth or kitchen paper. Cut the stems into thin slices, then cut each cap into four pieces.
3. Clean the stem onion or leek. Using as much of the green part of the stem onion as possible, or as little of the green part of the leek as possible, cut lengthwise into thin strips and cut these into 2 in (5 cm) lengths.
4. In a pan, bring the stock to the boil. Add the Japanese light soy sauce, mirin, sake or sherry with sugar and salt to taste. Bring back to the boil and stir well.
5. Slowly sprinkle in the rice so that the liquid continues to boil and boil rapidly for 1 minute. Reduce the heat, stir well and cover the pan. Simmer for 10 minutes.
6. Add the chicken, mushrooms and stem onion or leek to the rice. Replace the lid and simmer for 10-15 minutes until almost all the liquid is absorbed. Remove the pan from the heat and leave to stand, covered, for a further 5 minutes. Stir the contents of the pan with a large fork and serve in warmed bowls.

Shitagareimeshi
Rice with Sole and Carrots

00.15 plus standing time **00.40**

American	Ingredients	Metric/Imperial
6 (1 lb)	sole fillets	6 (450 g/1 lb)
6	small carrots	6
1 quart	dashi (see page 356)	1 litre/1 ¾ pints
1 tbsp	finely grated fresh root ginger	1 tbsp
4-5 tbsp	Japanese light soy sauce	4-5 tbsp
3 tbsp	Japanese dark soy sauce	3 tbsp
2-3 tbsp	mirin, sake or dry sherry with ½ tbsp sugar	2-3 tbsp
	salt	
1 cup	short grain rice, rinsed and dried	225 g/8 oz
4	Japanese stem onions or scallions (spring onions), cut into 1 ½ in (4 cm) lengths	4
1 tbsp	finely chopped coriander or parsley leaves	1 tbsp
4	tomato 'flowers'	4

1. Rinse the sole fillets under cold running water and dry with kitchen paper. Cut diagonally into thin strips about 2½ in (6 cm) long.
2. Clean the carrots, slice thinly lengthwise then cut into strips 2½ in (6 cm) long.
3. Bring the dashi to the boil. Add the root ginger, soy sauces, mirin, sake or sherry with sugar and salt to taste. Bring back to the boil.
4. Slowly sprinkle in the rice so that the liquid continues to boil. Cover and boil vigorously for 1 minute. Stir well, replace the lid, reduce the heat and simmer for 10 minutes.
5. Add the strips of sole, pieces of Japanese onion or scallions (spring onions) and the strips of carrot. Replace the lid and simmer for a further 10 minutes, until most of the liquid has been absorbed. Remove from the heat and leave to stand, covered, for 5 minutes. Stir with a large fork and spoon into four warmed bowls. Sprinkle with the finely chopped coriander or parsley leaves and garnish with the tomato 'flowers'.

Naganegigohan
Rice with Japanese Stem Onion

◢ 00.15   00.35 🍲
Serves 4

American	Ingredients	Metric/Imperial
3½ cups	dashi or vegetable bouillon (stock) (see page 356)	900 ml/1½ pints
3 tbsp	Japanese light soy sauce	3 tbsp
2 tbsp	Japanese dark soy sauce	2 tbsp
2 tbsp	mirin, sake or dry sherry with ½ tbsp sugar	2 tbsp
	salt	
½ lb	lean beef or pork, cut into 1½ in (4 cm) cubes	225 g/8 oz
1 cup	short grain rice, rinsed and dried	225 g/8 oz
12	Japanese stem onions or scallions (spring onions) cut into 1½ in (4 cm) lengths	12
½	red bell pepper, flesh cut into narrow strips 1 in (2.5 cm) long	½

1. In a pan bring the dashi or vegetable bouillon (stock) to the boil. Add the soy sauces, mirin, sake or sherry with sugar, and salt to taste.
2. Add the meat, stir well and bring back to the boil.
3. Slowly sprinkle in the rice so that the liquid continues to boil. Boil vigorously for 1 minute. Cover the pan, reduce the heat and simmer for 10 minutes until the rice is tender.
4. Add the Japanese onion or scallions (spring onions). Replace the lid and simmer for a further 12-15 minutes.
5. Sprinkle the strips of pepper on top, replace the lid and after ½ minute remove from the heat. Leave to stand for a further 8 minutes so that the pepper softens a little. Stir with a large fork and serve in warmed bowls.

Sakemeshi
Rice with Salmon and Japanese Stem Onion

◢ 00.10   00.30 🍲
plus standing time

American	Ingredients	Metric/Imperial
½ lb	salmon fillet	225 g/8 oz
	salt	
3½ cups	dashi (see page 356)	900 ml/1½ pints
3 tbsp	Japanese light soy sauce	3 tbsp
1-2 tbsp	Japanese dark soy sauce	1-2 tbsp
3 tbsp	mirin, sake or dry sherry with ½ tbsp sugar	3 tbsp
1¼ cups	short grain rice, rinsed and dried	275 g/10 oz
12	Japanese stem onions or scallions (spring onions) cut diagonally into 1½ in (4 cm) lengths	12
1	lime or lemon, in segments	1

1. Rinse the salmon under running cold water and dry with kitchen paper. Cut into finger width strips 2 in (5 cm) long. Sprinkle with salt to taste and leave to stand for at least 30 minutes.
2. Bring the dashi to the boil. Add the soy sauces, mirin, sake or sherry with sugar and salt to taste and bring back to the boil.
3. Slowly sprinkle in the rice so that the liquid continues to boil. Stir well and boil rapidly for 1 minute. Cover the pan, reduce the heat and simmer for 10-12 minutes, until the rice is tender.
4. Arrange the salmon and onion on top of the rice. Replace the lid and simmer for a further 6-8 minutes. Remove from the heat and leave to stand, covered for a further 5 minutes. Stir with a large fork and serve in four warmed bowls, garnished with the segments of lime or lemon.

Rice with Japanese stem onion

Awabimeshi
Rice with Abalones

00.15 Serves 4   **00.30**

American	Ingredients	Metric/Imperial
½ lb	canned abalones	225 g/8 oz
1	small young cucumber	1
3½ cups	dashi (see page 356)	900 ml/1 ½ pints
3 tbsp	Japanese light soy sauce	3 tbsp
1 ½ tbsp	Japanese dark soy sauce	1 ½ tbsp
2 tbsp	mirin, sake or dry sherry with ½ tbsp sugar	2 tbsp
1 tbsp	chopped coriander leaves or parsley	1 tbsp
1 tsp	lime or lemon zest	1 tsp
	salt	
1 ¼ cups	short grain rice, rinsed and dried	275 g/10 oz
3	finely chopped Japanese stem onions or scallions (spring onions)	3
1	lime or lemon, in segments	1

1. Drain the abalones and dry with kitchen paper. Cut into paper-thin slices.
2. Rinse and trim the cucumber. Halve and seed, if required. Cut the cucumber halves into ⅛ in (3 mm) slices.
3. Bring the dashi to the boil. Add the soy sauces, mirin, sake or sherry with sugar, coriander or parsley, lime or lemon zest, and salt to taste. Bring back to the boil.
4. Slowly sprinkle in the rice so that the liquid continues to boil. Boil vigorously for 1 minute and stir well. Cover the pan, reduce the heat and simmer for 10 minutes.
5. Add the abalone pieces and slices of cucumber. Replace the lid and simmer for a further 6-8 minutes until nearly all the liquid has been absorbed. Remove from the heat and leave to stand, covered, for 5 minutes. Stir with a large fork and serve in warmed bowls sprinkled with Japanese onions or scallions (spring onions) and garnished with segments of lime or lemon.

Kanimeshi
Rice with Crab and Scrambled Egg

00.10 plus standing time   **00.30**

American	Ingredients	Metric/Imperial
½ lb	crabmeat, thawed if frozen	225 g/8 oz
3¼ cups	skimmed dashi or chicken bouillon (stock) (see page 356)	750 ml/1¼ pints
3 tbsp	Japanese light soy sauce	3 tbsp
1½ tbsp	Japanese dark soy sauce	1½ tbsp
2 tbsp	mirin, sake or dry sherry with ½ tbsp sugar	2 tbsp
1	red chili, cut into very thin strips, or 1½ tsp sambal ulek or red chili oil	1
	salt	
1 cup	short grain rice, rinsed and dried	225 g/8 oz
4	eggs	4
1 tsp	sugar	1 tsp
1 tbsp	groundnut oil	1 tbsp
3	finely chopped Japanese onions or 1 tbsp finely chopped scallions (spring onions)	3

1. Pick over the crabmeat and cut into small pieces.
2. Bring the dashi or chicken bouillon (stock) to the boil.
3. Add the soy sauces, mirin, sake or sherry with sugar, red chili or substitute and salt to taste. Bring back to the boil.
4. Slowly sprinkle in the rice so that the liquid continues to boil. Boil vigorously for 1 minute then cover the pan. Reduce the heat and simmer for 10 minutes until some of the liquid has been absorbed and the rice is nearly cooked.
5. Add the crabmeat and simmer for a further 6-8 minutes. Remove from the heat and leave to stand, covered, for 5 minutes.
6. Beat the eggs in a bowl. Add a pinch of salt, the sugar and 2 tbsp water.
7. Heat the oil in a frying or omelette pan. Add the egg mixture and stir until the egg has nearly set but still moist on top. Remove the pan from the heat.
8. Stir the rice with a large fork and spoon into warmed bowls. Top with the scrambled egg and sprinkle with the chopped Japanese onion or scallions (spring onions).

*Left to right: Rice with abalones,
Rice with crab and scrambled egg,
Rice with smoked halibut and mushrooms*

Kunseihirameshi
Rice with Smoked Halibut and Mushrooms

00.10 plus standing time   **00.30**

American	Ingredients	Metric/Imperial
½ lb	mushrooms	225 g/8 oz
½ lb	smoked halibut (or other smoked fish)	225 g/8 oz
3½ cups	dashi (see page 356)	900 ml/1½ pints
3 tbsp	Japanese light soy sauce	3 tbsp
1 tbsp	Japanese dark soy sauce	1 tbsp
2 tbsp	mirin, sake or dry sherry with ½ tbsp sugar	2 tbsp
	salt	
	red chili oil	
1 cup	short grain rice	225 g/8 oz
3 tbsp	cooked peas	3 tbsp
3	finely chopped Japanese stem onions or scallions (spring onions)	3

1. Wipe the mushrooms clean with a damp cloth or kitchen paper. Cut the stems into thin slices and each cap into 4.
2. Cut the halibut into thin slices, then very thin strips.
3. Bring the dashi to the boil. Add the soy sauces, mirin, sake or sherry with sugar, salt to taste and a few drops of red chili oil. Stir well, bring back to the boil.
4. Slowly sprinkle in the rice. Boil for 1 minute, cover, reduce the heat and simmer for 10 minutes.
5. Add the mushrooms, replace the lid and simmer for a further 6-8 minutes, until some of the liquid is absorbed.
6. Add the peas and strips of halibut. Cover the pan and after ½ minute remove from the heat. Leave to stand, covered, for 5 minutes. Stir with a large fork then spoon into four warmed bowls and sprinkle with some finely chopped Japanese onion or scallions (spring onions).

Kakigohan
Rice with Mussels

00.20 Serves 4   **00.35**

American	Ingredients	Metric/Imperial
2¼ lb	mussels	1 kg/2¼ lb
	salt	
1 quart	dashi (see page 356)	1 litre/1¾ pints
3 tbsp	Japanese light soy sauce	3 tbsp
1½ tbsp	Japanese dark soy sauce	1½ tbsp
3 tbsp	mirin, sake or dry sherry with ½ tbsp sugar	3 tbsp
1 cup	short grain rice, rinsed and dried	225 g/8 oz
8	coarsely chopped Japanese stem onions or scallions (spring onions)	8
2-3	skinned tomatoes, cut into wedges	2-3

1. Rinse the mussels under running cold water, discarding any that are open or unusually heavy. Take the raw mussels out of their shells using an oyster knife, saving any liquid. Strain the liquid through a piece of wet muslin. Sprinkle a little salt over the mussels.
2. Add the mussel liquid to the dashi and bring to the boil.
3. Add the soy sauces, mirin, sake or sherry with sugar and some salt to taste. Bring back to the boil.
4. Slowly sprinkle in the rice so that the liquid continues to boil. Boil vigorously for 1 minute. Cover, reduce the heat and simmer for 10 minutes, until the rice is nearly cooked.
5. Arrange the mussels and the Japanese onions or scallions (spring onions) on top of the rice. Replace the lid and simmer for a further 6-8 minutes. Remove from the heat and leave to stand, covered, for a further 5 minutes. Stir with a large fork and serve in warmed bowls garnished with wedges of tomato.

Ebi no shogameshi
Rice with Shrimp (Prawns)

00.10 plus standing time   **00.25**

American	Ingredients	Metric/Imperial
¾ lb	peeled shrimp (prawns)	350 g/12 oz
1	crushed garlic clove	1
1-2 tsp	red chili oil or sambal ulek	1-2 tsp
2 tbsp	Chinese shrimp or crab sauce	2 tbsp
2 oz	fresh root ginger	50 g/2 oz
3½ cups	skimmed dashi or chicken bouillon (stock) (see page 356)	900 ml/1½ pints
3 tbsp	Japanese light soy sauce	3 tbsp
2 tbsp	Japanese dark soy sauce	2 tbsp
3 tbsp	mirin, sake or dry sherry with 1 tbsp sugar	3 tbsp
	salt	
1 cup	short grain rice, rinsed and dried	225 g/8 oz
2	finely chopped Japanese stem onions or scallions (spring onions)	2

1. Put the shrimp (prawns) into a bowl.
2. In a small bowl mix the garlic with the red chili oil or sambal ulek, shrimp or crab sauce and 1 tbsp of water.
3. Pour this mixture over the shrimp (prawns) and stir well to coat. Leave to stand for 30 minutes, stirring occasionally.
4. Peel the root ginger and cut into very thin slices and then into fine strips.
5. Bring the dashi or chicken bouillon (stock) to the boil.
6. Add the soy sauces, mirin or sake, sherry with sugar, salt to taste and strips of root ginger and bring back to the boil.
7. Slowly sprinkle in the rice so that the liquid continues to boil, stir well and cover the pan. Reduce the heat and simmer for 15 minutes.
8. Put the shrimp (prawns) on top and simmer for a further 2 minutes. Remove from the heat and leave to stand, covered, for a further 5 minutes. Stir with a large fork, spoon into warmed bowls and sprinkle with Japanese onions or scallions (spring onions).

Rice with mussels

Sabameshi
Rice with Mackerel and Bell Pepper

⏲ 00.15
plus standing time
00.40 🍲

American	Ingredients	Metric/Imperial
6 (1 lb 5 oz)	mackerel fillets	6 (600 g/1 lb 5 oz)
1 tsp	red chili oil or 1 ½ tsp sambal ulek	1 tsp
	seven-spice powder	
	salt	
2	small red bell peppers	2
1 ¼ quarts	dashi (see page 356)	1.25 litres/2 ¼ pints
4 tbsp	Japanese light soy sauce	4 tbsp
3-4 tbsp	Japanese dark soy sauce	3-4 tbsp
4 tbsp	mirin, sake or dry sherry with 1 ½ tbsp sugar	4 tbsp
1 cup	short grain rice, rinsed and dried	225 g/8 oz
4	finely chopped Japanese stem onions or scallions (spring onions)	4

1. Rinse the mackerel fillets under cold running water and dry with kitchen paper.
2. Mix the red chili oil or sambal ulek with a dash of seven-spice powder and a pinch of salt. Rub this mixture into the mackerel fillets and leave to stand for at least 30 minutes.
3. Cut the mackerel fillets diagonally into thin strips about 2½ in (6 cm) long.
4. Rinse and trim the bell peppers. Halve and seed, cut the flesh into thin strips about 2½ in (6 cm) long.
5. Bring the dashi to the boil. Add the soy sauces, mirin, sake or sherry with sugar and salt to taste. Bring back to the boil.
6. Slowly sprinkle in the rice so that the liquid continues to boil. Boil vigorously for 1 minute. Cover the pan, reduce the heat and simmer for 10-15 minutes.
7. Add the fish and strips of bell pepper. Replace the lid and simmer for a further 8 minutes. Remove from the heat and leave to stand, covered, for a further 5 minutes. Stir with a large fork, spoon into four bowls and sprinkle with the Japanese onion or scallions (spring onions).

Cook's tip: instead of mackerel other kinds of fish can be used to make this dish, for instance sole, turbot or brill. Filleted fresh eel, cut into pieces, also give successful results.

Rice with turbot and celery

Kareimeshi

Rice with Turbot and Celery

00.15 plus standing time		00.30

American	Ingredients	Metric/Imperial
1 lb	turbot fillets	450 g/1 lb
	salt	
2-3	celery sticks	2-3
1 quart	dashi (see page 356)	1 litre/1¾ pints
4 tbsp	Japanese light soy sauce	4 tbsp
2 tbsp	Japanese dark soy sauce	2 tbsp
3 tbsp	mirin, sake or dry sherry with 1 tbsp sugar	3 tbsp
1	small finely chopped red chili or ½ tsp red chili oil or 1½ tsp sambal ulek	1
	seven-spice powder	
1 cup	short grain rice, rinsed and dried	225 g/8 oz
2	finely chopped Japanese stem onion or scallions (spring onions)	2

1. Rinse the fish under running cold water. Dry with kitchen paper, cut into ¾ in (1.75 cm) cubes and sprinkle with a little salt. Leave to stand for 30 minutes.
2. Rinse the celery, topping and tailing if necessary. Cut into ¼ in (5 mm) wide strips.
3. Bring the dashi to the boil. Add the soy sauces, mirin, sake or dry sherry with sugar, chili or sambal ulek, salt to taste, and a dash of seven-spice powder. Bring back to the boil.
4. Slowly sprinkle in the rice so that the liquid continues to boil. Boil vigorously for 1 minute. Stir well, cover and simmer for 10 minutes.
5. Add the turbot and strips of celery. Cover and simmer for a further 8-12 minutes until the celery is tender. Remove from the heat and leave to stand, covered, for a further 5 minutes. Stir with a large fork, spoon into four warmed bowls and sprinkle with Japanese onion or scallions (spring onions).

Hamu to ebigohan
Rice with Ham and Shrimp (Prawns)

00.10 plus standing time **00.25**

American	Ingredients	Metric/Imperial
½ lb	raw ham, in thick slices	225 g/8 oz
3 ¼ cups	skimmed dashi or chicken bouillon (stock) (see page 356)	750 ml/1 ¼ pints
4 tbsp	Japanese light soy sauce	4 tbsp
2 tbsp	Japanese dark soy sauce	2 tbsp
4 tbsp	mirin, sake or dry sherry with 1 ½ tbsp sugar	4 tbsp
½ tsp	lime or lemon zest	½ tsp
	salt	
1 cup	short grain rice, rinsed and drained	225 g/8 oz
½ lb	peeled shrimp (prawns)	225 g/8 oz
8	Japanese stem onions or scallions (spring onions) cut into 1 ½ in/ 4 cm lengths	8
1 tbsp	finely chopped coriander or parsley	1 tbsp

1. Cut the ham into ¼ in × 1 ½ in (5 mm × 4 cm) strips.
2. Bring the dashi or chicken bouillon (stock) to the boil.
3. Add the soy sauces, mirin, sake or sherry with sugar, lime or lemon zest and salt to taste. Bring back to the boil.
4. Slowly sprinkle in the rice so that the liquid continues to boil. Stir well and boil vigorously for 1 minute. Cover the pan, reduce the heat and simmer for 15 minutes.
5. Add the strips of ham, shrimp (prawns) and Japanese onions or scallions (spring onions). Replace the lid and cook for a further 2 minutes. Remove from the heat and leave to stand, covered, for a further 5 minutes. Stir with a large fork and spoon into warmed bowls and garnish with chopped coriander or parsley.

Ebigohan
Rice with Shrimp (Prawns) and Broccoli

00.10 Serves 4 **00.30**

American	Ingredients	Metric/Imperial
½ lb	broccoli	225 g/8 oz
3 ½ cups	skimmed dashi or chicken bouillon (stock) (see page 356)	900 ml/1 ½ pints
3-4 tbsp	Japanese light soy sauce	3-4 tbsp
2 tbsp	Japanese dark soy sauce	2 tbsp
3 tbsp	mirin, sake or dry sherry with 1 tbsp sugar	3 tbsp
	salt	
1 ¼ cups	short grain rice, rinsed and dried	275 g/10 oz
½ lb	fresh peeled shrimp (prawns)	225 g/8 oz
1	skinned tomato, cut into wedges	1

1. Rinse the broccoli and cut the stalks diagonally into thin slices. Keep the florets separate.
2. Bring the chicken bouillon (stock) to the boil. Add the soy sauces, mirin, sake or sherry with sugar and salt to taste.
3. Add the pieces of broccoli stalk and bring back to the boil.
4. Slowly sprinkle in the rice so that the liquid continues to boil. Boil vigorously for 1 minute. Cover the pan, reduce the heat and simmer for 10 minutes.
5. Add the broccoli florets, replace the lid and simmer for a further 10-12 minutes until the rice is nearly tender.
6. Add the shrimp (prawns), replace the lid and after 2 ½ minutes remove from the heat. Leave to stand, covered, for 5 minutes. Stir with a large fork and serve in warmed bowls garnished with tomato wedges.

Torirebameshi
Rice with Chicken Liver and Bell Pepper

00.10 plus standing time **00.25**

American	Ingredients	Metric/Imperial
¾ lb	chicken livers	350 g/12 oz
1 ¼ cups	milk	300 ml/½ pint
1	red bell pepper	1
1	green bell pepper	1
3 ½ cups	skimmed dashi or chicken bouillon (stock) (see page 356)	900 ml/1 ½ pints
3 tbsp	Japanese light soy sauce	3 tbsp
2 tbsp	Japanese dark soy sauce	2 tbsp
3 tbsp	mirin, sake or dry sherry with ½ tbsp sugar	3 tbsp
	salt	
1 tsp	red chili oil or sambal ulek	1 tsp
	seven-spice powder	
1 cup	short grain rice, rinsed and dried	225 g/8 oz
2	finely chopped Japanese stem onions or scallions (spring onions)	2

1. Trim the chicken livers and rinse under cold running water. Soak the livers in the milk for 30 minutes to remove the bitter taste that is sometimes present. After soaking, rinse the livers again under cold running water, making sure all traces of milk are removed. Cut the livers into small pieces.
2. Rinse and trim the bell peppers. Halve and seed, cut the flesh into very thin strips about 1 ½ in (4 cm) long.
3. Bring the dashi or chicken bouillon (stock) to the boil.
4. Add both the soy sauces, mirin, sake or sherry with sugar, salt to taste, red chili oil or sambal ulek and a dash of seven-spice powder. Bring back to the boil.
5. Slowly sprinkle in the rice so that the liquid continues to boil. Boil rapidly for 1 minute. Cover the pan and simmer for 12 minutes.
6. Add the livers and strips of bell pepper and simmer for a further 4-6 minutes. Remove from the heat and leave to stand, covered, for 5 minutes. Stir with a large fork, spoon into warmed bowls and sprinkle with the Japanese onions or scallions (spring onions).

Sakana no gingami jaki

Fish and Vegetables in Foil

00.15 plus standing time   **00.20**

American	Ingredients	Metric/Imperial
4	Chinese cabbage leaves or paksoi	4
1 tbsp	groundnut or sunflower oil	1 tbsp
1½ lb	haddock, brill, turbot, sole or cod fillet	700 g/1½ lb
	salt	
2 tbsp	sake or dry sherry	2 tbsp
8	large peeled shrimp (prawns) thawed if frozen	8
4	Japanese mushrooms (shiitake)	4
12	gingko nuts	12
2-3 tbsp	Japanese light soy sauce	2-3 tbsp

1. Rinse the Chinese cabbage or paksoi and remove the thickest part of the stalks. Dry the leaves with kitchen paper.
2. Lay four sheets of aluminum foil on a work surface. Brush with a little oil and place the Chinese leaves on the foil.
3. Rinse and dry the fish and cut into 8 equal pieces. Sprinkle with a little salt and some sake or sherry and leave to stand for 15 minutes.
4. Set the oven to 200°C/400°F/Gas Mark 6.
5. Place the pieces of fish on the Chinese leaves.
6. Cut each shrimp (prawn) down the middle lengthwise. Remove the black thread. Place 2 shrimp (prawn) halves on each piece of foil.
7. Wash the Japanese mushrooms (shiitake) and cut into very small pieces. Sprinkle over the fish and shrimp (prawns). Put 3 nuts with each portion.
8. Sprinkle the whole with soy sauce. Fold over the foil to form a closed packet. Press to close.
9. Bake for 20 minutes in the center of the oven. Turn the packets over after 10 minutes. Serve wrapped in the packets, accompanied by Zarusoba.

1. Thread the sate sticks behind the gills and backbone

2. Small fish can be threaded on 3 sticks through the underside

3. Medium fish can be threaded in the same manner

Kinome jaki
Broiled (Grilled) Fish

00.15   **00.20**
plus marinating and standing time

American	Ingredients	Metric/Imperial
1 ½ lb	tuna fillet or other seafish, thawed if frozen	700 g/1 ½ lb
4 tbsp	Japanese light soy sauce	4 tbsp
4 tbsp	mirin, sake or dry sherry with 1 ½ tsp sugar	4 tbsp
2 tsp	very finely grated fresh root ginger	2 tsp
2 tbsp	groundnut oil	2 tbsp
2 tbsp	Japanese vinegar or other mild vinegar	2 tbsp
1-2 tbsp	sugar	1-2 tbsp
2 tbsp	Japanese dark soy sauce	2 tbsp
	pinch salt	
⅓	cucumber	⅓
2 tbsp	chopped pickled ginger (bottled or home made)	2 tbsp

1. Rinse the fish, dry on kitchen paper and cut into 4 equal pieces.
2. For the marinade mix together the light soy sauce, mirin, sake or dry sherry with sugar and root ginger.
3. Add the pieces of fish and leave to stand for up to 30 minutes, turning over regularly so that the marinade can penetrate on all sides.
4. Preheat a broiler (grill) until red hot. Brush the grid with a little oil to prevent the fish from sticking.
5. Make a dressing by mixing together the vinegar, sugar, dark soy sauce and salt. Stir until the sugar and salt have completely dissolved.
6. Rinse the cucumber, cut into thin slices and place in a bowl. Pour on the dressing and turn over a few times. Leave the cucumber in the dressing for 15 minutes. Drain in a strainer or colander.
7. Broil (grill) the fish for 6-8 minutes on each side, depending on the thickness of the fish. Baste very frequently with the remaining marinade.
8. Serve on warmed plates, sprinkle with chopped pickled ginger and garnished with cucumber slices.

Cook's tip: in Japan fish is broiled (grilled) over glowing charcoal in exactly the same way as food is barbecued in the West. The Japanese, however, never place the fish on a grid, but generally skewer it. The drawings show the various ways in which fish can be skewered.

Fish and vegetables in foil

Horaku-yaki
Broiled (Grilled) Sole

American	Ingredients	Metric/Imperial
4	sole fillets	4
1 tbsp	lemon juice	1 tbsp
2 tbsp	Japanese light soy sauce	2 tbsp
1 tbsp	mirin, sake or dry sherry with ½ tsp sugar	1 tbsp
½ tsp	ground ginger	½ tsp
8	small skinned tomatoes	8
	salt	
	a few sprigs parsley	

1. Rinse the sole fillets and dry with kitchen paper.
2. For the marinade mix together the lemon juice, soy sauce, mirin, sake or dry sherry with sugar and ground ginger.
3. Add the fish fillets and leave to stand for 30 minutes, turning regularly.
4. Halve the tomatoes, remove the seed and sprinkle the insides with a little salt. Place flat sides downward on a piece of kitchen paper and leave to drain for at least 10 minutes.
5. Cut each sole fillet lengthwise into 4 narrow strips. Roll up the strips and secure with wooden skewers.
6. Quickly broil (grill) the fish rolls until dark brown on both sides under a very hot broiler (grill). Baste the rolls continually with the remaining marinade while cooking.
7. Remove the wooden skewers and place the rolls inside the hollowed-out tomatoes.
8. Garnish the snacks with parsley. Serves 4 as a snack or starter.

Sake nanban-yaki
Broiled (Grilled) Salmon

American	Ingredients	Metric/Imperial
¾ lb	salmon fillet	350 g/12 oz
1 tbsp	lemon juice	1 tbsp
2 tbsp	Japanese light soy sauce	2 tbsp
1 tbsp	mirin, sake or dry sherry with ½ tsp sugar	1 tbsp
½ tsp	ground ginger	½ tsp
1	small cucumber	1
5 tbsp	hot dashi (see page 356)	5 tbsp
2 tsp	sesame oil	2 tsp
2 tbsp	mirin, sake or dry sherry with a pinch of sugar	2 tbsp
	salt	
1 tbsp	rice vinegar or other mild vinegar	1 tbsp
2	chopped scallions (spring onions)	2

1. Rinse the salmon and dry with kitchen paper. Cut into 8-12 finger-width strips.
2. For the marinade mix together the lemon juice, soy sauce, 1 tbsp mirin, sake or sherry with sugar and ground ginger.

3. Add the strips of salmon and leave to stand for 30 minutes, turning the strips frequently.
4. Rinse and trim the cucumber. Cut diagonally into 12 slices, each ¼ in/5 mm thick.
5. Mix together the dashi, sesame oil, remaining mirin, sake or sherry with sugar, a little salt and vinegar. Stir until the salt and sugar have dissolved.
6. Draw the slices of cucumber through the dressing and steep them in it for at least 10 minutes. Dry with kitchen paper and arrange on a large plate.
7. Roll up the strips of salmon. Secure them with wooden skewers and quickly broil (grill) until dark brown all over. Do not cook for longer than 5 minutes. Baste the fish continually with the marinade while it is cooking.
8. Remove the skewers and place a fish roll on each cucumber slice.
9. Sprinkle each roll with a little chopped scallion (spring onion) and serve immediately.

Broiled (grilled) salmon with teryaki sauce

Broiled (Grilled) Salmon with Teryaki Sauce

American	Ingredients	Metric/Imperial
4	salmon fillets	4
3 tbsp	sake or dry sherry	3 tbsp
2 tbsp	mirin or dry sherry with 1 tsp sugar	2 tbsp
4 tbsp	Japanese soy sauce	4 tbsp
1½ tsp	sugar	1½ tsp
1 tbsp	sesame oil	1 tbsp
1	bunch watercress	1
1 tbsp	groundnut oil	1 tbsp

1. Skin and bone the salmon fillets.
2. Put the sake or dry sherry, mirin or dry sherry with sugar, soy sauce and sugar in a basin. Stir until the sugar dissolves.
3. Add the sesame oil and beat vigorously into the mixture.
4. Transfer half the sauce into 4 small individual bowls.
5. Put the remaining sauce into a bowl and add the salmon fillets. Stir carefully to coat then leave to marinate for 15-20 minutes, turning occasionally.
6. Rinse and trim the watercress.
7. Preheat the broiler (grill) until very hot. Brush the grid with a little groundnut oil and broil (grill) the salmon fillets for 4-5 minutes on each side. Place a roasting tin underneath to catch the liquid and the marinade. Baste the fish with the liquid once or twice, during cooking.
8. Divide the watercress between 4 warmed plates. Arrange the salmon on top of the cress. Serve with the individual sauce dishes.

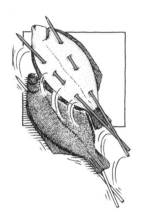

1. Sole and other flat fish should be threaded on to the sate sticks as shown to avoid damaging the fish.

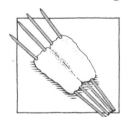

2. Salmon fillets should be threaded in this manner if very thick to keep in position during broiling (grilling).

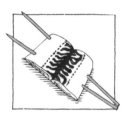

3. Another method of threading fish fillets with firm flesh on to sate sticks

4. This method of threading is suitable for very fresh fish and shorter cooking times.

Yosenabe

Poached Fish and Vegetables

00.10
Serves 4

00.10

American	Ingredients	Metric/Imperial
¼ lb	transparent vermicelli	125 g/4 oz
1 oz	spinach leaves	25 g/1 oz
1½ lb	mackerel or salmon	700 g/1½ lb
1 quart	dashi (see page 356)	1 litre/1¾ pints
4	sliced young carrots	4
6	sliced mushrooms	6
6	scallions (spring onions) cut into strips	6

1. Cook the transparent vermicelli as directed on the packet. Cut into small pieces and drain well in a strainer or colander.
2. Wash the spinach leaves and remove all the stalks.
3. Rinse the fish and dry with kitchen paper. Cut into large cubes.
4. Bring the dashi to the boil.
5. Add the carrot and boil for 2 minutes.
6. Add the mushrooms and scallions (spring onions). Boil for 1 minute.
7. Add the cubes of fish, reduce the heat and poach for up to 5 minutes.
8. Add the vermicelli and stir thoroughly.
9. Spread the spinach leaves on the bottom of warmed deep plates. Divide the contents of the pan between the plates and serve.

Cook's tip: Yosenabe may be regarded as a basic recipe for poaching all kinds of seafish. The Japanese are particularly fond of the combination of poached fish with vegetables and mushrooms. For an interesting variation ¼ lb (125 g/¼ lb) fresh peeled shrimp (prawns) can be added with the vermicelli.

Poached fish and vegetables

Niban dashi
Fish Bouillon (Stock) for Soups

	00.05	00.20
	makes 1½ quarts/1.5 litres	

American	Ingredients	Metric/Imperial
1 lb 2 oz	fresh sea fish bones and trimmings, (sole, turbot, brill)	500g/18 oz
3	slice fresh root ginger	3
1	coarsely chopped leek	1
1 tbsp	Japanese soy sauce	1 tbsp
1 tbsp	mirin, sake or medium dry sherry	1 tbsp

1. Rinse the bones and fresh sea fish trimmings under cold running water. Put in a saucepan and add a little over 1½ quarts (1.5 litres/2¾ pints) water. Bring slowly to the boil. Skim the surface very carefully a few times.
2. Add root ginger and leek. Cover the pan, reduce the heat and simmer for 16-18 minutes. Strain through a piece of wet muslin.
3. Add the soy sauce, mirin, sake or sherry.

Cook's tip: this fish bouillon (stock) is used almost exclusively in broths and soups.

Sakana ushiojiru
Clear Fish Soup

	00.02	00.05
	Serves 4	

American	Ingredients	Metric/Imperial
½ lb	sea fish fillets (turbot, sole or brill)	225 g/8 oz
4	scallions (spring onions)	4
1 quart	boiling fish bouillon (stock) (see page 384)	1 litre/1¾ pints

1. Cut the fish into 8-10 very thin slices and then into thin strips.
2. Chop the scallions (spring onion).
3. Divide the strips of fish and chopped spring onion into 4 warmed soup bowls.
4. Pour on the boiling fish bouillon (stock). Serve the soup immediately.

Hamaguri ushiojitate
Clear Mussel Soup

	00.15	00.10
	Serves 4	

American	Ingredients	Metric/Imperial
12-20	fresh mussels	12-20
1 (1 in)	cube dried seaweed (kombu)	1 (2.5 cm/1 in)
3-4	asparagus stalks (canned)	3-4
1 quart	fish bouillon (stock) (see page 384)	1 litre/1¾ pints
1 tsp	grated lemon zest	1 tsp

1. Clean the mussels thoroughly under running cold water. Discard any that are open or feel heavy.
2. Bring 1 quart (1 litre/1¾ pints) water to the boil.

3. Add the kombu and stir for 3 minutes. Remove the kombu and add the mussels. Boil until the shells have opened. Remove the mussels from the pan immediately with a skimmer. Leave to cool then remove the mussels from the shells.
4. Drain the asparagus stalks thoroughly, if canned. Cut into 1 in (2.5 cm) pieces.
5. Bring the bouillon (stock) to the boil.
6. Divide the mussels and pieces of asparagus between four warmed soup bowls. Sprinkle a little grated lemon zest over and pour on the hot bouillon (stock). Serve as hot as possible.

Sumashi wan
Bouillon (Stock) with Shrimp (Prawns)

	00.10	00.05
	Serves 4	

American	Ingredients	Metric/Imperial
4	large peeled shrimps (prawns)	4
1	carrot	1
1 (1 in)	cube soybean curd (tofu)	1 (2.5 cm/1 in)
1 quart	dashi (see page 356)	1 litre/1¾ pints
	salt	
	few sprigs watercress	

1. Cut the shrimps (prawns) in half, lengthwise and remove the black thread. Rinse under cold running water.
2. Scrape the carrot and cut lengthwise into thin slices and then into thin strips.
3. Slice the soybean curd (tofu) thinly.
4. Bring the dashi to the boil adding salt to taste. Add the shrimp (prawns), strips of carrot and slices soybean curd (tofu). Reduce the heat and simmer for 2 minutes.
5. Pour the soup into warmed soup bowls. Float the sprigs of watercress on top.

Cook's tip: as a basis for soups containing noodles the Japanese use dashi or chicken bouillon (stock) to which 4 tbsp of mirin sake or dry sherry and 4 tbsp of Japanese soy sauce are added per quart/litre. This basic bouillon (stock) is also used for cooking udon (Japanese wheat noodles) when the latter is served as an accompaniment to many dishes. This bouillon (stock) is called Kakijiru.

Misoshiru
Miso Soup

	00.03	00.05
	Serves 4	

American	Ingredients	Metric/Imperial
1 (1 in)	cube soybean curd (tofu)	1 (2.5 cm/1 in)
2	scallions (spring onions)	2
4	mushrooms	4
1 quart	dashi (see page 356)	1 litre/1¾ pints
2 tbsp	red bean paste (aka miso)	2 tbsp

1. Cut the soybean curd (tofu) into ½ in (1.25 cm) cubes.
2. Cut the scallions (spring onions) into thin strips.
3. Wipe the mushrooms clean with a damp cloth or piece of kitchen paper. Trim each stalk. Cut into thin slices.
4. Bring the dashi to the boil. Add the paste, soybean curd (tofu) and scallions (spring onions). Stir well.
5. Pour the soup into four warmed soup bowls and float the mushroom slices on top.

Nabeyaki udon
Soup with Noodles

00.06 **00.25**
Serves 4

American	Ingredients	Metric/Imperial
6	dried Japanese mushrooms or fresh shiitake	6
½ lb	thick noodles (udon)	225 g/8 oz
1 quart	dashi or chicken bouillon (stock) (see page 356)	1 litre/ 1¾ pints
4 tbsp	mirin, sake or medium dry sherry	4 tbsp
4 tbsp	Japanese soy sauce	4 tbsp
¼ lb	chicken breast fillet	125 g/4 oz
2 tbsp	sesame seed oil	2 tbsp
6	large shrimp (prawns) thawed if frozen	6
2	scallions (spring onions) cut into thin strips	2

1. Soak the dried mushrooms in boiling water for 30 minutes. Discard the stalks and cut the caps into thin strips.
2. Rinse the shiitake (if used) in plenty of cold water and cut into thin strips.
3. Cook the noodles as directed on the packet, in dashi or chicken bouillon (stock) to which mirin, sake or dry sherry and Japanese soy sauce have been added. They should be just undercooked (exactly as the Italians cook their pasta, al dente).
4. Remove the noodles from the liquid with a slotted spoon, drain them over the bouillon (stock) and transfer to a colander. Run cold water over them until completely cooled, drain well.
5. Cut the chicken breast into thin strips.

6. Heat the oil and quickly fry the shrimp (prawns) for 2 minutes. Leave the shrimp (prawns) to cool and peel them.
7. Bring the bouillon (stock) back to the boil and add the mushrooms, chicken and scallions (spring onions). Reduce the heat and simmer for 2 minutes.
8. Add the noodles, increase the heat and bring back to the boil.
9. Add the peeled shrimp (prawns) and stir. Serve in large warmed soup bowls.

Cook's tip: the soup with noodles lends itself to numerous variations. Instead of dried Japanese mushroom or fresh shitake, fresh mushrooms or oyster fungus cut into very thin slices may be used. The large shrimp (prawns) may be replaced with ¼ lb (125 g/4 oz) cooked chicken cut into very thin slices. The scallions (spring onions) give the soup a fresh and striking accent. They could be replaced by strips of leek. The Japanese have numerous further variations of soup with noodles. If dashi or chicken bouillon (stock) are used with added mirin sake, or dry sherry, soy sauce and noodles as a basis for such a soup for example, strips of fresh fish and chopped leek or scallions (spring onions) may be added. Other possible combinations are: strips of cooked ham with strips of red or green bell peppers — strips of pork with strips of fresh root ginger — strips of pork with black radish — strips of beef with coarsely chopped onion, leek or scallions (spring onions) — strips of beef with strips of white, green or savoy cabbage.

Clear mussel soup

Harusame tempura

Tempura

		00.10 plus marinating	00.30

American	Ingredients	Metric/Imperial
1½ lb	cod fillets	675 g/1½ lb
12	large shrimp (prawns) thawed if frozen	12
2 tbsp	Japanese dark soy sauce	2 tbsp
2 tbsp	mirin, sake or dry sherry with 1 tsp superfine (caster) sugar	2 tbsp
	salt	
3 tbsp	Japanese dark soy sauce	3 tbsp
2 tbsp	Japanese light soy sauce	2 tbsp
5 tbsp	sake or dry sherry with 1 tsp of superfine (caster) sugar	5 tbsp
	salt	
½ tsp	grated fresh root ginger pounded to a paste	½ tsp
¼ lb	transparent noodles (harusame)	125 g/4 oz
5 oz	cornstarch (cornflour)	150 g/5 oz
2	lightly beaten eggs	2
	oil for deep frying	

1. Rinse the fish under cold running water and dry with kitchen paper. Cut into finger width strips, 2 in (5 cm) long.
2. Peel the shrimp (prawns) and cut in half lengthwise. Remove the black thread.
3. In a small bowl stir together 2 tbsp dark soy sauce, 2 tbsp mirin, sake or dry sherry with 1 tsp caster sugar and salt to taste. Pour the mixture over the strips of fish and shrimp (prawns). Stir well and leave to stand for 20 minutes.
4. Mix together the remaining soys sauces ,sake or dry sherry, sugar, salt and root ginger.
5. Cut the harusame into ¼ in (5 mm) lengths.
6. Remove the fish from the marinade. Roll the pieces of fish and shrimps (prawns) in the cornstarch (cornflour), dip them into the lightly beaten egg and then coat with the harusame. Leave to stand for 5 minutes.

7. Heat the oil until very hot and add the fish 6 pieces at a time and shrimp (prawns), 4 at a time and fry for 1 minute, until golden brown. Drain the fish and shrimp (prawns) on kitchen paper and serve immediately. Serve the sauce separately.
Cook's tip: with the harusame serve gohan (see page 364)

Kimizu

Sauce for Salads

		00.05 plus chilling time	00.06

American	Ingredients	Metric/Imperial
3	egg yolks	3
	pinch salt	
1 tbsp	light soy sauce	1 tbsp
3 tbsp	rice vinegar	3 tbsp
1 tbsp	cornstarch (cornflour)	1 tbsp
½ tsp	wasabi or light French mustard	½ tsp

1. Blend all the ingredients to a smooth paste in a blender or mixer.
2. Transfer to a small pan and heat gently. Immediately the paste begins to thicken add 5 tbsp water, a few drops at a time, stirring constantly. Do not boil. Continue stirring, until a smooth, lightly thickened sauce has formed. Leave the sauce to cool completely, stirring occasionally.

Cook's tip: many Japanese cooks add 1-2 tbsp sesame seed oil to the sauce as a seasoning and stir the oil into the sauce immediately after the pan has been removed from the heat. Others add very finely chopped scallions (spring onions) and sometimes a little grated fresh root ginger, grated daikon or black radish to the Kimizu. In Japan, salads are served exclusively as light snacks. They are served ice-cold, garnished with cherry tomatoes, hard-cooked (hard-boiled) pullets or quails eggs and sprigs of curled parsley.

Left to right: Tempura,
Fish, shrimp (prawns) and vegetables

Sunomono
Cucumber Salad

	00.05 plus standing time	00.00

American	Ingredients	Metric/Imperial
1	green cucumber	1
2 tbsp	rice vinegar	2 tbsp
1 tbsp	sugar	1 tbsp
	good pinch salt	
½ tsp	finely grated fresh root ginger	½ tsp
	sprig dillweed or curled parsley	

1. Rinse and trim the cucumber. Halve lengthwise and seed it. Cut the flesh into moderately thin slices.
2. Mix the vinegar with the sugar, salt and root ginger, stirring until the salt and sugar have dissolved.
3. Pour the mixture over the cucumber slices and stir well. Leave to stand for 1 hour. Drain the cucumber salad in a strainer or colander.
4. Divide the slices between individual bowls and garnish with a sprig of dillweed or curled parsley.

Namasu
White Cabbage and Radish Salad

	00.10 plus chilling time	00.00

American	Ingredients	Metric/Imperial
¾ lb	white cabbage	350 g/12 oz
1	giant radish (daikon) or black radish	1
2	carrots	2
5 tbsp	kimizu sauce (see page 386)	5 tbsp

1. Clean the cabbage, remove any thick stalks and shred very finely.
2. Peel or grate the giant radish, cut into thin slices, then into narrow strips.
3. Scrape the carrots and cut into slices and then into julienne strips.
4. Put the salad vegetables into a large container with a few

quarts/litres cold water and plenty of ice cubes. Chill for 1 hour. Drain the vegetables in a colander.
5. Divide the ice-cold salad between four small bowls and spoon the sauce over.

Kywu sake
Cucumber Salad with Raw Salmon

	00.15 plus chilling time.	00.00

American	Ingredients	Metric/Imperial
¼ lb	thinly sliced raw salmon	125 g/4 oz
	salt	
1	small cucumber	1
4	lettuce leaves	4
4 tbsp	kimizu (see page 386)	4 tbsp
4	cherry tomatoes	4
4	hard-cooked (hard-boiled) quails eggs	4

1. Dry the salmon with kitchen paper. Sprinkle with a little salt and cut the slices into long thin strips.
2. Rinse and trim the cucumber. Halve lengthwise and seed it. Cut each half lengthwise into 6 long strips and then into pieces the same length as the strips of salmon.
3. Place a lettuce leaf on each plate.
4. Mix the kimizu with the strips of cucumber and spoon small mounds of cucumber on to each lettuce leaf.
5. Divide the strips of raw salmon equally between each portion. Chill until ice-cold. Garnish the salad with cherry tomato segments and quails eggs.

Kohaku mamasu
Daikon and Carrot Salad

	00.10 plus standing time	00.05

American	Ingredients	Metric/Imperial
½ lb	daikon or black radish	225 g/8 oz
½ lb	carrots	225 g/8 oz
4 tbsp	chicken bouillon (stock) or dashi (see page 356)	4 tbsp
4 tbsp	lemon juice	4 tbsp
1 tbsp	Japanese light soy sauce	1 tbsp
2 tbsp	superfine (caster) sugar or 1 tbsp honey	2 tbsp
	small pinch ve-tsin (optional)	

1. Put some ice cubes in a bowl of cold water. Add the daikon or black radish and soak for 30 minutes. Peel the radish and cut into thin strings 2½-3 in (6-8 cm) long and not more than ⅛ in (3mm) thick.
2. Peel the carrots and cut into long thin strings. Put them in the cold water at the same time as the radish so that both ingredients are at the same temperature when used.
3. Drain the radish and the carrot thoroughly in a strainer 5-10 minutes before use. Put them in a bowl and stir carefully.
4. Put all the remaining ingredients into a small pan (not aluminum) and heat gently until the sugar has dissolved. Leave to cool.
5. Pour the sauce over the salad and carefully toss together.

Tempura
Fish, Shrimp (Prawns) and Vegetables

	00. 15 plus standing time	00. 10

American	Ingredients	Metric/Imperial
16-24	large shrimp (prawns) thawed if frozen	16-24
1¾ lb	cod, turbot, brill fillets	800 g/1¾ lb
2 tbsp	lemon juice	2 tbsp
1 lb	trimmed mushrooms	450 g/1 lb
16	scallions (spring onions)	16
3-4	medium size onions	3-4
14 oz	canned lotus root, drained and sliced	400 g/14 oz
14 oz	canned baby corncobs, drained	400 g/14 oz
14 oz	canned bamboo shoots, drained and cut into strips	400 g/14 oz
6 tbsp	mirin, sake or dry sherry	6 tbsp
3 tbsp	Japanese light soy sauce	3 tbsp
3 tbsp	Japanese dark soy sauce	3 tbsp
1 tsp	grated fresh root ginger	1 tsp
	salt	
3 tsp	sugar	3 tsp
2 cups	sieved flour	200 g/7 oz
2	eggs	2
2 cups	groundnut or sunflower oil	450 ml/¾ pint
1¼ cups	sesame oil	300 ml/½ pint
1	grated daikon (giant radish)	1
4 tbsp	grated fresh root ginger	4 tbsp

1. Peel the shrimp (prawns) and halve lengthwise. Remove the black thread. Dry the shrimp (prawns).
2. Rinse the fish under cold running water and dry with kitchen paper. Cut into ¾ in×2 in (2 in×5 cm) slices. Sprinkle with a little lemon juice.
3. Wipe the mushrooms with a moist cloth and cut into ¼ in (5 cm) slices.
4. Cut the scallions (spring onions) into 2 in (5 cm) lengths.
5. Cut each onion into 8 segments and separate the layers.
6. Arrange the fish, shrimps (prawns), mushrooms, scallions (spring onions), onions, lotus root, corncobs and bamboo shoots on one or two dishes.
7. In a small pan bring the mirin, sake or sherry to the boil. Remove the pan from the heat and light the alcohol vapor over it. Allow the flames to go out, then add the soy sauces, 1 tsp root ginger, and a little salt and sugar to taste. Stir well and bring to the boil. Pour into individual bowls and keep warm.
8. Pour 1¼ cups (300 ml/½ pint) ice-cold water into a bowl. Add the sieved flour and salt and stir until a smooth batter is obtained. Add the eggs and beat with a small whisk. Leave to stand for 15 minutes. Serve in individual bowls.
9. Heat both oils in a pan. Transfer pan to a hotplate at the table.
10. Using a fork, each guest dips one or two ingredients into the batter, then the hot oil to fry until golden brown. Finally dipping into the sauce, which has been flavored to taste with daikon and root ginger.

Cook's tip: rice, noodles or one or more salads can be served with tempura. The following recipe is a good accompaniment to tempura. The vegetables used in the tempura recipe can also be varied, for example small broccoli florets, pieces of celery and other kinds of fungus as an alternative to the mushrooms specified.

Horenso no goma-a
Spinach Salad with Sesame Dressing

	00. 05 plus standing time	00. 02

American	Ingredients	Metric/Imperial
1¾ lb	spinach	800 g/1¾ lb
6 tbsp	white sesame seeds	6 tbsp
1½ tbsp	sugar	1½ tbsp
4 tbsp	Japanese dark soy sauce	4 tbsp
4 tbsp	dashi or chicken bouillon (stock) (see page 356)	4 tbsp

1. Rinse the spinach, drain and remove all stalks. Put in a colander and pour over several quarts/litres boiling water. Leave to drain.
2. Roast the sesame seeds in a dry pan until beginning to pop. Spread out on a cold plate to cool, grind finely in a mortar and put into a bowl.
3. Add the sugar, soy sauce and bouillon (stock), stirring until the sugar has dissolved. Beat well with a small whisk.
4. Put the drained spinach in a bowl. Pour the dressing over and carefully cover all the leaves with it.
5. Divide the salad between 8 small individual bowls, placing one by each guest's plate.

Cook's tip: because young leaf spinach is very tender, it is not really necessary to pour boiling water over it. It is sufficient to rinse the spinach and leave to stand in a bowl of hot water (75°C/150°F); the vegetable will then retain a slight crispness.

Sukiyaki: The sukiyaki is prepared at the table. No side dishes such as rice or mie are served with it, but these can be served after the sukiyaki, as is done in many Japanese restaurants. The meal is usually rounded off with Gohan (boiled rice: (see page 364) and pickles (see page 389). This is accompanied by Japanese tea, whilst with the sukiyaki warm sake and nowadays chilled beer are served.

Sukiyaki (Osaka no sukiyaki)

Fried Beef with Vegetables (Osaka)

00.30 Serves 8　**00.20**

American	Ingredients	Metric/Imperial
3¼ lb	slightly marbled beef (rump or topside)	1½ kg/3¼ lb
16	scallions (spring onions)	16
1 lb	drained canned bamboo shoots	450 g/1 lb
7 oz	fresh bean sprouts	200 g/7 oz
1¾ lb	mushrooms	750 g/1¾ lb
3	medium size onions	3
1	Chinese cabbage	1
1 (2 in)	cube soybean curd (tofu)	1 (5 cm/2 in)
¼ lb	transparent vermicelli (shirataki)	125 g/4 oz
	few sprigs watercress	
	Japanese light soy sauce	
	Japanese dark soy sauce	
	sake	
2 cups	beef bouillon (stock)	450 ml/¾ pint
	sugar	
8	eggs	8
¼ lb	beef suet	125 g/4 oz

1. It is essential that all the ingredients for the sukiyaki are as dry as possible, otherwise they will spatter during frying.
2. Dry the meat with kitchen paper and with a very sharp knife, cut into paper-thin slices.

Fried beef with vegetables (Osaka)

3. Rinse the scallions (spring onions) and cut into 2 in (5 cm) pieces.
4. Cut the bamboo shoots into rounds, slices or strips.
5. Rinse the bean sprouts in plenty of cold water. Remove the seedcases and leave to drain in a colander.
6. Wipe the mushrooms with a damp cloth or kitchen paper. Trim the stalks and cut the mushrooms into 2-3 pieces.
7. Peel the onions, cut each one into 8 segments and separate the layers
8. Rinse the Chinese cabbage and cut into finger-width strips 2-2½ in (5-6 cm) long. Dry thoroughly in a lettuce centrifuge.
9. Cut the soybean curd (tofu) into ¼ in (5 mm) pieces.
10. Prepare the vermicelli as directed on the packet. Drain thoroughly and cut into 2 in (5 cm) lengths.
11. Place all the ingredients, one at a time, on one or two large dishes. Garnish with a few sprigs of watercress.
12. Put small jugs containing soy sauces and sake, small bowls of bouillon (stock) and a bowl of sugar on the table.
13. Break the eggs into 8 bowls and place a bowl by each plate. Your guests should beat the egg themselves, using chopsticks, and add a little soy sauce, a few drops of sake and a little sugar, according to taste.
14. Heat a sukiyaki pan, electric wok or a deep cast iron pan and melt a little of the suet.
15. Add a little of each vegetable and stir fry for 2-3 minutes until beginning to color. Push the vegetables to the side of the pan.
16. Very quickly, stir fry 1-2 slices of meat for 20 seconds, until beginning to color. Add a little soy sauce, a little sake, a pinch of sugar and a few tbsp beef bouillon (stock). Stir well and bring to the boil.
17. Add a little vermicelli and 1-2 pieces of soybean curd (tofu). Stir and serve on warmed plates.
18. The guests – using their chopsticks – take the pieces of meat and vegetables and dip them into their individual sauces before eating.

Cook's tip: toward the end of the meal, add some bouillon (stock) to the remaining ingredients, bring to the boil and serve as soup. Serve small bowls with a few tbsp rice or boiled noodle and let the guests pour a few tbsp soup over. Thin slices or strips of pickled ginger (see page 389) and a crisp salad can also be served.

Sudori shoga

Pickled Ginger

00.10 makes 2 jars　**00.05**

American	Ingredients	Metric/Imperial
1 lb	fresh root ginger	450 g/1 lb
1¾ cups	rice vinegar	400 ml/14 fl oz
6 tbsp	sugar	6 tbsp
1 tsp	salt	1 tsp

1. Rinse the root ginger in cold running water. Place in boiling water for 1 minute and then rinse again in cold running water. Dry with kitchen paper and cut into coarse pieces.
2. In a pan, bring the vinegar and 5 tbsp water to the boil. Add the sugar and salt stirring continuously until they have dissolved.
3. Add the pieces of root ginger and bring back to the boil. Remove the pan from the heat immediately and leave to cool.
4. Transfer carefully to clean airtight jars. Seal, label and store in a cool dry place for up to 3 months.

Udon suki
Sukiyaki with Noodles and Fish

	00.40	00.30
	Serves 8	

American	Ingredients	Metric/Imperial
1½ lb	udon or soba noodles	675 g/1½ lb
2-3 tbsp	sesame oil	2-3 tbsp
2	cakes soybean curd (tofu) cut into ¼ in (5 mm) cubes	2
8	slices canned fish paste (kamaboko)	8
8	scallions (spring onions) cut into ½ in (4 cm) pieces	8
½ lb	canned, drained, sliced bamboo shoots	225 g/8 oz
1 lb	filleted eel	450 g/1 lb
8	large shrimp (prawns) thawed if frozen	8
¾ lb	large mushrooms	350 g/12 oz
1 lb	young spinach	450 g/1 lb
1 lb	chicken breast fillets	450 g/1 lb
6 tbsp	fresh grated root ginger	6 tbsp
6 tbsp	finely chopped scallion (spring onions) or leeks	6 tbsp
2	lemons cut into segments	2
1½ quarts	dashi (see page 356)	1.5 litres/2¾ pints
¾ cup	sake or medium dry sherry	200 ml/7 fl oz
1 tsp	superfine (caster) sugar	1 tsp
1¼ cups	Japanese light soy sauce	300 ml/½ pint

1. Prepare the udon or soba as directed on the packet. Cool in cold water. Leave to drain well in a colander and spread on a very large dish.
2. Heat 1-2 tbsp oil and stir fry the soybean curd (tofu) until golden on all sides. Drain in a colander and cool.
3. Arrange the soybean curd (tofu) on the udon or soba with the slices of fish paste, scallions (spring onions) and bamboo shoots.
4. Cut the eel fillets into 8-16 pieces and broil (grill) quickly until golden brown on both sides. Drain on kitchen paper and leave to cool.
5. Peel the shrimp (prawns), cut in two lengthwise and remove the black thread.
6. Wipe the mushrooms with a damp cloth or piece of kitchen paper. Trim the stalks and cut each mushroom into 4.
7. Rinse the spinach, drain and remove the stalks.
8. Cut the chicken breast fillets into ½ in (1.25 cm) cubes.
9. Place the pieces of broiled (grilled) eel, shrimp (prawns), mushrooms, spinach leaves and cubes of chicken, one at a time, on the bed of udon or soba.
10. Spoon a little root ginger and some chopped scallion (spring onion) into 8 small individual bowls, add a segment of lemon. Place one bowl next to each guest's plate.
11. Bring to the boil the dashi, sake or substitute, sugar and soy sauce. Put the pan of hot sauce on a hotplate on the table and place the dish of ingredients next to it.
12. Cook the shrimp (prawns) in the sauce for 2 minutes and serve.
13. Warm the grilled eel in the sauce and serve.
14. Continue to cook each ingredient for about 1 minute and serve individually. Cook the mushrooms and scallions (spring

onions) and spinach leaves for 2 minutes. Prepare the cubes of chicken and cook for 3-4 minutes.
15. When the last ingredients have been served, add the udon or soba to the sauce and warm through. Do not let it boil as it tends to become too soft. Serve the udon or soba with as much sauce as possible and invite your guests to add some grated root ginger and scallion (spring onions) to taste.

Wafu
Crab and Cucumber Salad

	00.20	00.02
	plus standing and chilling time	

American	Ingredients	Metric/Imperial
1	small cucumber	1
	salt	
1	small, washed head of lettuce	1
¼ lb	daikon (giant radish)	125 g/4 oz
3	finely chopped shallots or scallions (spring onions)	3
6 oz	canned crabmeat	175 g/6 oz
2-3 tbsp	white sesame seeds	2-3 tbsp
4-5 tbsp	dashi (see page 356)	4-5 tbsp
1-2 tbsp	Japanese salty soy sauce (shoyu)	1-2 tbsp
2 tbsp	mirin or sake or medium dry sherry with 1 tsp sugar	2 tbsp
	seven-spice powder	
	aji-no-moto (ve-tsin) (optional)	
8	small radishes	8
2	sweet-sour gherkins	2

1. Rinse the cucumber, dry and slice very thinly. Sprinkle with salt and leave to stand for 15 minutes. Rinse under cold water and leave to drain in a colander. Arrange the slices on some lettuce leaves.
2. Peel and slice the daikon very thinly. Put the slices on the cucumber in neat piles.
3. Sprinkle the shallots or scallions (spring onions) over the salad.
4. Drain the crabmeat, pick over and separate the pieces.
5. Arrange the leaves from the heart of the lettuce on a large flat dish.
6. Briefly roast the sesame seeds in a dry pan until light brown. Grind them in a mortar and transfer to a bowl. Add the dashi, soy sauce, mirin or substitute, sugar, a dash of seven-spice powder and aji-no-moto (ve-tsin) and stir well. Add salt to taste.
7. Pour half the sauce over the salad and serve the rest separately.
8. Garnish the salad with radish 'flowers' and gherkin 'fans'. Leave the salad to stand in a cool place for 30 minutes before serving.

Cook's tip: zucchini (courgettes) can be used in place of cucumber. Rinse and cut into ⅛ in (3 mm) slices. Blanch for 2 minutes in boiling water with a little salt or a dash of light soy sauce. Drain and cool before arranging the slices on the dish with the lettuce leaves. Shelled hazelnuts, Brazil or walnuts can be used in place of sesame seeds. Grind in a mortar and add them unroasted.

Sashimi is a typically Japanese first course or snack. For sashimi buy fish that is as fresh as possible. Keep the fish in a covered bowl in the refrigerator until just before use, and use it within 4-6 hours of purchase.

Sashimi

Sashimi

	00.20 Serves 4	00.00

American	Ingredients	Metric/Imperial
1 ¼ lb	fresh filleted fish (3-4 kinds) (sea bass, sea bream, salmon, tuna, haddock, cod, squid)	550 g/1 ¼ lb
	small quantities finely grated cucumber, daikon (giant radish) and carrot, chopped celery and curly parsley	
2 tbsp	dashi or chicken bouillon (stock) (see page 356)	2 tbsp
4 tbsp	Japanese salty soy sauce (shoyu)	4 tbsp
1 tsp	mirin, sake or (medium dry) sherry with a pinch of sugar	1 tsp

1. Using a very sharp filleting knife, cut the fish up in one of the following ways: (1) Hira giri (very flat slices). about ¼ in (5 mm) thick and 1 in (2.5 cm) long, depending on the shape of the fillets. (2) Usu zukuri (wafer thin slices). Put the fillet on a flat clean working surface or board and cut at 45° into slices as thin as possible. (3) Ito zukuri (in pieces): the best cutting technique for squid. Cut the squid into ¼ in (5 mm) pieces crosswise and then into equally wide slices lengthwise. (4) Kaku giri (½ in (1.25 cm) cubes): cut the fish into flat slices (as in (1)) and then into cubes.
2. Arrange the various fish on an oval or round dish.
3. Decorate with finely grated cucumber, daikon, carrot, chopped celery and sprigs of curly parsley.
4. Mix together the dashi or chicken bouillon (stock), soy sauce, mirin or substitute and sugar and serve separately in small individual bowls. Dip the fish pieces in the sauce before eating.

Cod with Chinese cabbage

Isobe sukuri

Sashimi in Seaweed

	00.20 Serves 4	00.03

American	Ingredients	Metric/Imperial
1 ¼ lb	fresh filleted fish (see basic sashimi recipe page 391)	550 g/1 ¼ lb
4-6	leaves dried seaweed (nori)	4-6

1. Prepare the fillets as described in Sashimi recipe, cutting the fillets into slices not more than ¼ in (5 mm) thick and about 6 in (15 cm) long.
2. Briefly toast the nori to produce the maximum aroma and color. Lay out on a bamboo mat or linen napkin.
3. Place a slice of fish along the length of the nori leaf (longer edge toward you) and firmly roll up the fish and nori. Repeat until all the nori has been used. Cut the rolls into 1 in (2.5 cm) wide slices.

Tsjirizu

Sashimi Sauce (I)

	00.05 plus cooling time	00.02

American	Ingredients	Metric/Imperial
2-3 tbsp	sake (rice wine)	2-3 tbsp
¼ lb	daikon (giant radish)	125 g/4 oz
3	chopped shallots or scallions (spring onions)	3
4 tbsp	Japanese salty soy sauce	4 tbsp
4 tbsp	lemon juice or wine vinegar	4 tbsp
	salt	
	seven-spice powder	

1. Warm the sake in a stainless steel pan (not aluminum) (do not boil). Remove from the heat and light the alcohol vapor, shaking the pan while the sake is burning. When the flames have gone out, pour into a small earthenware bowl and leave to cool (not in a refrigerator).
2. Peel the daikon and grate very finely on to a plate.
3. Add the daikon and shallot or scallion (spring onion) to the cooled sake.
4. Mix with the soy sauce, lemon juice or vinegar, a little salt and seven-spice powder, stirring continuously. Pour the sauce into small individual bowls and serve with sashimi.

Tosu shoyu

Sashimi Sauce (II)

00.02 plus cooling time   **00.05**

American	Ingredients	Metric/Imperial
5 tbsp	Japanese salty soy sauce (shoyu)	5 tbsp
1-2 tbsp	sake (rice wine)	1-2 tbsp
2 tbsp	dried chopped bonito (katsuobushi)	2 tbsp
	salt	
	seven-spice powder	
1-1 ½ tbsp	wasabi powder	1-1 ½ tbsp

1. In a small pan (not aluminum) mix together the soy sauce, sake, chopped bonito (katsuobushi), a little salt and seven-spice powder. Bring to the boil over moderate heat stirring continuously. Strain into a bowl and leave to cool slowly (not in a refrigerator).
2. Mix the wasabi with enough water to make a thick paste. Put a knife point of this spicy paste on to each plate. Stir thoroughly and taste. Be careful: add tiny quantities and always taste before you add extra wasabi to the sauce.

Nabemono (Single pan dishes) — Japanese cuisine includes many dishes which are a meal in themselves and are prepared in a single pan at the table.

Tara chirinabe

Cod with Chinese Cabbage

00.30 plus cooking at table   **00.15**

American	Ingredients	Metric/Imperial
1½ lb	cod fillets	675 g/1 ½ lb
8	large Chinese cabbage leaves	8
	salt	
1 lb	young spinach	450 g/1 lb
8	large mushrooms	8
8	scallions (spring onions) or 4 thin leeks	8
2 (2 in)	cakes of soybean curd (tofu)	2 (5 cm/2 in)
2 tbsp	sesame oil	2 tbsp
2 cups	boiled short grain rice (see page 364)	225 g/8 oz

1. Rinse the fish under cold running water and cut diagonally into 1 in (2.5 cm) strips.
2. Rinse the Chinese cabbage and cook in boiling salted water for 4 minutes. Cool rapidly in cold water. Drain in a colander.
3. Remove the thickest veins from the leaves but retain the original shape as far as possible. Spread the leaves out on a work surface or board.
4. Rinse the spinach leaves and remove all stalks and put the leaves in hot water (about 75°C/50°F) for 1 minute. Drain in a colander and press out as much water as possible. Divide the

spinach leaves into 8 portions and make into little rolls. Put the rolls on to the cabbage leaves. Roll the Chinese cabbage leaves round the spinach and secure with wooden cocktail picks.
5. Wipe the mushrooms with a damp cloth or kitchen paper and trim the stalks. Cut each mushroom into 2-3 pieces.
6. Clean the scallions (spring onions) or leeks and cut into 1¼-1½ in (3-4 cm) pieces.
7. Cut the soybean curd (tofu) into ¼ in (5 mm) cubes.
8. Heat the oil in a wok and stir fry the soybean curd (tofu) until golden on all sides. Drain on kitchen paper. Place in a bowl with cold water to cover and leave to stand for 15 minutes. Drain in a strainer.
9. Arrange all the ingredients, one at a time, on a large dish. Chill until ready to serve.
10. Prepare the rice and keep it hot. Prepare the sauce (recipe follows).
11. Cut the cabbage rolls into 1½ in (3 cm) slices, remove the cocktail picks. Arrange the slices on a dish with the other ingredients and place on the table.
12. Poach the fish in the sauce for 6-8 minutes and serve.
13. Heat the slices of stuffed cabbage in the bouillon (stock).
14. Boil the mushrooms for 2-3 minutes, followed by the scallions (spring onions) or leek and, to conclude the meal, warm the cubes of soybean curd (tofu) in the bouillon (stock).

Cook's tip: ensure there are little bowls of boiled rice on the table for each guest throughout the meal, and keep refilling them: in Japan it is considered wrong for a bowl to contain more than 3-4 tbsp of boiled rice. Tara chirinabe should be served with a ponzu sauce, which can be bought in bottles ready to use. You can also prepare the sauce yourself, but this takes at least three months!

Sauce and Stock for Tara Chirinabe

00.05 Serves 4   **00.00**

American	Ingredients	Metric/Imperial
¼ lb	roasted peanuts or 5 tbsp peanut butter	125 g/4 oz
1 tsp	sugar	1 tsp
1 tsp	Japanese rice vinegar or sherry vinegar	1 tsp
1 tbsp	Japanese dark soy sauce	1 tbsp
¾ cup	chicken bouillon (stock) (see page 356)	200 ml/7 fl oz
1½ quarts	dashi (see page 356)	1.5 litres/2 ¾ pints
2 tbsp	Japanese light soy sauce	2 tbsp
2 tbsp	mirin or sherry with 1 tsp sugar	2 tbsp

1. Grind the peanuts (if using) to a paste in a mortar or blender.
2. Put the paste or peanut butter in a pan and add the sugar, Japanese vinegar or sherry vinegar, Japanese dark soy sauce, chicken bouillon (stock). Bring slowly to the boil stirring continuously and simmer for 5 minutes. Leave to cool until just warm then spoon into small individual bowls.
3. Bring the dashi to the boil and add the Japanese light soy sauce and mirin or sherry with 1 tsp sugar. Put on a hotplate on the table.

Oysters from the sandbank

Kaki dotenabe

Oysters from the Sandbank

00.25 plus cooking at table | 00.10

American	Ingredients	Metric/Imperial
6 tbsp	*soy paste (red miso)*	*6 tbsp*
6 tbsp	*soy paste (white miso)*	*6 tbsp*
5 tbsp	*dashi (see page 356)*	*5 tbsp*
1 tbsp	*mirin or dry sherry with 1 tsp sugar*	*1 tbsp*
36	*large oysters*	*36*
1 tsp	*salt*	*1 tsp*
2	*coarsely chopped scallions (spring onions)*	*2*
1¾ lb	*mushrooms*	*350 g/12 oz*
½ lb	*Chinese cabbage*	*225 g/8 oz*
1½ quarts	*dashi (see page 356)*	*1.5 litres/ 2¾ pints*
2 tbsp	*Japanese light soy sauce*	*2 tbsp*
2 tbsp	*mirin or dry sherry with 1 tsp sugar*	*2 tbsp*
2 cups	*boiled short grain rice (see page 364)*	*225 g/8 oz*

1. Put the red and white miso into a bowl. Add 5 tbsp dashi and 1 tbsp mirin or sherry with sugar. Mix well with a fork until smooth.
2. Coat the inside of a glass pan with this paste, which represents the 'sandbank' from which the oysters are to be taken.
3. Open the oysters, set aside the oyster liquor. Remove the oysters from the shells and discard the beards. Place the oysters in a bowl with the oyster liquor.
4. Stir in the salt and scallions (spring onions).
5. Wipe the mushrooms with a damp cloth or kitchen paper. Trim the stalks and leave the mushrooms whole if they are small. Cut larger ones into 2-3 pieces.
6. Cut the Chinese cabbage into thin strips 2 in (5 cm) long.
7. Place all the ingredients on a dish.
8. Bring the remaining dashi to the boil and add the soy sauce and remaining mirin or sherry and sugar.
9. Put a hotplate on the table and place the glass pan containing the sandbank on it. Pour the boiling dashi slowly into the middle of the bowl. (While the oysters are poaching the miso paste is gradually absorbed into the bouillon (stock)).
10. Place the bowl of oysters on the table and put a small bowl of hot boiled rice next to each plate. Poach the oysters in the hot bouillon (stock), 6-8 at a time, for 2 minutes.
11. When the guests have all had their portions of oysters, add the mushrooms and boil gently for 2-3 minutes. Serve with a little of the liquid. Repeat with the Chinese cabbage.

Jodofu

Tofu with a Dip

00.15 Serves 4 | 00.10

American	Ingredients	Metric/Imperial
4	*slices fresh soybean curd (tofu)*	*4*
1½ quarts	*dashi or chicken bouillon (stock) (see page 356)*	*1.5 litres/2¾ pints*
1 (4 in)	*piece dried seaweed (kombu)*	*1 (10 cm/4 in)*
4-5	*shallots or scallions (spring onions)*	*4-5*
1 tbsp	*finely grated fresh root ginger*	*1 tbsp*
1½ tbsp	*dried bonito pieces (katsuobushi)*	*1½ tbsp*
¾ cup	*Japanese salty soy sauce (shoyu)*	*200 ml/7 fl oz*
2 tbsp	*mirin or dry sherry with 1 tsp sugar*	*2 tbsp*
3 tbsp	*dashi (see page 356)*	*3 tbsp*

1. Cut the tofu into 1 in (2.5 cm) cubes and put on a plate.
2. Bring 1½ quarts (1.5 litres/2¾ pints) dashi to the boil in a large pan. Rinse the kombu and add to the dashi. Add the tofu and simmer for 3 minutes.
3. Cut the cleaned shallots or scallions (spring onions) into very thin rings.
4. In a bowl mix together the shallots or scallions (spring onions), ginger and crumbled bonito.
5. Bring the soy sauce, mirin or sherry with sugar and 3 tbsp dashi to the boil in a stainless steel pan, stirring continuously. Remove from the heat.
6. Spoon the sauce into small individual bowls and garnish with pieces of ginger, shallot or scallion (spring onion), and katsuobushi.
7. Remove the tofu from the cooking water using a skimmer and put into a large warmed dish or small individual warm bowls.
8. Pour over a very small amount of bouillon (stock) over and serve the sauce separately with the tofu.

Cook's tip: to make the whole dish vegetarian, use a vegetable bouillon (stock) and leave out the katsuobushi.

Makunushi bento
Picnic Lunch

01.00
Serves 6

01.15

American	Ingredients	Metric/Imperial
1¾ quarts	dashi (see page 356)	1.75 litres/3 pints
1	medium size carrot	1
12	long green beans or French beans	12
12	snow peas (mange-tout) (optional)	12
1 tbsp	Japanese light soy sauce	1 tbsp
3 tbsp	herb vinegar or lemon juice	3 tbsp
1-1½ tbsp	sugar	1-1½ tbsp
18	small spinach leaves	18
3 tbsp	lightly crushed and lightly roasted white sesame seeds	3 tbsp
8 (4 in sq)	sheets of nori (seaweed)	8 (10 cm/4 in sq)
24	ginkgo nuts	24
2-3 tbsp	mirin or dry sherry with 2-2½ tsp white sugar	2-3 tbsp
2-3 tbsp	sugar	2-3 tbsp
4 oz	rice flour	125 g/4 oz
3-4	drops red vegetable food coloring	3-4
9 oz	cod fillets	250 g/9 oz
1 tbsp	cornstarch (cornflour)	1 tbsp
	salt	
12	oysters or large mussels	12
1	large lemon cut into 6 slices	1
12	medium size shrimp (prawns) thawed if frozen	12
2 tbsp	sake or dry sherry with 1 tsp sugar	2 tbsp
3-4 tbsp	light soy sauce	3-4 tbsp
12	small pork sausages	12
12	small heart lettuce leaves	12
4 tbsp	grated daikon (giant radish)	4 tbsp

1. Bring 1 cup (250 ml/9 fl oz) dashi to the boil.
2. Cut the carrot diagonally into 18 thin slices. Add the carrot to the dashi, bring back to the boil and cook for 4 minutes. Drain well. Keep the dashi.
3. Rinse, trim and string the beans, if necessary. Cut diagonally into 2 in (5 cm) lengths.
4. Rinse and string the snow peas (mange-tout) if necessary.
5. Bring the dashi back to the boil. Add the light soy sauce, beans and snow peas (mange-tout), cook for 5 minutes. Drain well.
6. Bring 3 tbsp herb vinegar or lemon juice to the boil in a small pan. Add 1-1½ tbsp sugar and stir until the sugar dissolves. Add the beans and mange-tout, cook for 1 minute. Remove the pan from the heat and cool.
7. Rinse the spinach leaves under running cold water. Put in a sieve or colander and steam over boiling water for 2 minutes.

Cool, then dry one at a time with kitchen paper. Toast the leaves for 2-4 seconds and place them, in threes, in one of the corners of the boxes.

8. Add 1 tbsp water to the sesame seeds. Stir thoroughly and divide into four equal portions.

9. Toast the sheets of nori for 2-4 seconds. Coat 4 sheets with the sesame paste and place the other 4 sheets on top. Roll up the double sheets and secure with wooden cocktail picks.

10. Bring 1¼ cups (300 ml/½ pint) water to the boil. Add the ginko nuts and boil for 2 minutes. Remove the nuts and plunge into a bowl of cold water. Shell and skin them.

11. In a small pan bring 2-3 tbsp mirin or sherry with sugar, 2 tbsp dashi and 3 tbsp sugar to the boil. Add the nuts and simmer for 2 minutes stirring continuously to coat the nuts with a glossy layer of sugar. Thread the nuts onto 6 wooden cocktail sticks.

12. Sieve the rice flour into a bowl. Add 1-2 tbsp water and knead to form a supple dough. Knead in enough red coloring to turn the dough light pink. Form the dough into six little balls and flatten them slightly.

13. Bring 1 cup (250 ml/9 fl oz) dashi to the boil. Add the dough balls, reduce the heat and simmer for 6-8 minutes.

Remove from the heat and cool the balls.

14. Chop the fish very finely, preferably in a blender. Mix in the cornstarch (cornflour) and a little salt. Steam for 12 minutes in a steamer then cool thoroughly.

15. Remove the shellfish from the shells without damaging them. Remove all impurites and cut them into 2-3 slices.

16. Cut each of the lemon slices into three equal pieces. Place each piece on a slice of oyster or mussel.

17. Bring 1 cup (250 ml/9 fl oz) dashi to the boil. Add the shrimp (prawns) and boil until the shrimp (prawns) are bright pink. Peel when cool.

18. Mix the sake, or dry sherry with sugar, with 3-4 tbsp of light soy sauce. If using sherry with sugar, stir until the sugar has dissolved. .

19. Add the shrimp (prawns) to the mixture for a few minutes, drain briefly then arrange them on salad leaves in the lunch boxes.

20. Cook the sausages for 12-15 minutes in the remaining dashi and leave to go cold.

21. Divide the dishes between the various lunch boxes lined with lettuce leaves.

22. Add the grated daikon and serve.

Picnic lunch

Dashi-maki Tamago
Japanese Omelette

00.10 makes 2 omelettes   **00.20**

American	Ingredients	Metric/Imperial
8	eggs	8
¾ cup	dashi or chicken bouillon (stock) (see page 356)	200 ml/8 fl oz
	pinch salt	
1½ tbsp	mirin, sake or dry sherry with 1 tsp sugar	1½ tbsp
½ tbsp	Japanese light soy sauce	1½ tbsp
3 tbsp	groundnut or sunflower oil	3 tbsp
1	very finely chopped daikon (giant radish)	1
3-4	drops soy sauce	3-4

1. Beat the eggs until thoroughly mixed.
2. Mix together the dashi, salt, mirin, sake or dry sherry and sugar and the soy sauce and stir into the eggs. Pour ½ the mixture into a jug.
3. Heat a rectangular Japanese omelette pan and oil lightly. Pour ⅓ of the mixture in the jug into the pan and tilt the pan so that the egg mixture covers the surface.
4. Cook the omelette gently, without browning, until set. Roll it up, away from you into a tight roll. Re-oil the pan.
5. Add ½ the remaining mixture in the jug to the pan, lifting the omelette to allow the mixture to coat the pan. Cook as before and roll up, rolling the first omelette inside the second.
6. Repeat with the remaining egg mixture in the jug, rolling the third omelette around the other two.
7. Turn the omelette out on to a bamboo mat or linen napkin and roll up firmly. Leave to stand for 10 minutes then cut into thick slices and serve sprinkled with daikon an few drops soy sauce. Repeat with the remaining egg mixture.
Cook's tip: tamago is sometimes served in combination with spiced rice. Tamago omelettes can also be stamped out into 2 in (5 cm) diameter circles or into small diamonds decorated with shrimp (prawn), cooked lobster, raw salmon, smoked salmon or eel, cooked crab or fish, cherry tomato, radish.

Sakana no kunsei iri omuretsu
Japanese Omelette with Smoked Fish

00.15   **00.20**
Serves 4 (2 omelettes)

American	Ingredients	Metric/Imperial
¼ lb	smoked fish (eel or salmon)	125 g/4 oz
2 tsp	Japanese light soy sauce	2 tsp
	few drops of lemon juice	
8	eggs	8
⅔ cup	dashi or light chicken bouillon (stock) (see page 356)	150 ml/¼ pint
	pinch of salt	
1½ tbsp	mirin, Chinese rice wine or dry sherry with 1 tsp sugar	1½ tbsp
1½ tsp	Japanese light soy sauce	1½ tsp
3 tbsp	groundnut or sunflower oil	3 tbsp
8	small lettuce leaves	8
1	lemon or lime, cut into 8	1

Japanese omelette with smoked fish

1. Chop or grind the smoked fish very finely, if necessary purée in a food processor to a smooth paste.
2. Add 2 tsp soy sauce and lemon juice to taste.
3. Make the omelettes as described in the recipe for Japanese omelette (see page 396). Before rolling the layers, spread with a thin layer of the smoked fish paste. Roll the omelettes in bamboo mats or linen napkins, leave to stand for 10 minutes then cut each roll into 4 equal pieces.
4. Arrange 8 lettuce leaves on a dish, and top with the omelette pieces with a piece of lemon or lime next to them.

Torinuku iri omuretsu
Japanese Omelette with Chicken

00.15   **00.20**
Serves 4 (2 omelettes)

American	Ingredients	Metric/Imperial
½ lb	chicken breast fillets	225 g/8 oz
2 tbsp	mirin, Chinese rice wine or dry sherry with 1 tsp sugar	2 tbsp
2 tbsp	Japanese light soy sauce	2 tbsp
8	eggs	8
⅔ cup	dashi or light chicken bouillon (stock) (see page 356)	150 ml/¼ pint
	pinch salt	
1½ tbsp	mirin, Chinese rice wine or dry sherry with 1 tsp sugar	1½ tbsp
1½ tbsp	Japanese light soy sauce	1½ tbsp
4	finely chopped scallions (spring onions) or 1 piece leek	4
3 tbsp	groundnut or sunflower oil	3 tbsp

1. Chop or grind the chicken very finely.
2. Bring 2 tbsp mirin, 2 tbsp soy sauce and 2 tbsp water to the boil in a small pan. Add the chicken, reduce the heat and simmer to reduce the liquid. Cool slightly and stir through a fine strainer.
3. Fry the omelettes as described in the recipe for Japanese omelette (page 396). Before rolling the layers of omelette, spread them with a thin coating of chicken paste and sprinkle with a little chopped scallion (spring onion) or leek. Roll them tightly into a bamboo mat or linen napkin. Leave to stand for 10 minutes.
4. Cut each omelette obliquely into four equal pieces and place in a dish. Garnish with the tails of scallions (spring onions) or leek.

Nori to sake iri omuretsu

Japanese Omelette with Nori and Salmon

00.15 00.20

Serves 4 (2 omelettes)

American	Ingredients	Metric/Imperial
5½ oz	salmon fillet	150 g/5½ oz
1-2 tbsp	tomato ketchup	1-2 tbsp
2 tsp	Japanese light soy sauce	2 tsp
6 (8 in)	sheets dried seaweed (nori)	6 (20 cm/8 in)
8	eggs	8
⅔ cup	dashi or light chicken bouillon (stock) (see page 356)	150 ml/¼ pint
	pinch of salt	
1½ tbsp	mirin, Chinese rice wine or dry sherry with 1 tsp sugar	1½ tbsp
1½ tsp	Japanese light soy sauce	1½ tsp
3 tbsp	groundnut or sunflower oil	3 tbsp
6	scallions (spring onions)	6
2-4	skinned tomatoes (optional)	2-4

1. Chop or grind the salmon very finely. If necessary purée in a food processor to make a smooth paste.
2. Add the tomato ketchup and 2 tsp soy sauce.
3. Toast the sheets of nori briefly.
4. Make the omelettes as described in the recipe for Japanese omelette. (see page 396)
5. Place a sheet of nori on to each omelette layer and spread as smoothly as possible with salmon paste. Roll the omelettes, cut each one into 4 and place in a dish.
6. Clean the scallions (spring onions) and cut into tails (see page 35, cooking techniques). Garnish the omelettes with the tails and tomato flowers (optional).

Shiitake iri omuretsu

Japanese Omelette with Mushrooms

00.15 00.20

Serves 4 (2 omelettes)

American	Ingredients	Metric/Imperial
½ lb	mushrooms	225 g/8 oz
2-3 tbsp	groundnut oil or sunflower oil	2-3 tbsp
2	scallions (spring onions) or shallots	2
1 tsp	Japanese light soy sauce	1 tsp
1 tbsp	finely chopped chives	1 tbsp
8	eggs	8
⅔ cup	dashi or chicken bouillon (stock) (see page 356)	150 ml/¼ pint
1½ tbsp	mirin, sake or dry sherry with 1 tsp sugar	1½ tbsp
	salt	
1½ tsp	Japanese light soy sauce	1½ tsp
3 tbsp	groundnut or sunflower oil	3 tbsp
	mushrooms caps (optional)	
	watercress (optional)	

1. Wipe the mushrooms clean with a damp cloth. Trim the stalks and chop or grind the mushrooms very finely.
2. Heat 2-3 tbsp oil in a wok and stir fry the onions until transparent. Add the mushrooms and stir fry over very moderate heat for 1 minute. Remove from the heat.
3. Add 1 tsp soy sauce and the chives. Cool slightly then stir through a fine strainer to a fairly smooth paste.
4. Make the omelettes as described in the recipe for Japanese omelette. (see page 396). Before rolling the layers spread with a thin coating of the mushroom paste. Roll up in a bamboo mat or linen napkin, leave to stand for 10 minutes.
5. Cut each omelette into 4 equal pieces and arrange on a dish. Garnish with mushrooms caps and sprigs of watercress.

Adzji tsulie gohan iri omuretsu

Japanese Omelette with Spiced Rice

00.15 00.20

Serves 4 (2 omelettes)

American	Ingredients	Metric/Imperial
2 cups	boiled short grain rice (see page 364)	125 g/4 oz
2 tbsp	mirin, Chinese rice wine or dry sherry with 1 tsp sugar	2 tbsp
2 tsp	Japanese light soy sauce	2 tsp
	salt (optional)	
24	spinach leaves	24
8	eggs	8
⅔ cup	dashi or light chicken bouillon (stock) (see page 356)	150 ml/¼ pint
	pinch of salt	
1½ tbsp	mirin, sake or dry sherry with 1 tsp sugar	1½ tbsp
1½ tsp	Japanese light soy sauce	1½ tsp
3 tbsp	groundnut or sunflower oil	3 tbsp
4	scallions (spring onions) cut into tails (optional)	4

1. Place the rice into a small pan, add 4 tbsp boiling water, 2 tbsp mirin or substitute, soy sauce, sugar and a pinch of salt and bring to the boil. Stir vigorously and simmer over very moderate heat until the rice has become slightly slushy. Cool, then purée the rice in a food processor.
2. Rinse the spinach leaves and remove the stalks. Steam the leaves over boiling water for 2 minutes. Dry the leaves, one at a time, with kitchen paper.
3. Make the omelettes as described in the recipe for Japanese omelette (see page 396).
4. Place 4 spinach leaves on to each layer of omelette, covering the whole surface, if necessary cut the spinach leaves to size. Spread a thin layer of the rice filling over the spinach. Roll up the layers in bamboo mats or linen napkins, leave to stand for 10 minutes. Cut each omelette into 4 equal pieces.
5. Place on a dish and garnish with tails of scallions (spring onions), (optional).

Tamago dofu
Steamed Omelette

00.05
Serves 4

00.40

American	Ingredients	Metric/Imperial
6	eggs	6
2¼ cups	dashi or chicken bouillon (stock) (see page 356)	500 ml/18 fl oz
3 tbsp	mirin, rice wine or dry sherry with 2 tsp sugar	3 tbsp
1	pinch of salt	1
3 tbsp	Japanese light soy sauce	3 tbsp
1 cup	dashi	250 ml/8 fl oz
3 tbsp	mirin, rice wine or dry sherry with 2 tsp sugar	3 tbsp
3 tbsp	Japanese light soy sauce	3 tbsp
1 oz	dried bonito flakes	25 g/1 oz
	grated lemon zest or chopped chives	

1. Carefully beat the eggs, not allowing them to become frothy.

2. Add 2¼ cups (500 ml/18 fl oz) dashi, mirin or substitute, salt and soy sauce. Stir well.

3. Line a rectangular baking tin 8 in (20 cm) wide with a piece of muslin. Pour the egg mixture into the tin and cover with aluminum foil. Make a small opening (½ in (1.25 cm)) in the center of the foil to enable the steam to escape.

4. Preheat the oven to 180°C/350°F/Gas Mark 4. Place the baking tin into a close fitting pan or roaster and pour enough water into it surround the tin. Place the pan or roaster on to a grid in the oven and cook for 30-35 minutes. To test whether the omelette is cooked pierce the center with a metal skewer, if the skewer emerges clean, the omelette is ready. Remove the baking tin from the oven and leave to cool. Carefully, lift the steamed omelette out of the tin and place on a plate. Cover with a second plate and turn the omelette.

5. Remove the muslin. Cut the omelette into 4 pieces and transfer to warmed plates.

6. In a small pan bring the dashi, remaining mirin, rice wine or sherry and light soy sauce to the boil.

7. Add the bonito flakes and bring back to the boil. Strain the sauce and spoon over each piece of steamed omelette. Garnish with grated lemon zest or chopped chives.

Left to right: Steamed omelette, Steamed omelette with crab, Steamed omelette with mushrooms

Kani no tamago mushi

Steamed Omelette with Crab

00.10 Serves 4 00.20

American	Ingredients	Metric/Imperial
1-2 tsp	*sesame oil*	*1-2 tsp*
¼ lb	*crabmeat, drained if canned, thawed if frozen*	*125 g/4 oz*
2	*finely chopped scallions (spring onions)*	*2*
1 tbsp	*Japanese light soy sauce*	*1 tbsp*
1 tbsp	*mirin, Chinese rice wine or dry sherry with ½ tsp sugar*	*1 tbsp*
6	*eggs*	*6*
5 tbsp	*dashi or light chicken bouillon (stock) (see page 356)*	*5 tbsp*
1 tbsp	*Japanese light soy sauce*	*1 tbsp*
½ tsp	*sugar*	*½ tsp*
	salt	
4	*light green lettuce leaves*	*4*
1	*lemon or lime, cut in to 4*	*1*

1. Brush the inside of 4 deep cups or flan cases with sesame oil.
2. Pick over the crabmeat, break into flakes and divide between the cups or flan cases.
3. Sprinkle with the scallion (spring onion) and then with a mixture of 1 tbsp soy sauce and 1 tbsp of mirin or substitute with sugar.
4. Beat the eggs in a bowl. Add the dashi, 1 tbsp soy sauce, ½ tsp sugar and a pinch of salt. Beat vigorously with a small whisk. Pour an equal amount of this mixture into each of the cups or flan cases and cover with aluminum foil. Make small holes in the foil to release the steam.
5. Place the flan cases in a steamer and steam for 20 minutes. Carefully, turn the omelettes on to warmed plates and garnish with lettuce leaves or lemon or lime quarters.

Chawan mushi

Steamed Omelette with Mushrooms

00.10 plus standing time 00.20

American	Ingredients	Metric/Imperial
1-2 tsp	*sesame oil*	*1-2 tsp*
¼ lb	*cleaned and finely chopped mushrooms*	*125 g/4 oz*
3 oz	*finely chopped chicken breast fillet*	*75 g/3 oz*
1 tsp	*sake*	*1 tsp*
1 tbsp	*Japanese light soy sauce*	*1 tbsp*
	salt	
2 tsp	*mirin, Chinese rice wine or dry sherry with a pinch of sugar*	*2 tsp*
6	*eggs*	*6*
5 tbsp	*dashi or chicken bouillon (stock) (see page 356)*	*5 tbsp*
1 tbsp	*Japanese light soy sauce*	*1 tbsp*
1 tbsp	*mirin, Chinese rice wine or dry sherry with ½ tsp sugar*	*1 tbsp*
	pinch of salt	
4	*small tomatoes, (optional)*	*4*

1. Brush the inside of 4 deep cups or flan cases with sesame oil.
2. In a bowl, mix the chopped mushrooms, chopped chicken, sake, 1 tbsp soy sauce, a pinch of salt and 2 tsp mirin or substitute with sugar. Leave to stand for 15 minutes. Stir well.
3. Beat the eggs in a bowl. Add the dashi, 1 tbsp soy sauce, 1 tbsp mirin or substitute with sugar and a pinch of salt. Beat thoroughly again.
4. Divide the mushroom mixture the cups or flan cases. Spoon an equal amount of the egg mixture into the cups or cases and cover with aluminum foil. Make small openings in the foil to release the steam.
5. Place in a steamer and steam for about 20 minutes.
6. Carefully turn the omelettes out of the cases on to small warmed plates. Garnish with tomatoes cut into "flowers."

Broccoli no tamago mushi

Steamed Omelette with Broccoli

⊐ 00.10
Serves 4

00.40

American	Ingredients	Metric/Imperial
6	eggs	6
⅔ cup	dashi or chicken bouillon (stock) (see page 356)	150 ml/¼ pint
3 tbsp	mirin, Chinese rice wine or dry sherry with 2 tsp sugar	3 tbsp
	pinch of salt	
3 tbsp	Japanese light soy sauce	3 tbsp
1 cup	dashi or chicken bouillon	250 ml/8 fl oz
3 tbsp	mirin, Chinese rice wine or dry sherry with 2 tsp sugar	3 tbsp
3 tbsp	Japanese light soy sauce	3 tbsp
½ lb	broccoli	225 g/8 oz
	salt	
1 tsp	mirin, Chinese rice wine or dry sherry with a pinch of sugar	1 tsp
1 tsp	Japanese light soy sauce	1 tsp
	a few drops of lemon juice	
4	cherry tomatoes (optional)	4

1. Prepare the steamed omelette and sauce as described in the recipe on page 398.
2. Rinse the broccoli and divide into small florets. Cut the broccoli stalks into ½ in (1.25 cm) pieces. Cook the broccoli stalks in boiling salted water for 5 minutes. Remove from the water and drain thoroughly in a colander. Add the broccoli florets to the same liquid, bring back to the boil and cook for 4 minutes. Drain thoroughly in a colander.
3. Just before covering with the aluminum foil sprinkle the egg mixture with the broccoli florets. Reserve a few for garnishing.
4. Rub the pieces of broccoli stalk through a fine strainer.
5. Add the remaining mirin or substitute with sugar, soy sauce, lemon juice and a pinch of salt and stir well.
6. After removing the omelette from the tin and removing the muslin, cut into 8 equal pieces.
7. Transfer the (double) pieces of steamed omelette to warmed plates and pour some sauce over each piece. Garnish with the reserved broccoli florets or with cherry tomatoes.

Kamaboko no tamago mushi

Steamed Omelette with Fish Paste

⊐ 00.05
Serves 4

00.40

American	Ingredients	Metric/Imperial
6	eggs	6
2¼ cups	dashi or light chicken bouillon (stock) (see page 356)	500 ml/18 fl oz
3 tbsp	mirin, Chinese rice wine or dry sherry with 2 tsp sugar	3 tbsp
	pinch of salt	
3 tbsp	Japanese light soy sauce	3 tbsp
1 cup	dashi	250 ml/8 fl oz
3 tbsp	mirin, Chinese rice wine or dry sherry with 2 tsp sugar	3 tbsp
3 tbsp	Japanese light soy sauce	3 tbsp
6 oz	sea fish fillets (turbot brill or halibut)	175 g/6 oz
2 tbsp	mirin, Chinese rice wine or dry sherry with 2 tsp sugar	2 tbsp
2 tsp	lemon juice	2 tsp
	salt	
	piece of leek, cut into rings or plumes	

1. Prepare the steamed omelette as described in the previous recipe.
2. Chop or grind (mince) the fish very finely.
3. Add 2 tbsp mirin or substitute, lemon juice and salt and stir well. Rub this mixture through a fine strainer, or use a food processor, to make a smooth paste.
4. Prepare the sauce also as described in the previous recipe.
5. Cut the omelette into 8 equal pieces. Spread 4 of these with the fish mixture and cover with the remaining pieces. Transfer the (double) pieces of omelette on to 4 warmed plates and pour the sauce over. Garnish, with rings or plumes of leeks (see page 35 cooking techniques).

Steamed omelette with broccoli

Takara mushi
Steamed Pumpkin

	00.10	01.00
	plus standing time	

American	Ingredients	Metric/Imperial
1 (3½ lb)	pumpkin	1 (1.5 kg/ 3½ lb)
2 tbsp	sake	2 tbsp
1 tsp	salt	1 tsp
6	eggs	6
5 tbsp	skimmed bouillon (stock) (see page 356)	5 tbsp
1 tsp	Japanese light soy sauce	1 tsp
1 tbsp	sugar	1 tbsp
¼ lb	cleaned and finely chopped mushrooms	125 g/4 oz
¼ lb	ground (minced) or finely chopped chicken breast fillet	125 g/4 oz
2 oz	ground (minced) or finely chopped raw ham	50 g/2 oz
2 oz	fresh or frozen peas	50 g/2 oz

1. Cut the top off the pumpkin. With a spoon, remove the seeds and a small amount of the soft flesh. Drain as much of the pumpkin juice as possible.
2. Mix the sake and salt in a small bowl, stirring until the salt has dissolved. Sprinkle over the pumpkin flesh and leave to stand for 30 minutes.
3. Bring several quarts/litres water to the boil in a large steamer. Place the pumpkin in the steamer with the opening facing downward and steam for 8-10 minutes. Remove the pumpkin and turn it over.
4. Beat the eggs in a bowl. Add the bouillon (stock), soy sauce and sugar and beat vigorously with a small whisk.
5. Mix the mushroom, chicken and ham in a bowl. Add a pinch of salt if necessary.
6. Fill the pumpkin with the mushroom mixture. Sprinkle with the peas and add the egg mixture. Stir, replace the top of the pumpkin and put the pumpkin in the steamer with the opening upward. Steam for 40-50 minutes.
7. Remove the top of the pumpkin and test the egg mixture has set with a skewer. The egg mixture has set if the skewer emerges clean.
8. Cut the pumpkin into 4 pieces and transfer to warmed plates.
9. Serve boiled rice or spiced rice separately.

Cook's tip: allow the fruit and its filling (such a pumpkin is suitable as a starter for 6 to 8 people) to cool off completely if you wish to serve it cold. Place the pumpkin in the refrigerator for 1 hour. Pumpkins can also be filled with other ingredients, provided that the instructions in the previous recipe are followed. For example, assuming a small pumpkin 3½ lb (1.5 kg) is used it can be filled
- with ½ lb/225 g coarsely grated cucumber and ½ lb/225 g chopped crabmeat or shrimp (prawns).
- with ¾ lb/350 g cooked and chopped oysters or mussels.
- with ¾ lb/350 g coarsely flaked salmon fillet and chopped scallions (spring onions) or leek.
- with ¼ lb/125 g quartered mushrooms and 3 oz/75 g finely diced, cooked ham. Add a mixture of 6 eggs, chicken bouillon (stock), soy sauce and sugar to the filling.

Hakusai tofu
Soybean Curd (Tofu) with Chinese Leaves

	00.05	00.00
	plus chilling time	

American	Ingredients	Metric/Imperial
½ lb	soybean curd (tofu)	225 g/8 oz
2	scallions (spring onions)	2
1 tbsp	finely grated fresh root ginger	1 tbsp
2 tbsp	Japanese light soy sauce	2 tbsp
2 tbsp	dashi (see page 356)	2 tbsp
2 tbsp	sake, mirin or dry sherry with 1 tsp sugar	2 tbsp
1	large Chinese leaf or 2 paksoi leaves, stalks cut into very thin strips	1

1. Chill the soybean curd (tofu) for at least 1 hour.
2. Cut the scallions (spring onions) into thin rings, chop 1 tbsp of these very finely.
3. Mix the scallions (spring onions) root ginger, soy sauce, dashi, sake, mirin or dry sherry with sugar, to a smooth paste.
4. Cut the tofu into 8 long pieces. Place 2 pieces on each plate and spoon a little paste on to each piece.
5. Divide the strips of Chinese leaves or paksoi over the dishes and sprinkle with the remaining scallions (spring onions). Serve as cold as possible.

Ao-togarashi tofu
Soybean Curd (Tofu) with Bell Pepper

	00.10	00.06
	Serves 4	

American	Ingredients	Metric/Imperial
2 (½ lb)	cakes soybean curd (tofu)	2 (225 g/8 oz)
3-4	medium size bell peppers	3-4
4	scallions (spring onions) or green shallots	4
2½ cups	chicken bouillon (stock)	600 ml/1 pint
3 tbsp	Japanese light soy sauce	3 tbsp
2 tbsp	sake	2 tbsp
2 tbsp	mirin or dry sherry with ½ tsp sugar	2 tbsp
4	eggs	4

1. Cut the soybean curd (tofu) into ¾ in (1.75 cm) cubes.
2. Rinse and trim the bell peppers. Halve and seed them and cut the flesh into thin strips.
3. Shred the scallions (spring onions) or green shallots.
4. Bring the bouillon (stock) to the boil, adding salt to taste. Add the soybean curd (tofu) and boil for 3 minutes.
5. Add the bell pepper and after 2 minutes the soy sauce, sake, mirin or dry sherry and sugar. Bring back to the boil.
6. Sprinkle the contents of the pan with half the scallions (spring onions) or green shallots and stir well.
7. Transfer to 4 shallow bowls. Break an egg into each bowl.
8. Sprinkle the remaining scallions (spring onions) or shallots around the yolk and serve immediately.

Gomoku tofu
Vegetables with Soybean Curd (Tofu)

00.06 — Serves 4

00.10

American	Ingredients	Metric/Imperial
¼ lb	young carrots	125 g/4 oz
½ lb	mushrooms	225 g/8 oz
½ lb	soybean curd (tofu)	225 g/8 oz
2 tbsp	Japanese light soy sauce	2 tbsp
2 tbsp	Japanese dark soy sauce	2 tbsp
2 tbsp	sake	2 tbsp
2 tbsp	mirin or dry sherry with 1 tsp sugar	2 tbsp
½ tbsp	white sugar	½ tbsp
4 tbsp	dashi or chicken bouillon (stock) (see page 356)	4 tbsp
¼ lb	cooked corn kernels	125 g/4 oz
¼ lb	cooked peas	125 g/4 oz
2 tbsp	lightly dry roasted sesame seeds	2 tbsp

1. Scrape the carrots and cut into 1 in (2.5 cm) julienne strips.
2. Wipe the mushrooms with a damp cloth or kitchen paper. Trim the stalks and cut the mushrooms into slices then thin strips.
3. Bring ¾ cup (200 ml/7 fl oz) water to the boil. Boil the carrots for 1 minute. Drain and cool in a strainer or colander.
4. Place the soybean curd (tofu) in a pan with boiling water. Boil for 3 minutes, then place the soybean curd (tofu) in a fine strainer. Drain and cool until completely cold. Rub it through the strainer and mix with both soy sauces, sake, mirin or sherry and sugar. Stir vigorously.
5. Bring the dashi or chicken bouillon (stock) to the boil in a pan. Add the carrots, mushrooms, drained corn and peas. Bring back to the boil and stir continuously until the bouillon (stock) has almost completely evaporated.
6. Divide the vegetables between 4 warmed plates and arrange the soybean curd (tofu) mixture next to it.
7. Sprinkle the sesame seeds over the vegetables and serve.

Tori no gomoku tofu
Soybean Curd (Tofu) with Chicken and Vegetables

00.10 — plus standing time

00.06

American	Ingredients	Metric/Imperial
2 (½ lb)	cakes soybean curd (tofu)	2 (225 g/8 oz)
¼ lb	chicken breast fillet	125 g/4 oz
4	dried Japanese mushrooms (shiitake)	4
4	scallions (spring onions) or green shallots	4
12	spinach leaves	12
1	egg	1
2 tbsp	Japanese light soy sauce	2 tbsp
2 tbsp	Japanese dark soy sauce	2 tbsp
2 tbsp	sake, mirin or dry sherry with 1 tsp sugar	2 tbsp
3-4 tbsp	sunflower oil or corn oil few celery leaves	3-4 tbsp

1. Cut the soybean curd (tofu) into ½ in (1.25 cm) cubes.
2. Chop or grind (mince) the chicken very finely.
3. Place the mushrooms in a bowl with boiling water to just cover. Leave to soak for 30 minutes. Remove them from the soaking liquid and reserve 3 tbsp. Discard the mushroom stalks and cut the caps into thin strips.
4. Cut the scallions (spring onions) or green shallots into 1 in (2.5 cm) pieces.
5. Rinse the spinach leaves and dry with kitchen paper.
6. Beat the egg and add both soy sauces, the sake, mirin or dry sherry with sugar.
7. Heat the oil in a frying pan or wok.
8. Add the chicken strips and stir fry until the chicken changes color.
9. Add the spinach leaves and scallions (spring onions) or shallots. Stir carefully and add the cubes of soybean curd (tofu). Stir fry over moderate heat until lightly colored.
10. Add the egg mixture and the mushrooms. Remove from the heat and stir well. Place the pan over very moderate heat

and continue stirring until the egg mixture has nearly set.
11. Serve in a warmed dish, garnished with celery leaves.
Cook's tip: in small individual bowls, serve separately a sauce of 2 parts Japanese light soy sauce mixed with 1 part sake, mirin or dry sherry and a pinch of fine (Japanese) wasabi.

Ebi no shiitake tofu

Fried Soybean Curd (Tofu) with Shrimp (Prawns) and Mushrooms

	00.12 Serves 4	00.06

American	Ingredients	Metric/Imperial
2 (½ lb)	cakes soybean curd (tofu)	2 (225 g/8 oz)
1	small green bell pepper	1
¼ lb	Japanese mushrooms (shiitake) or small mushrooms	125 g/4 oz
2	young carrots	2
1	egg white	1
1 tbsp	rice flour or cornstarch (cornflour)	1 tbsp
2 tbsp	light Japanese soy sauce	2 tbsp
1 tbsp	sake	1 tbsp
1 tbsp	mirin or dry sherry with ½ tsp sugar	1 tbsp
¼ lb	fresh peeled shrimp (prawns)	125 g/4 oz
1 tbsp	rice or cider vinegar	1 tbsp
2 tbsp	Japanese dark soy sauce	2 tbsp
4-5 tbsp	sunflower oil or corn oil	4-5 tbsp

1. Place the soybean curd (tofu) cakes on a piece of muslin. Fold the sides of the cloth over and with the flat of the hand press out as much liquid as possible. Cut each cake into 4 equal pieces.
2. Rinse and trim the bell pepper. Halve and seed it and cut the flesh into very thin strips, 2 in (5 cm) long.
3. Wipe the mushrooms with a damp cloth or kitchen paper. Trim the stalks, slice thinly, then cut the slices into thin strips
4. Scrape the carrots and cut obliquely into slices and then into thin strips.
5. Beat the egg white in a bowl until frothy. Add the rice flour or cornstarch (cornflour), 2 tbsp light soy sauce, sake and the mirin or dry sherry with sugar. Stir until smooth.
6. Stir in the bell pepper, mushrooms, carrots and shrimp (prawns) lightly.
7. Add the rice or cider vinegar to the dark soy sauce and divide this mixture between 4 individual bowls.
8. Spread the shrimp (prawn) mixture evenly over each piece of soybean curd (tofu). Leave to stand for 2-3 minutes.
9. Heat 2-3 tbsp oil in a frying pan or wok.
10. Place the soybean curd (tofu) pieces into the pan carefully, with the shrimp (prawn) mixture facing down. Fry for 3 minutes over moderate heat. Turn the pieces carefully with a spatula or a fish-slice.
11. Add the remaining oil and fry the pieces of soybean curd (tofu) for 2 minutes.
12. Divide the pieces between 4 warmed plates and serve bowls with the slightly sour soy sauce separately.

Left to right: Fried soybean curd (tofu) with shrimp (prawns) and mushrooms, soybean curd (tofu) with chicken and vegetables, Vegetables with soybean curd (tofu).

Chikuzen-ni
Chikuzen Chicken with Vegetables

◖▷ OO. 1O   OO. 1O ⬢
         plus soaking time

American	Ingredients	Metric/Imperial
1 lb	chicken breast fillets	450 g/1 lb
4	large dried Japanese mushrooms or (shiitake)	4
1 cup	chicken bouillon (stock) (see page 356)	250 ml/8 fl oz
¼ lb	canned, drained bamboo shoots	125 g/4 oz
2 tbsp	sunflower oil or corn oil	2 tbsp
3 tbsp	Japanese light soy sauce	3 tbsp
2 tbsp	Japanese dark soy sauce	2 tbsp
1 tbsp	sake	1 tbsp
1 tbsp	sugar	1 tbsp
3 oz	cooked snow peas (mange-tout)	75 g/3 oz

1. Dry the chicken with kitchen paper and cut into ¾ in (1.75 cm) cubes.
2. Place the mushrooms in a bowl with boiling water to just cover. Soak for 30 minutes. Discard the stalks and cut the caps into thin strips. Strain the soaking liquid through a piece of wet muslin.
3. Add the liquid to the bouillon (stock).
4. Cut the bamboo shoots into thin strips.
5. Heat the oil in a frying pan or wok and stir fry the chicken cubes for 2 minutes.
6. Add the mushrooms and after 2 minutes the bamboo shoots.
7. Stir well, then add the bouillon (stock) with the mushroom soaking liquid. Simmer over moderate heat until the liquid is reduced to ¼ of the original quantity.
8. Add both soy sauces, sake, sugar and snow peas (mange-tout). Stir well.
9. Transfer to warmed bowls and serve.

Tori jibu-ni
Braised Chicken with Chinese leaves

◖▷ OO. 1O   OO. 12 ⬢
         Serves 4

American	Ingredients	Metric/Imperial
1 lb	chicken breast fillets	450 g/1 lb
2 tbsp	sieved flour	2 tbsp
1	small head of Chinese leaves	1
	salt	
1 cup	dashi or chicken bouillon (see page 356)	250 ml/8 fl oz
6 tbsp	Japanese light soy sauce	6 tbsp
6 tbsp	mirin or dry sherry with 2 tbsp sugar	6 tbsp
1 tbsp	white sugar	1 tbsp
1-2 tsp	finely grated fresh root ginger	1-2 tsp

1. Dry the chicken with kitchen paper and cut into slices 2 in (5 cm) long, ¼ in (5 mm) thick.

Chikuzen chicken with vegetables

2. Dip each slice into the flour and shake off any excess.
3. Blanch 6 good Chinese leaves for 3 minutes in slightly salted water. Rinse under running cold water and drain. Place the leaves on top of each other, cut them widthwise into 4 equal pieces. Then cut them lengthwise into 4 pieces. Trim away the stalk if it is too thick. Put the Chinese leaves on to the bottom of a pan.
4. In another pan, bring the bouillon (stock), soy sauce and mirin or dry sherry with sugar to the boil. Dissolve the sugar. Pour half of this mixture into the pan containing the Chinese leaves and bring to the boil.
5. Add the chicken slices and simmer for 5-6 minutes, stirring and shaking the pan ocassionally, so that the chicken absorbs most of the liquid.
6. Divide the batches of Chinese leaves between 4 small warmed plates. Place the cooked chicken slices next to them.
7. Sprinkle the chicken with a finely grated root ginger and serve.

Torigan-ni
Chicken Balls in Ginger Sauce

◖▷ O. 1O   OO. 3O ⬢
         Serves 4

American	Ingredients	Metric/Imperial
¾ lb	chicken breast fillets	350 g/12 oz
3 oz	sea fish fillets (turbot, sole or brill)	75 g/3 oz
2	beaten eggs	2
½-1 tsp	salt	½-1 tsp
3 tbsp	sake	3 tbsp
4 tbsp	Japanese light soy sauce	4 tbsp
1½ tbsp	ginger syrup	1½ tbsp
1-1½ tbsp	sugar	1-1½ tbsp
2½ cups	chicken bouillon (stock)	600 ml/1 pint
2 tbsp	finely grated fresh root ginger	2 tbsp
5 tbsp	sake	5 tbsp
3 tbsp	mirin or dry sherry with ½ tsp sugar	3 tbsp
3 tbsp	Japanese light soy sauce	3 tbsp
2 tbsp	rice flour or cornstarch (cornflour)	2 tbsp

1. Purée the chicken and fish in a food processor. Rub the paste through a fine strainer.

2. Add the beaten eggs, and then the salt, 3 tbsp sake, 4 tbsp soy sauce, ginger syrup and sugar.

3. Mix thoroughly and then shape the mixture into small balls the size of walnuts.

4. Bring the bouillon (stock) to the boil, with the root ginger, 5 tbsp sake, mirin or dry sherry with sugar, and 3 tbsp soy sauce.

5. Add the chicken balls 5-6 at a time. Take care that the bouillon (stock) is kept at boiling point. Poach the balls until they float to the surface. Add another 5-6 balls. Continue until all the balls float on the surface. Then simmer, uncovered for 4 minutes over moderate heat.

6. Remove the balls from the pan and keep them warm.

7. Boil the bouillon (stock) quickly, reducing it to half the original quantity. Strain through muslin and bring to the boil again.

8. Mix the rice flour or cornstarch (cornflour) with 3 tbsp cold water. Stir into the bouillon (stock) and cook, stirring until the sauce thickens slightly.

9. Add the balls to the sauce and simmer for 3-5 minutes.

Butaniku no hiyashi-chiri

Summer Pork

American	Ingredients	Metric/Imperial
	00.10 Serves 4	02.40
2	large Japanese onions or 4 green shallots or 2 thin young leeks	2
2 oz	fresh root ginger	50 g/2 oz
	salt	
18 oz	boned pork loin with rim of fat	500 g/18 oz
4	chopped scallions (spring onions)	4

1. Clean the Japanese onions, green shallots or leeks and cut them into 2 in (5 cm) pieces.

2. Peel the root ginger thinly and cut into very thin slices.

3. Bring 2½ quarts (2.5 litres/4½ pints) water with a little salt added, to the boil in a suitable pan. Add the meat, bring back to the boil and simmer for 5 miniutes. Skim the surface carefully several times. Reduce the heat.

4. Add the pieces of onion, green shallot or leek and the root ginger slices. Cover the pan with a lid and braise very gently for 2½ hours. Remove the meat from the pan and rinse it quickly under running cold water until cooled. Replace it in the pan and leave to cool further in the braising liquid. Remove from the pan, drain, dry with kitchen paper and cut the meat into ¼ in (5 mm) slices.

5. Arrange the meat slices in an overlapping circle on a large flat dish.

6. Place the chopped scallions (spring onions) in the center and serve small individual bowls with ponzu sauce and wasabi separately.

Summer pork

Buta kaku-ni

Braised Pork

American	Ingredients	Metric/Imperial
	00.20 plus standing time	06.30
1 lb	smoked pork (bacon or raw ham)	450 g/1 lb
2 tbsp	sunflower oil or corn oil	2 tbsp
1 oz	fresh root ginger	25 g/1 oz
3¼ cups	dashi (see page 356)	750 ml/1¼ pints
½ cup	sake	125 ml/4 fl oz
1½ tbsp	mirin or dry sherry with 1 tsp sugar	1½ tbsp
2½ tbsp	Japanese dark soy sauce	2½ tbsp
1 tbsp	sugar	1 tbsp
6	scallions (spring onions) or shallots	6
9	snow peas (mange-tout)	9

1. Cut the smoked pork into strips 1½ in × ½ in (4 cm × 1.25 cm) ½ in (1.25 cm) thick.

2. Heat the oil in a frying pan or wok and stir fry the meat until golden brown all over.

3. Place the meat into a strainer or colander and slowly pour 2½ quarts (2.5 litres/4½ pints) boiling water over until all excess fat has been rinsed off. Drain the meat.

4. In a deep pan, bring 2 quarts (2 litres/3½ pints) water to the boil.

5. Peel the root ginger thinly and cut into thin slices.

6. Add these, together with the meat, to the boiling water. Cover the pan with a lid and reduce the heat. Simmer for 5-6 hours until the meat is very tender. Take care that the meat stays submerged while braising.

7. Remove the pan from the heat and transfer to a strainer or colander. Remove the root ginger slices. Drain the meat.

8. Place the meat in a clean pan with enough dashi to just cover. Leave to stand for 12 hours.

9. Bring the dashi to the boil, with the sake, mirin or dry sherry with sugar and soy sauce and sugar.

10. Cook the scallions (spring onions) or shallots in this liquid for 5-6 minutes. Remove and drain.

11. Cook the snow peas (mange-tout) in the same liquid for 3-5 minutes, then drain. Reserve 5 tbsp of the liquid and discard the rest.

12. Remove the meat from the pan. Add it to the contents of the second pan with the 5 tbsp reserved liquid. Bring it slowly to the boil. Simmer for 5 minutes.

13. Transfer the meat into warmed individual bowls. Arrange the scallions (spring onions) or shallots and the snow peas (mange-tout) around it and serve.

Nimame

Braised Soybeans

00.15 plus soaking time | 02.30

American	Ingredients	Metric/Imperial
1 cup	*dried soybeans*	*225 g/8 oz*
2-3	*young carrots*	*2-3*
	salt	
1 (5 in)	*piece dried seaweed (kombu)*	*1 (10 cm/5 in)*
2½ cups	*chicken bouillon (stock) (see page 356)*	*600 ml/1 pint*
1 tbsp	*sugar*	*1 tbsp*
1½-2 tbsp	*Japanese light soy sauce*	*1½-2 tbsp*
4 tbsp	*Japanese dark soy sauce*	*4 tbsp*

1. Pick over the soybeans. Rinse the beans several times in plenty of cold water and place them in a pan. Add 3 quarts (3 litres/5 pints) cold water. Soak for 12-16 hours. Discard any beans which float to the surface. Drain the beans in a strainer or colander, then rinse under plenty of cold running water.
2. Replace them in the pan with enough fresh cold water to cover well. Bring to the boil and cook steadily for 10 minutes. Drain and rinse them again under running cold water.
3. Cut the carrots lengthwise then into thin strips. Cook the carrot strips for 1-2 minutes in salted water. Rinse quickly in cold water and drain thoroughly.
4. Toast the kombu for 2 minutes then cut with a razor-sharp knife into ¼ in (5 mm) long strips and then into squares.
5. Add the squares to the bouillon (stock) and bring to the boil with a little salt, the sugar and both soy sauces.
6. Stir well and add the soybeans. Cover the pan with a lid and braise for 1½ hours. Stir well occasionally.
7. Add the carrot strips about 10 minutes before the end of the cooking time and braise in the soybean mixture until tender.
8. Serve the braised soybeans in small, warmed individual bowls.

Kinpira gobo

Braised Carrots

00.05 Serves 4 | 00.10

American	Ingredients	Metric/Imperial
12-20	*young carrots*	*12-20*
3-4 tbsp	*sunflower oil or corn oil*	*3-4 tbsp*
3 tbsp	*sake, mirin or dry sherry*	*3 tbsp*
3 tbsp	*Japanese dark soy sauce*	*3 tbsp*
2 tsp	*sugar*	*2 tsp*
½	*red chili*	*½*
	pinch seven-spice powder	

1. Select carrots of the same size. Scrape and cut into 2 in (5 cm) julienne strips.
2. Heat the oil in a frying pan or wok and stir fry the carrots for 3 minutes.
3. Add the sake, mirin or dry sherry, soy sauce and sugar.
4. Stir well and cook over very moderate heat until all the liquid has evaporated. Stir occasionally.
5. Rinse, trim and seed the chili. Cut the flesh into very thin strips. Sprinkle over the carrots and stir well.
6. Add seven-spice powder to taste.

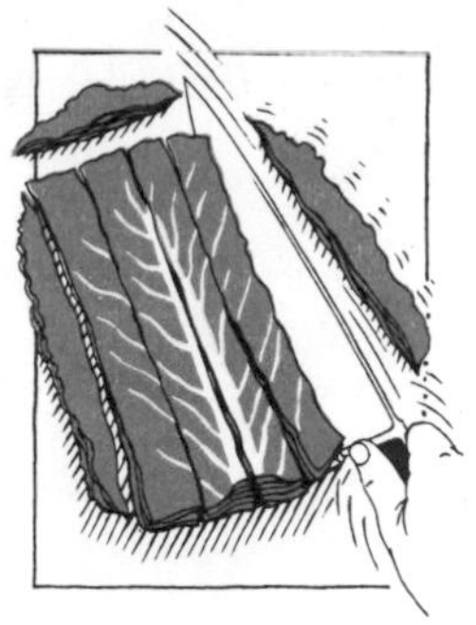

1. Lay six leaves in a stack. Trim the edges, then slice through cleanly into four pieces.

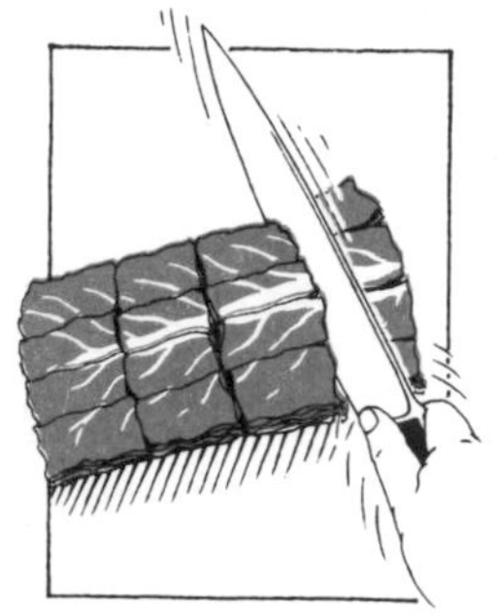

2. Hold the strips together and slice crosswise, into cubes.

7. Serve the carrots in small, individual bowls, arranged in the shape of fans.
Cook's tip: serve this dish warm or at room temperature. Slightly warmed sake in small warmed bowls is a tasty addition. Kinpira gobo can be kept in the refrigerator for 1 week.

Shiitake Kara-ni

Braised Mushrooms

00.05 plus soaking time | 00.12

American	Ingredients	Metric/Imperial
40-50	*dried Japanese mushrooms or ¼ lb (125 g/4 oz) medium size mushrooms*	*40-50*
3 tbsp	*sake*	*3 tbsp*
3 tbsp	*Japanese soy sauce*	*3 tbsp*
2	*shredded scallions (spring onions) or green shallots*	*2*

1. Soak the dried mushrooms in warm water for 4-5 hours. Strain through a piece of wet muslin and reserve the soaking liquid. Trim the stalks and cut into ¼ in (5 mm) strips.
2. Wipe fresh mushrooms with a damp cloth or kitchen paper. Trim the stalks and quarter.
3. Place the dried or fresh mushrooms in a pan with the mushroom soaking liquid or 5 tbsp water. Add the sake and soy sauce and bring to the boil. Reduce the heat, cover the pan and simmer for 7-8 minutes. Remove the lid and simmer, stirring occasionally, until almost all the liquid has evaporated.
4. Serve the mushrooms in small, individual bowls and sprinkle with a little shredded scallion (spring onion) or green shallot.

Nasu itame-ni

Fried or Braised Eggplant (Aubergine)

⬛▷ 00.10 00.30 🍲
Serves 4

American	Ingredients	Metric/Imperial
4	small or 2 large eggplants (aubergines)	4
5 tbsp	sunflower oil or corn oil	5 tbsp
1 tsp	red chili oil	1 tsp
2 cups	dashi or chicken bouillon (stock) (see page 356)	450 ml/¾ pint
1½ tbsp	sake, mirin or dry sherry with 1 tsp sugar	1½ tbsp
2½-3 tbsp	sugar	2½-3 tbsp
3-4 tbsp	Japanese dark soy sauce	3-4 tbsp

1. Rinse the eggplants (aubergines) Cut them lengthwise, then slice each half diagonally into slices ½ in (1.25 cm) thick. Dry the slices with kitchen paper.
2. Heat 1-2 tbsp oil in a large frying pan or wok.
3. Add a few drops of red chili oil, and place 2-3 slices of eggplant (aubergine) in the pan. Fry quickly for about 6 minutes over high heat until golden on both sides. Remove from the pan and drain on kitchen paper. Fry the remaining eggplant (aubergine) slices in the same way. Add a little oil.
4. Pour the dashi and chicken bouillon (stock) into a pan. Bring to the boil and add the sake, mirin or dry sherry with sugar, the sugar and the soy sauce.
5. Add the eggplant (aubergine) slices to the hot liquid. Reduce the heat and cover the pan. Simmer for 10-12 minutes.
6. Remove the lid and simmer for a further 5-7 minutes, during which time part of the liquid should evaporate.
7. Serve the eggplant (aubergine) slices arranged in shallow bowls. Pour a little of the braising liquid over them.

Nasu-ni

Fried and Braised Zucchini (Courgettes)

⬛▷ 00.05 00.25 🍲
Serves 4

American	Ingredients	Metric/Imperial
4	small or 2 large zucchini (courgettes)	4
5 tbsp	corn oil or sunflower oil	5 tbsp
1 tsp	red chili oil	1 tsp
2 cups	dashi or chicken bouillon (stock) (see page 356)	450 ml/¾ pint
1½ tbsp	mirin or dry sherry with 1 tsp sugar	1½ tbsp
3 tbsp	Japanese dark soy sauce	3 tbsp

1. Rinse the zucchini (courgettes), trim the ends and cut diagonally into ½ in (1.25 cm) slices. Arrange them into the original shape.
2. Heat 2-3 tbsp oil in a large frying pan or wok and add a few drops red chili oil.
3. Fry all the slices of 1 small zucchini (courgette) quickly for 5 minutes until golden on both sides. Drain on kitchen paper. Fry the remaining slices in the same way. Add a little oil if necessary. Drain on kitchen paper and thread onto wooden sate sticks in their original shape.
4. Bring the dashi or chicken bouillon (stock) to the boil.
5. Add the mirin or dry sherry with sugar and the soy sauce.
6. Place the sticks with the zucchini (courgette) slices in the liquid. Reduce the heat, cover the pan and simmer for 5-8 minutes. Remove the lid and simmer for a further 2-3 minutes during which time part of the liquid should evaporate.
7. Remove the zucchini (courgettes) from the pan. Transfer them, still on the sticks, to warmed plates.
8. Remove the sticks and pour 1-2 tbsp of the liquid over.

Fried and braised eggplant (aubergine)

Age tofu hakusai-ni
Braised Chinese Leaves with Soybean Curd (Tofu)

00.10 Serves 4   **00.15**

American	Ingredients	Metric/Imperial
1½	cakes soybean curd (tofu)	1½
1	small head of Chinese leaves	1
1¼ cups	dashi or chicken bouillon (stock) (see page 356)	300 ml/½ pint
2 tbsp	sake	2 tbsp
3 tbsp	Japanese light soy sauce	3 tbsp
1½ tbsp	sugar	1½ tbsp
1	Japanese onion or small leek	1
4-5 tbsp	sunflower oil or corn oil	4-5 tbsp
	few drops red chili oil	

1. Cut the cakes of soybean curd (tofu) horizontally into 2 slices. Then cut each slice into 2 equal pieces. Press out as much liquid as possible in a piece of muslin.
2. Warm the Chinese leaves and cut them into strips 1 in (2.5 cm) wide and 2 in (5 cm) long.
3. Heat the dashi or chicken bouillon (stock) and add the sake, soy sauce and sugar.
4. Clean the onion or leek and cut obliquely into 4 equal pieces.
5. Place the Chinese leaves in a pan with the bouillon (stock) and onion, or leek. Cover the pan with a lid and simmer for 2-3 minutes. Remove the lid and remove the pieces of onion or leek. Drain thoroughly in a strainer or colander.
6. Simmer the Chinese leaves for a further 4-5 minutes, during which time some of the stewing liquid should evaporate. Remove from the pan and drain well in a strainer or colander.
7. Heat the oil in a frying pan or wok. Add the red chili oil and fry the soybean curd (tofu) slices until golden on both sides.
8. Spoon a little of the leaves on to each plate or bowl. Cover with the slices of fried soybean curd (tofu) and arrange a piece of onion or leek on top.

Jaga-imo nikkorogashi
Braised Potatoes with Pork

00.07 Serves 4   **00.30**

American	Ingredients	Metric/Imperial
4	potatoes	4
1	large onion	1
4	fresh shiitake or 6 large mushrooms	4
1	medium size burdock root or 10 carrots	1
4-5 tbsp	groundnut oil or sunflower oil	4-5 tbsp
	few drops red chili oil	
4 oz	lean pork	125 g/4 oz
2½ cups	chicken bouillon (stock) (see page 356)	600 ml/1 pint
3 tbsp	Japanese dark soy sauce	3 tbsp
2½-3 tbsp	sugar	2½-3 tbsp

1. Choose potatoes of equal size. Peel and cut each into 2-3 equal pieces.
2. Clean the onion and cut it into 4-6 equal pieces and separate the layers.
3. Wipe the mushrooms with a damp cloth or kitchen paper. Discard the stalks and cut the caps into thin strips.
4. Scrape the burdock root or carrots and cut into very thin slices.
5. Heat the oil in a frying pan or wok and add a few drops red chili oil.
6. Stir fry the potato pieces for 2 minutes. Add the onion, meat and slices of burdock root or carrot. Stir until the meat has changed color and the onions are transparent.
7. Transfer to a deep pan and add the bouillon (stock), soy sauce and sugar. Bring to the boil. Cover the pan with a lid and reduce the heat. Simmer for about 15 minutes shaking the pan occasionally to baste with the braising liquid. Remove the lid and simmer for 7-8 minutes, during which some of the cooking liquid should evaporate.
8. Transfer to 4 warmed bowls and serve as hot as possible.

Jaga-imo miso-ni
Braised Potatoes in Miso

00.05 Serves 4   **00.25**

American	Ingredients	Metric/Imperial
6-8	potatoes	6-8
3½ cups	dashi or chicken bouillon (stock) (see page 356)	900 ml/1 ¼ pints
8-9 tbsp	white miso or 6 tbsp red miso	8-9 tbsp
6 tbsp	cooked peas	6 tbsp

1. Choose potatoes of similar shape. Peel and cut into 4-6 equal pieces. Bring to the boil in plenty of salted water. Boil for 10-12 minutes. Drain well.
2. Heat half the dashi or chicken bouillon (stock) and soak the miso in this.
3. Strain the mixture and add the remaining dashi or chicken bouillon (stock). Bring to the boil.
4. Add the potatoes. Cover the pan and simmer for 5 minutes over moderate heat. Remove the lid and simmer for 2-3 minutes.
5. Divide the potatoes between 4 warmed bowls.
6. Warm the peas in a little dashi or chicken bouillon (stock) and sprinkle over. Pour a little of the braising liquid over and serve.

Kiuri-ni
Braised Cucumbers

00.05 Serves 4   **00.30**

American	Ingredients	Metric/Imperial
2	medium size straight cucumbers	2
2½ cups	chicken bouillon (stock) (see page 356)	600 ml/1 pint
2 tbsp	mirin or dry sherry with 1 tsp sugar	2 tbsp
2½ tbsp	sugar	2½ tbsp
3 tbsp	Japanese light soy sauce	3 tbsp
2	dried chilies	2

1. Rinse the cucumbers and remove the ends. Cut each cucumber into 4 equal pieces and remove the seeds with an apple corer or small spoon.
2. Bring the bouillon (stock) to the boil. Add the mirin or dry sherry with sugar, the sugar and the soy sauce.
3. Add the crumbled, seeded chilies.
4. Cover the pan and simmer for 15 minutes. Strain the liquid through a piece of muslin and bring back to the boil.
5. Cut the cucumber pieces into ½ in (1.25 cm) slices. Do not sever completely.
6. Place the cucumber pieces into the liquid. Reduce the heat. Cover the pan with a lid and simmer for 7-8 minutes. Remove the lid and simmer for a further 4-5 minutes, during which time some of the liquid should evaporate. Remove the cucumber pieces from the liquid and drain.
7. Transfer to warmed bowls or plates and pull the pieces into a round shape. Spoon a few tbsp of the braising liquid over.

Cook's tip: braised cucumbers are delicious with chicken dishes.

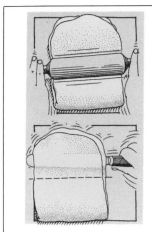

Roll the dough out then fold it over until it has a four fold thickness, trim the edges. Then with a sharp knife slice through to form long noodles.

Udon with egg

Teuchi udon

Home-made Udon

American	Ingredients	Metric/Imperial
2¼ lb	whole wheat flour	1 kg/2¼ lb
1½ oz	salt	40 g/1½ oz
2 cups	water	450 ml/¾ pint

00.15 plus standing time   00.10

1. Sieve the flour into a bowl and make a small well in the center.
2. Dissolve the salt in the water and pour into the well.
3. Stir from the middle outward and knead the mixture for 10 minutes into a firm but elastic dough. Add extra flour if the dough is not stiff enough.
4. Shape the dough into a ball and place in a bowl. Cover with a moist cloth. Leave to stand for 3-4 hours at room temperature. Moisten the cloth if it dries out.
5. Roll the dough out on a worktop or floured board until rectangular and about ¼ in (5 mm) thick.
6. Sprinkle the dough with some sieved flour and fold into 4 layers. Cut into extremely thin strips. Hang the strips on a stick or rolling pin. Leave to dry at room temperature for at least 20 minutes.
7. Cook the noodles in plenty of boiling water with salt if necessary. Add the noodles a little at a time to the boiling water and cook for 3 minutes or until 'al dente'.
8. Transfer to a colander and rinse it with cold water. Turn it over a few times with the hands and rinse again in cold water. Leave to drain.
9. Warm the noodles over steam just before serving.

Tamago udon
Udon with Egg

	00.20		00.10	
	plus standing time			

American	Ingredients	Metric/Imperial
2 ¼ lb	whole wheat flour	1 kg/2 ¼ lb
1 ½ oz	salt	40 g/1 ½ oz
2 cups	water	450 ml/¾ pint
2	egg yolks	2

1. Sieve the flour into a bowl and make a small well in in the center.
2. Dissolve the salt in the water.
3. Beat the egg yolks well with a small whisk. Add the water, beating continuously. Leave to stand for 5 minutes and stir well again.
4. Pour the egg mixture into the well in the flour and then proceed as for Home-made Udon.

Soba
Soba

	00.15		00.10	
	plus standing time			

American	Ingredients	Metric/Imperial
1 ½ lb	buckwheat flour	675 g/1 ½ lb
10 oz	whole wheat flour	275 g/10 oz
1 ½ oz	salt	30 g/1 ½ oz
2 cups	water	450 ml/¾ pint

1. Prepare the soba exactly as indicated in the recipe for udon.
2. Roll the dough into a rectangular shape with a thickness of about ¼ in (5 mm).
3. Fold into 4-5 layers and then cut into extremely thin strips.
4. Allow the strips to dry hanging from a stick or rolling pin for 20 minutes at room temperature.
Cook's tip: add egg yolks to the dough for soba, if liked. See recipe for udon with egg and do exactly as described there.

Above: Dashi bouillon (stock) for udon and soba (I), Below: Chicken bouillon (stock) for udon and soba

Cha soba
Cha Soba

	00.20		00.10	
	plus standing time			

American	Ingredients	Metric/Imperial
3 ¼ cups	water	750 ml/1 ¼ pints
2 tbsp	Japanese green tea	2 tbsp
2 ½ tsp	salt	2 ½ tsp
1 ½ lb	buckwheat flour	675 g/1 ½ lb
10 oz	whole wheat flour	250 g/10 oz

1. Bring the water to the boil. Pour 1 ¼ cups (300 ml/½ pint) boiling water into the teapot. Leave to stand for 1 minute. Remove the water from the teapot.
2. Place the tea leaves into the teapot and pour the remaining boiling water over. Leave to brew for 5 minutes.
3. Strain the tea. Dissolve the salt in the strained tea and leave to stand until completely cold.
4. Proceed as directed in the previous recipes replacing the water with the slightly salted tea.
Cook's tip: in Japan, dishes with udon, somen and soba are served in two different ways; in a bouillon (stock) or with a sauce which is used as a dipping sauce. In most cases, the warm udon or soba will be divided between the bowls at the table and the bouillon (stock) poured over. It is often left to the people at the table to sprinkle it with chopped Japanese onion, green shallot, leek or chives.

Kake-jiru (1)
Bouillon (Stock) for Udon and Soba

	00.00		00.08	
	Serves 4-6			

American	Ingredients	Metric/Imperial
1 ½ quarts	dashi (see page 356)	1.5 litres/2 ½ pints
2 tsp	salt	2 tsp
3 tbsp	Japanese light soy sauce	3 tbsp
3 tbsp	Japanese dark soy sauce	3 tbsp

Above: Tsuke-jiri (III)
Below: Tsuke-jiri (I)
Japanese dip sauce

1. Bring the dashi to the boil.
2. Add the salt and both soy sauces. Stir well and remove from the heat.
3. Strain the bouillon (stock) through a piece of wet muslin. Serve the bouillon (stock) warm or just warm.

Kake-jiru (II)
Bouillon (Stock) for Udon and Soba (II)

00.00 Serves 4-6   00.05

American	Ingredients	Metric/Imperial
1 ½ quarts	skimmed, strained chicken bouillon (stock)	1.5 litres/2 ½ pints
2 tsp	salt	2 tsp
4 tbsp	Japanese light soy sauce	4 tbsp

1. Bring the bouillon (stock) to the boil.
2. Add salt and soy sauce and stir well.
3. Remove the pan from the heat as soon as the salt has dissolved.
4. Serve the bouillon (stock) warm or just warm.

Tsuke-jiru (I)
Sauce for Udon, Soba and Somen (I)

00.02 Serves 4-6   00.05

American	Ingredients	Metric/Imperial
2 ½ cups	dashi (see page 356)	600 ml/1 pint
7 tbsp	Japanese dark soy sauce	7 tbsp
2 tbsp	mirin, sake or dry sherry with 2 tbsp sugar	2 tbsp
1 oz	dried bonito flakes	25 g/1 oz

1. Bring the dashi to the boil.
2. Add the soy sauce and mirin, sake or sherry with sugar.
3. Stir well, then sprinkle with the bonito flakes. Stir well. Immediately remove the pan from the heat.
4. Leave to stand for 10 seconds and strain the sauce through a piece of wet muslin.
5. Leave the sauce to cool to room temperature and serve in small individual bowls.

Tsuke-jiru (II)
Sauce for Udon, Soba and Somen (II)

00.05 Serves 4-6   00.08

American	Ingredients	Metric/Imperial
2 ½ cups	skimmed chicken bouillon (stock)	600 ml/1 pint
7 tbsp	Japanese dark soy sauce	7 tbsp
2 tbsp	mirin, sake or dry sherry with 2 tbsp sugar	2 tbsp
	seven-spice powder	

1. Bring the bouillon (stock) to the boil, then simmer until half the original quantity remains.
2. Add the soy sauce, mirin, sake or dry sherry with sugar and a pinch of seven-spice powder. Stir well.
3. Strain the sauce through a piece of wet muslin.
4. Serve the sauce just warm in small individual bowls.

Cook's tip: another method for preparing this sauce is to make a mixture of light and dark soy sauces, mirin, sake or dry sherry with sugar, garlic and a few drops of lemon or lime juice.

Tsuke-jiru (III)
Japanese Dip Sauce

00.05 Serves 4-6   00.00

American	Ingredients	Metric/Imperial
1-2	garlic cloves	1-2
3 tbsp	Japanese light soy sauce	3 tbsp
6 tbsp	Japanese dark soy sauce	6 tbsp
3 tbsp	mirin, sake or dry sherry with 1 ½ tbsp sugar	3 tbsp
1 tbsp	sugar	1 tbsp
½ tbsp	lime or lemon juice	½ tbsp

1. Crush the garlic and transfer on to a piece of wet muslin. Squeeze the liquid out. Exactly 1 tsp of this will be needed for the preparation of the sauce.
2. Mix the garlic juice with all other listed ingredients stirring, until the sugar has dissolved.
3. Serve the sauce in small individual bowls.

Kake udon
Udon in Bouillon (Stock)

00.05 Serves 4   00.10

American	Ingredients	Metric/Imperial
1 lb	home-made udon or ¾ lb/350 g /12 oz bought, dried udon	450 g/1 lb
4	Japanese onions or green shallots	4
1 ½ quarts	kake-jiru (see page 411)	1.5 litres/ 2 ½ pints
	seven-spice	

1. Boil home-made udon as described in the recipe on page 409. Bought udon is to be prepared as directed on the wrapper.
2. Drain the udon well in a colander after boiling. Rinse under running cold water and warm it again over steam, turning occasionally.
3. Divide the udon between large warmed soup bowls or domburi bowls.
4. Sprinkle with finely chopped onion or shallot and spoon warm bouillon (stock) over it.
5. Serve the seven-spice powder separately in tiny bowls.

Nabeyaki is a composite dish which can be treated as the base for many other dishes with udon as the main ingredient. A number of recipes follow which are all prepared in exactly the same way. The dishes should be served in small oven- proof individual bowls which can be covered with a lid.

Nabeyaki udon (I)

Udon Casserole with Salmon and Eggs

00.15 00.15
Serves 4

American	Ingredients	Metric/Imperial
1 lb	*home-made udon or ¾ lb/350 g/ 12 oz bought, dried udon*	*450 g/1 lb*
½ lb	*fresh salmon fillets*	*225 g/8 oz*
16-20	*large spinach leaves*	*16-20*
	salt	
1½ quarts	*kake-jiru (see page 411)*	*1.5 litres/ 2½ pints*
4	*eggs*	*4*

1. Boil the home-made udon as described in the recipe on page 409. Boil the dried udon exactly as indicated on the wrapper. Leave the boiled udon to drain well in a colander and then warm it over steam, turning occasionally.
2. Rinse the salmon under cold running water. Dry the fish with kitchen paper and divide into 16-20 equal pieces.
3. Rinse the spinach leaves under cold running water. Remove the stalks.
4. Sprinkle the salmon with salt. Wrap each piece of fish in a spinach leaf.
5. Divide the udon between 4 flame-proof bowls. Place the wrapped fish pieces on top and add the warm or just warm bouillon (stock). Make small wells in the center of the udon with a wooden spoon.
6. Break the eggs into the wells. Cover the bowls and cook for 2-3 minutes until the egg white has set.
7. Remove the lids from the bowls and serve immediately.

Nabeyaki udon (II)

Udon Casserole with Chicken, Mushrooms and Eggs

00.15 00.15
Serves 4

American	Ingredients	Metric/Imperial
1 lb	*home-made udon or ¾ lb/350 g/ 12 oz bought, dried udon*	*450 g/1 lb*
½ lb	*chicken breast fillets*	*225 g/8 oz*
12	*small mushrooms*	*12*
2	*chopped Japanese onions or green shallots*	*2*
½ quarts	*kake-jiru (2) (see page 411)*	*1.5 litres/2½ pints*
4	*eggs*	*4*

1. Boil home-made udon as described in the recipe on page 409. Cook bought, dried udon, as indicated on the wrapper. Leave the boiled udon to drain well in a colander and warm it again over steam, turning occasionally.
2. Dry the chicken with kitchen paper and cut into very thin strips.
3. Wipe the mushrooms with a moist cloth or a piece of kitchen paper. Trim the stalks, and quarter each mushroom.
4. Divide the udon between 4 flame-proof bowls and sprinkle with the strips of chicken, mushrooms and chopped onion or shallot. Add the warm or just warm bouillon (stock).
5. Bring slowly to the boil. Make small wells in the udon with a wooden spoon.
6. Break the eggs into the wells, cover the bowls and cook for 2-3 minutes until the egg white has set.
7. Remove the lids and serve immediately.

Nabeyaki udon (III)

Udon Casserole with Crab, Spinach and Eggs

00.15 00.15
Serves 4

American	Ingredients	Metric/Imperial
1 lb	*home-made udon or ¾ lb/350 g/ 12 oz bought, dried udon*	*450 g/1 lb*
½ lb	*crabmeat, thawed if frozen*	*225 g/8 oz*
¼ lb	*young spinach*	*125 g/4 oz*
1½ quarts	*kake-jiru (2) (see page 411)*	*1.5 litres/ 2½ pints*
4	*eggs*	*4*

1. Boil the home-made udon as described in the recipe on page 409. Cook dried udon as indicated on the wrapper. After boiling, drain in a colander and warm again over steam, turning occasionally.
2. Pick over the crabmeat and cut it into pieces.
3. Rinse the spinach in cold water. Remove the stalks. Stack 4-6 leaves on top of each other. Roll them tightly.
4. Divide the udon between 4 small flame-proof dishes and sprinkle with the pieces of crab and add the spinach rolls.
5. Pour over the warm or just warm bouillon (stock) and bring slowly to the boil. Make wells in the udon.
6. Break the eggs into the wells.
7. Cover the bowls and cook for 2-3 minutes, until the egg white has set.
8. Remove the lids and serve immediately.

Nabeyaki udon (IV)

Udon Casserole with Shrimp (Prawns) and Eggs

00.15 00.15
Serves 4

American	Ingredients	Metric/Imperial
1 lb	*home-made udon or ¾ lb/350 g/ 12 oz bought, dried udon*	*450 g/1 lb*
¼ lb	*fresh peeled shrimp (prawns)*	*125 g/4 oz*
2	*chopped Japanese onions or green shallots*	*2*
1½ quarts	*kake-jiru (1) (see page 411)*	*1.5 litres/ 2½ pints*
4	*eggs*	*4*

1. Boil home-made udon as described in the recipe on page 409. Cook dried udon as directed on the wrapper. Drain well and warm over steam, turning occasionally.

2. Divide the udon between 4 flame-proof dishes. Arrange the shrimp (prawns) on top and sprinkle with the onion or shallot.
3. Add the just warm bouillon (stock) and bring slowly to the boil. Make small wells in the udon with a wooden spoon.
4. Break an egg into the wells.
5. Cover the dishes and cook gently for 2-3 minutes, until the egg white has set.
6. Remove the lids and serve immediately.

Nabeyaki udon (VI)

Udon Casserole with Fish and Eggs

◤	00.15 Serves 4	00.15 ⌺

American	Ingredients	Metric/Imperial
1 lb	home-made udon or ¾ lb/350 g/ 12 oz bought, dried udon	450 g/1 lb
½ lb	white fish fillets (plaice, sole	225 g/8 oz
6	Japanese onions or green shallots	6
1½ quarts	kake-jiru (1) (see page 411)	1.5 litres/2½ pints
4	eggs	4

1. Boil home-made udon as described in the recipe on page 409. Cook dried udon as indicated on the wrapper.
2. Drain the udon well after boiling and warm it again over steam, turning occasionally.
3. Rinse the fish under cold running water. Dry with kitchen paper and cut them widthwise into thin strips.
4. Cut the onions or green shallots obliquely into strips the same length as the fish strips.
5. Divide the warm udon between 4 small flame-proof dishes. Arrange the strips of fish and onion over. Pour over the warm or just warm bouillon (stock).
6. Bring slowly to the boil. Make small wells in the center of the udon with a wooden spoon. Break an egg into the wells.
7. Cover the dishes and cook for a further 2-3 minutes, until the egg white has set.
8. Remove the lids from the dishes and serve immediately.

Cook's tip: add ¼ lb (125 g/4 oz) mushrooms to this dish for a variation. Cut the cleaned mushrooms into very thin slices. Sprinkle over the warm udon and add the fish and onion strips.

Nabeyaki udon (V)

Udon Casserole with Vegetables and Eggs

◤	00.15 Serves 4	00.15 ⌺

American	Ingredients	Metric/Imperial
1 lb	home-made udon or ¾ lb/350 g/ 12 oz bought, dried udon	450 g/1 lb
1	Japanese onion or medium size leek	1
¼ lb	spinach	125 g/4 oz
1	daikon (giant radish)	1
4 tbsp	cooked peas	4 tbsp
1½ quarts	kake-jiru (2) (see page 411)	1.5 litres/2½ pints
4	eggs	4

1. Boil home-made udon as described in the recipe on page 409. Prepare dried udon as instructed on the wrapper. Drain well and then warm again over steam, turning occasionally.
2. Cut the onion or leek lengthwise into very thin strips, then into pieces 2 in (5 cm) long.
3. Rinse the spinach in cold water. Drain and remove the stalks. Make stacks of 4-6 spinach leaves and roll them as tightly as possible.
4. Peel the daikon thinly and cut into very thin slices and then into strips 2 in (5 cm) long.
5. Divide the udon between 4 small flame-proof dishes. Sprinkle evenly with onion or leek, the daikon and peas and place the spinach rolls on top.
6. Pour over the warm or just warm bouillon (stock) and bring slowly to the boil. Make little wells in the udon with a wooden spoon.
7. Break an egg into each well. Cover the dishes and cook for 2-3 minutes, until the egg white has set.
8. Remove the lids and serve immediately.

Udon casserole with fish and eggs

Ankake udon (I)

Udon with Chicken, Crab and Peas

□►▽   00.15   00.20 ⌷
Serves 4

American	Ingredients	Metric/Imperial
1 lb	home-made udon or ¾ lb/350 g/ 12 oz bought, dried udon	450 g/1 lb
½ lb	chicken breast fillets	225 g/8 oz
¼ lb	crabmeat, thawed if frozen	125 g/4 oz
1½ quarts	kake-jiru (2) (see page 411)	1.5 litres/ 2½ pints
1½-2 tbsp	cornstarch (cornflour)	1½-2 tbsp
3	chopped green shallots or scallions (spring onions)	3
4 tbsp	cooked, drained peas	4 tbsp

1. Boil home-made udon as described in the recipe on page 409. Cook, dried udon as indicated on the wrapper. Drain well in a colander, then warm it again over steam, turning occasionally.
2. Dry the chicken with kitchen paper and cut it into very thin strips.
3. Pick over the crabmeat and cut into small pieces.
4. Bring the bouillon (stock) to the boil.
5. Mix the cornstarch (cornflour) with 3 tbsp cold water. Stir into the boiling bouillon (stock) and cook, stirring until it thickens slightly. Simmer for 2 minutes.
6. Divide the udon between 4 small flame-proof dishes. Sprinkle with the strips of chicken, the pieces of crab and the green shallot or scallion (spring onion).
7. Pour over the thickened bouillon (stock) and bring to the boil. Sprinkle with the peas.
8. Cover the dishes and cook for 3-4 minutes.
9. Serve the dishes, covered and remove the lids at the table.

Ankake udon (III)

Udon with Fish, Shrimp (Prawns) and Onions

□►▽   00.15   00.20 ⌷
Serves 4

American	Ingredients	Metric/Imperial
1 lb	home-made udon or ¾ lb/350 g/ 12 oz bought, dried udon	450 g/1 lb
¾ lb	white fish fillets (sole, plaice)	350 g/12 oz
1	Japanese onion or medium size leek	1
1	skinned tomato	1
1½ quarts	kake-jiru (1) (see page 411)	1.5 litres/2½ pints
1½-2 tbsp	cornflour (cornstarch)	1½-2 tbsp
¼ lb	fresh peeled shrimp (prawns)	125 g/4 oz

1. Boil home-made udon as described in the recipe on page 409. Cook dried udon as indicated on the wrapper. Drain well in a colander and warm it over steam, turning occasionally.
2. Rinse the fish under cold running water. Dry with kitchen paper and cut widthwise into thin strips.
3. Clean the onion or leek and cut lengthwise into very thin strips. Cut the strips into pieces the same length as the fish strips.

4. Halve the tomato. Remove the seed and the juice. Cut the flesh into tiny cubes.
5. Bring the bouillon (stock) to the boil. Mix the cornstarch (cornflour) with 5 tbsp cold water and stir into the boiling bouillon (stock). Cook, stirring until the bouillon (stock) has thickened.
6. Divide the udon between 4 small flame-proof dishes. Arrange the strips of fish on top and then sprinkle with the strips of onion or leek.
7. Pour over the bouillon (stock) and bring slowly to the boil. Sprinkle with the shrimp (prawns) and tomato cubes and cover the dishes. Simmer for 3-4 minutes.
8. Serve the dishes covered, remove the lids at the table.

Kitsune udon (I)

Udon with Soybean Curd (Tofu), Onion and Corn

□►▽   00.15   00.20 ⌷
Serves 4

American	Ingredients	Metric/Imperial
8 tbsp	Japanese dark soy sauce	8 tbsp
4 tbsp	mirin, sake or dry sherry with 2 tbsp sugar	4 tbsp
2-3	sheets dried soybean curd (aburage)	2-3
1 lb	home-made udon or ¾ lb/350 g/ 12 oz bought, dried udon	450 g/1 lb
1	Japanese onion or 4 scallions (spring onions) or 3 thin leeks	1
1½ quarts	kake-jiru (2) (see page 411)	1.5 litres/ 2½ pints
1½-2 tbsp	cornflour (cornstarch)	1½-2 tbsp
6 tbsp	cooked corn	6 tbsp

*Udon with soybean curd (tofu),
smoked pork and onion*

1. Bring ¾ cup (200 ml/7 fl oz) water to the boil in a small pan.
2. Add the soy sauce and mirin, sake or dry sherry with sugar. Stir, until the sugar has dissolved.
3. Reduce the heat and add the aburage. Cover the pan and simmer until most of the liquid has been absorbed by the aburage. Cut into ½ in (1.25 cm) cubes.
4. Cook the home-made udon as described on page 409. Cook the dried udon as instructed on the wrapper. Drain well in a colander and warm again over steam, turning occasionally.
5. Clean the onion, scallions (spring onions) or leeks. Cut the onion or scallions (spring onions) lengthwise into thin strips and then into 2 in (5 cm) pieces.
6. Bring the bouillon (stock) to the boil.
7. Mix the cornstarch (cornflour) with 5 tbsp cold water. Stir into the boiling bouillon (stock) and cook, stirring until the bouillon (stock) has thickened and is smooth. Simmer for 2-3 minutes.
8. Divide the udon between 4 small flame-proof dishes. Sprinkle with the cubes of soybean curd (tofu) strips of onion, scallions (spring onions) or leek and the corn.
9. Add the bouillon (stock) and cover the dishes, simmer for 4-5 minutes.
10. Serve the dishes covered and remove at the table.

Kitsune udon (III)
Udon with Soybean Curd (Tofu), Smoked Pork and Onion

	00.15 Serves 4	00.20

American	Ingredients	Metric/Imperial
3 tbsp	Japanese dark soy sauce	3 tbsp
2 tbsp	mirin, sake or dry sherry with 1 tbsp sugar	2 tbsp
1	sheet dried soybean curd (aburage)	1
1 lb	home-made udon or ¾ lb/350 g/ 12 oz bought, dried udon	450 g/1 lb
½ lb	smoked pork (raw ham)	225 g/½ lb
1	medium size Japanese onion green shallot or leek	1
1½ quarts	kake-jiru (1) (see page 411)	1.5 litres/2½ pints
1½-2 tbsp	cornstarch (cornflour)	1½-2 tbsp
2 tbsp	cooked peas	2 tbsp

1. Bring 4 tbsp water to the boil. Add the soy sauce and mirin, sake or dry sherry with sugar, stirring until the sugar has dissolved.
2. Place the sheet of aburage into the hot liquid. Reduce the heat and cover the pan and simmer until nearly all the liquid has been absorbed by the aburage.
3. Cut the aburage into ½ in (1.25 cm) cubes.
4. Cook the home-made udon as described on page 409. Cook dried udon as indicated on the wrapper. Drain and warm again over steam, turning occasionally.
5. Cut the pork into thin strips 2 in (5 cm) long.
6. Clean the onion, green shallot or leek and cut lengthwise into thin strips and then into 2 in (5 cm) pieces.

7. Bring the bouillon (stock) to the boil. Mix the cornstarch (cornflour) with 5 tbsp cold water. Cook, stirring until the bouillon (stock) is smooth and thick. Simmer for 2-3 minutes.
8. Divide the udon between 4 small flame-proof dishes. Sprinkle with the cubes of aburage, strips of pork, onion, green shallot or leek and the peas.
9. Pour over the bouillon (stock). Cover the dishes and bring slowly to the boil and simmer for 4-5 minutes.
10. Serve covered and remove the lids at the table.

Kitsune udon (II)
Udon with Soybean Curd (Tofu), Chicken and Mushrooms

	00.15 plus soaking time	00.20

American	Ingredients	Metric/Imperial
4	large dried Chinese mushrooms	4
4 tbsp	Japanese dark soy sauce	4 tbsp
2 tbsp	mirin, sake or dry sherry with 1 tbsp sugar	2 tbsp
1-1½	sheets dried soybean curd (aburage)	1-1½
1½ quarts	kake-jiru (2) (see page 411)	1.5 litres/2½ pints
¼ lb	chicken breast fillets	125 g/4 oz
1 lb	home-made udon or ¾ lb/350 g/ 12 oz bought, dried udon	450 g/1 lb
1½-2 tbsp	cornflour (cornstarch)	1½-2 tbsp
2	chopped Japanese onions or scallions (spring onions)	2

1. Put the dried mushrooms in a bowl with 1 cup (250 ml/8 fl oz) boiling water and soak for 30 minutes.
2. Bring 5 tbsp water to the boil. Add the soy sauce and mirin, sake or dry sherry with sugar, stir until the sugar has dissolved.
3. Place the sheets of aburage into the hot liquid. Reduce the heat. Cover the pan and simmer until most of the liquid has been absorbed by the aburage. Cut into into ½ in (1.25 cm) cubes.
4. Discard the mushroom stalks and cut the caps into thin strips. Strain the soaking liquid through wet muslin and add it to the kake-jiru.
5. Dry the chicken with kitchen paper and cut it into very thin strips.
6. Cook the home made udon as described on page 409. Cook dried udon as indicated on the wrapper. Drain and warm again over steam, turning occasionally.
7. Bring the bouillon (stock) to the boil.
8. Mix the cornflour (cornstarch) with 5 tbsp cold water. Stir into the bouillon (stock) and cook, stirring until the bouillon (stock) is smooth and thickened. Simmer for 2-3 minutes.
9. Divide the udon between 4 small flame-proof dishes. Sprinkle with the soybean curd (tofu) cubes, strips of chicken, mushroom and chopped onion or scallions (spring onions). Add the bouillon (stock).
10. Cover the dishes and simmer for 4-5 minutes. Serve still covered and remove the lids at the table.

Tai men

Udon with Fried Bream

American	Ingredients	Metric/Imperial
	OO. 15 *plus standing time*	OO. 1O
10 oz	home-made udon or ½ lb/225 g/ 8 oz bought, dried udon	300 g/10 oz
1½ lb	sea bream fillets	675 g/1½ lb
	salt	
3 tbsp	groundnut oil	3 tbsp
2¾ cups	Tsuke-jiru (1) (see page 411)	700 ml/1 pint
4-5	chopped green shallots or scallions (spring onions)	4-5

1. Cook home made udon according to the recipe on page 409. Cook dried udon as indicated on the wrapper. Drain well and warm again over steam, turning occasionally.
2. Rinse the fish under cold running water. Dry with kitchen paper. Rub with a little salt and leave to stand for 15 minutes.
3. Heat the oil in a frying pan or wok and fry until golden brown on both sides. Drain on kitchen paper.
4. Divide the udon between four individual flame-proof bowls and sprinkle with 5-6 tbsp warm Tsuke-jiru.
5. Cut the fish into small, equal pieces. Divide them between the udon in the bowls. Sprinkle with half the green shallots or scallions (spring onions).
6. Stir the remaining scallions (spring onions) into the remaining sauce.
7. Serve the sauce in small individual warmed bowls with the bowls with fish and udon.

Left: Udon with fried bream
Right: Udon with fried sole and root ginger

Udon with Fried Sole and Root Ginger

American	Ingredients	Metric/Imperial
	OO. 15 *plus standing time*	OO.2O
¾ lb	home-made udon or ½ lb/225 g/ 8 oz bought, dried udon	350 g/12 oz
6-8	sole fillets	6-8
	salt	
	pinch ground root ginger	
2 oz	piece fresh root ginger	50 g/2 oz
4-5 tbsp	groundnut oil	4-5 tbsp
3	drops red chili oil	3
1¾ cups	Tsuke-jiru (1) (see page 411)	400 ml/14 fl oz
4-6	chopped green shallots or scallions (spring onions)	4-6
1	skinned tomato	1

1. Cook home-made udon according to the instructions on page 409. Cook dried udon as indicated on the wrapper. Drain well in a colander and warm over steam, turning occasionally.
2. Rinse the fish under cold running water. Dry with kitchen paper. Rub lightly with salt and ground root ginger and leave to stand for 15 minutes.
3. Peel the root ginger thinly. Cut it, with a very sharp pointed knife, into paper thin slices and then into very thin strips.
4. Heat the oils in a frying pan or wok and fry the fish fillets until golden brown on both sides. Drain on kitchen paper.
5. Stir fry the strips of root ginger in the remaining oil, until golden brown. Remove from the pan and drain on kitchen paper.
6. Cut the fish obliquely into 20 equal pieces.

7. Divide the udon between four warmed bowls or deep plates. Sprinkle a few tbsp Tsuke-jiru over each bowl or plate. Sprinkle with the root ginger strips and arrange the fish pieces on top. Sprinkle with the chopped green shallot or scallion (spring onion) and garnish with tomato segments.

8. Serve the remaining Tsuke-jiru separately in small individual bowls.

Udon with Fried Mackerel and Spinach

	OO. 15 plus standing time	OO. 30

American	Ingredients	Metric/Imperial
1¼ lb	mackerel fillets	550 g/1¼ lb
	salt	
2 tbsp	lemon or lime juice	2 tbsp
½ lb	spinach	225 g/8 oz
¾ lb	home-made udon or ½ lb/225 g/ 8 oz bought, dried udon	350 g/12 oz
2	skinned tomatoes	2
4-5 tbsp	groundnut oil	4-5 tbsp
1¾ cups	Tsuke-jiru (1) (see page 411)	400 ml/14 fl oz

1. Rinse the fish under cold running water. Dry with kitchen paper. Dissolve a little salt in the lemon or lime juice and rub the mackerel fillets with this. Leave to stand for 15 minutes.

2. Rinse the spinach in cold water and drain. Remove the stalks. Make stacks of 12 leaves. Cut the stacks into thin strips.

3. Cook home-made udon according to the recipe on page 409. Cook the dried udon as indicated on the wrapper. Drain well.

4. Mix the drained udon with the strips of spinach and warm over steam, turning occasionally.

5. Halve the skinned tomatoes, remove the juice and the seed. Cut the flesh into cubes.

6. Heat the oil in a frying pan and wok and fry the mackerel fillets 2-3 at a time, until golden brown on both sides. Cut into 20 equal pieces.

7. Divide the udon with the spinach between 4 warmed bowls or deep plates.

8. Sprinkle a few tbsp Tsuke-jiru on to each bowl. Arrange the pieces of mackerel on top and sprinkle with the tomato cubes.

9. Serve the remaining Tsuke-jiru separately in individual small bowls.

Udon with fried mackerel and spinach

Ankake udon (II)
Udon with Duck, Shrimp (Prawns) and Corn

◖▷	00.15 Serves 4	00.20 ⌸
American	**Ingredients**	**Metric/Imperial**
1 lb	home-made udon or ¾ lb/350 g/ 12 oz bought, dried udon	450 g/1 lb
½ lb	lean duck breast fillets	225 g/8 oz
¼ lb	fresh peeled shrimp (prawns)	125 g/4 oz
1½-2 tbsp	cornstarch (cornflour)	1½-2 tbsp
1½ quarts	kake-jiru (2) (see page 411)	1.5 litres/ 2½ pints
3	chopped green shallots or scallions (spring onions)	3
4 tbsp	cooked, drained corn	4 tbsp
3	small mushrooms, cut into slices and then into strips	3

1. Boil the home-made udon as described in the recipe on page 409. Cook dried udon as instructed on the wrapper. Drain well and warm the udon over steam, turning occasionally.
2. Cut the duck into thin strips and the shrimp (prawns) into small pieces.
3. Mix the cornstarch (cornflour) with 3 tbsp cold water and stir into the boiling bouillon (stock). Cook, stirring until the bouillon (stock) thickens.
4. Divide the udon between 4 small flame-proof dishes and add the duck, shrimp (prawns), green shallots or scallions (spring onions) and the bouillon (stock).
5. Bring slowly to the boil and sprinkle with the corn and mushroom strips.
6. Cover the dishes and cook for 3-4 minutes.
7. Serve the dishes covered and remove the lids at the table.

Tsukimi udon (I)
Udon with Crab and Eggs

◖▷	00.15 Serves 4	00.20 ⌸
American	**Ingredients**	**Metric/Imperial**
1 lb	home-made udon or ¾ lb/350 g/ 12 oz bought, dried udon	450 g/1 lb
½ lb	crabmeat, thawed if frozen	225 g/8 oz
½ quarts	kake-jiru (1) (see page 411)	1.5 litres/2½ pints
1 tsp	Japanese red chili oil or 1 chopped red chili	1 tsp
3	chopped Japanese onions or green shallots	3
4	eggs	4

1. Cook home-made udon as described on page 409. Cook dried udon as indicated on the wrapper. Drain and warm again over steam, turning occasionally.
2. Pick over the crabmeat and cut into small pieces.
3. Bring the bouillon (stock) to the boil. Add the red chili oil or chopped chili and boil for 2-3 minutes.
4. Divide the udon between 4 small flame-proof dishes. Sprinkle with the crab and onion or green shallots. Add the bouillon (stock) and bring slowly to the boil.

5. Make small wells in the udon with a wooden spoon. Break an egg into each well.
6. Cover the dishes and simmer for 2-3 minutes, without stirring, until the egg white has set.
7. Remove the lids and serve immediately.

Tsukimi udon (II)
Udon with Salmon Strips and Eggs

◖▷	00.15 Serves 4	00.20 ⌸
American	**Ingredients**	**Metric/Imperial**
1 lb	home-made udon or ¾ lb/350 g/ 12 oz bought, dried udon	450 g/1 lb
½ lb	fresh salmon fillets	225 g/8 oz
1½ quarts	kake-jiru (2) (see page 411)	1.5 litres/2½ pints
3	chopped Japanese onions, green shallots or scallions (spring onions)	3
4	eggs	4

1. Cook home-made udon as described on page 409. Cook dried udon as indicated on the wrapper. Drain and warm again over steam, turning occasionally.
2. Rinse the fish under cold running water. Dry with kitchen paper and cut it into thin strips, 2 in (5 cm) long.
3. Bring the bouillon (stock) to the boil.
4. Divide the udon between 4 small flame-proof dishes. Sprinkle with salmon strips, chopped onion, green shallots or scallions (spring onions). Pour over the bouillon (stock). Bring to the boil slowly.
5. Make wells in the udon with a wooden spoon. Break an egg into each well.
6. Cover the dishes. Simmer for 2-3 minutes without stirring until the egg white has set.
7. Remove the lids and serve immediately.

Udon with Fried Chicken and Shrimp (Prawns)

◖▷	00.15 plus standing time	00.20 ⌸
American	**Ingredients**	**Metric/Imperial**
1 lb	chicken breast fillets	450 g/1 lb
	salt	
¾ lb	home-made udon or ½ lb/225 g/ 8 oz/ bought, dried udon	350 g/12 oz
4-5 tbsp	groundnut oil	4-5 tbsp
¼ lb	fresh peeled shrimp (prawns)	125 g/4 oz
1¾ cups	Tsuke-jiru (2) (see page 411)	400 ml/14 fl oz
3	chopped green shallots or scallions (spring onions)	3

1. Dry the chicken with kitchen paper and cut into very thin slices. Sprinkle with salt and leave to stand for 10 minutes.
2. Prepare home-made udon, according to the instructions on page 409. Cook dried udon as indicated on the wrapper. Drain well and warm it again over steam, turning occasionally.

3. Heat the oil in a frying pan or wok and stir fry the chicken slices for 2 minutes. Drain on kitchen paper.

4. Stir fry the shrimp (prawns) in the remaining oil for 1 minute. Sprinkle with a little salt if necessary and drain on kitchen paper.

5. Divide the udon between four warmed bowls or deep plates. Sprinkle with 2 tbsp Tsuke-jiru.

6. Sprinkle the shrimp (prawns) over and arrange the chicken slices on top. Sprinkle with the chopped green shallots or scallions (spring onions).

7. Serve the remaining sauce separately in small individual bowls.

Udon with Fried Ham and Mushrooms

American	Ingredients	Metric/Imperial
½ lb	raw ham	225 g/8 oz
½ lb	fresh button mushrooms	225 g/8 oz
¾ lb	home-made udon or ½ lb/225 g/ 8 oz bought, dried udon	350 g/12 oz
4-5 tbsp	groundnut oil	4-5 tbsp
	salt	
2 cups	Tsuke-jiru (2) (see page 411)	450 ml/¾ pint
3	chopped green shallots or scallions (spring onions)	3

1. Cut the ham into tiny cubes.

2. Wipe the mushrooms with a moist cloth or piece of kitchen paper. Trim the stalks and cut the mushrooms in half.

3. Prepare the home-made udon according to the recipe on page 409. Cook ready made udon as indicated on the wrapper. Drain well and warm it again over steam, turning occasionally.

4. Heat the oil in a frying pan or wok and stir fry the cubes of ham for 1 minute.

5. Add the mushrooms and stir fry for 3 minutes. Drain well.

6. Divide the udon between four warmed bowls or deep plates. Sprinkle with a few tbsp Tsuke-jiru. Sprinkle the ham and mushrooms over and the chopped green shallots or scallions (spring onions)

7. Serve the remaining Tsuke-jiru separately in small individual bowls.

Tori nanba udon

Udon with Chicken and Scallions (Spring Onions)

American	Ingredients	Metric/Imperial
1 lb	home-made udon or ¾ lb/350 g/ 12 oz bought, dried udon	450 g/1 lb
1 lb	chicken breast fillet	450 g/1 lb
8	green shallots or scallions (spring onions)	8
1 quart	kake-jiru (2) (see page 411)	1 litre/1¾ pints
	ground sansho or black pepper	

1. Cook the home-made udon according to the recipe on page 409. Cook dried udon as indicated on the wrapper. Drain well, warm again over steam, turning occasionally.

2. Dry the chicken and cut it into ½ in (1.25 cm) cubes.

3. Cut the green shallots or scallions (spring onions) into pieces 2 in (5 cm) long.

4. Bring the bouillon (stock) to the boil.

5. Divide the warm udon between 4 small individual flame-proof bowls.

6. Add the diced chicken and bouillon (stock) and simmer for about 8 minutes until the meat is tender. Skim the surface during simmering if necessary. Add the shallot or scallion (spring onion) and simmer for 1 minute. Stir occasionally.

7. Sprinkle with a little sansho or black pepper and serve.

Udon with fried ham and mushrooms

Udon with Fried Pork and Tomato

| ▬▷ | 00.15 | 00.20 🥘 |
| | Serves 4 | |

American	Ingredients	Metric/Imperial
1 lb	lean pork	450 g/1 lb
¾ lb	home-made udon or ½ lb/250 g/ 8 oz bought, dried udon	350 g/12 oz
	salt	
4-5 tbsp	groundnut oil	4-5 tbsp
3	skinned, diced tomatoes	3
1¾ cups	Tsuke-jiru (2) (see page 411)	400 ml/14 fl oz
5-6 tbsp	mirin, sake or dry sherry with 1-1½ tbsp sugar	5-6 tbsp
3	chopped green shallots or scallions (spring onions)	3

1. Dry the pork with kitchen paper and cut into thin slices.
2. Cook home made udon according to the recipe on page 409. Cook dried udon as indicated on the wrapper. Drain well and warm it again over steam, turning occasionally.
3. Sprinkle the meat slices with a little salt.
4. Heat the oil in a frying pan or wok and stir fry thr pork slices for 3 minutes. Remove from the pan with a slotted spoon and drain on kitchen paper.
5. Fry the diced tomato very briefly in the remaining oil and sprinkle with a little salt. Drain well.
6. Divide the udon between four warmed bowls or deep plates. Sprinkle with a few tbsp Tsuke-jiru mixed with the mirin, sake or sherry with sugar. Sprinkle with the diced tomato.
7. Arrange the meat slices on top and finally sprinkle with the green shallots or scallions (spring onions).
8. Serve the remaining Tsuke-jiru separately in small individual bowls.

Hiyashi somen

Somen with Shrimp (Prawns) and Mushrooms

| ▬▷ | 00.10 | 00.35 🥘 |
| | plus soaking time | |

American	Ingredients	Metric/Imperial
4	large dried Japanese mushrooms (shiitake) or Chinese mushrooms	4
3 tbsp	Japanese dark soy sauce	3 tbsp
3 tbsp	mirin, sake or dry sherry with 2 tbsp sugar	3 tbsp
4-6	large Chinese shrimp (prawns)	4-6
¼ lb	dried, bought somen	125 g/4 oz
1	small bunch watercress	1
1 cup	dashi or chicken bouillon (stock) (see page 356)	250 ml/8 fl oz
1¼ tbsp	mirin, sake or dry sherry with 1 tbsp sugar	1¼ tbsp
4-5 tbsp	Japanese dark soy sauce	4-5 tbsp

1. Put the dried mushrooms in a bowl with boiling water to just cover. Soak for 30 minutes.

2. Remove the stalks from the mushrooms. Strain the soaking liquid through wet muslin. Measure out exactly 5 tbsp and set aside.
3. Put the soaking liquid in a pan, add 3 tbsp soy sauce and 3 tbsp mirin, sake or dry sherry with the sugar and bring to the boil. Reduce the heat.
4. Place the mushroom caps into the liquid and simmer for 15 minutes. Leave to go cold.
5. Remove the mushrooms caps and cut into thin strips.
6. Bring some water to the boil in a saucepan. Add the shrimp (prawns) and keep the water just under boiling point. Cook for 3-4 minutes until pink and firm. Remove from the pan, rinse briefly under cold water and peel.
7. Cut the shrimp (prawns) lengthwise down the front, remove the black thread and flatten them slightly. Cut into ½ in (1.25 cm) pieces.
8. Prepare the somen as indicated on the wrapper. Drain well, and cool with plenty of cold water. Drain in a colander.
9. Pick over the water cress, trim, rinse and dry.
10. Divide the somen between four plates. Arrange the watercress at the sides, and the shrimp (prawns) and mushroom strips on top of the somen.
11. Put the dashi, remaining mirin, sake or dry sherry and remaining soy sauce in a pan and warm through. Leave to go cold. Serve the sauce separately in small bowls.

Torisomen

Somen with Chicken and Bell Peppers

| ▬▷ | 00.10 | 00.25 🥘 |
| | Serves 4 | |

American	Ingredients	Metric/Imperial
1 lb	chicken breast fillets	450 g/1 lb
	salt	
4 tbsp	groundnut oil	4 tbsp
¼ lb	dried, bought somen	125 g/4 oz
1	green bell pepper	1
1	red bell pepper	1
6 tbsp	chicken bouillon (stock) (see page 356)	6 tbsp
3 tbsp	Japanese light soy sauce	3 tbsp
3 tbsp	mirin, sake or dry sherry with 2 tsp sugar	3 tbsp
2 tsp	grated fresh root ginger	2 tsp
	few drops red chili oil	
	sprigs celery leaves	

1. Dry the chicken with kitchen paper and cut obliquely into thin slices. Sprinkle with a little salt.
2. Heat the oil in a wok or frying pan and fry the slices quickly until golden. Drain and leave to cool.
3. Prepare the somen as indicated on the wrapper. Drain well. Cool with with plenty of cold water and drain well in a colander.
4. Rinse, trim, halve and seed the bell peppers. Cut the flesh into very thin strips 2 in (5 cm) long.
5. Bring 1¼ cups (300 ml/½ pint) water to the boil in a pan. Add ½ tsp salt. Add the bell pepper strips and cook for 1½ minutes. Drain well and leave to cool.
6. Put the bouillon (stock), soy sauce, mirin, sake or dry sherry with sugar, root ginger and red chili oil into a saucepan. Bring slowly to the boil. Leave to cool.

Somen with salmon and daikon

7. Divide the somen between 4 small plates. Sprinkle with the bell pepper strips and arrange the chicken slices round it. Garnish with the celery leaves.
8. Serve the sauce separately in small individual bowls.

Sakesomen
Somen with Salmon and Daikon

▬▬◤ 00.10   00.25 🍲
plus chilling time

American	Ingredients	Metric/Imperial
1 lb	fresh salmon fillets	450 g/1 lb
	salt	
1 (3 oz)	piece daikon (giant radish)	1 (75 g/3 oz)
1 (3 oz)	piece cucumber	1 (75 g/3 oz)
¼ lb	dried, bought, somen	25 g/4 oz
6 tbsp	dashi (see page 356)	6 tbsp
2 tbsp	Japanese light soy sauce	2 tbsp
2 tbsp	Japanese dark soy sauce	2 tbsp
4 tbsp	mirin, sake or dry sherry with 2-3 tsp white sugar	4 tbsp
2 tsp	grated fresh root ginger	2 tsp
2	chopped green shallots or scallions (spring onions)	2
4	skinned tomatoes	4

1. Cut the salmon into very thin slices. Sprinkle with a little salt. Make stacks of 6 slices of salmon. Place a small board on to the salmon stacks and put a weight on top of the board. Cover with aluminum foil and chill for 1 hour.
2. Peel the daikon thinly and cut into thin slices and then into thin strips 1 in (2.5 cm) long.
3. Rinse the cucumber and cut obliquely into slices. Sprinkle with some salt and drain well in a colander, turning occasionally.
4. Prepare the somen as indicated on the wrapper. Drain well and cool with plenty of cold water. Drain well in a colander.
5. Put the dashi, soy sauces, mirin, sake or sherry with sugar and root ginger into a small pan. Bring slowly to the boil. Stir well and leave the sauce to get cold.
6. Cut the pressed salmon into extremely thin strips.
7. Divide the somen between 4 plates. Sprinkle with the salmon, daikon and the green shallots or scallions (spring onions).
8. Arrange the cucumber slices on the side and garnish with a tomato "flower".
9. Serve the sauce separately in small individual bowls.

Tempura soba (V)
Soba with Lobster and Green Shallot

▬▬◤ 00.10   00.20 🍲
Serves 4

American	Ingredients	Metric/Imperial
1 lb	cooked lobster, divided into 12 equal pieces	450 g/1 lb
	salt	
1 lb	home-made soba or ¾ lb/350 g/ 12 oz dried, bought soba	450 g/1 lb
1 cup	all-purpose (self-raising) flour	125 g/4 oz
1	egg	1
	pinch of salt	
4 tbsp	ice cold water	4 tbsp
	oil for deep-frying	
12	green shallots or scallions (spring onions), cut into 2 in (5 cm) pieces	12
1¾ cups	Tsuke-jiru (1) (see page 411)	400 ml/14 fl oz
1	small diced red bell pepper	1
1	lemon or lime, cut into 8 segments	1

1. Dry the pieces of lobster with kitchen paper and sprinkle with some salt.
2. Prepare home-made soba according to the instruction on page 410. Cook dried soba as indicated on the wrapper. Drain well, cool with cold water, drain and warm over steam, turning occasionally.
3. Sieve the flour into a bowl. Make a small well in the flour. Beat the egg and add a pinch of salt and 3-4 tbsp ice cold water, stirring continuously. Pour this mixture into the well. Stir from the center outward until a smooth and elastic batter is formed. If necessary, add 1-2 tbsp ice cold water.
4. Heat the oil until very hot.
5. Dip the pieces of lobster into the batter. Drain briefly over the bowl and fry 3-4 at a time, until golden brown.
6. Do the same with the pieces of green shallot or scallion (spring onion). Drain on kitchen paper.
7. Bring the sauce slowly to the boil, then keep warm over low heat.
8. Divide the soba between four warmed bowls or deep plates. Pour half the sauce over the soba and arrange the pieces of lobster and green shallots or scallions (spring onions) on top. Sprinkle with the diced bell peppers.
9. Serve the remaining sauce and lemon or lime segments separately in small individual bowls.

Tempura soba (I)
Soba with Chicken and Mushrooms

	00.10 Serves 4	00.20

American	Ingredients	Metric/Imperial
1 lb	home-made soba or ¾ lb/350 g/ 12 oz dried, bought, soba	450 g/1 lb
½ lb	chicken breast fillets	225 g/8 oz
½ lb	fresh mushrooms	225 g/8 oz
	oil for deep-frying	
1 cup	all-purpose (self-raising) flour	125 g/4 oz
1	egg	1
	pinch of salt	
4 tbsp	ice cold water	4 tbsp
3¼ cups	Tsuke-jiru (2) (see page 411)	750 ml/1¼ pints
3	chopped green shallots or scallions (spring onions)	3

1. Prepare home-made soba according to the instructions on page 410. Cook dried soba as indicated on the wrapper. Drain well, cool with cold water. Drain and warm it again over steam, turning occasionally.
2. Dry the chicken with kitchen paper and cut into strips 1 in×2 in (2.5 cm×5 cm).
3. Wipe the mushrooms with a moist cloth or piece of kitchen paper. Trim the stalks.
4. Heat the oil in a frying pan.
5. Sieve the flour into a bowl. Make a small well in the flour. Beat the egg and add a pinch of salt and 4 tbsp ice cold water, stirring continuously. Pour this mixture into the well in the flour. Stir from the center outward until a smooth, elastic batter is formed.
6. Dip the chicken strips into the batter. Drain briefly over the bowl and fry 4-5 at a time, until golden brown.
7. Do exactly the same with the mushrooms.
8. Bring the sauce slowly to the boil.

9. Divide the soba between four warmed bowls. Spoon over the sauce and arrange the strips of fried chicken and the mushrooms on top. Sprinkle with the chopped green shallots or scallions (spring onions).

Tempura soba (II)
Soba with Sole and Bell Pepper

	00.10 plus standing time	00.25

American	Ingredients	Metric/Imperial
4 (1 lb)	sole fillets	4 (450 g/1 lb)
	salt	
	ground root ginger	
1	red bell pepper	1
1	green bell pepper	1
1 cup	all-purpose (self-raising) flour	125 g/4 oz
1	egg	1
	pinch of salt	
4 tbsp	ice cold water	4 tbsp
1 lb	home-made soba or ¾ lb/350 g/ 12 oz dried, bought soba	450 g/1 lb
	oil for deep frying	
3¼ cups	Tsuke-jiru (1) (see page 411)	750 ml/1¼ pints
1	bunch of watercress	1
1	lemon or lime, cut into 8 segments	1

1. Rinse the fish under cold running water and dry with kitchen paper. Cut each fillet lengthwise into 4 strips. Sprinkle with some salt and ground ginger and leave to stand for 15 minutes.
2. Rinse, trim, halve and seed the bell peppers and cut lengthwise into strips 1 in (2.5 cm) wide and 2 in (5 cm) long.
3. Sieve the flour into a bowl. Make a small well in the flour. Beat the egg and add a pinch of salt and 4 tbsp ice cold water, stirring continuously. Pour this mixture into the well and stir from the center outward until the batter is smooth and elastic. If necessary, add 1-2 tbsp ice cold water.

4. Cook home-made soba according to the instructions on page 410. Cook dried soba as is indicated on the wrapper. Drain well, cool with cold water and drain again. Warm the soba again over steam, turning occasionally.

5. Heat the oil in a wok or frying pan until very hot.

6. Dip the sole strips in the batter. Drain briefly over the bowl and then fry 4-5 at a time, until golden brown.

7. Do the same with the bell pepper strips.

8. Bring the sauce slowly to the boil.

9. Spoon the soba into four warmed bowls or deep plates. Pour half of the sauce over the soba, then arrange the strips of fish and bell pepper on top and garnish with watercress sprigs.

10. Serve the remaining sauce and lemon or lime segments separately in small individual bowls.

Tempura soba (III)
Soba with Salmon and Asparagus

◤	00.10 plus standing time	00.20

American	Ingredients	Metric/Imperial
1 lb	fresh salmon fillets	450 g/1 lb
	salt	
12	green asparagus	12
1 cup	all-purpose (self raising) flour	125 g/4 oz
1	egg	1
	pinch of salt	
4 tbsp	ice cold water	4 tbsp
3¼ cups	Tsuke-jiru (1) (see page 411)	750 ml/1¼ pints
1 lb	home-made soba or ¾ lb/350 g/ 12 oz dried, bought soba	450 g/1 lb
	oil for deep-frying	
1	box cress	1

1. Rinse the salmon under cold running water. Dry with kitchen paper and cut into 12 equal strips. Sprinkle with some salt and leave to stand for 15 minutes.

2. Peel the asparagus from the tip to the bottom. Trim the stalks and put the asparagus into boiling salted water and boil them for 15 minutes precisely. Drain and cool in a colander. Cut each asparagus into 3 equal pieces and dry with kitchen paper.

3. Sieve the flour into a bowl. Make a small well in the flour. Beat the egg and add a pinch of salt and 4 tbsp ice cold water, stirring continuously. Pour this mixture into the well in the flour and stir from the center outward until a smooth and elastic batter is formed. If necessary, add 1-2 tbsp ice cold water.

4. Bring the sauce slowly to the boil and keep warm over low heat.

5. Prepare the home-made soba according to the instructions on page 410. Cook dried soba as indicated on the wrapper. Drain well and cool with cold water. Drain and warm it again over steam, turning occasionally.

6. Heat the oil in a wok or frying pan until very hot.

7. Dip the salmon strips into the batter and drain briefly over the bowl and fry the salmon strips, a few at a time until golden brown.

8. Do the same with the asparagus.

9. Divide the soba between four warmed bowls or deep plates. Pour half the warm sauce over the soba and then arrange the fish strips and pieces of asparagus on top.

10. Add a little cress here and there.

11. Serve the remaining sauce separately in small individual bowls.

Left to right: Soba with chicken and mushrooms,
Soba with sole and bell pepper,
Soba with salmon and asparagus

Soba with chestnuts and ham

Tempura soba (IV)

Soba with Mushrooms and Scrambled Egg

00.15 Serves 4   **00.25**

American	Ingredients	Metric/Imperial
1 lb	home-made soba or ¾ lb/350 g/ 12 oz dried, bought soba	450 g/1 lb
1 lb	small fresh mushrooms	450 g/1 lb
3	medium size eggs	3
	salt	
1 tbsp	mirin, sake or dry sherry with 1 ½ tbsp sugar	1 tbsp
3 tbsp	groundnut oil	3 tbsp
1 cup	all-purpose (self-raising) flour	125 g/4 oz
1	small egg	1
	salt	
	oil for deep frying	
3¼ cups	Kake-jiru (11) (see page 411)	750 ml/1 ¼ pints
2	chopped green shallots or scallions (spring onions)	2

1. Prepare home-made soba according to the recipe on page 410. Cook dried soba as indicated on the wrapper. Drain well. Cool with cold water, drain again and warm over steam, turning occasionally.
2. Wipe the mushrooms with a moist cloth or kitchen paper and trim the stalks.
3. Beat the eggs, add 2 tbsp water, a pinch of salt and the mirin, sake or sherry with sugar.
4. Heat the oil in a small frying pan. Pour the egg mixture into it and keep stirring until it has set. Remove the frying pan from the heat.
5. Sieve the flour into a bowl. Make a small well in the flour. Beat the egg and add 2-3 tbsp ice cold water. Pour this mixture into the well together with a pinch of salt. Stir from the center outward until a smooth and elastic batter is formed. If necessary, add 1-2 tbsp ice cold water.
6. Heat the oil until very hot.
7. Bring the stock to the boil.

8. Dip the mushrooms in the batter. Drain, briefly over the bowl and fry them 5-6 at a time until brown. Remove from the pan and drain on kitchen paper.
9. Divide the soba between four bowls or deep plates. Pour over part of the stock, sprinkle with the scrambled egg and arrange the mushrooms on top. Sprinkle with the green shallot or scallion (spring onion).
10. Serve the dish as warm as possible and serve the remaining bouillon (stock) separately in individual bowls.

Tempura soba (VII)

Soba with Chestnuts and Ham

00.10 Serves 4   **00.25**

American	Ingredients	Metric/Imperial
¾ lb	cooked canned chestnuts	350 g/12 oz
½ lb	cooked ham	225 g/8 oz
1 lb	home-made soba or ¾ lb/350 g/ 12 oz dried, bought soba	450 g/1 lb
1 cup	all-purpose (self-raising) flour	125 g/4 oz
1	large egg	1
	pinch of salt	
5-6 tbsp	ice cold water	5-6 tbsp
	oil for deep frying	
3¼ cups	Kake-jiru (11) (see page 411)	750 ml/1 ¼ pints
2	chopped green shallots or scallions (spring onions)	2

1. Drain the cooked chestnuts thoroughly. Dry each individually.
2. Cut the ham into finger-width slices, 2 in (5 cm) long.
3. Prepare home-made soba according to the instructions on page 410. Cook dried soba as indicated on the wrapper. Drain well, cool with cold water. Drain in a colander and warm over steam, turning occasionally.
4. Sieve the flour into a bowl. Make a small well in the flour. Beat the egg and add 5-6 tbsp really ice cold water. Pour this mixture together with a pinch of salt into the well. Stir from

the center outward until a smooth, elastic batter is formed. If necessary, add 1-2 tbsp cold water.

5. Heat the oil in a wok or frying pan until very hot.

6. Bring the bouillon (stock) to the boil.

7. Dip the chestnuts in the batter and fry them, 2-3 at a time, until golden brown.

8. Do the same with the strips of ham. Drain on kitchen paper.

9. Divide the soba between four warmed bowls or deep plates. Pour over some of the bouillon (stock). Arrange the chestnuts and ham strips on top. Sprinkle with the chopped green shallot or scallion (spring onion).

10. Serve the dish as warm as possible. Serve the remaining bouillon (stock) separately in small individual bowls.

Tempura soba (VIII)

Soba with Lamb and Eggplant (Aubergine)

◄─▷ 00.10   00.25
Serves 4

American	Ingredients	Metric/Imperial
1 lb	lean lamb	450 g/1 lb
1	medium size eggplant (aubergine)	1
	salt	
	ground sansho-pepper or black pepper	
1 lb	home-made soba or ¾ lb/350 g/ 12 oz dried, bought soba	450 g/1 lb
1 cup	all-purpose (self-raising) flour	125 g/4 oz
1	large egg	1
	salt	
5-6 tbsp	ice cold water	5-6 tbsp
	oil for deep-frying	
3¼ cups	Kake-jiru (1) (see page 411)	750 ml/1 ¼ pints
2	chopped green shallots or scallions (spring onions)	2

1. Dry the meat with kitchen paper and cut into ¼ in (5 mm) slices.

2. Toast the eggplant (aubergine) for a 2-3 minutes under a hot broiler (grill), turning until the skin is completely black. Cool, remove the black skin and cut obliquely into ½ in (1.25 cm) slices.

3. Sprinkle the slices of meat and eggplant (aubergine) with some salt and sansho-pepper.

4. Prepare home-made soba according to the recipe on page 410. Cook dried soba as indicated on the wrapper. Drain and cool with cold water. Drain in a colander and warm again over steam, turning occasionally.

5. Sieve the flour into a bowl. Make a well in the flour. Beat the egg and add 4-5 tbsp ice cold water. Pour this mixture into the well with a pinch of salt. Stir from the center outward until a smooth, elastic batter is formed. If necessary, add 1-2 tbsp ice cold water.

6. Heat the oil in a frying pan or wok until very hot.

7. Bring the bouillon (stock) to the boil.

8. Dip the lamb slices into batter. Drain briefly over the bowl, then fry quickly in the hot oil until golden brown.

9. Do the same with the eggplant (aubergine) slices. Drain on kitchen paper.

10. Divide the warm soba between four warmed bowls or deep plates. Pour over some of the bouillon (stock) and

arrange the slices of meat and eggplant (aubergine) on top. Sprinkle with the green shallot or scallion (spring onion).

11. Serve as warm as possible. Serve the remaining stock separately in warmed small individual bowls.

Tempura soba (VI)

Soba with Tuna, Beans and Onions

◄─▷ 00.10   00.25
plus standing time

American	Ingredients	Metric/Imperial
1 lb	tuna fillets, divided into 12 equal pieces	450 g/1 lb
	salt	
	ground black pepper	
	ground root ginger	
¼ lb	long green beans (string beans)	125 g/4 oz
1	large onion	1
4	cherry tomatoes	4
1 lb	home-made soba or ¾ lb/350 g/ 12 oz dried, bought soba	450 g/1 lb
1 cup	all-purpose (self raising) flour	125 g/4 oz
	pinch of salt	
5-6 tbsp	ice cold water	5-6 tbsp
	oil for deep-frying	
3¼ cups	Kake-jiru (1) (see page 411)	750 ml/1 ¼ pints
1½ tsp	cornstarch (cornflour)	1½ tsp
1 tbsp	chopped scallion (spring onion) or chives	1 tbsp

1. Dry the pieces of tuna with kitchen paper. Sprinkle with some salt, a pinch of ground pepper and ground ginger and leave to stand for at least 15 minutes.

2. Rinse and top and tail the green beans. Dry with kitchen paper.

3. Clean the onion and cut it into 8 equal parts.

4. Make each cherry tomato into a flower.

5. Prepare home-made soba according to the recipe on page 410. Cook dried soba as indicated on the wrapper. Drain well. Cool with cold water, drain in a colander and warm again over steam, turning occasionally.

6. Sieve the flour into a bowl. Make a small well in the flour. Beat the egg and add a pinch of salt and 5-6 tbsp ice cold water. Pour this mixture into the well. Stir from the center outward until you a smooth, elastic batter is formed. If necessary, add 1-2 tbsp really ice cold water.

7. Heat the oil in a frying pan or wok until very hot.

8. Bring the bouillon (stock) to the boil.

9. Mix the cornstarch (cornflour) with 1 tbsp cold water and thicken the Kake-jiru with it, stirring continuously. Keep warm.

10. Dip the pieces of tuna fish into the batter. Drain briefly over the bowl, and fry 3-4 pieces at a time, until golden brown.

11. Do the same with the beans and onions. Drain on kitchen paper.

12. Divide the soba between four warmed bowls or deep plates. Pour some of the stock over, arrange the pieces of tuna fish, beans and the onion on top. Garnish with tomato flowers and sprinkle with a little chopped green shallot or scallion (spring onion) or finely chopped chives.

13. Serve the remaining Kake-jiru in warmed bowls.

Shabu shabu is the name for a special dinner at which the dishes are cooked in bouillon (stock) at the table. Shabu shabu can be compiled as simply or as extensively as you wish.

Shabu shabu (I)

Shabu Shabu with Beef and Mushrooms

◄▬▬▷ 00.25   00.00 ◄▭
plus chilling and cooking at table

American	Ingredients	Metric/Imperial
8	dried Japanese mushrooms (shiitake or matsutake) or Chinese dried mushrooms	8
1 lb	tender beef, eg. sirloin steak in one piece	450 g/1 lb
8	Japanese stem onions, scallions (spring onions) or shallots	8
½ lb	fresh mushrooms	225 g/8 oz
¼ lb	fresh oyster mushrooms	125 g/4 oz
¼ lb	canned bamboo shoots	125 g/4 oz
¼ lb	soybean curd (tofu)	125 g/4 oz
	pine sprigs or chrysanthemum flowers	
4 tbsp	Japanese soy sauce	4 tbsp
1½ quarts	dashi or chicken bouillon (stock) (see page 356)	1.5 litres/2¾ pints
	sesame and horseradish sauces (see page 427)	
1-2 tbsp	mirin or 1 tsp red chili oil	1-2 tbsp

1. Put the dried mushrooms in a bowl and cover generously with boiling water. Leave to soak and cool completely. Remove and discard stems and cut the caps into long thin strips.
2. Put the meat in the freezer compartment of the refrigerator for 30 minutes to stiffen. Cut across the grain into paper-thin slices and arrange on a large dish.
3. Place the strips of soaked mushroom next to the meat.
4. Clean the Japanese onions, scallions (spring onions) or shallots and cut diagonally into 1½ in (4 cm) pieces. Place beside the soaked mushrooms.
5. Wipe the fresh mushrooms clean with a damp cloth or kitchen paper. Trim the stalks then cut the mushrooms into medium slices. Arrange next to the Japanese onions, scallions (spring onions) or shallots.
6. Clean the oyster mushrooms in the same way and cut into long thin strips. Place next to the other mushrooms.
7. Drain the bamboo shoots and cut into long thin strips. Place next to the oyster mushrooms.
8. Cut the soybean curd (tofu) into ½ in (1.25 cm) slices.
9. Garnish the ingredients on the dish with a pine sprig or 1-2 chrysanthemums.
10. Add the soy sauce to the dashi or chicken bouillon (stock), heat it and transfer to a fondue pan on a hotplate on the table. The guests use a pair of chopsticks to take the ingredients from the serving dish and hold them in the hot bouillon (stock), (special small skimmers can also be used for this). The meat should not be held in the bouillon (stock) for more than ½ minute. Then the piece of meat is dipped into one of the sauces and placed on the plate. Cook the soaked mushrooms, scallions (spring onions) and soybean curd for 1-1½ minutes.

Shabu shabu with beef and vegetables

(spring onions) or shallots for 1 minute. Boiled noodles or rice may be served separately.
11. At the end of the meal add 1-2 tbsp mirin or 1 tsp red chili oil to the stock and pour into warmed bowls as a soup.

Cook's tip: in Japan a bouillon (stock) is by no means always prepared for Shabu shabu. Very often the (fondue) pan is filled with boiling water and a stick of seaweed (kombu) allowed to 'stew' in it for a few minutes, and sometimes some Japanese soy sauce (shoyu) or salt is added.

Shabu shabu (II)

Shabu Shabu with Beef and Vegetables

◄▬▬▷ 00.30   00.00 ◄▭
plus chilling and cooking at table

American	Ingredients	Metric/Imperial
1 lb	tender beef eg. sirloin steak in one piece	450 g/1 lb
8	Japanese stem onion, scallions (spring onions) or shallots	8
8	large Chinese cabbage leaves	8
4	celery sticks	4
2	large carrots	2
¼ lb	canned bamboo shoots	125 g/4 oz
¼ lb	soybean curd (tofu)	125 g/4 oz
2	skinned tomatoes or 4 red chilies	2
	sprig of pine	
4 tbsp	Japanese light soy sauce	4 tbsp
1½ quarts	dashi or chicken bouillon (stock) (see page 356)	1.5 litres/2¾ pints
	sesame and horseradish sauces (see page 427)	
1-2 tbsp	mirin or 1 tsp red chili oil	1-2 tbsp

1. Put the meat in the freezer compartment of the refrigerator for 30 minutes to stiffen. Cut across the grain into paper-thin slices and arrange on a dish.
2. Clean the Japanese onions, scallions (spring onions) or

shallots and cut diagonally into 1½ in (4 cm) pieces. Place them by the meat.

3. Wash the cabbage leaves, roll up tightly and tie with cotton thread. Blanch for 3 minutes in salted boiling water then rinse under cold running water. Remove the cotton thread and cut the rolls into 1 in (2.5 cm) strips. Place next to the Japanese onions, scallions (spring onions) or shallots.

4. Clean the celery stalks. String if necessary and cut into 1 in (2.5 cm) pieces. Arrange next to the rolls of cabbage.

5. Peel and trim the carrots. Rinse and cut diagonally into thin slices. Place next to the celery.

6. Drain the bamboo shoots and cut into strips. Arrange next to the carrot.

7. Cut the soybean curd (tofu) into slices about ½ in (1.25 cm) thick. Arrange next to the bamboo shoots.

8. Garnish the ingredients on the dish with for example, tomato or chili flowers or a sprig of pine.

9. For remaining method, follow the method for Shabu Shabu in the previous recipe.

Shabu shabu (III)

Shabu Shabu with Lamb and Beans

	00.25	00.00
	plus chilling and cooking at table	

American	Ingredients	Metric/Imperial
1 lb	lamb, preferably with a strip of fat on it	450 g/1 lb
8-12	Japanese stem onions, scallions (spring onions) or shallots	8-12
½ lb	string beans or French beans	225 g/8 oz
12	large fresh mushrooms	12
¼ lb	canned bamboo shoots	125 g/4 oz
½ lb	soybean curd (tofu)	225 g/8 oz
4 tbsp	Japanese light soy sauce	4 tbsp
1½ quarts	dashi or chicken bouillon (stock) (see page 356)	1.5 litres/2¾ pints
	sesame and horseradish sauces (see page 427)	
1-2 tbsp	mirin or 1 tsp red chili oil	1-2 tbsp

1. Put the meat in the freezer compartment of the refrigerator for 30 minutes to stiffen. Cut across the grain into paper-thin slices and arrange these to overlap on a large dish.

2. Clean the Japanese onions, scallions (spring onions) or shallots and cut diagonally into 1½ in (4 cm) pieces. Place next to the meat.

3. Wash the beans, stringing if necessary, and cut into 1½ in (4 cm) lengths. Cook for 3 minutes in salted boiling water. Drain and cool rapidly in cold water. Drain again and arrange next to the Japanese onions, scallions (spring onions) or shallots.

4. Wipe the mushrooms clean with a damp cloth or kitchen paper, trim the stalks and cut the mushrooms into thin slices. Arrange next to the beans.

5. Drain the bamboo shoots and cut into thin strips. Arrange next to the mushrooms.

6. Cut the soybean curd (tofu) into slices and place next to the bamboo shoots.

7. Follow the method for Shabu shabu 1 (page 426) for the completion of the dish at table.

Gome dare

Sesame Sauce

	00.00	00.10
	plus cooling time	

American	Ingredients	Metric/Imperial
3-4 tbsp	white sesame seeds	3-4 tbsp
4 tbsp	dashi or chicken bouillon (stock) (see page 356)	4 tbsp
2 tsp	Japanese light soy sauce	2 tsp
½ tsp	Japanese dark soy sauce	½ tsp
1 tsp	mirin or dry sherry with ½ tsp sugar	1 tsp

1. Toast the sesame seeds in a dry frying pan over moderate heat, shaking the pan continuously, until golden brown. Turn on to a large cold plate, leave to cool then grind in a mortar.

2. Stir in the dashi or chicken bouillon (stock), soy sauces and mirin or dry sherry with sugar. Continue stirring until a smooth sauce forms.

Wasabi joyu

Horseradish Sauce

	00.05	00.00
	plus standing	

American	Ingredients	Metric/Imperial
1½ tsp	wasabi powder	1½ tsp
2 tbsp	dashi or chicken bouillon (stock) (see page 356)	2 tbsp
4 tbsp	Japanese dark soy sauce	4 tbsp
2 tbsp	Japanese light soy sauce	2 tbsp
1 tbsp	mirin or dry sherry with ½ tbsp sugar	1 tbsp

1. Make up the wasabi powder with cold dashi or chicken bouillon (stock).

2. Stir in the soy sauce and mirin or dry sherry and sugar. Leave to stand for 15 minutes for the flavor to develop.

Shabu shabu with lamb and beans

Shabu shabu (IV)

Shabu Shabu with Mixed Meat and Cucumber

00.40 00.00
plus chilling and cooking at table

American	Ingredients	Metric/Imperial
½ lb	beef	225 g/8 oz
½ lb	lamb	225 g/8 oz
¼ lb	pork	125 g/4 oz
8	Japanese stem onions, scallions (spring onions) or shallots	8
1	large cucumber or 2 zucchini (courgettes)	1
½ lb	piece pumpkin	225 g/8 oz
½ lb	spinach	225 g/8 oz
¼ lb	soybean curd (tofu)	125 g/4 oz
	a few pine sprigs (optional)	
1-2	tropical flowers eg. orchids (optional)	1-2
5-6 tbsp	Japanese light soy sauce	5-6 tbsp
2 quarts	dashi or chicken bouillon (stock) (see page 356)	2 litres/3 ½ pints
	sesame and horseradish sauces (see page 427)	
1-2 tbsp	mirin or 1 tsp red chili oil	1-2 tbsp

1. Put the meat in the freezer compartment of the refrigerator for 30 minutes to stiffen. Cut across the grain into paper-thin slices and arrange one kind at a time on a large dish.
2. Clean the Japanese onions, scallions (spring onions) or shallots and cut diagonally into 1 ½ in (4 cm) pieces. Place next to the meat.
3. Rinse and trim the cucumber or zucchini (courgettes). Halve and seed, cut each half into three long strips. Cut the strips into 1 ½ in (4 cm) pieces. Place next to the Japanese onion, scallions (spring onions) or shallots.
4. Peel and seed the piece of pumpkin, cut the flesh into 1 in (2.5 cm) cubes. Cut each cube into 3 slices. Arrange, overlapping, next to the cucumber or zucchini (courgettes).
5. Wash the spinach several times then dry the leaves with kitchen paper as thoroughly as possible. Make small stacks each of 8 small leaves. Remove the stalks and secure the leaves by pushing wooden cocktail picks through the middle. Arrange next to the slices of pumpkin.
6. Cut the soybean curd (tofu) into ½ in (1.25 cm) slices and overlap them next to the spinach.
7. Garnish the ingredients on the dish using pine sprigs and one or more tropical flowers, (optional).
8. Proceed at table as for Shabu shabu (1) (page 426).

Left to right: Shabu shabu with mixed meat and cucumber, Shabu shabu with mixed meats, snow peas (mange-tout) and eggplant (aubergine)

Shabu shabu (V)

Shabu Shabu with Mixed Meats, Snow Peas (Mange-tout) and Eggplant (Aubergine)

00.45 **00.00**

plus standing and cooking at table

American	Ingredients	Metric/Imperial
½ lb	beef	225 g/8 oz
½ lb	lamb	225 g/8 oz
½ lb	chicken breast fillets	225 g/8 oz
½ lb	snow peas (mange-tout)	225 g/8 oz
	salt	
8	Japanese stem onions, scallions (spring onions) or shallots	8
2	small eggplants (aubergines)	2
12	large fresh mushrooms	12
3 tbsp	meat bouillon (stock)	3 tbsp
1 tbsp	sesame oil	1 tbsp
2 tbsp	finely chopped chives	2 tbsp
1 tbsp	red chili oil	1 tbsp
2 tbsp	mirin, sake or dry sherry with ¾ tsp sugar	2 tbsp
	freshly ground pepper	
2-3 tbsp	Japanese light soy sauce	2-3 tbsp
2	medium size onions	2
¼ lb	soybean curd (tofu)	125 g/4 oz
1-2	small (blue) irises (optional)	1-2
5-6 tbsp	Japanese soy sauce	5-6 tbsp
2 quarts	dashi or chicken bouillon (stock) (see page 356)	2 litres/3 ½ pints
	sesame and horseradish sauces (see page 427)	
1-2 tbsp	mirin or 1 tsp red chili oil	1-2 tbsp

1. Put the meat in the freezer compartment of the refrigerator for 30 minutes to stiffen. Cut across the grain into paper-thin slices, all of the same size and thickness. Arrange the slices of meat, one kind at a time, on a dish so that they overlap.
2. Rinse the snow peas (mange-tout), trim the ends and string if necessary. Blanch for up to 2 minutes in salted boiling water. Cool quickly in cold water. Drain, dry with kitchen paper and arrange on the dish next to the meat.
3. Clean the Japanese onions, scallions (spring onions) or shallots. Cut diagonally into 1½ in (4 cm) lengths and place next to the snow peas (mange-tout).
4. Rinse the eggplants (aubergines), remove the ends and cut into ¼ in (5 mm) slices. Sprinkle with salt and leave to drain in a colander for about 15 minutes. Dry with kitchen paper and arrange next to the Japanese onions, scallions (spring onions) or shallots.
5. Wipe the mushrooms clean with a damp cloth or kitchen paper. Trim the stalks then cut the mushrooms into ¼ in (5 mm) slices. Put these in a bowl.
6. In a small bowl mix the meat bouillon (stock) with the sesame oil, chives, red chili oil, mirin or sherry with sugar, 3 tbsp soy sauce and some salt and pepper. Pour this mixture over the mushrooms and stir several times. Arrange the slices of mushroom next to the eggplant (aubergine).
7. Clean the onions. Cut each into 8 and separate the layers. Place the pieces of onion next to the mushroom.
8. Cut the soybean curd into ½ in (1.25 cm) slices and arrange next to the onions.
9. Garnish with 1-2 blue irises or similar flowers (optional)
10. For the further preparation of this dish and how to eat it see Shabu shabu (1) pages 427.

At first sight Karibayaki very much resembles Shabu shabu. The ingredients are presented in exactly the same way, and are also cooked in the hot stock at the table in the same way. But the ingredients are different, especially those for the stock, so that Karibayaki is not as suitable for special occasions as Shabu shabu.

Karibayaki (I)
Boiled Beef with White Radish (Daikon) Sauce

00.30   00.00

plus cooling and cooking at table

American	Ingredients	Metric/Imperial
1 lb	tender beef, eg. sirloin steak, in one piece	450 g/1 lb
4	Japanese stem onions, scallions (spring onions) or shallots	4
½ lb	canned bamboo shoots, well drained	225 g/8 oz
½ lb	small mushrooms or canned straw mushrooms	225 g/8 oz
1	pine sprig (optional)	1
1-2	small blue irises (optional)	1-2
1¼ lb	white radish (daikon)	575 g/1¼ lb
2 tbsp	Japanese light soy sauce	2 tbsp
1 tbsp	Japanese dark soy sauce	1 tbsp
1 tbsp	mirin or dry sherry with ¾ tsp sugar	1 tbsp
	salt	
2½ cups	mirin or dry sherry with 2 tbsp sugar	600 ml/1 pint
1¼ cups	sake	300 ml/½ pint
5 tbsp	Japanese light soy sauce	5 tbsp
2 tbsp	Japanese dark soy sauce	2 tbsp

1. Put the meat in the freezer compartment of the refrigerator for 30 minutes to stiffen. Cut into thin slices about ⅛ in (3 mm) thick. Arrange on a dish so that they overlap.
2. Clean the Japanese onions, scallions (spring onions) or shallots and cut diagonally into 1½ in (4 cm) pieces. Place these next to the meat.
3. Cut the drained bamboo shoots into ¾ in (1.75 cm) squares. Arrange so they overlap, next to the Japanese onions, scallions (spring onions) or shallots.
4. Wipe the mushrooms with a damp cloth or kitchen paper. Trim the stalks. Place the mushrooms next to the bamboo shoots. If using straw mushrooms ensure they are well drained.
5. Garnish the ingredients with a pine sprig and 1-2 small blue irises.
6. Finely grate the white radish (daikon). Spoon on to a double thickness piece of muslin. Fold the cloth over and squeeze out as much liquid as possible – at least 5-6 tbsps is needed.
7. Add 2 tbsp light and 1 tbsp dark soy sauce, 1 tbsp mirin or dry sherry with sugar and a little salt and stir until the salt has dissolved. Divide the sauce between four small individual bowls.
8. Bring to the boil the remaining mirin, or dry sherry with sugar, the sake and remaining soy sauces and add salt to taste.
9. Put the pan on a heater on the table. Place the dish of ingredients next to it and place the little bowls of sauce by the plates. Using chopsticks, small skimmers or long fondue forks,

the guests should hold the ingredients in the boiling bouillon (stock) until cooked. Allow ½ minute for the meat, 10-20 seconds for the straw mushrooms and 1-1½ minutes for all the other ingredients. Dip the ingredients in the sauce before eating.
Cook's tip: if good white radish (daikon) is not available, make the sauce using wasabi powder. To do this make up 1 tbsp of wasabi powder with 5 tbsp of water. Continue stirring until a smooth mixture is obtained, then add the other ingredients mentioned for the sauce.

Karibayaki (II)
Boiled Beef with Beans and White Radish (Daikon) Sauce

00.35   00.00

plus chilling and cooking at table

American	Ingredients	Metric/Imperial
1 lb	tender beef, eg. sirloin steak, in one piece	450 g/1 lb
4	Japanese stem onions, scallions (spring onions) or shallots	4
¾ lb	thin string beans or French beans	350 g/12 oz
½ lb	canned bamboo shoots, well drained	225 g/8 oz
1	red bell pepper	1
1	green bell pepper	1
	tomato flower and watercress	
1¼ lb	white radish (daikon)	575 g/1¼ lb
2 tbsp	Japanese light soy sauce	2 tbsp
1 tbsp	Japanese dark soy sauce	1 tbsp
2 tbsp	mirin or dry sherry with 1½ tsp sugar	2 tbsp
	salt	
2½ cups	mirin or dry sherry with 2 tbsp sugar	600 ml/1 pint
1¼ cups	sake	300 ml/½ pint
5 tbsp	Japanese light soy sauce	5 tbsp
2 tbsp	Japanese dark soy sauce	2 tbsp

1. Put the meat in the freezer compartment of the refrigerator for 30 minutes to stiffen. Cut into thin slices ⅛ in (3 mm) thick. Arrange on a dish so they overlap.
2. Clean the Japanese onion, scallions (spring onions) or shallots and cut diagonally into 1½ in (4 cm) pieces. Place next to the meat.
3. Clean and trim the beans, cut into 1½ in (4 cm) pieces. Blanch in salted boiling water for up to 5 minutes. Cool rapidly in cold water, drain and place next to the Japanese onions, scallions (spring onions) or shallots.
4. Cut the drained bamboo shoots into ¾ in (1.75 cm) squares. Arrange, overlapping, next to the beans.
5. Rinse and trim the bell peppers. Halve and seed, cut the flesh into 1½ in × ½ in (4 cm × 1.25 cm) strips. Place next to the bamboo shoots.
6. Garnish the ingredients on the dish with a tomato 'flower' on a bed of watercress.
7. Prepare the sauce and bouillon (stock) as described in the recipe for Karibayaki (1).

Soboro
Beef with Soybean Curd (Tofu)

00.20 Serves 4   00.10

American	Ingredients	Metric/Imperial
4 tbsp	groundnut oil	4 tbsp
10 oz	coarsely chopped or ground (minced), lean beef	275 g/10 oz
1	finely chopped large onion	1
2	finely chopped Japanese stem onions, scallions (spring onions) or shallots	2
1	crushed garlic clove	1
½ lb	coarsely chopped soybean curd (tofu)	225 g/8 oz
2	small carrots, cut into julienne strips	2
	salt	
3 tbsp	Japanese light soy sauce	3 tbsp
1 tbsp	Japanese dark soy sauce	1 tbsp
2 tbsp	mirin or dry sherry with ½ tsp sugar	2 tbsp
2	lightly beaten eggs	2
2 tbsp	finely chopped coriander or parsley leaves	2 tbsp

1. Put all the ingredients on the table in bowls of appropriate sizes.
2. Heat the oil in a deep frying-pan. Add the meat, turning it several times.
3. Add the onion, Japanese onions, scallions (spring onions) or shallots and garlic. Stir.
4. Add the soybean curd (tofu) and stir once more.
5. Add the carrot, some salt, soy sauces and mirin or dry sherry with sugar. Stir again and briefly remove from the heat.
6. Add the lightly beaten eggs stirring well and put the pan back on the heat. Continue stirring until the eggs have set.

7. Just before spooning the mixture on to the plates, sprinkle with 2 tbsp finely chopped coriander or parsley leaves. Serve immediately on warmed plates, accompanied by bowls of boiled rice.

Niku no miso yaki
Beef in Red Bean Sauce

00.10   00.00 plus chilling and cooking at table

American	Ingredients	Metric/Imperial
1 lb	tender beef, eg. sirloin steak, in one piece, with a strip of fat on	450 g/1 lb
3 tbsp	red soy paste (miso aka miso)	3 tbsp
2 tbsp	Japanese light soy sauce	2 tbsp
1 tbsp	Japanese dark soy sauce	1 tbsp
2 tbsp	mirin or dry sherry with 1½ tsp sugar	2 tbsp
1½ tbsp	finely grated fresh root ginger	1½ tbsp
2	finely chopped Japanese stem onions, scallions (spring onions) or shallots	2
2 tbsp	groundnut oil	2 tbsp

1. Put the meat in the freezer compartment of the refrigerator for 30 minutes to stiffen, or almost thaw frozen meat, cut into ⅛ in (3 mm) slices. Cut the slices into strips about ¾ in (1.75 cm) thick.
2. In a bowl thoroughly mix the miso, soy sauces, mirin or dry sherry with sugar, root ginger and Japanese onions, scallions (spring onions) or shallots. Cover the strips of meat with the sauce and leave to stand for 5 minutes. Stir thoroughly and leave to stand for a further 5 minutes.
3. Heat the oil in a deep frying-pan which has been placed on a heater on the table. Add the meat and the marinade and stir continuously for 2-3 minutes until the meat has lost its original color. Serve immediately, accompanied by boiled rice in individual bowls, and Japanese light soy sauce in small separate individual bowls.

Boiled beef with white radish (daikon) sauce

Buta teriyaki (I)
Broiled (Grilled) Pork (I)

00.20 plus standing and chilling times   **00.05**

American	Ingredients	Metric/Imperial
14 oz	tender pork, eg. tenderloin (fillet)	400 g/14 oz
1 tbsp	very finely grated fresh root ginger	1 tbsp
1	finely chopped medium size onion	1
4 tbsp	Japanese light soy sauce	4 tbsp
1-2 tbsp	Japanese dark soy sauce	1-2 tbsp
5 tbsp	mirin or dry sherry with 1½ tsp sugar	5 tbsp
	salt	
8	cherry tomatoes	8
8	small onions (silverskin)	8
1-2	large lettuce leaves	1-2

1. Put the meat into the feeezer compartment of the refrigerator for 20-30 minutes then cut across the grain into ⅛ in (3 mm) slices.
2. In a bowl mix together the root ginger, onion, soy sauces, mirin or sherry with sugar and a pinch of salt.
3. Put the slices of meat in this marinade and stir. Leave to stand for at least 1 hour, stirring thoroughly from time to time.
4. Wash the tomatoes and remove the stalks.
5. Clean the onions.
6. Put 8 small wooden grill sticks (sate sticks) into cold water for 20 minutes, or they will quickly burn during broiling.
7. Remove the meat from the marinade, fold the slices double and thread on to the sticks. Complete each stick with an onion and a cherry tomato. Broil (grill) the meat for 5 minutes on a barbecue or under a hot broiler (grill), turning the sticks regularly and brushing once or twice with the marinade. Put the sticks on a platter lined with lettuce leaves.

Cook's tip: serve the Japanese 'sates' as part of a meal which must always include a vegetable dish. Boiled rice, or mie boiled and then, if wished, fried in a very small amount of oil, will go very well. These Japanese 'sates' can also be served as a snack between meals or accompanied by a glass of wine.

Right: Broiled (grilled) pork (I)

Buta teriyaki (II)
Broiled (Grilled) Pork (II)

00.10 plus standing time   **00.12**

American	Ingredients	Metric/Imperial
4 (4 oz)	boned loin pork chops	4 (125 g/4 oz)
1	very finely shredded small onion	1
1	very finely shredded garlic clove	1
1 tsp	finely grated fresh root ginger	1 tsp
1 tbsp	soft brown sugar	1 tbsp
3 tbsp	Japanese light soy sauce	3 tbsp
1½ tbsp	Japanese dark soy sauce	1½ tbsp
3 tbsp	mirin or dry sherry with 2 tbsp sugar	3 tbsp
4	skinned small tomatoes	4
1-2	pine sprigs, optional	1-2

1. Dry the meat with kitchen paper.
2. In a mortar or food processor, grind the onion, garlic, root ginger and sugar to a smooth paste.
3. Add the soy sauces and mirin or dry sherry with sugar.
4. Thickly coat the pork chops with the mixture and leave to stand for 30 minutes-1 hour. Coat the chops again, turning so that they are all evenly covered. Leave for a further 30 minutes. Remove as much of the marinade from the meat as possible, using the back of a knife.
5. Broil (grill) the chops for 10-12 minutes over a barbecue or under a hot broiler (grill), turning after 6-7 minutes. Serve on warmed plates, garnished with small tomato 'flowers' and 1-2 pine sprigs (optional).

Cook's tip: in Japan, the boiled rice served in preheated individual bowls with this dish will be decorated with a sprinkling of grated orange zest. A little seaweed (iziki), which can be obtained in Japanese shops and in delicatessens, also gives white rice a very attractive appearance.

Center: Broiled (grilled) pork (III)

Buta teriyaki (III)
Broiled (Grilled) Pork (III)

	00.10	00.10
	plus standing time	

American	Ingredients	Metric/Imperial
1 lb	streaky pork steaks	450 g/1 lb
3 tbsp	Japanese light soy sauce	3 tbsp
1½ tbsp	Japanese dark soy sauce	1½ tbsp
2 tbsp	mirin or dry sherry with 1½ tsp sugar	2 tbsp
1 tbsp	soft brown sugar	1 tbsp
1 tsp	grated lime or lemon zest	1 tsp
2 tbsp	lime or lemon juice	2 tbsp
2	very finely shredded Japanese stem onions, scallions (spring onions) or shallots	2
3 tbsp	groundnut oil	3 tbsp
1-2	lemon or orange slices	1-2

1. Dry the meat with kitchen paper and cut into strips 2½ in (6 cm) long and ¾ in (1.75 cm) thick.
2. In a bowl mix the soy sauces, mirin or dry sherry with sugar, soft brown sugar, lime or lemon zest, lime or lemon juice, Japanese onions, scallions (spring onions) or shallots and 1-1½ tbsp oil. Stir until the sugar has dissolved.
3. Add the meat to this marinade and leave to stand for 1 hour, turning occasionally.
4. Brush a griddle or broiler (grill) pan with oil. Heat the griddle or pan and add the strips of meat, coating them several times during cooking with the remaining marinade. Cook the strips of meat for up to 10 minutes, turning them regularly to cook evenly on all sides.
5. Divide the strips of meat between four warmed plates and garnish with lemon and orange slices.

Cook's tip: serve a ginger sauce separately (see page 433) to which 1 tbsp strained orange juice, per person, is added.

Below: Broiled (grilled) pork (II)

Shoga joyu
Ginger Sauce

	00.05	00.00
	plus standing time	

American	Ingredients	Metric/Imperial
2 tsp	very finely grated fresh root ginger	2 tsp
1 tbsp	mirin or dry sherry with ¾ tsp sugar	1 tbsp
2 tbsp	dashi (see page 356)	2 tbsp
4 tbsp	Japanese dark soy sauce	4 tbsp

1. Mix the root ginger with the mirin or sherry and sugar and dashi.
2. Grind in a mortar, or food processor to a smooth paste. Mix in the soy sauce and leave to stand in a cool place for about 30 minutes before serving.

Butaniku no kyuriitame
Pork with Cucumber

	00.15	00.20
	Serves 4	

American	Ingredients	Metric/Imperial
¾ lb	lean pork in one piece	350 g/12 oz
1	large cucumber	1
4 tbsp	groundnut oil	4 tbsp
1 tsp	finely grated fresh root ginger	1 tsp
2 tbsp	Japanese light soy sauce	2 tbsp
1 tbsp	Japanese dark soy sauce	1 tbsp
2 tbsp	mirin, sake or dry sherry with 1½ tsp sugar	2 tbsp
1	small shredded onion	1
1	small red bell pepper	1
1	small green bell pepper	1
½	green chili	½
1½ tsp	cornstarch (cornflour)	1½ tsp
	shredded scallions (spring onions), shallots or lemon grass, optional	

1. Dry the meat with kitchen paper. Slice it thinly across the grain and then into thin strips.
2. Rinse and trim the cucumber. Halve and seed, cut diagonally into thin slices and then into thin strips.
3. Heat the oil in a heavy-based pan or wok. Fry the meat until golden brown, turning continually, and then remove as much of the oil as possible from the pan.
4. Add the root ginger and cucumber strips, stir.
5. Add the soy sauces, mirin, sake or sherry with sugar, shredded onion and ¾ cup (200 ml/7 fl oz) boiling water. Bring to the boil and cover the pan. Reduce the heat and simmer for 10-12 minutes.
6. Rinse and trim the bell peppers and chili. Halve and seed, cut the flesh into thin strips. Add to the contents of the pan and simmer for a further 3 minutes.
7. Mix the cornstarch (cornflour) with 1 tbsp cold water and stir into the contents of the pan. Cook, stirring until the liquid has thickened slightly.
8. Spoon into a warmed dish and garnish with scallions (spring onions), shallots or blades of lemon grass.

Pork with broccoli

Brokkori to butaniku
Pork with Broccoli

	00.15	00.15
	Serves 4	

American	Ingredients	Metric/Imperial
4-8	large fresh mushrooms or oyster mushrooms	4-8
1 tbsp	cornstarch (cornflour)	1 tbsp
1	lightly beaten egg	1
1½ tbsp	mirin, sake or dry sherry with 1 tsp sugar	1½ tbsp
1½ tbsp	Japanese light soy sauce	1½ tbsp
1 tbsp	Japanese dark soy sauce	1 tbsp
	salt	
2	shredded scallions (spring onions) or shallots	2
¾ lb	lean coarsely ground (minced) pork	350 g/12 oz
¾ lb	cleaned broccoli	350 g/12 oz
5 tbsp	groundnut oil	5 tbsp
2 tbsp	Japanese light soy sauce	2 tbsp
2 tbsp	mirin, sake or dry sherry with 1½ tsp sugar	2 tbsp
½-1 tbsp	Japanese mustard	½-1 tbsp

1. Wipe the mushrooms clean with a damp cloth or kitchen paper and chop finely.
2. Mix the cornstarch (cornflour) with 2 tbsp lightly beaten egg.
3. Add this with 1½ tbsp mirin, sake or sherry with sugar, 1½ tbsp light and 1 tbsp dark soy sauce, salt, chopped scallions (spring onions) or shallots and the finely chopped mushrooms to the pork. Mix well and divide the mixture into 12 portions. Form each portion into meatballs.
4. Cut the broccoli stalks into ¾ in (1.75 cm) pieces. Keep the broccoli florets separate. Cook the broccoli stalks in boiling salted water for 3-4 minutes. Add the broccoli florets and boil for a further 2 minutes. Drain well.
5. Heat the oil in a heavy-based pan or wok and fry the meatballs until golden brown on all sides.
6. Add the broccoli and ¾ cup (200 ml/7 fl oz) boiling water, simmer for 2-3 minutes.

7. Using a slotted spoon or skimmer, remove the meatballs and broccoli from the pan and put into a warmed dish.
8. Boil the remaining liquid in the pan rapidly to reduce the quantity to 4 tbsp.
9. Add the remaining soy sauce, mirin, sake or sherry with sugar and Japanese mustard. Stir vigorously and serve the sauce in small individual bowls.

Cook's tip: the sauce can be enhanced by stirring in 1 tsp finely grated fresh root ginger, bringing to the boil and simmering for 4-5 minutes.

Butanikudango
Pork with Apple and Mushrooms

	00.30	00.10
	plus standing time	

American	Ingredients	Metric/Imperial
4	large dried mushrooms	4
¾ lb	lean pork in one piece	350 g/12 oz
1	large apple	1
2	scallions (spring onions) or shallots	2
1	lightly beaten egg	1
2 tbsp	sake or dry sherry with 1½ tsp sugar	2 tbsp
	salt	
3 tbsp	cornstarch (cornflour)	3 tbsp
	groundnut oil for deep-frying	
1-2	lettuce leaves	1-2
3 tbsp	Japanese light soy sauce	3 tbsp
3 tbsp	sake or dry sherry with ½ tsp sugar	3 tbsp
2 tbsp	mirin	2 tbsp
1 tbsp	Japanese mustard	1 tbsp
	salt	

1. Put the dried mushrooms in a bowl with boiling water to just cover. Leave until the mushrooms have swelled up and the liquid cooled. Discard the stalks and cut the caps first into thin strips, then into shreds.

2. Dry the pork with kitchen paper. Slice very thinly across the grain, then into thin strips and into shreds.

3. Peel the apple and remove the core. Cut the apple first into slices, then into thin strips, then into shreds.

4. Shred the scallions (spring onions) or shallots.

5. Mix all the above ingredients in a bowl and stir in the lightly beaten egg, 2 tbsp sake or sherry with sugar, a little salt and 1 tbsp cornstarch (cornflour). Cover and chill for about 20 minutes.

6. Divide the mixture into 12 portions. Form each portion into a ball and roll in the remaining cornstarch (cornflour).

7. Heat the oil in a frying pan until very hot. Quickly fry the balls a few at a time until golden brown on all sides. Drain on kitchen paper.

8. Line a dish with lettuce leaves and arrange the balls on it. Serve immediately.

9. Mix together the soy sauce, remaining sake or sherry with sugar, mirin and Japanese mustard, adding a little salt to taste. Serve the sauce in small individual bowls.

Butaniku no seroriitame

Pork with Celery

American	Ingredients	Metric/Imperial
¾ lb	lean pork in one piece	350 g/12 oz
4	large dried Japanese or Chinese mushrooms	4
4	celery sticks, scraped if necessary	4
4 tbsp	groundnut oil	4 tbsp
1 tsp	finely grated fresh root ginger	1 tsp
2 tbsp	mirin, sake or dry sherry with 1 ½ tsp sugar	2 tbsp
2 tbsp	Japanese light soy sauce	2 tbsp
1 tbsp	Japanese dark soy sauce	1 tbsp
1	egg	1
1	egg yolk	1
	salt	
2	scallions (spring onions), cut into ½ in (1.25 cm) pieces	2
1	skinned tomato	1

1. Dry the meat with kitchen paper. Cut across the grain into thin slices and then into strips.

2. Put the mushrooms in a small bowl with boiling water to just cover. Set aside until the liquid is cold. Discard the stalks and cut the caps into thin strips.

3. Cut the celery stalks diagonally into thin strips.

4. Heat the oil in a heavy-based pan or wok. Stir fry the meat until golden brown, and remove as much of the oil as possible.

5. Add the root ginger, strips of mushroom, mirin, sake or sherry with sugar, soy sauces and ⅔ cups (150 ml/¼ pint) boiling water. Stir well and bring to the boil. Reduce the heat, cover and simmer for 10-12 minutes.

6. Add the strips of celery and simmer for a further 3-4 minutes.

7. Lightly beat the egg and egg yolk in a small bowl. Add 1 tbsp water and a little salt. Stir this into the contents of the pan, adding the pieces of scallions (spring onions) or shallots. Immediately remove the pan from the heat. Stir well and transfer to a warmed dish. Garnish with tomato 'flower' and serve.

Butanikudango no nasunitsuke

Pork with Eggplant (Aubergine)

00.15 plus chilling time — 00.15

American	Ingredients	Metric/Imperial
2 tsp	cornstarch (cornflour)	2 tsp
1	egg	1
1 tbsp	Japanese light soy sauce	1 tbsp
1 tbsp	Japanese dark soy sauce	1 tbsp
2 tbsp	mirin, sake or dry sherry with 2 tsp sugar	2 tbsp
	salt	
1	finely shredded small onion or shallot	1
½ tsp	finely grated fresh root ginger	½ tsp
¾ lb	lean ground (minced) pork	350 g/12 oz
¾ lb	eggplant (aubergine)	350 g/12 oz
4 tbsp	groundnut oil	4 tbsp
¾ cup	warm chicken bouillon (stock)	200 ml/7 fl oz
2 tbsp	Japanese light soy sauce	2 tbsp
2 tbsp	mirin, sake or dry sherry with 2 tsp sugar	2 tbsp
1 tsp	cornstarch (cornflour)	1 tsp
1	skinned tomato	1
1	sprig coriander or parsley	1

1. Mix the cornstarch (cornflour) with 2 tbsp lightly beaten egg. Add this mixture, with 1 tbsp light and 1 tbsp dark soy sauce, 2 tbsp mirin, sake or sherry with sugar, a little salt the onion or shallot and root ginger to the ground (minced) pork. Mix well, cover and chill for about 20 minutes.

2. Divide the mixture into 12 portions and shape into balls.

3. Wash the eggplant (aubergine) and remove the ends. Cut lengthwise into four equal strips and cut these into pieces. Place in a colander and sprinkle with some salt. Leave to drain for 15 minutes, turning occasionally.

4. Heat the oil in a heavy-based pan or wok. Stir fry the meatballs a few at a time until golden brown on all sides.

5. Add the pieces of eggplant (aubergine) and stir fry for 3 minutes.

6. Remove as much oil as possible from the pan. Add the warm chicken bouillon (stock) and bring to the boil.

7. Reduce the heat, cover and simmer for 5 minutes. Remove the meatballs and pieces of eggplant (aubergine) from the pan using a slotted spoon or skimmer. Keep hot.

8. Boil the remaining cooking liquid rapidly, until no more than 5 tbsp remains. Strain the liquid and add the remaining soy sauce and mirin, sake or dry sherry with sugar and bring to the boil. Add salt to taste.

9. Mix the remaining cornstarch (cornflour) with 1 tbsp cold water and stir into the pan. Cook, stirring until the sauce thickens slightly.

10. Divide the meatballs and pieces of eggplant (aubergine) between 4 warmed plates. Garnish with a tomato 'flower' and a sprig of coriander or parsley. Pour a little of the sauce over the dish and serve the rest separately in small individual bowls.

Azuki no serada

Carrot Salad with Red Beans

American	Ingredients	Metric/Imperial
5 oz	scraped carrots	150 g/5 oz
1	small sweet-sour dessert apple	1
2 tbsp	dashi or chicken bouillon (stock) (see page 356)	2 tbsp
½ tbsp	Japanese light soy sauce	½ tbsp
½ tbsp	Japanese dark soy sauce	½ tbsp
½ tbsp	Japanese rice vinegar, lime or lemon juice	½ tbsp
1 tbsp	mirin, sake or dry sherry with 1 tsp sugar	1 tbsp
2 tbsp	canned or bottled red beans	2 tbsp
4	small lettuce leaves	4
4	radishes	4

00.15 — Serves 4 as side dish — 00.00

1. Cut the carrots into thin slices lengthwise and then diagonally into thin strips.
2. Peel the apple, remove the core and cut the apple first into slices and then into thin strips.
3. Mix together the dashi or chicken bouillon (stock), soy sauces, rice vinegar or lime or lemon juice and mirin, sake, or dry sherry with sugar. Pour ¾ of the dressing over the strips of carrot and the remainder over the apple.
4. Put a small heap of carrot on each of 4 small plates, arrange the strips of apple on top and spoon the red beans over.
5. Garnish with a small lettuce leaf and a small radish rose.

Tomato no tsukemono

Sweet Tomato Salad

00.15 — plus standing time — 00.00

American	Ingredients	Metric/Imperial
12	small under-ripe tomatoes	12
3 tbsp	coarse sea salt	3 tbsp
2 tbsp	lime or lemon juice	2 tbsp
2 tbsp	dashi or chicken bouillon (stock) (see page 356)	2 tbsp
1 tbsp	Japanese rice vinegar	1 tbsp
1½ tbsp	white sugar	½ tbsp
1 tbsp	mirin, sake or dry sherry with 1 tsp sugar	1 tbsp
1-2	sprigs curly leaved parsley	1-2

1. Plunge the tomatoes into a pan of boiling water for 30-40 seconds. Immediately plunge them into a bowl of ice- cold water containing ice cubes. Leave the tomatoes until cold.
2. Skin the tomatoes and with the point of a knife remove the stalks. Dry the tomatoes with kitchen paper and place in a bowl.
3. In another bowl mix the sea salt with the lime or lemon juice and an equal quantiy of cold water, stirring until the salt has dissolved. Add to the tomatoes and leave for 12 hours, stirring every 2 hours.

Carrot salad with red beans

4. Just before serving, drain the tomatoes and dry with kitchen paper.
5. Mix the dashi or chicken bouillon (stock), vinegar and sugar with the mirin, sake or sherry with sugar and roll each tomato in the mixture. Cut each tomato into 6 segments and put on small plates. Serve garnished with sprigs of curly-leaved parsley.

Ebi to kiwi no sarada

Kiwi Fruit with Shrimp (Prawns)

00.10 — Serves 4 as side dish — 00.00

American	Ingredients	Metric/Imperial
3	firm kiwi fruits	3
1 tbsp	lime or lemon juice	1 tbsp
2 tbsp	dashi or chicken bouillon (stock) (see page 356)	2 tbsp
½ tbsp	Japanese light soy sauce	½ tbsp
½ tbsp	Japanese dark soy sauce	½ tbsp
1 tbsp	mirin, sake or dry sherry with 1 tsp sugar	1 tbsp
	salt	
6 oz	peeled shrimp (prawns)	175 g/6 oz
4	long, crisp lettuce leaves	4
4	scallions (spring onions) or shallots	4
4	cherry tomatoes	4

1. Peel the kiwi fruits thinly and cut lengthwise down the middle and then into thin slices. Lay the slices of kiwi fruit in an overlapping semicircle in the middle of each plate.
2. Mix the lime or lemon juice with the dashi or chicken bouillon (stock), soy sauces and mirin, sake or sherry with sugar. Add a little salt to taste. Pour the dressing over the shrimp (prawns) and stir several times.
3. Put the shrimp (prawns) on the plates next to the slices of kiwi fruit.
4. Garnish with lettuce leaves, scallions (spring onions) or shallots, cut into blades and small 'flowers' of cherry tomatoes.

Cook's tip: serve the kiwi and shrimp (prawn) salad with dishes which include fried or grilled fish.

Piman no sarada

Mixed Salad with Bell Pepper and Onion

00.20 plus standing time — 00.03

American	Ingredients	Metric/Imperial
4	*bell peppers, preferably of different colors*	4
2	*medium size onions*	2
2 tbsp	*coarse sea salt*	2 tbsp
2 tbsp	*dashi or chicken bouillon (stock) (see page 356)*	2 tbsp
2 tbsp	*Japanese light soy sauce*	2 tbsp
1 tbsp	*Japanese dark soy sauce*	1 tbsp
2 tbsp	*mirin, sake or dry sherry with 1 ½ tsp sugar*	2 tbsp
1 tbsp	*white sugar*	1 tbsp
1 tsp	*Japanese mustard*	1 tsp
1 tbsp	*Japanese rice vinegar*	1 tbsp
	pinch seven-spice powder	
½ tsp	*grated fresh root ginger*	½ tsp
1	*finely chopped hard-cooked (hard boiled) egg*	1
1 tbsp	*finely chopped parsley*	1 tbsp

1. Rinse and trim the bell peppers. Halve and seed, cut the flesh into very thin strips 1½-2 in (4-5 cm) long.
2. Clean the onions and cut each one into 8-10 segments. Separate the layers of each segment.
3. Cook the strips of bell pepper and onion in boiling water for 3 minutes.
4. Dissolve the salt in 2¼ cups (500 ml/8 fl oz) cold water, stirring continuously.
5. Remove the bell peppers and onion from the boiling water with a skimmer and plunge into the cold salt solution. Stir and set aside for 6-8 hours. Drain in a colander for 30 minutes.
6. Mix the remaining ingredients, except the egg and parsley.
7. Put the drained peppers and onions in a bowl, pour the dressing over and toss lightly. Leave to stand for 30 minutes then stir just before serving.
8. Serve the salad in mounds on small plates, garnished with a little finely chopped hard-cooked (hard-boiled) egg around the salad and a little finely chopped parsley on top.

Kyuridango no tsukemono

Pickled Cucumber

00.20 plus standing time — 00.00

American	Ingredients	Metric/Imperial
1	*large green cucumber*	1
1	*small bunch of black grapes*	1
3 tbsp	*coarse sea salt*	3 tbsp
2	*small dried red chilies*	2
1 ½ tbsp	*white sugar*	1 ½ tbsp
2 tbsp	*dashi or chicken bouillon (stock) (see page 356)*	2 tbsp
1 tbsp	*mirin, sake or dry sherry with 1 tbsp sugar*	1 tbsp

1. Rinse and trim the cucumber. Halve and seed, make small balls from the cucumber flesh using a melon baller.
2. Peel the grapes and carefully remove the pips, retaining their shapes as far as possible.
3. Mix together the grapes and cucumber balls.
4. Rinse a jar or bowl with boiling water and add ⅓ of the balls. Sprinkle with salt and crumbled red chili. Fill the bowl or jar layer by layer in this way. Add 1¼ cups (300 ml/½ pint) water, cover and leave for 6 hours. Carefully stir several times.
5. Cover the jar or bowl again and stand in a cool place for 2-3 days, stirring the contents each day.
6. Just before use drain the contents of the jar or bowl in a colander and put them in a bowl.
7. Mix the white sugar with the dashi or chicken bouillon (stock) and mirin, sake or sherry with sugar. Pour this mixture over the cucmber balls and grapes, and stir carefully several times. Serve the dish in small bowls.

Kako no kyabetsusarada

Cabbage Salad with Oysters

00.15 Serves 4 as side dish — 00.05

American	Ingredients	Metric/Imperial
½ lb	*white cabbage*	225 g/8 oz
12	*oysters*	12
1 tbsp	*mirin, sake or dry sherry with 1 tsp sugar*	1 tbsp
½ tsp	*Japanese light soy sauce*	½ tsp
1 ½ tbsp	*lime or lemon juice*	1 ½ tbsp
1 ½ tbsp	*Japanese light soy sauce*	1 ½ tbsp
1 ½ tbsp	*Japanese dark soy sauce*	1 ½ tbsp
	sugar	
	pinch wasabi powder	
	piece red bell pepper (optional)	
	piece green bell pepper (optional)	

1. Clean the cabbage, removing the stalk and outer leaves. Cut into very fine strips.
2. Open the oysters using an oyster knife, reserve the liquid and put it in a pan. Take the oysters out of the shells.
3. To the liquid in the pan add the mirin, sake or sherry with sugar, and ½ tsp Japanese light soy sauce. Bring to the boil.
4. Add the oysters, stir several times then remove the pan from the heat. Drain the oysters in a sieve or colander.
5. Mix together the lime or lemon juice, remaining soy sauces, sugar, and wasabi powder and pour over the white cabbage. Toss several times and divide the salad between 4 small plates, arranging the oysters next to it. Garnish with a few strips of red and green bell pepper (optional).

Cook's tip: the recipe for salad with white cabbage and oysters can also be prepared with other ingredients for example, substitute iceberg lettuce for the white cabbage and mussels for the oysters.

Masurumu no karashi
Salted Mushrooms with Mustard Dressing

00.10 plus standing time   **00.00**

American	Ingredients	Metric/Imperial
¾ lb	large fresh mushrooms or oyster mushrooms	350 g/12 oz
3 tbsp	coarse sea salt	3 tbsp
2 tbsp	lime or lemon juice	2 tbsp
2 tbsp	dashi or chicken bouillon (stock) (see page 356)	2 tbsp
2 tbsp	Japanese light soy sauce	2 tbsp
2 tbsp	mirin, sake or dry sherry with 2 tsp sugar	2 tbsp
½ tbsp	mustard powder	½ tbsp
	pinch wasabi powder	
1 tbsp	finely chopped chives (optional)	1 tbsp
1-2	sprigs of curly leaved parsley	1-2
1-2	small tomatoes	1-2

1. Wipe the mushrooms clean with a damp cloth or kitchen paper. Trim the stalks then slice the mushrooms very thinly.
2. Dissolve the salt in 3¼ cups (750 ml/1¼ pints) water. Add the lime or lemon juice and place the mushrooms in the liquid. Stir well several times and set aside for 6-8 hours, stirring occasionally.
3. Mix together the remaining ingredients except the chives, parsley and tomatoes.
4. Drain the mushrooms in a colander for 30 minutes then put them in a bowl and pour the dressing over. Stir well and leave to stand for 20 minutes.
5. Stir well just before serving. Spoon on to small plates and sprinkle with some chives (optional). Garnish with sprigs of curly leaved parsley and 'flowers' of small tomatoes.

Nasu no karashi
Salted Eggplant (Aubergine) with Mustard Dressing

00.10 plus standing time   **00.00**

American	Ingredients	Metric/Imperial
1	large eggplant (aubergine)	1
4 tbsp	coarse sea salt	4 tbsp
2 tbsp	lime or lemon juice	2 tbsp
2 tbsp	dashi or chicken bouillon (stock) (see page 356)	2 tbsp
2 tbsp	Japanese light soy sauce	2 tbsp
1 tbsp	Japanese dark soy sauce	1 tbsp
3 tbsp	mirin, sake or dry sherry with 1 tsp sugar	3 tbsp
3 tbsp	white sugar	3 tbsp
1 tbsp	mustard powder	1 tbsp
1-2	sprigs of coriander or parsley	1-2
1-2	tomatoes	1-2

1. Wash the eggplant (aubergine) and remove the ends. Cut lengthwise into four strips, then cut the strips into finger-width slices.
2. Dissolve the salt in 3¼ cups (750 ml/1¼ pints) water, stirring continuously.
3. Stir in the lime or lemon juice and add the pieces of eggplant (aubergine). Stir well several times and set aside for about 8 hours, stirring occasionally. Drain in a colander for 30 minutes.
4. Mix together the dashi or chicken bouillon, soy sauces, mirin, sake or dry sherry with sugar, sugar and mustard powder. Stir until the sugar has dissolved.
5. Put the pieces of eggplant (aubergine) in a bowl and pour the dressing over. Stir once or twice and leave to stand for 20 minutes. Stir once more then divide the salad between 4 small plates and garnish with sprigs of coriander or parsley and tomato 'flowers'.

Sake no daikonsarada
Radish (Daikon) Salad with Cucumber and Salmon

00.20 plus standing time   **00.05**

American	Ingredients	Metric/Imperial
6 oz	raw salmon fillet, preferably from the tail section	175 g/6 oz
2 tbsp	lime or lemon juice	2 tbsp
	salt	
¼ lb	radish (daikon)	125 g/4 oz
½	cucumber	½
2 tbsp	dashi or chicken bouillon (stock) (see page 356)	2 tbsp
2 tbsp	Japanese light soy sauce	2 tbsp
1 tbsp	Japanese dark soy sauce	1 tbsp
2 tbsp	mirin, sake or dry sherry with 1 tsp sugar	2 tbsp
1 tbsp	dried shredded bonito (katsuobushi)	1 tbsp
	seven-spice powder	
1 tsp	wasabi powder	1 tsp
	few blades of lemon grass or scallions (spring onions) or shallot cut into blades	

1. Rinse the salmon and dry with kitchen paper. Mix together 1 tbsp lime or lemon juice and 1 tsp salt and rub into the fish. Leave to stand for 10 minutes.
2. Peel the white radish (daikon), cut into thin slices and then into very thin strips 1½ in (4 cm) long.
3. Rinse and trim the cucumber. Halve and seed, thinly slice the halves.
4. In a small pan mix together the dashi or chicken bouillon (stock), soy sauces, mirin, sake or sherry with sugar, bonito, seven-spice powder and wasabi. Add 2 tbsp water and bring to the boil stirring continuously. Remove from the heat and leave to stand (not in the refrigerator) until completely cold. Strain the liquid. Pour ½ the strained dressing over the cucumber and toss several times.
5. Arrange the cucumber slices in overlapping semicircles on the plates. Put the strips of white radish (daikon) in the rest of the dressing and sprinkle over 1 tbsp lime or lemon juice.

6. Dry the salmon again with kitchen paper and cut into thin strips 1½ in (4 cm) long. Very carefully combine the strips of salmon with the strips of white radish (daikon). Divide them into 4 portions and arrange in the cucumber semi-circles.
7. Garnish with blades of lemon grass or scallions (spring onions) or shallots.

Inarihorenso
Spinach Salad with Soybean Curd (Tofu)

00.20   **00.05**
Serves 4 as side dish

American	Ingredients	Metric/Imperial
1 lb	spinach, stalks removed	450 g/1 lb
2	sheets dried, fried soybean curd (aburage)	2
2 tbsp	sesame seeds	2 tbsp
1½ tbsp	Japanese light soy sauce	1½ tbsp
1½ tbsp	Japanese dark soy sauce	1½ tbsp
1 tbsp	mirin, sake or dry sherry with 1 tsp sugar	1 tbsp
1 tbsp	Japanese rice vinegar	1 tbsp
	salt	
	seven-spice powder (optional)	

1. Rinse the spinach thoroughly. Bring a large pan of water to the boil and plunge the spinach into it for ½ minute. Drain in a colander and press out as much water as possible.
2. Plunge the sheets of aburage into a pan of boiling water for ½ minute. Drain and cut into strips.
3. Heat a dry frying pan and toast the sesame seeds over moderate heat until they start to jump. Do not allow to brown. Spread the seeds on a cold plate to cool. Grind the sesame seeds in a mortar.
4. Add the soy sauces, mirin, sake or sherry with sugar, and vinegar, a little salt and some seven-spice powder to taste.
5. Press the spinach leaves down hard again. Take them out of the colander as a thick 'wad' and put them on a board. Shape the spinach into a square, ½ in (1.25 cm) thick. Cut it into 4 triangles, put one on each plate and spoon over some of the sesame dressing. Arrange the strips of aburage next to it.

Hakusai no tsukemono
Pickled Chinese Leaves

00.20   **00.00**
plus standing time

American	Ingredients	Metric/Imperial
1 lb	Chinese leaves	450 g/1 lb
3 tbsp	coarse sea salt	3 tbsp
3 tbsp	raisins	3 tbsp
4-5	small dried red chilies	4-5

1. Clean the Chinese leaves. Remove the root end and cut the leaves into broad strips.
2. Rinse a large glass bowl or jar with boiling water. Put ¼ of the Chinese leaves in the bowl or jar and sprinkle with 1 tbsp salt, 1 tbsp raisins and 2 crumbled red chilies.

Pickled cabbage with prunes

3. Fill the bowl or jar layer by layer in this way with cabbage, salt, raisins and dried chilies. Add 1 cup (250 ml/8 fl oz) cold water. Put a saucer or small plate on top and weight it down. Cover with a lid, aluminum foil or cling wrap and leave for 12 hours at room temperature.
4. Remove the weight and the saucer or plate and stir the contents. Cover, put the Chinese leaves in a cool place and leave for 4-6 days. Stir the contents once each day.
5. Just before serving cut the pickled Chinese leaves into thin strips. Use as a garnish for grilled fish or meat.

Kyabetsu no tsukemono
Pickled Cabbage with Prunes

00.20   **00.00**
plus standing time

American	Ingredients	Metric/Imperial
1	small white cabbage	1
4-6	prunes	4-6
3 tbsp	coarse sea salt	3 tbsp
3-4	small dried red chilies	3-4

1. Remove most of the cabbage stalk and outer leaves. Cut the cabbage into thick strips.
2. Remove the stones from the prunes and shred the flesh.
3. Rinse a bowl or jar with boiling water. Place ¼ of the cabbage in the bowl or jar and sprinkle 1 tbsp of salt and ⅓ of the finely chopped prunes on. Then sprinkle on 1 crumbled chili, with the seeds removed. Fill the jar layer by layer in this way, then add 1 cup (240 ml/8 fl oz) cold water.
4. Put a small plate or saucer on the contents of the jar or bowl and weight it down, cover and leave the jar or bowl for 12 hours at room termperature.
5. Remove the weight and the saucer or plate. Stir the contents several times, cover and leave for 4-6 days in a cool place. Stir the contents once each day.
6. Cut the cabbage into thin strips just before serving.

Cook's tip: in the same way prepare pickled white cabbage with dried and then shredded apricots or with (blue) raisins.

Kari no serorisarada
Celery Salad with Crab

00.15 Serves 4 as side dish **00.05**

American	Ingredients	Metric/Imperial
1 (¾ lb)	head celery	1 (350 g/ 12 oz)
	salt	
1 tbsp	lime or lemon juice	1 tbsp
5 oz	white crabmeat, thawed if frozen	150 g/5 oz
1 tbsp	lime or lemon juice	1 tbsp
1 tbsp	Japanese light soy sauce	1 tbsp
1 tbsp	Japanese dark soy sauce	1 tbsp
1 tbsp	mirin, sake or dry sherry with 1 tsp sugar	1 tbsp
2 tbsp	dashi or chicken bouillon (stock) (see page 356)	2 tbsp
½ tsp	wasabi powder	½ tsp

1. Remove and tough outside stalks from the celery. Trim the other stalks, reserving any green leaves to garnish the salad. If necessary, scrape the stalks. Cut diagonally into finger-width strips.
2. In a pan bring 1 quart (1 litre/1¾ pints) water to the boil. Add 1 tbsp salt and 1 tbsp lime or lemon juice. Boil the celery strips for exactly 3 minutes. Drain and cool in a colander.
3. Pick over the crabmeat and cut into thick slices.
4. Mix together the remaining lime or lemon juice, soy sauces, mirin, sake or sherry with sugar, dashi or chicken bouillon (stock) and wasabi powder.
5. Draw the drained strips of celery through the dressing and place in mounds on the plates. Arrange the slices of crab in a semicircle around them and garnish with the reserve celery leaves.

Daikon-croshi sasami
Radish (Daikon) Salad with Chicken

00.15 Serves 4 as a snack **00.00**

American	Ingredients	Metric/Imperial
½ lb	white radish (daikon)	225 g/8 oz
½ lb	smoked chicken	225 g/8 oz
2	scraped carrots	2
4 tbsp	kimizu (see page 386)	4 tbsp
4	cherry tomatoes	4
1-2	sprigs of curly leaved parsley	1-2

1. Peel the white radish (daikon), slice thinly then cut into thin strips.
2. Cut the chicken into thin strips.
3. Cut the carrots first lengthwise into slices and then into thin strips. Put all the vegetables in a bowl and lightly stir in the sauce.
4. Divide the vegetable salad between 4 small bowls and top with the strips of chicken. Garnish with the cherry tomatoes cut into 4 and sprigs of curly leaved parsley.

MENU

Marinated leg of lamb
Cucumber and mushroom salad
Steamed eggs with ginger

Marinated Leg of Lamb

00.15 plus marinating **00.20**

American	Ingredients	Metric/Imperial
1½ lb	boned leg of lamb	675 g/1½ lb
2 tbsp	Japanese light soy sauce	2 tbsp
2 tbsp	Japanese dark soy sauce	2 tbsp
3 tbsp	mirin, sake or dry sherry with 1-1½ tbsp sugar	3 tbsp
1 tsp	sansho pepper	1 tsp
3 tsp	lime or lemon juice	3 tsp
4 tbsp	cornstarch (cornflour)	4 tbsp
	groundnut oil for frying	
	salt	
	few coarsely chopped shallots or scallions (spring onions)	
3 tbsp	Japanese light soy sauce	3 tbsp
3 tbsp	mirin, sake or sherry with 1½ tsp sugar	3 tbsp
3 tbsp	dashi (see page 356)	3 tbsp
¼ tsp	finely ground daikon (radish) or wasabi powder	¼ tsp

1. Dry the meat with kitchen paper. Cut into 1½ in (4 cm) cubes.
2. In a bowl, mix together 2 tbsp light and 2 tbsp dark soy sauce, 3 tbsp mirin, sake or dry sherry with sugar, sansho pepper, lime or lemon juice and 2 tbsp water. Stir until the sugar has dissolved. Put the meat into the marinade and stir well. Leave to stand for 12 hours, turning occasionally.
3. Dry the meat with kitchen paper and toss in the cornstarch (cornflour) to coat, shaking off any surplus.
4. Heat the oil in a wok until very hot. Stir fry the cubes of meat, 5-6 at a time, until golden brown. Drain on kitchen paper.
5. Sprinkle with a little salt and roll through the chopped shallots or scallions (spring onions). Arrange the meat on warmed plates.
6. In a bowl, mix together the remaining soy sauce, mirin, sake or sherry with sugar and dashi. Stir in the daikon or wasabi powder and serve separately in individual bowls.

Cucumber and Mushroom Salad

American	Ingredients	Metric/Imperial
	00.10 plus standing time	**00.00**
1	cucumber	1
8	large mushrooms	8
4 tbsp	white wine vinegar	4 tbsp
	few drops red chili oil	
3 tbsp	superfine (caster) sugar	3 tbsp
½ tsp	salt	½ tsp
1 tsp	finely grated fresh root ginger	1 tsp
1 tbsp	finely chopped coriander or parsley	1 tbsp

1. Rinse the cucumber, trim the ends and halve lengthwise. Remove the seeds and cut the flesh into ⅛ in (3 mm) slices.
2. Wipe the mushrooms with a damp cloth or kitchen paper. Remove the stalks and cut the caps into ⅛ in (3 mm) slices.
3. Mix together the cucumber and sliced mushrooms.
4. Mix together the vinegar and chili oil, 2 tbsp cold water, sugar, salt and root ginger. Stir well until the salt and sugar have dissolved.
5. Spoon the sauce over the salad and toss carefully. Leave to stand for 1 hour. Put the salad in a colander and drain well.
6. Arrange the salad on individual side plates and sprinkle with a little chopped coriander or parsley to garnish.

Steamed Eggs with Ginger

American	Ingredients	Metric/Imperial
	00.10 Serves 4	**00.12**
2 tbsp	finely grated fresh root ginger	2 tbsp
3 tbsp	sugar	3 tbsp
3 tbsp	sake, mirin or sherry with 1 ½ tsp sugar	3 tbsp
1 tbsp	cornstarch (cornflour)	1 tbsp
6	eggs	6
1 tbsp	sesame oil	1 tbsp
4	mint leaves	4
4	small red fruits	4

1. In a bowl, mix together the root ginger, sugar, sake or substitute, 2 tbsp water and the cornstarch (cornflour). Stir until the sugar has dissolved.
2. Lightly beat the eggs, then whisk them for 30 seconds. Quickly beat in the sweet root ginger mixture.
3. Divide the mixture between 4 souffle or similar dishes, lightly brushed with oil. Each dish should be ⅔ full.
4. Cover each dish with aluminum foil.
5. Bring several quarts/litres of water to the boil in a steamer. Place the dishes in the perforated part of the pan, cover and steam for 10-12 minutes.
6. Remove the dishes from the steamer and remove the foil.
7. Serve, in the souffle dishes garnished with a mint leaf and a small red fruit. The dessert is generally eaten lukewarm.

This short glossary of some unfamiliar ingredients will explain spices, flavorings and sauces, mentioned in the recipes for the true flavor of many Asian dishes. Substitutes or home-made versions of many of these are given in the recipes, as access to Oriental food stores may not be equally easy for all cooks. In addition a list of suppliers of ingredients, some of whom offer mail order service is given at the end of the book.

Aburage: thin sheets of fried soybean curd, used in Japanese cookery. Usually sold frozen.

Agar-agar: a setting agent extracted from seaweed and used in a similar way to gelatin. Gelatins can be used but give a different texture.

Aji-no-moto: see monosodium glutamate.

Amchur: ground, dried green mango, used to give an acid flavor to Indian dishes.

Anise pepper: see Szechwan peppercorns.

Asafoelida: an evil smelling extract of a type of fennel, used in minute quantities as a flavoring in many Indian dishes.

Atta: fine whole wheat flour used to make Indian breads. Substitute whole wheat flour.

Bamboo shoots: sold canned. Once opened they can be stored in the refrigerator in a bowl of water, changed daily, for up to 1 week.

Black beans: small, black soybeans that have been fermented with salt and spices. Used in Chinese cookery to give a rich, savory flavor to stir fried and braised dishes. Unused beans can be stored in the refrigerator, in a sealed container, for up to 3 months.

Blachan: see dried shrimp paste.

Bonito: a type of tunny fish which is dried and used by the Japanese as a basic flavoring for soups and bouillons (stocks).

Candle nuts: used as a flavoring and thickening in Indonesian and Malaysian cooking, where they are known as kemiri nuts. Brasil or Macadamia nuts can be used as a substitute.

Cardamom: an expensive spice used to flavor many Indian dishes, both sweet and savory. Choose pale green pods with scented, sticky seeds.

Chilies: there are numerous varieties of chilies, varying considerably in degrees of 'hotness'. Use all chilies with caution and handle carefully, washing the hands afterwards to avoid burning the eyes and sensitive skin. The seeds are the hottest part and can be discarded if preferred. Ground chili is made from dried red chilies mixed with other herbs and spices, different brands varying in 'hotness'.

Cassia: see cinnamon.

Cinnamon: cinnamon sticks are rolls of thinly shaved bark from the cinnamon tree. Cassia is the bark of a similar tree and has a similar but less subtle flavor. Use cinnamon for sweet dishes, cassia or cinnamon for savory dishes. Ground cinnamon quickly loses its flavor so buy in small quantities and use quickly.

Cloves: dried flower buds of a tropical evergreen tree grown in South East Asia. Sold whole and ground.

Coconut milk: a creamy, white liquid extracted from the meat of coconuts, not the liquid found inside the nuts. Easily made at home from fresh or dried coconut (see page 310) and also available as a packet mix, canned and frozen.

Coriander: dried coriander seeds are an important ingredient in curry powders. The fresh leaves, easily grown at home, are a vital ingredient and garnish for many Indian, Chinese and South East Asian dishes.

Cumin: a vital ingredient in curry powders. The seeds look similar to caraway but the flavor is totally different.

Curry leaves: dried, glossy leaves, added to curries. Often available in specialist food stores.

Curry powder: although widely available, authentic recipes do not use ready made curry powders. However, as an introduction to Indian food, it may be worth sampling a few before buying a full selection of spices. Some spice mixtures and spice pastes for specific purposes, such as garam masala, are used in recipes.

Dahi: see yogurt

Daikon: see giant radish.

Dashi: a clear broth, made from dried bonito and kombu, a type of seaweed. The broth is essential in Japanese cooking. A packet mix is available.

Daun salam: aromatic leaf used in Indonesian cooking. Similar in flavor to curry leaves, but larger in size. Curry leaves can be substituted.

Dried shrimp paste: a strongly pungent paste made from pounded dried shrimp. It is used in small quantities to add a distinctive savory flavor to many dishes in most South East Asian countries.

Five spice powder: Chinese spice mixture made from ground star anise, szechwan peppercorns, fennel seeds, cloves and cinnamon. It is fragrant, spicy and slightly sweet. (see page 51) The mixture is also available in whole spice form from Chinese food stores and is used when a more subtle effect is required.

Garam masala: an Indian spice mixture added at the end of cooking or used as a garnish. There is no standard mixture but it usually contains warm flavored spices such as black pepper, cardamom, cinnamon, cumin, cloves and nutmeg. Ready ground garam masala is widely available but it is easily made at home (see page 310) and the flavor is best when the mixture is freshly ground.

Giant radish: also known as mooli or daikon, this large radish is widely used in India and Japan. It has a mild flavor and is widely available. Turnip can be substituted.

Ginger: fresh root ginger is vital to most Asian dishes. Ground root ginger cannot be used as a substitute. Leftover ginger can be frozen and grated straight from the freezer. Alternatively store in a small jar, covered with dry sherry, in the refrigerator.

Hoisin sauce: a dark, red-brown sauce made from soybeans with garlic, vinegar, sugar and spices. Sometimes sold as 'barbecue' sauce and often used as a sauce for Peking duck in Chinese restaurants. Refrigerate after opening the can or bottle.

Jaggery: see palm sugar.

Ketyap benteng asin: Indonesian salty soy sauce.

Ketyap benteng manis: Indonesian sweet soy sauce.

Lemon grass: a scented grass used in South East Asia as a flavoring. Available fresh, dried and ground. No real substitute but strips of lemon zest can be used to give an idea of the flavor if necessary.

Lotus root: the root of a type of white lily used as a decorative vegetable in Chinese and Japanese cooking. Readily available canned, sometimes fresh.

Matcha: powdered green tea used for the traditional tea ceremony. Produced by very tedious and expensive processes.

Mirin: Japanese rice wine, sweeter than sake and used only for cooking. Dry sherry with a little sugar can be substituted.

Miso: paste made from cooked, fermented soybeans. Various colors (white, red, brown and beige) and degrees of saltiness. Japanese thick soups usually based on miso stirred into dashi. One of Japan's most important staple diet foods, eaten by every Japanese, every day.

Mocha: rice cakes made by pounding glutinous rice and shaping it into balls or squares. Grilled and eaten with soy sauce. Essential ingredient in Ozoni, a thick vegetable soup eaten particularly at Chinese New Year.

Monosodium Glutamate: white crystals, like coarse salt. Used as a flavor enhancer, extensively in Chinese cooking. Unnecessary additive to good food. Readily available in supermarkets, chemists and Asian grocers. Also known as aji- no-moto (Japan) and ve-tsin (China).

Mooli: see giant radish.

Mushroom, dried Chinese and Japanese: very fragrant, intensely flavored. Expensive but incomparable flavor. No substitute. Soak before using.

Mustard seeds: black, brown or white seeds, used as a flavoring spice. Fry in very hot oil before use, to release the full flavor.

Nam pla: salty, matured fish sauce equivalent to trasi etc. Tastes similar to salty soy sauce.

Nori: dried seaweed, one of the most popular flavorings, garnishes and decorations in Japanese cooking. Sold in thin sheets. It must be toasted before use.

Okra (Bhindi): available fresh and canned, all year. Common name — ladies fingers. Green, slender, tapering pods with white flesh and small edible seeds. Wipe clean, trim and cook. Avoid any with black spots. Fresh ones are best, canned ones tend to be slimy and stringy.

Oyster sauce: not oyster flavored sauce. Chinese flavoring sauce, made from oysters cooked in soy sauce and brine.

Paksoi: spinach-like vegetable, with white stems and green leaves. Available fresh in Chinese food shops and some supermarkets.

Palm sugar: also known as jaggery or goela djawa. Dark, strongly flavored sugar with a bitter taste. Obtained from the sap of coconut and palmyrah palms. Sold in round flat cakes. Use soft brown sugar if unobtainable.

Panch Phcra (Panch Phoran): combination of 5 aromatic seeds - black mustard seed, cumin, black cumin, fenugreek and fennel. Used whole to add characteristic flavor to many Indian dishes. There is no substitute.

Pandanus (screwpine): flat green leaves used as a flavoring and coloring in Malay and Indonesian sweet dishes. Crush or boil leaves to release color and flavor. It is as popular as vanilla is in the West. Vanilla can be substituted in some recipes.

Panir: soft milk cheese used in desserts and vegetarian dishes. Available from Indian grocers, easily home made (see page 310). Full-fat soft cheese or other soft cheeses can be used as a substitute.

Peanuts (groundnuts): used mainly in South East Asian cooking. Legumes, with the 'pods' being produced underground. Grown in India, USA and African countries. In nearly all recipes peanuts are roasted before use – either in cool oven or by dry-frying. They must be roasted enough to remove the raw flavor – insufficiently roasted nuts will not keep. Pressed to produce peanut, groundnut or arachide oil. Rub roasted nuts in a cloth or between the fingers to loosen skins, then winnow, using fan (or blowing).

Plum sauce: spicy, sweet, hot Chinese sauce made from plums, chilies, vinegar, spices and sugar. Used as a dip. Sold in cans and jars. Keeps indefinitely when open.

Poppadums: crisp, very thin Indian breads made from dried dal. Sold in packets in various flavors. Grill or deep fry to serve.

Prahoc: fishy flavoring made from fish heads – dried in the sun, pounded and fermented. The liquid is taken off each day - this is prahoc sauce.

Red bean paste: thick, reddish-brown paste made from puréed, sweetened red beans (asuki beans). A very popular filling for sweet dishes. Sold in cans and jars.

Sake: rice wine, usually served warm. A fermented liquor made from rice. Smooth, mellow taste. 17% alcohol content. Brandy or sherry can be substituted for use in cooking.

Sambal ulek: combination of chilies and salt. (see page 128) Used in cooking or as an accompaniment. Sold in oriental grocers.

Sansho pepper: ground seeds of sansho tree used as a Japanese seasoning.

Santen: see coconut milk.

Sesame oil: extracted from toasted sesame seeds, this is different from sesame oil sold in health food shops. Buy from Chinese food stores or specialist stockists. Used in small quantities for flavoring, not as a cooking medium. Indian (til ka tail) – light, colorless oil, not like Chinese sesame oil.

Sesame seed paste: Chinese version is not the same as the Middle Eastern tahini. Made from toasted sesame seeds, it is brown and nutty. Substitute – peanut butter with added sesame seed oil, not tahini.

Sesame seeds: used mostly in Korean, Chinese and Japanese food and in sweets in South East Asia. Black sesame, another variety, is used in Chinese desserts and as a flavoring mixed with salt in Japanese food. Toasted sesame seeds – dry roast in a very hot pan to brown before the seeds become oily.

Seven-spice pepper: grainy mixture of ground chili, black pepper, dried orange peel, sesame seeds, poppy seeds, slivers of nori seaweed and hemp seeds. Sold in Japanese food shops. Used as a seasoning and condiment.

Sharks fin: very expensive. Sold dried, in processed and unprocessed form, processed is less expensive. Considered by the Chinese to be the ultimate in gastronomy.

Shiitake: Japanese mushrooms. Grown commercially on oak-related wood. Fresh — dark brown velvety caps (with white fissures sometimes). Dry well. Sold fresh in some oriental stores and supermarkets. Usually sold dried in cellophane packs (1 oz) containing 8-10 mushrooms. Soak in warm water for 3-5 hours before use. Soaking water can be used as bouillon (stock).

Shirataki: translucent noodles used in Sukiyaki. Made from the starch of a tuberous root. Sold in cans or plastic sachets, ready for use. Rinse before use.

Shoyu: Japanese soy sauce. Lighter and thinner than the Chinese type. Light-colored soy sauce is used to avoid darkening a light-colored dish; saltier than the dark type.

Shrimp (Prawns), dried: small shrimp (prawns) dried to use for flavoring soups and savory dishes. Soaked and ground before adding to sauces. Strongly flavored but milder than dried shrimp paste.

Soba: Japanese buckwheat noodles

Somen: Japanese noodles can be bought in packets or made at home

Soy sauce: light soy sauce, used for cooking. Lighter in color, more salty and thinner. Dark soy sauce, used mainly as a condiment. Slightly sweet. Used for 'red-cooked' dishes. Sweet soy sauce (ketyap manis), use dark Chinese soy sauce with added brown sugar. Mushroom soy sauce — flavored with mushrooms during last stage of processing.

Star anise: star shaped fruit with aniseed flavor. Available in Chinese shops. Also available ground. Ingredient of five spice powder.

Sweet bean sauce/paste: yellow bean sauce made from crushed yellow bean paste, sweetened with sugar. Traditional dipping sauce for Peking duck, although hoisin sauce is more commonly used in the West as it is more easily available.

Sweet soybean paste: red-bean paste. Sold in cans and jars, used as a dip or sauce. Brushed on Mandarin pancakes, used as a base for sweet sauces.

Szechwan peppercorns: Chinese pepper, Anise pepper. Dried, red-brown berries, sold by weight.

Tamari: looks like thick soy sauce. Made from soybeans it is cultured and fermented like miso. Used as a dipping sauce, in Japanese cooking, as a base for basting sauce such as Yakitori sauce and as an ingredient in sushi dipping sauces.

Tamarind water: acid water extracted from tamarind pulp, add to curried dishes to give a sour taste. Lemon juice can be used as a substitute, but is not the same.

Temeh: fermented bean paste, made by innoculating the curd with a mould.

Terasi/trasi: dried shrimp paste. Vital ingredient in many Indonesian and South East Asian recipes. Usually toasted before use. Shrimp sauce (bottled, from Oriental grocers) or a little anchovy essence can be used as a substitute.

Turmeric: rhizome of the ginger family, this is the mainstay of commercial curry powders. Colors food yellow but must not be used as a saffron substitute. Usually sold ground but also available as fresh roots. (Used fresh in Indonesia and Malaysia).

Udon: Japanese noodles can be bought in packets.

Varak: silver (or gold) leaf. Extremely thin sheets of beaten silver, used as a garnish on special occasions. Edible. Sold in some Indian and Pakistani grocers shops. Packed between sheets of paper to protect it. Store in airtight container to prevent tarnishing.

Vinegar: milder than Western vinegars. Chinese: Chinkiang - thick and fragrant, low vinegar content. Red vinegar — low vinegar content, often used as a dip. Rice vinegar — used for cooking and pickling vegetables. Japanese: rice vinegar + special 'sushi vinegar'. Cider vinegar can substitute for rice vinegar.

Wakami: seaweed used in Japanese cooking. Sold dried, it must be soaked before use. Used in soups and vinegared relishes.

Wasabi: pungent green horseradish used by the Japanese. Available in cans — powdered like dry mustard. Reconstituted with cold water. Also sold, made up, in tubes. Usual accompaniment to raw fish dishes.

Water chestnuts: sometimes available fresh. Peel away the skin before use. Usually canned. Store in fresh water in refrigerator for 7-10 days.

Wine Chinese: Kao-liang liqueur — very strong spirit made from Sorghum. Moutai wine — spirit made from wheat and sorgham. Shaahsing wine — popular wine made from fermented glutinous rice and yeast. Mei-kuei-lu wine — made from Kao- liang liqueur and rose petals. Substitute sake or dry sherry. Substitute mirin or sweet sherry for sweet rice wine.

Wonton wrappers: sold fresh. Small squares of fresh noodle dough available in Chinese grocery shops. Sold by weight - about 90 wrappers/pound. Can be frozen after filling but best not to freeze unfilled and they don't thaw very well.

Wood ears: small bracken fungus, cultivated in China and Japan. Available dried — soak in warm water for 20 minutes before use. Larger than cloud ears, often black on top and white underneath. Used more in soups than in stir fried dishes. Store dried wood-ears in an airtight tin.

Yellow bean sauce: very similar to black beans, but lighter in color. Use in the same way as black bean sauce. Sold in cans. A major Chinese seasoning. Store in covered jar in refrigerator.

Yogurt: Dahi in India, essential in Indian cookery, used as a marinade, flavoring and sauce ingredient. Greek-style yogurt or yogurt based on goat's milk can be substituted.

ENGLISH
RECIPE INDEX

CHINA

INDONESIA

MALAYSIA

KOREA

SINGAPORE

SRI LANKA

BURMA

INDIA AND PAKISTAN

JAPAN

Useful Addresses

US
House of Spices
76-77 Broadway
Jackson Heights, NY 11372

India Food and Gourmet
110 Lexington Avenue
New York, NY 10021

Wing Wing Imported Groceries
79 Harrisson Avenue
Boston, Massachusetts 02111

Wing On Co.
1005 Race Street
Philadelphia, PA 19107

Haig's Delicacies
642 Clement Street
San Francisco, California

Bezjian's
4725 Santa Monica Boulevard
Los Angeles, California

UK
Loon Fung Provisions
31 Gerrard Street
London W1

Nippon Food Centre
193 Upper Richmond Road
London SW15

Cheong-Leen Supermarket
4-10 Tower Street
London WC2

Chung Nam Provisions
162 Bromsgrove Street
Birmingham 5

Yau's Chinese Foodstore
9 St Mary's Street
Southampton

Chung Ying Supermarket
63 Cambridge Street
Glasgow

AUSTRALIA
Korean, Japanese and Chinese Food Store
14b Oxford Street
Sydney, New South Wales 2000

Hong Oriental Pty Ltd
206 Little Bourke Street
Melbourne, Victoria 3000

Orient Import
406a Brighton Road
Brighton, South Australia 5048

Global Foods
493 Albany Highway
Victoria Park, Western Australia 6100